ITALIAN MODERNISM:
Italian Culture between Decadentism and Avant-Garde

Edited by Luca Somigli and Mario Moroni

Italian Modernism offers a historiographic and theoretical reconsideration of the concepts of *decadentismo* and the avant-garde within the Italian critical tradition. The essays in this volume focus on the confrontation between these concepts and the broader notion of international modernism, understood as the complex phase of literary and artistic practices as a response to the epistemes of philosophical and scientific modernity at the end of the nineteenth century and in the first three decades of the twentieth.

This study is the first attempt in English to provide a comprehensive examination of Italian literary modernism. The volume documents how the previous critical categories employed to account for the literary, artistic, and cultural experiences of the period have provided only partial and inadequate descriptions, and have prevented a fuller understanding of the complexities and the interrelations among the cultural phenomena of the time. Provocative and wide-ranging, *Italian Modernism* will be of interest not only to Italianists but to specialists in a variety of fields, including comparative literature, fine arts, and cultural studies.

(Toronto Italian Studies)

LUCA SOMIGLI is an associate professor in the Department of Italian Studies at the University of Toronto.

MARIO MORONI is the Paul and Marilyn Paganucci assistant professor in the Department of French and Italian at Colby College.

ITALIAN MODERNISM

Italian Culture between
Decadentism and Avant-Garde

Edited by
LUCA SOMIGLI and MARIO MORONI

A Rebecca,
con amicizia e Stima,
Mario

UNIVERSITY OF TORONTO PRESS
Toronto Buffalo London

© University of Toronto Press Incorporated 2004
Toronto Buffalo London
Printed in Canada

ISBN 0-8020-8828-7 (cloth)
ISBN 0-8020-8602-0 (paper)

Printed on acid-free paper

Toronto Italian Studies

National Library of Canada Cataloguing in Publication

Italian modernism : Italian culture between decadentism and avante-garde/
editors, Luca Somigli and Mario Moroni.

(Toronto Italian studies)
Includes bibliographical references and index.
ISBN 0-8020-8828-7.   ISBN 0-8020-8602-0 (pbk.)

1. Modernism (Literature) – Italy.   2. Italian literature – 20th century –
History and criticism.   3. Italian literature – 19th century – History
and criticism.   4. Literature and history – Italy – History – 20th century.
5. Literature and history – Italy – History – 19th century.   I. Somigli,
Luca   II. Moroni, Mario, 1955–   III. Series.

PQ4088.173 2003   850.9'112   C2003-906908-7

Publication of this book was made possible by a Senate Research Grant from
Victoria University, University of Toronto.

University of Toronto Press acknowledges the financial assistance to its
publishing program of the Canada Council for the Arts and the Ontario Arts
Council.

University of Toronto Press acknowledges the financial support for its
publishing activities of the Government of Canada through the Book Publishing Industry Development Program (BPIDP).

Contents

Acknowledgments

The publication of this volume was made possible by a generous Senate Research Grant from Victoria University.

The essays by Antonio Saccone and Keala Jewell are published with permission of, respectively, Pendragon editore and The Pennsylvania State University Press.

The editors would like to thank Patrizia Di Vincenzo and Christine Sansalone for their assistance in translating some of the material into Italian, and Marisa Ruccolo for her help in compiling the index.

Foreword: After *The Conquest of the Stars*

Étoile mourante, hélas! À demi-nue et toute flexueuse
avec sa chair moite et verdissante!
...
Elle m'inonda de ses larmes d'amour,
l'inconsolable Étoile de mon Rêve!

> F.T. Marinetti, *La Conquête des étoiles* (1902)

[A dying Star, alas! Half-naked and supple
with her flesh drenched and livid!
...
She flooded me with her love tears,
the inconsolable Star of my Dream!]

> F.T. Marinetti, *The Conquest of the Stars* (1902)

Italian Modernism marks a significant turn in the development of contemporary research – in Italy, the United States, and elsewhere – on modern Italian literature. Italianists in Italy are often content to rehearse the (undeniable but in itself not very interesting) fact that in Italian literature the category of 'modernism' has never been really at home. The editors of this book (Mario Moroni and Luca Somigli), on the other hand, have finally decided to take the logical next step: to acclimatize this category in the landscape of contemporary critical discourse on modern Italian literature, thus making this territory more accessible and comparable with the general panorama of other European (as well as non-European) literatures.

One might think such an effort pleonastic for a literature that, thanks in part to Filippo Tommaso Marinetti and his Futurist movement, has been one of the creators of the very idea of modernism. But Italian literature (both in its primary language and in its critical metalanguage) is paradoxical. Indeed, I know of no other great literature in the modern period that has demonstrated the same amount of self-criticism (at the limit of defeatism) cultivating, at least at the level of traditional popularizing statements, a less-than-positive, and reductive, image of whole periods of its own history, including the late Renaissance and Baroque, Romanticism, and (until recently) that peculiar mixture of Symbolism and Futurism that gave birth to Italian modernism. One might say that, traditionally, Italian literature has not seemed very interested in the idea of 'selling' itself, as far as its history after the end of the sixteenth century is concerned.

It is high time to abandon this suicidally selective and hardly communicative attitude. Italianists should reclaim the continuous greatness and international relevance of the literature they study, from its origins to today, including its conflictual and ambiguous situation during the period of the Fascist dictatorship (it is not the least of the above-noted paradoxes that this overdue vindication of the importance of Italian modernism comes about at the initiative of two expatriate Italian scholars).

The problem with the implementation of the category of modernism at this point in time, however, is that the development of a large critical literature has revealed the ambiguities and uncertainties connected to it, so that a unified theory of modernism is no longer possible or even desirable. (All the essays in this book are of high scholarly quality; the most stimulating among them are the ones that show a critical attitude towards their own categories, and the future development of those categories.)[1] The most we can hope for in the present situation is the elaboration of some general perspectives on modernism, rather than formal definitions of the phenomenon.

For instance, we can look at modernism as a locus of paradox – 'the paradox of an art freed in principle and yet neutralized in practice. It is this paradox which provides the context for, and in a general way defines, the phenomenon of modernism in art' (Adamson, 222) – so that modernism would appear to be a particularly apt vehicle for the generally paradoxical nature of Italian culture and society. This kind of tension can be further specified in socio-political terms: 'Committed politically to leading an aestheticization of the public sphere that challenged all parties, left and right, that failed to face up to the crisis of values in the social and political world, the early modernists were also committed culturally to a politicization of art. Cultural against actually existing politics, they were also political against actually existing cultures' (Adamson, 223). In this vein, we can also have recourse to some of those broad categories, like 'bourgeoisie' and 'capitalism,' that seem to have taken the place of theological concepts in the secular religion of modern times, observing, for instance, that in this period a division develops in 'the field of artistic production along a major fault line, separating industrial literature, which obeys the demands and rules of the marketplace, from high art, which finds in the rejection of the norms of bourgeois society its own validation. It is this critical and at times radically anti-bourgeois thrust that defines, in broad strokes, modernist literature.' At the same time, this 'oppositionality' may grow in opposite directions, from the reactionary to the revolutionary (Somigli, 310 ff.).

On the other hand, and leaving aside for the moment the political problem, it is sobering to note that the critique that is appropriately aimed at the old-fashioned category of decadentism could also be applied to modernism: 'Despite a large bibliography, Italian *Decadentismo* appears to be, in fact, an excogitation *a posteriori*, developed by critics to explain cultural phenomena and attitudes that were simply *contemporary* to each other and that seemed to lie beyond the realm of other possible designations' (Moroni, 66). Indeed, it is hard to find a category in literary history that could not be subject to the same criticism, whether or not we accept 'the principle of concomitance rather than disjunction' (Ceserani, 38). In the field we are dealing with here, the basic inadequacy of intellectual(istic) categories for describing concrete literary phenomena could be summarized by stating that, if a label like 'decadentism' is misleading, 'modernism' is always already belated, and 'postmodernism' is premature. But, before slipping into a Wildian cynicism or a post-Crocean irrationalism with respect to the application of these and similar critical categories, an important distinction should be maintained: whereas 'decadentism' is irremediably compromised by its moralistic and ideological connotations, 'modernism' can and should be salvaged because of its more descriptive and detached tone. Admittedly, the term sends us back to the essentially mysterious nature of the concept of time, as debated at least from Saint Augustine to Bergson (see also the discussion in note 2), but it is still functional to a hermeneutic circulation of knowledge, by virtue of which the specific texts studied in this book throw some light on what we might mean by modernism, at the same time as the modernist emblem plausibly defines a general mental landscape.

Perhaps we should be more mindful of the fact that the rhythm of history is very slow. This is one of the realities of life that the arrogantly noble utopianism of modernist avant-gardes tries to ignore – or rather, valiantly (and uselessly) fights against. Not only have we, at the beginning of the third millennium, still to come fully to terms with thinkers like Heidegger: we have still to come to terms with his predecessor Nietzsche, *his* predecessor Kierkegaard, and *his* predecessor Hegel (whom not even Kierkegaard succeeded in exorcizing and laying to rest).

History might be said to move very slowly, or, conversely, human events may be regarded as a mere blip in the history of the cosmos. But these two apparently contrary views are actually united by the same consequence, in the way we look at historical events, or historical events look at, as well as to, us, in what might be called the ethos of history. That is, no single historical event at bottom matters very much, because it is always part of a slow and complex evolution, *and* because its scale, with regard to universal reality, is infinitesimal.[2]

Italian literature – or more precisely, Italian literary thought – is perhaps one of the most impressive international illustrations of this slow movement (we return to the Italian paradoxes). When Italian literature ceased to be the moving force of European literature, many Italian literary thinkers began to play what can be called the game of the past (a game that Marinetti among others found exasperating): that is, they uttered a series of sophisticated 'No's' to the ideas and movements that came from abroad, especially from Northern Europe. For instance, Leopardi brilliantly eluded the issue of Romanticism (which is the whole issue of early modern, or premodern, literary thought) in the name of the Classic tradition; later, Vincenzo Cardarelli and (more subtly) Giuseppe Ungaretti, elegantly circumnavigated the issue of modernism in the name of Leopardi and Petrarch. But then, what is the issue of modernism? Or, more ambitiously, what is the philosophy of modernism? Put in this form, the question is of course too vague. Let me try to clarify it.

When I ask about the philosophy of modernism, I am not (primarily) asking what is the philosophical system which is most representative of modernism – an interesting question but a very difficult one to answer. There is no single philosophy of modernism but several competing ones with conflicting claims, from the heretical trends of modern Christianity (it is not by chance that the term 'modernismo' in Italian cultural history has a para-Catholic reference) to the heretical trends of modern Judaism (Freud's thought being perhaps the prime instance) to the various trends of that quintessentially modern heresy – the heresy of modernity – that is Marxism. (More or less radical forms of heresy are the driving forces of modern philosophical and theological thought.) Nor am I (foremostly) asking what is the philosophical system that is best suited to interpret modernism *a posteriori* – another interesting question, and again, one that is difficult to answer, because the misleadingly uniform rhetoric of 'postmodernism' obscures several different and competing philosophies – which are, by and large, the more or less thoroughly updated versions of the philosophies of modernism (the slow rhythm of history, again). For instance, Marxist trends tend to survive, somewhat sheepishly, in ideologies like feminism and cultural studies, while on the other hand Christian trends, Catholic or not, seem to have, with honorable exceptions, renounced even the attempt to elaborate some new perspective on world culture and literature. The Judaeo-Christian rhetoric has become a thoroughly secularized rhetoric, leading to a reductive view of modernism, since 'Mysticism – its definition, and the appropriation of its power – is at the heart of the modernist crisis. This is the crucial intuition that literary modernism, in particular in its decadent and symbolist roots, brings to religious modernism' (Wittman, 131).

When I ask what the philosophy of modernism is the question I propose is more modest, but perhaps also more ambitious, than the ones just evoked. More modest, because I do not presume to identify, much less to privilege, a single full-fledged philosophical system; more ambitious, because I am thinking of nothing less than a general characterization of the mental tone or atmosphere of modernism.

The philosophy of modernism is a form of erosion, or subtle vulgarization (a necessary oxymoron), of philosophy – a 'filosofia bruciata,' as I have called it elsewhere; where 'bruciata' means neither 'burned out,' nor, at the other extreme, 'burning': rather, it refers to a desertified, scorched-earth kind of thought.[3] This 'filosofia bruciata' consists essentially in a questioning of philosophy as a consistent, non-contradictory system – a kind of degradation of philosophy as systematic thought. The philosophical tone of modernism is one of indifference towards the principle of non-contradiction – an indifference that does not bother with the niceties of Hegelian dialectics. The enduring, and disquieting, legacy of modernism is its dizzying capacity for simultaneously saying everything and the contrary of everything – and the champion of modernism is appropriately Futurism, which creates the rhetoric of the avant-garde on the international scene thanks mostly to its frightening ability to juggle aporias (I listed some of them elsewhere). This relaxed attitude towards consistency characterizes modernism not only in the cultural but also in the socio-political sphere; indeed, such a philosophical (or post-philosophical, or para-philosophical)) strategy can be called a form of vulgarization because it powerfully represents the philosophy of the man in the street, who (to limit myself to one example that is particularly relevant to the rhetoric of modernism) has become adept at employing the term 'bourgeois' with a tone of ironic superiority in the same breath in which (s)he extols the elements of bourgeois conformism.

Having sketched the answer to one ambitious question, I will be so bold (the intellectual restlessness, not to say recklessness, of modernism encourages such boldness) as to ask another, equally daring, one: What is next? Postmodernism has turned out to be, by and large, a coda to modernism; and since one of the distinctive features of modernism is the speed (some might say, the unseemly haste) with which it consumes the various positions and attitudes which it itself creates, postmodernism in its wake seems to have exhausted itself almost as thoroughly as modernism. The question 'What is next?', in the continuous fast-forward rhythm of (post)modernism, thus translates into 'And what now?'

Well, the 'returns to order' are always possible: after all, Italy can rightfully boast that she, after having given birth to the first great avant-garde movement in Europe, generated the first great reaction in Europe against that very movement ('ritorno all'ordine' is originally an Italian expression). We could then search the current artistic and intellectual landscape for signs of such 'returns,' and we would be sure to find some significant such signs. But there is always something predictable and predetermined about these findings, although specialized research along these lines enriches our detailed knowledge of the period.

Perhaps the story that awaits us – the story of which we are already a part – is more simple than that, and it has to do, once again, with the slow rhythm of history. Literary history is not necessarily made up of successive, clearly distinguishable, movements that we can characterize as opposite to one another, thus remembering them more easily. There is undeniably a vivaciousness and an excitement in the way a historian (literary or not) is able to show how, say, the correction even of one year in the dating of a novel or play or painting can modify our view of the work in question and of its position in a given cultural context. But at the same time there is something slightly absurd about all this – something hurried and a bit hysterical – a spectacle that the avant-garde (I think for instance of Futurist theatre) is so good in both exalting and demystifying.

Literary history should resist the pull of Futurism's fascination with velocity, and insert modernism into the rhythm of a long and slow view of history. There is a 'multiplicity that only certain cultures possess by virtue of their longevity and their "long view"' (Jewell, 367). My previous reference to Hegel was also meant to suggest that in literature we are still absorbing the end-of-the-eighteenth-century shock of Romanticism; so that the abbreviation used above – (post)modernism – is not simply a play on words. It is important to ask 'can we also think of modernism as a critical anticipation of exactly those themes and metaphors which structure the self-understanding of postmodernism?' (Somigli, 335). This formula is a way of ensuring that statements like 'As a modernist, then, de Chirico already behaves as a postmodernist' (Hirsh, 410) do not sound like parodies of themselves.

What is at stake, in this historiographical slowing down, is nothing less than the chance of properly *contemplating* single works of art. This idea of contemplation is clear with regard to the visual arts (as exemplified in this book especially by Giorgio de Chirico's paintings), but it concerns, in a more important because not self-evident way, the literary texts as well; and the category of listening (which I developed elsewhere) is the auditory equivalent of the visually based experience of contemplation. In fact, the appreciation of any kind of work of art is at heart a synesthetic experience, which is particularly enhanced in the act of reading. Reading a page is also a way of *looking* at the words, and through them at the referred images (this act of looking at the words as concrete objects is particularly important in the perception of poetic texts); it is also a way of *listening* to the oral discourse that underlies the page. This comprehensive view of the act of reading makes it clearer that ideas of listening to the whispered discourse of a painting, or contemplating the architecture of a musical piece, are something more than fancy images: they are cognitively significant metaphors.

Contemplation allows us to develop an ontological perspective on texts, and generally on works of art and culture. Now, (post)modernism is perhaps the most articulate challenge to such a contemplative attitude towards the work of art – a contemplation that (to repeat) brings to the fore the ontology of the work. Future work on modernism, then – in the wake of innovative collections like the present one – might also take the form of an effort to, so to speak, save modernism from itself. And it is not by chance that the strongest philosophical advocate in the twentieth century of the ontological look at works of art and culture is Heidegger, that resolutely anti-modern(ist) thinker. What I am elaborating is an attitude of slowing down – taking one's time, in order to develop a long view of the texts. Such a long view makes it possible for the critic to calibrate more carefully the real achievements of the period, to see that the most significant works, authors, movements sometimes turn out to be those which, to a fast-moving view, may appear marginal and out of step.

The most glaring example of such an equivocation in modern Italian literature (see note 5) is the case of Gabriele d'Annunzio, still too often the object of a historiographical and esthetic myopia which relegates him to some sort of nineteenth-century archaeology, or flattens his extraordinary achievements with a pseudo-sociological approach. The truth (that Marinetti, for instance, anxiously intuited) is that the genial Symbolist experimentation of d'Annunzio is essentially what makes modernism possible in Italian literature. D'Annunzio was 'among the first writers in Europe to explore the labyrinthine link between eroticism, the unconscious, the body, temporality, myth, and the death drive' (Re, 103.)

The critic, then, can never relax his or her guard against the recurrent temptations of reductionism and determinism: there is no necessary, unified, privileged connection between the single works of art, philosophy, and so forth created in a given historical period and the main features which, by accretion and sedimentation, are most often used in elaborating the traditional narrative about that period.[4]

Such a fruitful dis-connection (which does not mean, of course, the lack of any relationship) deserves to be underscored, because philosophico-literary historiography must constantly defend its phenomenological detachment against the encroachment of unilateral political posturings. For instance, the darkest period in modern European history witnessed a richness of divergent philosophical, theological, critical systems (and anti-systems) of thought: the uncompromising reflections of Antonio Gramsci, Piero Gobetti, Simone Weil, Walter Benjamin, and Dietrich Bonhoeffer; the uncompromised theologizing of Karl Barth and others; the more-or-less uncompromised philoso-

phizing of Benedetto Crose et al.: the brilliantly compromised meditations of Giovanni Gentile and Martin Heidegger, etc.; the turbidly
compromised conceptions of Julius Evola, etc. This list is partial and
discontinuous, but not haphazard; while clearly insufficient, it is nevertheless necessary as a starting point for an honest assessment. There
is no easy lesson, no facile moralizing or ideologizing, to be drawn
from this uneasy coexistence.

In fact, the historical connections of modernism are as broad as they
are disquieting: modernist literature coexists with the formation of
modern imperialism and with the birth of the two totalitarian systems
that tragically renewed for the twentieth century the dramatic urgency
of that Stendahlian title, *The Red and the Black*; and nowhere is that
coexistence more intimate and perplexing than in Italy, the birthplace
of one of the two totalitarian creatures. At first sight, modernism, with
its rhetoric of fragmentation, would seem to be intrinsically opposed
to the forcible and forced rhetoric of unification implicit in the very
term 'totalitarianism.' The actual situation is considerably more complex, and only now – now that we have apparently left the twentieth
century behind – have we begun to analyse the full extent of that
complexity. I say 'apparently' because we will not come out of the
Novecento until we develop a phenomenologically detached view of it,
and we will not attain such a view until we achieve full distance from
both forms of totalitarianism. The politically correct focus on 'such
monsters as Fascism, Nazism, and racism' (Ceserani, 45) is both too
broad and too narrow. It is too broad because the term 'racism' (eroded
by current opportunisms and partisan squabbles) no longer identifies
clearly enough that distinctive modernist horror, the genocide of the
Holocaust, and too narrow because it no longer seems possible (as it
often was for Italian literary historiography, until recently) to keep
totalitarian communism out of that monster list, or to euphemize and
personalize the issue by salvaging communism and reserving the blame
for 'Stalinism.'

These implications and entanglements are not to be conceived in a
deterministic perspective: there is no straightforward cause-and-effect
relationship between Fascism, Nazism, imperialism, and communism
on the one hand and philosophico-literary modernism on the other.
What is called for is an analysis that respects the full complexity of the
web of interrelationships. Before being shot for his collaborationism,
the critic and novelist Robert Brasillach hinted at the poetic nature of
two of the above-listed monsters, twinning Fascism and communism

as 'the poetry of the twentieth century.'[5] One does not have to agree with this hyperbolic, unilateral, and ultimately desperate idea, but one should also not be too shocked by it. The suggestion is not completely irrational, not so much because of the enduring importance of so many compromised poets (Bertolt Brecht, Ezra Pound), but rather because poetry, if not monstrous, is at least irreducible to morality. (This is one of the features that poetry has in common with religion – one of the genealogies of theological modernism being Kierkegaard's famous analyses of the divarication between religion and morality.) My proposal is actually very modest: I am simply suggesting that the literary historian (as any other historian) cannot adequately criticize one of the two totalitarian formations of the twentieth century while remaining entangled in the principles of the other totalitarian formation.

Returning to Italy, this extreme laboratory of modernity: to speak of the modernistic nature of Fascism is not the same thing as alleging a fascistic nature of modernism; the former connection is hard to deny, the latter is demonstrably false. It seems to me that politically interested and interesting literary analyses of Italian modernism at the heart of the twentieth century have passed through two phases, a puritanical phase and a purist one. In the first, puritanical, phase, a simplistic opposition is developed between the category 'Fascism' and the category 'culture,' as if they were incompatible – hence the rhetoric about Italian culture 'under' Fascism. The fact that this strategy was originally understandable because of certain political and social conditions[6] does not make it any the less inadequate. This black-and-white (or black-and-red) assessment has by and large been superseded by a more subtle kind of analysis, purist rather than puritanical (some of whose best results are represented by American scholarship on these issues). This more sophisticated criticism is aware of the complexity of the Fascist phenomenon, but seems to be very concerned with the danger of contagion, as if it were still worried about what has been called, with an effective alliterative label, 'the fascination with Fascism,' evoking the picture of an 'innocent' (see below) passerby hypnotized and dominated by the relentless, icy gaze of some witch or magician. Hence, the minute dissection of literary and generally esthetic productions, to extract from them something that is often described as the 'stain' or 'taint' of Fascism.

But the immersion in the diverse landscape of Italian modernism reflected in this rich collection has reinforced an idea that had been for some time developing in the mind of one observer: the time has come to abandon excessively hygienic, or quarantine-oriented, preoccupations, and to study Italian culture – literature, philosophy, the arts, and so forth – as it develops above, under, and through Fascism (the Italian attribute 'trasversale' may be useful here). This phenomenologically descriptive and detached critique requires in turn a detachment from (to repeat) all forms of totalitarian *Novecento* ideologies. European scholars, justifiably worried by the European origins of these more-or-less-poetic monstrosities, may take refuge, and pride, in that other, much more reassuring European creation rooted in the Enlightenment, that is, liberalism.[7] Liberalism has a rich history in non-extremist Italy: beside the already-quoted Gobetti and Croce, one thinks, for example, of those modern forms of Catholic thought of which Antonio Fogazzaro's essayistic novels are one of the first modernist poetizations.

But here American (or American-based) scholars and critics would seem to have a great advantage with respect to their European counterparts, because the enlightened origins of their cultural history (which are, of course, European) excluded any direct conspiration in the creation of those monster-poetics, although America felt their deep effects. It is as if the American critics might vindicate, in the study of modernism as well as of other cultural formations, a strong and critically articulated position of *innocence*: not innocence as a synonym of naiveté (still a widespread European cliché about Americans in general), but innocence as a form of hard-gained purity.

The situation, however, turns out to be considerably more complicated than that, if we look at the actual interaction of the primary and secondary forms of rhetoric. American innocence (both in the weak and the strong variant of the concept) is irremediably compromised by the evolution of American imperialism, which from the late nineteenth century to the present runs parallel to the history of American (post)modernism. This large problem cannot be dealt with here,[8] and in any case one has to insist on the absence of deterministic cause-and-effect relationships. But the point is that the American critical look at modernism, as well as other cultural phenomena, is at bottom not any the more innocent than the European one. As already noted with respect to the apparent opposition between the logic of modernism and that of totalitarianism, there would seem to be a deep contrast between the apparently 'soft' category of modernism – with its connotations of anarchic individualism, e(s)th(et)ic rebelliousness, fluidity, cosmopolitan nomadism – and the prima facie 'hard' category of empire, with its connotations of tight political organization, economic rationalization, and systematic application of military power. There is indeed a truth to this contrast, and one could trace a whole history of opposition between, for instance, the modernist style in Italy and the imperial ambition that found its broadest, but not its first, expression during the Fascist period.[9] And yet, once again (as in the case of modernism and totalitarianism), the actual rhetorical interaction is more complicated.

There is indeed a whole dimension of modernistic literature – its aggressive utopianism, its energetic celebration of strength and decisiveness, its scorn for conformism, social mores, etc. – that lends itself to the celebration of empire, whether it be the 'reactionary' Italian empire, the 'revolutionary' Russian empire, or the 'democratic' American empire (phenomenological descriptivism is here more important than ever). But modernism's capacity for simultaneously expressing contrary notions (a capacity explicitly theorized by Marinetti), is revealed also in its ambivalent attitude towards violence and its celebration of both the 'hard' machines glamorized by Futurism and various type of 'soft' machines.[10] Finally, the American connection between modernism and imperialism is more subtle. American modernism, with its open-space and generously experimental rhetoric seems to have realized a kind of philosophical master move: the hollowing out, so to speak, of the American empire, freeing it from its self-consciousness as empire. The American empire, then, is perhaps the first in world history that resolutely refuses to conceptualize itself as an empire; and this refusal (as Europeans find hard to accept) is not so much a form of hypocrisy – a Machiavellian gesture in the degraded sense of the term – but a deep conviction that importantly modifies the style and perhaps the substance of this empire. The consequence is that the basic imperial style, from ancient Rome to Great Britain to Fascist Italy, appears archaic with respect to the American style even as it begins to take shape in the time of Theodore Roosevelt. In other words, the American empire has a distinctively modernist style. This is of course a larger history than the one covered in the present book; but the basic importance of *Italian Modernism* lies in my opinion in the way in which this collection encourages thought, exploration, and criticism.

Paolo Valesio
Yale University

NOTES

1 One should distinguish a secondary rhetoric (the metalanguage of criticism) from a primary rhetoric: the creatively structured use of language in literature, philosophy, and so forth (the distinction, as in all such cases, is significant but relative – as proved by that indispensable and hybrid genre, the essay). Any structured use of language has an unavoidable ritual quality about it, so that, to come to the case in point, the rituals of modernistic literature – its recurrent invocations and evocations, its tics and tricks – are parallel by analogous rituals in modernistic criticism. This is inevitable, and it is even a good thing (recurrences confer a certain compactness and recognizability on a whole field of discourse, just as they confer it on a single poem), but it is also good occasionally to question the traditional citational hierarchies within a given critical rhetoric. Certain authors are over-cited (and we know who they are), while others are under-cited. To confine myself to just one example: the study of the great modernist obsession with repetition should, so to speak, repeatedly insist on its basic genealogy, that bewildering philosophico-epistolary novel by 'Constantin Constantius,' *Repetition: A Venture in Experimental Psychology* [1843] (see Kierkegaard, *Fear and Trembling*). The problem goes beyond specific philologies and genealogies; as an economist (quoted in the *New York Times*, 26 July 2003, B9) noted a quarter-century ago: 'Research reflects prevailing moods at least as much as it influences them.'

2 'What we formerly called history is ended – an intermediary moment of five thousand years between the prehistoric centuries in which the globe was populated and the world history which is now beginning. Three millennia, measured by the preceding era of man's existence and by future possibilities, are a minute interval. In this interval men may be said to have gathered together, to have mustered their forces for the action of world history, to have acquired the intellectual and technical equipment they needed for the journey which is just beginning' (Jaspers 103–4). The initial part of this passage is more convincing than the last, although one might be tempted to say that this idea of 'the journey which is just beginning,' originally enunciated in the 1950s, is prophetic with respect to the hopes and aspirations of contemporary mankind. But this is precisely the problem: always applicable, this futuristic idea risks being irrelevant – like the eloquent utterances of the Biblical prophets (only they were not naively intent on predicting the future, nor on moralizing about the present: they tried instead to attain an ontological position outside of history). The

ambiguity of the quoted passage is pertinent to the question of modernism. 'Modernism' is an essentially *deictic* term: it really makes sense only with respect to the existential position of the subject who uses it (which is a fortiori true also of 'postmodernism').

3 I insist on this Italian expression, 'filosofia bruciata,' in its original form: the metalanguage of modernism is too narrowly dominated by the imperial claims of the French and English languages. Apropos of this contemporary and international 'questione della lingua': the fact that all the essays in this book are written in (or at least translated into) English has obvious advantages, but it also confronts us with an unavoidable ambiguity, as we miss the epistemological flavour of the secondary Italian rhetoric (see note 1) applied to the primary Italian rhetoric. But the interplay of advantages and disadvantages may reserve some surprise (if the present non-native writer may venture an observation on English usage): while the 'native' American essays are clearly more lively in their idiomatic-stylistic implementation, they tend also, at times, to be prone to jargon and to be a bit self-conscious.

4 'It is a far remove from the opinions held generally in a given epoch to the content of the philosophical works created in that epoch' (Jaspers 142). To return to the distinction mentioned in note 1: what we actually face in any given period of literary history is not one secondary rhetoric paralleling one primary rhetoric, but conflicting *rhetorics*, on both the secondary and the primary level. This may sound obvious: how else would literary scholarship progress, if not by virtue of fruitful disagreements and successive readjustments? Or (to put it in a less reverent and more Wildian way): How else would individual scholars in the humanities justify their grant applications, and universities with strong humanities components, their fund-raising efforts? What is less obvious – and here lies the real challenge of rhetoric as a discipline – is the possibility of a meta-rhetoric that would analyse and evaluate, in each given case, the turbulent chorus of secondary and primary rhetorics.

5 For the full quotation, see my *Gabriele d'Annunzio* (27–8).

6 The conditions I refer to have essentially to do with Italy's defeat in the Second World War, one of whose results on the cultural plane is a peculiar, and slightly perverse, coupling of the triumphalistic ideology of the victors with the victimistic ideology of the vanquished. The Italian author who perhaps expresses in the most effective way the mixture of tragedy and grotesqueness which marks the peculiarity of this ideological marriage is Curzio Malaparte.

7 It is useful to keep in mind that, in European political discourse, 'liberal' is a synonym, rather than an antonym, for 'moderate.'

8 Suffice it to cite a serious and ambitious analysis like that undertaken by Hardt and Negri in *Empire*. This analysis, however, still did not leave the oppressive *Novecento* atmosphere behind, because it is entangled in one of its two master-pseudo-narratives or monster-poetics. The book that opens with a scornful dismissal of an early-nineteenth-century social theory as 'a fantastic utopia' (6) ends more than four hundred pages later with a contradictory statement (echoing Marx's *Communist Manifesto*) that is a bit sinister and also a little pathetic: 'This is the irrepressible lightness and joy of being communist' (413). We remain in a situation of sad symmetry with the disparate and desperate hyperboles exemplified by the quotation from Robert Brasillach.

9 One instance of this is Aldo Palazzeschi's, *Due imperi .... mancati* (the four ellipses belong to the original title).

10 There is a rhetorical strain connecting a modernist title like Gertrude Stein's *Tender Buttons: Objects, Food, Rooms* (originally published in semi-private form by a very small New York publishing house, Claire Marie, in 1914) to a 'postmodernist' title like *The Soft Machine*, by William Burroughs, originally published in Paris in 1961 by the adventurous Olympia Press. One thinks also of Surrealist-style paintings (the most popular ones are those by Salvador Dalí) that represent melting machines.

WORKS CITED

Hardt, Michael, and Antonio Negri. *Empire*. Cambridge: Harvard UP, 2000.

Jaspers, Karl. *Way to Wisdom: An Introduction to Philosophy*. 2nd ed. Trans. Ralph Manheim, intro. Richard M. Owsley. New Haven and London: Yale UP, 1951.

Kierkegaard, Søren. *Fear and Trembling; Repetition*. Ed. and trans. Howard V. Hong and Edna H. Hong. Princeton: Princeton UP, 1983.

Palazzeschi, Aldo. *Due imperi .... mancati*. Florence: Vallecchi, 1920.

Valesio, Paolo. *Gabriele d'Annunzio: The Dark Flame*. Trans. Marilyn Migiel. New Haven and London: Yale UP, 1992.

Contributors

Walter L. Adamson teaches modern European intellectual history and the history of modern Italy at Emory University. He is the author of *Avant-garde Florence: From Modernism to Fascism* (1993), which won the American Historical Association's Marraro Prize for the best book in Italian history. He has also written numerous articles on European modernism, fascism, and Marxism, and is currently at work on a book devoted to avant-garde intellectual responses to commodity culture in Europe, 1900–1950.

Enrico Cesaretti currently is an assistant professor of Italian at the University of Virginia. After receiving his PhD in Italian from Yale University, he held positions at the University of Michigan and Wake Forest University. His research concentrates mostly on nineteenth- and twentieth-century Italian literature. He is the author of *Castelli di carta: Retorica della dimora tra Scapigliatura e Surrealismo* (2001) and articles on Tommaseo, the Scapigliati, and Futurism.

Remo Ceserani is professor of comparative literature at the University of Bologna. He also taught at universities in Milan, Berkeley, Genoa, and Pisa and was a visiting professor at numerous other universities. He has edited, with Lidia De Federicis, a well-known anthology for the study of literature, *Il materiale e l'immaginario* (Turin, 1979–95). Among his most recent publications are *Raccontare la letteratura* (1990), *Il romanzo sui pattini* (1990), *Treni de carta* (1993; new edition 2002), *Il fantastico* (1996), *Viaggio del dottor Dapertutto* (1996), *Raccontare il postmoderno* (1997), *Lo straniero* (1998), *Guida allo studio della letteratura* (1999), and *Guida breve allo studio della letteratura* (2003). He was for six years the president of the Italian association of comparative literature.

Allison Cooper is a lecturer in the Department of French and Italian at Colby College. Her research and teaching interests include Italian modernism and the avant-garde, technology and the self in early twentieth-century Europe, and Italian cinema. She is currently working on a book-length study of the effects of the Great War on painting and literature in Italy.

Cristina Della Coletta is an associate professor of Italian in the Department of Spanish, Italian, and Portuguese at the University of Virginia. She has published numerous articles on modern and contemporary Italian literature, particularly historical fiction, fiction-to-film adaptation theories, and cultural and women's studies. Della Coletta is the author of *Plotting the Past: Metamorphoses of Historical Narratives in Modern Italian Fiction* (1996). She received numerous grants and awards such as the NEH Horace W. Goldsmith Distinguished Teaching Professorship at the University of Virginia (2002–5), and the University of Virginia/Terza Università de Roma Research Grant (2001). She is currently completing a book on exotic narratives in late-nineteenth and early-twentieth-century Italy.

Manuela Gieri is Associate Professor of Italian and Cinema Studies at the University of Toronto, where she is also an associate member of the Centre for Comparative Literature and the director of the Graduate Program in Semiotics. She has published extensively in scholarly journals and edited volumes on Italian cinema, Luigi Pirandello, and contemporary Italian women's writing. In recent years, she has authored a volume on Italian cinema entitled *Contemporary Italian Filmmaking: Strategies of Subversion* (1995), and with her dear friend, the late Professor Gian Paolo Biasin, she has co-edited *Luigi Pirandello: Contemporary Perspectives* (1999).

Thomas Harrison is Professor of Italian at UCLA and specializes in nineteenth- and twentieth-century aesthetics. He is the author of *1910: The Emancipation of Dissonance* (1996), and *Essayism: Conrad, Musil, and Pirandello* (1992), and the editor of *Nietzsche in Italy* (1988) and *The Favorite Malice: Ontology and Reference in Contemporary Italian Poetry* (1983).

Jennifer Hirsh recently completed her PhD in the Department of History of Art at Bryn Mawr College. She is currently Visiting Assistant

Professor in the Department of Art at Oberlin College, where she teaches courses on modern and contemporary art and architecture. She has published previously on de Chirico as well as on other aspects of modern Italian art and architecture, and on postwar cinema.

Keala Jewell is the Paul D. Paganucci professor of Italian Studies at Darmouth College, where she teaches Italian language and literature, as well as in the comparative literature and the gender and women's studies programs. She holds a PhD from the University of Wisconsin, Madison. She edited *Monsters in the Italian Literary Imagination* (2001) and co-edited *The Defiant Muse: Italian Feminist Poems from the Middle Ages to the Present* (1986), and authored *The Poiesis of History: Experimenting with Genre in Postwar Italy* (1992). Her most recent book, *The Art of Enigma: The de Chirico Brothers' Politics of Modernity* (2004), focuses on the intersections of literature and art history.

Mario Moroni is the Paul and Marilyn Paganucci Assistant Professor of Italian at Colby College. He has published a book on Antonio Porta and another on subjectivity in the poetics of modernity entitled *La presenza complessa* (1998). His articles on nineteenth- and twentieth-century Italian and European literature have been published in many magazines in Italy, the United States, and Canada.

Lucia Re, who received her PhD in comparative literature from Yale, has taught Italian literature and culture at the University of California in Los Angeles since 1982. Her book *Calvino and the Age of Neorealism: Fables of Estrangement* (1990) was awarded the MLA Marraro prize for the best book in Italian studies in 1990–2. She has received a National Endowment for the Humanities Fellowship and a Getty Senior Research Grant. Her current research and scholarly interests include the relationship between Futurism, Fascism, and feminism, gender issues in nineteenth- and twentieth-century literature and art, and comparative theories of gender and feminism. She has recently completed a book entitled *Women and the Avant-Garde*.

Antonio Saccone is professor of modern and contemporary Italian literature at the Università di Napoli Federico II. His major studies include the monographs *Massimo Bontempelli: Il mito del '900* (1979), *Marinetti e il futurismo* (1984), *L'occhio narrante: Tre studi sul primo Palazzeschi* (1987), *Carlo Dossi: La scrittura del margine* (1995), *Futurismo*

(2000), and *"La trincea avanzata" e "la città dei conquistatori": Futurismo e modernità* (Liguori, 2000), as well and as numerous essays on Ungaretti. He has also contributed to the *Manuale di Letteratura Italiana* published by Bollati Boringhieri. He has been a visiting professor at Yale University and at the Sorbonne.

Luca Somigli is Associate Professor of Italian Studies at the University of Toronto. He is the author of *Legitimizing the Artist: Manifesto Writing and European Modernism, 1885–1915,* and the co-editor of *The Literary Journal as a Cultural Witness* (1996) and of a volume of the *Dictionary of Literary Biography* entitled *Italian Prose Writers, 1900–1945* (2002). He has published numerous essays on Italian modernist authors, including Marinetti, Bontempelli, Savinio, and Primo Conti.

Paolo Valesio is Professor of Italian Language and Literature at Yale University. In 1997 he founded the journal *Yale Italian Poetry (YIP),* which he continues to direct. He is the coordinator of the Yale Poetry Group and is the American correspondent of the Milan-based monthly *Poesia.* Valesio is a poet, literary critic, essayist, and narrator. His critical works include *Gabriele d'Annunzio: The Dark Flame* (1992) and 'The Most Enduring and Most Honored Name' in *Filippo Tommaso Marinetti, Selected Poems and Related Prose* (2002). His fourteen published collections of poetry include the bilingual edition of *Every Afternoon Can Make the World Stand Still / Ogni meriggio puo' arrestare il mondo* (2002) and the trilingual volume (Italian with English and Spanish translations) *Volano in cento* (2002).

Laura Wittman is Assistant Professor of Italian and Comparative Literature at the University of California, Santa Barbara. She has published articles on Marinetti and Futurism, Benedetta Marinetti, Ungaretti, and Sereni. Her main research interest is the intersection of poetics, religion, and politics in modern Italy and France. She is currently at work on a book on the changing understanding of mysticism, and its relation to Modernism, in Italy and France at the last turn of the century.

ITALIAN MODERNISM

Italian Culture between Decadentism and Avant-Garde

Modernism in Italy: An Introduction

LUCA SOMIGLI AND MARIO MORONI

Modernism and Modernity

In introducing a special volume of the journal *Annali di Italianistica* on postmodernism in Italy, the editor Dino Cervigni noted the difficulty of dealing with such a category from the perspective of a cultural tradition in which modernism remains at best a vague and under-determined concept. Obviously, the issue is not that Italian culture has not gone through a 'modernist' phase – though the terms of that 'modernism' are precisely what need to be addressed – but rather that the word, if not the phenomenon itself, has until recently had very little purchase in the context of Italian arts and letters. In fact, it is arguably because of the 'importation' of postmodernism, first via the discourse of architecture and then that of philosophy, that it has been necessary to consider to what, precisely, postmodernism can be said to be *post*. The '-ism' in postmodernism is a suffix traditionally linked in Italian cultural discourse with specific and localized phenomena such as Decadentism, *Crepuscolarismo*, Futurism, and Hermeticism – in other words, with what Walter Binni would have called 'poetics' – and the term itself has raised some eyebrows, since from the beginning 'postmodernism' has been received as a more ambitious program – even, famously, a 'condition' – rather than the merely artistic project of a group or school. Investigation of the relationship between this supposed condition and the cultural production that characterizes it has led to conclusions that will appear familiar to scholars of Anglo-American modernism. For instance, Romano Luperini's blistering attack of postmodernism, from a Marxist perspective not unlike that of Fredric Jameson in *Postmodernism, or the Cultural Contradictions of Late*

Capitalism, was founded upon a distinction between postmodernity as 'a historical period, namely the age which began roughly forty years ago and which is characterized by the electronic and computer science revolution' and postmodernism as 'the ideology and the artistic tendencies which accept the self-representation of postmodernity' ('Bilancio di un trentennio' 7). However, in his analysis of certain contemporary cultural products, such as the works of the poets associated with the journal *Baldus*, Luperini also suggests the possibility of a critical instance that uses the tools of postmodernity to break down its monologic discourse. Thus, Luperini's reading of postmodern culture recalls similar descriptions of modernism, which also emphasize openness. Modernism, too, brings into focus the contradictions of modernity. Its celebratory dimension – most famously exemplified by what has been called Futurist 'modernolatry,' that is, the exaltation of progress and of industrial technology – is accompanied by a series of antagonistic and critical strategies which recent Anglo-American scholarship has brought into focus. For instance, Marshall Berman, in *All That Is Solid Melts into Air*, defines modernism as 'any attempt by modern men and women to become subjects as well as objects of modernization, to get a grip on the modern world and make themselves at home in it' (5), while for Astradur Eysteinsson modernism can be understood as 'an attempt to *interrupt* the modernity that we live and understand as a social, if not "normal," way of life' (6).

This is not to say, of course, that the term 'modernism' itself is foreign to Italian literary historiography and theory. Rather, what we want to suggest is that there have been historical reasons for its limited application. It is precisely because of its relative neutrality – its 'foreignness' to the Italian tradition, if you will – that modernism can serve as a less ideologically charged term to define a range of cultural experiences between the turn of the twentieth century and the Second World War. In other words, and to anticipate some of our conclusions, far from attempting to interpret modernism as a monolithic notion, yet another of the many '-isms' already canonized by cultural history, we use it as an 'open' or 'weak' epistemological category to access the constellation of cultural phenomena which reflect, in complex and contradictory ways, on the experience of modernity in Italy.

We must consider, first of all, the fact that in Italy, as in France, the term 'modernism' was introduced at the beginning of the twentieth century to indicate the religious movement within the Catholic Church which sought to 'democratize' its structures and, most importantly, suggested an 'evolutionary' view of dogma, which was, as Dennis Mack Smith puts it, 'not formulated once and for all, but could be expected to grow organically and change to suit the times' (202). Fiercely condemned by Pope Pius X in his 1907 encyclical *De modernistarum doctrinis* (also known as *Pascendi dominici gregis*), which associated modernism with 'the most blasphemous and most scandalous things that could be imagined from the perspective of Christian religiosity and tradition: [...] materialism, rationalism, atheism, anti-Catholicism and anti-Christianity' (Saresella 74), modernism was nevertheless influential for Catholic intellectuals who sought a closer relationship with the social reality of their time. It is certainly possible to establish links between it and a broader literary modernism, not only through such figures as the novelist Antonio Fogazzaro, discussed in Laura Wittman's essay, who were directly influenced by the debate within the Church, but more generally through the spiritual meditations of several writers of the period preceding the First World War, who saw both the necessity for a spiritual renewal after the crisis of nineteenth-century positivism and the loss of faith in the power of positivist science – and therefore also of its literary declensions, such as 'verismo' – but who were also unwilling to accept the institutional strictures of the Catholic church. It is in the light of a dialogue with the modernist instances of Catholicism that one can read the experience of writers such as Giovanni Papini, Piero Jahier, or Scipio Slataper, for whom writing becomes the central activity in an ethical and moral quest in which the Church represents a negative, repressive model and in which the desire for a more intimate relation with one's fellow human beings is ideologically sublimated by nationalism or a form of 'regionalist' solidarity.

We leave to Remo Ceserani's contribution a more thorough theoretical discussion of modernism. Here, we simply want to suggest that a broader notion of modernism as a constellation may account for the diversity of the cultural production of the period under consideration. In order to do this, it is necessary to examine the ways in which the period has been theorized within Italian literary historiography. The problem, as we see it, is that the most influential or simply the most common attempts to account for the cultural experiences between (to use two convenient sign posts) Carducci's late neo-Classicism and post-war neo-realism have employed overdeter-mined categories which have limited their range of application and obscured the common roots of the various forms of cultural production of the period. Here we will consider the two most common historiographic categories, Decadentism and the avant-garde.

As Walter Binni noted in his highly influential study *La poetica del decadentismo* (1936), by the 1930s the debate on the moral and ideological implications of the term 'Decadentism,' clearly related to its etymological origins, had relaxed to the point that it now seemed possible 'to consider Decadentism historically, to separate it from the abstract concept of decadence, to give it the same historical value that we give to "romanticism." Let us remember that even the term "romantic" can be used to indicate a more or less pathological character' (6). Binni's invocation of Romanticism was not casual, since at the time of his writing an established critical tradition considered *Decadentismo* as an excessive manifestation of the most extreme aspects of Romantic individualism and *superomismo*. According to Benedetto Croce, whose influence on this issue was especially long-lasting, Decadentism was first and foremost one of the currents of contemporary art which precipitated the more general crisis of Romanticism. As he wrote in the entry on 'Aesthetics' for the *Encyclopædia Britannica*,

> The crisis of the romantic period [...] asserted an antithesis between *naïve* and *sentimental* poetry, *classical* and *romantic* art, and thus denied the unity of art and asserted a duality of two fundamentally different arts, of which it took the side of the second, as that appropriate to the modern age, by upholding the primary importance in art of feeling, passion and fancy. [...] Later, it was thought that the disease had run its course and that romanticism was a thing of the past; but though some of its contents and some of its forms were dead, its soul was not: its soul consisting in this tendency on the part of art toward an immediate expression of passions and impressions. Hence it changed its name but went on living and working. It called itself 'realism,' 'verism,' 'symbolism,' 'artistic style,' impressionism, 'sensualism,' 'imagism,' 'decadentism,' and nowadays, in its extreme forms, 'expressionism' and 'futurism.' (268–9)

As we can see, and as Matei Calinescu has convincingly argued in *Five Faces of Modernity*, Croce makes an implicit distinction between a suprahistorical notion of 'decadence,' denoting a general sense of decline in several realms of modern life (moral, political, religious, and aesthetic), and a historical *Decadentismo* which, from being singled out as one of the post-Romantic '-isms,' finally comes to include a range of artistic and literary movements later canonized as modernist or avant-garde. Thus, Crocean thought casts its shadow over both uses of the term – the moral and the historical – and makes it difficult to differentiate them clearly.

The use of Decadentism as a period term has been such that an informed reader like Calinescu, in discussing Elio Gioanola's 1972 study, entitled precisely *Il Decadentismo*, could say that it 'might be taken by an English reader [...] as one more introduction to literary modernism' (219). And yet clearly this is not a perfect fit, if only because it remains difficult to escape the value judgment implicit in the term. Even Binni, the first advocate for the 'historicization' of the notion of Decadentism, could not avoid this problem. Thus, his book concludes on what we might call an 'optimistic' note, which serves at the same time to declare the experience of Decadentism at an end. According to Binni, Eugenio Montale and Giuseppe Ungaretti, the 'new poets' who have learned and interpreted in a personal way the lesson of the 'foreign poetics' of what we could call modernism (from Baudelaire to Valéry to Apollinaire), also consign Decadentism to history: the new poets 're-affirm the human values, the serene song, which brings them back to the core of our most intimate tradition. All we intend to do is to indicate the new period as the conclusion of Decadentism and the birth of a new poetry – Italian, yes, but experienced, European' (137). Aside from the fact that it sets up an implicit hierarchy of values in the experience of modern Italian poetry, this *caesura* between Decadentism and post–First World War poetry, and, in another permutation, between Decadentism as an uncritical appropriation of European tendencies and the new poetry as its critical re-elaboration, further conceals or denies the dialogic relationship that links the authors of so-called Decadentism to their successors, and to the broader landscape of European modernism. Consider, for instance, the question of the poet's role in bourgeois society: if Baudelaire had announced the loss of the 'halo,' the auratic quality of the work of art and of its producer, Italian modernism, from D'Annunzio to the *Crepuscolari* to the Futurists to Montale and Ungaretti and the Hermetics, can be read as the articulation of a series of responses to that crisis. The *Crepuscolare* Guido Gozzano's famous renunciation of the title of poet is certainly related to the loss of the social function of art and to the breach between the aesthetic and the praxis of life which, according to Peter Bürger, characterizes late-nineteenth-century aestheticism. Cristina Della Coletta's reading of Gozzano's travel writings shows that the epic mode, which allowed the poet to construct a coherent narrative of his civilization, appears no longer practicable. The poet's role is thus ambiguously positioned between the posturing of the aesthete and the materialism of the bourgeois. In 'La Signorina Felicita, ovvero la felicità' [Miss Felicita, or Happiness], he famously writes:

> Oh! questa vita sterile, di sogno!
> Meglio la vita ruvida concreta
> del buon mercante inteso alla moneta,
> meglio andare sferzati dal bisogno,
> ma vivere di vita! Io mi vergogno,
> sì, mi vergogno d'essere un poeta! (191)

> [Oh! This sterile, dream-like life!
> How better the rough, concrete life
> Of a good merchant concerned with money
> How better to be whipped on by need
> and yet live life! I am ashamed
> yes, ashamed, of being a poet!]

Yet, this impossibility of assuming the role, the *persona*, of the poet constitutes the direct link between – in Binni's terms – a decadent experience like that of *crepuscolarismo* and its supposed overcoming in a poet like Montale, who in *Ossi di seppia* [The Bones of Cuttlefish] finds himself forced to admit the purely negative – yet necessary – role of the poet in modern society:

> Non domandarci la formula che mondi possa aprirti,
> sì qualche sillaba storta e secca come un ramo.
> Codesto solo oggi possiamo dirti,
> ciò che *non* siamo, ciò che *non* vogliamo. (*Tutte le poesie* 29)

> [Do not ask us for the formula which could open worlds for you,
> yes, some twisted syllable and dry like a branch.
> This alone nowadays can we tell you,
> what we are *not*, what we do *not* want.] (*The Bones of Cuttlefish* 29)

Thus, Decadentism is problematic as a historical category, because it parcels Italian literature at the turn of the century in such a way that it erases the complex relationship, between the pre- and the post-war period, of the different articulations of the question of the role of intellectual and literary labour and of the writer him/herself in modern society. It is equally problematic as a conceptual/aesthetic category insofar as it involves a moral judgment on the validity of certain literary experiences which has traditionally functioned to repress them (as in the case of D'Annunzio). Indeed, in the last two decades the fortune of the term 'Decadentismo' has declined significantly, so much so that Paolo Giovannetti, in one of the most recent monographs on the problem, could conclude his study by writing that 'nowadays, the idea that for over a century world art has been decaying after reaching the apogee of its aesthetic and cognitive greatness in the middle of the last century is seen as an absurdity, as nothing more than a polemical exaggeration' (99).

'Avant-garde' proves similarly problematic. Here, too, we are confronted with a series of partially overlapping applications of the term. 'Avant-garde,' of course, tends to project a certain cultural experience beyond the borders of the national literary debate and to insert it in the context of a broader European phenomenon articulated in a series of movements, from Futurism in Italy and Russia to Vorticism in England to Surrealism in France. But the notion of avant-garde, like that of Decadentism, also entails a certain parcelling of the literary landscape. The term 'avant-garde' has been applied to those movements which have sought to break openly with the conventions of the literary traditions and, in particular, have confronted both the reification of language in bourgeois literature and the institutional roles constructed by the conventions of literary communication. Futurist *serate*, Dada *happenings*, Surrealist exquisite corpses, and so forth may demonstrate the same sense of uncertainty with respect to the question of 'what is a poet' found in the stanzas of Gozzano and Montale quoted above, but they also entail a radically different relationship with the institution of literature, as Bürger has explained.

A further, specifically Italian, question needs to be considered, given the fact that, within the Italian tradition, the historical avant-garde has been identified with the Futurist movement. Because of the links between Futurism and Fascism, and also as a result of the cultural hegemony of neo-realism after the Second World War, the notion of avant-garde found itself eclipsed until it was resurrected by the neo-avant-garde of the late 1950s and the 1960s as a specifically stylistic option which at the same time articulated a critical and antagonistic relationship between the artist and bourgeois society. Thus in Italy more than anywhere else the avant-garde has been associated with a practice of writing which aims at deconstructing the formative and normative power of language, and which is carried out at the level of expression. It cannot easily account, on the other hand, for all those cultural phenomena, especially in the wake of the First World War, which sought to establish a dialogic relation with tradition, or at least to mediate between the necessity of giving formal expression to the sense of alienation and futility of artistic practice and the desire to recuperate in a critical fashion, the cultural tradition. Thus, movements such as Hermeticism, *Novecentismo*, or *arte metafisica*, and figures such as Massimo Bontempelli, Alberto Savinio, Giorgio de Chirico, and even Luigi Pirandello or Italo Svevo, whose relationship with the cultural tradition entails neither the epigonistic mode of decadence nor the rebellion associated with the avant-garde, but who are nevertheless involved in a debate with both experiences, are either cut off from a general discourse on the characteristics of the culture of the first half of the century or interpreted (Binni's reading of Ungaretti and Montale above is an example) as returning to traditional forms of aesthetic experience after the iconoclastic moment of the avant-garde. In this latter construction, the 'system-immanent critique' (to use Bürger's term) opposing the avant-garde to the traditional institutional sites that mediate between the work of art and its public is simply suppressed from the unfolding of literary history by re-establishing a continuity that by-passes the avant-garde and connects the new poetry of the post-war period to the lyrical tradition and, at best, to the less emphatic aspects of D'Annunzio's oeuvre and the more melodious strains of *Crepuscolarismo*.

The critical commonplace that Futurism was responsible for an enormous amount of propaganda material – especially manifestos – but for very few 'important' works is typical of this inability to read the key moment of the avant-garde in terms of its own challenge to the institution of aesthetics: the separation between art and life which Futurism repeatedly called into question is precisely what is reasserted through the very gesture of distinguishing between the work of art and the act of propaganda, the aesthetic object to be contemplated and the 'event' (the *serata futurista*, the concert of noise-tuners, the pamphleteering activity) which brings the audience into the performance and exchanges the place of the receiver with that of the producer. But, as was well known by those artists who, after the First

World War, sought to re-establish a suitable distance between the artist and the public, between the sphere of the aesthetic and the praxis of life, the work of restoration cannot simply be a matter of returning to the pre-avant-garde tradition. It must also involve an engagement with the practical and theoretical questions raised by the avant-garde itself, as Antonio Saccone demonstrates in his study of Ungaretti's poetic theory. It is significant, of course, that the return to order should be carried out, in many instances, by artists who had gone through the experience of the avant-garde. For the artists who came to intellectual maturity during the war, like Ungaretti himself, a confrontation with the avant-garde, in one or another of its configurations, was often unavoidable, whether that meant militancy in Futurism (from Aldo Palazzeschi to Mario Sironi to Bontempelli) or a loose affiliation with '-isms' still on the margins of the national culture, like Surrealism (Savinio or de Chirico) or the adoption of techniques borrowed from the avant-garde itself (as, for instance, in the case of Pirandello). Bontempelli acknowledged as much in a programmatic essay in his journal *900* [The Twentieth Century], when he wrote of the Futurist leader F.T. Marinetti:

> Marinetti ha conquistato e valorosamente tiene certe trincee avanza tis-sime. Dietro esse io ho potuto cominciare a fabbricare la città dei conquistatori. Evidentemente, la trincea è più 'avanzata': ma non tutti ci possono andare ad abitare. (25)

> [Marinetti has conquered and bravely holds some very advanced trenches. Behind him I was able to begin building the city of the conquerors. Obviously, the trench is more 'advanced,' but not everybody can go and live there.]

More generally, the work of reconstruction characterizing the post-war *ritorno all'ordine* can be understood as a response to the Futurist challenge to the aesthetic and as an attempt to translate the Futurist destructive *élan* into a constructive program. The success of Fascism, whose rise accompanied the *ritorno all'ordine*, was due, among other things, to the fact that it was able to do precisely what the avant-garde had sought to do: it managed to close the gap between art and life by aestheticizing the everyday, and to eliminate the antithesis between producer and recipient by turning each individual into an extra on the stage of the spectacles of the regime. Indeed, one of the most original moves of Fascism was to appropriate the anti-institutional discourse of the avant-garde and to mediate it with that of its moderate epigones.

By adopting the notion of modernism as it has developed in the critical debate on the cultural crisis of modernity, we intend to contribute to a broader understanding of the period under study. If we interpret modernity as the ground of formation of epistemes of knowledge centred on the Enlightenment categories of reason, social emancipation, and scientific progress, whose beginnings can be found in the eighteenth century and culmination in the nineteenth and early twentieth centuries, modernism can then be considered as the network of cultural responses – at times openly antagonistic, at others characterized by a much greater ambiguity – which reflect upon, react to, and seek to articulate alternatives to the triumph of the institutions of modernity. Modernism thematizes a series of issues that are central to an understanding of the culture of the period, such as the relationship between the artist and the institutions of culture; the relationship between the artist and tradition and the question of cultural memory; the role of the sacred, the mythical, and the metaphysical vis-à-vis the positivist discourses of modernity; the status of technology within modern society and its effect on the production, circulation, and reception of the work of art; the tension between the homogenizing power of modernity and the persistence of local cultural traditions; the emergence of the counterdiscourses of marginalized groups questioning the coherence and unity of modern culture; the rejection of realism and the emergence of new modes of representation. Modernism thus allows us to bring into significant relation experiences which have traditionally been kept separate in Italian criticism, but it also makes it possible to show the links between the various manifestations of late-nineteenth- and early-twentieth-century Italian culture and the more general European context. In this sense, what we call modernism is related to what others – for instance, Giovanni Dotoli in *La nascita della modernità* or Fausto Curi in *La poesia italiana d'avanguardia* – have recently called '*modernità letteraria* [literary modernity].' We think, however, that the term 'modernism' has the advantage of being more clearly distinguished from modernity, a term loaded with historiographic and sociological implications.

We believe that we are not alone in our undertaking. In fact, in the last few years a new comparative and international perspective on the notion of modernism appears to have emerged, as Edward Mozejko indicated in an article published in 1998. Of course, the Anglo-American modernist tradition has been discussed in relation to its European counterparts in a variety of forums – for instance, at the international conference held at the University of Antwerp in 1993, and in the volume *Modernism 1890–1930*, edited by Malcolm Bradbury and James McFarlane in 1976, a critical and historiographic attempt to discuss such artistic currents as Symbolism, Expressionism, and Impressionism. However, these discussions did not permit an in-depth study of specific issues and texts concerning Italian culture between the turn of the nineteenth century and the early decades of the twentieth. This is precisely the gap that this volume aims to fill.

The Cultural-Historical Framework

As we have argued above, modernism must be understood in its complex network of relations and reactions to modernity. Such an understanding requires knowledge of the particular cultural-historical framework of the period. Thus, we intend to outline the features of modernity in Italy between 1861, when the question of the political formation of the nation gave way to that of the creation of a national culture and identity, and the mid-1930s, when the cultural protectionism fostered by the now-consolidated Fascist regime became pervasive and weakened the ties linking Italian modernism to its European counterparts.

The annexation of the city of Rome by Italy on 20 September 1870, and the transfer of the capital of the kingdom from Florence to Rome in 1871, marked the realization of the program of Italian unity and independence initiated in 1861 with the proclamation of the Kingdom of Italy, and it opened a long and complex phase of construction of a unified state. The intellectual group that best represented a commitment to the major issues of modernity – which in Italy meant not only the process of modernization of economic and productive structures and of everyday life, but also an evolution from the heroic and idealistic values of the *Risorgimento* to the constitution of a culture suitable to the new state – was that of the so-called Hegelians in Naples, represented by Bertrando Spaventa (1817–1883) and Francesco De Sanctis (1817–1883). Their cultural politics consisted of connecting the Italian philosophical and literary tradition with Hegelian dialectical historicism in order to generate the necessary conditions for the emergence of a new type of Italian intellectual, one capable of forging an Italian cultural identity. The legacy of the Neapolitan School was extremely influential, shaping the intellectual formation of such philosophers as Benedetto Croce (1866–1952) and Giovanni Gentile (1875–1944).

When Prime Minister Camillo Cavour – the key figure in the process of political unification – died in 1861, unification remained incomplete. Cavour's political heirs, the so-called Right, had to integrate the peninsula into a single state. This was a different and less heroic task than the struggle for independence which had characterized the *Risorgimento*. During its tenure in power the Right was dogged by the serious political opposition of the Left. The Left was composed of former followers of Giuseppe Mazzini, who had joined the Piedmontese camp in the 1850s to make unification possible. The old *Risorgimento* question of whether Italy should be united as a monarchy or a republic constituted the original distinction between these two political groups and persisted in the newly formed kingdom.

Prior to 1870, the major issue dividing Left and Right was that of Rome. The Left, influenced by its anticlerical and revolutionary origins, criticized the Right's timid Roman policy. In addition, the two groups fought over issues such as tax policies, and the Left insisted that the Right neglected Italy's pressing social problems and failed to widen the country's electoral base. The Left gained support in the South of Italy because of resentment of the Right's perceived 'Piedmontization' of the area, as well as the poor treatment of Garibaldi's volunteers after unification, the free-trade regime that crippled the region, and the frequent use of police to quell social agitation. The Left's constant hammering and the South's decisive support produced a major change in the 1874 elections. While the Right preserved a slight majority, parliamentary arithmetic opened the possibility of negotiations that would produce an eventual majority of the Left. Neither the Left nor the Right was a 'party' in the modern sense; both were divided into many groups, centred on prominent individuals, which could suddenly shift their political allegiance.

Finally, on 18 March 1876, a cabinet of the Right headed by Marco Minghetti lost a crucial vote on the question of taxation of wheatmilling. A government of the Left replaced Minghetti, and in November new elections were held. The new interior minister, Giovanni Nicotera, brought the government's power to bear in favour of the Left. As a result, the Right lost most of its seats in the Chamber, and the Left took control of the Italian government. Following this political change a dramatic separation ensued between those intellectuals who accepted the institution of the monarchy and those who wanted to continue pursuing a republican and radical agenda, especially in the city of Milan. Alberto Asor Rosa has described this division in terms of its ideological implications: among the intellectuals who accepted the monarchy, the dominant ideology would shift from the old progressivism of the *Risorgimento* to a form of social conservatism that found expression in the literary works of such authors as the novelist Giovanni Verga and the nationalist poet Giosuè Carducci. The more radical group would instead mature the impulse that moved bourgeois intellectuals in the direction of the common people, in the conviction that only by embracing their values and needs could Italian culture find a solution to Italy's problems as a young nation. However, both intellectual blocks were united by a common aversion to the tradition of Catholic thought, especially after Pope Pius IX condemned all trends of contemporary philosophy and their corresponding political ideologies in 1864, in his encyclical *Quanta cura* and the document entitled *Sillabo*. The Pope had demanded from believers an absolute respect for Christian dogma and a strong opposition to the political unification of Italy. Thus the ideological ground for Italian intellectual groups was comprised of a combination of anticlericalism, atheism, and positivism. More complex attempts to mediate between the principles of positivist science and liberal politics on the one hand, and the Catholic Church on the other, were frustrated by the Church's sweeping condemnation of modernism.

In the cultural and literary realms, the combination of anticlericalism, atheism, and positivism generated, in turn, two different, if not opposing, tendencies within the original social conservative intellectual attitude. The prevalence of a scientific mentality favoured the formation of a naturalistic literature, whose major representative was the Sicilian novelist Giovanni Verga. The main goal of this trend was the application of the methods of the exact sciences to literary production. The demand for national autonomy, in contrast, encouraged a revival of the culture of pre-Romantic Classicism. There is no doubt that this second tendency prevailed in Italian popular opinion, and Carducci, its major representative, was loved and admired as a spiritual guide by generations of Italians.

It remains difficult to formulate a definitive judgment about this period in Italian culture. In general, it may be argued that the lay, scientific mentality often represented the means by which the leading intellectual groups legitimated the survival of the dominant class in Italian society, which it considered an inarticulate and impersonal entity to be guided according to a series of mechanical laws. The Darwinian theory of evolution, with its emphasis on the survival of the fittest, could be used to justify the supremacy of the ruling class.

In Italy, positivist culture and ideology found a particular application. Asor Rosa has argued that the positivist attempt to reduce intellectual intervention in reality to the determination of the rational mechanisms that regulate it appeared to be inadequate for the task that a dominant ideology was supposed to undertake. Positivism ended up as a tool of the leading political group, the *Sinistra Storica* (historical Left), which believed that the future of Italy could be based on an absolute trust in the elements of progress. Thus the idealist and spiritualistic critiques of positivism in Italy came to represent a critique of the contemporary political climate. The reaction to positivist culture and ideology, in fact, assumed the form of a resurgence of idealism. Two philosophers dominated the idealist revival: Croce and Gentile. These two authors and their works influenced Italian culture, including its Marxist components, throughout the twentieth century. Croce and Gentile shared the belief that contemporary Italian culture ought to be connected with the historicist tradition, from Gianbattista Vico to Francesco De Sanctis, the nationalist tradition of Vincenzo Gioberti, and Hegelian philosophy. Each of these traditions tended to look at life in terms of organicism and complexity rather than in terms of fixed structures and the pseudo-scientific concepts of positivism. Croce and Gentile also tended to reject the purely materialistic principles of Marxism in favour of a more inclusive conception of history founded on the creative and autonomous activity of the human spirit, although both were profoundly influenced by Marxist principles, which remained the basis of their approach to society through the categories of material conditions and economics.

Croce and Gentile also shared the conviction that philosophy was a superior form of science, compared to which the natural sciences appeared as pseudo-sciences – an attitude that generated the prejudice and diffidence towards scientific thought which would characterize Italian cultural discourses throughout the twentieth century. Finally, Croce and Gentile strongly believed that their views and principles ought to be linked to a specific cultural politics, and that they ought not to be used in a spontaneous way, but should instead be deployed within a struggle among ideas, according to a strategy. In other words, Croce and Gentile's was not a form of speculative idealism; rather, they theorized what was called 'militant idealism.' The tool for this militancy, and for the collaboration between the two philosophers, was the journal *La critica* [Criticism], founded by Croce in 1903. Over the years, Croce and Gentile's thought intersected with that of young Italian intellectuals, in particular that of the Florentine group led by Giovanni Papini (1881–1956) and Giovanni Prezzolini (1882–1982). Walter Adamson demonstrates in his essay in this volume that Papini and Prezzolini were committed to elaborating adequate cultural responses to and solutions for the need for change in both Italian culture and politics at the very beginning of the twentieth century. The organ for the expression of this intersection of tendencies and interests was the journal *La Voce* [*The Voice*] (1908–14).

In order to grasp the complexity of Italian culture in the period between the 1880s and the First World War, it is necessary to consider the works and the influence of Croce vis à vis those of another major figure, Gabriele D'Annunzio (1863–1938). Interestingly, both the philosopher and the poet/novelist shared the same point of departure: modern Italian poetry as it was articulated by Carducci's Classicism. Carducci's enormous influence on Italian literature at the end of the nineteenth century may best define the difference between it and other contemporary European modernist experiences, and neither Croce nor D'Annunzio could conceive literary modernity outside the context of Classicism. For Croce, however, Carducci represented the ideal fulfilment of the values of the *Risorgimento*, namely, the love of freedom and patriotism, whereas for D'Annunzio Carducci was the master of poetic form, as well as the prophet (or *vate*) of a new Italian nation, unfortunately run by people whom D'Annunzio considered second-rate politicians. Carducci came to represent the bard of a high poetry characterized simultaneously by the praise of beauty and the passion for national ideals and glory. It was precisely with respect to D'Annunzio and his works that Croce outlined the theory of Decadentism, whose formation as both a conceptual and a historiographic notion is the subject of Mario Moroni's essay.

If the decade 1890–1900 was characterized by a series of literary experiences defined as *post-carducciane*, new and more ambitious forms of literary experimentation marked the decade 1900–10. But even this phase was influenced by the works by Croce published in that decade and immediately after, in particular, *Estetica* [Aesthetics] (1902), *L'intuizione pura e il carattere lirico dell'arte* [Pure Intuition and the Lyric Character of Art] (1908), *Breviario di estetica* [Manual of Aesthetics] (1912), and *Il carattere di totalità dell'espressione artistica* [The Total Character of Artistic Expression] (1917). Croce's notion of art was based on the concept of 'pure intuition,' which implied the negation of intellectual knowledge and practical objectives in the process of artistic creation. In some respects, Croce's conception was close to the 'decadent' view of art; the philosopher displayed a Classicist conception of style, however, and a strong interest in the ethical nature of the sentiments expressed in the work of art. The complexity of Croce's influence on early-twentieth-century Italian culture and literature consists in the fact that it was innovative and conservative at the same time. The philosopher emphasized the importance of creative subjectivism, along with some of the principles of literary modernism, but he also opposed the forms of expression of that very same European modernism, since he saw in its experiments an attempt to overturn the balance between idea and form. This largely accounts for Croce's lack of understanding and appreciation of the European avant-garde, including Italian Futurism. At the same time, the influence of Croce contributed to the rebellion of the young authors against the two major father figures, Giovanni Pascoli and D'Annunzio, in that Croce himself strongly criticized the former for expressing confused sentiments and the latter for his aestheticism and sensuality.

Practically every young Italian writer and poet of the early twentieth century faced the challenge of overcoming the influence of Pascoli and D'Annunzio, and of Carducci before them. This struggle generated three major cultural and literary experiences: *Crepuscolarismo*, Futurism, and *Frammentismo*. In the works of the two major representatives of *Crepuscolarismo*, Guido Gozzano (1883–1916) and Sergio Corazzini (1886–1907), poetry is confronted by the reality of the modern world. These poets acknowledged the illusory nature of any celebratory or vitalistic use of poetic language and denounced the fracture between the high tone of art and the frantic pace that characterized contemporary reality. They responded to this situation by adopting a colloquial language, which did not mask or falsify the experience of modern reality, but, unlike the Futurists, they avoided any form of participation in or celebration of that same reality.

On the opposite end of the cultural spectrum there was, of course, Futurism. In the 'Founding Manifesto' of 1909, Marinetti outlined the movement's unconditional acceptance of the features of modern civilization: its technology, the exasperated dynamism of human and verbal relationships, the mechanicity and automatism of images, and the break with past modes of expression and of existence. Futurism was also characterized by a wide-ranging intervention in the cultural and political arena. Its openly nationalistic rhetoric established from the beginning a connection between the production of literary and artistic artifacts and a broader project of renewal and regeneration for the nation. Futurism viewed the question of national identity as an open one, which could not be solved simply by appealing to the inherited cultural tradition – to what the Futurists vituperated as the 'cemeteries' of the museums, the cities of art, and the literary canon. By presenting itself as not limited to a specific domain but involved in all realms of art (a long-established tradition even considers Futurist art rather than literature as its highest achievement) and in life in all its various aspects – politics, economics, architecture, fashion, and even cooking – Futurism was the first movement in Italian culture to question the validity of the category of the aesthetic and to seek a new mediation between it and life praxis. Nationalism provided the overarching ideology within which this mediation could be accomplished.

The authors of *La Voce* expressed a rather different attitude towards the function of literature and its formal structures. This group of young writers such as Scipio Slataper (1888–1915), Piero Jahier (1884–1966), Carlo Michelstaedter (1887–1910), and Giovanni Boine (1887–1917) developed a 'fragmented' style of lyrical and ethical content embodied in short poetic or prose pieces. The experimentation of the writers of *La Voce* can be considered a parallel avant-garde with respect to Futurism. *Frammentismo* rejected the Futurist collective spirit and its programmatic purpose, as well as its cult of modernization. The fragmented style of the *'vociani'* tended to implode into an investigation of the self and its problematic relationship with the world, animated by an intense moral and ethical tension, which Thomas Harrison identifies as the features of 'expressionist modernism' and which differentiates it from the historical avant-garde.

The First World War represented a turning point for Italian culture and Italian intellectuals. There were those who, like Croce, opposed the intervention of Italy in the war, but found themselves isolated. Most of the intellectual sector justified the war according to its own point of view, and used the war to support and confirm its agenda. D'Annunzio and his followers were looking for both the glories of Italy and an opportunity for an adventure that would exalt the qualities of the individual hero. The nationalists represented the front line of interventionism and recruited intellectuals such as Prezzolini, Papini, and Soffici. Marinetti and the Futurists welcomed the war as a form of ethical and biological activity, in the hope that a new generation of men would be born out of the bloodshed, a generation of younger, more dynamic, and stronger Italians.

In terms of more specific political groups, the right-wing socialist reformists, led by Bissolati and Bonomi, thought that the war would consolidate the unstable relationship between the masses and the ruling class. Even the Socialist Party, the only organized mass party in Italian politics, which was officially against intervention in what it considered a capitalist war, found itself divided over the issue. The so-called leftist socialist revolutionaries, led by Benito Mussolini, hoped that the war would provide a healthy education in violence and fighting, leading to a revolution. Even progressive democrats like Gaetano Salvemini tended to justify the war ideologically, conceiving it as the continuation and final stage of the historical process of the *Risorgimento*. They also supposed that the peasants, who had hitherto contributed little to the construction of a strong national consciousness and identity, might acquire political maturity via the sacrifice and sense of unity generated within the common experience of the battlefield. Finally, the irredentists, including the Triestine writer Scipio Slataper, fought for the annexation of their native region to the territory of Italy.

In spite of their various motivations and hopes, the war ultimately had the same function for everyone: it shattered the illusions of those who had believed that it could constitute a means for social emancipation and political education, and reinforced instead the militaristic and authoritarian tendencies already present in certain quarters of the ruling class and in public opinion. In the meantime, the war had taken the lives of major representatives of the Futurist movement, including the painter Umberto Boccioni and the architect Antonio Sant'Elia, along with the *vociano* Slataper. Even for those who survived, the war was a traumatic experience. For instance, Giuseppe Ungaretti's poetry, written in the years after the war, was imbued with a sense of human life as tragedy; this sense of tragedy led the author to a religious experience that would colour his poetry for the rest of his life.

As Luperini argued in *Il Novecento*, the signs of a sense of tragedy came from practically the entire intellectual front. Apart from the historical events of the war, there seemed to have been a death of the very role of the intellectual, who could no longer continue to operate in a space which could guarantee both artistic autonomy and an influence on the cultural-political sphere. The general sense of discontent which developed in public opinion after the war required the ruling class to channel the explosive tension by configuring not only political, but also cultural and moral solutions for the future. In this historical scenario, intellectuals found themselves confronting a reality in which the war had reinvigorated the masses of workers and peasants, but, in obvious reaction, had also strengthened the subversive agenda of the revolutionary Right. In addition, the war had promoted the rise of the middle class, which was pervaded by strong anti-socialist feelings and resented the working-class movement which emerged in the aftermath of the war.

It is within what can be defined as a crisis of liberal culture – a culture of which Croce was the major representative – that we can see how Italian intellectuals were forced to abandon their autonomous space and to side with one or the other of the two antagonistic political solutions which would characterize Italian society until the consolidation of the Fascist regime. For the intellectuals it was, essentially, a question of choosing between socialism and bourgeois reaction, between social democracy and a rigid classist social structure. A parallel alternative between two antagonistic solutions emerged in the realm of art and literature: one could either follow the trend of the dominant ideology or live in a separate realm of 'pure' literary and artistic experience. In such a cultural and political atmosphere, the intellectual group around the journal *Lacerba* moved from one alternative to the other, first exalting art as a totalizing activity, and later championing, with an analogous exclusiveness, interventionist and hawkish politics. When Papini closed the publication of *Lacerba* at the onset of the war, he made it very clear that an autonomous ideological space was no longer practicable. In other words, on the one side there was literature, on the other politics.

It is only within this framework that we can understand the 'restoration' which characterized Italian culture after the First World War; it was not simply a return to tradition, but the institutionalization of the separation between art and literature and politics. This institutionalization retrieved from the past not so much content, or the social role of the intellectual, but rather traditional forms and styles, as well as the exaltation of the dignity and the rigour of literary studies. The post-war years in Italy represented a turning point of major consequence. The war plunged the intellectual and artistic avant-garde into a state of crisis and Futurism itself lost its original strength and was absorbed into the Fascist reaction.

Thus, while the war inspired a call for a return to order, the dynamics of this return were complex. In the so-called *pittura metafisica* – which originated in the city of Ferrara at the beginning of the war (1914–15) with the encounter of Giorgio De Chirico, his brother Andrea (known as Alberto Savinio), and the painters Filippo de Pisis and Carlo Carrà – the issue was the return to Classicism in the visual arts. These painters interpreted the restless cultural and artistic experimentation of the late nineteenth and early twentieth century as a sign of the unstated need of a generation to return to its origins, to the great principles of classical art. According to this assessment, the attempt to destroy, which had characterized the early avant-garde, was a necessary stage of this rediscovery and return to tradition. Thus, the painters of the *arte metafisica* interpreted the rebellious and anarchistic attitudes of artists and writers as forms of individualism and Messianism, which had eventually been smashed by the brutal reality of the war. After that tragic turning point those very attitudes were converted into a form of nationalism which climaxed with the violent manifestations of the early Fascist groups. In other words, Metaphysical artists were looking back to a sense of order available in the classical tradition and, at the same time, sounding a warning signal to other intellectuals against the trap of false Fascist rebellion, into which many had fallen by giving their support to the new regime.

Another aspect of this complex situation is represented by the intellectual group around the journal *La Ronda* [The Patrol] (1919–23). The goal of these intellectuals was, essentially, to bring the cultural debate back to an exclusively literary dimension. They rejected the principle that literary and artistic expressions were the symptom of something outside the realm of art itself. In this respect, they were indifferent to any ideological discourse. To a certain extent, the editors of *La Ronda* did not reject politics and its practice per se but refused, rather, to believe that the man of letters was able to intervene in the realm of politics. The best way to define the transition we have described above would be to say that from an antagonistic and anarchistic mode of modernism, Italian culture in the 1920s moved towards what may be called a traditionalist modernism.

In the same years as this complex transition from the avant-garde to the return to order, play-writing and theatrical productions remained sites of experimentation. From the beginning, the Futurists theorized a series of profound changes in the traditional theatrical space. They proposed the abolition of popular genres, such as farce, pochade, drama, tragedy, and comedy, in favour of new theatrical devices including segments of free dialogue, simultaneous scenes, dramatized poems, mises en scène of sensations, illogical discussions, and music hall entertainment, to name just a few. This revolution in theatrical performance remained, for the most part, at the level of pure intentions. The influence of Futurist ideas was pervasive, however, and generated a series of interesting outcomes in the years of the First World War and those immediately following. A particularly important tendency was the so-called *teatro grottesco* [grotesque theatre], a true new wave in the realm of Italian theatre, which lasted only a few years but had a profound historical and technical impact. Its major representative was Luigi Chiarelli (1884–1947) who, in his best-known work, *La maschera e il volto* [The Mask and the Face] of 1916, explored one fundamental theme: the contrast in contemporary society, at all levels of everyday life, between social conventions and external appearances on the one hand and the inner reality of human feelings on the other. This theme had its cultural and indirect political counterpart in the contrast between social bourgeois conventions and the uncanny and disturbing dimension of what lies beneath these conventions. After having started his career as a fiction writer, the playwright, director, and Nobel Prize–winner Luigi Pirandello (1867–1936) devoted his work to further exploration of this theme, beginning with the war years. Pirandello's theatrical characters are constantly engaged in the task of unmasking the system of conventions and prejudices behind which people protect themselves. But once the uncanny dimensions of life are revealed, the world becomes too complex and problematic to be managed, and it appears absurd to those no longer accustomed to reasoning according to social and logical conventions.

We have just delineated the cultural-political and ideological setting in which the essays of this volume are inscribed, and to which the various authors with whom the contributors deal gave different – and sometimes opposing – responses and reactions. We would like to conclude this section of the introduction with some reference to the period of the consolidation of the Fascist regime, when Italian culture lost much of its international dimension.

Benito Mussolini came to power after the Fascist 'March on Rome' on 28 October 1922. The political victory of Fascism was welcomed by the Italian bourgeoisie and accepted by the monarchy. Both these political forces saw in the advent of Fascism the end of a period of turmoil and dissatisfaction generated by the difficult post-war social and economic conditions. They also saw Fascism as providing protection against the spectre of socialism, in the wake of the Russian Revolution of 1917. But the increasing restrictions, the censorship, and the persecution of the opposition perpetrated by the regime progressively blocked the free circulation of ideas and any form of open cultural debate. Under these conditions, Italian culture lacked the basic elements for continuation of the avant-garde projects that had characterized the first two decades of the century. A small number of intellectuals decided to go into exile outside of Italy; others tried to organize forms of cultural opposition from within the country, risking incarceration and confinement. Many, however, attempted to find forms of compromise or co-existence with the Fascist regime, some driven by an actual sympathy for it, and others seeing compromise as a means to survive and to keep doing their work. Even projects sponsored by intellectuals apparently integrated into the regime, such as Massimo Bontempelli's *Novecentismo*, whose journal *900* was initially published in French and with an editorial board which included European intellectuals of the calibre of James Joyce and Georg Kaiser, were quickly quashed if they seemed to threaten the regime's nationalistic cultural policy. It was in this scenario of oppositional discourses, condescending attitudes, and the supposed neutrality of art that one of the most influential literary poetic practices in twentieth-century Italian culture emerged: Hermeticism.

At the theoretical and stylistic level, Hermeticism further elaborated the idea of the *vociani* that poetry constitutes a privileged, alternative form of experience, and a means for the exploration of the hidden and uncanny reality beneath the paradigm of knowledge established by science and rational thought. Taking up the lesson of major poets such as Ungaretti and Montale, hermetic poetry tried to free the poetic word from any conventional and intellectual meaning, as well as any predictable sentimental effect, in order to return it to an original sense of purity and of evocative power, that is, to a new form of poetic absolute. Poetry was then understood as a way to access the depth of the human soul, at the expense of historical reality which, under Fascism, was characterized by totalitarianism and repression. Hermeticism can be considered as one of the most influential attempts to recover individual freedom in a time of objective lack of political freedom, and it configured itself as a poetic of the crisis of the contemporary individual subject. The textual obscurity that resulted in this poetry was thus an extreme modernist act of estrangement performed at a time when Italian culture and society were moving towards isolation from the international community and away from the roots of that same modernist impulse.

The Essays

We open the volume with an essay by Remo Ceserani which outlines, from a comparative perspective, the cultural context for the volume as a whole. Ceserani emphasizes the lines of continuity and the faults that run across the landscape of modernity from the beginning of the nineteenth century to the middle of the twentieth. His reading of the Italian cultural situation in relation to the broader European context of modernity – of which he identifies certain recurrent themes, such as that of the individual and of the nation – is especially important to the general aim of this volume, as it shows both the usefulness of general categories like modernism in bringing into relief the homologies and the influences among European literatures, and, at the same time, the necessity of grounding these general categories in terms of specific local experiences. The pages devoted to the critic and writer Giacomo Debenedetti, an author peripheral to most histories of modernism, provide a case study of the theoretical issues Ceserani explores.

The other essays follow a chronological sequence which helps to trace the complex path that leads from modernism to postmodernism. This path, however, need not be a linear one. Here we would like to indicate some thematic itineraries that cut across the volume. The first itinerary deals with the reconsideration of some of the historiographic and critical categories which orient the discourse on the period under consideration. Mario Moroni analyses Italian *Decadentismo* in the light of the discourses of literary criticism which generated and defined it, through the works of such leaders of the Italian cultural scene in the 1890s as Vittorio Pica, Arturo Graf, and Gian Pietro Lucini, up until the appropriation of the ideas of decadence and Decadentism by idealist and Marxist thought in the works of Benedetto Croce and Georg Lukács. Moroni's essay is based on the initial assumption that notions such as Decadentism are cultural discourses developed according to criteria and strategies of appropriation and rearticulation within different cultural projects and at different stages of the history of literary criticism and ideas.

Laura Wittman's essay reconsiders the cultural phenomenon of Catholic modernism within the broader context of cultural and literary modernism. Unlike most scholars of cultural modernism, Wittman does not separate the religious/mystical and the cultural sides of the debate. Instead, she positions the phenomenon of mysticism at the heart of the modernist crisis, and as the critical intuition that literary modernism brought to religious modernism. Wittman argues that in the years before the turn of the twentieth century in Western Europe, literature and poetics became the locus of a reflection on the 'death of God,' and on the need for a new mystical practice severed from dogma and from philosophical abstraction. It is precisely at this juncture that Antonio Fogazzaro, for example, used literary language to critique the language of the project of theology.

Thomas Harrison explores the works of an unlikely assortment of literary figures – Giuseppe Ungaretti, Luigi Pirandello, Eugenio Montale, and Carlo Michelstaedter, as well as others associated with the journal *La Voce* – in the light of Lukács's essay, 'Aesthetic Culture' (1910). Reading these Italian authors through the framework of Lukács's essay, Harrison describes a form of anti-aestheticist, eccentric writing which he calls 'expressionist modernism,' as distinct from the historical avant-garde.

Walter Adamson proposes an alternative physical location for a reflection on modernism: not its canonized historical capital, Paris, but, rather, the city of Florence. He argues that in the 1910s both an avant-garde counter-culture and a potent working-class and peasant-based opposition made the Tuscan city the centre for the elaboration of a modernist cultural-political discourse, in which artists and intellectuals who came after the heyday of aestheticism articulated a refusal to pursue either politics or culture in isolation from each other.

A second motif is that of the relationship between modernism, the literary tradition, and the question of memory. Enrico Cesaretti challenges the commonly accepted critical interpretation of Futurism as a mere repudiation of the past and suggests that Marinetti's narrative production, especially *Gli indomabili* [The Untameables] (1922), *Spagna veloce e toro futurista* [Fast Spain and Futurist Bull] (1931), and the autobiographical *Il fascino dell'Egitto* [The Appeal of Egypt] (1933), demonstrate that Marinetti's perception of and relationship with the category of time is not univocally antagonistic. The identification, in these texts, of a rhetoric of nostalgia and memory, which Cesaretti discusses in light of Bergson's ideas about the concepts of space and time, betrays Marinetti's fascination with the past and his ambivalence with respect to change and modernity.

Antonio Saccone's essay is a study of the complex influence of Futurism on Giuseppe Ungaretti, who was, with Eugenio Montale, the most influential figure in the transition of Italian poetry from the avant-garde to Hermeticism. As Saccone points out, in the years between 1920 and 1930 Futurism constituted a crucial, albeit negative, point of reference of a poetics in which the Futurist celebration of the moment, of an artistic practice which was consumed in the present of its performance, was tempered by a recovery of the poetic tradition, and of the philosophical line which privileged the question of memory (Bergson in particular). The poetic word thus becomes the instrument through which memory and modernity can find a precarious balance.

Yet another itinerary is that of the gradual awareness and coming into focus of the contradictions of the 'universal subject' on which the Western culture of modernity is centred. The emergence of organized feminism in England, Italy, and other European nations, and the encounter with the colonial 'other,' produced a reconsideration of traditional categories of gender and race. Lucia Re's study of the relationship between two celebrated actresses whose fame reached mythical proportions at the turn of the century – Sarah Bernhardt and Eleonora Duse – and two writers whose work is crucial to the articulation of the aesthetics of Decadentism – Oscar Wilde and Gabriele D'Annunzio – makes an important contribution to our understanding of the debate on gender roles at the turn of the century. For Re, the actresses, with their glamour and success, and their ability to assume a multiplicity of roles, represented a radical challenge to nineteenth-century notions of domesticity and of a stable and familiar female subjectivity. Their mobile and 'nomadic' identities, which spill from the stage to the world, turning the actresses into fascinating and alluring divas, are peculiarly in tune with the cult of artificiality of the decadent poetics of Wilde and D'Annunzio. Precisely because of this conjunction, Duse and Berhardt, as the performers through whom the work of art finds its completion on the stage, also present a threat to the myth of the individual originality of the artist to which both authors subscribe.

In her essay on Paola Masino, Allison Cooper argues that *Monte Ignoso* provides an original look at Italy's post–First World War return to order. The novel seems ultimately to suggest that while the return to order so ardently desired by figures like Bontempelli, Carrà, and Sarfatti might provide an illusion of cultural stability and epistemological certainty, these would come at the expense of the individual – particularly the female individual, for whom the order of the past traditionally meant self-sacrifice and denial. Masino conveys this through an experimental style which shows the influence of European modernists like Joyce and Woolf, as well as Breton and his fellow surrealists.

The theme of the gladiator is the concern of Keala Jewell's essay on Giorgio De Chirico, who is studied here not only as a painter but also as a writer. His figures, both heroic and tragic, caught in repose as well as in moments of struggle, become the site of intersection of conflictual discourses of gender, power, heroism, and tradition. Tradition, in particular, constitutes a crucial problem for De Chirico, since his aesthetic project seeks to find a point of contact between it and modernity in an Italian landscape in which, as Jewell writes, 'the classical lives on in the present in uncanny ways' (352). Moreover, the potential nationalist implications of such an aesthetic reflection are an important reminder of the close relationship between art and politics in modernism.

Cristina della Coletta's essay on Guido Gozzano's Indian narratives provides a further example of how the modernist literary discourse dealt with 'otherness.' In his travel journal Gozzano resorts to quotations and erudite allusions to account for the otherwise difficult task of writing about the exotic and elusive reality of colonial India. Gozzano's self-reflexive textual strategy – or, in Della Coletta's own words, his 'criticism in action' – reveals that employing 'meta-textual' practices to account for the 'other' is not unique to the postmodernist discourse.

Finally, several essays address the very notion of modernism and the issue of the continuity/discontinuity between it and postmodernism. In her essay on Pirandello, Manuela Gieri situates the theory of humour of the Sicilian playwright in relation to the theory of laughter of Charles Baudelaire. Both Baudelaire and Pirandello identify in laughter/humour a modern form of knowledge which results from the awareness of the profound interconnection of comedy and tragedy. Moreover, this double nature of humour reproduces the internal redoubling and contradictoriness, the split condition of the modern subject. The transition from Romanticism to modernism is marked, according to Gieri, by a rejection of the figure of the tragic hero who can recompose his/her internal divisions, who is replaced on the stage by the Pirandellian *raisonneur*.

Luca Somigli's essay considers modernism as a critique of modernity, or, to be specific, as the cultural production which confronts and brings into relief the existential and social effects of technological and capitalist modernity. More importantly, he suggests that postmodernism, far from being a rupture with the horizon of modernism, is still firmly ensconced within it: for Somigli, both modernism and postmodernism constitute answers to the fundamental problem of modernity, namely, the question of what happens to the real in a social environment governed by exchange, in which no moment of authenticity or truth is available to halt the circulation of signs and products. The theme of simulation in Massimo Bontempelli's play *Minnie la candida*, which Somigli examines in detail, links the work to a well-established modernist literary tradition and at the same time looks forward to the postmodern motif of the simulacrum.

Jennifer Hirsh, like Jewell, considers De Chirico's paintings, although she concentrates on his later, 'post-metaphysical' canvases, which appropriate not only the studied monuments that had characterized his previous works, but also artistic styles ranging from Renaissance and Baroque to his own signature Metaphysical rhetoric. Focusing on De Chirico's entire pictorial project, Hirsh's essay reconsiders the painter's works as symptomatic of a melancholic condition of mourning. De Chirico's confrontation with the iconic traces of no longer recoverable histories is thus a declension of a larger modernist thematic, the inability to deal with the loss of meaning. By looking at the works of Andy Warhol and Mike Bidlo, two contemporary artists who repaint De Chirico, Hirsh finally considers the 'uncanny' return – and repetition – of modernist nostalgia in postmodernist art, thus bringing the volume, and the reader, full circle to the question of the continuity of modernism and postmodernism with which we began.

WORKS CITED

Asor Rosa, Alberto. *Sintesi di storia della letteratura italiana*. Florence: La Nuova Italia, 1983.

Berman, Marshall. *All That Is Solid Melts into Air*. New York: Penguin Books, 1982.

Binni, Walter. *La poetica del Decadentismo*. 1936. Florence: Sansoni, 1996.

Bontempelli, Massimo. *L'avventura novecentista*. Ed. Ruggero Jacobbi. Florence: Vallecchi, 1974.

Brand, Peter, and Lino Pertile, eds. *The Cambridge History of Italian Literature*. Cambridge: Cambridge UP, 1996.

Bradbury, Malcolm, and James McFarlane, eds. *Modernism 1890–1930*. Harmondsworth: Penguin, 1976.

Bürger, Peter. *Theory of the Avant-Garde*. Trans. Michael Shaw. Minneapolis: U of Minnesota P, 1984.

Calinescu, Matei. *Five Faces of Modernity*. Durham, NC: Duke UP, 1987.

Cervigni, Dino. 'The Modern and the Postmodern: An Introduction.' *Annali d'Italianistica* 9 (1991): 5–31.

Croce, Benedetto. 'Aesthetics.' 1929. *The Encyclopædia Britannica. Canadian Centennials Private Edition. A New Survey of Universal Knowledge*. 14th ed. Toronto: Encyclopædia Britannica of Canada, 1934. 1: 263–72.

Curi, Fausto. *La poesia italiana d'avanguardia. Modi e tecniche*. Naples: Liguori, 2001.

Di Scala, Spencer. *Italy: From Revolution to Republic*. Boulder, Co: Westview P, 1995.

Dotoli, Giovanni. *Nascita della modernità. Baudelaire, Apollinaire, Canudo, il viaggio dell'arte*. Fasano: Schena, 1995.

Duggan, Christopher. *A Concise History of Italy*. Cambridge: Cambridge UP, 1994.

Eysteinsson, Astradur. *The Concept of Modernism*. Ithaca and London: Cornell UP, 1990.

Fokkema, D., and E. Ibsch, eds. *Modernist Conjectures: A Mainstream in European Literature 1910–1940*. New York: St Martin's Press, 1993.

Gioanola, Elio. *Il Decadentismo*. Rome: Studio, 1977.

Giovannetti, Paolo. *Decadentismo*. Milan: Bibliografica, 1994.

Gozzano, Guido. *Poesie*. Milan: Rizzoli, 1977.

Jameson, Fredric. *Postmodernism or, the Cultural Logic of Late Capitalism*. Durham: Duke UP, 1991.

Luperini, Romano. 'Bilancio di un trentennio letterario (1960–1990) e ipotesi sul presente.' *Scrittori, tendenze e conflitto delle poetiche in Italia (1960–1990)*. Ed. Rocco Capozzi and Massimo Ciavolella. Ravenna: Longo, 1993. 7–13.

– *Il Novecento*. 2 vols. Turin: Loescher, 1981.

Mack Smith, Dennis. *Modern Italy: A Political History*. Ann Arbor: U of Michigan P, 1997.

Montale, Eugenio. *The Bones of Cuttlefish*. Trans. Antonino Mazza. Oakville, ON: Mosaic P, 1983.

– *Tutte le poesie*. Ed. Giorgio Zampa. Milan: Mondadori, 1984.

Mozejko, Edward. 'Literary Modernism: Ambiguity of the Term and Dichotomy of the Movement.' *Canadian Review of Comparative Literature*. Mar.–June (1998): 123–43.

Petronio, Giuseppe, and Vitilio Masiello. *La produzione letteraria in Italia.*
    Vol. 4. Palermo: Palumbo, 1993.
Riall, Lucy. *The Italian Risorgimento*. London and New York: Routledge, 1994.
Saresella, Daniela. *Modernismo*. Milan: Bibliografica, 1995.

PART I

Modernism in Context

1 Italy and Modernity: Peculiarities and Contradictions

REMO CESERANI

New Proposals for the History of Modernity

New attitudes among historians are slowly changing our perception and interpretation of the historical events of the last two centuries. According to this general shift in historical interpretation, two great transformations radically altered the social and cultural life of Europe: one at the turn of the eighteenth century, the other in the 1950s and 1960s. While their impact and timing varied slightly from country to country, these epochal changes altered both European cultural life and literary production. Many smaller changes and transformations have, of course, also occurred, including the beginning of industrialization in France during the 1830s and the subsequent industrialization of Germany and Italy; the two world wars and other significant, even symbolic, periods of political turmoil and confrontation (e.g., 1848, 1870, 1969); the great technological inventions, from steam power to electricity to the internal combustion engine and systems of digital communication; and advances in the fields of art and literature, such as the emergence of the avant-garde movements in the early twentieth century.[1] Nevertheless, there seems to be some agreement among the new historians that European societies experienced only two major changes in the last two centuries, to which we have given the names of, respectively, modernity and postmodernity. From this perspective, it seems to me that the interesting and lively discussion prompted by the proposal of British historian Eric Hobsbawm to consider the twentieth century as a 'short' century confirms the growing awareness that the historical shift of the 1950s was an epochal one in its dimension and significance, characterized by the transition to the economic phase of late capitalism and transformations in the fields of technology, ideology, collective behaviour, and culture.

Views such as Hobsbawm's require some qualifications. First, historical changes in human societies do not have the same physical concreteness as, for instance, the transformations in the surface of the earth through geologic eras, which tend to leave strata whose age can be measured according to the quantity of carbon monoxide present in each of them. It is we, the observers from a later time, who interpret the past, identify the signs of a smaller or larger change; distinguish between different styles of life, cultural atmospheres, and historical conditions; and try to recapture the specific quality of a period by giving it a name. Second, while the historical conditions of a certain age exert great influence on the people who live within it, this does not mean that a single human being, or even a community or group of people, cannot work against the dominant culture of the age. Finally, each new period of time is bound to have a different view and to give a different interpretation of the preceding periods; each period writes a different history of its past, subjecting the existing histories to revisions and adjustments.

The process of historiographic revision of the entire period of modernity has been prompted mainly by a change in our methods of research and tools of interpretation. Our attitude is further influenced by the fact that, as we look at the great *tournant du siècle* between the eighteenth and the nineteenth century, and at the complexity of its various manifestations, we see it from the new perspective that comes after experiencing another epochal change, probably similar in scope: the shift from modernity to postmodernity.

What appears sufficiently clear to us now is that, in spite of the many changes and leaps forward that have been typical of modernity – and which have contributed an intrinsic feature to its view of the world – there was a continuity, a coherence in the cultural background, between men such as Diderot, Rousseau, and Friedrich Schlegel, who lived in the late eighteenth or early nineteenth century, and men such as Nietzsche, Marx, Freud, Joyce, Svevo, and Musil, who lived in the second part of the nineteenth or in the twentieth century. Their historical experiences, notwithstanding all possible large and small crises and phases of internal change, have something in common. With enthusiasm or horror, or both, they lived in and represented through their writings the historical age of modernity. They experienced its triumphs and disasters, advances and tragedies, achievements and breakdowns, the utopian projects for changing the world, and the frustrations of a world that had changed in ways contrary to their expectations.

It is high time that we consider all aspects and ramifications of the age of modernity. Within the span of that long period a number of intellectuals and writers, usually in the minority, called themselves 'modern' or 'modernist,' feeling at one with society's transformations. Some of them proclaimed: *'il faut être moderne.'* Some wrote in their diaries, at a certain date (usually at the beginning of the twentieth century), 'today I perceive that I am modern' and 'in this period I feel that the human character has radically changed.' Many of them assembled in groups, founding movements that looked hopefully towards the future. Interestingly, some of the writers and intellectuals who were extremely active in the most advanced phases of the period, and especially those who took part in some of the movements of the avant-garde, deliberately denied any relationship with the initial phase of modernity and especially with the Romantic movement. They often represented Romanticism as fundamentally extraneous to modernism and inevitably connected with tradition and the past. T.S. Eliot, for instance, felt that he belonged to modernism (although he cherished, especially in his later years, a strong sense of tradition), but was aggressively hostile to Romanticism and Romantic poetry, which he accused of being sentimental, subjective, and expressionistic, and far removed from the symbolistic objectivity of modern poetry. Today we find ourselves beyond those differences and those simple choices. We feel that there are more similarities than differences between, on the one hand, Wordsworth, Hölderlin, Pushkin, Hugo, and Leopardi and, on the other, Baudelaire, Rilke, Eliot, and Montale. In spite of the closed forms of the first group versus the open forms of the latter, weary conformity to tradition versus clamorous experimentations with the new, departures from and reversions to the past, the nostalgic return to Romanticism and the parodic mimicries of it, we feel that, on the whole, the same general cultural atmosphere held together the artistic manifestations of modernity.

Today, the historiographic problem for anyone who wishes to study the age of modernity from the beginning of the nineteenth century to the middle of the twentieth century is not so much that of establishing the various intermediate phases, the successive modifications and ruptures (which have been at times both important and impressive), as it is drawing the general profile and meaning of the age as a whole.

Resorting to the principle of concomitance rather than disjunction, the literary historian of modernity tries to establish the links that connect all the different phenomena: socio-economic, cultural, ideological, political, or artistic and musical, as well as literary.

The recent debates about modernism have revolved precisely around these issues. Scholars, that is, have attempted to determine whether or not the various forms of change were concomitant. Was there, for example, a relationship of temporal coincidence between, on the one hand, great socio-economic events such as the Industrial Revolution, which began in England and gradually spread to other European countries, and which resulted in enormous changes in the means and modes of production, building methods, use of the work force, and the relationship to the market and, on the other, great ideological-political events like the French Revolution and the many revolutions throughout Europe that followed, which created an entirely new individual and collective phenomenology, a new way for thinking of oneself as citizen, new forms of organization along currents of thought, movements, and political parties, and a new method of acting politically in offices, clubs and cafés, in the squares and on the streets? Scholars also considered whether there was a relationship between the great socio-economic events, political activities, and the new cultural models, the new languages, and the new rhetorical systems that spread throughout the world. Is it possible, for example, to speak of an artistic and imaginative revolution parallel to and concomitant with the economic and political revolutions that punctuated the entire period, producing projects of social reform and utopian change that often crumbled under the difficulties and harsh experiences that characterized modernity? After so many efforts to change the world, and to make it new and human, in the end it was discovered that nature – that very nature so idealized and beloved by the Romantics – had been so widely colonized by man, so conquered and placed in the service of machines, production, commerce, and the design of power, that nothing remained of it. Nature had become, in its totality, culture.

Romanticism as the First Phase in the Formation of a Consciousness of Modernity. The Interpretation of Paul De Man: Allegory and Symbolism

In the lively debate that has characterized the historical and interpretive work of recent decades, Paul de Man has held a prominent position. It is to him that we owe the great effort of rereading the entire period of modernity. He, and the other, chiefly American, critics who followed his lead, brought many texts that we previously classified as Romantic works of the early nineteenth century into the principal canon of the literature of modernity.[2] Paul de Man's book *The Rhetoric of Romanticism*, a collection of his most mature inquiries into the subject, is of great importance. However, another of his books, a collection of essays written much earlier, strikes me as particularly moving, given its pioneering spirit: *Romanticism and Contemporary Criticism*. This collection brings together the texts of several seminars given by de Man in 1967 at Princeton University, inaugurating the critical process of rereading the Romantics as the first among the moderns, that is, of rereading Rousseau, Hölderlin, and Wordsworth as spiritual brothers of the future Baudelaire, Rimbaud, and Yeats, among others. It is particularly interesting to see him at work in these lectures, which consist of tentative ideas and working hypotheses. Among other things, one feels that in certain moments we are very close to positions that touch the deep motivations of de Man's drama, which exploded after his death in 1983. When de Man speaks of the nostalgia that Hölderlin, one of first great Romantic poets, felt for Greece, it is impossible not to recall Heidegger's well-known pages on the same theme. Unfortunately, it is equally impossible not to recall certain official stances of Nazism, a certain racist and nationalist mythology founded on the ancient Indo-European (or Aryan) past of the German peoples. In these pages, we feel that de Man is in trouble, that he is working laboriously against an ideology that is also his own, and which involves him deeply. We also know that, in a confused way, that sort of nationalist ideology has its own connection with the deeper phenomena of modernity, precisely in their Romantic variant: the search for roots, the invention of the past, and nationalism.

It is interesting to observe how, when dealing with Hölderlin, Rousseau, and others, de Man tries to find their contradictions and internal lacerations. He tries, in other words, to make them modern. And he does this with writers usually considered nostalgic for moments in history dominated by unitary models. Those poets and writers, having found themselves living in an era of alienation, in a world in which the gods of religion had abandoned the earth, adopted the rhetorical discourse of symbolism and assumed the task of bringing them back in the form of grand images and mytho-poetic creations.

De Man wishes to demonstrate that the great Romantic poets of the early nineteenth century, having experienced the epochal leap and the interior rupture of modernity, were modern in every respect. In the

Princeton lecture dedicated to Hölderlin, for example, he pauses at a famous lyric, 'Der Rhein' (1802).[3] The poem describes the conflict between the forces of nature and destiny that drive the Rhine to flow towards the North Sea, and a deep mythological and symbolic force that acts in an opposite direction, expressing itself through the river's great curves and tortuous bends. This latter force would instead push it south, towards Greece, to rediscover the far-off, ideal conjunction between Germany and Hellas.

De Man and others who have followed his example – I could cite Geoffrey Hartman, an American scholar who was very close to de Man and studied the English Romantic poet William Wordsworth at length, among others[4] – have conducted thematic and rhetorical studies, collecting a whole series of recurring symbolic images of splitting and laceration.[5] Moreover, these critics introduced a distinction between a rhetoric of allegory and one of symbol, borrowed from the German critic Walter Benjamin, that proved to be fundamental in their studies. Benjamin occupies a central place in all the itineraries of historiographic revision of which I am speaking, not only for the connection he instituted between allegory and modernity in *Ursprung des deutschen Trauerspiels* [The Origin of German Tragic Drama],[6] but also as the greatest scholar of modernity, as it is represented in the emblematic events of its capital, Paris, and in the combination of technological innovation and the disintegration of man's perceptive structures, of utopian and revolutionary impulses, tragedies, and catastrophes.

According to de Man's interpretation, *symbolism* is one of the two possible discursive strategies and rhetorical reactions to the modern experience of rupture. It is an attempt to repair, with rhetorical figures and poetic images of recomposition, the fracture between man and nature, between man's reasoning self-consciousness and the lost richness of his inner life. The symbol is, within the experience of modernity, a poetic procedure capable of 'bringing the gods back to earth,' of substituting the signs of laceration with those of a reconstructed unity. *Allegory* would be an alternative rhetorical procedure, also present in modernity and available to the poets of this period. It too begins with the great Romantics, who use it to point out the laceration, and to express it in forms and images. Allegory keeps the separate entities distinct, renounces any nostalgic attempt at recomposition, and is bitterly pessimistic and lucidly catastrophic.

It is clear that, for de Man, symbolism and allegory are two closely associated, but different, rhetorical modalities of representing the themes of modernity. However, allegory is clearly preferable to de Man, because it represents rather than masks the modern experience of laceration. Rousseau, for example, according to de Man's interpretation, is not a theorist of a pantheistic union of man with nature, but a theorist of alienation. Rousseau often makes use of allegorical representation and morally charged landscape in *La Nouvelle Héloise* [The New Heloise], for example, as de Man has maintained in his well-known essay, 'The Rhetoric of Temporality.' Following this interpretative itinerary, de Man even manages to uncover the themes of laceration and doubt in poets we would be inclined to consider perfect exponents of symbolism, such as Yeats.

Following the example of de Man and the earlier ideas of Walter Benjamin, critics are rereading and re-interpreting the principal figures of the nineteenth century. Even the French Symbolist poets do not escape this revision, as Baudelaire himself, despite his poetics of 'correspondences,' is considered a fundamentally allegorical poet.[7] Because of this widespread revision, perhaps the time has come for us in Italy to apply these new interpretative instruments not only to the recognized protagonists of late modernity, such as Montale, but also to some of his nineteenth-century predecessors, such as Foscolo, Leopardi, Pascoli, and d'Annunzio, who experienced the turmoil of the new era and tried to give expression to it. Though I have mentioned mainly the poets, rereading novelists in this new light would probably also be rewarding.[8]

The New Structures of the Imaginary in the Age of Modernity

In any attempt to reconstruct the general structures of the imaginary of any historical period (what we could call the dominant 'cultural models,' to use Iurii Lotman's anthropological terminology), one must pay special attention to the system of literary genres and rhetorical forms. Every literary period is characterized by a different hierarchical situation of the various modes and genres. In every new historical period the literary imagination assumes a new shape. New modes and genres are invented, while older ones are elevated to higher expressive or representative tasks, lowered, manipulated and parodied, or removed altogether from the literary system. Writers use new modes and genres of representation to explore new fields of personal or social experience and to recognize new strategies of knowledge, persuasion, or narration.

There is a sharp distinction between the systems of literary modes and genres that dominated the eighteenth and nineteenth centuries. It is widely known, for example, that during the eighteenth century the satiric or the didactic poem occupied a position of great prestige in many European national literatures, while the elegy, the love lyric, and the pastoral poem enjoyed a relatively lower standing. After the great divide at the turn of the century, lyric poetry assumed the highest hierarchical position and some narrative genres (such as the novel of manners, that of adventure and experience, the *Bildungsroman*, the love romance, etc.) attained a position of great importance in the new literary landscape. The transformation of the whole system was governed by both external and internal dynamic forces. One internal force was the dominant presence of two literary modes during the eighteenth century, the 'pathétique sentimental' or 'melodramatic' (to use Peter Brooks's terminology in *The Melodramatic Imagination*) and the 'ironic-parodic' and, in the nineteenth century, of the 'mimetic-realistic' and the newly found 'fantastic' modes.[9]

Another aspect that must be taken into account is the system of literary themes that characterize the production of the two periods. In other words, we must not only consider the way in which those texts speak, but also what they say. It is not difficult to discover, for instance, that the literary production of the early nineteenth century contains some obsessively recurrent themes. It is also characterized by interesting links between those literary themes and features and representative attitudes found in the material life of the period, in its socio-economic structures, ideological stances, and collective sensibility.

An important thematic cluster that has given form and substance not only to single works, but to entirely new literary genres, involves the new conception of the human individual. This conception is connected, of course, with a new social figure who had entered into the world of economic transactions: the modern capitalist and entrepreneur, who assumed a central position in society. This new figure considered himself capable of making his own economic fortune and believed that the very process of creating that fortune could constitute his entire aim in life. A novel human type had made his appearance in the world, one who thought in completely new terms of his relationship with labour, profit, and money. The archetypal literary figure of this new human being is Robinson Crusoe, a symbolic if not an allegorical embodiment of the bourgeois man, able to survive on a desert island, relying on his hard work, faith in God, intelligence, and skills, but also on some indispensable tools that Defoe providentially put at his disposal after the wreck of the ship and the death of all of his companions. From that moment on, Crusoe's only aim on the island was to enter into a relationship with nature, colonizing, transforming, and possessing it, exploiting it for his own sustenance and, ultimately, for the accumulation of great wealth.

It might be useful to recall, in this connection, *The Legitimacy of the Modern Age*, an important book by a contemporary German philosopher, Hans Blumenberg.[10] Blumenberg elaborates an interesting concept in reference to the human subject: self-assertion [*Selbstbehauptung*], which he at times presents as a sort of self-programming. According to Blumenberg, modern man is programmed to assert himself, to adapt to the various conditions of reality, to develop all his potentialities and achieve all his goals. The primary goal of modern man would no longer be simple biological survival, but a programmed acquisition of knowledge. Crusoe's reaction to his new environment at the beginning of his adventure, however, is not simply an attempt at biological maintenance and survival. Any such attempt would have been destined to fail. Virtually all the eighteenth-century sailors who were shipwrecked on a deserted island met with madness and death. Only Crusoe survived; as a fictional embodiment of modern man, he was endowed with a program of self-assertion.

Is it possible to establish a link between Blumenberg's concept of self-assertion (138) and some of the new themes and forms of the cultural and literary products of the early nineteenth century? I would say yes. We need only look at a few of the literary genres resulting from the great change at the turn of the nineteenth century and at the new dominant position accorded to lyric poetry. In lyric poetry, the individual subject occupies centre stage and represents the writer's projections, aspirations, difficulties, and failures in his attempts to govern his relations with nature and society and to control the internal world of his thoughts and passions. As for the narrative genres, we need only think of the significant position achieved by the new genre of the *Bildungsroman*, the novel of education, which tells the story of a character who not only slowly builds up his fortune and position in the world, but also asserts and forms his own self.[11] Blumenberg's program of self-affirmation becomes the novelistic plot of a process of self-education. From Goethe's *Wilhelm Meister* to Flaubert's *L'Education sentimentale* [Sentimental Education], from Dickens's *David Copperfield* to Nievo's *Confessioni di un italiano* [The Confessions of an Italian] –

and absorbing strains from the picaresque tradition, the novel of manners, and the sentimental romance – the *Bildungsroman* came to occupy a particularly prominent position in the system of genres of the Romantic imagination.

And yet literature is not only the place in which we apply, in our imaginary explorations of the world, the dominant ideological and epistemological schemes; it is also the locus of criticism, ambiguities, and contradictions. In literature our positive and triumphant representative strategies activate at the same time as those dominated by a sense of drama and defeat. The great Romantic literature of the nineteenth century, besides placing the lyrical 'I' at its centre or inventing the frame for the stories of self-education of the new individual subject, also produced a whole series of forms and structures which represented failures in the programs of self-assertion and attempted to understand the crises that could befall such programs. On the one hand, there is a powerful 'I' that creates its own path and progress on the basis of a linear and consistent development, imposes a story on its own biological being. Although its body might change and become mutilated or ill, although the cells that constitute it might die or become transformed and renewed, it represents itself in the form of identity and continuity according to a precise internal logic. On the other hand, there is a weaker 'I,' which conceives itself in terms of discontinuities, breaches, and sudden changes of direction, internal fragmentation and lacerations. These experiences are the origin, in the literature of the nineteenth century (especially that written in the fantastic mode), of two other types of representation. One of these types takes the subject of the program of self-assertion to its logical extreme and transforms itself into the monomaniacal 'I,' the obsessed mind; the other sends the divided self into action, splitting the subject into two different natures or characters, into Dr Jekyll and Mr Hyde. From the first attitude spring the texts, so common in the literature of the time, which elaborate the theme of madness, especially of the obsessive, paranoid type; from the second attitude derive the texts that have as their central theme the double, the split and alienated subject.

Another relevant theme, which is connected to the one I have just spoken of, is that of the rapid development, in the period under consideration, of the concept of the individual nation, expressing a new need for self-representation and self-assertion on the part of the various peoples who wished to have their voices heard. There is a clear parallel between the program of self-assertion of individual subjects within the new bourgeois society and the program of self-assertion for individual nations. Here again it is possible to determine a link between social, political, and ideological attitudes and the establishment of the literary themes and the special role of literature in the overall history of culture. At this time, the various peoples and nations of Europe, and progressively of other continents as well, began a search for their roots and identity through the recovery, and in many cases the invention, of their past history, traditions, symbols, and myths. The Scots thus invented their own folklore, composed of kilts, bards, hornpipes, and square dances; the Germans restored their medieval castles and romantic locales and revived the stories and scenarios of the Nibelungen saga; the French, Spaniards, and Provençaux recovered their medieval kings, lords, and troubadours; and the inhabitants of Tuscany invented their cultivated landscape of cypresses and olive trees, of small country houses with, in a niche in their façades, a small madonna by Luca della Robbia. Literature, music, and the arts contributed substantially to the establishment of the new mood, producing poems, collections of stories, fairy tales and legends, historical novels, historical paintings, and operas with strong patriotic subjects and vivid, colourful backdrops. The folkloric and nationalistic imaginary is a typical product of the modern age,[12] both in its strong positive potential as an instrument contributing to the shaping of the past and the destiny of each nation, and in its dangerous negative potential as a set of cultural products that, in the cyclical crises and conflicts of the world economy, nourished and gave birth to such monsters as Fascism, Nazism, and racism, with their inevitable massacres, transplantation of entire populations, and ethnic cleansings. The role of literature has not always been a progressive and illuminating one.

Another important theme gained a central place in the social and cultural life of the period, and even more in the system of themes and forms of literature: romantic love. This theme is interesting because it is a clear example of the driving influence of literature in shaping the ideas and behaviour of whole societies. Passionate love, together with other types of human love (*l'amour plaisir* or *l'amour libertin*, homoerotic or Platonic love, among others), has been present in human societies as a great cultural model at different stages of their development. Passionate love as a form of experimentation and exploration was pervasive in the European societies of the eighteenth century, as Niklas Luhman has shown in his interesting study, *Liebe als Passion*. But that special version of passionate love that is, to my mind, romantic love, has some very peculiar and specific traits that differentiate it from previous models. It is characterized, first of all, by the couple's strong element of self-programming. Two people choose each other on the basis of a deep and mysterious affinity: 'that person,' they say, 'is my soulmate, whom I have finally encountered.' The program of the couple is that of building a new and indissoluble unity out of two separate bodies and souls. It is not surprising, of course, that such a program enters into a state of conflict with some social structures (traditional marriage, for instance, based on economic interest), and with the temporal dimension of history (individual events, changes of feelings, careers, etc.). Romantic love is an imperious driving force that does not accept compromises and, unlike some other traditional models of love, also invests in marriage – a marriage of love – again opening up conflicts with other social forces, such as the expectations of the original families and differences in class origins.

Nineteenth-century literature is an enormous experimental field for exploring all the aspects and consequences of romantic love, from the sublimating drives of lyric poetry to the dramatic or even tragic complications of the various love triangles, quadrangles, and other geometric combinations to the comic or grotesque consequences of all possible intrigues. I need not mention the many texts that elaborate the theme, from its early enthusiastic but ultimately dramatic representation in Goethe's *Die Leiden des jungen Werther* [The Sorrows of Young Werther], Benjamin Constant's *Adolphe*, or Ugo Foscolo's *Le ultime lettere di Iacopo Ortis* [The Last Letters of Jacopo Ortis]. I also do not need to mention the close, almost inevitable, connection between the theme of love and that of death in those and subsequent texts. Two perfectly similar souls, which could unite like two drops of water, often encounter external or even internal obstacles to the accomplishment of their dream (failure of communication, social constraints, differences in the intensity and orientation of passion); in many cases death seems the only way to make eternal the bond that has been established. This accounts for the enormous success in the Romantic age of the story of Romeo and Juliet, or of Tristan and Iseult, particularly in Wagner's version, in which, before the silence of death, the music intervenes to give shape to the unifying ideal of two bodies and two souls that have become one.

Not all the literary texts, of course, have represented in positive terms the theme and ideal of romantic love in its sublime or dramatic or tragicomic aspects. One of the roles of literature, as we have seen, is to question the cultural models, to examine them critically and explore their contradictions. This has happened also with romantic love, whose limits and possible aberrations have been exposed, especially in certain texts of the fantastic: the excesses of casting one's individual passion onto an object of desire that is unworthy or fails to notice such attention, the imaginary projection or substitution of the human object of love with a portrait, a statue, a fetish, or even, as in Gautier's novelette *Spirite*, a ghost.

Modernity and Italian Society, Culture, and Literature

Authors of nineteenth- and twentieth-century Italian cultural and literary histories were long guided by a widely influential model of interpretation and reconstruction, deeply rooted in the nineteenth-century conception of the national character (or *Geist*) of each nation. The most prestigious example was probably the *History of Italian Literature* by Francesco De Sanctis (1870–1), considered by many a European masterpiece.[13] Others, recognizing its strong narrative construction, see it as the best Italian *Bildungsroman* of its century (its subject being the education not of a single individual but of an entire nation).[14] De Sanctis's history, and many similar ones – some of which were more decidedly idealistic (*geistesgeschichtlich*), or, at times, naturalistic and even evolutionistic along biological models – have coined certain historical partitions and tags common in the educational handbooks and the critical jargon of Italy even today, such as *Risorgimento* and *Rinascimento* (rebirth, renaissance, new rising), *Rinnovamento* (renewal), *Decadenza* and *Decadentismo* (decadence, decadentism), *Restaurazione* (restoration), and *Resistenza* (resistance).

The most popular story of the Italian political, cultural, and literary *Risorgimento* has a very simple plot, based on the idea of the recovery and renewal of a cultural and political identity that took place in the nineteenth century, with the revival of an ancient and noble tradition and the foundation of a *nuova Italia* [new Italy]. The real historical development was much more complicated and can best be represented by images of contradiction, problems left unsolved, and a certain fortuitousness in the historical events. However, a number of ideological simplifications and constraints were employed for many years in official explanations and interpretations.

It would be difficult to find another country in nineteenth-century Europe that presented so many contradictions. Italy was traditionally divided into parts that not only had different political systems, but often quite dissimilar economic and social organizations and cultural traditions. In many regions and states the process of modernity was very slow in dominating the scene; yet in certain Italian cities, during the eighteenth century, groups of intellectuals formed around important figures with European connections and developed some of the ideas of the Enlightenment. In the early nineteenth century, the Romantic movement that developed in Milan and in other cities of the North was characterized by a moderation and timidity that distinguished it from its more daring counterparts in the rest of Europe. Yet some of the protagonists of the intellectual and literary life of the time, such as Alessandro Manzoni, Giacomo Leopardi, Carlo Cattaneo, Ippolito Nievo, Francesco De Sanctis, Cesare Lombroso, and Vilfredo Pareto, enjoyed a stature that placed them at the same level as many intellectuals in other countries. After political unification, a general backwardness hindered the progress of Italy as a whole. The economic and cultural gap that affected many regions, especially the South, was an obstacle to true progress, although some of the best intellectuals and writers of the time came from those same backward regions (philosophers such as Benedetto Croce and Giovanni Gentile, historians such as Pasquale Villari or De Sanctis, writers such as Giovanni Verga, Luigi Capuana, or Federico De Roberto, etc.). Another contradiction is the fact that, in spite of the presence of conservative and retrograde elements in much of the country's intellectual culture, the contribution of Italians to avant-garde movements and to various facets of modernism, starting with Futurism, was of the utmost importance.

A rewriting of Italian literary history along the lines suggested by the general revision of the history of modernity would probably give some interesting results. Even authors like Manzoni and Leopardi, who have been the object of much critical appraisal and deep study, might profit from such a reconsideration. Manzoni's great novel *I promessi sposi* [The Betrothed] (1840) has an experimental (and therefore modern) quality that would place it at the crossroad between various narrative modes: the historical novel in the vein of Walter Scott, the romance in the vein of Richardson and Diderot, the *Bildungsroman* with some picaresque episodes around the character of Renzo, and even at times the comedy of errors and mischief in the vein of Mozart and Da Ponte's *Don Giovanni*. Critics such as Raimondi have already begun to move in those interpretive directions.[15] Leopardi continues to be undervalued in many general surveys of nineteenth-century European poetry, in spite of the fact that, as many scholars have shown, his lyrics, together with the prose of the *Operette morali* and the impressions, observations, and memories recorded in his *Zibaldone*, prove him to be a very modern man. His insights are original and the quality of his thought bold and paradoxical. At times, he seems to elaborate some of the most striking ideas of Diderot; at other times, he seems to anticipate those of Nietzsche.[16]

I would be inclined to include, among the examples of indisputable modernity in Italian literature, two poets, Carlo Porta and Giuseppe Gioacchino Belli, who expressed themselves in the dialect of Milan and of Rome, respectively, adopting the language of the comic mode, mingled with touches of the dramatic, the realistic, and the grotesque. They, of course, have been systematically excluded from the traditional canon for not using the language of the literary tradition and of the nation that was in the process of unifying itself. Comparing them with other European poets and writers who chose to express themselves in a local language rather than a national one – for instance, Ludwig Thoma in Bavaria or Frédéric Mistral in Provence – it is obvious that there is nothing of the easily nostalgic and picturesque or comic in their texts. The vigour of their expressionistic language and of their powerful representation of human feelings, obsessions, and ideas bring to mind some of the best pieces in Gaetano Donizetti's *Don Pasquale* or Giuseppe Verdi's *Falstaff*.

The traditional canon tends to leave out not only the poetry of Porta and Belli, but also two books that had a strong impact on the general public of modern Italy and were fundamental in shaping its language and imagination – although in almost opposite fashions, confirming once more the contradictions at the heart of the new society and culture. I am referring to Edmondo De Amicis's *Cuore* (1886) and Carlo Lorenzini's (also known as Collodi) *Pinocchio* (1883).

The first work was instrumental in building the symbols of power and some of the ideological premises of the new nation, such as the ethics of sacrifice, obedience, and solidarity, the importance of education and work, admiration for individual acts of heroism, and respect for the authorities. *Cuore* takes the form of a school diary, kept by a less than brilliant young student at an elementary school in Turin. It contains Dickensian portraits of teachers and schoolmates, many of them coming from other regions of the country, but all of them equally engaged in the hard work of transforming themselves into educated citizens of the newly unified state. Themes such as a strong vein of violence and perversity hidden behind the exhibited goodness of De Amicis's characters and a disturbing echo of many of Italy's social problems (poverty, unemployment, emigration, criminality)[17] arise from the political unconscious of the book to enliven it and make it more complex and ambiguous than readers could have expected from its confessed ideological aims. *Pinocchio*, a masterpiece of narrative invention, human psychology, and language, can also be considered a true parody of the many educative programs, in the form of the *Bildungsroman*, for young Italians. The parody is surprisingly modern in its simplicity and efficacy. Through the adventures, rebellions, and transgressions of the wooden puppet Pinocchio, Collodi lays bare, with lightness and humour, the hypocrisies of such important institutions as the school, the administration of justice, the police, the entertainment industry, and so forth.

In many cases the new themes and forms of modernity came to Italy somewhat late, softened or distorted from the most advanced literatures of the time, especially French, English, and German. Some themes of European Romantic poetry can be found even in an outspoken adversary of the Romantics, such as Giosue Carducci or, in a more sympathetic and Symbolist version, in the poetry of Giovanni Pascoli. Some of the most daring, and modern, aspects of Baudelaire's poetry can be detected in the imitations of a *scapigliato* like Emilio Praga. The fantastic inventions of Hoffmann, Gautier, Dickens, and Poe, for instance, were taken up by other *scapigliati* such as Iginio Ugo Tarchetti, Camillo, and Arrigo Boito. Giovanni Verga, though he added a personal and original touch, emulated the narrative experiments of the French novelists, from Balzac to Flaubert to Zola, and his greatest novels, *I Malavoglia* (1881) and *Mastro Don Gesualdo* (1889), were admired by D.H. Lawrence. Other novelists, such as Capuana and De Roberto, likewise emulated Europeans. The greatest specialist in recycling all types of modern European literature, from Flaubert to Maupassant, Zola to Dostoevsky, Huysmans to Swinburne, and Nietzsche to Tolstoy, in prose and poetry, was probably Gabriele D'Annunzio. But D'Annunzio's modernity is more evident in his way of life, his enormously successful public image, and his ability to exploit the trends and whims of the new bourgeoisie than in his writings.

The true rupture, the real leap into modernity, occurred comparatively late in Italian literature, but once made it was so bold and advanced that the literary establishment of the country had some difficulty recognizing it. This was less true of poetry (for Ungaretti and

Montale were soon recognized as the most important voices of the new century) than of narrative prose and the theatre. The extraordinary importance of Italo Svevo's *La coscienza di Zeno* [Zeno's Conscience] (1923) was first recognized by non-Italian readers, such as James Joyce or Valéry Larbaud; Pirandello had to resort to audiences in other countries to find recognition, because the experimental quality of his short stories, novels, and theatrical pieces aroused the hostility of Benedetto Croce and most of his followers.

Many Divides within a Period of Great Divides: The Year 1922

I have spoken, in the first part of this essay, of the two epochal changes that, according to historians, radically transformed the social and cultural life of Europe (including Italy) and of the many smaller shifts that took place in the nineteenth and twentieth centuries, some of which were perceived as important and of great historical impact. Now the question is: what do we make of the secondary changes, especially those connected with some great symbolic event, such as the revolutions of 1848; the Paris Commune; the outbreak of the First World War; or the appearance of major works such as Marx and Engels's *Communist Manifesto*, Baudelaire's *Fleurs du mal*, Darwin's *Origin of the Species*, Nietzsche's *Birth of Tragedy*, Wagner's Ring cycle, Freud's *Interpretation of Dreams*, the manifestos of Futurism or Surrealism, Joyce's *Ulysses*, Svevo's *Coscienza di Zeno*, and Pirandello's *Sei personaggi in cerca d'autore* [Six Characters in Search of an Author]?

It seems to me that once we are aware that one of the main characteristics of modernity was the desire to change and renew the world, to prepare the future and be ahead of one's time, dates associated with secondary changes are bound to acquire a significance within the general movement of history. Many of those dates were perceived as marking shifts of enormous importance by both observers and protagonists of cultural life at the time. They have equally acquired a remarkable significance for historians.

One date that is not often seen as particularly significant or symbolic, but which has some interesting features, especially from the point of view of Italian literary history, and which symbolizes the establishment of full modernism in the cultural atmosphere of the twentieth century, is 1922. Many will claim that it is too late in comparison with other dates (1900, 1905, 1914, or others) that have been considered as particularly crucial. Yet, a student of English modernism such as Harry Levin has identified this year as particularly capable of representing the culminating moment of modernism, calling it the 'annus mirabilis' in the history of the entire movement. The same date was singled out by Italian critic Giacomo Debenedetti, who, as we shall see, can be considered the true 'critic of modernity' in Italy. The chronicler and historian of modernism, Debenedetti was himself immersed in modernity as a writer and intellectual, with a deep interest in psychoanalysis and Marxism, a constant involvement in the political and cultural events of his time, and a dedication to practical activities such as the foundation of journals and little magazines and the editorial direction of publishing houses.

In listing some of the most important events of 1922, we might use the words of Debenedetti, who, when he happened to study a later date in the development of modernism in Italy, resorted to a metaphoric image to represent his way of proceeding. To him it was inevitable, in order to understand a year's significance, to look not only at the year in question but also at the preceding and the following ones: 'To act in the same way as when one cuts the trunk of a tree and looks at the rings in it, at the sap that mounts from the bottom, coming from what was before, and rising toward what will come after' (*Il romanzo*, 60–1). If we apply the same procedure to the year 1922, we soon discover that it really was, on the European scene, the 'annus mirabilis' of which Levin speaks. The year saw the publication, to start with, of James Joyce's *Ulysses* and T.S. Eliot's *The Waste Land*. It was the year in which Rainer Maria Rilke composed his *Duineser Elegien* [Duino Elegies], and the *Sonette an Orpheus* [Sonnets to Orpheus] (due to be published the following year), and in which appeared the second part of Marcel Proust's *Sodome et Gomorrhe* [Sodom and Gomorrha] (preceded in 1920 by *Le côté de Guermantes* [The Guermantes Way] and in 1921 by the first part of *Sodome et Gomorrhe*) and Virginia Woolf's *Jacob's Room*. It was the year of D.H. Lawrence's *Aaron's Rod*, and Hermann Hesse's *Siddharta*, and the year in which Kafka wrote *Das Schloß* [The Castle]. It was the year of Bertold Brecht's debut, with *Baal* and *Trommeln in der Nacht* [Drums in the Night], the year of the first international congress of avant-garde artists in Düsseldorf; the year of Georg Grosz's trip to the Soviet Union and of the publication of his *Ecce homo*, the folder of drawings that raised a scandal resulting in a court trial. Henry Bergson's *Durée et simultaneité* [Duration and Simultaneity], Ludwig Wittgenstein's *Tractatus*, and Oswald Spengler's *Untergang des Abendlandes* [The Twilight of the West] were also published in 1922. Public radiobroadcasts had officially begun a year earlier. In the history of cinema, it was the year in which the film *Doktor Mabuse*, by Fritz Lang, was distributed. Lang followed in the footsteps of Robert Wiene's *Das Kabinett des Doktor Caligari* [The Cabinet of Doctor Caligari], released in 1921. The year was also marked by the first release of Dziga Vertov's 'Kino-Pravda,' and by the triumphant European tour of Charlie Chaplin, with his new films. *The Kid*, released in 1921, captured the spirit of the time. 1922 was the year immediately following the first production of Alban Berg's *Wozzeck* and Mayakovsky's *Mystery-Bouffe*. Various cities staged Eugene O' Neill's *Anna Christie*. Pirandello's *Sei personaggi* (staged for the first time in Italy in 1921) opened in New York City and London in 1922, while *Enrico IV* opened in his native Italy.

But how is 1922 distinguished in the chronology of Italian literature? It was the year of the 'Esposizione d'arte italiana futurista' and of Vinicio Paladini's 'Appello agli intellettuali,' published after the appearance in *Ordine nuovo* [New Order] in 1921 of an article by Antonio Gramsci that bluntly asked the question, 'is Marinetti a revolutionary?' In 1921, Giuseppe Antonio Borgese had published *Rubé* and Umberto Saba his *Canzoniere*. In 1922 Svevo finished writing *La coscienza di Zeno*, due to come out the following year, Enrico Pea published *Moscardino*, and Giani Stuparich his memoir on Scipio Slataper. A year later, in 1923, Bruno Cicognani's *La Velia* would appear in stores, and Borgese would collect his essays on contemporary Italian literature, previously published in the literary journal, *I libri del giorno*. Borgese's catchword was 'it is time to construct' and he supported the works of Federigo Tozzi, the Sienese writer who died in 1920, the year in which his *Ricordi di un impiegato* [The Recollections of a Clerk] had been published (his novels were published just after his death, *Tre croci* [Three Crosses] in 1920, *Il podere* [The Farm] in 1921, and *Gli egoisti* [The Egoists] in 1923).

In the notes for his courses at the University of Rome, published as *Il romanzo del Novecento*, Giacomo Debenedetti paid much attention to 1921–2 and declared that date as marking the beginning of the history of the 'modern' novel in Italy. He described those years as the moment in which the narrative genre disengaged itself from 'the non-narration, the pseudo-narration or even the sabotage of any narration' (60–1) once customary in literary circles. As he argues, 1922 was also the year in which, following the recent discovery of Verga, the Italian novel and short story 'painfully disengaged themselves from the schemes of the tradition of Verismo' (112). Yet, as we all know, 1922 was a crucial and important year mainly in the history of 'modern' Italian poetry: it witnessed the debut of Eugenio Montale, who published the seven pieces of *Accordi* [Chords] and the poem 'Riviere' in *Primo tempo*, a literary journal founded that same year in Turin by four very young men: Sergio Solmi, Giacomo Debenedetti, Mario Gromo, and Emanuele F. Sacerdote.

But 1922 – this is what I wanted to come to at last – was also the year in which Giacomo Debenedetti made his debut as a critic. Apart from participating in the foundation of *Primo tempo* and writing his first essays (on Croce's style, Saba, Montale, Boine, Michelstädter),[18] Debenedetti had his first contacts with writers and intellectuals outside Turin, and in the first months of 1923 he wrote his long story 'Amedeo.' To the miraculous quality of the year's literary and artistic production in Europe we can compare something that appears perhaps even more miraculous: the extraordinary certainty with which the young critic who grew up in Turinese intellectual circles made his choices of taste and decided, for himself and for others, which were the truly important events, authors, and works of the literature of his time. In his critical choices, he appears to be in perfect consonance with the tastes and the emergent choices of modernism. Franco Brioschi has spoken, referring to this precocious certainty, of 'the divining-rod of a dowser' (Introduction ix).

What helped to place Debenedetti in immediate sympathy with the sensibility and taste of modern times was his keen awareness that modern poetry and fiction – in their structure, rhetorical stance, and style, and in their use of the appropriate objective correlatives – should give expression to the typical cognitive and existential experiences of modernity. These experiences can be identified with the 'sentiment of laceration,' the 'dissociation of sensibility,' the loss of coherence, weight, and depth of the subject, and attention to the fragment and the detail.

This laceration was existential but also sociological and philosophical, and it took the form of a break with teachers and colleagues, people who were refined in their literary tastes but also conservative, traditional, and faithful to the dominant model of Benedetto Croce's aesthetics. Against the Crocean canon, which explicitly excluded much of contemporary European literature on the grounds that it was morally decadent and aesthetically impure, an alternative canon had to be constructed. Debenedetti set to work and carried out this task with extraordinary self-assurance and intuition, devising a canon that included all the works that today we consider the true classics of modern literature. An interesting evocation of that moment of rebellion and the foundation of a new canon can be found in the autobiographical pages of 'Probabile autobiografia di una generazione,' his 'Prefazione 1949' to *Saggi critici* (first edition, 1929), which are generally admired for their narrative tone:

> Mattini all'Università di Torino, dei quali posso testimoniare di persona: sotto i portici del cortile, vaporassero le nebbie dell'inverno col loro sapore di seltz, o il sole degli aprili e dei maggi levigasse di ceruleo le colonne, o fiammeggiasse quello estivo sui giorni d'esame, chi ora con la macchina del tempo potesse tornare a quei mattini sentirebbe di che cosa si discorreva. Croce e Gentile, Gentile e Croce, il grande duello. [...]
>
> In una fase di maggiore maturità, questa situazione si vede rispecchiata nei *Quaderni del carcere* di un più anziano di noi, Antonio Gramsci. Lui aveva già distaccato, dal fondo comune dove ancora le nostre adolescenze si arrovellavano, una sua autobiografia, e con che segno incisa. Eppure, quando si trovò in prigione, solo col proprio cervello, sul punto ormai di formulare la sua autonoma filosofia della prassi, anche lui constatò la necessità di pagare pedaggio a Croce. E per quanto concerne le questioni dell'arte, nelle *Lettere dal carcere* si noterà che la materia dei giudizi è tutta di lui, Gramsci, la struttura invece di quei giudizi, il modo di motivarli risentono ancora lo strumentale crociano. S'è detto Gramsci: cioè un uomo che intimamente aveva già attuata la 'rottura.'
>
> 'Rottura' sarebbe stata anche per noi la parola, ma la conoscevamo male e non sospettavamo che si potesse applicare alla nostra situazione di giovanotti divisi tra l'amore dell'arte e l'assillo di trovare la ragione sufficiente di questo amore. (Amare senza capire ci sarebbe parso libertinaggio, un perdere la vita, noi che eravamo nati per giuste nozze. Si traggano le conseguenze, anche biografiche, di una simile situazione.). I più anziani e più saggi [...] ci chiamavano, con garbata impazienza, problemisti. Effettivamente, come succede a coloro che si spendono in una serie di gesti coatti e maniache superstizioni, perché incapaci di commettere il gesto che corregga i loro rapporti con la vita, così anche noi ci esercitavamo a volgere tutto in problemi, a suscitare da tutto un problema, per deficiente coraggio di quella rottura, che era il nostro vero problema, tutt'insieme tipico e immaturo. (*Saggi* 107–8)

> [Mornings at the University of Turin, which I can personally recall: under the arcades of the courtyard: winter fogs dissolving, with their taste of soda-water, or April or May suns that washed the columns and coloured them sky blue, or summer sun that blazed on exam days. If anyone could now, with

the help of a time-machine, go back to those mornings he could hear the topics of our conversation: Croce and Gentile, Gentile and Croce, the great duel. [...]

In a more advanced phase, that situation is reflected in the *Prison Notebooks*, by someone who was a bit older than us, Antonio Gramsci. He had already separated his autobiography (and with what originality!) from the common background in which we, with our adolescent persons, still tormented ourselves. Yet, when he found himself in a prison, alone with his mind, on the threshold of formulating his own philosophy of praxis, he also felt that it was necessary to pay his toll to Croce. As for art, it is easy to observe that, in his *Letters from Prison*, while the subjects under examination are all of his own choice, the structure of his judgments and the ways of motivating them are influenced by the critical instruments of Croce. And that was Gramsci, a man who in his inner self had already consummated the 'rupture.'

'Rupture' was to be the word for us as well, but we did not know it well enough and we did not suspect that it could be applied to our situation of young men divided between the love of art and the anguish of finding sufficient ground for that love. (To love without understanding would have seemed to us libertinism, a way of spoiling our life – we who believed that we had been born to celebrate a just marriage. You can draw all possible conclusions, including the biographical ones, from such a situation). The oldest and wisest among us [...] used to call us, with well-mannered impatience, *'problematisti.'* And in fact, as it happens to those who waste themselves in a series of compulsive gestures and obsessive superstitions because they are unable to make the gesture that would set right their relationship with life, so we too applied ourselves to turn everything into a problem, to stir up a problem from everything, as we lacked the courage for that rupture, which was our true and only problem, at once typical and immature.]

In 'Amedeo,' a 'critical short story' written by Debenedetti in 1923, the necessity of a 'rupture,' of a 'laceration' also breaks into – although it is impossible to say whether truly or wishfully – the short circuit of the day of the protagonist in the shape of a message from the outside, or from destiny, a circular letter from America. However, Amedeo, a 'slothful man' – a sort of Eliotian Prufrock in his adolescent years – remains enclosed in the narrow circle of his conscience, of his ways of behaving dominated by the repetition compulsion, of the image that others have of him, and that he himself has of his 'immanent destiny.'

Debenedetti not only represented the dismembering of the human character into many fragments in his own narrative experiments, he also analysed it in the works of other writers, especially of the great modern writers who were dear to him. Among the many instances in which he has expressed himself on this subject, I would like to quote from 'Commemorazione provvisoria del personaggio uomo,' in which the image of the narrow circle appears once again: 'For the human character [*personaggio-uomo*] a new hard life had begun: he can be found intact only at the point in which the circle closes its circumference and the beginning coincides with the end. He appears, a name and a civil status is imposed on him, then he disperses into a myriad of corpuscles that drive him out from the stage, and he is called back only when he is needed to glue together his tiny fragments' (*Saggi* 1290–1).

Debenedetti analyses the new phenomenology of the character in many works of contemporary European literature, such as those of Proust, Joyce, and Musil, and in works of modern Italian literature, such as those of Svevo and Tozzi. He also finds examples in the work of Boris Pasternak. These include the separate destinies of the two main characters of *Doctor Zhivago* and the encounters dominated by the law of chance. When they meet, the narrator does not care to tell us what new forces have driven them towards their meeting:

> All this can be translated into a metaphor that might go behind its simple metaphoric range, taken from the language of nuclear physics. Pasternak lets us assist to the collision of the atoms that unchains the reaction, he gives us, in wonderful pages of lyric descriptions of the landscape, the exact location of the collision point, in wonderful pages of dramatic narration, the sight and scene of the chain reaction and its effects; he cannot give us the trajectories of the atoms that concur to it, the journey they have taken to come to the collision-point; for, exactly as in physics, their trajectories elude any possible calculation and to reconstruct it by supposition would be, for his aims, totally unessential. The important thing is that they have met. ('A proposito di "Intermezzo"' 57)

Debenedetti surprisingly discovers the same phenomenology in a writer who fully belongs to the Italian nineteenth century: Niccolò Tommaseo. Because of his strong adherence to the Catholic orthodoxy and his classical taste, at first sight Tommaseo would seem extremely remote from the experience of modernity. Yet Debenedetti succeeds, in a manner reminiscent of the more recent reinterpretation of the Romantics carried out by de Man, in transforming Tommaseo, on the basis of his internal contradictions, his tormented biography, the mixture of passions and rigours in his character, the fragmentary and experimental elements in his writing, into a sort of bearded grandfather of the writers immersed in the crisis of modernity. Tommaseo was a writer 'without a destiny,' a man 'at the disposal of circumstances' (*Niccolò Tommaseo* 19). His life was a true odyssey, 'but an odyssey with many landings and no final landing at Ithaca' (123). His *Memorie poetiche* [Poetic Recollections] place him alongside Joyce and Dylan Thomas's *Portraits* and the autobiographical memoirs of many other modern writers. In order to uncover the secret of that proto-modern life, the critic must embark on a search for details, hints, clues, Freudian slips of the tongue, and unrestrained repetition compulsions.

But, like every great critic and interpreter of modernity, Debenedetti knows, explores, and invents strategies to heal the laceration and overcome the dispersion of life into innumerable fragments. His ways for proceeding to a tentative reconstruction of the lost unity of the subject are based on examples taken from the great literature of modernity. They include 1) memory as the space in which the details project themselves and attain a unity, the 'intermittences of the heart' suggested by Proust; 2) the hermeneutical space and the experience of epiphany, which elevate details to an absolute meaning, suggested by Joyce; 3) the use of a supporting structure for the variety and disparity of the details, such as the one offered by a mythic story in Joyce's *Ulysses*; 4) the model offered by the Marxist interpretation of history, which finds a meaning for the single detail in the general, dramatic, and grandiose frame of class struggle; 5) the symphonic poem and the musical drama surging from the mystic gulf of the orchestra, according to the Wagnerian model, which draws the catastrophic explosion of the detail within the intricate web of the musical themes and the thunder of Destiny. In the critical work of Debenedetti there are numerous examples of each one of these categories, confirming the extraordinary, persistently modern quality of his criticism.

NOTES

1 There are detailed accounts in my *Raccontare la letteratura* (109–8) and *Guida allo studio della letteratura* (359–91). I am also making extensive use of my essay, 'The New System of Literary Modes in the Romantic Age.'

2 On the problem of Romanticism it might be useful to revisit the debate
  between Arthur Lovejoy ('On the Discrimination of Romanticism')
  and René Wellek ('The concept of Romanticism in Literary History').
  Among the more recent introductions, see also Lilian Furst's two studies,
  Romanticism and *Romanticism in Perspective*, and Marcello Pagnini's *Il
  Romanticismo*.
3 De Man, *Romanticism and Contemporary Criticism* 134–6.
4 By Hartmann, see in particular *The Unmediated Vision*, *The Unremarkable
  Wordsworth*, and *Wordsworth's Poetry*.
5 I have the impression that, with due caution, a similar argument could be
  made for Giacomo Leopardi in Italy.
6 See also Luperini, 'Costruzione di una "Costruzione".'
7 See Jauß.
8 Interesting attempts at an allegorical reading of Verga, Pirandello, and
  Montale can be found in some recent essays by Luperini; see *Storia di
  Montale*, *Simbolo e costruzione allegorica in Verga*, and *L'allegoria del moderno*.
9 On the fantastic, see Todorov, Bessière, Jackson, and my *Il fantastico*.
10 Another important contribution is Berman's *All That Is Solid Melts Into Air*.
11 See Moretti.
12 See Bhaba.
13 See, for example, Wellek, *A History of Modern Criticism* (4: 125). Wellek
   writes, 'All three, De Sanctis, Belinsky, and Taine, absorbed Hegelian
   historicism and romantic aesthetics and transformed them for the needs
   of their time and place, preserving their essential truths and thus handing
   them on to the twentieth century. But De Sanctis' achievement far
   transcends his historical role: in spite of lapses into didacticism and
   emotionalism, he wrote what seems to me the finest history of any
   literature ever written.'
14 See my *Raccontare la letteratura* (20).
15 See Raimondi's *Il romanzo senza idillio* and *La dissimulazione romanzesca*.
16 See Brioschi, *La poesia senza nome*, Nietzsche, and Negri.
17 Turin, the city of De Amicis and the protagonists of *Cuore*, was, after all,
   the home of Lombroso.
18 'Turin 1922' could be the title of this chapter in the history of modern
   Italian culture. Among the cities that are entitled to be considered
   symbolic centres of modernity – such as Paris, London, and New York
   and the equally important and plausible Berlin, Vienna, Prague, Saint
   Petersburg, Copenhagen, and Chicago – one could include Milan and
   Turin and, in a more or less relevant way, Florence, Rome, and Trieste. To
   legitimate the city's claim one must only recall the highly contradictory,
   and for this very reason dynamic and interesting, case of Turin's basic

economic structure. The city, very traditional in many of its features, was suddenly overtaken, from about 1903, by a rapid process of transformation, which in a few years turned it into an industrial city of factories and workers. This rapid modernization pushed Turin's citizens towards both a nostalgic and provincial attachment to the tradition of nineteenth-century *'piemontesismo'* and daring and cosmopolitan innovations. In cultural life, the city was characterized by the double presence of an elitist and a largely popular culture. There were academic circles connected with the deeply rooted tradition of nineteenth-century positivism and scientism together with centres of spiritualism or humanitarian socialism, along with important schools of historians and economists imbued with a respect for a scientific method of ascertaining the facts (people like Gaetano De Sanctis, Achille Loria, Luigi Einaudi, Francesco Ruffini, and Gioele Solari). There were also groups, born within the academy but driven by interior needs for spiritual and moral renewal, who searched for contact with other groups in Italy from different social strata, such as the followers of Neapolitan philosopher Benedetto Croce (himself connected with Piedmont through his wife's relatives), Antonio Gramsci's supporters and his political enterprise, and those gathered around Piero Gobetti, a brilliant mind and great organizer of culture (until they were all stopped by the Fascist regime). To understand the importance of Turin as a capital of modernity in Italy it might be necessary to add a few other events: the international exhibition of modern decorative art of 1902, the formation of local Futurist groups (with such artists as Fillia, Nicola Djulgheroff, and Medardo Rosso), the birth in the city of the first experimental and industrial cinema in Italy, and the key role of the Italian automobile and its first trade mark: the FIAT.

WORKS CITED

Benjamin, Walter. *Ursprung des deutschen Trauerspiels*. Frankfurt: Suhrkamp, 1963.
Berman, Marshall. *All That Is Solid Melts Into Air: The Experience of Modernity*. New York: Simon and Schuster, 1982.
Bessière, Irene. *Le récit fantastique: la poétique de l'incertain*. Paris: Larousse, 1974.
Bhaba, Homi, ed. *Nation and Narration*. London and New York: Routledge, 1990.

Blumenberg, Hans. *The Legitimacy of the Modern Age*. Cambridge: MIT P, 1983.

Brioschi, Franco. 'Introduction.' *Personaggi e destino. La metamorfosi del romanzo contemporaneo*. By Giacomo Debenedetti. Milan: Il Saggiatore, 1977.

– *La poesia senza nome: Saggio su Leopardi*. Milan: Il Saggiatore, 1980.

Brooks, Peter. *The Melodramatic Imagination*. New Haven: Yale UP, 1976.

Ceserani, Remo. *Il fantastico*. Bologna: Il Mulino, 1996.

– *Guida allo studio della letteratura*. Bari: Laterza, 1999.

– 'The New System of Literary Modes in the Romantic Age.' *The People's Voice. Essays on European Romanticism*. Monash Romance Studies, 4. Ed. A. Ciccarelli et al. Melbourne: School of European Languages and Culture, Monash University, 1999. 7–25.

– *Raccontare la letteratura* Turin: Bollati-Boringhieri, 1990.

Debenedetti, Giacomo. *Niccolo Tommaseo*. Milan: Garzanti, 1973.

– 'A proposito di "Intermezzo".' *L'approdo letterario* 13.39 (1967): 5–18.

– *Il romanzo del Novecento*. 2nd ed. Milan: Garzanti, 1987.

– *Saggi*. Ed. Alfonso Berardinelli. Milan: Mondadori, 1999.

De Man, Paul. 'The Rhetoric of Temporality.' 1969. *Blindness and Insight*. Minneapolis: U of Minnesota P, 1983.

– *Romanticism and Contemporary Criticism*. Baltimore: Johns Hopkins UP, 1993.

Furst, Lilian R. *Romanticism*. London: Methuen, 1976.

– *Romanticism in Perspective: A Comparative Study of Aspects of the Romantic Movements in England, France, and Germany*. London: Macmillan, 1979.

Hartman, Geoffrey. *The Unmediated Vision: An Interpretation of Wordsworth, Hopkins, Rilke, and Valéry*. New York: Harcourt Brace, 1966.

– *The Unremarkable Wordsworth*. Minneapolis: U of Minnesota P, 1987.

– *Wordsworth's Poetry: 1787–1814*. Cambridge: Harvard UP, 1987.

Hobsbawm, Eric. *The Age of Extremes: The Short Twentieth Century, 1914–1991*. London: Abacus, 1995.

Jackson, Rosemary. *Fantasy: The Literature of Subversion*. London and New York: Routledge, 1988.

Jauß, Hans Robert. 'Baudelaire's Rückgriff aud die Allegorie.' *Studien zum Epochenwander der ästhetischen Moderne*. Frankfurt: Suhrkamp, 1989.

Levin, Harry. 'What was Modernism?' *Refractions: Essays in Comparative Literature*. New York: Oxford UP, 1966.

Lovejoy, Arthur. 'On the Discrimination of Romanticism.' *Essays on the History of Ideas*. Baltimore: Johns Hopkins UP, 1948.

Luhmann, Nicholas. *Liebe als Passion. Zur Codierung von Intimität*. Frankfurt: Suhrkamp, 1982.

Luperini, Romano. *L'allegoria del moderno*. Rome: Riuniti, 1990.
- 'Costruzione di una "Costruzione": Il "Baudelaire" di Benjamin, il moderno, l'allegoria.' *Allegoria*. 1.3 (1989): 7–35.
- *Simbolo e costruzione allegorica in Verga*. Bologna: Il Mulino, 1989.
- *Storia di Montale*. Rome and Bari: Laterza, 1986.
Moretti, Franco. *The Way of the World: The Bildungsroman in European Culture*. London: Verso, 1987.
Negri, Antimo. *Interminati spazi ed eterno ritorno*. Florence: Le lettere, 1994.
Nietzsche, Friedrich. *Intorno a Leopardi*. Ed. G. Galimberti. Genoa: Il Melangolo, 1992.
Pagnini, Marcello. *Il Romanticismo*. Bologna: Il Mulino, 1986.
Raimondi, Ezio. *La Dissimulazione romanzesca, la antropologia manzoniana*. Bologna: Il Mulino, 1997.
- *Il romanzo senza idillio: saggio sui 'Promessi sposi.'* Turin: Einaudi, 1974.
Tiedermann, Rolf. *Das Passagen-Werk*. Frankfurt: Suhrkamp, 1982.
Todorov, Tzvetan. *The Fantastic: A Structural Approach to a Literary Genre*. Ithaca, NY: Cornell UP, 1975.
Wellek, René. 'The Concept of Romanticism in Literary History.' *Concepts of Criticism*. New Haven: Yale UP, 1960.
- *A History of Modern Criticism, 1750–1950*. Vol. 4. Cambridge: Cambridge UP, 1965.

PART II

Decadence and Aestheticism

2 Sensuous Maladies: The Construction of Italian *Decadentismo*

MARIO MORONI

Introduction

In this essay I will consider Italian *Decadentismo* as a critical and historiographic category, in the light of the literary criticism which generated and defined it. I will begin with its first formulations in the context of French late-Romanticism, and then turn to the articulations of – and reactions to – the notions of decadence provided by such protagonists of the Italian cultural scene in the 1890s as Vittorio Pica, Arturo Graf, and Gian Pietro Lucini. I will conclude by discussing the reappropriation of the ideas of decadence and Decadentism by Idealist and Marxist thought in the works of Benedetto Croce and Georg Lukács.

I have chosen to deal with works of criticism on *Decadentismo*, rather than specific literary texts canonized as *Decadenti*, in the conviction that it is necessary to reconsider *Decadentismo* as a cultural discourse which has developed according to criteria and strategies of appropriation and rearticulation of the notion within different cultural projects and at different stages of the history of literary criticism and ideas.

Decadence: A Retrospective Look

In a general way, one may say that the term '*Decadentismo*' has been used by critics and historiographers to define the most varied aspects of art and literature of the second half of the nineteenth century. For a long time the term bore a negative connotation and covered practically any breaking of traditional models, any form of crisis and contradiction that characterized European culture in the transition from the nineteenth to the twentieth century. Italian Idealist culture has, in fact, applied the label of *Decadentismo* to all the literary experiences that questioned or shattered the forms of communication of Classic and Romantic culture. Later on, I will suggest that the Idealist cultural discourse appropriated the descriptive connotations of weakening and decadence that had emerged within post-Romantic culture, in order to transform them into strong critical and historical categories through which Idealism itself was able to invalidate those cultural discourses that went beyond the parameters of its own project. In other words, Italian *Decadentismo*, unlike Romanticism, lacks accurate terms of reference in both its conceptualization and periodization. Despite a large bibliography,[1] Italian *Decadentismo* appears to be, in fact, an excogitation *a posteriori*, developed by critics to explain cultural phenomena and attitudes that were simply *contemporary* to each other and that seemed to lie beyond the realm of other possible designations.

To begin with, however, I would like to consider briefly certain premodern features of the term 'decadence.' The Latin term *'decadentia'* – from which the corresponding terms *'décadence'* (French), *'decadenza'* (Italian), 'decadence' (English), and *'Dekadenz'* (German) originated – appeared in the Middle Ages, but the idea of decadence has a much longer history. Matei Calinescu reminds us that the myth of decadence existed, albeit in various forms, among the majority of ancient cultures.[2] The destructive power of time and decline were among the major motifs in all mythical and religious traditions. Essentially, each civilization tended to consider itself inferior and less fortunate than that of the previous age. Calinescu argues that ancient Greece perceived itself as already in a state of decadence, and the same may be said about all the other civilizations which developed before the Western world formed its notions of modernity and progress. One may even think of Plato as the first Western philosopher to organize an ontology based on the idea of decadence. Plato's theory of ideas implied a metaphysical concept of decadence (or degeneration), especially when he described the relationship between the real models of things (perfect and immutable) and their shadows manifesting themselves in the realm of perception. In this realm everything is subjected to a form of decadence, that is, the corruption of time and change.[3] This idea is also reflected in the Christian myth of Eden as well as in the classical one of the Golden Age.

Within the limits of this brief retrospective on decadence, it is necessary to look at the formation of the modern meaning of the term 'Decadentism' (*Decadentismo* in Italy) in its artistic and literary context. This term, proposed for the first time in 1886 by Anatole Baju – who later replaced it with *'décadisme'* – was soon forgotten in France. On 10 April 1886, Baju published the first issue of *Le Décadent* which was supposed to be the official organ of *décadisme* or *décadentisme*. But Baju's literary movement did not have a following, and its creator endured the same fate as other founders of short-lived journals or magazines which claimed the critics' attention only to the extent that they were considered precursors of Symbolism. French dictionaries eventually suppressed the term, and today it appears only in essays dealing with Symbolism.[4]

What interests me is the uncertain status of the notion of Decadentism. Norbert Jonard has pointed out that even today it would be very difficult to define the concept on the sole evidence of the Parisian journals of those years. Not even Baju's journal allows us to grasp any defined principle or a consistent cultural program.[5] Baju himself claimed that his mission did not consist in constructing the new but, rather, in destroying what was old in order to prepare the ground for the great literature of the twentieth century.[6]

A significant date for the phenomenon referred to as Decadentism is 1884. In that year a number of literary works were published which had resonance precisely because they would eventually be interpreted through the notion of Decadentism. The paradigmatic case remains J.K. Huysmans's *A Rebours*, which represented the model according to which the connotative aspects of Decadentism would be articulated. The main character of the novel, Jean Floressas des Esseintes, is the last descendant of a noble family. He withdraws from society to a bizarre hermitage, after having unsuccessfully tried to assuage his inner dissatisfaction and his boredom with life through vice. He wants to escape from contemporary capitalist and rationalist bourgeois society. The hermitage reflects his troubled soul; the place and its furnishings correspond to the most refined and perverse needs of an extreme form of aestheticism, based on the conviction that if the main characteristic of civilization is a progressive departure from nature, then the search for the individual lifestyle must rely upon artificial stimuli which provide subtle and hallucinative sensations, in preparation for the full achievement of an artificial life lived against the stream, or *a rebours*, with respect to the vulgarity of everyday life.

At this early stage in the formation of the decadent discourse we can already see two distinctive aspects of that differentiated experience with respect to the modes of everyday life and perception which would later characterize the notion of Decadentism. Experience is articulated from the very beginning as a true *counterdiscourse*, indicated in the title of the novel itself; that same experience is also articulated as a morbid condition, so much so that Huysmans's novel was defined by many critics as the documentation of a neurosis.

In fact, it was precisely the newborn psychological theories, indebted to the Darwinian ones on the evolution of the species, that allowed literary critics to label as neurotic those works which showed signs of alternative discourses. The recent medical discoveries had expanded the notion of decadence to the sphere of the individual psyche. Paul Bourget wrote that modern man, in his frantic lifestyle, bore the marks of diminished muscular energy and exacerbated nervousness, manifested through his frail limbs, the overexcited features of his face, and his excessively intense look.[7]

The term 'nervousness' existed previously, but by 1860 'neurosism' had also appeared, soon to be replaced by 'neurosis,' to indicate the disorder which, in the eighteenth century, had been called 'nervous illness,' and which, along with mental alienation, had gained ground in the field of medicine.[8] Max Nordau would later transfer the studies on mental disorders into the realm of artistic expression in his *Degeneration* (1892).[9] Although I am not going to deal extensively with Nordau's work in this essay, I would like to mention just one among his formulations which is significant for my reconsideration of Decadentism. Nordau interpreted as a pathological symptom of degeneration what would, in fact, become a typical expressive device of modernist and Symbolist poetry: synesthesia, consisting in the fusion of two distinct perceptive spheres, such as hearing and vision, in a single image:

In any case, it is an evidence of diseased and debilitated brain activity, if consciousness relinquishes the advantages of the differentiated perception of phenomena and carelessly confounds the reports conveyed by the particular senses. It is a retrogression to the very beginning of organic development. It is a descent from the height of human perfection to the low level of the mollusc. To raise the combination, transposition, and confusion of the perceptions of sound and sight to the rank of a principle of art, to see futurity in this principle, is to designate as progress the return from consciousness of man to that of oyster (142).

It was precisely the two complementary connotations of alternative discourse and malady and weakening that would generate a permanent ambivalence around a series of artistic and literary works canonized as 'decadent.'

The fictional character of des Esseintes remains probably the most extreme and emblematic representative of the decadent condition. In this scenario, the expressive forms conveying a neurotic and morbid dimension should be considered as attempts to articulate a discourse of differentiation of the artistic individuality with respect to the dynamics of everyday life and ordinary communication. They are a series of attempts ranging from the individual anarchist protest to the aesthetic gesture understood as transgression to the representation of forms of mental and/or physical alienation, indicating the inadaptability of both mind and body to a reality which demonstrates more and more advanced features of scientific, technological, and bureaucratic modernization.

One may argue, therefore, that *Decadence* was the expression of the writers' consciousness of their estrangement from and superiority to social norms considered corrupted and aberrant. To the pseudo-sanity of the bourgeois code, the writers opposed forms of moral and spiritual 'decadence' which they considered as the only viable option left to express their humanity. The term 'decadence' implicitly reflects the inversion of value – from negative to positive – that the authors attributed to the very idea of decline.

The 'decadent' style itself indicated the need for artistic and literary languages to refer totally and obsessively to themselves, in an attempt to validate their self-enclosed code against external reality and history at large. Here I would like to repropose what Marina Paladini Musitelli has suggested, that Italian *Decadentismo* appears to have been constructed for the purpose of indicating a variety of signs of an epochal *crisis* of values, rather than signs of a *critique* of those values.[10] I would add that in so-called *Decadentismo*, the signs of crisis and those of critique are inevitably correlated and complementary. In the last decade of the nineteenth century in Italy, however, the idea of decadence was constructed and conveyed primarily as a crisis rather than a critique.

Between Sensualism and Mysticism: The Reception of Decadence in Italy

The initial impact of Italian literary criticism on the notion of Decadentism is revealed in a series of articles by Vittorio Pica in *La Gazzetta letteraria* of Turin, devoted to contemporary French literature, later collected in his *Letteratura d'eccezione* (1899). From the beginning, the approach of Italian critics was characterized by an appropriation of the notion of decadence because of the idea of decline and decay that it conveyed, with the consequent emphasis on the condition of epochal crisis. Although Pica was an attentive interpreter of decadence, he was ultimately trying to explain the psychological origin of what seemed to be a state of mind rather than attempting to define an actual cultural critique of contemporary society. Certainly Pica acknowledged the value of such a critique, which he considered a reaction to the progress of the century, but in looking at the critique as a form of decline he attributed it to an objective psychological degradation and to the lack of willpower caused by phenomena of organic degeneration. In his essay on Paul Verlaine, but with general reference to the decadent writers, Pica wrote:

Fluttuanti tra il sensualismo e il misticismo, costoro non trovano mai pace, e nella loro irrequietudine angosciosa e irragionevole, domandano ai sensi una somma voluttà che essi in nessun modo possono dare e non ottengono che lo spasmo; [...] Ed in questi sforzi vani, folli, innaturali, si esaurisce quel pò di energia che posseggono, ed essi ripiombano, abbattuti ed esausti, in una triste e inguaribile lassitudine. Quel bisogno che, chi più chi meno, ciascuno di noi prova, di sottrarsi alle uggiose miserie della vita quotidiana, di volontariamente esiliarsi dal nostro mondo, per vivere di una vita extra-umana, di una vita immaginaria e celestiale, quel bisogno che in noi è eccezionale, in costoro diventa di tutti i giorni, di tutte le ore, e rappresenta uno stato normale, per quanto patologico. (44)

[Fluctuating between sensualism and mysticism, these people never find peace, and in their painful and unreasonable restlessness, they demand of their senses a supreme voluptuousness which they are not able to provide in any way, so they do not obtain anything but spasm; [...] And in these vain, crazy, and unnatural efforts, they spend what little energy they have, and they fall back, disheartened and exhausted, to a sad and incurable lassitude. That need that each of us feels, some more some less, to evade the boring miseries of everyday life, to voluntarily exile ourselves from our world, in order to live an extra-human life, an imaginary and celestial life, that need that in us is exceptional, in these people becomes a daily thing, an hourly thing, and represents a normal state, though a pathological one.][11]

In Pica's critical discourse, the diagnosis – at times a colourful one – based on explicit reference to medical pathology, coexists with the realization that, in fact, some specific connotations of an actual cultural discourse were emerging among the so-called *decadenti*. While Pica discusses an objective physical exhaustion of energy, accompanied by lassitude, he also seems to identify the modality of estrangement from epochal values and from forms of representation related to the sphere of everyday life. This is particularly true when he talks about the attempt to avoid the misery of everyday life, but also when, in the conclusion of his analysis, Pica writes: 'Data la concezione ultra-aristocratica dell'arte, dato il profondo disprezzo per la vita ordinaria, dato l'eccezionale stato psicologico, che son venuto ora determinando, quali opere scriverà un poeta e quale particolare estetica ne scaturirà? [Given the ultra-aristocratic conception of art, given the profound contempt for ordinary life, given the exceptional psychological state, which I have been defining, what works will a poet write and what particular aesthetics will spring from all this?]' (45).

The contempt for ordinary life and the exceptional condition that Pica points out here correspond precisely to some of the ideas discussed by Friedrich Nietzsche in his *The Birth of Tragedy*. According to the German philosopher, in the aesthetic sphere the individual subject frees itself from the conventions of perception and behaviour typical of everyday life. It is a moment when the subject loses itself, and therefore represents a departure from a rational foundation, along with a separation from ordinary communicative practice.[12] Elsewhere in *The Birth of Tragedy*, Nietzsche writes about the overcoming of the ordinary limits of existence through the Dionysiac state, which, once exhausted, inspires a sense of nausea for everyday life.[13] Pica identified exclusively as loss of energy, or clinical exhaustion, the same phenomenon that in Nietzsche's work was addressed as an issue of aesthetics and epistemology.

It is important to remember the extent to which the influence of the German philosopher generated, in artistic and literary works of the turn of the last century, a loss of interest in everyday linguistic practices, shifting the focus towards that 'aestheticism' detached from life, which was, in fact, the result of an extreme attempt to radicalize the critique of subject-centred reason. Nietzsche's critique implied that art was able to provide the subject with access into the Dionysiac dimension, which represented a radical alternative to the values produced by the reason and morality founded on scientific and philosophical modernity.

Another witness and critic of the phenomenon under examination, Arturo Graf, focused on some essential points in relation to the function of art as a way of access to a differentiated sphere. In his essay

'Preraffaeliti, simbolisti ed esteti' (1897),[14] Graf identified the attempt to open this way of access in the artist and writer's obscure languages and refusal of communication. He analysed both features in terms of 'immagini che si dissolvano prima d'essersi in tutto formate, [...] pensieri indefiniti che passino in una specie di luce crepuscolare e sottentrino l'un l'altro senza mai collegarsi tra loro [images that dissolve before they are completely formed, [...] undefined thoughts that pass through a kind of twilight and replace one another without ever linking up or coordinating with one another]' (310). Graf's evaluation of the cultural phenomenon was negative overall, but I am interested in verifying the accounts of certain dynamics from within the writings of those who were their close observers, as when Graf delineates the Symbolist gesture of responding to the restrictive code of social reality by working at the renewal of the soul and the deepening of human feelings, with the consequent expansion of the perceptive sphere.

Graf's critical discourse remains tied to the positivist confidence in contemporary reality and to the deep conviction that the task of art was that of operating in harmony with the forces of modernity, not of withdrawing from them. Both Pica and Graf interpreted the cultural expressions associated with decadence through the restoration of that hierarchy previously overturned by the French poets, therefore contradicting the latter's critical operation and reaffirming the fundamental positivist values of contemporary society.

But in the relationship between the French and the Italian cultural contexts, we are confronted with an issue of cultural politics. Graf and other Italian critics tended to want to preserve the Renaissance Italian tradition from the influence of the French decadent climate. In the same years of the publication of Graf's essay in *Nuova Antologia*, another literary magazine began publication: *Il Convito*. It is still considered one of the official organs of Italian *Decadentismo*, and yet in its articles we can find expressed a profound aversion for the attitude of some of the most important French writers of that time, interestingly because of their polemic employment of an oppositional code of values, which negated any possible positive value. Paradoxically, the editors of *Il Convito* interpreted the French writers' response to positivist culture as a sign of crisis that confirmed the corrupting influence of positivism itself, in the sense that decadence was seen as one of positivism's constitutive aspects. From this perspective, an author like Paul Verlaine was considered both a victim of positivist culture and an agent of that very epochal malady. It is no coincidence that Giulio

Aristide Sartorio, in his article 'Nota su D.G. Rossetti pittore' (1895), formulated an opposition between French Decadentism and Pre-Raphaelitism. According to Sartorio, the latter was distinguished from the former by virtue of its recovery of the best aspects of the art of the past:

> Ora la rivoluzione prerafaellita pittoricamente lontana dai tentativi deca-
> denti da cui è afflitta la Francia artistica, creò ed ebbe viva efficacia per
> l'appoggio che chiese nella sua opera alla tradizione dei primitivi Italiani e
> Fiamminghi e non s'agitò a fondare l'impero dei simboli nuovi i quali non
> associandosi a nessuna abitudine, a nessun senso plastico l'avrebbero
> condotta o all'abuso di allegorie o alla vana ricerca di tecniche fantastiche.
> (141–2)

> [The Pre-Raphaelite revolution, pictorially far from the decadent attempts
> which afflict the art in France, looked for and found effective life because it
> seeked the support of the ancient Italian and Flemish traditions, and did not
> get wrapped up in founding the empire of new symbols which, not being
> associated with any custom or any plastic meaning, would have led either
> to the abuse of allegories or to the vain search for fanciful techniques.]

At first, Sartorio's claims may be read merely as pertaining to the realm of art criticism, but they extend far beyond it, to the point of articulating a cultural and moral condemnation of the elaboration of new artistic techniques. They are a clear critique of Symbolist aesthetics, of its waste of cognitive and creative energy in trying to establish new symbols, which would not be viable and recognizable within the acquired codes of reception anyway.

Sartorio's critical move remains paradigmatic of *Il Convito*'s cultural politics as a whole. Once the opposition was established between the Pre-Raphaelites and the French decadents, the editors of the magazine were able to configure their cultural project in anti-positivist terms but, at the same time, to avoid expressing the crisis and critique of the discourse of modernity – which the editors still considered essential for the progress of society, in spite of its positivist development – by linking back to the progressive trajectory of the entire course of human history.

In the case of *Il Convito* we are confronted with a more complex cultural situation than that explicitly confident in positivist values, conveyed in the works of Pica and Graf. The aestheticist principles expressed in the magazine opposed the breaking with tradition and its official values. We can see now how the wish for the revival of Italian culture and civilization's greatest ideals from the past constituted an objective prejudice against the acceptance of those cultural and aesthetic attitudes that characterized *Decadentismo*. Thus, in Italy, the anti-positivist reaction manifested itself in the form of a recovery of the humanist tradition, understood as an alternative to that process of barbarization which, according to the editors of *Il Convito*, was represented by the progressive cultural homogenization that Italy was undergoing at the end of the nineteenth century.

One exception to the situation I have described above is exemplified by the works of the poet and critic Gian Pietro Lucini. In the introduction to his book of poetry *Libro delle figurazioni ideali* (1894),[15] he formulated the principles of his own Symbolist poetics, as well as the relationship between Symbolism and Decadentism, which Lucini called *decadenza*. According to the poet, *decadenza* was the process of the destruction of aspects of ancient culture, which allowed new expressions of artistic and political avant-gardes to emerge. Lucini therefore saw the decadent condition as a necessary stage within an inevitable process of transformation:

> Ma il punto sta nel vedere dove in verità esiste decadenza: o in noi o negli altri o in nessuno? E però sgraziatamente ci siamo detti decadenti e, non essendolo forse, resteremo. Decadenti però non in quanto all'opera, ma in quanto alla vita: decadenti, perché ogni cosa che ne circonda, scienza, religione, forma politica, economia, si tramutano, né il tramutarsi è senza una fine, né la fine è senza una morte od una rovina: né senza morte o putredine havvi nuova vita. (4–5)

> [But it is important to see where decadence really resides: in ourselves or in others or in nobody? Yet, unfortunately, we called ourselves decadent and we will remain such, although we may not be decadent at all. In any case, we would not be decadent with respect to our artwork, but with respect to life, because everything around us is subject to change: science, religion, political forms, economics, but change comes to an end, and that end is not without death and ruin: nor is a new life possible without death and rottenness.]

In the debate on Decadentism of 1890s Italy, Lucini was among the few to define *decadenza* as an almost accidental term used to describe the whole of contemporary cultural phenomena, therefore distancing it from the various definitions of malaise and malady discussed above. Lucini acknowledges the arbitrariness of the terms *decadenza* and *decadente* and accepts both with a tone of resignation, but he also points out that the phenomenon is historically necessary. Lucini believed that a transformative force was at work within history, and that this force was accessible to the knowledge of the Symbolist poet. Decadence thus existed only as a transitory stage destined to be overcome by a future social renewal.

In the same years the adjective *decadente* officially entered the terminology of Italian literary criticism. For instance, Amedeo Morandotti, in his 1895 review of D'Annunzio's novel *Le vergini delle rocce*, published in *Critica sociale*, talked about decadence, in spite of the writer's attempt to represent a kind of Latin renaissance.[16] In his analysis of contemporary art in the same magazine in 1900, Giuseppe D'Angelo similarly discussed an isolated, sensual, and shrewd art, which had stopped being inspired by society, in order to withdraw into the artist's individual self.[17]

The social and political engagement of the editors of *Critica sociale* allowed them to acknowledge in D'Annunzio's work that process of evasion of everyday life that Pica and Graf had also delineated but, again, their analysis focused mainly on the signs of crisis in nineteenth-century ideals. Because of their strong moral prejudices, these analyses were unable to account for the cultural and epistemological significance of either the breaking of the harmonious relationship between art and life or the artist's withdrawal into himself or the effects of such a rupture on the modes of representation typical of that harmonious relationship and its consequences within the realm of aesthetics.

Thus, Italian literary criticism at the end of the nineteenth century, from Pica to the intellectuals of *Critica sociale*, identified the features of contemporary art and literature with those of an actual decadence and, in doing so, prepared the ground for the use and canonization of the term *decadentismo*. The term became a convenient label by which all the various artistic expressions of the late nineteenth century could be classified. Despite the cultural debates that characterized the 1890s, and despite the objective differences between, for instance, French Decadentism and English Pre-Raphaelitism, all of these movements appeared to be *decadenti*. The result of this cultural situation was the construction of an essentially moralistic term (*Decadentismo*). From our own contemporary critical perspective, the difficulty of setting specific terms of reference for a *beginning* and an *end* of the decadent phenomenon becomes readily apparent. Attempting this kind of periodization means risking subjection to the same moralistic logic that generated it, in that the periodization itself would arrive at an *end* only at the moment of the hypothetical overcoming of the very condition of decadence, which means the moment when the lost harmonious relationship between art and life is restored. Following this logic, until that moment of restoration, the art and literature of our century and, possibly, of the centuries to come, will continue to be irremediably *decadenti*.

To return to the debate on the decadentism of the 1890s, we have seen that in spite of the open opposition to positivist culture, Italian critics and intellectuals were not willing to abandon the values of the Italian humanist tradition in favour of new modes of representation that they perceived as decadent. The editors of *Il Convito* thus retained a certain deference for a national poet like Giosuè Carducci, or for the Classicist dimension conveyed by certain aspects of D'Annunzio's work. Not until the work of the critic and philosopher Benedetto Croce would we see a full development and historiographic legitimation of the category of *Decadentismo* as referring to the culture and literature of the turn of the century.

Italian Idealism and *Decadentismo*

In his famous essay 'Di un carattere della più recente letteratura' (1907), Croce attributed to D'Annunzio, Pascoli, and Fogazzaro the origin of what he defined as the *fabbrica del vuoto* (industry of the void).[18] According to Croce, this industry characterized modern literature as a whole. But on reading this essay, one realizes that for Croce the responsibility for the condition of decadence, or moral void, that characterized art and literature at the end of the nineteenth century was to be found in the previous twenty-year period (1865–85). According to him, positivism had generated within itself the new forms of malaise and mysticism; analogously, the political opposition to socialism had blocked the progress of civilization and created forms of imperialism and attitudes of aristocracy.[19] From this situation of opposite extremes Croce deduced that art would never be able to return to the old ideals once those forms of reaction were consumed. In this essay Croce was not yet explicitly condemning turn–of-the-century culture, and it remains the first document in which *Decadentismo* is referred to as a moment in the Italian context.

Beyond the works more specifically devoted to *Decadentismo*, including the six volumes of *Letteratura della nuova Italia* (1929) and the essays collected in *Poesia e non poesia* (1935), one may say that Croce's entire critical project was concerned with *Decadentismo*, in that he tended to set it up as an exemplary object of polemics. Croce dealt with a series of moral and intellectual attitudes, defining them as decadent far beyond their strictly literary significance, to the point that he identified them as objective obstacles to the foundation of a cultural civilization. Such a civilization was supposed to be dominated, or directed, by what can be defined as a form of absolute historicism. On a more personal level, Croce saw in these attitudes the opposite of what he had been educated to consider as art and poetry. Thus, he embarked on a life-time battle against such cultural phenomena as mysticism, Catholicism, aestheticism, imperialism, and others, which he identified as forms of contemporary irrationalism.[20]

According to Croce, these irrational cultural forms were characterized, on the philosophical level, by the abandoning of thought, understood as a power able to dominate reality; on the artistic and literary level, by moral faults such as insincerity and the creation of void; and, finally, at the political level, by the lack of trust in the values of freedom. Croce looked at Carducci as the first poet who had revealed to him the greatness of poetry, and it is no coincidence that in the essay that concludes *Poesia e non poesia*, Croce greets the poet of his youth with the same words that Carducci himself had dedicated to Torquato Tasso: 'D'Italia grande, antica, l'ultimo vate or viene! [The last prophet of great, ancient Italy now comes!]' (340). If Carducci was the last poet, the broad cultural meaning that Croce instituted for *Decadentismo* becomes clear: after great poetry there can be only decadence, that is, the decline of the great original values of tradition.

But with regard to the notion of *Decadentismo* it is necessary to consider other Crocean propositions, such as the distinction between ideal Romanticism – that is, philosophical Idealism – and practical Romanticism made in his *Storia d'Europa nel secolo decimonono*, published in 1932. Here Croce brought the issue of *Decadentismo* into the realm of the philosophy of history. According to the critic the decadence that characterized contemporary literature had to be linked back to the negative effects of what he called *romanticismo pratico*, as opposed to *romanticismo teoretico*. The latter was, for Croce, a constructive cultural attitude, which had been elaborated within the major philosophical discourses of the first half of the nineteenth century. It consisted in the capacity to make the ideals of the age of Enlightenment work in the present time, provided that they were freed from the abstractions that had limited them in the past.[21] Croce conceived of theoretical Romanticism as the necessary precursor to Idealistic philosophy, as well as to the project of political liberalism. It was the essential feature of what he called the religion of freedom, which in the nineteenth century had led to the recovery of national identities and to the emancipation of peoples. In Italy, in particular, it had represented the political project that founded the process of the *Risorgimento* and the unification of the country.[22]

Croce defined as *pratico* that Romanticism characterized by private and individual choices, and in this definition he reproposed the psychological and pathological connotations of decadence.[23] It was the Romantic malady, a form of neurosis provoked by lack of faith, which, at the same time, struggled to find faith, generating a sense of anxiety that, in the words of Croce himself, was related to 'l'impotenza di ciò fare o di soddisfarsi in quelle [fedi] che a volta a volta venivano asserite o di tenerle ferme come principî del pensare e del vivere [the inability to take action or to find satisfaction in those [faiths] that were asserted at different times or to hold on to them as principles of thinking and living]' (48–9).

According to Croce, all the great Romantic authors experienced a crisis of this kind – the major examples were Goethe and Manzoni – but they had been able to overcome it by virtue of superior ideals, which had allowed them to achieve a detached dimension. By superior ideals, Croce meant civil and collective commitments, the capacity to link one's private vicissitudes to public events, without any conflict between the two spheres.[24] The neurotic condition relating to practical Romanticism was, for Croce, at the origin of the decadent crisis. It is not by chance that he contrasted the malady of many poets with the sanity of Carducci.[25] The latter was a virtuoso of artistic form, but also a *vate*, that is, an advocate and popularizer of collective political values.[26]

It has to be said, however, that in many passages of his analysis of nineteenth-century history Croce thought, paradoxically, that the century had not been a 'decadent' one, that the literature produced by decadent authors such as D'Annunzio, Pascoli, and Fogazzaro developed within a society which, as a whole, was not decadent.[27] Croce's position can be explained by considering that he was trying to delineate a movement towards progress within nineteenth-century European society. He believed that if the world was advancing towards the triumph of the religion of freedom, then the writers who conveyed pessimistic and degraded images in their works were wrong, meaning that they did not conform to the ideals of liberalism. Croce was thus instituting a notion of decadent literature that worked against his own political project. In order to do so, he reshaped the idea of decadence – with the connotations of neurosis and malady that it had acquired within the positivist pathological terminology – in the realm of the philosophy of history.

Although writing from a Marxist perspective, Georg Lukács arrived at a condemnation of contemporary art that, in many respects, resembles Croce's. Like Croce, the Hungarian philosopher worked within a historiographic notion of decadence. And like Croce, he delineated a specific period in cultural history against which to evaluate previous and subsequent stages of artistic production. For Lukács, the paradigmatic model was represented by the so-called Age of Realism, or that group of works of fiction published between the second half of the eighteenth century and the first half of the nineteenth century. According to the philosopher, realist fiction had been able to expose the internal contradictions of Western society, and to represent the scenarios of class struggle which characterized it. The narrative technique of 'representation' was the tool for observing reality in all its empirical and concrete details, and for grasping the directions in which history was evolving.

In his *The Meaning of Contemporary Realism*, published in 1957, Lukács defined the expressive result of 'representation' with the term 'typicality.' This result consists of a representation in which the concrete data of reality and of the ideal – therefore of the particular and of the universal – are combined.[28] In Lukács's analysis, after having being put in a state of crisis by the proletariat, the middle class had produced fewer and fewer literary works able to provide a totalizing image of society. In fact, its works were often limited to portraying fragments of reality, unrelated to one another, or even to representing forms of un-reality constituted by the authors' individual ghosts, as in the case of Marcel Proust. It was precisely in that increasing fragmentation of the middle-class authors' representative ability that Lukács identified decadence. From his perspective, decadent literature was a mistake. The proletariat and the Communist party were supposed to acquire the best artistic products elaborated within the culture of the middle class, and realist fiction had been, so far, the highest result. Thus, for Lukács, to argue against decadence meant to argue for social progress and to defend the principles of artistic realism.[29]

Lukács saw the works of the great realist authors (e.g., in Germany, Thomas Mann) as growing out of a given society and 'mirroring' that society. But the 'mirroring' is not based on the artistic accumulation of facts, impressions, or experiences, but, rather, on a dialectical totality comprised of mediations and contradictions. In this way the realist work of art exposes the process of social interaction that underlies the actual existence as it is subjectively experienced by individuals. The function of the 'mirroring' is, therefore, that of stripping away the ideological veils of the existing society, as the difference emerges between the way society *actually functions* and the way it *merely appears*. Class contradictions determine – and are affected by – the way in which society *appears* in its particular aspects, but this is also an *essence*, which is to be analysed in order for a potential classless society to become manifest. In Expressionism, Lukács found, instead, an emotional, unreflexive subjectivist mode of apprehending reality. The philosopher's basic objection to Nietzsche's notion of the liberation of subjectivity and its relativization becomes apparent in his critique: Nietzsche's philosophy made it impossible for reality to be analysed.

Conclusion

Both the Crocean and the Lukácsian critiques have worked as powerful critical and historiographic *master narratives* for the formulation and canonization of the notion of Decadentism.[30] It is also apparent that any reconsideration of Italian *Decadentismo* must necessarily come to terms with these two master narratives. They convey two influential and conflicting ideologies and philosophies of history. One is bourgeois and liberal, in which the history of the nineteenth century is characterized by a progressive spreading of Romantic values, destined to be fulfilled within Idealist culture and in the monarchic political system founded on middle-class private property; the other is Marxist, and its aim is to provoke the advent of a socialist revolution able to end capitalist oppression and to reconcile mankind with itself, within a classless society.

In terms of literary criticism and historiography, Croce and Lukács divided two major literary genres between them: the former focused on decadence in poetry, the latter on its manifestation in fiction. In addition, their works generated practically all the subsequent studies on *Decadentismo* in Italy. Francesco Flora (1925) and Luigi Russo (originally 1919) both confirmed the interpretation of *Decadentismo* as a form of degeneration. For the former, it was the last degenerate manifestation of Romanticism; for the latter, it was the final degeneration of that very ancient tendency of the man of letters to separate thought from action. Luciano Anceschi (1936) employed decadent art's autonomy and separation from history and society as a tool within the broader anti-Fascist cultural discourse of the 1930s, where the autonomy itself represented a viable category for the anti-Fascist intellectual's own estrangement from forms of collaboration with the Fascist regime. Another attempt to rescue *Decadentismo* from previous condemnations is represented by Binni (1936). On the Marxist side, Carlo Salinari argued that the culture of Italian *Decadentismo* essentially projected the sense of political and moral bewilderment of the post-*Risorgimento* generation. Its authors, unable to acquire an authentic consciousness of the contradiction they had experienced, generated a series of utopian aspirations and other mystifying responses to epochal problems. For his part, Arcangelo Leone de Castris explained the culture of *Decadentismo* in terms of ideological responses to the discomfort felt by intellectuals, resulting from the progressive erosion of the traditional role of men of letters in modern industrial society.

My reconstruction of the cultural dynamics that lie behind the formation of Italian *Decadentismo* has shown that one cannot think of it as merely a neutral literary category. This realization may motivate today's scholars to consider the broader issue of the status of those cultural, critical, and historiographic discourses which, over time, have contributed to generate canonical categories such as *Decadentismo*. It seems fair to say that, in the last twenty years, the need to reconsider and interrogate a series of cultural discourses that were previously taken for granted has been generated by the increasing questioning of all forms of ideological constructions, inside and outside of literary studies. That certain notions and periodizations within literary history may be subjected to further analysis and reassessment seems completely legitimate. Such reassessment is important to grasp their inherently discursive nature, and to broaden critical reflections on literary criticism and historiography understood as cultural practices.

NOTES

1 Among the contributions published in the last forty years aimed at
   providing critical and historiographical information about *Decadentismo* as
   a general phenomenon, see Scrivano, Seroni, Ghidetti, Annoni, and, in
   English, Calinescu, in particular 211–21; for more theoretical accounts see
   Bobbio, Gianola, and Roda.
2 See his chapter 'Versions of Decadence,' esp.151.
3 Ibid., 152.
4 Among the various poetic circles wherein the magazines were born, the
   first was that of the *Hydropathes*, founded on 5 October 1878 by Emile
   Goudeau. He edited this magazine from 22 January 1879 through 12 May
   1880; he then belonged to the group called *Hirsutes* from September 1881
   through April 1883. Goudeau left this circle as well and, in January 1882,
   became the chief editor of *Le Chat Noir*, a journal aimed at publishing the
   works performed in the homonymous cabaret, which opened in December 1881. In 1883 a group of dissidents from *Le Chat Noir* followed Charles
   Cros, who founded the group *Les Zutistes* (from *zut*, accident); four
   months later this circle disappeared, to be replaced by *Les Jemenfoutistes*
   (from *je m'en fous*, I don't care) led by Léo Trézenik, who in the previous
   year had launched the magazine *La Nouvelle Rive Gauche* (9 November
   1882), which changed its name to *Lutèce* in March 1883. After a successful
   series of publications that lasted almost four years, the magazine ended
   its activity. For an exhaustive reconstruction of Decadentism in France see
   Jonard, in particular 196–212.
5 See Jonard (199).
6 See *Le Décadent*, 10 Apr. 1886, 1.
7 Ibid. Bourget (2: 215).
8 The term 'neurosis' was coined at the end of the eighteenth century by the
   Scotch doctor William Cullen, who used it to define a wide range of
   disorders that could not be explained by organic injuries. It was defined
   more specifically only in 1851, in France, by Claude Marie Stanislas
   Sandras.
9 Barbara Spackman has dealt effectively with the role of Nordau and
   Cesare Lombroso as critics of decadence, though underestimated ones
   (see, in particular 2–3, 6–8, 10–12, and 30–1).
10 See Paladini Musitelli (222).
11 All translations from Italian are mine unless otherwise indicated.
12 See Nietzsche (36–8).

13 Ibid., 60.
14 Now in *Foscolo, Manzoni, Leopardi*.
15 Now in *Scritti critici* (3–11).
16 See 350.
17 See 176.
18 See *La Letteratura della nuova Italia* 191.
19 Ibid., 189–92.
20 Ibid., 196–7.
21 See 57–9.
22 See the chapter, 'La religione della libertà' (11–30).
23 Ibid., 59–65.
24 Ibid., 71.
25 See 340.
26 With regard to the role of the poet as *vate*, there is the issue of Croce's ambivalent relationship with D'Annunzio. The critic expressed a relative approval of him, which can be explained by D'Annunzio's peculiar ability to link his artistic ideals to his public role, especially in the realm of oratory. One instance of Croce's approval of D'Annunzio's wartime oratorical ability can be found in the essay 'L'ultimo D'Annunzio,' in *La letteratura della nuova Italia* (6: 252–4).
27 *La letteratura della nuova Italia* (4: 11) and *Storia d'Italia dal 1871 al 1915* (173–4).
28 See, in particular, 42–6.
29 The philosopher's elaboration on the issue of decadence began when he actively contributed to the so-called *Expressionismus Debatte*, which took place in the context of a broader debate on anti-Fascist art, after the congress held in Paris in 1935. The debate was based on the search for 'socialist realism,' in order to find an orientation for socialist art and culture. Within this cultural and political framework, German Expressionist art was analysed and criticized from three different points of view by three major figures in the contemporary German cultural scene, Lukács himself, Ernst Bloch, and Bertold Brecht. For an extensive account of this debate, see Bronner.
30 Here I understand master narratives in Jean-François Lyotard's terms, in *La Condition postmoderne*, as those philosophical discourses that produce the legitimation of their own status. Lyotard uses the term 'modern' to designate any science that legitimates itself with reference to a meta-discourse, making an explicit appeal to some grand narrative (see the 'Introduction' in the English edition of *The Postmodern Condition* xxiii).

84   Mario Moroni

WORKS CITED

Anceschi, Luciano. *Autonomia ed eteronomia dell'arte*. Milan: Garzanti, 1976.
Annoni, Carlo. *Il Decadentismo*. Brescia: La Scuola, 1982.
Baju, Anatole. 'Le Décadisme.' *Le Décadent* 20 Nov. 1886: 1.
Binni, Walter. *La poetica del decadentismo*. Florence: Sansoni, 1996.
Bobbio, Norberto. *La filosofia del decadentismo*. Turin: Chiantore, 1944.
Bourget, Paul. *Essais de psychologie contemporaine*. 2 vols. Paris: Plon-Nourrit, 1912.
Bronner, Stephen Eric. 'Expressionism and Marxism: Towards an Aesthetic of Emancipation.' *Passion and Rebellion*. Ed. Stephen E. Bronner and Douglas Kellner. New York: Universe Books, 1983. 411–53.
Bürger, Peter. *Theory of the Avant-Garde*. Trans. Michael Shaw. Minneapolis: U of Minnesota P, 1984.
Calinescu, Matei. *Five Faces of Modernity*. Durham, NC: Duke UP, 1987.
Croce, Benedetto. *La letteratura della nuova Italia*. Vol. 4. Bari: Laterza, 1929.
– *Poesia e non poesia*. Bari: Laterza, 1935.
– *Storia d'Europa nel secolo decimonono*. Milan: Adelphi, 1991.
– *Storia d'Italia dal 1871 al 1915*. Milan: Adelphi, 1991.
D'Angelo, Giuseppe. 'L'apostasia politica di Gabriele D'Annunzio.' *Critica sociale* 10.11 (1900): 174–6.
Flora, Francesco. *Dal romanticismo al futurismo*. Milan: Mondadori, 1925.
Ghidetti, Enrico, ed. *Il Decadentismo*. Rome: Riuniti, 1976.
Gianola, Elio. *Il Decadentismo*. Rome: Studium, 1977.
Graf, Arturo. *Foscolo, Manzoni, Leopardi*. Turin: Loescher, 1955.
Jonard, Norbert. 'Alle origini del Decadentismo. Il termine e il significato.' *Problemi* 59 (1980): 196–220.
Leone de Castris, Arcangelo. *Il Decadentismo italiano*. Bari: Laterza, 1995.
Lucini, Gian Pietro. *Scritti critici*. Ed. Luciana Martinelli. Bari: De Donato, 1971.
Lukács, Georg. *The Meaning of Contemporary Realism*. Trans. John and Necke Mander. London: Merlin Press, 1963.
Lyotard, Jean-François. *The Postmodern Condition: A Report on Knowledge*. Trans. Geoff Bennington and Brian Massumi. Minneapolis: U of Minnesota P, 1984.
Morandotti, Amedeo. 'Il superuomo (Intorno alle *Vergini delle rocce*).' *Critica sociale* 5.22 (1895): 350–2.
Nietzsche, Friedrich. *The Birth of Tragedy and The Case of Wagner*. Trans. Walter Kaufmann. New York: Vintage Books, 1967.

Nordau, Max. *Degeneration*. Lincoln and London: U of Nebraska P, 1993.

Paladini Musitelli, Marina. 'Il concetto di Decadentismo nella critica italiana.' *Problemi* 59 (1980): 221–45.

Pica, Vittorio. *Letteratura d'eccezione*. Genoa: Costa & Nolan, 1987.

Roda, Vittorio. *Decadentismo morale e decadentismo estetico*. Bologna: Pàtron,1966.

Russo, Luigi. *Il tramonto del letterato*. Bari: Laterza, 1960.

Salinari, Carlo. *Miti e coscienza del decadentismo italiano*. Milan: Feltrinelli, 1960.

Sartorio, Giulio Aristide. 'Nota su D.G. Rossetti pittore.' *Il Convito* II (1895): 121–50.

Scrivano, Riccardo. *Il decadentismo e la critica*. Florence: La Nuova Italia, 1963.

Seroni, Adriano. *Il Decadentismo*. Palermo: Palumbo, 1964.

Spackman, Barbara. *Decadent Genealogies*. Ithaca, NY, and London: Cornell UP, 1989.

3 D'Annunzio, Duse, Wilde, Bernhardt: Author and Actress between Decadence and Modernity

LUCIA RE

At the end of the nineteenth century and in the first decade of the twentieth, the actress, more than the actor, assumed a fundamental role in the theatre. It was the figure of the prima donna that attracted crowds and galvanized critics at a time when the theatre was still (indeed, more than ever) the principal form of mass spectacle and entertainment. Sarah Bernhardt (1844–1923) and Eleonora Duse (1858–1924) in particular achieved fame of mythic proportions. The triumphant era of Bernhardt and Duse coincided with the years in which suffragism and organized feminism developed in Europe, while the role of women and the relationship between the sexes became hotly debated topics on and off stage.

The figure of the prima donna occupied a particularly ambiguous and complex position in the context of the turn-of-the-century debate on women. Actresses, and above all *mostri sacri* like Bernhardt and Duse, who were also women-impresarios with their own companies, and controlled all the details of their productions, became symbols of the '*new woman*' and of a woman's ability to be independent and professionally successful.[1] These were the only women who were sometimes referred to as 'geniuses' in an age in which being a 'genius' was tantamount to being male. Appearing publicly at the center of the stage and under everyone's gaze, actresses had an aura of independence, professionalism, and sexual liberation that seemed to personify the antithesis of Victorian puritanism and bourgeois gender values (and, in Italy, of Catholicism and the patriarchal family values of the new nation). True female virtue required a woman to devote herself exclusively to the domestic sphere, to the home, and to a limited circle of family relationships. As a public figure, commercialized and exposed to the gaze and the desire of all, the actress in the culture of the fin-de-siècle, even when she was mythologized and adored, was thus perceived to be dangerously close to the figure of the prostitute. The actress, like the prostitute, represented a perverse reduction of the feminine to the status of commodity, and she stood in opposition to the myth of the angel of the house.[2]

To be sure, the actress's capacity to interpret a variety of different roles – including deeply immoral ones – desecrated the Victorian myth of the feminine nature. Yet even more unsettling was the implication that there was no fixed, recognizable, familiar, and reassuring female identity. It was this undoing of the very notion of gendered identity (and, as we shall see, of identity itself), that made the actress such a disturbing figure. In Henry James's novel *The Tragic Muse* (first edition 1890), the actress Miriam Rooth appears as a kind of monster in the eyes of one of the male protagonists, Peter Sherringham. More than the actress's suspected promiscuity, it is Miriam's ability to assume different personalities and different roles that renders her monstrous: 'It struck him abruptly that a woman whose only being was "to make believe," to make believe that she had any and every being that you liked, that would serve a purpose, produce a certain effect, and whose identity resided in the continuity of her personations, so that she had no moral privacy, as he phrased it to himself, but lived in a high wind of exhibition, of figuration – such a woman was a kind of monster, in whom of necessity there would be nothing to like, because there would be nothing to take hold of' (151).[3] Yet Peter believes that he loves Miriam, and in order to express his love he tries (unsuccessfully) to convince her to abandon the stage and marry him. Marriage, he presumes, will make her normal and real, and cure her monstrous lack of identity.

The actress's apparent flouting of both Victorian puritanism and traditional bourgeois notions of identity made her, at least in appearance, an almost emblematically decadent figure. She was certainly useful, almost *necessary* to Wilde and D'Annunzio's decadent aesthetics. Wilde and D'Annunzio both seem in fact to have been at least partial models for the aesthete Gabriel Nash, a character in James's *The Tragic Muse*, who turns out to be no less disturbing and 'monstrous' than the actress Miriam Rooth. The disturbing monstrosity of 'decadent aesthetics' is indeed in many ways similar to that of the actress. Both are deeply indebted to the myths of Romantic and Victorian identity, and yet at the same time they are also profoundly modernist. Oscillation between Romanticism and modernism is in fact character-istic of Wilde and D'Annunzio's aestheticism, and of most of the great European decadence. In this oscillation, the deconstruction, inversion, and even disintegration of Romantic ideological categories, styles, and myths are often followed by a return of the same, albeit in phantasma-goric, estranged or uncanny forms.[4]

The affinity between the dandy and the woman actress/seductress intuited by Henry James is one of the key themes of D'Annunzio's *Il piacere* (1889). Andrea Sperelli's mysterious lover, Elena Muti, has all the characteristics considered to be typical of an actress (even though she is only a seductress). She is a woman in whom spontaneity and artifice are impossible to distinguish. She seduces with the continuous metamorphosis of her appearance and has no identity of her own, fixed and recognizable above the hypnotic variety of her forms. But rather than recoiling from her monstrosity, the novel embraces it and extends it to the male protagonist, as in a play of mirrors. A series of parallels between Elena and Andrea Sperelli renders the two charac-ters reflections of one another.

D'Annunzio's portrayal of Foscarina in the novel *Il Fuoco* (published in 1900 after a long and complex writing process) is the clearest ex-ample of how the figure of the actress becomes central to decadent/modernist aesthetics, to the point of being one of its most effective and seductive icons. Foscarina is modelled directly on Eleonora Duse, D'Annunzio's collaborator, lover, and principal international interpreter (as well as generous financer) in the years between 1895 and 1904. Foscarina's other name in the novel, Perdita, was one of D'Annunzio's nicknames for Duse. The name evokes one of Shakespeare's characters in *The Winter's Tale*, but it also alludes to the semantic sphere of *loss, losing, losing oneself,* and even *perdition, ruin,* and *dissolution.* D'Annuzio plays with all of these connotations in the text. As an actress, Foscarina/Perdita loses her selfhood in the fictional identity of multiple others. In the eyes of the male protagonist – the aesthete and visionary play-wright Stelio Effrena, based on D'Annunzio himself – the actress's body is like a palimpsest, a text through which he can glimpse traces of all the passions represented on stage and aroused in the audiences of the past. Yet, in a replay of the Victorian stereotype (which man-ages entirely to mask the truth about the financial relationship be-tween D'Annunzio and Duse), the actress's body is also associated with that of the prostitute, the courtesan or 'lost woman' who promis-cuously displays and sells herself:

[Q]uella donna solitaria e nomade [...] pareva portare per lui nelle pieghe delle sue vesti raccolta e muta la frenesia delle moltitudini lontane dalla cui bestialità compatta ella aveva sollevato il brivido fulmineo e divino dell'arte con un grido di passione o con uno schianto di dolore o con un silenzio di morte; una torbida brama lo piegò verso quella donna sapiente e disperata in cui egli credeva scoprire i vestigi di tutte le voluttà e di tutti gli spasimi, verso quel corpo non più giovane, ammollito da tutte le carezze e rimasto ancora sconosciuto per lui. (*Il Fuoco* 222).

[[T]hat lonely, nomadic woman [...] seemed to carry with her in the folds of her silent garments memories of distant multitudes whose basic bestiality had been stirred to frenzy by the impact of her magnificent, divine artistic skills exemplified in a cry of rage, a shriek of agony or the silence of death itself. An obscure desire drew him towards that wise, desperate woman in whom he believed he could discern traces of every kind of voluptuousness and pain, towards that body which was no longer young, made soft by the endless caresses yet still unknown to him.] (*The Flame* 27)[5]

Foscarina is not merely a reincarnation (as Mario Praz maintained) of the synthetic *femme fatale*, the eternal, promiscuous courtesan of Flaubert and Pater's sadistic fantasies. Rather, she is a character in which the myth of the synthetic femme fatale is melded with that of the modern 'divine actress,' whose ability to make infinite characters come alive and to excite the crowd is an object of marvel, desire, and envy for Stelio Effrena. In possessing the body of the actress, Stelio imagines that he can make her power his own and incorporate it into his own future work for the theatre and its ever-growing mass audience.

The years of D'Annunzio's tormented composition of *Il Fuoco* were also the years of his equally tormented relationship with Duse and with the theatre. This complexity is reflected in the novel. It was largely under the influence of Duse's mystique that D'Annunzio – who previously shared the general contempt of intellectuals for the modern theatre, deemed to be an inferior, degraded art form fit only for the entertainment of the bourgeoisie and the uneducated masses – began to write for the stage for the first time, rapidly producing a remarkable series of major texts: *La città morta* (begun in 1896), *Francesca da Rimini* (1901), and *La figlia di Jorio* (1903). In 'Alla divina Eleonora Duse' (the poem solemnly placed at the beginning of *Francesca da Rimini*) D'Annunzio accords the actress not only the role of an inspirational muse, but also that of an essential emblem of the innovative power of his own art. It must be said, however, that Duse was for D'Annunzio much more than an emblem or a muse in the traditional sense of the word. She was a decisive factor in his theatrical vocation, and it was through her that D'Annunzio became acquainted with a kind of acting that was both original and modern.

The gestural art for the expression of deeper, inner feelings and emotions that Duse invented revealed to D'Annunzio the possibility of a new kind of tragedy that could be classical (the urge for the classical was sparked by D'Annunzio's formative journey to Greece in 1895) and yet at the same time modern in a psychological and political sense. D'Annunzio betrays this in the second part of *Il Fuoco*, when he describes the way in which Stelio lovingly and almost vampirically takes possession of Foscarina's art and pours it into the theatrical work he is conceiving, the play 'La vittoria dell'uomo' (which corresponds exactly to D'Annunzio's first major play, *La città morta*). Duse also took it upon herself to look after all the practical aspects of the staging of D'Annunzio's plays, thus making his theatrical debut possible. Their projects for a renewal and an ennoblement of the decayed art of the theatre met with scepticism, and it was hard to find producers as well as theatres and actors willing or able to do D'Annunzio's plays, whose potential for financial success was rather dubious. D'Annunzio himself, even as he saw in the theatre the only possible means for a true diffusion and politicization of art and strove for theatrical glory, felt a strong sense of disgust for theatrical audiences and the very idea of staging his own works.[6]

Wilde had adored Bernhardt since the seventies, when the actress first arrived in England. In what has become a legendary episode, he welcomed her with his arms full of lilies. After the staging of *Phèdre* in London in June 1879, Wilde published a sonnet dedicated to Bernhardt that began, 'How vain and dull this common world must seem/To such a One as thou,' presenting the actress as a reincarnation of that mythical Greek world, which, due in part to the central role of homosexuality in it, had a fundamental hold on Wilde's imagination. For Bernhardt, or, in any case, under the influence of her myth, Wilde wrote his most famous play, *Salomé*, a text that by itself would be sufficient to place Wilde among the greatest modernists. This play inspired infinite other works, including Richard Strauss's musical drama by the same title.

A closer scrutiny of Wilde and D'Annunzio's overall vision, however, shows that for these two authors the image of the actress also has a profoundly negative and potentially devastating power. While it is part of decadent and proto-modernist aesthetics (an aesthetics that seems to appropriate it and absorb it completely, apparently without leaving any residue), the figure of the actress undermines decadent aesthetics from within, to the point of demolishing its very foundations. How can this occur?

Although they employed very different styles, the great international actresses at the end of the nineteenth century shared a tendency to express themselves mainly through the exhibition of their bodies: poses, gestures, and the intonation of their voices. This style, completely based on exteriority, on sounds and appearances (which explains why these actresses could be praised and worshipped by a public that could not understand the language in which they acted) was intrinsically similar to the decadent aesthetics of the dandy as well as to D'Annunzio's aesthetics of pleasure. The actress, like the dandy and the aesthete, brought the modern theatricalization and textualization of the body and of appearances into the limelight, and through her elaborate use of costumes, make-up, and sets, she valorized the pose, the mask, and artifice.[7]

In the diva system of the end of the century, what the actress wore, the calculated way in which she moved, and the sound and tonality of her voice were the essential elements of her *style* and of the set of semiotic conventions (that she herself created) through which she operated. Bernhardt and Duse broke away from the naturalistic, Romantic, and positivist schools of acting and from the grand classical tradition which (especially in France) imposed on the actors a precise conventional code of stage communication. Each situation and each feeling required specific gestures and tones meticulously laid out in acting manuals. Bernhardt and Duse studied and constructed their own code and their own 'character.' It was the general opinion of Bernhardt and Duse's audiences that both actresses, however different, gave the unmistakable imprint of their personal style to the characters they played. In all their roles they remained faithful to a consciously constructed image of themselves, and each role was a seductive variation of this persona.[8]

What is particularly remarkable about Bernhardt is how she appropriated a creation of the male Romantic-decadent imaginary, the 'femme fatale,' rewriting it for herself and reinventing it to develop her own unmistakably new and modern mask. According to Jules Lemaître, Bernhardt 'does what no one had dared to do before her: she performs with her whole body ... This is, I believe, the most surprising innovation of her practice: in all her characters she pours not only her soul, her intelligence, and her physical grace, but also all her sex.'[9] What made Bernhardt fascinating for women (starting with actresses like Duse and Ellen Terry) was precisely the fact that she always dared to be, above all, herself. She adapted each role to her own image (instead of adapting herself to the roles) and thus visibly contradicted the clichés regarding female passivity, pliability, and weakness. Bernhardt appeared strong and irrepressible, a timeless, irresistible figure, and at the same time the incarnation of the new woman. Bernhardt's unrestrained, imperious, and sensual image seemed strangely artificial and abstract. She was a sensation in England and the United States, where she appeared as the shameless negation of female decorum. Her style seemed the opposite of the elegance and moderation usually recommended to 'serious' actresses in order to give them some respectability and avoid the suspicion of promiscuity perennially associated with women of the theatre.

Duse, on the other hand, paradoxically triumphed by elaborating a style that deliberately deconstructed the nineteenth-century Romantic and positivist mystique of the prima donna. She eliminated grandiose gestures and melodramatic exhibitions and invented an expressive minimalism comprised of small signs and nuances which required great concentration and attention, surprising the audience with breathtaking performances. A particularly affected aspect of Duse's image was what could be called 'the artifice of the non-artifice': her proverbial and highly mannered 'naturalness,' 'spontaneity,' and 'nudity,' along with her famous rejection of make-up. This rejection was in reality a calculated use of stage make-up and powder in order to create a 'natural' effect of 'authentic' pallor that stood in contrast to the bright rouges and the glaring hair-dyes characteristic of Sarah Bernhardt.[10] It was from their respective stylistic coherence that both actresses derived their power as divas.

Duse's expressive, silent use of her body, and her great gestural and somatic repertoire, were universally admired. She became famous for her hand gestures, her nervous excitement, her intense gaze, and her ability to appear as if she were 'in a trance.' This style deeply influenced D'Annunzio in the creation of many of his tragic characters, with results that, as we shall see, were often paradoxical. But Duse also influenced D'Annunzio's understanding of spectacle and performance in other ways. From the early years of his gossip columns, D'Annunzio had been particularly taken by Duse's style because it was based on the careful manipulation of appearances and images. He was struck by the way in which female spectators in particular experienced the diva's charm and attempted to imitate her in real life by adopting the same hairstyles and gestures.[11] The mechanisms of the diva's theatrical power of seduction fascinated D'Annunzio, who, in attempting to make it his own, clearly understood its political potential.

One of the essential elements that make up the decadent-modernist aesthetics is style, that unmistakable appearance that the aesthete gives to all his creations, including clothing, the body, and the rituals of daily life. These become an integral component of the oeuvre, of the author's system or 'corpus,' and are simultaneously utilized to publicize and 'sell' the work of art. The protagonist of the novel *Le vergini delle rocce*, Claudio Cantelmo, echoing a topic widely analysed by D'Annunzio in various other works of the nineties, talks about the necessity of giving to himself and to his words and actions 'l'impronta costante di un medesimo stile [the constant imprint of the same style]' (22). And it is precisely through style (in the images, in the rhetorical *dispositio* and in the *elocutio*) that the word itself becomes theatrical and 'spectacular,' capable of seducing the audience and eventually the crowd. Claudio Cantelmo's political-aesthetic (and utopian) vision is inseparable from the sense of the need to seduce the crowd and 'the masses' through spectacle. This intuition is fully developed in the (profoundly theatrical) scene of Stelio Effrena's speech in the Palazzo Ducale in *Il Fuoco*, and by D'Annunzio himself in the 'Discorso della siepe,' pronounced in front of his constituency in Pescara on 22 August 1897.

Throughout the long scene at the Palazzo Ducale and in the prelude to the speech, Stelio is described not only as a skilful improviser and speaker, but also by terms usually used by critics to evoke the actress's magnetism on stage, especially that of Eleonora Duse. Stelio has 'per tutto il corpo una specie di contrattura convulsiva che rispondeva alla tensione estrema del suo spirito [a kind of convulsive contraction throughout his body that responded to the extreme tension of his spirit]' (*Il Fuoco* 217). Between speaker and audience there is 'comunicazione elettrica [electric communication]' (*Il Fuoco* 241), and 'nella comunione tra la sua anima e l'anima della folla un mistero sopravveniva, quasi divino [in the communion between his own soul and the soul of the crowd a mystery was happening, something that was almost divine].' Stelio's gestural ability, the mobility of his face and of his gaze, his capacity to use his body and the musical beauty of the voice to seduce the crowd, are also highlighted (*Il Fuoco* 239–41/ *The Flame* 43–5). Thus, through a process of role shifting and role inversion, D'Annunzio puts Stelio in the actress's place, and vice versa.[12] In this long sequence, which occupies almost the entire first part of the novel, the actress is part of the audience, or, rather she is at the head of it. She is charmed, tamed, and seduced by the speaker's power, while Stelio, who has taken possession of the actress's usual role, appears alone at the centre of the stage. He is the object of both women's and men's admiration and, at the end, receives the 'il vasto applauso scrosciante [immense, thundering applause]' (*Il Fuoco* 257/*The Flame* 61).

Nietzsche's *Birth of Tragedy* and *Gay Science*, and the aesthetic theories of Angelo Conti (and, through him, Walter Pater's), were, to be sure, fundamental sources for D'Annunzio's vision of the theatre and of style. No less important, however, was the influence of Duse. D'Annunzio tried to master and politicize the Dusian technique that emphasized the seductive theatricality of body, gaze, and diction. This is not only true of D'Annunzio's works for the stage and of some of his fiction, but also of D'Annunzio as a personage. D'Annunzio as *divo* as well as D'Annunzio as a seducer of the crowd (and thus a precursor of Mussolini, even though the latter degraded his techniques, demagogically popularizing them as D'Annunzio had feared) is not an autonomous creation, but (like everything in D'Annunzio's work) a skilful mimesis and transformation of a pre-existing strategy, that of the great actress.[13]

Like Wilde, D'Annunzio paid much attention to the market and to the theatre as a means of mass communication and circulation. The use of divas like Bernhardt and Duse, however, does not merely satisfy the authors' desire to entrust their works to actresses who could fill the theatres, but also signals their wish to absorb the strength and seductive power of the divas. The divas' qualities were to be incorporated as essential elements of the authors' own style and work. The gender ambiguity, usually attributed not only to Wilde, but also, despite his acclaimed and publicized heterosexuality, to the image of D'Annunzio '*divo*' (caricatures often depicted him as a feminine being, a man-woman) is caused, at least in part, by the association made by audiences between the diva-like strategies of D'Annunzio's dandyism and the image of the seductive actress. With the advent of cinema, it became common to see in the silent-movie divas mere imitators of D'Annunzio and his iconography, ironically forgetting that the origin of D'Annunzio's '*divismo*' is to be found precisely in the divas of the theatre, particularly Duse. Undoubtedly, however, in approaching the real theatre for the first time, D'Annunzio was not simply inspired by Duse but also exploited the diva, and the diva system, to try to launch the myth of himself and his work for the stage.

Wilde, for his part, lived for the theatre. He assiduously attended performances in even the lowest English theatres and became one of the most appreciated playwrights of the eighties and nineties. He theatricalized his own existence on the basis of the rigorous stylistic rules of dandyism (which he created), and transformed late Victorian society into a stage for himself and his performances. The political dimensions of this theatricality, less noticeable but no less corrosive than D'Annunzio's, have been studied by Regina Gagnier in *Idylls of the Marketplace*. Wilde lived and practised the message of his narrative essay, 'The Portrait of Mr. W.H.,' according to which not only life, but all art, is 'to a certain degree a mode of acting' (Wilde 937). Wilde made acting, according to a certain rigorous style and technique, into a privileged aesthetic and existential model of modernity. In 'The Portrait of Mr. W.H.' Wilde recalls, with subtle irony and considerable nostalgia, that for the other great era of the theatre, the Shakespearian era, the paradigmatic model of acting was a male one, and female roles were usually played by young men dressed as women. In the modern era gender relationships on stage have been inverted, and it is the actress, not the actor, who dominates the stage and dresses up as a man. Bernhardt was particularly famous for her roles '*en travesti*' (among them Hamlet and Lorenzaccio) and for her ability to switch easily from a female to a male role. This fluidity in the actress's gender identity was an essential element of her modernity. In the Elizabethan theatre, there was no such fluidity, and male actors who took on female roles were exclusively specialized in those parts (as were the actors performing on the stages controlled by the Papal States in Italy). The fluidity of the actress's gender roles corresponds to a decadent and modernist 'theatrical' vision of identity, typical of both Wilde and D'Annunzio (as well as Nietzsche). No longer fixed or stable, this theatrical identity is constructed as a perpetual slippage among various masks and disguises, poses and positions.[14]

Without a doubt, Wilde's most alarming text in this respect is *Salomé*. Written in 1891 in French (perhaps to evade censorship, which was generally less careful and less strict with texts written in foreign languages), the play was blocked by the Lord Chamberlain's office in June 1892, when Sarah Bernhardt had already started rehearsing it at the Palace Theatre. At the centre of Wilde's drama there is not only an actress/diva in the primary part, but also a character whose role is a sort of *mise-en-abîme* of the actress/diva's own image. Salomé is the object of the desire and of the collective and voyeuristic vision of the other characters of the drama. She is a skilful and fascinating actress, whose body and voice are carefully controlled. She uses them to seduce whoever looks at her and listens to her. The seduction on stage, which is ultimately deadly, is thus mirrored and duplicated off stage in the seduction of the audience. This disturbing breach of the fourth wall certainly contributes to the strange effect of modernity produced by this apparently 'antique' and almost quaintly obsolete drama, based on a well-known biblical story. The play has a transgressiveness that extends well beyond the decadent exoticism of Moreau's painting of Salomé, and explains the often violent and censorial reaction by critics and spectators, as well as the fascination that the drama held for the avant-garde.[15]

Maeterlinck has often been cited as *Salomé's* principal stylistic source, especially for its repetitive and incantatory language and its obsessive theme of vision. But, as Kerry Powell points out, there is a precise correspondence between the by-then mythical image of the actress/diva Sarah Bernhardt (in her most typical roles), and the character of Salomé.[16] When writing *Salomé*, Wilde used an extremely repetitive, monotone, and mechanical language and created a hieratic musical effect, in almost perfect syntony with the psalm-like monotony that distinguished Bernhardt's style of speech.[17] In addition, the character of Salomé, with her femme-fatale violence, her hieratical poses, and her hysterical agitation, is, as has been noted, a variant (even though wild and untamed) of the typical characters played by Bernhardt and created or adapted for her by Sardou or Dumas *fils*. Fedora, Gismonda, Theodora, Tosca, and Césarine all resemble one another and were essentially vehicles for the actress to display her technical ability. Even Racine's Phèdre, as played by Bernhardt, ended up looking and sounding like the same character. Wilde's Salomé was so typical in certain aspects (perhaps that is why she became *mythical*), that Bernhardt planned to wear the same seductive costume (only slightly modified) that she had worn when playing Cleopatra.

The character of Salomé created by Wilde may be the most concrete demonstration of the correspondence, or, we could say, the syntony, between certain aspects of Wilde's aestheticism and dandyism and the figure of the actress/prima donna.[18] By sexualizing this biblical character, Wilde launched a fierce attack against Victorian puritanism; Salomé, with her indomitable strength and sexual intensity, was a profoundly subversive character destined to be – as in fact she was – censured in England, even though she was speaking French. Just how much Salomé's effect was linked to the style and the body of Bernhardt, or to the actress's mythical power as femme fatale, is demonstrated by the fact that when, at the beginning of 1892, Wilde (putting himself literally *in the place* of the actress) gave a private reading of his text to a friend, the artist and costume-designer Graham Robertson, it seems that the effect of the cues – especially the scenes in which Salomé speaks lasciviously to Jokanaan's decapitated head – was irresistibly comical.

Wilde denied having written *Salomé* under the great actress's spell: 'My play was in no sense of the words written for this great actress. I have never written a play for any actor or actress, nor shall I ever do so. Such work is for the artisan of literature, not the artist' (*Letters* 336). On this occasion, as on numerous others, Wilde proved himself an excellent actor. The role of the great artist was the most suited to Wilde's desires, even if his work (no less than D'Annunzio's) is in some ways that of an artisan: a smart recycling and reworking of fragments, plots, and words from the works of others. Wilde said that Bernhardt was 'the greatest artist on any stage,' and that to hear during rehearsal his own words recited by the most beautiful voice in the world was 'the greatest artistic joy that is possible to experience.'[19] It is clear that Wilde fulfilled himself aesthetically *through* the actress; he spoke through the actress's voice and body. Yet (and this is the fundamental point), whose words did the actress recite? They were certainly Wilde's words, but they were also the echo, the repetition, the recycling, the reworking of the voice of that inimitable character who was Sarah Bernhardt on stage.

Many of those who left written testimonies of the experience of attending one of Bernhardt's performances have spoken of a shiver; Bernhardt was not only electrifying, but she also provoked within the spectators a sense of horror (however pleasurable). This was certainly due to the stories of passionate, tragic, violent, and deadly female characters, like Sardou's Cleopatra and the numerous other exotic and oriental femme fatales interpreted by her 'in series.' The shiver was a reaction to witnessing all the taboos of femininity violently broken upon the stage and to the display of uncontrolled desires that were thought to be perverse and unnatural in a woman. The phallic woman, armed and cruel (or disguised) is in a certain sense *not* a woman; yet one cannot say that she is therefore a man. Rather, she exhibits a sexual ambiguity, a 'dangerous' oscillation.

The women played by Bernhardt, and Bernhardt herself, were repeatedly compared by critics to *wild* animals – tigers, panthers, lionesses, etc. – or to mythical monsters – sphinxes, chimeras, or medusas. There was something monstrous about them, something inhuman and unnatural, as well as deadly, that rendered them sisters to the disturbing, but also beautiful, Dorian Gray. It was precisely this wild, monstrous, and thus spectacular aspect, 'against nature,' that constituted the great actress's dangerous charm for Wilde and D'Annunzio. One can surely hypothesize that they both identified, at least partially, with the transgressive and ambiguous sexuality of Bernhardt's characters.

Wilde's *Salomé* debuted in Paris in 1896, produced by the avant-garde director Aurélien Lugné-Poe at the Théâtre de l'Oeuvre, with Lina Muntz in the part of Salomé.[20] Two years later D'Annunzio 'betrayed' Duse, 'his' Beatrice/actress, and gave Bernhardt his first play to do in Paris: *La Ville morte*. Competing with Wilde, he tried to pretend he had written it in French, something he only did with *Le Martyre de Saint Sébastien* (in many respects a very Wilde-like text), a play written ten years after Wilde's death and first performed in Paris in 1911, accompanied by the music of Claude Débussy and with the famous dancer Ida Rubinstein in the role of Saint Sebastian. On the other hand, in 1897, in Naples, Wilde tried unsuccessfully to convince Duse to interpret *Salomé*. Duse did not act in French, and it would have been difficult to reproduce the original effect in an Italian translation. In addition, there was the issue of Duse's rivalry with Bernhardt, who was in any case Wilde's favourite.[21] Duse, who was an attentive reader and very cautious about accepting new roles, may have thought that Wilde's text was not appropriate for her style. Years later, however, upon reading *De Profundis*, she was very moved.

Bernhardt and Duse often performed the same plays, sometimes even in the same city and during the same week (for example, *La Dame aux camelias* and *Heimat* [*Casa paterna*] by Sudermann). But they brought to their respective performances their own unique techniques and style. Bernhardt had developed a technique that made her the epitome of tireless sexual energy and enchanting female 'artificiality' whose signs – in addition to a fluted, monotonous, and hypnotically repetitive voice and spasmodic movements of the body – were audacious and majestic poses, make-up, jewellry, and exotic dresses. She gave the terrifying impression of being 'all body,' all appearance and artifice. Bernhardt was the *synthetic* femme fatale par excellence, but in the double sense of the word: a synthesis of all the femmes fatales and a synthetic product, obtained artificially. She was also famous – with her artificial red hair and her cosmetics – for appearing ageless, a sort of eternal sphinx. Apparently, she was able to take on the roles of young women even at the age of seventy. And she continued to act after the famous amputation of one of her legs, with a 'monstrous' stoicism that rendered her even more legendary.

Duse had created herself in contrast to Bernhardt, after having seen and carefully studied her during Bernhardt's Italian tour in 1882. Duse tried to render her characters the incarnation of naturalness, sincerity, and depth. As noted above, she created the impression of not using make-up, exposing her famous paleness, her thick, Medusa-like and almost uncontrollable hair (held only by a few hair clips and deliberately messy) and her neck without any jewellery, expressively rigid and arched. Even in the style of her clothes (big and long Greek tunics, with soft folds and wide sleeves that accentuated arms and hands during their intense gesturing), she cultivated an image of anti-artificiality, and of being natural.[22]

Entering or exiting a scene, Bernhardt would often assume statuesque poses which were not part of the text, thus giving the audience a chance to admire and applaud her. (Traces of this technique can be found in the out-of-character poses of the silent-film divas.) Avoiding Bernhardt's artificial and out of character poses, Duse specialized instead in entering the stage almost unnoticed, taking only a few humble and sometimes shuffled steps, or even turning her back to the public. She used pauses and silence (often disproportionately extended) to let the audience contemplate and decipher her expression, the extreme mobility of her face, and, most of all, her famous intense gaze. The mysterious meaning which seemed implicit in even the slightest quivering of her lips and eyelids, made Duse's face legendary. Display of the signs of aging, including wrinkles and white hair, eventually became a part of her proverbial and tragic image. This had a particular significance for D'Annunzio, who saw in her the embodiment of one of his obsessive themes, that of the tragedy or 'evil' of time.[23]

All witnesses and commentators agree that Duse had the ability to evoke, through sudden movements of her body, gestures, voice, and especially through the manipulation of poses, immobility, silences, and of her gaze, the sense of something authentic coming up from within. She was thus able to charm and almost hypnotize the audience. She gave the illusion of an emotional depth and of contrasting passions that acted upon her body. Her anguish and vision were perceived as coming from a hidden depth. D'Annunzio himself, when narrating in a transparently autobiographical way in *Il Fuoco* how Stelio builds the character of the blind woman in 'Vittoria dell'uomo' (in other words, Anna in *La città morta*) under the influence of Foscarina (in other words, Duse), provides a precise description of the novelty and evocative effectiveness of Duse's technique, to which he gives credit for having 'fecundated' his intellect: 'Egli [...] l'amò per le inattese visioni [...] il senso misterioso degli eventi interiori, ch'ella gli comunicava con le vicende dei suoi sembianti. Si stupì che le linee d'un volto, le movenze di un corpo umano potessero toccare e fecondare così fortemente l'intelletto' (*Il Fuoco* 470) ['[H]e loved her for the unexpected visions [...] the mysterious sense of inner happenings that she communicated to him with the changes in her appearance. He was astonished that the lines of a face, the movements of a human body could so touch and fertilize the mind'] (*The Flame* 264). In the same passage Stelio goes immediately from admiration for the actress to self-admiration, with a mirror-like effect of overturning and inversion (a key process in the novel as a whole). He is under the illusion that he has created her and that she is his character: '– Ah, io t'ho creata!, io t'ho creata! – le gridò illuso dall'intensità dell'allucinazione' (470) ['Ah, I have created you! I have created you!' he cried, deceived by the intensity of his hallucination'] (264). This scene is not only a demonstration of D'Annunzio's narcissism, it is also testimony to how much Duse/Foscarina was able to create the illusion of visualizing the ghosts that belonged to the unconscious not only of her characters, but of those who watched her.

Duse's technique seems to be the product of her profoundly modern and idiosyncratically feminist analysis, or, one can almost say, of her *psychoanalysis* of the characters, which contributed to her enormous success among women. Talking about her characters in an 1884 letter, Duse wrote:

Io non guardo se hanno mentito, se hanno tradito, se hanno peccato – se nacquero perverse – purché io senta che esse hanno pianto – hanno sofferto o per mentire o per tradire o per amore [...] io mi metto con loro e per loro e le frugo, frugo non per mania di sofferenza, ma perché il compianto femminile è il più grande e dettagliato, è più dolce e più completo che non il compianto che accordano gli uomini.

[I do not look to see if they have lied, if they have betrayed, if they have sinned – if they were born perverse–as long as I feel that they have cried – they have suffered either to lie or to betray or for love [...] I place myself with them and for them and I search them, I search them not out of an obsession with pain, but because women's lament is greater and more detailed, sweeter and more complete than the lament of men.][24]

What stands out in this description of the way in which Duse approached her characters is the use of the term 'lament' ('*compianto*'). Duse's analysis is not cold and dispassionate, nor does she completely identify with the character. Hers is a sympathetic approach, a crying together or next to the character. The cathartic or curative, and at the same time aesthetic, effect of Duse's interpretations seems to derive from this splitting in two, and from the empathy she feels for her characters' pain. It is an effect comparable to that of the ancient literary genre of the complaint or *planctus*, of which Duse seems to want to offer a modern equivalent.

In her acting, Duse projected an image of constrained intensity, alternating with moments of sudden, subtle agitation. This technique represented a radically new style compared to the majestic and exterior grandiosity of nineteenth-century Italian acting, and it created the impression that through the actress's body one could 'see' or glimpse into the depths of the unconscious, with its conflicts and contradictions.[25] Duse's style contrasted strikingly with that of the greatest Italian actor of the time, Ermete Zacconi, with whom she had often acted, even in some of D'Annunzio's plays. While Duse strove for delicate expressive details, Zacconi completely exteriorized his characters (for example, Leonardo in *La città morta*). Following the Lombrosian theory of deforming passions, excess, and criminality, Zacconi's characters were pathologically over-excited beings with exaggeratedly contorted movements and facial expressions.

Duse's proverbial naturalness, however, was not perceived as the mark of a healthy female animal nature, but, on the contrary, as the surfacing of an inner malady, a sort of gigantic neurosis. Duse's famous modernity corresponds to her ability to put on stage a kind of woman considered to be deeply neurotic and 'hysterical.' This was the nature of 'modern' woman and, indeed, of modernity itself.[26] The fascination of Duse's modern style is comparable (and was actually compared) to that exercised by the spectacle and enigma of female hysterics.[27] It is no coincidence that psychoanalysis and Freud's theory of the unconscious, which made a crucial contribution to the creation of modernity, were born in part through the contemplation of female hysterics. Lacan's association between woman and the unconscious has its roots there as well. Fetishized woman becomes a symptom of the unconscious according to Lacan, or rather, she *is*, in the last analysis, the unconscious. One can thus explain the fascination that Duse held for some of the greatest modernist writers, including James Joyce, Rainer Maria Rilke, Hugo von Hofmannsthal, Federico García Lorca, and Luigi Pirandello.

On the great stage of the collective imaginary at the end of the nineteenth century, Duse and Bernhardt stood on opposite and complementary sides of the spectrum of femininity. They represented the entire range of the feminine, and its oscillation between antithetical and archetypal categories fundamental to decadent and modernist aesthetics. They stood for woman as oscillation between nature and artifice, surface and depth, body and psyche (and the unconscious), animality and spirituality, aggressiveness and suffering, timelessness (eternal femininity) and temporality. The very dubiousness, the uncertainty of sexual difference, of what is masculine and what is feminine – so important not only for psychoanalysis, but also for Joyce, Rilke, Lorca, and all great modernist writers – seemed to be embodied by the two actresses. Others, like Réjane, Ellen Terry, and Irma Gramatica, were admired, and were exceptional performers on European stages, but none of them reached the mythical-archetypal proportions or generated the international interest obtained by Duse and Bernhardt.

It is not surprising, then, that Wilde and D'Annunzio, although attracted to other actresses, were particularly fascinated by the two divas. For D'Annunzio in particular (who was among the first writers in Europe to explore the labyrinthine link between eroticism, the unconscious, the body, temporality, myth, and the death drive), Duse was a revelation whose depth and importance have not been sufficiently studied. Unfortunately, analysis of the relationship between the two has remained, with few exceptions, on an anecdotal biographical level.[28]

All of D'Annunzio's theatre is, as has been noted, a theatre of women,[29] not only because of the high number of female protagonists or heroines, but because the characters that display the most depth and intensity are indeed women who 'steal the scene' from the male protagonist (this also happens in *Il Fuoco*, as we shall see). In this theft of the male scene, the female becomes profoundly problematic and ambiguous, and gender roles are confused and inverted. The myth of the virile man and of the superman disintegrates, and, in a typical end-of-the-century inversion, the male tends to become female and the female male.

In *La ville morte* or *La città morta*, for example, it is Anna who, with her courage and lucidity, appears most 'virile' compared to Leonardo (the mad archeologist, discoverer of the treasures of the house of Atreus, who incestuously loves his sister and kills her) and Alessandro (the frustrated superman and writer who is Anna's sterile and impotent husband). Even according to Angelo Conti, Anna is the real protagonist of this tragedy.[30] D'Annunzio makes an interesting use of this female character, and of the sexual and gender ambiguity connected to the image of the actress as *mostro sacro*. Through Anna, D'Annunzio exploits the myth of the *mostro sacro* by turning it upside down or inverting it; Anna is indeed a monster, but a monster of purity. Ironically, she is blind, even though she secretly has the keys to man's hidden identity, like the sphinx in the myth of Oedipus. In re-appropriating the plot of the Greek tragedy and modernizing it, D'Annunzio inverts and finally conflates the gender roles, attributing to Anna both the role of Oedipus and that of the sphinx.[31]

Critics, scandalized if not horrified by D'Annunzio's heroines, and most of all by the protagonists of *La Gioconda* and *La Gloria* (both plays were written for Duse), talked about 'superwomen,' destructors of men, inhuman and sexually deviant beings. Even the legendary Max

Beerbohm, in reviewing for the *Saturday Review* the London version of *La Gioconda* staged at the Lyceum Theatre in 1900, seemed to lose his famous irony by declaring that Duse's performance had deeply disturbed him: 'My prevailing impression is of a great egoistic force ... In a man I should admire this tremendous egoism very much indeed. In a woman it only makes me uncomfortable. I dislike it. In the name of art, I protest against it' (qtd. in Weaver 231).[32]

For D'Annunzio, Duse (and to a lesser extent Bernhardt) was truly a revelation of modernity, not only in her style of theatricalization of the body but also in the fundamental theme of temporality, and the complex and contradictory relationship between the unconscious, temporality, and *eros*, that her acting technique disclosed and illuminated. D'Annunzio venerated Duse until his death. In the Vittoriale study, he wrote until the end in front of a marble bust of the actress, but he kept it covered with a veil. For D'Annunzio had an extremely agonistic relationship with Duse (in a Bloomian sense), aimed at obscuring her influence in the public's and perhaps his own eyes.[33] He tried to contain her energy while making it his own. He resisted in particular the threatening originality of her interpretations, and sought to obfuscate it in various ways. According to witnesses and critics, in fact, the suggestive power of Duse's technique and interpretive inventiveness would often overshadow the texts, sometimes eclipsing them completely. Mirella Schino, for example, states that Duse: 'tended to use the empty moments of the character and of the text to get herself to a stage of strong but cold emotional intensity; it was a dramatic situation unconnected to the story that was being told on stage, yet it became the focus of the performance, instead of the text or the character' (232–3). Even Verga, whose *Cavalleria rusticana* Duse brought to triumph (she refused, however, other roles inspired by *Verismo* that she considered excessively crude and violent, such Capuana's *Giacinta*), felt that the actress *destroyed*, rather than glorified his text.[34]

Although he was only a few years younger than Duse (she was born in 1858 and he in 1862), D'Annunzio promoted an image of himself as a young poet and innovative genius in contrast to the older actress, oppressed by the weight of time and experience. This allowed him to allegorize their relationship as a link between the past and the future, between the great traditional repertoire (impersonated and transmitted by her) and the modern theatre which was to be born from their encounter. As Gerardo Guerrieri wrote, the novel *Il Fuoco* 'is the story of a duel between the sexes, but even more of a duel between two opposed fantasies of power and possession unleashed against each other' (*Eleonora Duse. Nove saggi* 192). Stelio/D'Annunzio wants to take possession of the woman to 'tame' her, and this fantasy of erotic possession is nothing but the author's desire to absorb and incorporate into his own work the strength and the temporal depth emanating from the actress's body, which he admits he envies deeply (*Il Fuoco* 449).

To Stelio/D'Annunzio, who adorns himself with the title of 'multanime [multi-soul]' and dreams of transcending 'il male del tempo [the evil of time],' the actress appears as one who really does have 'mille anime [a thousand souls]' and 'mille maschere [a thousand masks]' (*Il Fuoco* 343/*The Flame* 143). Through her classical roles (from Antigone to Cassandra, Fedra, Medea, Cleopatra, Mirra, Giulietta, and infinite others, according to D'Annunzio's vast list), the actress miraculously resurrects the past. She thus embodies simultaneously the evil of time and its negation. The actress's body is a body-text that synthesizes and brings back to life the aesthetic sense of the works interpreted on stage:

Così in una vastità senza limiti e in un tempo senza fine pareva ampliarsi e perpetuarsi il contorno della sostanza e dell'età umana; pur tuttavia non da altro se non dal moto di un muscolo, da un cenno, da un segno, da un lineamento, da un battito di palpebre, da una tenue mutazione di colore, da una lievissima reclinazione della fronte, da un fuggevole gioco di ombre e di luci, da una fulminea virtù espressiva irradiata dalla carne angusta e frale si generavano di continuo quei mondi infiniti d'imperitura bellezza [...] Così la Vita e l'Arte, il passato irrevocabile e l'eternamente presente, la facevano profonda, multanime e misteriosa; magnificavano oltre i limiti umani le sue sorti ambigue. (*Il Fuoco* 283–4)

[Thus in unlimited space and endless time the shape of human age and substance seemed to widen and be extended, and infinite worlds of lasting beauty could be generated simply by the twitch of a muscle, by a sign, a gesture, a profile, a tremor of the eyelids, a slight change in colour, the faintest of frowns, a fleeting play of light and shadow, a flash of expressive power in that thin, frail flesh. [...] Life and Art, irrevocable past and eternal present had made her profound, mysterious, many-souled; her ambiguous destiny had been magnified beyond ordinary human limits.] (*The Flame* 84–5)

Rather than timeless, Duse's habitual repertoire was actually rather dated (in contrast with her brilliant and very modern performances). It did not include any classics, but consisted mostly of texts by Sardou and Dumas *fils* (she also played Cleopatra, but it was an adaptation from Shakespeare that Boito had written expressly for her). These texts allowed her to be the sole protagonist, and to fill the theatres. She hoped to find in D'Annunzio a modern Italian writer of great literary value who would still give her space as the absolute prima donna, without any rivals, in accordance to the system to which she was accustomed. But she found that space only when she returned to Ibsen. In 1891, Duse had been the first in Italy, and then in Russia, to perform his scandalous and revolutionary play, *A Doll's House*; she did not revisit Ibsen's dramas until the end of her partnership with D'Annunzio. The texts that D'Annunzio wrote for her, modern and even visionary in some respects, were not made to glorify the image of Duse as the sole attraction on the stage. *La città morta*, for example, required a solid and well-trained ensemble with actors capable of reciting D'Annunzio's complex text, and a real director. Duse was neither able nor, apparently, willing to organize such a professional company, as Bernhardt already had.[35] Even Bernhardt, however, soon abandoned D'Annunzio's play. When Duse finally staged *La città morta* with Ermete Zacconi in 1901, the company's training and the production were sorely lacking, and the clash between Duse's restrained, visionary style and Zacconi's histrionics was disastrous.[36]

D'Annunzio's dramas and *Il Fuoco* can, in some respects, be read as attempts on D'Annunzio's part to showcase Duse's power and her modernity as an actress; but they also reflect the agonistic dialectics between the poet and the diva. The affirmation of the poet in the theatre required that the mythical Duse be contained and strictly controlled in her roles, making her symbolically subordinate to the author's authority. During rehearsals, D'Annunzio gave the most detailed and pedantic stage directions in the history of the Italian theatre, and he eventually took care of all the details, from lights to fabrics to the smallest gestures and movements on stage. This happened especially in the sumptuous staging of *Francesca da Rimini*, which was considered to be the height of the collaboration between the poet and the actress, but apparently also marked the height of the tension between them (Schino 226). According to critics and audience, the results of the partnership were highly disappointing, not only, as has often been said, for the substantial lack of theatricality of D'Annunzio's plays (they were based too much on words and images, leaving little space for action), but also for the way in which they were staged (before *Francesca*), without the support of a professional ensemble and professional, modern direction. Duse alone could not make D'Annunzio's texts work on stage. Indeed, according to Guerrieri, the disaster of *La Gloria* was caused, at least in part, by the actress's irresponsibility or (one can assume) by her sense of agonism and resentment towards the author, which led her, perhaps unconsciously, to sabotage the production.[37]

The first of D'Annunzio's dramas in which Duse appeared was *Sogno d'un mattino di primavera* [Dream of a Spring Morning] in June 1897 in Paris. It is a particularly revealing play with regard to the relationship between author and actress. The drama echoes Shakespeare in its title and alludes to Ophelia's madness (filtered through various Pre-Raphaelite interpretations) as well as Juliet's tragedy (Juliet was, according to legend, Duse's first role, at the age of fourteen); D'Annunzio thus presents himself as heir to the most illustrious classical tradition.[38] But the perspective of the drama is already psychoanalytical and very modern. The tone is that of a discourse fluctuating between the oneiric and the analytical. The protagonist (known as 'La Demente'), is the victim of a trauma that caused her to lose her memory: her young lover was killed in her arms, and she spent an entire night covered by his blood and his body. Her language is filled with delirious images through which we occasionally gain access to a deeper level of unconscious truth. In making explicit the character's unconscious and bringing it to the surface of the text, D'Annunzio literally takes the actress's place and deprives her of her power of analysis. His language pre-empts Duse's work, making it redundant. In her interpretations of Dumas *fils* and of Sardou's popular dramas, the penetration and disclosing of the character's unconscious was an original invention, an interpretative creation by the actress who worked on the texts, and who in a certain sense rewrote them through her body. In *Sogno* D'Annunzio seems to have learned Duse's lesson all too well, to the point that his discourse has usurped hers.

In *Sogno d'un mattino di primavera* even the striking invention of the vegetable mask, the green mask made of leaves and grass which, according to D'Annunzio's detailed and peremptory stage directions, the Demente must wear on her face, has an ambiguously agonistic role. The function of the green mask is symbolically to display and emphasize Duse's famous naturalness, but to display it means also in

a sense to 'un-mask' it; to call attention to the fact that Duse's naturalness is nothing but a mask, a technical artifice. Even more ironically,
by covering her face the mask prevents Duse from displaying *her own*
mask, the carefully constructed facial mimicry that rendered every
feature, every movement of her eyes and lips, profoundly meaningful.
In D'Annunzio's text, the expression of the character's complexity is
entrusted entirely to the allegorical mask and to the richness of the
poetic words that the author has written for her. There is almost no
space left – without incurring the risk of excessive emphasis that Duse
so detested – for her famous calculated gesticulation, her technique of
somatic expressiveness, and her analytical search for the character's
hidden depth. Everything has already been brought to the surface by
the author. Paradoxically, then, a text inspired by and written for Duse
ends up dispensing with those very technical elements that constituted the actress's greatness and modernity, making them superfluous.

It was precisely the actress's *technique*, her stylistic greatness, that
made her appear strangely disturbing and even dangerous to the author, like a double-edged weapon. The mixture of pleasure and terror
inspired by Bernhardt and Duse's performances seemed to be caused
not only by their gender ambiguity, but also by the technical virtuosity of their style, or rather by their style *as* technique. Bernhardt had a
dreadful effect because, according to George Bernard Shaw's somewhat malevolent description, she was like a monstrous acting machine. Her body appeared simultaneously wild and perfectly controlled;
her voice enhanced the sound of single words and yet rendered them
almost incomprehensible and estranged from their context. This 'wild
delivery,' as it was repeatedly called, had something uncanny about it,
something profoundly disquieting.[39] Bernhardt and Duse both (even if
in different ways) seemed to be machines, or, one could say, *deae ex
machina*, divine and inhuman incarnations of an artifice, a *techne* or
technique that was opposed to 'nature,' and to the familiar and reassuring image of woman connected to the body's natural rhythms, and
to maternity.

In 1897, the year in which Wilde saw her perform, a Parisian critic
compared the movements of Duse's body to the 'frenzied movements
of the cinematograph' (qtd. in Molinari 121). In the same year Adelaide
Ristori noticed that Duse's gestural technique rendered her similar to
an *automaton*, with a strange and hypnotic toughness and mechanical
stiffness.[40] The modernity of Duse's style (notwithstanding its notable
variations) was often described by emphasizing her amazing technical

control over body and voice. Being simultaneously natural and artificial, she provoked in the spectator the alarming sense that the artificiality and the technique of performing (or of pretending to be something or someone) were not at all different from actually or 'naturally' being it (a notion which subsequently became a commonplace of Pirandello's theatre). The critics often reacted to this uncanny dialectic of artifice and naturalness by denying that Duse was really a woman, or that she was a sane and healthy woman. She was, they claimed, 'all nerves and no heart' (Molinari 122), the epitome of neurosis and hysteria. This was due in part to her great repertoire, which included the transgressive heroines of Ibsen's *A Doll's House* and *Hedda Gabler*, widely believed to be neurotics or hysterics. The characters and the actress were identified as belonging to a single, degenerate type: the modern woman. It was in the role of Hedda Gabler that Duse reached the apex of monstrosity: 'in her silent poses [...] the actress's eyes assumed the stone-like stare of the Sphinx' (Molinari 151). In the Greek version of the myth, obsessively rehearsed in the decadent-modernist imaginary, the sphinx is, like the actress, a kind of machine, a sort of sterile and lethal automaton; she is an artificial 'device' that mechanically repeats her deadly riddles on the walls of Thebes.[41]

The myth that the actress (associated in this respect with the perversion of modernity itself) was a sterile machine, a 'technical' rather than a human or natural entity, was widespread in Europe during the second half of the nineteenth century and it even finds echoes in Pirandello. In *Il Fuoco*, D'Annunzio dwells on the subject of the great actress's tragic sterility. Foscarina is obsessed by the impossible desire to have a child with Stelio: 'l'istinto originale del suo sesso si risvegliava nel suo grembo sterile. [...] Ella sentiva la sua sterilità interno ai suoi, fianchi come una cintura di ferro [the original instinct of her sex reawakened in her sterile womb. [...] She could feel her barrenness around her thighs like an iron band]' (*Il Fuoco* 456–7 / *The Flame* 252–3). But, in another typical gender-role inversion, D'Annunzio instead attributes to the actress the power of making Stelio 'fecondo.'[42] The gestating Stelio feels inside of him the tremors and movements of the play/creature, just like a mother feels the foetus move in her uterus: 'L'animatore, con un altro brivido, sentì sussultare entro di sé l'opera che egli nutriva, ancora informe ma già vitale [With another shiver, the Creator felt the still unformed but vital work that he was nourishing within him stir again]' (*Il Fuoco* 282 / *The Flame* 84; cf. also *Il Fuoco* 244, 342, and *passim*). Duse herself (who at the age of twenty-four gave birth to a daughter, Enrichetta, to whom she remained deeply attached her whole life) sometimes considered herself degenerate and without maternal instinct. Her alleged bisexuality and her relationships with younger actresses contributed to the myth of Duse as a 'non-woman,' or an unnatural and false woman, a degenerate body-machine.[43]

The mechanistic, technical, and inhuman aspect of the figure of the actress would also seem to fit perfectly with both Wilde and D'Annunzio's aesthetics, but in reality this is only partially the case. Wilde, like D'Annunzio, delighted in technique and artificiality, and resisted everything natural, spontaneous, and authentic. Like D'Annunzio, he provocatively maintained the superiority of the artificial and upheld the paradoxical authenticity of the mask. For the mask, as Giovanna Franci noted, is not the role but the persona of the dandy (31). Yet both authors remained essentially faithful to the Romantic myth of the originality of the author's individual genius. And it was exactly this myth that, albeit in different ways, Bernhardt and Duse undermined and even destroyed on stage.

The terror and revulsion that spectators experienced when confronted with Salomé's character constitute the other side of the pleasure and joy that Wilde felt when Bernhardt recited his words. Yet even Wilde was in some ways deeply uneasy with Bernhardt's rendering of Salomé. Being a veritable reciting machine and a technical wonder, Bernhardt rendered the origin of the words irrelevant. She used the words only to project her own voice and to articulate her own body and mask. The author was entirely forgotten, his authority erased. The power of the actress implicitly demolished the myth and the authority of the author – any author – as an original creative genius. The importance of genius itself seemed under question: Bernhardt triumphed playing Cleopatra, but the Cleopatra of Sardou's adaptation, not Shakespeare's version. The body of the actress eclipsed the author's genius and made it seem to vanish. But there was more: in the divine Sarah's consistent voice and intonation, the authors' words began to seem like, as often they really were (especially in the cases of Wilde and D'Annunzio), repetitions and echoes of other authors' words: Wilde sounded like Sardou or Dumas *fils*. Even Duse was accused of 'betraying' the texts (which she studied and annotated obsessively) by her long pauses and by taking excessive advantage of silences and 'empty' moments in order to show off the famous expressiveness of her body and gestures. This uncanniness of the actress as prima donna, and her subversion of the myth and authority of the creative genius (traditionally assumed to be male), constitute an important but as of yet scarcely studied part of the complex battle of the sexes fought on the wider stage of turn-of-the-century society.

It is therefore not surprising that Wilde and D'Annunzio, while professing an infinite admiration for the image of the great actress, felt an equally profound resentment that assumed precise textual forms. Both authors staged a symbolic revenge against the actress: Wilde in the novel *The Picture of Dorian Gray*, and D'Annunzio particularly in *Il Fuoco*. In *The Picture of Dorian Gray*, before Dorian can have the stage all to himself, become the main actor, and play his part of dandy under the influence of Lord Henry Wotton (who is his brilliant creator and, in a sense, stage director, in addition to being Wilde's double), the actress must be suppressed, and with her, the suspicion that Wilde's art may not be original. Wilde does this by employing his favourite and most effective weapon: paradoxical and ironic reversal. The actress may indeed be a threat to the originality and the importance of the dandy, but since she is a mechanical being completely devoid of originality, her threat is banal and tautological. The actress to whom Dorian takes a fancy (significantly named Sibyl Vane, or 'vain sibyl,' both names, incidentally, that are echoed in D'Annunzio's novels) is demolished without pity by Henry. When Dorian calls her a 'genius' and 'sacred' (just as Bernhardt and Duse were often described) Henry replies: 'My dear boy, no woman is a genius. Women are a decorative sex. They never have anything to say, but they say it charmingly. Women represent the triumph of matter over mind' (192).

In order to demolish the image of the actress, Henry identifies her with the feminine sex in general; the actress is a woman, ergo she cannot be a genius, nor can she have anything original to say. Essentially, everything the actress says and that renders her so desirable and fascinating on the stage, originates literally from another source: the author of the text she recites. Henry explains that what Dorian believes he loves in Sibyl does not belong to Sibyl at all, but rather to the authors, especially Shakespeare, recited by her mechanically, like an empty and passive automaton. Sibyl's nature is, like that of her mother (also an actress and suspected to be a prostitute) rooted in 'shallowness and vanity' (214). When Sibyl, falling in love with Dorian, reveals the banality and emptiness of her being, exposes, in essence, her *non*-being, Dorian is revolted by it and Sibyl kills herself in desperation. This death is a parody of the tragic deaths of the great actresses, and it confirms Wotton's hypothesis: women (and thus actresses) neither have nor do anything original: it is only the male imagination that cloaks them in the mystery and charm attributed to them.

Women are thus 'sphinxes without secrets': this epigrammatic definition of the female sex by Henry Wotton (derived from Baudelaire), cites, among other things, the title of an 1887 story by Wilde, 'The Sphinx Without a Secret.' The theme of this story is specifically the mysterious and fascinating appearance of femininity that conceals only a banal and boring reality: a chronic lack or emptiness. One must then ask the question: is the expression 'sphinx without secrets' simply the equivalent of saying *false* sphinx, sphinx only in appearance (which would render the phrase synonymous with the name of Sibyl Vane, 'vain sibyl')? This is the most obvious interpretation, but one could also hypothesize another, according to which the sphinx is false because her secrets are false; in other words, the tragic secret of Oedipus's identity, and especially of his sexuality, are false.[44] Wilde's discourse would seem to question a fundamental aspect of the modern mythology of identity and of obligatory heterosexuality that was, precisely in the years of Wilde's trials and of his imprisonment, the object of heretical investigation in the work of Sigmund Freud.

In reality, as much as Wilde's aphorism may look ahead and as much as it may be the cause of some perplexity, behind the idea of the woman-actress as 'sphinx without secrets,' lie perhaps, above all, the stereotypes of a positivist Victorian culture. Behind Wilde lurk Darwin and Havelock Ellis, more than Freud. In particular, the Darwin of *The Descent of Man* (1871) suggested that women, inferior to man in all the arts, were naturally passive, emotional, and incapable of original thought or action, and therefore that they had a natural tendency to repeat, suffer, and imitate, in addition to being easily excitable (563–4). This made them dangerously weak and potential victims of disastrous passions and degenerations of the primitive-regressive kind, but it also rendered them particularly adept at receiving the civilizing influence of man, and at being guided towards the proper path of maternity and tender family relationships. The same female passivity, rapidity of perception, and capacity to imitate also formed the basis of the generally acknowledged notion according to which women excelled more than men in the theatre and at the art of acting. Havelock Ellis, whose theories were profoundly influenced by Lombroso and Mantegazza, wrote: 'There is at least one art in which women may be said not merely to rival but naturally to excel men: this is the art of acting' (437).[45] Women, according to Havelock Ellis, are potentially great actresses because all women, with their emotional explosiveness, their excitability, and their narcissism, as well as their habit of imitating and behaving according to prescribed roles, are *instinctively* actresses even in normal life.

Ellis cites Bernhardt and Duse as examples of the indisputable preeminence of women in the theatre, but he does so only to discredit the myth that these actresses are geniuses, or that they possess genius (a quality that Ellis attributes exclusively and systematically to men). It is not difficult to find the organic basis of woman's success in acting, Ellis states, suggesting that what Bernhardt and Duse had done was simply what all women were able to do. The character Sibyl Vane, and in particular the way in which she passively falls under Dorian Gray's influence, ultimately committing suicide, gives concrete form to these commonplace ideas about femininity and about the art of the actress, according to which the two terms – woman and actress – are essentially interchangeable.[46]

D'Annunzio's case is strangely similar to that of Dorian Gray. In *Il Fuoco*, Stelio Effrena, like Dorian Gray, falls in love with an actress and he makes her fall in love with him by exalting her greatness, only to then proceed, in what he passes off as a search for and an unveiling of the truth, to make her go away and vanish from the scene (something that fortunately, in Duse's case, notwithstanding the trauma and the public humiliation of *Il Fuoco*, did not happen in reality). For Foscarina, as for Sibyl Vane, the end is a voluntary disappearance, and thus a kind of suicide. Foscarina sadly says: 'Io partirò, io scomparirò, me ne andrò a morire lontano [I shall go away, I shall disappear, I shall go far away and die]' (*Il Fuoco* 416/*The Flame* 213), using a phrase that, with a few variations, becomes for her a musical motif throughout the novel, along with 'Bisogna che io muoia ... [I must die ...]' (*Il Fuoco* 328, 381/*The Flame* 130, 180, and *passim*). At the same time, Stelio – like and with D'Annunzio – strongly reaffirms the myth of his own originality: 'Io non verso la mia sostanza in impronte ereditate. La mia opera è d'invenzione totale. Io non debbo e non voglio obbedire se non al mio istinto e al genio della mia stirpe [I am not pouring my essence into inherited moulds. My work is completely new. I can't and won't obey anything except my own instinct and the genius of my race]' (*Il Fuoco* 494/*The Flame* 287).

As Cesare Molinari (among others) said, in the course of her collaboration with D'Annunzio (concurrent with the composition of *Il Fuoco*), the diva was increasingly deprived of her central position, and ultimately of her power and her mystique. D'Annunzio insisted that the words in the text could not be sacrificed. To exalt the musicality of D'Annunzio's texts, Duse rendered her diction more melodic, and she made her physical presence more abstract and stylized. Critics noticed the improvement in the clarity of Duse's diction, but they did not appreciate the actress's new D'Annunzian style. They found it affected and thought it represented a lamentable loss of Duse's famous naturalness (Valentini, *Il poema visibile* 74, 223–4). In the last production in which D'Annunzio and Duse collaborated, *Francesca da Rimini* (staged after the publication of *Il Fuoco*), the actress appeared 'paralysed' to Luigi Pirandello (Pirandello 379).

'The tendency toward self-annihilation, toward disappearance' (Molinari 177), became the actress's new stylistic mode in her D'Annunzian roles. In *La Gioconda*, Silvia, the protagonist (played by Duse), sacrifices her hands in order to save her husband Lucio's statue. Duse thus became symbolically disabled on stage, deprived of the famous expressive hands that represented the quintessence of her technique. In the last act, Duse, famous for being able to communicate with even the slightest movements of her body, and with her voice reduced to an intense whisper, was literally immobilized like a statue, reduced to a completely mute presence at the back of the stage. In addition, the bipolar structure of the play, in which there are not one but two female protagonists, undermined the monological diva system.

This is made even more explicit by the fact that the younger and prettier Gioconda (the fascinating but deadly model of Lucio's veiled sculpture, an 'imperious and pure' sphinx) is characterized by traits that, according to various interpreters, seem to be directly inspired by Duse's own acting style.[47] Gioconda is like Duse, an actress capable of expressing great depths through her body and her gaze, yet Duse cannot be Gioconda:

> Ella è sempre diversa. [...] Ogni moto del suo corpo distrugge un'armonia e ne crea un'altra più bella. [...] A traverso la sua mobilità passa un torrente di forze oscure come i pensieri passano negli occhi. [...] La vita degli occhi è lo sguardo, questa cosa indicibile, più espressiva d'ogni parola, d'ogni suono, infinitamente profonda eppure istantanea come il baleno, più rapida ancora del baleno, innumerevole, onnipossente: insomma *lo sguardo*. Ora immagina diffusa su tutto il corpo di lei la vita dello sguardo. [...] Un battito di palpebre ti trasfigura un viso umano e ti esprime un'immensità di gioia e di dolore. (*La Gioconda* 274–5)

[She is always different. [...] Each movement of her body destroys a harmony only to create another, more beautiful one. [...] Through her mutability flows a stream of obscure forces, like thoughts passing through the eyes. [...] The life of the eyes is the gaze, this unspeakable thing, more expressive than any word, any sound, infinitely deep and yet instantaneous, like a flash, faster than a flash, innumerable, all-powerful: in short, *the gaze*. Now imagine all over her body the life of the gaze. [...] A quick glance transfigures a human face and expresses an immensity of joy and pain.]

Locked into the role of Silvia, Duse thus found herself painfully divided and reproduced, ironically, in a character that she could not interpret. The entire course of D'Annunzio's relationship with Duse seems to have taken place under the sadistic insignia of division, impairment, or purification. D'Annunzio's containment of the actress's power was based on a kind of exorcism of the body. As Franca Angelini noted, the characters D'Annunzio created for Duse 'are all under the sign of a mutilation, that of the hands and the eyes, which were her most striking expressive resources.' The mouth and voice are also suppressed. Before offering her body to the flame in a final purifying ritual, Mila di Codro is a presence almost entirely without a voice in *La figlia di Jorio*, lacking the 'noblest sign' of Duse's art, 'the art of speech' (72). It is therefore not surprising that Duse, after much agonizing, ended up not taking the part, officially due to illness. But by then *Il Fuoco* had already been published and, in a letter to D'Annunzio, Duse had already denounced the book as a lie.[48]

The actress's body served as an irreplaceable source of inspiration (even beyond *La Figlia di Jorio*), yet it is progressively devalued and vilified. In *Il Fuoco* it becomes the object of 'orrore' and 'disgusto' (278), and it is finally removed from the scene once the fecundation is over: 'Ella stessa camminando sentiva l'estrema leggerezza del suo passo e in sé qualcosa di sparente, come se il corpo fosse per mutarsi in una larva [As she walked, she could feel the extreme lightness of her step and sense that in herself something was disappearing, as though her whole body were about to change into a wraith]' (*Il Fuoco* 441/*The Flame* 237). It will be Stelio's turn now, as he gets ready to give birth to his play 'La vittoria dell'uomo,' to appear dazzling in his 'corpo voluttuoso [sensuous body]' (*Il Fuoco* 468/*The Flame* 261). His is an appropriation or, rather, a final expropriation of the mythical body of the diva and of its power of signification. The expropriation culminates in the violent scene of vampire-like 'scopophilia' when the actress 'conobbe un altro modo d'esser posseduta [encountered another way to be possessed]:' 'come a stilla a stilla la sua stessa anima entrasse nella persona del dramma, e i suoi aspetti, le sue attitudini, i suoi gesti, i suoi accenti, concorressero a formare la figura dell'eroina. [...] Si chiuse e si contrasse, sotto lo sguardo dell'indagatore, come per impedirle di penetrarla e di rapirle quella vita segreta [drop by drop her soul [was] entering into the character of the drama, and her features, her stance, her gestures, her tone of voice were combining to create the figure of the heroine. [...] She retreated into herself, contracted herself, under his enquiring gaze, as though to prevent him penetrating her and stealing away her secret life]' (*Il Fuoco* 469/*The Flame* 262–3).

In the self-gratifying and narcissistic fantasy of D'Annunzio's novel (where Duse is depicted just as D'Annunzio wanted her), an uncontrollable masochism is attributed to the actress, along with the urge to offer herself, to serve and to suffer, modelled after Wagner's Kundry. Foscarina's desire for death and disappearance is the ultimate and necessary consequence of her masochism. Even though he is given female qualities, in the novel Stelio does not lose his sadistic inclination. On the contrary, the text exalts his manly sadism and violence. Through the act of creation, he appropriates the actress's mythical body for himself. The most vivid emblem of this creative sadism is the image of Stelio as he attacks Foscarina's body 'come se volesse percuoterla per trarne scintille [as though he wanted to strike sparks from her]' (*Il Fuoco* 472/*The Flame* 265). At the end of the novel, Foscarina 'disappears' as a lover from Stelio's horizon (just as D'Annunzio wished Duse would disappear), but she starts, 'compagna virile e volenterosa [a virile and eager companion],' her American tour, intending to use the profits to finance 'La vittoria dell'uomo.'

Some have interpreted Mila di Codro's immolation as the emblem of Duse's sacrifice of her art for D'Annunzio's theatre. The sacrifice was also financial. Duse did not bring *La figlia di Jorio* to the stage because, after the failure of *Francesca*, she was not financially able to put on D'Annunzio's new tragedy and risk financial ruin.[49] She agreed at first to appear in ten exceptional performances in Virgilio Talli's company, but even this deal fell through in the end. *Il Fuoco* had already irreparably damaged the relationship between Duse and D'Annunzio, and Duse's reaction demonstrated that she was not such a masochist, or as virile and willing a partner, as D'Annunzio had hoped.[50]

The relationship between Duse and D'Annunzio had always been primarily agonistic, but *Il Fuoco* exposed it as never before. In a letter written after reading *Il Fuoco* Duse says that she wanted to 'smash [D'Annunzio's] head open.'[51] Other testimony indicates, however, that Duse, in love with the poet, initially approved of the novel and perhaps even contributed to the draft of the manuscript, making corrections and additions.[52] Paradoxically, Duse emerges triumphant from the novel. Foscarina is surely the greatest role D'Annunzio ever wrote for her, so much so that the novel contributed decisively to defining Duse's myth in the world. Nonetheless, the novel is totally centred on an attempt to reduce the actress to the role of a mere instrument, a means through which the masculine genius expresses itself. Stelio is the artificer, the fire that forges, Foscarina is 'la vivente materia atta a ricevere i ritmi dell'arte, a essere foggiata [living material ready to receive the rhythms of art, to be shaped]' (*Il Fuoco* 372/*The Flame* 171). He affirms the values of domination and of creation; she represents the feminine and passive values of submission, devotion, instinct, sacrifice, and suffering. Her entire character is built to highlight the connection of femininity with passion, passivity, and pain. She will be 'lo strumento mirabile [the marvelous instrument]' (*Il Fuoco* 249/*The Flame* 53), the 'divulgatrice' (249; 278) of Stelio's work. Even her genius is nothing but an instinctive form, an 'arte involontaria [involuntary skill]' (*Il Fuoco* 208/*The Flame* 14), almost a biological form of possession (which implies passivity). The great actress is 'prey' to her own roles, and the passion that she feels and transmits is the unconscious passion of a maenad, of a woman dominated by a divine force, by an atavistic or bestial memory, that comes from outside her, and therefore is instinctive and uncontrolled. The knowledge of the actress is the product of the 'eterna servitù della natura [...] destinata a soggiacere nelle improvvise convulsioni del suo sesso [eternal servitude of nature [...] destined to succumb to the unexpected traumas of her sex]' (*Il Fuoco* 304/*The Flame* 105). In *Il Fuoco*, no trace remains of Duse's famous technique, of her interpretive and analytical genius, or of the intensely calculated style through which she created a hypnotic effect of depth, suffering, and empathy on the stage.

In order to appropriate the figure of the actress for himself, even D'Annunzio resorted to the stereotypes about femininity and women that were circulating in the European cultural context. If Darwin and Havelock Ellis are behind Wilde, behind D'Annunzio stand Lombroso and Mantegazza. Mantegazza had asserted in *Fisiologia della donna* that even though women are incapable of creating something new or original, there is in them a type of instinctive and intuitive memory of the collective past: 'woman is stronger than us in rapid intuition, because she is richer in congenital memories' (2: 192).[53] The few women artists who have existed over the ages, Mantegazza claims, 'have drawn the best of their inspiration from their unconscious psyche' (2: 202). From this he deduces their inferiority.

In *Il Fuoco* D'Annunzio highlights how much Foscarina is the passive receptacle of ancient passions (mostly erotic passions), even as she makes them come back to life on the stage. D'Annunzio emphasizes that this condition of passivity, which allows her to be a great actress, also renders her ineluctably inferior to Stelio. For as an author and 'attore del suo stesso dramma [actor in his own drama]' (*Il Fuoco* 367/*The Flame* 166), Stelio is not passive, but active; he consciously knows how to produce, control, and manipulate the passions of those who listen to him.

But in contrast to Wilde, D'Annunzio, even while he exalts the male genius (i.e., himself), periodically recognizes, almost with humility, the actress's modernity, her greatness, and her 'libero genio [free genius]' (*Il Fuoco* 284/*The Flame* 86). She appears to him as the one who has truly penetrated and revealed, through her interpretation of countless roles, the complexity and profundity of not only an immense theatrical and literary repertoire, but also of the question of identity. For Duse brings into the limelight the tenuous difference between self and other. She subtly insinuates that it is through acting, and through the fabrication of a discourse and of a role, that one creates a reality that one can (at least temporarily) call one's own. In Foscarina/Perdita's multiple roles, the illusion of a unique and authentic identity is lost, and a simulated, nomadic, labyrinthine and decidedly modern identity emerges.

NOTES

This is a revised and updated version of an essay that first appeared in Italian in *MLN* vol. 117, 1 (Jan. 2002): 115–52, under the title 'D'Annunzio, Duse, Wilde, Bernhardt: il rapporto autore/attrice fra decadentismo e modernità.'

1 For further details on Duse and Italian feminism, and in particular Sibilla Aleramo, see Laura Mariani's 'Eleonora Duse e Sibilla Aleramo: un teatro per "la donna nuova".'

2 In Europe, the theme of the promiscuity and corruption of the actress or 'stage woman' reached an archetypal codification in Zola's novel *Nana* (1880). Nana, a courtesan, reaches theatrical glory (even though she does not know how to act, sing, or dance) through the public exhibition of her flesh. In the course of the novel, the corruption of and by her flesh takes on epic proportions and becomes the emblem of the corruption of modern society by materialism and commodification. As actresses' biographies and memoirs of the late nineteenth and early twentieth century repeatedly demonstrate, all the 'serious' actresses had to defend themselves from the influence of the 'Nana archetype.' The issue of actresses' morality was debated during the first national congress of Italian women in 1908. The actress Virginia Marini (an interpreter of Ibsen) and the playwright Teresa Sormanni participated in that debate, along with the feminist Giuseppina Lemaire. (Cf. Mariani (209) and Consiglio Nazionale delle donne italiane, *Atti del I Congresso Nazionale delle Donne Italiane, Rome 24–30 April 1908*, Rome, 1908).

3 I thank J. Hillis Miller for drawing my attention to the importance of this novel.

4 For further details on the genetic relationship between Decadence and modernism, see the interesting study conducted by David Weir in *Decadence and the Making of Modernism*. Unfortunately, Weir gives a rather superficial reading of both Wilde and D'Annunzio. Of the latter's work, he considers only *Il piacere*, substantially subscribing to Mario Praz's outdated understanding of D'Annunzian aesthetics in *La carne, la morte e il diavolo nella letteratura romantica* (1930).

5 Cf. also the passage in which Foscarina, after giving herself to Stelio, feels lost and denigrates herself in front of him as a 'creatura corrotta, la carne di voluttà, l'avanzo degli amori avventurosi, l'attrice vagabonda che è nel suo letto come sulla scena, di tutti e di nessuno [corrupted being, a leftover from occasional passions, a vagabond actress who belongs to everyone and yet to no one in bed just as on stage]' (*Il Fuoco* 339/*The Flame* 140).

6 For the history of the staging of D'Annunzio's early plays, and of the complex relationship between D'Annunzio and Duse, see Valentina Valentini's careful study, *Il poema visibile*.

7 See Felski (110–11), for a brief but interesting and useful discussion of the image of the actress (with particular reference to Wilde). Felski attributes

the tendency towards artifice and the mask to all modernism, but, in my opinion this represents an excessive broadening of a tendency that actually belongs specifically to decadent-modernist aesthetics. For example, in Pirandello the theme of the mask is everywhere, but it is expressed as a drama or even a tragedy of modernity, without the positive connotations found in the decadents. Pirandello was obsessed with Duse, whose style he greatly admired, thinking it a miracle of naturalness, naked truth, and inner depth. On the other hand, he deeply resented D'Annunzio and his theatre, which he bitterly criticized for lacking depth, and for what, according to him, was total and empty 'exteriority,' the purely superficial game of poses and verbal forms, which were not at all suited to Duse. See 'Più che un'attrice' (the text originally appeared in German in *Eleonora Duse*, edited by B. Segantini and F. Mendelssohn, Berlin, 1926). Pirandello tried in vain to convince Duse to work for him: the actress always refused. In 1923 she even declined to do *La vita che ti diedi*, which Pirandello had written especially for her, but in which there were three important female roles (evidently too many), two of which were mothers. To make up for Duse's absence, according to Daniela Bini (121), Pirandello tried to convince *his* actress, Marta Abba, to interpret many of Duse's roles, and, in a certain sense, to 'become' Eleonora Duse for him.

8 Robert Horville states that 'Bernhardt had a tendency to repeat her roles endlessly, blending them with each other or blending them with herself.' He cites the critic Gabriel Boissy, who complained that 'the basic fault of Madame Sarah Bernhardt is in never adapting herself to a role but adapting the role to herself and playing herself all the time' (42).

9 Cited in Guerrieri (25). Horville (51) instead attributes this observation to Anatole France.

10 The most illuminating text concerning these differences of style is still George Bernard Shaw's famous essay of 1895, 'Duse and Bernhardt.' For a modern and very useful interpretation, see John Stokes, Michael R. Booth, and Susan Bassnett, *Bernhardt, Terry, Duse* and Kelly Powell's 'A Verdict of Death: Oscar Wilde, Actresses and Victorian Women' in *The Cambridge Companion to Oscar Wilde*, edited by Peter Raby. See also Powell's *Oscar Wilde and the Theater of the 1890s*.

11 See the piece published in *La Tribuna* entitled '31 gennaio 1888. Cronaca delle arti,' now in *Scritti giornalistici* (1043).

12 Rendered feminine in his role as a seducer, Stelio also assumes Salomé's serpentine and swaying aspect: 'Ella si lasciava sedurre ... Eravi in lui

qualcosa di ondeggiante e di volubile e di possente [She let herself be seduced ... There was something swaying and mutable and powerful in him]' (*Il Fuoco* 213). For further information on inversion as a rhetorical process typical of literary decadence, see Barbara Spackman's interesting essay 'Inversions.'

13 The most disturbing and explicit version of the link between woman-diva and the seductive, dangerous spectacularization of politics can be found in the historical tragedy *La Gloria*, staged by Duse in Naples in 1899.

14 For the theme of the mask in Nietzsche, see Gianni Vattimo's *Il soggetto e la maschera*.

15 For example, after the first performance in London, which finally took place privately (with Millicent Murby in the main role) in May 1905, Max Beerbohm – generally in tune with Wilde's dandyism – wrote that the drama was 'too horrible for definite and corporeal presentment,' complaining in particular about the scene in which Salomé kisses the dead Jokaanan's lips, during which 'we suffer qualms of physical disgust,' while at the same time the scene 'destroyed all our illusion' (*Saturday Review*, 13 May 1905).

16 Kerry Powell, 'Salomé, the Censor, and the Divine Sarah,' in *Oscar Wilde and the Theatre of the 1890s* (46).

17 According to Powell, 'So exaggerated is the ritualistic style of Salomé, in fact, that its language comes dangerously near to a travesty of the speech which was the hallmark of the actress Wilde most admired' (48). On Bernhardt's voice see also Horville.

18 Thus Richard Ellmann's famous false interpretation seems in part justified, at least symbolically. Ellmann claimed that the picture reproduced on page 428 of his biography, *Wilde*, was a portrait of Wilde dressed up as an actress in the role of Salomé, and not, as was proved by Marvin Holland in 1994, the image of a woman, the Hungarian opera singer Alice Guszalewicz, photographed in the role of Salomé in Cologne in 1906.

19 *Pall Mall Budget*, 30 June 1892, 947; *The Letters of Oscar Wilde* (156).

20 Wilde was still in prison, and Bernhardt had lost all interest in acquiring – in spite of Wilde's explicit request – the rights to the drama, because the deal seemed financially insecure to her.

21 A letter of 23 November 1897, addressed to Robert Ross, indicates that Wilde had asked Duse's ex *impresario* and *capocomico*, Cesare Rossi, to ask Duse to read *Salomé* in a translation written for the occasion. A letter of early December to the editor Leonard Mithers confirms that Duse was

reading the text (which, however, she did not find suited to her): 'Eleonora Duse is now reading *Salomé*. There is a chance of her playing it. She is a fascinating artiste though nothing to Sarah' (*Letters* 664, 683, 695).

22 The most indepth and iconographically rich studies of Duse's style are Cesare Molinari's *L'attrice divina*, Gerardo Guerrieri's *Eleonora Duse. Nove saggi*, and Guerrieri's catalogue of the Treviso show, *Eleonora Duse e il suo tempo 1858–1924*. See also *Divina Eleonora*, edited by Fernando Bandini. Very useful are the biographies by William Weaver (*Duse*), and Giovanni Pontiero (*Eleonora Duse: In Life and Art*).

23 For further details on this topic see Paolo Valesio's *Gabriele D'Annunzio*.

24 Letter to Francesco D'Arcais, 4 Aug. 1884, in Camillo Antona Traversi (387).

25 Even Guerrieri (*Eleonora Duse. Nove saggi* 25) notices that Duse's sincerity technique corresponds to the actress's new way of accessing the subconscious, suggesting also that Stanislavsky's method was deeply influenced by her technique. For further information on how Duse's acting technique created the impression of surfacing from the unconscious, see Susan Bassnett, 'Eleonora Duse,' in Stokes, Booth, and Bassnett (141).

26 The extremely detailed, technical description of Duse's style by Adelaide Ristori (the greatest actress of the generation preceding Duse's) is very interesting in this regard. It was included in a letter to Count Giuseppe Primoli, published in French in *Galois* (26 May 1897). I cite from the Italian version reproduced in Guerrieri (*Eleonora Duse. Nove saggi* 68): 'La Duse si è creata da sé la propria *maniera*, un convenzionalismo tutto suo, che affascina, per cui, essenzialmente, è la *Donna moderna* con tutte le sue malattie di nevrosi, d'anemia, e con tutte le sue conseguenze, e perciò nel suo repertorio ha introdotto, con molta sagacia, una completa collezione di questi tipi anomali [Duse has created for herself her own *manner*, a fascinating set of conventions through which she is essentially *Modern Woman* with all her illnesses – neurosis, anemia – and all their consequences. Therefore she has introduced in her repertoire, with great adroitness, a complete collection of these anomalous types].' On the association between neurosis and modernity at the end of the century, see Molinari's interesting comments (111–12).

27 See, for example, the passage in the best-selling memoir *La Duse* by the actor Luigi Rasi, who worked for a long period of time with Duse (first edition, Bemporad 1901): 'La Duse, al primo tempo della sua grandezza, possedeva al sommo la faccia che noi vediamo il più spesso nelle malattie generali del sistema nervoso, e particolarmente nelle grandi nevrosi: *la faccia convulsiva*. L'occhio agitato da tremiti impercettibili, si recava

rapidamente in direzioni opposte; le guance passavano con incredibile rapidità dal rossore al pallore; le narici e le labbra fremevano; i denti si serravan con violenza, e ogni più piccola parte del volto era in movimento. [...] La persona poi, a significar ben compiuta l'espressione del tipo, avesse guizzi serpentini, o abbandoni profondi, rispondeva perfettamente con l'azione e contrazione delle braccia, delle mani, delle dita, del busto, all'azione e contrazione del volto. E perciò, forse, la grande artista riusciva insuperabile nella rappresentazione dei personaggi a *temperamento isterico* [In her first great phase, Duse possessed to the utmost the face that we see most often in conjunction with illnesses of the nervous system, and particularly in cases of serious neuroses: *the convulsive face*. With eyes agitated by imperceptible tremors, she would move quickly in opposite directions; her cheeks changed with incredible rapidity from blushing to pallor; the nostrils and lips quivered, the teeth clenched violently, and even the smallest part of her face was moving. [...] Her body, perfectly displaying the full expression of that type – whether through serpentine wriggling or profound abandon – responded perfectly through the contraction of arms, fingers and chest, to the contractions of the face. This is perhaps why the great artist was unbeatable in the interpretation of characters with an *hysterical temperament*]' (27).

28 Unfortunately the majority of the letters D'Annunzio wrote to Duse were destroyed by Duse's daughter, Enrichetta, who claimed it was her mother's wish (cf. Pontiero 380). The small volume *Carteggio D'Annunzio-Duse*, edited by Piero Nardi, contains only the crumbs of what, one might suppose, was a substantial and complex correspondence. Other letters written by Duse were published in Molinari, Guerrieri (*Eleanora Duse. Nove saggi*), Weaver and Pontiero, and, edited by Emilio Mariano in 'Il 'patto di alleanza' fra Eleonora Duse and Gabriele D'Annunzio,' and in 'Undici lettere di Eleonora Duse a Gabriele D'Annunzio.' See also Mariano, *Sentimento del vivere ovvero Gabriele D'Annunzio* (148–73) and, for the letters pertaining to the theatrical productions, the precious volume by Valentina Valentini, *La tragedia moderna e mediterranea*. Other, unpublished letters are still in the Vittoriale archives.

29 See Luisetta Elia Chomel's *D'Annunzio. Un teatro al femminile*. Chomel, however, does not attach much significance to the influence Duse had on D'Annunzio, seeing her only as an element, and not a determining factor, in D'Annunzio's theatrical formation.

30 'La città morta' in *Il Marzocco*, 23 Jan. 1898.

31 For the notion of overturning the Oedipus complex into its feminine version through the character of Anna, see also Paolo Valesio, 'Il coro

degli Agrigentini,' in *Quaderni del Vittoriale* (Nov.–Dec. 1982) and then in *Gabriele D'Annunzio: The Dark Flame*, esp. 53 and 222.

32 Weaver, perhaps too generously, thinks instead that Beerbohm is being ironic here, at least in part.

33 See Harold Bloom's *Agon*.

34 See also Hugo von Hoffmansthal's opinion in 'Duse in the Year 1903,' in *Gabriele D'Annunzio e Eleonora Duse*: 'In this actress lives such a soul that any work recited by her falls apart due to the sublimity of her gestures. And she stands alone [with] her great emotions, that, in an unprecedented way, have become corporeal forms, her way of walking, standing still, raising her head, the magic of her hands' (87–8).

35 Between the end of September and the beginning of October 1896, Duse wrote to D'Annunzio (with her usual underlinings for emphasis): 'La verità è che *oggi* non ho con me né *i due attori* né *la donna* che occorrono al dramma. Ma se questa grande gioia tu *non me la rubi* [...] non dispero affatto poter cercare – e *trovare* – qualcosa di *quasi* fattibile [The truth is that *today* I have with me neither *the two male actors* nor the *actress* that are needed for ther play. But *unless you rob me* of this great joy. [...] I do not despair of being able to look for and *find* something *almost* feasible].' But D'Annunzio, being impatient, had already contacted Bernhardt. Writing to Herelle, the translator, he claimed (probably to win the favour of the actress) that he had written the drama inspired 'dai fantasmi dei suoi gesti [by the phantoms of her gestures].' Duse's letter and D'Annunzio's are published in Valentini, *La tragedia* (114–18).

36 For information on the first staging of *La città morta* and of D'Annunzio's other plays interpreted by Duse, see Valentini's *Il poema visibile*. According to Guerrieri (*Eleonora Duse. Nove saggi* 103), even the first staging of *La Gioconda* and *La Gloria* were disastrous. This last tragedy was, according to him (and not Duse), 'mandata al massacro [send to the slaughter],' apparently with Duse's unconscious help, and definitively buried (cf. also 138 and 148). The situation started to change when D'Annunzio decided to direct his own productions, beginning with *Francesca da Rimini*, and especially when he hired a real director, Virgilio Talli, for *La figlia di Jorio*.

37 Valentini (*Il poema* visibile 200) hypothesizes that the failure to produce *Sogno di un tramonto d'autunno* in 1897 (the second of the 'Sogni' written by D'Annunzio for Duse) was caused not only by the impossibility of finding the ten actresses suited for the tragedy (the official reason given by Duse), but also by Duse's unconscious resistance to the role of Gradeniga, the mature *dogaressa* who is abandoned by her lover for a younger and prettier woman, Pantea.

38 The text also evokes, in D'Annunzio's typical intertextual weaving, Boccaccio's story of Isabetta in the fourth day.

39 D.H. Lawrence's reaction, after 'La Dame aux camélias' in 1908, is typical: 'Sarah Bernhardt was wonderful and terrible. [...] Oh, to see her, and to hear her, a wild creature, a gazelle with a beautiful panther's fascination and fury, sobbing and sighing like a deer sobs, wounded to death, and all the time with the sheen of silk, the glitter of diamonds, the moving of men's handsomely groomed figures around her! [...] She represents the primeval passion of woman, and she is fascinating to an extraordinary degree' (cited in John Stokes, 'Sarah Bernhardt,' in Stokes, Booth and Bassnett, 55).

40 The great actress's critical intervention appeared in Le Galois, Paris, 26 May 1897 (Cf. note 26).

41 The more explicit and ironic version of this mythical sphinx's 'macchinismo' is certainly the pièce by Jean Cocteau entitled La Machine infernale (1934).

42 The definition of 'fecondo' according to the Dizionario della Lingua Italiana Devoto Oli, is 'Di femmina atta alla riproduzione (contrapposta a sterile) [Of female apt for the purpose of reproduction (opposed to sterile)].'

43 On Duse's bisexuality, and in particular her relationship with Lina Poletti, see Sibilla Aleramo, Lettere d'amore a Lina, and Mariani (217). See also the Taccuini 1915–1921 by F.T. Marinetti (189–90), for a fairly detailed (but not necessarily trustworthy) discussion of the lesbian relationship between Duse and the young actress Enif Robert, who was in the company with Duse in 1908–9, and then again after the diva's post-war return to the stage. Robert supposedly recounted the episode herself to the author. There is also an allusion to the relationship with Duse in Robert's autobiographical novel written with Marinetti's collaboration, Un ventre di donna (1919). In his biography, Weaver denies that there is proof of Duse's bisexuality, but Bassnett (in Stokes, Booth, and Bassnett 167) notes that the affectionate relations between Duse and the young women usually called 'adopted daughters' by biographers almost always ended with extraordinary mutual hostility and bitterness. According to Bassnett this indicates that there is still biographical work to be done on this question.

44 The 'real' sphinx, with authentic secrets, is, in Regina Gagnier's allegorical interpretation of the short poem 'The Sphinx' (written by Wilde between 1874 and 1894 and dedicated to the young Marcel Schwob) Wilde himself. In the sphinx Wilde secretly represents his own transgressive sexual fantasies in order to seduce and excite the imagination of the young Schwob (44–5). Wilde's gravestone at Père Lachaise, sculpted by Jacob

Epstein in 1912 but immediately censured by the French authorities, was a fantastical and syncretic interpretation of an Assyrian and Egyptian sphinx, of masculine sex, endowed with prominent genitalia (which remained covered until the First World War). See Belford (309–10).

45 The first edition of *Man and Woman* was published in 1890.

46 It is important to note that probably neither Wilde nor D'Annunzio believed in these stereotypes, but they made spectacular use of them in order to reinforce the myth of their own originality. The friendship between Wilde and Ada Leverson, together with some of Wilde's opinions concerning women's rights, indicate how complex and contradictory his position concerning women was.

47 See Luigi Rasi's comments in *La Duse* (41).

48 D'Annunzio himself was ambivalent about giving Duse the part of Mila, even though he wrote it for her. Duse's letter about *Il Fuoco* is published in Weaver, who also tells of the complex vicissitudes surrounding the production of *La figlia di Jorio*.

49 Ironically, however, *La figlia di Jorio*, due in part to the compromises with folkloric sketch-writing and with melodrama, was a great success. Irma Gramatica's interpretation, however, was not convincing, and the actress was soon replaced by the young Teresa Franchini (cf. Valentini, *Il poema visibile* 303).

50 See the letter that Duse wrote to D'Annunzio in August 1901. This letter is in the Guerrieri archive and was published in Valentini, *La tragedia moderna* (172–5). In this letter Duse, even though she declares that she is willing to continue the artistic collaboration, expresses strong doubts about *Francesca* and again confronts D'Annunzio with the lies that are in the novel, sarcastically defined as a 'Galeotto libro' that completely overturned the truth.

51 Letter from London, 22 May 1900, now in the Vittoriale archives, cited in Molinari (270).

52 See Antogini (321). D'Annunzio himself, remembering in *Il libro segreto* (1935) what a tragedy it had seemed to him to 'lose Perdita,' states that Duse read the manuscript of *Il Fuoco* page by page while it was being written and that the suspicion that the novel might contain 'contempt' for her arose much later, when she began listening to the 'terribly base insinuations of a few English, German and French women' (*Prose di ricerca* 679).

53 Lombroso and Mantegazza's views of women were widespread even in the Anglo-Saxon world. In James's *The Tragic Muse*, Sherringham often seems a victim of these same prejudices in his relationship with his

beloved, the actress Miriam Rooth, but the novel belies them (at least in part), meticulously clarifying the role of technique and study in the construction of the great actress's 'genius.'

WORKS CITED

Aleramo, Sibilla. *Lettere d'amore a Lina.* Ed. Alessandra Cenni. Rome: Savelli, 1982.

Angelini, Franca. *Teatro e spettacolo del primo Novecento.* Rome and Bari: Laterza, 1988.

Antona Traversi, Camillo. *Eleonora Duse. Sua vita, sua gloria, suo martirio.* Pisa: Nistri-Lischi, 1936.

Antogini, Tom. *Vita segreta di D'Annunzio.* Milan: Mondadori, 1938.

Bandini, Fernando, ed. *Divina Eleonora. Eleonora Duse nella vita e nell'arte.* Venice: Marsilio, 2001.

Belford, Barbara. *Oscar Wilde: A Certain Genius.* New York: Random House, 2000.

Bini, Daniela. *Pirandello and His Muse.* Gainesville: UP of Florida, 1998.

Bloom, Harold. *Agon. Towards a Theory of Revisionism.* New York: Oxford UP, 1982.

Chomel, Luisetta Elia. *D'Annunzio. Un teatro al femminile.* Ravenna: Longo, 1997.

Consiglio Nazionale delle donne italiane. *Atti del I Congresso Nazionale delle Donne Italiane, Rome 24–30 April 1908.* Rome, 1908.

D'Annunzio, Gabriele. *The Flame.* Trans. Susan Bassnett. London: Quartet Books, 1991.

– *Il Fuoco.* D'Annunzio, *Prose di romanzi* 195–518.

– *La Gioconda. Tragedie sogni e misteri.* Milan: Mondadori, 1949. 231–340.

– *Prose di ricerca.* Vol. 2. Milan: Mondadori, 1947.

– *Prose di romanzi.* Vol. 2. Ed. Niva Lorenzini. Milan: Mondadori, 1989.

– *Scritti giornalistici 1882–1888.* Milan: Mondadori, 1996.

– *Le vergini delle rocce.* D'Annunzio, *Prose di romanzi* 1–193.

Darwin, Charles. *The Descent of Man and Selection in Relation to Sex.* New York: D. Appeton & Co, 1896.

Ellis, Havelock. *Man and Woman: A Study of Human Secondary Sexual Characteristics.* 1890. London: A.C. Black, 1930.

Ellmann, Richard. *Wilde.* New York: Vintage, 1988.

Felski, Rita. *The Gender of Modernity.* Cambridge: Harvard UP, 1995.

Franci, Giovanna. *Il sistema del dandy. Wilde-Beardsley-Beerbohm (Arte e artificio nell'Inghilterra fin-de-siècle).* Bologna: Patron, 1977.

Gagnier, Regina. *Idylls of the Marketplace: Oscar Wilde and the Victorian Public.* Stanford: Stanford UP, 1986.

Guerrieri, Gerardo. *Eleonora Duse e il suo tempo 1858–1924.* Treviso: Canova, s.d. [1974?].

– *Eleonora Duse. Nove saggi.* Ed. Lina Vito. Rome: Bulzoni, 1993.

Hoffmansthal, Hugo von. *Gabriele D'Annunzio e Eleonora Duse.* Brescia: Shakespeare & Company, 1984.

Horville, Robert. 'The Stage Techniques of Sarah Bernhardt.' Trans. Eric Salmon. In *Bernhardt and the Theater of Her Time.* Ed. Eric Salmon. Westport, CT: Greenwood Press, 1984. 35–65.

James, Henry. *The Tragic Muse.* London: Rupert Hart Davis, 1948.

Mantegazza, Paolo. *Fisiologia della donna.* 2 vols. Milan: Treves, 1893.

Mariani, Laura. 'Eleonora Duse e Sibilla Aleramo: un teatro per "la donna nuova".' *Svelamento. Sibilla Aleramo: una biografia intellettuale.* Ed. Annarita Buttafuoco and Marina Zancan. Milan: Feltrinelli, 1988. 208–25.

Mariano, Emilio. 'Il "patto di alleanza" fra Eleonora Duse e Gabriele D'Annunzio.' *Nuova Antologia* 1801 (Jan. 1951): 3–16, and 1802 (Feb. 1951): 144–53.

– *Sentimento del vivere ovvero Gabriele D'Annunzio.* Milan: Mondadori, 1962.

– 'Undici lettere di Eleonora Duse a Gabriele D'Annunzio.' *Quaderni dannunziani* 10–11 (1958): 27–40.

Marinetti, Filippo Tommaso. *Taccuini 1915–1921.* Ed. Alberto Bertoni. Bologna: Il Mulino, 1987.

Molinari, Cesare. *L'attrice divina. Eleonora Duse nel teatro italiano fra i due secoli.* Rome: Bulzoni, 1985.

Nardi, Piero, ed. *Carteggio D'Annunzio-Duse.* Florence: Le Monnier, 1975.

Pirandello, Luigi. 'Più che un'attrice.' *Antologia del grande attore.* Ed. Vito Pandolfi. Bari: Laterza, 1954. 373–9.

Pontiero, Giovanni. *Eleonora Duse: In Life and Art.* Frankfurt and New York: Peter Lang, 1986.

Powell, Kerry. *Oscar Wilde and the Theater of the 1890s.* Cambridge: Cambridge UP, 1990.

Raby, Peter, ed. *The Cambridge Companion to Oscar Wilde.* Cambridge: Cambridge UP, 1997.

Rasi, Luigi. *La Duse.* 1901. Rome: Bulzoni, 1986.

Schino, Mirella. 'La Duse contro il teatro del suo tempo.' Afterword. *La Duse.* By Luigi Rasi. Rome: Bulzoni, 1986.

Shaw, George Bernard. 'Duse and Bernhardt.' 1859. *Dramatic Opinions and Essays with an Apology.* London: Constable & Co., 1917.

Spackman, Barbara. 'Inversions.' *Perennial Decay: On the Aesthetics and Politics and Decadence*. Ed. Liz Constable, Dennis Denisoff, and Matthew Potolsky. Philadelphia: U of Pennsylvania P, 2000. 35–49.

Stokes, John, Michael R. Booth, and Susan Bassnett. *Bernhardt, Terry, Duse: The Actress in Her Time*. Cambridge: Cambridge UP, 1988.

Valentini, Valentina. *Il poema visibile. Le prime messe in scena delle tragedie dannunziane*. Rome: Bulzoni, 1993.

– *La tragedia moderna e mediterranea. Sul teatro di Gabriele D'Annunzio*. Milan: Franco Angeli, 1992.

Valesio, Paolo. *Gabriele D'Annunzio: The Dark Flame*. New Haven and London: Yale UP, 1994.

Vattimo, Gianni. *Il soggetto e la maschera: Nietzsche e il problema della liberazione*. Milan: Bompiani, 1974.

Weaver, William. *Duse*. San Diego, New York and London: Harcourt Brace Jovanovich, 1984.

Weir, David. *Decadence and the Making of Modernism*. Amherst: U of Massachusetts P, 1995.

Wilde, Oscar. *Complete Works of Oscar Wilde*. London: Collins, 1966.

– *The Letters of Oscar Wilde*. Ed. Rupert Hart-Davis. New York: Hartcourt, Brace & World, 1962.

– *The Picture of Dorian Gray. The Portable Oscar Wilde*. Ed. Richard Aldington and Stanley Waintraub. London and New York: Penguin Books, 1981.

4 *Omnes velut aqua dilabimur*: Antonio Fogazzaro, *The Saint*, and Catholic Modernism

LAURA WITTMAN

Il Santo come espressione delle idee proprie del modernismo è stato un vero insuccesso. Io non parlo, s'intende, del valore artistico del romanzo, parlo del suo valore filosofico, che è nullo. [...]

Non mancano, è vero, nel *Santo*, sprazzi magnifici di una religiosità evolutissima. [...] Ma in genere la concezione della santità che vi predomina [...] il programma limitato di riforma cattolica che vi è esposto, non possono rispecchiare integralmente il nostro pensiero. [...]

Benedetto si dibatte nella resistenza tenace alle seduzioni della donna amata e sospirata; sembra voler martoriare le sue carni, nella più crudele delle astensioni, e come compenso alla sua castità di psicopatico, si abbandona agli eccessi di un ascetismo morboso che soffoca la vita normale dei sensi in una ipersensibilità e in un parossismo permanente di maniaco. Noi non concepiamo così la vita interiore e non lanciamo anatemi sulle gioie intense dell'amore.[1]

[As an expression of the ideas of modernism, *The Saint* has really been a failure. I am not speaking, of course, of the artistic value of the novel, but of its philosophical value, which is non-existent. [...]

It is true that there are magnificent glimpses of a highly evolved religious sense in *The Saint*. [...] But in general the concept of sainthood that predominates, [...] the limited program of Catholic reform that is proposed, cannot be a faithful rendition of our thought. [...]

Benedetto struggles tenaciously to resist the seductions of the woman he loves and desires; he seems to want to punish his flesh with the most cruel of abstentions, and in compensation for his psychopathic chastity, he abandons himself to a morbid asceticism that suffocates the normal life of the senses with hypersensitivity and the constant paroxysms of a maniac.

This is not how we understand the inner life, nor do we consider the intense joys of love anathema.]

Je crois qu'on ne saurait trop insister sur le caractère moral et religieux dans le sens mistique [sic] du mouvement qu'on appelle modernisme et qui est loin d'avoir l'organisation intellectuelle qu'on lui attribue. Mon Benedetto est bien plus un mystique qu'un intellectuel. C'est ce caractère là qu'à Rome on redoute le plus et qui est le plus difficile à frapper. [...] Il faut que [...] je fasse mon chemin, *inter deforme obsequium et obrutam contumaciam.*[2]

[I believe we cannot insist too much on the moral and religious character, in a mystical sense, of the movement called modernism, which is far from having the intellectual organization attributed to it. My Benedetto is far more of a mystic than an intellectual. This is the personality most feared in Rome, and the one that is hardest to condemn. [...] I must [...] make my way *inter deforme obsequium et obrutam contumaciam.*]

Mysticism – its definition, and the appropriation of its power – is at the heart of the modernist crisis. This is the crucial intuition that literary modernism, in particular in its decadent and symbolist roots, brings to religious modernism.[3] For in the years before the turn of the twentieth century in Western Europe, literature and poetics became the locus of a sustained reflection on the 'death of God' and on the need for a new mystical practice severed from dogma and from philosophical abstraction. And Antonio Fogazzaro (his own sense of antagonistic respect for the Church notwithstanding)[4] stands at a turning point where literature explicitly critiques not the project of theology but its language. As an inheritor of French Symbolism, he was interested in capturing the voices of nature and the occult workings of the unconscious; as in the case of Huysmans, Fogazzaro's conversion to Catholicism was intrinsically connected to this aesthetic meditation, which in turn coloured his religiosity. As an Italian modernist writer (at the very beginnings of modernism), he would refuse the stark choice famously evoked by d'Aurevilly as the only alternative left after the conclusion of Huysmans's *A Rebours* [Against Nature] – 'the barrel of a gun or the foot of the cross' – preserving for literature (if not for his own personal life) an ambiguous space between the sacred and the secular.[5] Ultimately, Fogazzaro's mystical poetics of epiphanic visibility and sentimental transparency – emblematized by the quest for a renewed vision of sainthood evoked in the work of fiction most directly associated with religious modernism, Fogazzaro's *The Saint* (*Il Santo*, 1905)[6] – questioned traditional religious and philosophical discourse. This not only shaped his contentious and contested association with Catholic modernism but also revealed that an aesthetic problem lay at the core of Catholic modernism's by now rather well-established contradictions.[7] To understand the nature of this aesthetic problem, and to elucidate its consequences for modernist poetics, will require a complex sense of how Fogazzaro's *imagery* deflects and renews, and perhaps even undercuts, the terms of the modernist crisis.

In particular, I will examine the imagery of water that runs through *Little World of the Present* (*Piccolo mondo moderno*, 1901, depicting the pre-conversion youth of the future saint, Piero Maironi)[8] and *The Saint* (Maironi's journey towards sainthood under the name of Benedetto), signifying their aesthetic continuity and suggesting that it stems from a metaphorical meditation on the process of purification – a meditation in which water bears at once the fluidity and the narcissism of immanent contemplation and the ubiquity and the power of contradiction of spiritual vision. Water's natural processes, indissolubly one with its imaginative and spiritual qualities, here become the paradigm for, perhaps the source of, a knowledge that is decidedly not intellectual, but experiential and personal.[9] Purification is not only at the heart of Maironi's spiritual quest as it develops in Fogazzaro's two novels, it is also the overarching metaphor for the experience that, as one body, the Church should seek – at least in Fogazzaro's particular view of modernism, which not everyone shared. For if Ernesto Buonaiuti – one of the major Italian exponents of Catholic modernism – rejects *The Saint*'s 'limited program,' the dichotomy he sets up between 'non-existent' 'philosophical value' and 'highly evolved religious sense' only apparently finds confirmation in Fogazzaro's opposition of 'mystical' to 'intellectual.' Fogazzaro clearly contends that much of the philosophical value of modernism (literary *and* religious) comes from its engagement with mysticism. Where Buonaiuti sees a 'morbid' (he almost says *decadent* – there is clearly an aesthetic divide here) conflict between the spirit and the flesh, Fogazzaro evokes a suffering struggle towards *askesis*, a struggle that attempts to reconcile the philosophical and the religious under the aegis of mystical practice rather than intellectual theory.[10] Fogazzaro's crucial intuition is that art may provide a language for this suffering *askesis* where systematic theology and philosophy have failed[11] – that spiritual purification through mystical practice has become an aesthetic problem. Maironi's spiritual journey not only through the temptations of adultery, but also through a superficial and mechanical religiosity, is thus guided, more than by his ambiguous 'vision' (in which he sees himself in dialogue with the Pope, and then dying in Franciscan poverty at the foot of a pine tree),[12] by the roar and inarticulate voice of the Aniene river (which runs near the monasteries of San Benedetto and Santa Scolastica at Subiaco).[13] If *The Saint* is an 'ascetic and disciplinary' novel,[14] it is because it pulls back from the sentimental mysticism of *Little World of the Present* and attempts to purify it, just as Fogazzaro's aesthetic meditation seeks to distil the essence of modernism's mystical crisis.[15]

[Benedetto] salì per la petraia [...] fino alla croce del vertice, incoronata di stelle. [...] Gelava, gelava sempre più. [...] lo slancio della volontà gli venne meno senza movere il cuore inerte e mancò in uno stupido ascoltare del rombo eguale dell'Aniene. [...] Sentiva in sè il vaporare di un veleno, sentiva un'assenza di amore, un'assenza di dolore, un tedio, un peso, l'aggravarsi di un assopimento mortale. [...] Quali viluppi di serpi gli si attorcigliavano ai piedi simulando l'innocenza dell'erba? [...] Il rombo dell'Aniene questo? No, il ruggito dell'Abisso trionfante. [...] Un lampo aperse le nubi. [...] Il suo corpo giaceva immobile nel vento del temporale, come un corpo schiantato, fra il dibattersi delle ginestre e il mareggiare dell'erba. [...] Sentiva una levità strana delle membra, una spossatezza fisica piacevole, una infinita dolcezza interna. (*S* 71–5)[16]

[[Benedetto] climbed the rocky slope [...] to the star-crowned cross on its summit. [...] It grew colder, ever colder [...] his effort of will weakened and could not move his sluggish heart; he remained inert, absorbed by the even roar of the Aniene. [...] He felt weariness, a great weight, the advance of a mortal drowsiness. [...] What tangles of serpents wound themselves around his feet simulating innocent grass? [...] Was this the roar of the Aniene? No, it was the scream of the triumphant Abyss. [...] A flash of lightning rent the clouds. [...] His body lay motionless under the rushing thunderstorm, shattered, between the straining gorse and the waves of grass. [...] He felt a strange lightness in his limbs, a pleasant exhaustion, an infinite sweetness.]

How can a river's roar on a starry night transform deathly cold into infinite sweetness? What is at stake in this passage, and indeed in Fogazzaro's musical prose, is the relationship between grace and form.

For the conflict between ineffable experience and the need to express and understand it in terms that are inevitably external to it could be adopted as a definition of mysticism that encompasses different religions and historical periods.[17] The degree to which the terms shape the experience is a question of form, whereas the extent to which the experience is genuinely manifested, in terms that now acquire intrinsic meaning, is a question of grace. In most types of traditional religious mysticism, this conflict is resolved precisely through the specificity of a single revealed tradition, which guarantees that the aesthetic aspects of religious practice – ritual, liturgy, art of meditation – will derive from grace. Hence conflict erupts as soon as the hegemony of a specific tradition (and especially its aesthetic hegemony) is questioned. In the West, the monastic aesthetic of Franciscan mysticism is accepted at first with difficulty, and after the Reformation and the Counter-Reformation, mysticism for the first time becomes a practice that is distinct from other types of spiritual experience, and is increasingly perceived as threatening by the representatives of tradition.[18] The modernist crisis is a further step in this evolution, and a radical one. For lack of a better way of putting it, mysticism now becomes distinct from *any* type of revealed religious experience, and seeks to become autonomous, in particular through the creation of its own independent aesthetics. Here, religious modernism intersects with literary modernism insofar as the latter asserts the autonomy of the pure aesthetic experience in an attempt to grasp a determinedly non-religious epiphany.[19] Fogazzaro's Maironi, in his mystical and ascetic nature, hence incarnates a double impulse: first, there is the desire to create a form that is derived directly from grace, without the mediation of any revelation; second, there is the growing sense that the perfection or the purity of form *is* grace – that mystical experience is contained in its manifestation, in its epiphany.

This double and contradictory impulse is what divides the modernists from within. It is also at the heart of their individual experiences of spiritual turmoil. Specifically, to the degree that religious modernism can be defined as a single movement, it is characterized by the will to reform Christianity from within, to derive from the Christian tradition itself – the crucial question is *how* – principles of change that will ensure a continuing link between spirituality and modernity. To this question, which is at the intersection of grace and form, of inspiration and historicism, of personal conversion and philosophical immanentism, there are many answers. The historiography of religious modernism tends to group them chronologically and geographically, roughly as follows.[20] Modernism is said to begin with the development of scientific inquiry, and in particular with its application to the 'humanities' (in anthropology, psychology, critical history, linguistics), which resulted in radical changes in biblical exegesis in the last quarter of the nineteenth century. Alfred Loisy's work is at the apex of this development, which is also found in the early phases of Buonaiuti's thought. For Loisy and Buonaiuti, a renewal of dogma and liturgy is to be sought in an ever more accurate reading of the canonical texts of the tradition. In Italy this work of historical criticism is flanked by a movement for social renewal, headed by Romolo Murri; here renewal is seen as the extension of Christian principles to political life, and as the democratization of the Church hierarchy. In France, the historical phase is soon followed by a philosophical inquiry – Maurice Blondel is its central figure, and very influential on Buonaiuti's mature thought – that rejects the neo-Thomism promulgated by the Church, but tries at the same time to overcome the impasse of Kantian metaphysics. In Blondel's philosophy of action, and his 'method of immanence,' renewal takes place in man's increased consciousness, which allows his action to become, through its own impulse, more and more in conformity with grace. In England, William James's pragmatism adds to this a sense of religion as a cultural construction 'in the making' that must be constantly built up and renewed by experience. Through the figure of George Tyrrell, the inquiry focuses more on individual spirituality and sees renewal as the result of a unique personal experience of conversion or illumination. In France, Henri Bremond and Louis Laberthonnière in turn placed the emphasis on the history of 'religious sentiment' as a spiritual evolution. Looking less at the 'high' mysticism of a few privileged individuals, they seek renewal in a more choral sense of progressive conversion, which they link to Newman's idea of 'development.' In the same vein, Edouard Le Roy focuses specifically on the language of dogmatic propositions, and argues that their symbolic form must be renewed in order for them to remain in conformity with the spirit. Common to all of these contrasting views of renewal, what is specifically modernist is the typically mystical tension between redefining old paradigms through experience and asserting that experience itself is the new paradigm. It is very much this personal aspect of the modernist conflict – the contention between grace and form within the quest for renewal – that Fogazzaro's work seeks to illuminate.

Ma poi questa gerarchia d'idee ferme con impero non è tutto l'uomo. Sotto di essa vi è in lui una moltitudine di altre idee, una moltitudine di pensieri che continuamente si muovono e si modificano per le impressioni e l'esperienza della vita. E sotto questi pensieri vi ha un'altra regione dell' anima, vi ha l'Inconscio dove facoltà occulte lavorano un lavoro occulto, dove avvengono i contatti mistici con Dio. Le idee dominanti esercitano autorità sul volere dell'uomo giusto, ma tutto l'altro mondo del suo pensiero ha pure una importanza immensa perché attinge continuamente alla Verità con l'esperienza del reale nell'esterno, con l'esperienza del Divino nell'interno, e quindi tende a rettificare le idee superiori, le idee dominanti, in quanto il loro elemento tradizionale non è adequato al Vero; è per esse una perenne fonte di fresca vita che le rinnova, una sorgente di autorità legittima fondata sulla natura delle cose, sul valore delle idee, più che sui decreti degli uomini. (*S* 177)

[Yet this hierarchy of firmly grounded opinions does not constitute the whole man. Below it there are in him a multitude of other thoughts, a multitude of other ideas, that are continually changed and modified by the experiences and impressions of life. And below these thoughts there is another region of the soul, there is the unconscious, where occult faculties work at an occult task, where a mystical contact with God takes place. Dominant ideas exercise authority over the will of the upright man, but all that other world of thought is of immense importance as well, for it continually derives Truth from the experience of what is real externally, and from the experience of the Divine internally, and therefore tends to rectify the superior ideas, the dominant ideas, insofar as their traditional form is not adequate to the Truth; it is to them a perennial fountain of fresh life that renews them, a source of legitimate authority derived from the nature of reality and the value of ideas, not from the decrees of men.]

Because he constantly brings the conflict back to the personal level that is beneath ideas, which can only be caught in the shifting and indistinct voices of the Aniene, Fogazzaro's place with respect to the different strands of modernism outlined above has been the subject of much controversy. Initially, of course, *The Saint* was put on the Index, ostensibly because of its rejection of a dogmatically established division between the damned and the saved,[21] and no doubt also because of its extensive depiction, in chapter 2, of a meeting of reformers, which includes theologians, Protestants, priests, and intellectuals, and was modelled on the meetings Fogazzaro attended at the house of Pio

Molajoni in Rome.[22] Fogazzaro portrays with ironic finesse the mixture of calculation, generous impulse, intellectualism, and deep religious feeling that different participants bring to this meeting, and in doing so he gathers together for the first time the different strands of what was later to be called modernism.[23] At the time, this was read as an attempt to gather the voices for social reform, for personal asceticism, for philosophical renewal, and for dogmatic and liturgical evolution into a single movement, joined by the presence of the spirit made visible in Benedetto's transfiguration. Fogazzaro's interest in reconciling Darwinism with a spiritual evolution that would lead to perfection at the end of time was associated with the immanentism of modernist philosophy, and even with the idea that revelation was a purely cultural construction, whose development was inspired perhaps, but not designed in its every turn, by the spirit.[24] The modernists gathered around the journal *Il Rinnovamento* [The Renewal], from Murri to Papini to Gallarati Scotti, hence defended Fogazzaro, though some were disappointed by his acceptance of the Index's condemnation.[25] From this disappointment emerged a sense that Fogazzaro was a 'moderate' modernist, and Benedetto's association with the Benedictine don Clemente, with his obedience, anti-intellectualism, and humble mystical sentiment, was taken as an implicit condemnation of the philosophical components of modernism – to the point that years later, Catholic critics would even defend Fogazzaro as a 'non-Modernist reformer.'[26] More typical, however, is the view promulgated by Gallarati Scotti's rather biased *La Vita di Antonio Fogazzaro* [The Life of Antonio Fogazzaro] (1920), which holds that because Fogazzaro was not an intellectual (a judgment that prefigures the ideological suspicion he fell under first from the Catholic right and then from the Marxist left), and because he was so focused on the intimate drama of the flesh and the spirit (a judgment that echoes Croce's distaste for what he saw as an unaesthetic confusion of the hot eroticism of emotions and the cold eroticism of ideas), he was only able to grasp the lower, more simply emotional or sentimental aspects of modernism, and lapsed into terrible confusion when it came to philosophical, theological, or political discussion.[27] At best, Fogazzaro is associated with a call for moral renewal that finds a sincere, if troubled, expression in his art, which has little or nothing to do with the modernist program, with its serious doubts concerning faith itself, and with its general intellectual confusion.[28] What has been seriously overlooked is the extent to which, in his work, Fogazzaro searched – experimentally, as only the practice of writing can do – for his position in the modernist meeting. Benedetto's absence from the debate depicted in chapter 2 – or better, his removal to the garden, where the voices of nature and the unconscious are heard[29] – is not a sign that he will in some occult fashion synthesize those conflicting voices, nor does it indicate that he will offer a more moderate, or more moral, alternative. Rather, it is the fluctuation in the novel – is Benedetto the saint we are waiting for? and what does it mean to say he is a saint? – that constitutes a genuine meditation on the very nature of modernism, both religious and artistic.

E comprendo come l'Arte, che attinge le proprie ispirazioni dall'inconscio, crei, quando prende a soggetto il dolore che non ha visibile causa, forme di bellezza sovrumana perché la intuisce occultamente nell'ordine che collega la dissonanza intermedia del mondo presente a due mondi sovrumani appunto, a un mondo passato di splendore e di colpa dove si è dischiuso il seme del piangere, a un mondo futuro sulla cui soglia il dolore conduce le creature rifatte splendide per esso e spira. E [...] comprendo pure che [la Intelligenza ordinatrice dei mondi] abbia disposto l'Arte anche a render voluttuosa non la sofferenza ma l'idea del soffrire; così che gli uomini [...] almeno per un momento sentano quel desiderio indistinto d'infinito, quell'amore che punge il pellegrino di Dante [...] *se ode squilla di lontano / Che paia il giorno pianger che si muore.* Indefinibile palpito, pieno di rimpianti e di aneliti, ricordo di un tempo felice trascorso, presentimento di un tempo felice venturo, anello sensibile di due mondi inaccessibili al senso.[30]

[And I understand how Art, which takes inspiration from the unconscious, when it takes for its subject suffering that has no visible cause, creates overwhelming beauty, for it glimpses it darkly in the order that connects the intermediate dissonance of the present world to two supreme worlds: a past world of splendour and sin where the source of tears overflowed, and a future world to which suffering leads the creatures made by it once again resplendent as it wanes. And [...] I also understand that [the ordering Intelligence of the worlds] has disposed Art to make voluptuous, not suffering itself, but the idea of suffering; so that men [...] at least for an instant might feel that indefinite desire for the infinite, that love that spurs Dante's pilgrim. [...] *If he doth hear from far away a bell / That seemeth to deplore the dying day.* Indefinite palpitation, full of regrets and desires, memory of a happy time long gone, presentiment of an imminent happiness, sensible ring uniting two worlds inaccessible to the senses.]

This meditation is not so much *about* mysticism as the defining issue of modernism, as it is itself an attempt to *make modernism mystical* by developing for it an aesthetic that joins grace and form, that gathers together 'the experience of what is real externally' and 'the experience of the Divine internally' to bring us into contact with a 'perennial fountain of fresh life that renews.' The very possibility of sainthood is here expressed in a new language that puts into doubt our ability to circumscribe it abstractly or to understand it fully; and this doubt is an integral part of Fogazzaro's modernism, not an element of confusion.[31] The Romantic genealogy of Fogazzaro's 'indistinct infinite' and his sublime sense of 'suffering' should not blind us to his intimate sense of the 'intermediate dissonance' which can become the 'sensible ring' uniting us to another world.[32] While echoing Foscolo's 'dissonant harmony,'[33] Fogazzaro's aesthetic of 'dissonance' responds specifically to modernist concerns, and in doing so reveals itself to be on that literary edge between decadence and modernism where art sought to assert its spiritual autonomy. In particular, Fogazzaro's insistence on the unconscious as the place of 'a mystical contact with God' and his correlation of art's liberation of its 'occult faculties' and the transformation of dissonance into the link between two worlds implies that a new language of sainthood will contend with an unknown that is within the self, and will do so on its own terms – that is, in terms that are themselves partially obscure. The infinity of natural contemplation, be it gently ironic as in Leopardi, or terrible in its mobile eternity as in Foscolo, breaks against an invisible barrier here; something in Benedetto's night of temptation comes between 'strange lightness' and 'shattered' 'body' not to divide but to unite them. Fogazzaro's art thus constantly searches for what is on the edge of the visible, and the musicality of his prose dissolves the appearance of suffering in an attempt to make palpable another suffering – 'the source of tears' – a nameless cry that longs for another, as yet formless, fulfilment.[34]

Il mormorio della pioggia, il rombo dell'Aniene profondo avrebbero detto a Jeanne uno sconsolato compianto di tutto ciò che vive sulla terra e ama. A don Clemente dicevano un consenso pio della creatura inferiore con la creatura supplice al Padre comune. Benedetto non li udiva. (S 95–6)

[The murmur of the rain, the deep roar of the Aniene would have spoken to Jeanne the disconsolate cry of all that on the earth lives and loves. To don

Clemente they spoke the pious consent of the inferior creature and the
supplicant creature to their common Father. Benedetto did not hear them.]

How, then, can a river's roar on a starry night transform deathly
cold into infinite sweetness? Benedetto's journey of purification could
be described as the attempt to hear what lies within the sounds of the
Aniene, and to decipher the invisible words inscribed upon its fluid
surface. Emblematically caught between don Clemente's faith and
Jeanne's scepticism (for she is at once the femme fatale who tempts
him and the other he must relate to), Maironi does not hear what they
hear, for he follows a voice that is far more ambiguous and indistinct.
Indeed, he inhabits from the beginning a liminal space, on the edge of
silence: he is an orphan, of parents one Catholic and one Protestant; he
is married, but his insane wife is confined to an asylum; he lives in the
temporary riches of his wife's family, away from the humble house
where he was born; he is supported politically by the Catholics but
has socialist leanings; and, most crucially, he longs to escape this world
yet at the same time rushes forth to redeem it. As Fogazzaro wrote,
'Lui in teoria vive per l'altro mondo, in pratica per questo non per
goderlo male, ma per goderlo onestamente! [In theory *he* lives for the
other world, but in practice he lives for this one, not to enjoy it badly,
but honestly!]' (*LWP* 20), and as don Giuseppe warns, 'bisogna restar
nel mondo e bisogna uscirne (*LWP* 106) [we must stay in the world
and we must not be of the world].' His choice of the name *Benedetto* no
doubt reflects the battle with lust he shares with Saint Benedict, as
well as his retreat into silence; yet it also echoes the 'benedictus qui
venit' describing Christ's followers, which implies that as he tries to
hear the voice that would guide him he is ceaselessly in the process of
becoming Benedetto.

Maironi's story has as its imaginative origin the Benedictine abbey
of Praglia. Here, as a boy on the verge of adolescence, he experienced
mystical ecstasies, and thought he had a religious vocation; and though
he turned away from it, it left him with the sense of an unfinished
mission, with an obscure 'reproach' (*LWP* 124). And here he returns,
at the opening of *Little World of the Present*, seeking comfort from two
intertwined temptations that he has just confessed to don Giuseppe,
not with relief but with disappointment (*LWP* 110). For after years of
battle to remain faithful to his demented wife, he feels himself all at
once falling in love with Jeanne Dessalle; at the same time the pious

practices of his wife's wealthy family and of his ambitious political supporters seem to him ever more hypocritical. He becomes more and more convinced that faith is an artifice imposed by education, and even admits: 'Per un pezzo mi sono rifiugiato nelle ragioni di credere che avevo nel mio proprio cervello, nel mio proprio cuore; adesso non mi sento più sicuro neppure lì [For a long time I took refuge in the reasons my own mind provided to justify my faith; now I no longer feel certain even of them]' (*LWP* 98). With this in his heart, he heads for Praglia beneath a rain he does not notice (*LWP* 111), just as later he will not hear the Aniene, feeling that 'il monastero [...] adesso lo respingeva da sé, muto [the monastery [...] pushed him away, mutely]' (*LWP* 124). And thus here, as his journey begins in earnest, the seductions of water, and its warnings, will gush forth with a force he cannot contain.

Jeanne is at Praglia, dressed 'nello stesso mantello, col collare di *skunk* [in that same cloak, with the *skunk* collar]' (*LWP* 113), with the same serious look of voluptuous maturity that had caught Maironi the first time he had seen her, years before, on a train. She extorts a confession from him. Asking their guide for a glass of fresh water, she contrives to be alone with Piero in a cell where she insists on the purity of her love for him: 'La purificherei meglio io che il digiuno e le preghiere nel deserto, [...] Mi dica che mi vuol bene, mi dica che non mi abbandona! Non mi faccia morire! [I would purify you better than fasting and prayer in the desert, [...] Tell me you love me, tell me you won't abandon me! Don't make me die!]' (*LWP* 127), she insists, just as:

'Signora, l'acqua' disse il custode dietro a loro.
Jeanne si alzò dal parapetto, livida, con gli occhi rossi, prese la tazza.
'Si c'était du poison' diss'ella, volta a Maironi, 'faudrait-il boire?'
Nei grandi occhi magnetici erravano tristezza e tenerezza infinite.
'Je crois que non' mormorò egli malgrado sé, in una vertigine, pallido come se gli mancasse la vita.
Gli occhi di Jeanne s'illuminarono di un lampo inesprimibile di sorriso.
'Quest'acqua è torbida' diss'ella al custode attonito. Porse la tazza fuori dal parapetto, verso l'acqua pian piano fino all'ultima goccia, guardandola, sorridendo, mormorando: 'Che gioia, che gioia, che gioia!' (*LWP* 127)[35]

['Madam, your water,' said the guardian behind them.
Jeanne rose from the parapet, livid, her eyes red, and took the cup.

'If it were poison,' she said, turning to Maironi, 'should I drink it?'
Her big magnetic eyes were full of sadness and infinite tenderness.
'I believe not,' he murmured almost unwillingly, caught by vertigo, pale
as though life had drained out of him.
Jeanne's eyes filled with the inexpressible flash of a smile. 'This water is
cloudy,' she said to the astounded guardian. She held the cup over the
parapet, pouring out the water very slowly, drop by drop, looking at it,
smiling, murmuring: 'What joy, what joy, what joy!']

Jeanne here emblematically refuses to drink the bitter cup that Christ
accepted in his night at Gethsemane (Matt. 26: 42), and by turning
Piero into the instrument of her refusal, she draws out from him a
tacit admission of doubt far greater than the one he confessed to don
Giuseppe. As he will later articulate:

'Sai, vi è nell'anima mia un tale polverìo di rovine ancora in moto, che non
so bene che cosa sia caduto e che cosa resti in piedi. Credo di credere ancora
in Dio, questo sì, ma non nel Dio che mi hanno insegnato. Quello l'ho sepolto a Praglia. Era già mezzo morto dentro di me, anche prima: stavo però
ancora nel vischio delle mie vecchie abitudini mentali. [...] Una volta ho
pensato: "Se venisse un altro San Francesco! Se venisse un altro
Sant'Agostino!" Adesso so che non verranno.' (*LWP* 169)

['You know, my soul is so filled with shattered swirling ruins, that I cannot
tell what has fallen and what remains standing. I believe that I believe in
God, still, yes, but not in the God they have taught me. He was already half
dead within me, before: but I was still caught in my old mental habits. [...]
One day I thought: "If only a new Saint Francis came! a new Saint Augustine!" Now I know they will never come.']

Not only does Maironi's 'I believe that I believe' make evident the
modernity of Fogazzaro's meditation on modernism,[36] it also radically
redefines spiritual thirst. For this thirst has now become so formless –
the ruins of faith are like the ruins of Praglia – that the living water it
seeks can be turned to poison by a mere conceit. And in this first
moment of vertigo, Piero does not so much admit that he thirsts for
Jeanne, as he reveals that he does not know the nature of his thirst: 'I
believe not' echoes 'I believe that I believe.' By pouring out the water,
Jeanne thus poisons him more surely than if she had offered it to him

(like Saint Benedict, he will eventually survive this attempt at poisoning), for in her gesture she imposes her interpretation of his thirst upon him – just as her Venus-in-furs coldness is an interpretation of purification that only exacerbates his desire (*LWP* 159).[37] Her slowness in pouring out the cup drop by drop accentuates her triumphant and controlling sensuality, but also underscores the affinity of this water with rain and, more importantly, with tears. For if Fogazzaro's art searches for 'the source of tears' – the living source that so pervades the work of a writer in many ways close to Fogazzaro, Georges Bernanos, where it is the visible sign of grace's action[38] – Jeanne's gesture deliberately empties that source, reducing tears to a purely natural event.

Minutes later, she beckons him to the monastery's spring:

'Non so mai come chiarmarla' diss'ella, piano. E soggiunse forte: "Cosa è scritto qui? Mi spieghi." Piero le tradusse il motto latino scolpito dentro l'arco, al di sopra del vaso marmoreo:
OMNES VELUT AQUA DILABIMUR
E chinandosi come per guardare lo squisito marmo, susurrò:
'Chiamami amore.'
Ella non rispose; egli rimase chino celando il fuoco del viso.
'Poveri fratùcci!' esclamò Dessalle [Jeanne's brother, Carlino] alle loro spalle. 'Son passati tutti davvero, eh? Ma ditemi un po': quel motto li' come va preso? Dev'essere epicureo, dentro quella gioia di fregi, quel sorriso dello scettico Cinquecento! Mangiamo, beviamo e godiamo fin che ci è tempo, eh?' (*LWP* 130)

['I never know what to call you,' she said quietly. And she added, out loud:
'What is written here? Explain it to me.' Piero translated the Latin inscription that was inside the arch, over the marble basin:
OMNES VELUT AQUA DILABIMUR
And leaning forward as though to admire the exquisite marble, he murmured: 'call me love.'
She did not answer; he continued to lean, hiding the fire that had rushed to his face.
'Poor little monks!' [Jeanne's brother, Carlino] Dessalle exclaimed behind them. 'They all passed away, eh? But tell me now: how should we take that maxim? It must be Epicurean, with all those glorious friezes, that sceptical *Cinquecento* smile! Let's eat, drink and enjoy ourselves while we can, eh?']

Again, and more forcefully, the dispersion of water is an ambiguous sign upon which Jeanne, for the moment at least, imposes an interpretation that Piero seems to accept: as he finally proffers the word she has deliberately, in her withdrawing way, not yet said, he implicitly rejects the ascetic aspiration in the spring's tears in favour of a more sensual suffering and a more earthly love. Yet already in this scene his love is not her love. Carlino's ironic carpe diem is strident against the somber melancholy of the inscription, whose power both he and Jeanne seem to ignore, whereas Piero's love emerges from it shrouded with despair. For him this love is more fatal than death, and we are reminded (as surely he is) that *dilabor* echoes the use of *labor* in Virgil's description of the souls who as 'folia lapsa cadunt' in Book VI of the *Aeneid*, just before Aeneas glimpses Dido. Further, he glimpses her 'as one who sees, or thinks to have seen, the moon rising through the cloud, all dim' (VI, 610). This detail too re-emerges in Fogazzaro's text, as Jeanne flits over to another inscription, 'completur cursu,' next to a 'crescent moon': Piero's lyrical impetus, still coloured by the rhetoric of divine love, is to say, 'Significa [...] l'anima mia che si volge a te e tutta s'illumina, si compie nella luce tua [It means [...] that my soul turns to you and brightens, finding its fullness in your light].' But Jeanne interrupts him: 'Non importa; mi dica che mi ama! [It doesn't matter; tell me you love me!]' (*LWP* 131). Again the dissonance between her lightness and laughter and Piero's anguished abandon is evident; the image also prefigures Piero's horror, towards the end of *Little World of the Present*, at what the consummation of his passion would have brought, as he contemplates the moon and now anxiously calls out, 'Padre mio, sei tu in quel pianeta? [My Father, are you in that planet?]' (*LWP* 354).[39]

This dissonance is articulated again by Carlino, who on the way home imagines the foundation of a new religion at Praglia:

> 'Non importa. Una religione nuova! Poniamo, se vuole, la religione mia, ch'è la religione del dubbio, una religione che invece di obbligarci a credere quello che non si può sapere, ci proibisce di negarlo e c'impone il dubbio, il quale è infinitamente più sapiente e utile della fede, perché ci dispone a tutte le possibilità! Ed è anche più poetico!'
> Maironi scattò con una violenza strana.
> 'No, no, sia tutto per o sia tutto contro! Neghi piuttosto! Dica che l'uomo creò Iddio perché gli fece comodo! Oppure dica che il Dio della religione è una maschera del Dio vero e che Lei non vuole adorare le maschere! Oppure si ribelli. [...] Dica questo se Le piace, ma non quello che ha detto!' (*LWP* 133)

['It doesn't matter. A new religion! Let's say, my religion, which is the religion of doubt, a religion that instead of forcing us to believe that which we cannot know, prevents us from negating it and imposes doubt upon us; doubt, which is infinitely wiser than faith, for it opens up all the possibilities! and more poetic too!'

Maironi shuddered with unusual violence.

'No, no, be all for it or against it! Deny it! Say that man created God because it suited him! Or say that the God of religion is a mask and you don't want to adore a mask! Or rebel. [...] Say this if you like, but not what you just said!']

What Carlino describes is terrifyingly close to Maironi's 'I believe that I believe,' hence his anger, followed by an even darker abandon to a passion for Jeanne that seems ever more arid with despair. Yet there is a difference, a difference in tone, or in form, in which the very essence of modernism is at stake – a difference that Maironi cannot yet, in his aridity, hear, but which Fogazzaro carefully modulates. For Carlino's aestheticism, which Jeanne shares, at least in the beginning, is here very seductive, and in appearance much more coherent than Maironi's struggles with self-deception and contradiction. Yet Carlino's conclusive remark, coming after long and superficial disquisitions on the beauty of the abbey's frescoes, rings like a warning against conflating the aesthetic vibration of doubt and the deeper suffering at the source Maironi's lyricism. There is nothing wrong with the way Carlino defines his new religion, Fogazzaro implies, nothing a modernist would ultimately disagree with; it is the way he practises it, rather, that condemns him to find at the end of it nothing but his own self-satisfied scepticism. For Carlino is comfortable with his doubt and proud of its intellectual clarity (which he mistakes for poeticity) – much more so than Jeanne, who perceives 'quanto è triste di non aver dentro di sé niente di fermo, niente di assoluto [how sad it is not to have anything within the self that is firm or absolute]' (*LWP* 169). However, her sadness is still entirely material whereas we perceive in Maironi's anger the suffering of spiritual loss, we hear the offended spirit crying out, echoing the melancholy of the waters.

Piero Maironi is impelled to seek the source of this cry, and thus indissolubly tied to Jeanne, who calls it forth, as she seduces his inexpressible anguish, endowing it with the dangerous sensuality and the palpable beauty of form. Yet as the novel progresses, Maironi is led further and further astray, not only by the slightly frivolous life of Jeanne and Carlino, but by his own political ambition; he leaves the Church and seeks to define on his own terms a more genuine social justice and personal morality. Most telling, perhaps, he seeks to drown his growing anxiety in an apparently selfless gesture – giving away most of his property because it had been acquired by his family if not illegally, at least rather unjustly – a gesture which nonetheless procures him 'un sottile piacere d'orgoglio [a subtle outburst of pride]' (*LWP* 314), which becomes even more visible when he tells Jeanne of his decision and is disappointed at her lack of admiration (*LWP* 327). A crucial encounter takes place, this time, at Vena di fonte alta, another spring where the waters speak their mysterious message.

Jeanne is tormented by what she (rightly) perceives as Piero's 'pride' (*LWP* 315) in condemning her lifestyle and her sensuality, and she is wounded by his 'scorn' for her love.

> 'Vuole aspettar un poco?' diss'ella affranta dallo sgomento e dallo sforzo. [...] Piegarono a destra in un picciol cavo ombreggiato di noci dove convergono altri sentieri e chiama con fioca dolente voce una sottile polla dell'Acqua Barbarena. [...] Piero fece sedere Jeanne sull'orlo della vasca. Non aveva tazza, raccolse l'acqua della polla con le mani. Ella bevve, impresse la bocca nella commessura delle palme, ebbe un singhiozzo arido e alla domanda di lui se desiderasse bere ancora, scosse il capo senza levarlo. Egli disgiunse le mani adagio adagio, le ne sfiorò il viso pietosamente ed ella subito se lo coperse con le proprie. (*LWP* 328–9)

> ['Shall we wait a minute?' she asked, crushed by fear and effort. [...] They turned to the right towards a little shady hollow of walnut trees where various paths meet and the faint weeping voice of one of the Acqua Barbarena's springs calls out. [...] Piero made Jeanne sit on the edge of the marble basin. He did not have a cup, and gathered the water in his hands. She drank, pressing her mouth to his joined palms, and sobbed dryly; when he asked if she wanted more to drink, she shook her head and did not raise it. He drew his hands apart slowly, pitifully brushing them against her face, as she suddenly covered it with her own palms.]

The pastoral setting, the absence of a glass, their isolation in this cove surrounded by fog all suggest (rather Romantically, again) that here the voice of nature will be heard without mediation, without cultural conceits, as the very name of the 'Acqua Barbarena' implies. Piero's gesture is one of apparently innocent sensuality,[40] but Jeanne's dry sobs (again, withholding tears) signify an unquenchable thirst that seems to penetrate Piero's fingers, as they linger on her face.

La tristezza delle cose pareva conscia di quel silenzio doloroso. 'Dio, Dio!' gemette Jeanne, sottovoce. 'Oggi' soggiunse dopo un altra pausa 'se quest'acqua fosse veleno non Le chiederei se la dovrei bere.' Piero la guardò, attonito. Appena ella ebbe detto amaramente, come parlando a se stessa, 'Neppure si ricorda!' gli venne in mente Praglia, il bicchier d'acqua sparso.

'Sí' diss'egli, commosso. 'Mi ricordo. Neppur oggi Le direi di bere.'

Ella sospirò: 'Per pietà, forse.'

'Oh no!'

Jeanne ebbe un sussulto di speranza, ma poi ripeté malinconicamente: 'Sí, sí, per pietà.'

Parole calde parvero salire alle labbra di lui e arrestarsi. Non ne uscirono che queste: 'Non lo dica!' Jeanne si voltò sul fianco e con la punta dell'indice tracciò sull'acqua la parola: *pietà*. [...] Jeanne ripeteva: 'Vada, vada!' senza muoversi.

'Ma non posso' diss'egli 'lasciarla così!' E soggiunse teneramente: 'Vieni, vieni, forse un giorno ...'

'Forse un giorno ...?' diss'ella in un lampo di dolcezza e di amore.

'Forse un giorno ci sarà fra noi quella concordia di anime che può giustificare una unione stretta.'

Esprimeva egli il proprio pensiero oppure lo avevano quelle apprensioni vaghe tratto più in là? Jeanne tornò a oscurarsi, mormorò scuotendo incredula il capo:

'Pietà.'

Egli si guardò attorno, si chinò, le pose sui capelli un bacio e sussurrò: 'No, cara, speranza.' (*LWP* 330–1)

[The sadness of nature seemed conscious of that painful silence. 'God! God!' Jeanne softly moaned. 'Today,' she added after a pause, 'if this water were poison I would not ask you if I should drink it.' Piero looked at her, surprised. Just as she said bitterly, as though to herself, 'He doesn't even remember!' he remembered Praglia, and the glass of water poured out drop by drop.

'Yes,' he said, moved. 'I remember. Still today, I would tell you not to drink.'

She sighed: 'Out of pity, perhaps.'

'Oh, no!'

Jeanne felt surge of hope, but then repeated sadly: 'yes, yes, out of pity.'

Hot words seemed to rush up to his lips and stop there.

Only these escaped: 'Do not say it!' Jeanne turned on her hip and with the

tip of her index finger traced upon the water the word: *pity*. [...] Jeanne
repeated again without moving: 'Go! Go!'

'But I cannot leave you like this,' he insisted, adding tenderly: 'Come,
come, maybe someday ...'

'Maybe someday ...?' she said with a flash of tenderness and love.

'Maybe someday there will be between us that agreement of souls that
can justify a close union.'

Were these his true thoughts or had vague apprehensions pushed him
beyond his intentions? Jeanne's expression darkened again, and she shook
her head incredulously: 'Pity.'

He looked around, bent over, kissed her hair and whispered:

'No, dear, hope.']

To try to capture this thirst is like writing a word on water: no
sooner is it written than the waters close themselves over it again, and
we perceive only a continuing ripple, a dispersion that calls for an
interpretation. Much like the inscription at Praglia, the word written
by Jeanne overwhelms the two lovers with a somber melancholy that
neither of them grasps, though they both try to decipher the destiny it
spells out for them.[41] The pity Jeanne hears is not 'the sadness of
nature' but a far more human and selfish sense of disappointment; the
hope Piero offers is far more vague and self-deceptive than the 'hot
words' arrested at the edge of his lips. In their double inability to
understand, or perhaps more important, genuinely to feel pity,
Fogazzaro's modernist sense of writing on water emerges; it becomes
even more evident when compared to Dante's use of the same image:[42]

L'acqua ch'io prendo, giammai non si corse:
[...]
    Voi altri pochi che drizzaste il collo
Per tempo al pan degli angeli, del quale
Vivesi qui, ma non sen vien satollo
    Metter potete ben per l'alto sale
Vostro naviglio, servando mio solco
Dinanzi all'acqua che ritorna equale. (*Paradiso* II, 7, 10–15)

[The sea I sail has never yet been passed;
[...]
    Ye other few who have the neck uplifted

Betimes to th' bread of Angels upon which
One liveth here and grows not sated by it,
    Well may you launch upon the deep salt-sea
Your vessel, keeping still my wake before you
Upon the water that grows smooth again.]

There is a 'wake' here that some can follow, and preserve, and repeat: the continuity of tradition, even within an innovation as radical as Dante's *Commedia*, is preserved to the degree that Dante's faith deliberately inscribes itself, again and again, in that tradition (the extent to which poetic creation is a contrary impulse, and Dante's awareness of this tension, notwithstanding).[43] For Fogazzaro, the continuity of tradition has been almost completely severed; there is not even the barest trace of a 'solco' for Piero and Jeanne to follow, only the most subterranean voice persists. As Benedetto will explain much later to his followers:

Udite una figura. Pellegrini assetati si accostano a una fonte famosa. Trovano una vasca piena di acqua stagnante, ingrata al gusto. La scaturigine viva è sul fondo della vasca, non la trovano. Si volgono mesti a un cavatore di pietre che lavora in una cava vicina. Il cavatore offre loro acqua viva. Gli chiedono il nome della sorgente. 'È' la stessa vasca' dice. 'È tutta, nel sottosuolo, una sola corrente. Chi scava, trova.' I pellegrini sitibondi siete voi, il cavatore oscuro sono io e la corrente occulta nel sottosuolo è la Verità cattolica. La vasca non è la Chiesa, la Chiesa è tutto il campo corso dalle acque vive. (*S* 176)

[Hear this parable. Thirsty pilgrims draw near to a famous fountain. They find a basin full of stagnant water, disgusting to the taste. The living spring is at the bottom of the basin, but they cannot find it. Sadly they turn for aid to a worker from a nearby quarry. The quarry worker offers them living water. They ask him the name of the spring. 'It is from the same basin,' he says. 'Underground, it is all one and the same stream. He who digs, finds it.' You are the thirsty pilgrims, and I am the humble quarry worker and the hidden underground current is Catholic Truth. The basin is not the Church; the Church is the whole field in which the living waters flow.]

At Vena di fonte alta, Piero and Jeanne are pilgrims lost in this vast field; there is no quarry worker to help them (and indeed, the optimism of the parable is temporary, for there is no certainty, even in *The*

Saint, that Benedetto will be that quarry worker): the water flows, and again they cannot decipher its voice.

> Allora le due anime salite sulle labbra si dissero tale una cosa che poi, quando le labbra si disgiunsero, gli occhi non sostennero di guardarsi. [...] Ambedue, attratti e respinti, trepidavano.
> Intanto si era levato un vento molesto che soffiava loro la nebbia in viso. [...] ecco Rio Freddo, il pauroso confine del paradiso verde di Vena, la valle dell'Ombra della Morte. Jeanne mise il piede sopra un lastrone sporgente fra gli abissi. Piero l'afferrò alla vita ed ella si rovesciò indietro nelle sue braccia, chiudendo gli occhi. La strinse a sé, la coperse, tacendo sempre, di carezze così violente, che Jeanne, atterrita, supplicò:
> 'No, no, no!' (*LWP* 332; 333–4)

> [Then their two souls raised up to their lips said to each other such a thing, that when their lips parted, their eyes could not sustain the vision. [...] Repulsed and attracted they both waited in trepidation.
> Meanwhile a sudden harsh wind blew fog in their faces [...] here was Rio Freddo, the fearful border of the green paradise of Vena, the valley of the Shadow of Death. Jeanne put her foot on a flat rock overhanging the abyss. Piero caught her by the waist and she fell backwards, closing her eyes. He held her tightly, and still silent, covered her with caresses so violent that she, terrified, begged:
> 'No, no, no!']

This is also a parable: this time, a warning about what it means to try to incarnate the inexpressible word the waters conceal. For the pilgrims Piero and Jeanne are here tempted to plunge into the 'basin full of stagnant water' to find the 'green pastures' and the 'still waters' of David's Psalm (23:2). But the fog rises up in their faces, and the 'valley of the shadow of death' (Ps. 23:4) is upon them, and they are afraid, though they do not recognize it. Once again, Fogazzaro uses the imagery of tradition to evoke, not without awe and not without fear, the discontinuity of tradition. Yet against this discontinuity, against Piero and Jeanne's sublime fall into the abyss of Rio Freddo, something intervenes to interrupt the illusory infinity of nature, the water's endlessly equal return – something quite undefineable. After they return to the hotel, Piero is ready to abandon himself to the violent caresses born under the shadow of death; he waits for all to be dark and quiet so he can steal away to Jeanne's room:

Piero si buttò in un seggiolone davanti alla finestra aperta, alle stelle tremolanti là in faccia sopra un nero culmine di bosco, immaginando la cosa detta senza parole da labbro a labbro, sentita sull'orlo degli abissi di Rio Freddo [...] La cosa era fatale forse; [...] Non senza rifiutare ascolto ai deboli richiami della coscienza, non senza un oscuro disprezzo di se stesso, si stese a terra per vedere, prima di aprir l'uscio, se fra l'uscio e il pavimento entrasse lume, se la lampada a petrolio del corridoio ardesse ancora. Era spenta. Si rialzò palpitando. (*LWP* 337–8)

[Piero threw himself onto the big chair in front of the open window, facing the stars trembling over the tip of the forest, imagining the thing said without words, lip to lip, on the edge of the abyss of Rio Freddo [...] The thing was fatal perhaps; [...] Not without refusing to hear the weak calls of his conscience, not without an obscure scorn for himself, he lay down upon the floor to see if light came through the bottom of the door, if the oil lamp in the hall was still lit. It was not. He got up, quivering.]

It has often been pointed out that Piero does not overcome this temptation; rather, he is prevented from consummating his passion for Jeanne by a jealous admirer of hers, who hears the slight noise Piero makes and walks out into the hallway. Then fate has it that on this very night Piero's wife, near death but suddenly lucid, calls him to her from the sanatorium; his shame, his horror, and his loss all flow into the vision that will guide his transformation into Benedetto. Prefiguring some of the accusations that were levelled at Fogazzaro himself, a doctor suggests that this vision is the result of sick nerves, of circumstance and not providence. Yet providence moves in this modernist novel like the imagery that moves the unconscious: unnamed, unnameable, but somehow penetrating, generating action.[44] Not only is it crucial that Piero cannot claim this night as a victory over himself, it is also significant (spiritually) that he does not grasp the import of his own gestures. For if the unconscious is where mystical contacts act, his prone immobile posture face down on the floor is also and already one of penitence, as though his body could not but act out and reflect that 'obscure scorn' his mind denies. It prefigures his 'shattered' 'body' in another night of temptation (*S* 75; see above), and even more, his body 'flattened to the ground' (*S* 95) in the cell at Subiaco, where he will pray just before he encounters Jeanne for what would be the next to the last time. And indeed, from this moment at the end of *Little World of the Present* to the end of *The Saint*, this will be

Piero's hidden and emblematically ascetic posture, even as he is first unaware of it, and then tries to make it his own, on the way to a consent he will never possess – a consent whose meaning must remain obscure even to him.

When Benedetto and Jeanne meet again (for the first time in *The Saint*) after the night of temptation at Vena, the inexpressible word of the waters seems to have received a new form, just as Piero has acquired a new name. But once again, modernistically, Fogazzaro reveals how the forms of tradition are broken by the very life that is at their source. Jeanne has followed Piero into one of the cloisters at the monastery of San Benedetto:

> Benedetto si recò alle labbra l'indice della sinistra e tese l'altro alla parete fronteggiante il balcone aperto sui carpineti del Francolano e sul fragore del fiume profondo. Nel mezzo della parete nereggiava, grande, la parola:
> SILENTIUM.
> Per secoli, da quando quella parola era stata scritta, mai voce umana si era udita là dentro. Jeanne non guardò, non vide. A lei bastò quell'indice alle labbra di Piero per serrar le sue. Ma non bastò a costringerle il pianto in gola. Guardava guardava lui con le labbra strette e le sdrucciolavano sul viso lacrime silenziose. [...] La grande, nera parola imperatoria, grave di ombre e di morte, trionfava sulle due anime umane, ruggendo contro a lei dal balcone lucente le anime belluine dell'Aniene e del vento.
> (*S* 110)

> [Benedetto drew his left index finger to his lips and pointed the other to the wall in front of the balcony, which opened onto the ravines of the Francolano and the deep roar of the river. In the middle of the wall, the word was large and dark:
> SILENTIUM.
> For centuries, since that word had been written, never had a human voice been heard here. Jeanne did not look, did not see. Piero's finger on his lips was enough to silence her. But it could not keep her tears within her breast. She looked and looked and silent tears fell over her tight lips. [...] The great, dark, imperious word, heavy with shadows and death, triumphed over those two human souls, even as the violent souls of the Aniene and the wind roared up against the scintillating balcony.]

As Paolo Valesio has pointed out, mystical silence is taken to an 'animistic' level in this scene, a level of indistinct natural existence that precedes (ontologically) any kind of mystical ascent; at this level, the dark, imperial colour of the word also evokes Dante's *Inferno* (III, 10: 'parole di colore oscuro, [words in sombre colour],' and implies 'the ambiguity of Fogazzaro in front of his world.'[45] Thus the word that is at the centre of the mystical tradition and its gnosis, written now not on water but in the very place where that mystical tradition begins, radiates a darkness far deeper even than mystical unknowing. (Though perhaps their source is one: this is very much what is at stake in modernism.) For here the soul does not go out into the dark in search of its lover; here the dark absorbs everything. Jeanne's tears are bitter, and their darkness seems to flow through her and break her, even as she drinks in and obscures Piero's very soul. Faced with this Pascalian dark silence, Piero recommends to Jeanne Pascal's *pari:* 'act as though you had faith,' he tells her, 'for me.' Yet he himself seems to walk in a darkness that no *pari* can redeem:

> Se con l'autorità dei grandi mistici mi dico che ho torto di avere tanto affetto alle dolcezze spirituali, di soffrire tanto per la loro privazione, mi rispondo che hanno torto i mistici, che nello stato di grazia sensibile si cammina sicuri e che invece in questa notte spirituale senza stelle il cammino non si vede, non c'è altra regola che ritrarre il piede quando si sente il molle dell'erba, e che ciò non basta, ch'è anche possibile di porlo adirittura, il piede, nel vuoto. (*S* 170)

> [If with the authority of the great mystics I tell myself that I am wrong to long for spiritual delights, and to suffer so much when they depart, I answer myself that the mystics are wrong, that in a state of sensible grace we can walk with a sure foot, and that instead in this spiritual night without stars we cannot see the path, there is no other rule but to withdraw our feet when we feel the softness of the grass, and even this is not enough, since we might at any moment step into the void.]

Such emptiness is more frightening even than Jeanne's bitterness, for it leaves no place for love. And love, like 'the softness of the grass' is at once 'green paradise of Vena' and 'whole field in which the living waters flow': 'to withdraw [his] feet' is thus the last and the greatest temptation to which Piero will be subject. (And here we also see that it is not possible to read Fogazzaro as a 'moderate' modernist, one for whom a quiet asceticism would be enough, as it was for don Clemente.)[46]

How can a river's roar on a starry night transform deathly cold into infinite sweetness? On his deathbed, Piero dreams a dream that will lead him to the greatest abandon:

Egli si vide in faccia un colossale muraglione di marmo. [...] Ed ecco fra le urne [...] sei giovani donne bellissime; [...] e con lo stesso armonioso gesto delle braccia ignude tendere a lui dall'alto, piegando il busto, sei scintillanti coppe d'argento. [...] Dalle loro labbra non usciva parola e tuttavia gli era evidente che le sei giovani gli offrivano nell'argento un liquore di vita, di salute, di piacere. [...] Le sei danzatrici piegarono a un punto le coppe verso di lui, sei mobili nastri di liquore rigarono l'aria. 'Come io' pensò il dormiente scambiando persone nella memoria turbata 'a Praglia.' E tutto scomparve, e si vide davanti Jeanne. Ritta in piedi, chiusa nel mantello verde foderato di *skunk*, ombrata il viso dal grande cappello nero, ella lo guardava come lo aveva guardato a Praglia nel momento del primo incontro. Ma stavolta il dormiente vide una rispondenza fra la gravità di quello sguardo e la gravità dei volti delle danzatrici, vide con lo spirito la parola silenziosa delle sette anime: povero uomo, tu ora conosci il tuo doloroso errore, tu ora sai che Dio non è. La gravità degli sguardi non era che tristezza di pietà. [...] E il dormiente fu invaso da questa presunta evidenza nuova che Dio non è. Era una vera e propria sensazione fisica, un gelo diffuso per tutte le membra, movente lento al cuore. Egli prese a tremare, a tremare e si destò. [...] Benedetto mormorò con gli occhi sbarrati: 'Padre! – Padre! – Padre!' (*S* 271–2)

[He saw himself, confronted by a colossal marble wall. [...] And now between the urns six beautiful maidens appeared; [...] with the same harmonious movement of their bare arms, bending their bodies forward, they offered him from their elevation, six shining silver goblets. [...] No word fell from their lips, but nevertheless he knew that the six maidens were offering him, in those six silver goblets, an elixir of life, of health, of pleasure. [...] At last the six dancing maidens inclined the goblets towards him, and six flowing ribbons of liquor streamed through the air. 'Just as I did, at Praglia!' the sleeper thought, confusing persons in his clouded mind. Then everything disappeared, and he saw Jeanne before him. Erect, wrapped in her green cloak lined with *skunk*, her face in the shadow of her black hat, she gazed at him as she had done at Praglia, at the moment of their first meeting. But this time the sleeper saw a correspondence between the gravity of this gaze and the serious faces of the dancers, he saw the silent word of those seven souls: poor man, now you see your grievous error, now you know that God is not. Those grave gazes held only the sadness of pity. [...] And the sleeper was invaded by this new presumed evidence that God is not. It was a genuine physical sensation, a diffuse icy cold taking over his limbs, moving to the heart. He started to tremble, and tremble, and suddenly awakened. [...] Benedetto murmured, with an unseeing stare: 'Father! – Father! – Father!']

Surrounded by the seven deadly sins, Piero finally dares to love. In his dream, he sees himself as Jeanne, when on that day at Praglia she poured out the bitter cup, the 'source of tears,' in a proud gesture of seduction that was never to bring her the happiness she desired. And, like Jeanne, he regrets having poured out what at the time seemed 'cloudy water' but now in the dream shimmers like the 'elixir of life, of health, of pleasure.' Almost becoming Jeanne, only half-dreaming, he is finally seduced by pleasure and takes on her despair: accepting the pity in her gaze, he accepts the pity of the beautiful yet funereal young women who reveal that pleasure is poured out only once, and that death comes without any possible redemption. Living out Jeanne's unbelief, with a love that is compassionate unto death itself, Piero traverses a spiritual death – the icy certainty that 'God is not.' And he lives out this unbelief bodily first of all, just as bodily he had given in to penitence, prone on the floor – as though the body were awake where the spirit slept, awake to a suffering too formless for words. Here Piero gets to the heart of pity, and love, making his own the 'silent word' the waters had covered over, accepting the 'word heavy with shadows and death' of the abyss that would overcome their two souls. His cry of 'Father! – Father! – Father!' is interrupted by the 'unfortunately foolish voice' (*S* 272) of the nun who continues as though reciting the *Pater*, 'who art in Heaven'; but his silence is eloquent enough for us to intuit the rest: 'why hast thou forsaken me?' (Matt. 27:46; Mark 15:34). The cry of dereliction was prefigured by Psalm 22:1, just as the extent of Piero's abandon was prefigured in the inscription at Praglia, which is from Psalm 22:14: 'I am poured out like water, and all my bones are out of joint.' The hidden meaning of *dilabimur*, emphasized by the shift to a plural form, is the inscription of both Piero and Jeanne's doubt in Christ's suffering, not – here is the essence of Fogazzaro's modernism – in his resurrection.[47] Ultimately, the vision of Christ that emerges from Piero's identification with him in *The Saint* is indeed radical, though not, in retrospect, entirely uncanonical, in its claim that Christ's humanity could – and did – entirely obscure his divinity (albeit temporarily). For this vision unites the mystical unknowing of religious modernism and the pure epiphanic emptiness of literary modernism in a single experience of having lost any and all claims to transcendence.

Piero's dereliction is thus also the abandonment of 'his' vision as a final explanation and fulfilment of 'his' life, and the abandonment, we might even say, of 'his' sainthood, in favour of the formless pity and the dark love he had glimpsed in his night of temptation on the edge of the Aniene. We see here the 'animism' evoked by Valesio (a more accurate term than 'pantheism,' for which modernism was often condemned):

> [...] quieta fonte interna di un indistinto amore. [...] Nel mormorio della pioggia senza vento, piana, piana, nella voce grande dell'Aniene, nella riposata maestà dei monti, dell'odore selvaggio della petraia umida, nello stesso proprio cuore, Benedetto sentiva un Divino confuso alla creatura, un'ascosa essenza di paradiso. Sentiva di fondersi con le anime delle cose come piccola voce in un coro immenso, di essere uno con la montagna odorante, uno con l'aria beata. Incertezze, dubbi, ricordi della mistica Visione gli si sciolsero nel profondo abbandono alla Divina Volontà. (S 75–6)

> [...] calm inner source of indistinct love. [...] In the murmur of the rain without wind, so gentle, in the great voice of the Aniene, in the quiet majesty of the mountains, in the sharp odour of the wet rocks, in his own heart, Benedetto felt the Divine confused with the creature, he felt a hidden essence of paradise. He knew himself fused with the soul of all things like a little voice in an immense chorus; he was one with the fragrant mountain, with the blessed air. Uncertainties, doubts, memories of his mystical Vision disappeared in his profound abandon to the Divine Will.]

At his moment of agony, Piero will thus resist the temptation to have himself carried outside to die under the pine tree he saw in his vision (S 283). And this returns us once more to Praglia, and to the moon. The lunar inscription 'completur cursu' had been for Piero a sign of his own fulfilment through his passion for Jeanne; we understand now that he later also took it as a sign that he was to fulfil his vision. In this, he is again like Dante who, when he compares his words to a wake swiftly erased in the flow of water, finds himself in the heaven of the moon, where he 'dentro all'error contrario [corre] / A quel ch'accese amor tra l'omo e il fonte [in error opposite / To that which kindled love 'twixt man and fountain [runs]]' (*Paradiso* III, 17–18):

Dante mistakes the faces of the blessed that emerge darkly from the moon (like Dido's shade in Virgil) for his own reflection, just as Piero mistook his vision for an image of his own destiny. But it is only by not forcing his vision into narcissistic self-completion that Piero finally allows it to have meaning for others – for the 'persons attracted to Christ but repulsed by Catholicism' (*S* 186), for those who continue to pray 'for the forgiveness of those who cannot be forgiven,'[48] for all those for whom the dark colour of silence is more eloquent than words.

And perhaps also for Jeanne. *The Saint* famously closes with her passionate embrace of the crucifix held by Piero as he dies (*S* 287), in a closure that isn't one – 'completur cursu' remains obscure – and that again brings out the ambivalence between sacred and profane love that neither of them can master. But before that moment Jeanne steps out into the rain and passes under the pine tree of Piero's vision, on her way to a fountain with a 'marble edge' like that of Praglia:

'Caro, caro, come ti potrei io ingannare?' Aveva lottato più volte col proprio scetticismo imperioso e sempre invano. Uno slancio di dedizione alla fede, lo sapeva, non sarebbe stato durevole. [...] Pioveva tanto dirotta-mente, il cielo, corso tuttora di tempo in tempo dal tuono, era tanto fosco che prima delle sei, quella sera di febbraio, pareva già quasi notte. Jeanne entrò come stava, a capo scoperto, nella pioggia fitta e fredda. [...] Passò dal gran pino che guarda il Celio e [...] si condusse alla fonte che un avello antico raccoglie nel pendio ripido fra una cintura di mirti [...] sedette sull'orlo marmoreo della vasca. Era possibile di affogare lì dentro? Avrebbe cercato di morire se non ci fosse Carlino? Pensieri vani; non vi si trattenne. Attese, attese, sotto la pioggia fredda, con gli occhi e l'anima fermi alla finestra lucente. (*S* 285–6)

['Dear, dear, how could I mislead you?' She had struggled more than once with her imperious scepticism but in vain. A sudden outburst of faith, she knew, would never last. [...] It was raining so hard that the sky, filled with thunder, was so dark that even before six, on the summer evening, it already seemed to be night. Jeanne entered the thick and cold rain as she was, without a hat. [...] She passed the great pine tree that looks over the Celio and [...] she came to the fountain that fills an ancient sarcophagus on the steep slope between rows of myrrh [...] she sat on the marble edge of the basin. Could one drown in there? Would she have tried to die if Carlino had not been there? Empty thoughts; she did not cling to them. She waited, and waited, under the cold rain, with her eyes and soul firm on the shining window.]

Here in her own way, in her own heart, Jeanne discovers the abandon and the pity signified by the inscription *omnes velut aqua dilabimur*. For this is a baptismal rain which, significantly, Jeanne *enters*, rather than *going out into* – here is her moment of decision where again the body, or more accurately the whole person and not simply the abstracting mind, leads. Surrounded by the perfume of myrrh, she lets herself be consumed and consents to a perishing, to a dispersion, to a loss that is plural – she lets herself be divided by the suffering of life and the infinite possibility of love, accepting, finally, the vanity of her own thoughts. *Dilabimur* here becomes the modernist cry of dereliction, agony understood in the dimension of a personalist existentialism where it is constantly the subject of hermeneutic reflection, and never the object of dialectical certainty.[49] In other words, '*dilabimur*,' as it is finally lived out by Jeanne, offers no claim to transcendence (or to its radical absence), no epiphany, positive or negative, but only the assertion that human finitude itself is a question, a cry of abandonment, that we share. Open to this cry, Jeanne's love is all waiting, for she accepts it, finally, as a question without an answer, a passion suffered without certainty, yet lived, not only with Piero, but with all that strives, and lives, beneath the dark rain. And she waits, like Eliot in 'East Coker,' eyes and soul firm but empty, having let go of her thoughts, without hope, but not without a window of light in the darkness:

> For I said to my soul, be still, and wait without hope
> For hope would be hope for the wrong thing: wait without love
> For love would be love of the wrong thing: there is yet faith
> But the faith the love and the hope are all in the waiting
> So wait without thought, for you are not ready for thought:
> So the darkness shall be light, and the stillness the dancing.[50]

NOTES

1 Buonaiuti (115–18).
2 Fogazzaro to von Hügel, in Bedeschi (346).
3 It is worth noting that the term 'modernism', though first used by Spanish and Latin American writers, comes to describe a religious, philosophical, literary, and social *movement* for the first time in the 1907 encyclical *Pascendi dominici gregis*, where it is thoroughly condemned by the Pope.

The relation of this 'religious' (in fact far broader) modernism to literary
and cultural modernism is all the more difficult to elucidate in that
'literary and cultural Modernism,' particularly in Italy (as this volume
attests) and France, is still in need of definition. The Anglo-American
understanding of modernism, even when referring only to England and
America, makes what I believe is too stark a distinction between the
'religious' and the 'literary' (see Lease); the distinction breaks down most
clearly in Italy, however, where the opposition of modernism to decadence (and its 'religiosity') is undermined by the concept of
'decadentismo' as *part of* modernism (see Calinescu).

4 Valesio (448).

5 Huysmans (37): Huysmans approvingly cites this comment by
d'Aurevilly in his preface to the novel, written twenty years after its
initial publication (hence after Huysmans's conversion). There is a very
marked divide in French literature from this period on between Catholic
writers, and secular writers, which does not have an equivalent in Italy.

6 *The Saint* was published in 1905 and put on the Index in 1906; though
modernism as a movement was not explicitly named until 1907,
Fogazzaro's novel, as we shall see, was explicitly associated with (religious) modernist ideas from the beginning; yet paradoxically, since that
time, as modernism has come to be defined not by its condemnation by
the Church, but by its historians, Fogazzaro's work has been perceived as
more and more marginal to mainstream religious modernism, and more
typical of *Decadentismo* and thus, in an Italian context, literary modernism.

7 See Colin for an extensive analysis of the contradictions of modernism in
France.

8 I translate *Piccolo mondo moderno* as *Little World of the Present* since the
story of Maironi's parents, *Piccolo Mondo Antico*, is translated as *Little
World of the Past*; I do not use the title of the published translation of
Piccolo mondo moderno, *The Sinner*, because it introduces a false dichotomy
between the two novels. Nonetheless I base my translations of
Fogazzaro's novels on Fogazzaro, 1906 and 1907; all other translations are
my own.

9 See Bachelard for the connection of imagery and knowledge; for the
definition of personal knowledge, see Polanyi. See Hollywood, for a
brilliant argument in favour of embodied knowledge.

10 'Bien amère et angoissante la situation de ceux qui se trouvent isolés,
comme moi, entre un fanatisme qui nie le Christ pratiquement et un
criticisme qui le nie théoriquement [Bitter and anguished is the situation
of those who are isolated, like I am, between a fanaticism that denies

Christ in practice, and a criticism that denies him in theory],' Fogazzaro to von Hügel, in Bedeschi (347). Fogazzaro sought in particular to reconcile science and religion under the aegis of a Newmanian notion of development that he saw as similar to Darwinism, and which he tied to a progress of consciousness through the movement of the unconscious which could also be grasped in parapsychology. Valesio also stresses Fogazzaro's silentiary understanding of the spirit (see Valesio, 422, 448).

11 See Fogazzaro's *Il dolou nell'arte* for his theoretical exposition of this point.

12 The location is Franciscan though his habit is Benedictine (Saint Francis is often depicted praying in the wilderness, whereas Saint Benedict is associated with the cave in which he lived as a hermit).

13 The monastery of San Benedetto at Subiaco is considered the place of origin of Western monasticism, since it is located where Saint Benedict's cave was; it has been a place of pilgrimage ever since, and appears in the works of Gabriele d'Annunzio and Giuseppe Ungaretti as well as Fogazzaro's.

14 Valesio (422).

15 Fogazzaro has often been accused of being a 'sentimental' writer, whose lack of intellectual clarity went along with a large female readership; yet his reflection on the role of passion in spirituality and in mysticism especially is far from being narcissistic or escapist, as the term might imply. See Pullini.

16 Hereafter *The Saint* will be abbreviated *S* and the page numbers will be given in the text; likewise, *Little World of the Present* will be abbreviated *LWP*.

17 See the etymology of *mystic* in *muein*, to be silent.

18 See de Certeau.

19 Note that the argument for autonomy is very different from claiming that the experience is 'atheistic' or 'profane,' for these spheres define themselves in opposition to the religious, whereas mysticism tries to overcome or get outside of this opposition. For the modernists, the trick is to do this while remaining within a redefined Christian tradition. See Harries on how this dovetails with a search an autonomy of the aesthetic.

20 My brief summary of religious modernism draws from Bedeschi, Colin, Guasco, Jodock, Kurtz, Loome, Poulat, and Ranchetti.

21 It was put on the Index on 4 April 1906, in particular because of the opinion evident in the passage quoted in note 48, below, which suggests that even a non-believer might be saved. See Gallarati-Scotti (424).

22 These were meetings of religious reformers of various types; they were attended, among others, by von Hügel who is said to be the model for the thinker in *The Saint*, Giovanni Selva. See *S* xi.

23 As mentioned, the term was used to define a movement in the encyclical *Pascendi*; however, it was already being used polemically in 1904 in various journals: see the precise chronology in the appendix of Ranchetti.

24 Benedetto is respectful of Church dogma to the extent that it does not go against what he perceives to be Christian charity in its most immediate experiential level; see again the passage in note 48, but also his willingness to hear, admittedly, in rather forced circumstances, the confession of a dying man who mistakes him for a priest and is much comforted (Fogazzaro is here revisiting Boccaccio's famous opening story of the *Decameron*, the novella of Ser Ciappelletto).

25 Fogazzaro agreed to eschew all further publications of the work, and accepted the Church's judgment in his outward actions at least; for someone like Buonaiuti this was to give up the battle entirely.

26 See Caronti for this argument.

27 See Pullini for an overview of criticism, and the discussion of Fogazzaro in Croce.

28 See Bo and especially Romanato for this view of Fogazzaro.

29 Fogazzaro plays with the 'selva' or wilderness of the mystic versus 'Selva,' the thinker here: for him both must tend towards the same perfection. At the same time, Benedetto is also *alter Christus* here, as Porcelli, argues: while he is awake, the others, in their debates, sleep.

30 Fogazzaro, (*Dolore nell'arte* 73–5). The expression 'seme del piangere' or 'seed of weeping/source of tears' appears in *Purgatorio* XXXI, 46; 'incognito indistinto' or 'indefinite infinite' is from *Purgatorio* VII, 81; the Dante citation is from *Purgatorio* VIII, 5–6.

31 Hence the question about what defines the saint is not a sign of religious moderation, as Porcelli suggests; rather, it is a radical attempt to redefine sainthood and our ability to understand it – in the tradition of the 'fols en Christ' as described by Yannaras.

32 'Indistinto ... infinito' echoes Leopardi's 'L'infinito' as well as Dante.

33 Foscolo's 'armonia dissonante' can also be said to have Christological parallels in Jacopo Ortis: see Terzoli (75).

34 See Kierkegaard's notion that one cannot know the true source of suffering. In a tradition within Catholic literature, this is symbolized by the ineffable source of tears, as seen in particular in Bernanos and Claudel, but also Valéry. *Il seme del piangere* is of course also the title of a more recent collection of poems that meditate on spirituality, by Giorgio Caproni.

35 Jeanne's use of French is a sign of her social class (and her desire not be understood by their tour guide) but also of the geographical origin of her scepticism.

36 See Vattimo, whose title, *Credere di credere*, echoes Fogazzaro; but see also Unamuno, for a more poetic meditation on the same themes.

37 See Deleuze on Sacher-Masoch and the deliberate coldness of the 'Venus in Furs,' which provokes desire: Jeanne is repeatedly described as distant and mysterious in her fur cloak. For the connection between masochism, formlessness, and mystical experience, see Hollywood (51–9).

38 Bernanos and Fogazzaro share a sense of suffering or agony as *dramatic* in the sense explored by Balthasar in *Le Chrétien Bernanos* and in *The Glory of the Lord*.

39 The image also recalls Piero's earlier temptation during a lunar eclipse, *LWP* 172.

40 As such it recalls the image of 'bere l'acqua nel cavo della mano' in d'Annunzio's *Poema paradisiaco*; Fogazzaro's 'paradiso verde di Vena' is also reminiscent of d'Annunzio's closed garden.

41 This recalls Bernanos again, and his repeated assertion that the 'repentance' of tears can precede actual understanding.

42 See Keats's epitaph, 'Here lies one whose name was writ in water' (apparently borrowed from the play *Philaster*, or *Love Lies-Ableeding*, written by Beaumont and Fletcher in 1611, which included the line: 'All your better deeds / Shall be in water writ'). The image of the trace or wake written in water appears in Dante's Heaven of the Moon, which again, quite specifically as we shall see, prefigures Piero's 'grande pianeta' and his ambiguous vision.

43 For the tension between poetic creation and the aesthetic, on the one hand, and prayer, on the other, see Bremond and Kierkegaard.

44 Here Fogazzaro takes up of the Manzonian problem of providence: Piero's night of temptation must be related to the night of the 'innominato' in *I Promessi Sposi*. Later, Piero's interrogation will echo the exchange between Fra Cristoforo and the 'innominato,' and both recall Christ's interrogation by Pilate, as noted by Valesio (422).

45 See Valesio (423–4) for an analysis of this ambiguity. Also note the shift between 'rombo' or 'fragore,' which describes the Aniene's roar most often, and 'ruggito,' in the quotation above (4), where it is associated with 'l'Abisso trionfante.'

46 Valéry's assertion that Christ should have been subjected to the temptations of love is one side of this radical stand; Bernanos' repeated dramatizations of agony are the other – asceticism as the terrifying 'bouche noire' of Donissan in *Sous le soleil de Satan:* his 'TU VOULAIS MA PAIX' in all caps at the end of the novel echoes the ambiguity of Fogazzaro's SILENTIUM.

47 See Wyschogrod for the association between sainthood and a shared experience of suffering.

48 See one of the passages that the Church most objected to:

'Non si tratta di me' disse. 'Io credo, sono cattolica. E' mio padre che ha vissuto così ed è morto così e ... se sapesse! ... hanno persuaso anche mia madre ch'egli non ha potuto salvarsi!'
Mentr'ella parlava, rade gocce, grosse, cominciarono a battere, fra i lampi e i tuoni, sulla via. [...]
'Mi dica, mi dica' implorò, alzando finalmente il viso 'che mio padre è salvo, che lo ritroverò in Paradiso!'
Benedetto rispose:
'Preghi.'
'Dio! Solo questo?'
'Si prega forse per il perdono di chi non può essere perdonato? Preghi.'
(*S* 143–4)

['I am not talking about myself,' she said. 'I believe, I am Catholic. It's my father, he lived that way and died that way and ... if only you knew! ... they persuaded even my mother that he could never have been saved!'
As she spoke, a few, heavy drops began to fall, between the lightening and thunder, upon the road. [...]
'Tell me, tell me,' she implored, finally raising her face 'that my father is saved, that I will find him in Paradise!'
Benedetto answered:
'Pray.'
'My God! Only this?'
'Does one pray for the forgiveness of those who cannot be forgiven? Pray.']

The modernity of Fogazzaro's modernism is evident here too: a very similar episode to the one above occurs in the recent biography of Padre Pio, in Allegri (515). Overall, it would be interesting to explore how recent hagiographies of Padre Pio (who began his activities not too long after *The Saint* was published, and was just canonized in the spring of 2002) both imitate and 'correct' Fogazzaro's view of sainthood.

49 Colin (263, 281); as well as Ricoeur, *Soi-même comme un autre* and 'Expérience et langage'.

50 'East Coker,' *Four Quartets*, in Eliot (126).

164   Laura Wittman

WORKS CITED

Allegri, Renzo. *La vita e i miracoli di Padre Pio (Le stigmate, i miracoli, il mistero)*. Milan: Mondadori, 1999.

Bachelard, Gaston. *La Poétique de la rêverie*. Paris: Presses Universitaires de France, 1960.

Balthasar, Hans Urs von. *Le Chrétien Bernanos*. Trans. Maurice de Gandillac. Paris: Éditions du Seuil, 1956.

– *The Glory of the Lord, vol. IV, The Realm of Metaphysics in Antiquity*. Trans. Brian McNeil, C.R.V., Andrew Louth, John Saward, Rowan Williams, and Oliver Davies. Edinburgh: T. and T. Clark, 1989.

Bedeschi, Lorenzo. 'Fogazzaro e il Modernismo in un Carteggio inedito di von Hügel.' *Antonio Fogazzaro*. Ed. Enzo Noè Girardi, Carlo Marcora, and Attilio Agnoletto. Milan: Franco Angeli, 1984. 327–50.

– *Modernismo italiano: voci e volti*. Cinisello Balsamo, Milan: San Paolo, 1995.

Bernanos, Georges. *Sous le soleil de Satan*. Paris: Plon, 1982.

Bo, Carlo. 'Fogazzaro, voce e silenzio.' *Antonio Fogazzaro*. Ed. Enzo Noè Girardi, Carlo Marcora, and Attilio Agnoletto. Milan: Franco Angeli, 1984. 11–21.

Bremond, Henri. *Prière et poésie*. Paris: Grasset, 1926.

Buonaiuti, Ernesto. *Lettere di un prete modernista*. Rome: Libreria Editrice Romana, 1908.

Calinescu, Matei. *Faces of Modernity: Avant-Garde, Decadence, and Kitsch*. Bloomington: Indiana UP, 1977.

Caronti, Luigi. 'Fogazzaro riformista ne *Il Santo* non modernista.' *Fogazzaro, Subiaco e 'Il Santo'*. Cinisello Balsamo, Milan: Edizioni Paoline, 1989.

Certeau, Michel de. *La Fable mystique: XVIe–XVIIe siècles*. Paris: Gallimard, 1982.

Colin, Pierre. *L'audace et le soupçon: La crise du modernisme dans le catholicisme français, 1893–1914*. Paris: Desclée de Brouwer, 1997.

Croce, Benedetto. *La letteratura della nuova Italia saggi critici*. Bari: Laterza, 1947–57.

Dante, Alighieri. *The divine comedy*. Trans. Henry Wadsworth Longfellow. Boston: Jefferson Press, 1909.

Deleuze, Gilles. 'Coldness and Cruelty.' In Sacher-Masoch, Leopold von, and Gilles Deleuze, *Masochism: Coldness and Cruelty followed by Venus in Furs*. New York: Zone Books, 1989.

Eliot, T.S. *The Complete Poems and Plays, 1909–1950*. New York: Harcourt, Brace, 1950.

Fogazzaro, Antonio. *Il dolore nell'arte, discorso.* Milan: Baldini, Castoldi, 1901.
– *Piccolo mondo moderno.* 1901. Milan: Mondadori, 1982.
– *The Saint.* Trans. M. Agnetti Pritchard. New York: G.P. Putnam, 1906.
– *Il Santo.* 1905. Milan: Mondadori, 1970.
– *The Sinner.* Trans. M. Agnetti Pritchard. New York and London: G.P.
  Putnam's Sons, 1907.
Gallarati-Scotti, Tommaso. *Vita di Antonio Fogazzaro.* 1934. Milan: Mondadori,
  1982.
Guasco, Maurilio. *Modernismo: i fatti, le idee, i personaggi.* Cinisello Balsamo:
  San Paolo, 1995.
Harries, Karsten. *The Broken Frame.* Washington, DC: Catholic University of
  America Press, 1989.
Hollywood, Amy M. *Sensible Ecstasy Mysticism, Sexual Difference, and the
  Demands of History.* Chicago: U of Chicago P, 2002.
Huysmans, Joris Karl. *A Rebours.* 1883. Paris: Pocket, 1999.
Jodock, Darrell. *Catholicism Contending with Modernity: Roman Catholic
  Modernism and Anti-Modernism in Historical Context.* Cambridge and New
  York: Cambridge UP, 2000.
Kierkegaard, Søren. *Fear and Trembling: Repetition.* Ed. Howard V. Hong and
  Edna V. Hong. Princeton: Princeton UP, 1983.
– *Il giglio nel campo e l'uccello nel cielo.* Rome: Donzelli, 1998.
Kurtz, Lester R. *The Politics of Heresy: The Modernist Crisis of Roman Catholi-
  cism.* Berkeley: U of California P, 1986.
Lease, Gary. 'Modernism and "Modernism".' *Journal for the Study of Religion* 1
  (1999): 2–23.
Loome, Thomas Michael. *Liberal Catholicism, Reform Catholicism, Modernism.*
  Mainz: Matthias-Günewald, 1979.
Polanyi, Michel. *Personal Knowledge: Towards a Post-Critical Philosophy.*
  London: Routledge and Kegan Paul, 1958.
Porcelli, Bruno. 'Note sul romanzo del Fogazzaro.' *Momenti dell'antinatura-
  lismo Fogazzaro, Svevo, Corrazzini.* Ravenna: Longo, 1975. 17–52.
Poulat, Emile. *Critique et mystique. Autour de Loisy ou la conscience catholique et
  l'esprit moderne.* Paris: Centurion, 1984.
Pullini, Giorgio. 'Antonio Fogazzaro.' *Dizionario Biografico degli Italiani.* Rome:
  Istituto della Enciclopedia italiana, 1960–. 252–7.
Ranchetti, Michele. *Cultura e riforma religiosa nella storia del modernismo.* Turin:
  Einaudi, 1963.
Ricoeur, Paul. 'Expérience et langage dans le discours religieux.'
  Phénoménologie et théologie. Paris: Criterion, 1992. 15–39.

– *Soi-même comme un autre*. Paris: Seuil, 1990.

Romanato, Gianpaolo. 'Buonaiuti, Fogazzaro e il Modernismo.' *Antonio Fogazzaro*. Ed. Enzo Noè Girardi, Carlo Marcora, and Attilio Agnoletto. Milan: Franco Angeli, 1984. 351–60.

Terzoli, Maria Antonietta. 'Jacob alter Christus.' *Il libro di Jacopo: scrittura sacra nell'Ortis*. Rome: Salerno, 1988.

Unamuno, Miguel de. *Comparative and Critical Edition of San Manuel Bueno, martir*. 1933. Chapel Hill: Dept. of Romance Languages, University of North Carolina, 1973.

Valesio, Paolo. *Ascoltare il silenzio. La retorica come teoria*. Bologna: Il Mulino, 1986.

Vattimo, Gianni. *Credere di credere: E' possibile essere cristiani nonostante la Chiesa?* Milan: Garzanti, 1988.

Wyschogrod, Edith. *Saints and Postmodernism*. Chicago: U of Chicago P, 1990.

Yannaras, Christos. *La liberté de la morale*. Trans. Jacques Touraille. Geneva: Labor et Fides, 1982.

5 Overcoming Aestheticism

THOMAS HARRISON

Interviewer: Let us return to the main theme. You said earlier that you gave up aesthetics because you had begun to be interested in ethical problems. What works resulted from this interest?
Georg Lukács: At that time it did not result in any written works. My interest in ethics led me to revolution.

Some ninety years after it was written, Georg Lukács's 'Aesthetic Culture' (1910) has at last appeared in English. The importance of this essay lies not only in its pointed critique of fin-de-siècle European aestheticism, but also in its defence of a strange new art which never took hold. Almost contemporaneous to the more egregious pronouncement of F.T. Marinetti (1909), the Hungarian manifesto had no real disciples – unless, of course, we read them into it, gathering under the Lukácsian aegis an unlikely assortment of figures who hardly had an inkling of what he wrote: such disparate writers as Giuseppe Ungaretti and Luigi Pirandello, Eugenio Montale and Carlo Michelstaedter, not to mention half a dozen young writers associated with the Florentine journal *La Voce* [The Voice]. One measure of the fecundity of Lukács's essay is that it suggests commonality among writers who do not fit neatly together, who occupy a more or less liminal space in the evolution of twentieth-century letters. Too late for turn-of-the-century aestheticism, they also came too early for most avant-garde festivities. They forged their writings eccentrically, without stylistic or intellectual benediction, stepping out and away from a familiar cultural legacy in a manner that was uncertain, unpopular, and unaccompanied.

Lukács's essay points to one aspect of that step: its ethical urgency, its anti-aestheticist turn. Implicitly or explicitly, Pirandello, Ungaretti, Montale, the *vociani*, and select other early-twentieth-century Italian writers declared themselves 'post-D'Annunzian,' believing that something crucial to art had been lost in the image of the artist-hero, something once enabling rhetoric to bridge the distance between the individual imagination and vast intellectual plights. To these anti- or post-aestheticists, a number of theoretical crises seemed to be handled, even settled, too easily by the epistemologies of Decadence, Impressionism, and Symbolism. Art appeared too quickly emancipated, not sufficiently burdened, by the divorce between things as they might be in themselves and things as we tend to value them. Following the aestheticist season, in convulsive writings that did not warm up to their Futurist cousin, the climate was quite the opposite. Nineteenth-century crises found new twentieth-century aggravations. And their complications unfolded in all directions.

If Lukács suggests a logic to post-D'Annunzian writings, these writings themselves make us suspect that the quarrel with aestheticism is ultimately internecine – a problem internal to aestheticism instead of the outside attack the Hungarian intended it to be. More importantly, they exemplify a number of post-aestheticist practices that go far beyond Lukács's critique. The real question after Lukács is where do these practices leave us? In attempting to answer that question, this study will cross the following waystations: (I) the details of Lukács's argument against aestheticism, bolstered by analogous positions in Carlo Michelstaedter's *La persuasione e la rettorica* [Persuasion and Rhetoric], (II) the place, on the Lukácsian spectrum, of Italian writers who are in greater or lesser sympathy with it, and (III) the tacit aestheticism of even these new forms of anti-aestheticism. My conclusion, however, in (IV), will be that the guiding ambitions of anti-aestheticism have an ethical charge that cannot be fully accounted for by Lukács's essay, but rather only by the scriptorial dilemmas of this lost generation.

I

The Lukács of 1908–16 is not the Marxist we know from works like *The Historical Novel*. That intellectual conversion occurs after his *Theory of the Novel* (1916) and is permanently affirmed in *History and Class Consciousness* (1923). When he wrote 'Aesthetic Culture,' as well as his most lyrical, stunning, and fertile work, *Soul and Form* (1910–11), Lukács was an unusual breed of nihilistic idealist. More particularly, he found himself in the thick of hostilities with many artistic and intellectual currents of pre-war Europe. Nowhere is this as evident as in 'Aesthetic Culture.'

The argument of the essay is essentially that Impressionists, decadents, and aestheticists (Lukács cites almost no names, but it is easy to imagine whom he has in mind as the heirs of *l'art pour l'art*) have converted life, experience, ideas, and values into a matter of mere images. They consider these issues for thought (not to mention the entire culture in which they are housed) as imaginative constructs. They generate aesthetic methodologies from a basic intuition that perceptions and desires name no objective or pre-given condition of being. What we have here is a turn away from a realist, materialist epistemology, which follows from a Kantian sense of the merely apparent, or not noetically reliable, nature of the phenomenal world and which reaches its apogee in Nietzschean meditations of the 1880s. Its result is a volatization of the real, propelled by the thought that experience and truth are but effects of the lens through which *homo ludens* views them. The ontological platform for this aestheticism becomes early-twentieth-century vitalism, or *Lebensphilosophie*, whose prime proponent is the German philosopher Georg Simmel (1858–1918).

What aestheticism ends up authorizing, for Lukács, is spiritual superficiality, which is now no longer distinguishable from lasting, deep, universal perception. With superficiality comes the appeal of diversity, plurality, and inconstancy of viewpoint. The tools of art – once signifying means – become self-justifying ends. At the same time, the ends of art are themselves only means: means to the creation or illustration of states of mind. Aestheticism is governed by an ethos of pleasure, sensuality, and mood. Its *idée fixe*, writes Lukács, is an apparently 'accidental and unanalyzed connection ... between the spectator and the object of his gaze' – a connection, incidentally, rigorously analysed at the time by the new disciplines of phenomenology and psychology. But Lukács is exclusively concerned with art; he does not take aestheticist science seriously. Aesthetic culture thus arose 'the moment this psychic activity was extended to the totality of life, when the totality of life became a succession of continuously changing moods, when objects ceased to exist because everything became merely an inducement to a mood. It arose when all constancy disappeared from life, because moods do not tolerate permanence and repetition; when all values vanished from life, because value is ascribed only to possibilities that occasion the mood ('Aesthetic Culture' [hereafter AC] 370–1). At this point how things make one feel becomes the proper measure of their value. At this point we get Gabriele D'Annunzio (also unnamed by Lukács), at least D'Annunzio as an ethos and myth, which is to say hedonism, irrationalism, will to power, exquisite sensibility, rhetorical effervescence, and an image of man as *imaginifico*. All experiences then become 'mere material in the hands of the uniquely sovereign artist. It is all one whether he paints a picture, writes a sonnet, or lives his life.' Ethics – the question of the *conduct* of life, or the conduct of life *as question* – relinquishes its function to aesthetics, to 'the art of life, making art out of life' (AC 371).

Rejections of the D'Annunzian myth were legion in the years surrounding the First World War, even if they were generally more ambivalent than Lukács's. There was, however, one intellectual who, also without naming D'Annunzio, was just as sweeping and categorical in his opposition. Carlo Michelstaedter, an Italian from the fringes of the Austro-Hungarian Empire, fully agreed with his compatriot about both the inherent insufficiencies of aestheticism and how to compensate them. Michelstaedter did not live long enough to develop his ideas into a systematic philosophy; he died at age twenty-three, leaving little more than his university dissertation, *La persuasione e la rettorica*. Yet this work resonates with the same passion and resolution of the pre-war Lukács, issuing into a defence of such abstractions as soul, form, persuasion, and tragic experience against their demonized, aestheticist opposites.

Read back to back with Lukács's 'Aesthetic Culture,' the *rettorica* denounced by Michelstaedter – the wiles of desire and moral shiftiness, the interpretive fallacies of language and signs, but apparently also such timeless failings in the structure of experience as becoming and change, anxiety and insecurity – appears to be a quality hypertrophied in the age the two thinkers inhabit. After all, it was post-Nietzschean philosophy that allowed for this shiftiness, emphasizing as it did that being is a play of becoming, where stability of knowledge is a chimera, where belief is an offshoot of desire and morality a crutch of self-interest. The 'benevolent and prudent' idol of his time, writes Michelstaeder, is 'the god of *philopsychia*' (a Platonic term: 'love of life'). The light this god provides to help us orient ourselves 'is *pleasure*' (*La persuasione*, 50), leading people to favour experiences that produce an adulatory echo of the only *fundamentum inconcussum* of Being which is the 'I':

E nello stesso tempo le *sue* cose che lo attorniano e aspettano il suo futuro, sono *l'unica realtà* assoluta indiscutibile – col suo bene e il suo male, il meglio e il peggio. Egli non dice: 'questo è per me', ma 'questo è'; non dice: 'questo mi piace', ma 'è buono' ... (*La persuasione*, 52)

[And at the same time the things of *his* that surround him and await his future are the *only* absolutely unquestionable *reality* – with its good and its evil, its better and its worse. He does not say: 'this is for me,' but 'this is'; he does not say 'this pleases me,' but 'this is good' ...]

In this 'rhetorical' manner of living, real is what serves one's interests and good what casuistically attaches to pleasure. Michelstaedter's rhetoricians are Lukács's aesthetes, taken by the sensations of things instead of their broader purposes, applying 'principles of artistic enjoyment – or better, a fraction of them' to life at large (AC 371). The ethical result is 'complete passivity,' 'enslavement to the moment,' 'inability to create or act' (AC 371).

What this rhetorical-aesthetic demeanour lacks is lasting intention, conviction, autonomous decision, deep knowledge of self and other. Michelstaedter calls it 'persuasion.' Persuaded types can be found throughout the pages of *La persuasione*: Socrates, Christ, Tolstoy, Heraclitus, Beethoven, and Leopardi – enough at least to convey a sense of their moral and imaginative high-mindedness. Not only are these figures endowed with a creative vision of human processes as a whole; they also accompany that vision with the courage for belief and the passion to give it form. Just how such form differs from the procedures of rhetoric is spelled out by Lukács.

Form, a key concept in the early Lukács, is an imaginative coordination of disparate sensations. It distills, selects, or abstracts a semantic unity to which they belong. Form conveys deep structures and patterns, the more resolutely the stronger and clearer its contours. Unlike labile signs and impressions, form presents a firm picture of being, steady enough to let its identities be perceived. The semiotics of such form becomes definitive, though its reach diminished, in Lukács's later aesthetics, especially in his doctrine of art as a revelation of individualities, types, and intellectual partisanship (see his 'Art and Objective Truth'). Here, instead, in the essay from 1910, Lukács's *formal* alternative to aesthetic decadence remains vague, described by terms more focused on the motivations or effects of form, such as power, mastery, domination, strength, and judgment (an interesting catalogue of these terms can be found on AC 372). The suspicion may easily arise that this anti-aestheticist platform is supported by nothing so much as a phobia of weakness, passivity, and feminization all too common in the era of Otto Weininger's *Sex and Character* (1903). Be that as it may, Lukács's essay speaks much less to the concrete qualities of (anti-aestheticist) form than to its raison d'être, characterized as ontological vision and moral direction. Form is both the origin and the *telos* of artistic creation, both its cause and objective. Indeed, it is the very flowering of the human spirit, arising from inner spiritual necessity like 'the unity of a growing plant' (AC 372). What is given features by form is 'the intensity of the will or the inner strength of the soul' (AC 375).

Form is thus the antithesis of mere rhetoric. Even as Lukács's discussion of form does not offer *formal*, or stylistic, alternatives to the arts of Impressionism and decadence, so it proposes an alternative *function* of art – namely, the articulation of a spiritual realm (the human self or truth) *underlying* perceptual impressions. Indeed, this is the only deep and worthwhile sense that the phrase 'aesthetic culture' can have in Lukács: 'the forming of the soul,' where the literal aesthete instead 'applies the concept of form to life' (AC 377). That is, the material of the aesthete's art is superficial: impressions, perceptions, moods of an empirical 'I.' When art truly plumbs innerness and subjectivity, however, claims Lukács, it reaches a domain that transcends all feelings and moods, a reality that is finally impersonal, external, and universal. That is why art in Lukács as well as in Michelstaedter can never stray far from the realm of the ethical – which is its working material. 'What is truly individual in the depths of one's soul goes beyond the mere individual,' writes Lukács (AC 376). Or, in the words of a close heir to the pre-Marxist Hungarian (Theodor Adorno), 'works of art, and that includes the so-called individualistic ones, speak the language of a "We," not of an "I"' (*Aesthetic Theory*, 240).[1]

What seems to be an *epistemological* opposition to aestheticism/rhetoric – to its narrow ontological reach – is therefore *moral*, where morality is understood not as a codification of conduct, but as a creative, imaginative stipulation of human motivation. Lukács and Michelstaedter deem the styles and practices they attack to be counterproductive of valuation. And how could it be otherwise, if rhetors view values as psychologically and culturally relative, as ciphers of fleeting appearance and self-interest? Growing as they do *out of* the instabilities of time, Michelstaedter and Lukács's artistic forms are also designed to *offset* those same instabilities, not to comply with their transitory logic. Belief, in art, fights the lures of opinion, the continual fascinations of the image. It seeks its own persuasion.

If this notion of art does not find a particularly sympathetic ear a hundred years later it is because we lean more readily to the positions of postmodernist thinkers like Gianni Vattimo to the effect that art does not 'establish what endures' as much as it loosens constrictions, weakens moral and ideological holds, or undoes firm visions of life. But on the eve of the First World War the stakes in the aesthetic debate were considerably higher than they are today. Art's impending break with its age-old functions of social instruction and communicable intention was to many an alarming prospect. 'Perhaps at no other time,' worried Lukács in 1910,

> has art meant so little as it does today to those people on whom culture depends. There is something deeply professionalized about the effects of art today: writers write for writers, and painters paint for painters – or rather for would-be writers and painters. They hardly have a 'message' (which they moreover refuse with conscious pride). Only the professionals may enjoy their values, and their main effects are confined to the garrets. [...] Soon people come to believe that art is not really necessary, or rather (how similar bourgeois contentment is to aesthetic hedonism!) that it is only for passing a few free hours pleasantly, for a pleasing thrill or a dulling caress of their tired nerves. (AC 372–3)

Easy as it is to recognize the one-sidedness of this portrait, it is just as easy to overlook the fact that Lukács's objections have continued unabated in one guise or another for a century. The question around the time of the First World War was whether contemporary art was squandering its ethical and philosophical potential; and if so, whether there was any way to recoup the loss. It was a question posed not by the avant-garde proper, which largely exacerbated the rift between aesthetics and ethics, but by figures on its fringes. In Italy those figures included Pirandello, Ungaretti, Montale, and a community of writers for *La Voce* in Florence.[2] Especially in that country, the eve of the war represented a stressful post-D'Annunzian moment, obliging all poets, novelists, and essayists to measure their styles against the aestheticism condemned by Lukács and epitomized by the work of Europe's most commanding bard.

II

The journal *La Voce* never hid the ethical motivations of its editorial choices. In fact, the entire rationale for this Florentine publication, founded by Prezzolini in 1908, was to exhort the arts to their broadest and most fundamental task: that of shaping culture. 'But what does "culture" mean?' Antonio Gramsci was to ask years later:

> Significa indubbiamente una coerente, unitaria [...] 'concezione della vita e dell'uomo', una 'religione laica', una filosofia che sia diventata appunto 'cultura', cioè abbia generato un'etica, un modo di vivere, una condotta civile e individuale. (Gramsci, 3: 2185–6)

> [Undoubtedly it signifies a coherent, unitary [...] 'conception of life and humanity,' a 'secular religion,' a philosophy that has indeed turned into 'culture,' which is to say, has generated an ethics, a manner of living, conduct that is both civic and individual.]

La Voce pursued aesthetic culture in the 'good' sense of *Bildung* – *coltura* – enlisting the best minds of the country to rethink the applications of poetry, morality, the visual arts, political systems, economy, psychological analysis, and sociology. The journal lacked an official philosophical credo; on the contrary, the very variety of its contributors, from Benedetto Croce to Giovanni Gentile and Prezzolini himself, rendered a monolithic stance such as Lukács's or Michelstaedter's anything but desirable. And yet within that discursive pluralism many *vociani* were no less idealistic in their purposes than the two ethicists, committed to furnishing their generation with an artistic mission and spiritual definition. To their minds, these were one and the same.

The *Voce* project inspired a series of philosophical charges against modernism, decadence, liberalism, and intellectual impressionism; in practice it also distilled itself into an insistence on the virtues of sincerity and authenticity in writing. From this followed the self-avowed vacillations, fragmentation, and heterogeneity of *vociani* texts; their studied suspension between poetry and prose; their effort to discover exemplary truths through the practice of *autobiografismo*. Creative works produced in this vein in the years between 1910 and 1912 ranged from Giovanni Papini's *Un uomo finito* [A Man Finished] to Scipio Slataper's *Il mio Carso* [My Carso], from Ardengo Soffici's *Lemmonio Boreo* to Piero Jahier's 'La famiglia povera' and 'Il paese della vacanze.' Here is a sample from the aphoristic exclamations of Giovanni Boine's *Frammenti* (1914–15):

28) Sedetti al tramonto su d'una soffice proda contro il sole a scaldarmi, ma si levò subito dopo un gelido vento e fu la notte.
29) Perché io sono triste ora? Ma perché io sono gioioso? Non intendo la ragione della notte e del giorno.
30) S'io godo della mia gioia e dico 'così ogni mia ora' ecco d'un tratto mi si leva dentro l'amarezza del pianto, come nebbia da una nera palude.
31) Come vuoi ch'io prometta se non so del domani? Non intendo che cosa sia promessa. (Boine 262)

[28) I sat at sunset on a soft bank across from the sun to warm myself, but immediately thereafter an icy wind rose up towards me and it was night.
29) Why am I unhappy now? Yet why am I joyful? I do not understand the reason of night and day.
30) If I take pleasure in my joy and say, 'thus each and every one of my hours,' why all of a sudden there rises up within me the bitterness of tears, like fog from a black swamp.
31) How do you want me to promise if I have no notion of tomorrow? I do not understand what a promise is.]

The interest of these earnestly titled 'fragments,' as of so many creative writings issuing from *La Voce*, lies in honesty and passion of conscience, in a tentative, questioning mood, in the effort to unify emotional and intellectual experience. Aesthetic practice no longer subsumes or sidesteps ethics by definition; on the contrary, it is summoned to stretch out beyond itself. The complexities that follow from this project can be sensed from the need of Boine's protagonist, at the end of the novel *Il peccato* [Sin] (1914), to reconcile the contradictions between dynamic, irrational being and firm, understandable form:

Egli ondeggiava fra questa abbondante tragico-gioiosa concezione del mondo come di uno scatenato torrente; tripudio violento e barbarico dove la misura è fuor della misura come in una musica dove la melodia ti nasca dal disaccordo cozzante [...] ondeggiava fra questo esaltamento baccante ed un attento, preciso governo dell'anima, un quasi avaro sempre cosciente sforzo di ordine. Spiritualizzare fino alla sillaba, controllare ogni tuo atto, non disperdere nulla come se d'ogni cosa tu dovessi in giudizio dar conto: fabbricare fuscello a fuscello, economizzare dentro a te lentamente lo Spirito. (Boine, 71)

[He wavered between this abundant tragic-joyous conception of the world as of an unleashed torrent; a violent and barbaric jubilation where limits are without limit as in a music whose melody is born from clashing discord [...] he wavered between this Bacchic exaltation and an attentive, precise management of the soul, an almost stingy, ever conscious effort at order. To spiritualize right up to the syllable, to control each one of your acts, to squander nothing as though, in judgment, you had to give an account of each thing: to construct straw by straw, economize slowly within you the Spirit.]

This 'abundant' conception of the world is that of an 'unleashed torrent' where the young man is compelled to engage in a 'conscious effort at order,' seeking a 'precise management of the soul.' The entire responsibility is then implicitly transferred over, in the guise of a duty, to the 'you' of the reader. The very suspension of this narrative ending marks out the new tasks of ethics.

Another Vocian moralist, as literary history has chosen to call them, finds his signature style in the opening rather than closing words of his main work. Before Scipio Slataper allows *Il mio Carso* (1912) to get underway, he must rehearse his quest for a style:

Vorrei dirvi: Sono nato in Carso, in una casupola col tetto di paglia annerita dalle piove e dal fumo. C'era un cane spelacchiato e rauco, due oche infanghite sotto il ventre, una zappa, una vanga, e dal mucchio di concio quasi senza strame scolavano, dopo la piova, canaletti di succo brunastro.

Vorrei dirvi: Sono nato in Croazia, nella grande foresta di roveri. D'inverno tutto era bianco di neve, la porta non si poteva aprire che a pertugio, e la notte sentivo urlare i lupi. Mamma m'infagottava con cenci le mani gonfie e rosse, e io mi buttavo sul focolaio frignando per il freddo.

Vorrei dirvi: Sono nato nella pianura morava e correvo come una lepre per i lunghi solchi, levando le cornacchie crocidanti. Mi buttavo a pancia a terra, sradicavo una barbabietola e la rosicavo terrosa. Poi son venuto qui, ho tentato di addomesticarmi, ho imparato l'italiano, ho scelto gli amici fra i giovani più colti; – ma presto devo tornare in patria perché qui sto molto male. (Slataper 37)

[I would like to tell you: I was born in the Carso, in a cabin with a straw roof blackened by rain and smoke. There was a raspy and raucous dog, two geese muddied at the belly, a hoe, a spade, and from the nearly strawless pile of manure little channels of brownish juice ran off after the rain.

I would like to tell you: I was born in Croatia, in the great oak forest. In winter everything was white with snow, you couldn't open the door but a crack, and at night I heard the cries of wolves. Mother bundled my swollen red hands with rags, and I threw myself at the fireplace whimpering from the cold.

I would like to tell you: I was born in the Moravian plains and ran like a hare along the long furrows, raising croaking crows to flight. I threw myself belly first to the ground, tore out a beetroot and gnawed it dirt and all. Then I came here, tried to domesticate myself, learned Italian, chose the most educated youths for friends; – but soon I must go back to my homeland for here I am fairing very ill.]

If you take away the intrusions of the *vorrei dirvi*, the narrative reads as a precious, sophisticated, aestheticist sensorium of childhood experiences. But by the fourth paragraph this litany of sensuous descriptions of a mythically natural childhood comes to rest in the decision to reject this same mode of presentation. To pursue such a manner of writing, Slataper suggests, would be to allow himself inordinate poetic licence and make him lose his true reader:

Vorrei ingannarvi, ma non mi credereste. Voi siete scaltri e sagaci. Voi capireste subito che sono un povero italiano che cerca d'imbarbarire le sue solitarie preoccupazioni. È meglio ch'io confessi d'esservi fratello ... (Slataper 37–8)

[I would like to deceive you, but you wouldn't believe me. You are sly and wise. You would immediately understand that I am a poor Italian trying to render barbaric his solitary worries. Better that I should confess to being your brother ...]

This transformation of *dirvi* into *ingannarvi* is an extended, self-conscious clearing of the throat. It is a preterition amounting to the claim that 'I *could* give my life a D'Annunzian cast, but I won't.' (As with Boine, the intertexual significance of the word *barbarico* is overdetermined.) 'Ma la lingua batte dove il dente duole [The tongue prods the tooth that hurts],' as they say, for throughout *Il mio Carso* the Triestine never quits wavering between sensational conceits and more humble efforts to bare the ostensibly simply truths of his soul. Like Michelstaedter, Slataper does not live long enough to seize on a 'method' for the ethico-aesthetic program he hesitatingly maps out in his autobiography; he dies on the front in 1915. The autobiography remains his *Bildungsroman*, telling us how he got where he currently is, no less than his palinode, wending a way between proclivities to self-indulgence and stoic commitments to suprapersonal responsibilities. By the end of the work Slataper no longer addresses the readers of the opening pages in a desiring, optative mood (*vorrei dirvi*) but in a resolute, communal, declarative sentence: *vogliamo amare e lavorare* [we want to love and work]. And yet the tension between aestheticist desire and intellectual conviction has hardly been laid to rest:

> Ah, fratelli come sarebbe bello poter esser sicuri e superbi, e godere della propria intelligenza, saccheggiare i grandi campi rigogliosi con la giovane forza, e sapere e comandare e possedere! Ma noi, tesi di orgoglio, con il cuore che ci scotta di vergogna, vi tendiamo la mano, e vi preghiamo d'esser giusti con noi come noi cerchiami di esser giusti con voi. Perché noi vi amiamo, fratelli, e speriamo che ci amerete. Noi vogliamo amare e lavorare. (Slataper 152–53)

> [Ah, brothers, how beautiful it would be to be able to be firm and haughty, and enjoy one's own intelligence, plunder the great luxuriant fields with one's youthful strength, and know and command and possess! But we, filled with pride, seared by our hearts in shame, offer you our hand, and beg you to be fair with us as we try to be fair with you. For we love you, brothers, and hope you will love us. We want to love and work.]

Henceforth – the writer would like to believe – his life will leave intemperate self-assertion behind for love and work. But the rhetoric is still one of desire (*bello, amare*), even if the new object of desire is ethical conviction and spiritual pietism, of a type not altogether different from what we find in Michelstaedter and the Lukács of 'On Poverty of Spirit' (1911; now in *The Lukács Reader*). As the initial, first person singular of *Il mio Carso* cedes to an all-encompassing plural (*noi*, doubled by 'brothers'), the book consciously traces 'the passage from an aestheticist and individualist idea of existence to an ethical vision of social relations and roles' (Damiani's note; Slataper 37–8).

Stylistically remote though the poets Ungaretti and Montale are from the moralists of *La Voce*, they are even more anti-aestheticist. First, the representative status of their poetry – what type of person it claims to exemplify, to whom and to what purpose it speaks – is extremely pared down. The authorial persona acts neither as a medium of super-abundant imagination (the D'Annunzian model) nor as a generational exemplum (Slataper and Boine). Rather, it denotes a precise, literal, fragile being in dramatic confrontation with the overwhelming effects of phenomenal presence. Even when the result is called *godimento* [pleasure], as in the following poem by Ungaretti, and is as transcendent as any pleasure in D'Annunzio, it has a decidedly alarming effect:

Mi sento la febbre
di questa
piena di luce

Accolgo questa
giornata come
il frutto che si addolcisce

Avrò
stanotte
un rimorso come un
latrato
perso nel
deserto ('Godimento,' Ungaretti, *Vita d'un uomo* 70)

[I feel the fever
of this
flood of light

I gather this
day like
fruit that sweetens
Tonight
my remorse
will be like a
dog's bark
lost in the
desert] (Ungaretti, *Selected Poems* 45)

The distance Ungaretti assumes from 'aesthetic' occasions of poetry can be further sensed by juxtaposing the links he and the older bard draw between their utterances and nature. D'Annunzio writes:

I miei carmi son prole
delle foreste,
altri dell'onde,
altri delle arene,
altri del Sole,
altri del vento Argeste
Le mie parole
sono profonde
come le radici
terrene
altre serene
come i firmamenti
... ('Le stirpi canore,' D'Annunzio 411–12)

[My songs are offspring
of the forest,
others of the waves,
others of the sands,
others of the Sun,
others of the Mistral wind
My words
are deep
as the earthly
roots
others serene
as the firmament
...]

and goes on to add another ten correlatives. Ungaretti writes:

Come questa pietra
del San Michele
così fredda
così dura
così prosciugata
così refrattaria
così totalmente
disanimata

Come questa pietra
è il mio pianto
che non si vede

la morte
si sconta
vivendo ('Sono una creatura,' Ungaretti, *Vita d'un uomo* 41)

[Like this stone
of S. Michele
so cold
so hard
so dried
so totally
dispirited

Like this stone
is my lament
that is not seen

Death is
paid off
by living] (Ungaretti, *Selected Poems*, trans. 23)

To paraphrase a comparison I have drawn elsewhere ('D'Annunzio's Poetics'), the semantic results could hardly be more dissimilar. In likening his voice to natural phenomena, Ungaretti singles out a cold, hard inanimate rock. D'Annunzio speaks of his voice through signs already invested with poetic significance. Ungaretti conceives of his speech as *pianto*, D'Annunzio as *canto*. The natural counterparts of Ungaretti's poetry are refractory and inanimate; D'Annunzio's are exquisite, vigorous, vague, and pungent (*prole delle foreste, ispide, vergini, funebri*). Ungaretti compares his cry – or rather the suppression of his cry – to one clear and distinct object. D'Annunzio compares his songs not to a single precise phenomenon but to eighteen nebulous ones (*firmamenti, dumi confusi, rugiade dei cieli, asfodeli dell'Ade*). Here lie two wholly different ontologies of poetic perception. For Ungaretti the phenomenal world is a signifying end in itself (even if a virtually unfathomable one); for D'Annunzio it is a signifying means. The status of one voice is antithetical to the other.

Montale's scriptorial project is even more anxious than Ungaretti's. It aims at identifying, through those *ossi di seppia* [cuttlefish bones] that are his poems, the poet's relationship with a speechless time and place. Everything in Montale boils down to a question of essence, or of essential questionability: how to exist, how to act, how to speak up for the taciturn foundations of the material world. Nothing could be more foreign to the dull, raw, inexplicable events that this poet feels called on to witness, and to his sense of the feckless nature of writing, than the suggestive, allusive, and gratifying impressions of the aestheticists. Not incidentally, in Ungaretti and Montale the question of *how* to speak is as perplexing as that of what to say; and this so-called hermetic dilemma – which may be the *sine qua non* of creative writing pure and simple – is apparently the least troublesome question of all to the voluble aestheticist.

The subjectivity of Montale and Ungaretti is less secure than D'Annunzio's. Hovering above the shocks of the First World War, it is easily wounded, elegiac, mistrustful of all empirical effects. A proto-existentialist account of artistic motivation like that of Lukács applies far better to these poets than D'Annunzio: The modern artist wrests form from a confrontation with 'his own rootlessness, his incoherent and disconnected existence, and the unbearableness of such a life as his, the only content of which could be to express something, the deepest commonality with other people' (AC 374). The driving problem here, as in Ungaretti and Montale, is *how* to experience one's subjectivity, how to experience and express it – in the interests of public relevance.

The problematic was never far from the mind of Luigi Pirandello, whose 'being-in-the-world' was even more removed from the integrities of aestheticism than were the lyrical concentrations of an empty 'I.' Split and deluded, divorced from its every pragmatic function, the subjectivity of Pirandellian characters is utterly unable to entrust itself to moods, sensations, and turns of phrase. Phenomenal appearances prove so unreliable that they threaten the very foundations of aesthetic creation. Accordingly, the categorical imperative of the Sicilian's writing is negative: It operates to dismantle human scripts of significance (and then enable, if possible, less illusory intellectual constructions). The prime interest of Pirandellian writing is to uncover those problems *repressed* by aesthetics – for example, the mechanics of interpersonal understanding, the continuity of perception from moment to moment, irreconcilable intellectual claims – that *complicate* the practice of ethics.

After this act of dismantling, the task that remains is to 'rewrite the script.' A life so metaphysically conflicted as to place no store in individual intuition requires a complex and very supple new hermeneutic. This need to rewrite the script, which is implicitly affirmed by all the other post-D'Annunzian writers discussed so far – shows that even one of the least aestheticist Italian writers of the century still harbours the opponent within him. For by definition this rewriting is an aesthetic operation, even if now, as Lukács advises, it should be applied to the plotting of a life rather than an articulation of mood. Despite appearances, we are, with Pirandello, Montale, Ungaretti, Slataper, Boine, and Michelstaedter, in the company of aestheticists after all. In ways that have yet to be analysed, their battle against aestheticism is waged from within.

III

Pirandello's Henry IV, Mattia Pascal, and 'six characters in search of an author' are fixated on an operation that Michelstaedter and Lukács would like to view as aestheticism's opposite but is not. The higher 'form' after which these characters hanker is essentially the most pliant possible guise of Lukács's 'soul,' a proper articulation of relations between self and fluctuant world. Ultimately this project is just as subjectivist as what it criticizes: It assigns the responsibility of self- and world-making to individual, creative egos, as though it were all a matter of artistic creation.

How was it, Lukács reasons, that 'the admirers of "form" killed form, the priests of *l'art pour l'art* paralyzed art' (AC 372)? It happened because these admirers and priests 'were not aesthetes enough, not aesthetes in a sufficiently deep and consistent way ... they did not apply the essence of art to life' (AC 377). They killed form by giving up its highest ambition. 'Change your life!' – that, as Rilke and Sartre will later say, is the ultimate injunction of art. It is not ethics that should collapse into aesthetics, but vice versa. Notwithstanding their virtuosity in forming 'art out of life,' nineteenth-century aesthetes utterly abandoned the 'heroism of forming oneself' (AC 378).

Different though this formation of self might be from a mere voicing of moods, desires, and imaginative impressions, both ideas follow one and the same imperative to treat experience in the manner of art. In one case the imperative suscitates a spirit of revelry, in the other the feeling of a limitless burden. Each harkens to different verses in the 'master text' of aestheticism which are the works of Nietzsche: dance and freeplay, on the one hand, the weight of self-and-world positing, on the other. The new aversion, then, is to the *values* of aestheticism, not the *aestheticism* of values, which are still deemed the province of art. The procedural difference of Lukács's generation vis-à-vis that of impressionists and decadents lies in *what* they would have artists come to terms with – not the relativities and mobilities of reality but its intractabilities, its unarticulated teleologies, the objectives and orders without which it is not worth living. 'The aesthetes' world view,' states Lukács, 'is oblivious of the disharmony of things and their embittered struggles' (*Lukács Reader* 150). The late-nineteenth-century fascination with perceptual differences has succeeded only in making everything in the world undifferentiated and indifferent; 'since we "understand and empathize" with everything, there are no longer any irreconcilable conflicts' (*Lukács Reader* 150). For Lukács and Michelstaedter, instead, these conflicts are the tragic substance of the projects of persuasion/form. If formation of self and world is not to be reduced to a chimera, it must be predicated on an irreducible *dissonance* between self and world. It must also acknowledge that art has no means to abolish or harmonize that dissonance. All it can do, perhaps, is make the strife comprehensible, clarifying the tasks it sets.

Post-aestheticist form is thus charged with grappling with intellectual and existential knots. This may explain why self-formation remains an insoluble dilemma in writers like Pirandello. In real historical dramas the play of masks and perspectives and delusions can never come to rest; it constitutes the very tension of life, an ethical problem that art must call to mind.

This 'ulterior aestheticism' of writers in Lukács's generation must be measured by the practice of each. It is clear, for example, that the *vociani*'s program of putting imagination in the service of cultural resurgence amounts to a Nietzschean project to apply one's artistry to the conduct of history (or essentially a more sober form of D'Annunzianism). It is even harder to exclude Ungaretti and Montale from the aestheticist camp in light of the chosen mode of their *poiesis*. Is not the lyric poet constitutionally responsive to the very moods, sensations, and nuances of each 'art of surfaces' reproved by Lukács (AC 379)? This is why Lukács gravitates towards novelists and playwrights for true examples of form (Dostoevsky, Thomas Mann, Shakespeare, Paul Ernst), or, like Michelstaedter, towards mystics and romantics (Meister Eckhart, Schiller, Keats, and the late Michelangelo). From Michelstaedter's perspective it is hard to understand how any poet could escape the charge of being irrecuperably committed to rhetoric. Assuming that Michelstaedter did allow for poetic persuasion (and he does value Leopardi and Petrarch, though primarily for their philosophical thought), and assuming that Ungaretti and Montale did pass his test, one would still want to know how that happens. The scriptorial 'I' of Ungaretti may be embarked on a more strenuous project than the D'Annunzian one, conceiving of itself *more* as a project, and less as a given; its world may be harder and more laden with disturbance. Yet the art of both poets follows one and the same rule of semantic epiphany, where the 'truth' of each fleeting instant – whether deep or shallow, negative or positive, withholding or manifest – is conveyed through a surface (the word, a mere eloquent word).

Montale presents a simpler but more puzzling case. Explicitly denouncing the effusive, exotic rhetoric of the D'Annunzian model as well as its vatic, romantic claims (for example, in 'I limoni'), he still does not turn, Mengaldo notes, to a crepuscular alternative ('aestheticist' in its very pretensions of anti-aestheticism, an anti-poetry dialectically enslaved to the elevated style it overturns). Nor does Montale follow Lukács's recommendations, cultivating more universal and lasting forms than those of impressionistic verse. Clear and definitive form is precisely what this poet considers himself *least able* to achieve ('Non chiederci la parola che squadri da ogni lato/ l'animo nostro informe ... [Don't ask me for words that might define / our formless soul ...]' Montale 40–1). If soul by definition is what possesses no form of its own, then it can only submit to one at the cost of irremediable distortion. In Montale the final and true object of poetic speech remains extralinguistic. He is marooned in negative aesthetics: 'Codesto solo oggi possiamo dirti, / ciò che *non* siamo, ciò che *non* vogliamo [All we can tell you now is this: / what we are *not*, what we do *not* want]' (ibid.).

The quarrel against aestheticism ultimately spares no sign or form whatsoever. Its destiny is unspeakability, unformability. And this implication is deeply imbedded in Lukács's and Michelstaedter's own notions of form and persuasion, whose contents are so rarefied as to lie all but beyond the reach of representation. They can never be more than *partially* communicated (through rhetoric), which also means betrayed.

IV

What is taking shape here is not a deconstruction, or even a critique of the critique. It is a logic imbedded in the travails of aesthetic theory at a particular moment in time. Even if anti-aestheticism arises *out of* aestheticism – and runs into an aporia – it is not thereby cancelled out. It preserves its own measure of integrity. It possesses, as we have already found, its own forms of practice. Instead of the dithyrambic, phenomenological adventures of the decadents, we get writings that are ethically knotted, speleological, analytic. Language moves vertically more than horizontally. Semantics becomes difficult, signs abysmal. Words participate not in a *pleroma* of being but a vacuum; they are caught up in a 'fall' in which poems turn out to be happy swerves (Lucretius's *clinamen*). Post-aestheticists are riveted by the covertness and withheldness of being, the experience of truth as *a-letheia* (Heidegger). Historical singularities and incommensurabilities replace the aesthetes' interchangeabilities and synonymies, the symbolists' assimilations, ventriloquisms, and synaesthesias. The bases are also laid for a whole series of new problems in ethics (addressed most in keeping with this new spirit by Ludwig Wittgenstein).

How should we understand these new practices if they aspire neither to the subjective impressionism of the decadents nor to the domineering new classicism advocated by Lukács and Michelstaedter? They wend a third way between them. Indeed, this third formal configuration is intuited by Lukács himself at the end of the essay that concerns us here. After praising Michelangelo for doing exactly what Lukács has proposed throughout the piece – namely, converting 'the soul of the marble' into the form of a statue – he makes a surprising confession: Twentieth-century soul can find no such equivalence in form. That was a privilege of bygone times, when things perhaps stood stiller, or experience was easier to understand. In the current era, instead, 'the forming of the soul' can never be 'a final product but [only] an endless process' (AC 377). It has been a long time, Lukács comments, since one could honestly believe in the 'creative precedence of art over culture' and the 'soul's world-moving power. [...] Today such a belief is possible only at the price of shutting one's eyes, at the cost of narrow-mindedness or conscious self-deception [...] today, after all we know, any attempt to realize this illusion, once seemingly believable, must become comic' (AC 375).

Formal closure is out of reach. But if that is so, what is Lukács advocating in the way of post-aestheticist practice? To all appearances he is asking that art and life be practiced *as though* world-moving forms were still achievable. Those dedicated to the 'heroism of forming oneself,' or to voicing the relation between life and self, lack such formative power and they know it. Yet that changes nothing in their goal. Such people 'create no culture, but live life so as to deserve culture. Their sphere of life could be best defined by one of Kant's deepest categories, the "as if," the "als ob"'; what they practice is a 'heroism without expectation,' an unfulfillable motivation that 'sanctifies life' (AC 378). Beneath the edifying tones of these words lies this intuition: The true partisan of form is one who, disabused of all romantic illusions, must be viewed as an essayist – pursuing a project whose goal, form, is out of reach. No doubt that is why in the same year as 'Aesthetic Culture' Lukács adds a crucial new study to his aesthetic investigations, penning a preface to his *Soul and Form* called 'The Essay as Form.'[3] At this stage in his thinking, Lukács's most pondered account of form sees it as the production of a relentless commitment to an unappeasable principle of formation, a commitment which cannot settle on its object of vision any more than it can choose its appropriate lens. Neither poem nor play nor novel, this formative process can only be called an essay – a tentative, ongoing formulation, an open, inconclusive attempt, a search for the proper means and ends of knowledge.

How well does this paradigm fit the work of Pirandello, Ungaretti, and others? Does their work, too, amount to a struggle *on behalf of* form, endlessly shuffling between fluctuant intuition and impliant discursive moulds? On this score Pirandello is very explicit. He situates his work at the very junction of experience and language (which he terms life and form). The practical result is that instead of writing conventional, mimetic drama he writes a drama of *seeking* the conventions (e.g., *Six Characters in Search of an Author*). Instead of writing a fictional biography – say, of a man called Mattia Pascal – he writes of the man's *efforts* to write a biography. Similar endeavors occur in almost all his mature works, each probing and essaying how thought might best be brought to expression, how truth can be articulated if it defies every form it is given.

Montale, too, notwithstanding his distance from both D'Annunzio and Lukács, writes eloquently about the space between them – of the comfortless search for a credible idiom, of unyielding burdens of understanding, of poetic sallies into regions of intellectual unclarity ('Il fuoco che non si smorza/ per me si chiamò: ignoranza [the name of unquenched fire / for me was – *ignorance*]' from 'Ciò che di me sapeste,' Montale 54–5). With Slataper, Ungaretti, and others of their tragic generation one can find comparable indications of this same intellectual intermediacy. They stand at the very border between form and flux, in that trench that *divides* persuasion from rhetoric, intuition from expression, speechless happening from articulate meaning. This intermediate locus – which no modernist art escapes, but to which some closes its eyes – is a type of scriptorial no man's land. It measures up to the distance of its intellectual ambition no less than to that of the shelters it has abandoned. Here, at the very border of hostile territories, is where an essayistic art takes up its position, represented by many post-D'Annunzian writers in Italy and other countries who came of age around the First World War.

NOTES

1 Incidentally, Adorno's only reference to D'Annunzio in his vast *Aesthetic Theory* bolsters the Lukácsian polemic against aestheticism: The 'commodity character (which gave art works the illusion of a being in themselves) ... was achieved ... by people like Oscar Wilde, Gabriele D'Annunzio and Maurice Maeterlinck – all of them precursors of the culture industry. With the growth of subjective differentiation and the intensification and expansion of aesthetic stimuli came the shift to market-oriented cultural production. Attuning art to ephemeral individual responses meant allying it with reification. As art became more and more similar to physical subjectivity, it moved more and more away from objectivity, ingratiating itself with the public. To that extent, the code-word of *l'art pour l'art* is the opposite of what it claims to be' (339).

2 As it turns out, both Michelstaedter and Lukács were active in Florence in the same years as the *Voce* group – in 1906–9 and 1911, respectively. In fact, Lukács and his friend Lajos Fülep founded the Hungarian journal *A Szellem* (1911) on the model of the admired *Leonardo*, the brainchild of Giuseppe Prezzolini and Giovanni Papini, with whom Fülep and Lukács were in contact. See Kadarkay's biography and Lukács's *Epistolario*.

3 A comment by the eighty-six-year-old Lukács in 1971 about his commitment to essay writing reaffirms its intermediate function between formal closure and aestheticist multiplicity. It is around 1908, he notes, that his 'period of essay writing begins. My need: to grasp the many-sidedness of the phenomena (which do not yield to abstract theories). A feeling for the simultaneity of the various aspects of individual phenomena and the wish to seek out non-mechanical ways of connecting them with broad general substances (totalities).' This essayism, he wants it known, bespoke 'not a rapprochement with the dominant (in many ways, of course, positivist)

impressionism, indeed rather a sharpening of the contrast, because in the final analysis I aimed at objectivity (a much more emphatic stress on laws) ... my argument went directly against impressionism (i.e. modern subjectivism)' (Lukács, *Record of a Life* 150).

WORKS CITED

Adamson, Walter L. *Avant-Garde Florence: From Modernism to Fascism.* Cambridge.: Harvard UP, 1993.

Adorno, T.W. *Aesthetic Theory.* Ed. Gretel Adorno and Rolf Tiedemann. Trans. C. Lenhardt. London and New York: Routledge & Kegan Paul, 1986.

Anceschi, Luciano. *Da Ungaretti a D'Annunzio.* Milan: Il Saggiatore, 1976.

Arato, Andrew, and Paul Breines. *The Young Lukács and the Origins of Western Marxism.* New York: Seabury P, 1979.

Bini, Daniela. *Carlo Michelstaedter and the Failure of Language.* Gainesville: UP of Florida, 1992.

Bobbio, Norberto. *La filosofia del decadentismo.* Turin: Chiantore, 1944.

Boine, Giovanni. *Il peccato, Plausi e botte, Frantumi, altri scritti.* Ed. Davide Puccini. Milan: Garzanti, 1983.

D'Annunzio, Gabriele. *Poesie.* Ed. Federico Roncoroni. Milan: Garzanti, 1978.

Gramsci, Antonio. *Quaderni del carcere.* Ed. Valentino Gerratana. 4 vols. Turin: Einaudi, 1975.

Harrison, Thomas. 'D'Annunzio's Poetics: The Orphic Conceit.' *Annali d'Italianistica* 5 (1987): 60–73.

– *Essayism: Conrad, Musil & Pirandello.* Baltimore and London: Johns Hopkins UP, 1992.

– *1910: The Emancipation of Dissonance.* Berkeley: U of California P, 1996.

Kadarkay, Arpad. *Georg Lukács: Life, Thought, and Politics.* Cambridge, MA, and Oxford, UK: Blackwell, 1991.

Lukács, Georg. 'Aesthetic Culture.' *Yale Journal of Criticism*, vol. 2, no. 2 (1998): 365–79. The essay is also included in *The Lukács Reader*, 146–59. I have amended some of my citations (from the former translation) after consulting the latter.

– 'Art and Objective Truth.' In *Writer and Critic and Other Essays.* New York: Grosset & Dunlap, 1970. 25–60.

– *Epistolario 1902–1917.* Ed. Eva Karadi and Eva Fekete. Trans. Alberto Scarponi. Rome: Riuniti, 1984.

– *The Lukács Reader.* Ed. Arpad Kadarkay. Oxford: Blackwell, 1995.

– *Record of a Life: An Autobiographical Sketch*. Ed. István Eörsi. Trans. Rodney Livingstone. London: Verso, 1983.
– *Soul and Form*. Trans. Anna Bostock. Cambridge: MIT Press, 1974.
Michelstaedter, Carlo. *La persuasione e la rettorica*. Ed. Sergio Campailla. Milan: Adelphi, 1982.
Mengaldo, Pier Vincenzo. *La tradizione del Novecento: Da D'Annunzio a Montale*. Milan: Feltrinelli, 1975.
Montale, Eugenio. *Cuttlefish Bones*. Trans. William Arrowsmith. New York and London: Norton, 1994.
Prezzolini, Giuseppe, Emilio Gentile, and Vanni Scheiwiller, eds. *La Voce 1908–1913: Cronaca, antologia e fortuna di una rivista*. Milan: Rusconi, 1974.
Rilke, Rainer Maria. *Duino Elegies*. With English translations by C.F. MacIntyre. Berkeley: U of California P, 1961.
Sartre, Jean-Paul. *Qu'est-ce que la littérature?* Paris: Gallimard, 1948.
Slataper, Scipio. *Il mio Carso*. Ed. Roberto Damiani. Trieste: Edizioni 'Italo Svevo,' 1988.
Ungaretti, Giuseppe. *Selected Poems*. Trans. and ed. Allen Mandelbaum. Ithaca and London: Cornell UP, 1975.
– *Vita d'un uomo. Tutte le poesie*. Ed. Leone Piccioni. Milan: Mondadori, 1969.
Vattimo, Gianni. 'The Shattering of the Poetic Word.' *The Favorite Malice: Ontology and Reference in Contemporary Italian Poetry*. Ed. and trans. Thomas Harrison. New York: Out of London P, 1983. 223–35.
Weininger, Otto. *Sex and Character*. New York: AMS Press, 1975.

6 Transtextual Patterns: Guido Gozzano Between Epic and Elegy in 'Goa: "La Dourada"'

CRISTINA DELLA COLETTA

Quipping about George Orwell's 'equals,' Gerard Genette once argued that if all literary works are hypertextual, some are definitely more so than others (9). Defined as 'any relationship uniting a text B [...] to an earlier text A' (5), hypertextuality is, in Genette's taxonomy, a subcategory of transtextuality, which he more broadly identifies as 'the textual transcendence of the text [...] all that sets the text in a relationship, whether obvious or concealed, with other texts' (1).[1] Guido Gozzano's Indian narratives, with their wealth of direct and indirect references to a common literary patrimony, belong to Genette's category of quintessentially transtextual works. Published in several newspapers and periodicals between 1914 and 1916, the majority of these narratives became part of a volume entitled *Verso la cuna del mondo: Lettere dall'India*, which Giuseppe Antonio Borgese edited and published in 1917, shortly after Gozzano's death.[2] If, in the wake of Borgese's philological rigour, critics have identified the provenance of most of Gozzano's borrowings, his borrowing strategies as well as these strategies' ideological implications remain unexplored.[3]

Concentrating on one of Gozzano's Indian narratives, 'Goa: "La Dourada,"' I shall examine how Gozzano self-consciously exploited the notion of literature's inherent transtextuality.[4] By direct quotations and erudite allusions (the intertextual level, in Genette's definition), Gozzano pays homage to numerous literary models, while submitting some of the cited or evoked texts to the transformative powers of parody. Parody, in Gozzano, implies a commentary on the text or the genre that is being parodied: a kind of 'criticism in action' (Genette's metatext) that spans beyond textual analysis to contain other art forms, such as architecture and painting. The massive presence of other texts

within 'Goa: "La Dourada,"' a narrative devoted to the writer/
traveller's first encounter with Goa, raises a provocative question: What
is the place of novelty and exotic distance, both experientially and
textually, in the modernist sensibility? While Gozzano argues that all
writing is essentially rewriting, and that unique and original experiences are no longer accessible in the modern world, he also contends
that this sense of novelty and distance can be experienced in a mediated, yet ultimately contradictory manner, through other people's
words.

Gozzano's engagement with Luis de Camões's epic poem, *The
Lusiads*, reveals how modern readers can imaginatively relish, yet must
analytically overturn, the original scope of the epic genre, that of sing-
ing the heroic beginnings of nations and heroes. Gozzano's own
counter-epic, which describes his wanderings in the old city of Goa,
exploits parody to both evoke and dismantle the epic paradigm on
thematic as well as formal levels. However, Gozzano is unable to fully
embrace the pluralistic and anti-authoritarian implications of his own
parodic move: while bluntly reversing them, Gozzano remains nostalgically attached to the concepts of purity, originality, and absolute
distance, of the epic genre. To overcome his own predicament, Gozzano
abandons epic altogether and chooses the elegy of the defeated, rather
than the victors' epic song, as the only apt tune for modernity. No
longer tempted by the disruptive powers of parody, Gozzano ends up
admitting that it is through mere repetition and borrowed words that
he can vicariously recover the sense of distance, the *aura*, of a city
which remembers, with sadness and nostalgia, the great and the powerful of a glorious age which has long disappeared. A victim of his
own contradictions, Gozzano concludes his narrative quest for 'the
sense of novelty' ('il senso della *cosa nuova*' 20) and for exotic distance
with an act of homage: by repeating verbatim a sonnet by José Maria
De Heredia, which he imagines devoted to Goa's melancholic backward gaze at its monumental past, Gozzano glosses over the unre-
solved and paradoxical status of novelty in the modernist canon.

Although based on his 1912 trip to India, Gozzano's Indian narratives demonstrate that, for him, India is not so much a concrete space
to be experienced in the first person as a literary construction to be
discovered, primarily, in other people's books. The 'discovery' of India, in other words, does not proceed from the unmediated contact
between the European intellectual and a specific ethnographic and

geographic reality. Rather, it results from this intellectual's journey across the broad regions of the exotic imagination, and produces a fertile textual space where the creative energies of various generations of Western interpreters are compelled to intersect. At the frontier between reality and invention, Gozzano's India demonstrates that it can be known only in a mediated manner, as the place of an encounter between direct experience and literary appropriation.[5] India, for Gozzano, remains an experience in the second degree, which inspires him to create a verbal mosaic made with the tesserae extracted from various narrative texts.

Catalyst of diffused ideological orientations and elegant popularizer of assorted cultural materials, Gozzano sees India as an open page waiting to be rewritten: a palimpsest, accessible only to those who are able to read through the layers and extrapolate new meanings from the subtle variations on the already said.[6] Flaunting, then, what Philippe Lejeune would term the palimpsestuous nature of writing, Gozzano opens his piece on Goa by explicitly tracing some important textual coordinates:

Andare a Goa, perché? I perché sono molti, tutti indefinibili, quasi inconfessabili; parlano soltanto alla mia intima nostalgia di sognatore vagabondo. Perché Goa non è ricordata da Cook, né da Loti, perché nessuna società di navigazione vi fa scalo, perché mi spinge verso di lei un sonetto di de Heredia, indimenticabile. (19)

[Go to Goa? Why? There are many reasons, all indefinable, indeed almost impossible to admit; they simply speak to my deepest longings as a wandering dreamer. Because Goa is not mentioned by Cook or Loti; because it is the port of call for no shipping company; because an unforgettable sonnet by Heredia urges me thither.] (Marinelli 76)[7]

Gozzano's narrative journey starts out by refuting his two most obvious narrative models. The first is the model provided by the famous Cook tourist guidebooks, which supply Gozzano with all the practical, extratextual references to places, itineraries, locations: a gold mine of concrete data on which to construct his often forged real-life itineraries.[8] The second model, which stands in opposition to the first, is that repository of exotic descriptions and stylistic refinements which constitutes the most massive intertextual presence in all of Gozzano's

Indian narratives, Pierre Loti's *L'Inde (sans les Anglais)*. Gozzano's journey to Goa, then, appears to find its inspiration in personal, nostalgic reminiscences:

> [...] pochi nomi turbavano la mia fantasia adolescente quanto il nome di Goa: Goa la Dourada.
> Oh! Visitata cento volte con la matita, durante le interminabili lezioni di matematica, con l'atlante aperto tra il banco e le ginocchia. [...] Il viaggio sull'atlante mi pare la realtà viva, e pallida fantasia mi sembra questo cielo e questo mare; cielo e mare di stagno fuso, limitato da una fascia di biacca verde: la costa del Malabar. (19)

> [...] few names captured my adolescent imagination as powerfully as Goa: *Goa A Dourada.*
> I visited it with my pencil a hundred times during never-ending math lessons, with my atlas open between desk and knees. [...] To me the voyage over the pages of the atlas seems to be living reality, and this sea and sky, pale imaginings – sea and sky of molten tin, bordered by the Malabar coast, a strip of green.] (Marinelli 76–7)

Gozzano's wavering between imaginative seductions (following a regressive trajectory, towards the personal past of the daydreaming schoolboy), and the appeal of the reality principle (the ship's progressive motion towards Goa), is only apparent. For the lover of poetic revisions and of imagined worlds, Goa is already fixed in its colonial cliché, that of the 'Golden Goa,' the Rome of the East, the paradise-city 'rich on trade and loot' (Scammel 243) constructed by so many narratives from 1510, the date of Alfonso de Albuquerque's conquest, onwards (Pearson 14–39). Even the Malabar coastline, in its chromatic motionlessness, is already a painting. It is not surprising that Gozzano inverts the relationship between art and life, invention and reality: he is capitalizing on one of the clichés of the decadents' poetics, as popularized by Oscar Wilde's famous aphorism: 'Life imitates Art far more than Art imitates Life' (82). If no original experience is possible – if the world, even the exotic world, is never to be approached directly but is accessible only through the mediation of reproduced forms and borrowed words – the pressing question at this point regards the modality of this experience in the second degree:

> Termina oggi il viaggio intrapreso a matita sull'atlante di vent'anni or sono, termina a bordo di questa tejera sobbalzante, una caravella panciuta, lunga

trenta metri, alla quale è stata senza dubbio aggiunta la prima caldaia a vapore che sia stata inventata. Ma tutto questo è indicibilmente poetico e mi compensa della vuota eleganza dei grandi vapori moderni dalle cabine e dalle sale presuntuose di specchi e di stucchi impero e Luigi XIV, dall'odore di volgarissimo *hôtel*, dove è assente ogni poesia marinaresca, ogni senso della *cosa nuova* e dell'*avventura*. Qui tutto è poetico, e la mia nostalgia può sognare d'essere ai tempi di Vasco De Gama, di navigare alle *Terrae Ignotae*, alle *Insulae non repertae*. (20)

[Today my voyage traced on an atlas twenty years ago is coming to an end, coming to an end upon this heaving teapot, a caravel with a rounded hull, thirty meters in length, in which has been installed what is doubtless the first steam engine ever invented. Yet this is all unutterably poetic, and more than compensates for the specious elegance of the great modern steamships with their cabins and presumptuous staterooms filled with mirrors à la Louis XIV and à la Bonaparte, which smell like ordinary hotels, without the slightest trace of seafaring poetry, a sense of [novelty and of] adventure.

Here everything is poetic. I can imagine myself living during the age of Vasco da Gama, sailing to *terrae ignotae* and *insulae non repertae*.] (Marinelli 77)[9]

Apt vessel for Gozzano's poetic journey, the antiquated caravel offers a fantastic escape into that remote past in which sailing towards the unknown was, geographically, intellectually, and aesthetically, still a possibility.[10] Although modernity is succumbing to the sterile comforts of mass tourism, with its commodified goods and mechanically reproduced forms, Gozzano's voyage into Vasco da Gama's past allows him to experience an original sense of wonder: Gozzano's 'senso della *cosa nuova*' – the 'aura' which, according to Walter Benjamin, modernity has lost (220–3): 'The concept of aura [...] may usefully be illustrated with reference to the aura of natural [objects]. If, while resting on a summer afternoon, you follow with your eyes a mountain range on the horizon or a branch which casts its shadow over you, you experience the aura of those mountains, of that branch. [...] We define the aura [...] as the unique phenomenon of a distance, however close it may be [...] [T]he contemporary decay of the aura [...] rests on two circumstances, ... namely the desire of contemporary masses to bring things "closer" spatially and humanly, which is just as ardent as their bent toward overcoming the uniqueness of every reality by accepting its reproduction' (222–3).

Unlike Benjamin, Gozzano sees novelty as something that has not entirely disappeared from the space of modernity: it survives in it, albeit in a paradoxical form. We live, Gozzano implies, in an aging world, where absolute originality is impossible, and where the imperial entrepreneurship of travel agencies like Thomas Cook & Son, the inventors of mass tourism, have successfully erased all sense of exotic distance. In this world, even novelty is an experience in the second degree, resulting from the self-conscious stirring up of acquired notions, mnemonic traces, and stored images, which cannot lay claim to, but only evoke, a sense of novelty. Novelty has become the site of a paradox in that the new (the authentic, the original, the first, and so forth) can only be perceived in a mediated manner, by carefully listening to, and attempting to repeat, the archaic words which first expressed this sense of novelty and remote distance.

If Goa offers herself already framed by a set of aesthetic codes and literary conventions, the problem for Gozzano is to identify, by means of concrete experiments, what hermeneutical system (and what literary discourse among those inherited from a century-long tradition), is most suitable for re-presenting Goa today. Only thus can he restore – with all the ambiguity of a secondhand claim to originality – the aura that once enshrouded it. Gozzano's reference to *Terrae Ignotae* and *Insulae non Repertae* semantically redoubles the concept of absolute novelty while formally estranging it in the distance evoked by the Latin quotation. Mediated, perhaps, by the epic pages of Virgil's *Aeneid*, (the 'ignotae [...] terrae' of Canto V, 793–5), Gozzano's first encounter with Goa occurs through one of the *Aeneid*'s hypertexts:

> [Leggo] *Os Lusiadas*, le *Lusiadi*, [in] un'edizione arcaica sucidissima, con in calce la *real alvaira*: la licenza dei superiori. Non conosco il portoghese e non mi giova ad avvicinarmi il poco spagnuolo che so, ma i versi sono così armoniosi, così perfette le rime che alla fine d'ogni strofe capisco esattamente ciò che il poeta ha voluto dire. [...] Il libro è tra i capolavori più completi che il Rinascimento abbia dato alla letteratura europea. È l'opera nazionale portoghese, quanto sopravvive, ohimé, di tutta la grandezza coloniale dei giorni splendidi. Non per nulla, e non indegnamente, Camões fu detto il Tasso del Portogallo. (22)

> [[I read] *Os Lusíadas*, The Lusiads, the immortal epic poem by Camões, an incredibly soiled old edition with the *alvará régio*, the permissions of the licensers, at the bottom of the title page. I do not know Portuguese and find

the little Spanish I have of scant help, yet the verses are so harmonious and the rhymes so perfect that at the end of each strophe I feel I understand exactly what the poet has meant. [...] Os Lusíadas is one of the most perfect masterpieces of the European Renaissance. It is the Portuguese national literary work – alas, all that survives of the colonial greatness of those splendid days. With good reason, and not undeservedly, Camões was called the Portuguese Tasso.] (Marinelli 79)

The epic code opens the doors of Goa, and this code is so comprehensive and familiar, in its fixed codification, that the linguistic barrier does not prevent Gozzano from fully comprehending it. The poem is universally enjoyable and understandable because of its classical sense of poetic harmony. Epic poems sing the world of the great national beginnings, of the magnificent acts of foundation made by a country's patriarchs and heroes.[11] Origin of contemporary reality, this world is, in its arcane perfection, also utterly detached from the present: 'an absolute epic distance separates the epic world from contemporary reality' (Bakhtin 13). Epic poets share with their readers the sense of reverence for the grand and inaccessible reality of their magnificent forefathers:[12]

The epic world is an utterly finished thing not only as an authentic event of the distant past but also on its own terms and by its own standards; it is impossible to change, to re-think, to re-evaluate anything in it. It is completed, conclusive, and immutable, as a fact, an idea and a value. This defines absolute epic distance. One can only accept the epic world with reverence; it is impossible to really touch it for it is beyond the realm of human activity, the realm in which everything humans touch is altered and re-thought. This distance exists not only in the epic material, that is, in the events and the heroes described, but also in the point of view and evaluations one assumes toward them; point of view and evaluation are fused with the subject into one inseparable whole. [...] The epic world is constructed in the zone of an absolute distanced image, beyond the sphere of possible contact with the developing, incomplete and therefore re-thinking and re-evaluating present. (Bakhtin 17)

As in hagiographic and memorialistic writing, the epic representation follows the rules of idealization. Only what is worthy of being transmitted to posterity is remembered, after being elevated into the realm of *sublimitas*. As Bakhtin points out, the absolute past is an evaluative category, and epic concepts such as 'founder,' 'beginning,' 'first,' are valorized temporal concepts, because it is in this past that the source of everything good for all later times is to be found. By definition, the epic discourse cannot be re-examined or re-evaluated: bordering on the sacred, it allows only one interpretation, that which is offered by tradition, and only one attitude, that of a respectful and admiring reverence. Source of all values, and guarantor of the laws of contemporary reality, the epic past becomes an absolute category. Events and heroes belonging to it are fixed *sub specie aeternitatis*. Distanced from the present, and liberated from any risk of contact or revision, they are static and complete.

In 'Goa: "La Dourada,"' the epic discourse is evoked in a context that deliberately puts these presuppositions into a state of crisis. The sublimity of the skies does not attract Gozzano as much as the depths of the Pedrillo's hold, with its jumble of sundry wares:

> Oggi sono sceso nella stiva. Quanta merce disparata abbiamo con noi! Pianoforti, macchine da scrivere, biciclette, balle di cotone a fiorami vivacissimi per le belle dei coloni, tre casse enormi, dove viaggia, divisa in tre parti, una statua gigantesca di San Francesco Saverio [...] e un'infinità di sacchi pieni di cocci: cocci di stoviglie raccattati in tutti gli spazzaturai occidentali, frantumi a colori vivi. [...] (21)

> [Today I went into the hold. What a collection of ill-assorted cargo it contains! Pianos, typewriters, bicycles, bales of cotton cloth with vivid floral patterns for colonial belles, three enormous crates containing a huge statue of Saint Francis Xavier disassembled into three parts [...] and an endless number of sacks filled with bits of broken pottery. Broken crockery is collected by street sweepers all over the West, vividly colored fragments. [...]] (Marinelli 78)

An act of homage to one of the most common stylistic devices of the epic, the catalogue, Gozzano's *enumeración caótica*, with its obvious pluralizing and multiplying effects, hardly creates that sense of democratic aggregation that Leo Spitzer saw operating in the post-Whitmanian examples of this device. Discussing Paul Claudel's ode, 'La Muse qui est la Grâce' (1913), Spitzer argued that if the pre-modern *Katalogdichters* such as Rabelais or Quevedo still respected distinctions between different realms of Nature, the modernist cataloguers enumerate things 'detached from their frames' ('Interpretation' 206) and liberated from contextual hierarchies of relevance, in order to celebrate the fullness of the world:

> The whole and the part, the far and the near, the concrete and the abstract, the important and the inconsequential, can all appear side by side, because the are fused in Claudel's vision. Claudel [...] is able to accept [the confusion of our world] without letting himself be distracted from the essentials: he can depict an apparent disorder, for he sees it in a higher order. His faith remains unshaken. Evidences of this same faith that can so easily accept the juxtaposition of part and whole can be found in any Catholic church, where a painting representing a single scene from the life of Christ [...] may hang side by side with one which represents the totality of God (the Trinity). And the juxtaposition of the sublime with the trivial [...] is paralleled by the arrangements of those medieval towns in which, from out the midst of booths and shops and sheds, there emerges the Gothic spire – or, perhaps by the medieval mysteries in which comic and solemn scenes are made to alternate. ('Interpretation' 206–7)

A contemporary of Claudel, Gozzano uses the same device in a very different manner. His enumeration does not evoke any sense of exuberant equality (Spitzer's 'democracy of things'; 'La enumeración' 288). There is no Whitmanian homogenizing intent in Gozzano's random cataloguing techniques, nor is there Claudel's thrill in the diversity of the world. Without Claudel's totalizing framework, in Gozzano a sense of incongruity prevails, as does fragmentation, *caotismo*, and waste. The sacred (the saint's statue) is, and remains, juxtaposed with the profane in a context (the Pedrillo's hold) that is bound to debase the sacred rather than elevate the profane. The gigantic statue of Saint Francis Xavier cut into thirds visualizes the divorce of the parts from the whole, thus denying that union of the macro- and the microcosmic which Spitzer saw as the core of Claudel's Christian vision, as well as of Whitman's neo-pagan pantheism. The divided statue also represents the modern fragmentation of that epic hero who used to be, as Bakhtin aptly put it, 'all of one piece' (35). Embodying the unity of universal and individual spheres, the epic hero gave form to the whole epic world, and the epic world recognized itself in its hero: 'And I'm resolved my inmost being / shall share in what's the lot of all mankind,' in the eloquent words of Goethe's Faust (2: 46–7). No longer believing in its own giants, and no longer able to produce, a unifying and totalizing view of reality, the West that Gozzano depicts can only

ship its material surplus abroad, and export its own spiritual debris.
The hero of Camões's *Lusiads*, Vasco da Gama, undergoes a similar
fate. After all it is 'in the kitchen, between a cask of bananas and a tin
of preserves' that Gozzano finds the soiled copy of *The Lusiads*:

> Tutti gli elementi delle grandi epopee sono ricordati intorno alla figura
> dell'eroe: Vasco De Gama, e intorno alla sua gesta: la scoperta delle Indie
> orientali. Eppure non so leggerlo senza un sorriso d'irriverenza. La figura
> dell'Ulisside portoghese è così grottesca, camuffata secondo l'ossessione
> classicheggiante del tempo: sembra di vedere gli stivali, il robone logoro
> d'un pirata medioevale spuntare sotto la corazza, il casco clipeato delle
> reminiscenze omeriche e virgiliane. [...]
> Ed ecco Didone, camuffata da Ines de Castro, [...] e il Ciclope, parodiato
> dal gigante Adamastorre. (22)

> [All the elements of the great epic are brought in to serve the figure of the
> hero, Vasco da Gama, and his discovery of the East Indies. Still, I am unable
> to read it without an irreverent smile. The figure of the Portuguese Ulysses
> is so grotesque, filled in according to the classicizing mania of the times: one
> can almost see the boots, the patched outfit of a medieval pirate showing
> underneath his cuirass and the helmet that echoes of Homer and Virgil. [...]
> Now we have Dido disguised as Inês da Castro, [...] and the Cyclops,
> parodied by giant Adamastor.] (Marinelli 79–80)

Measured against its Homeric and Virgilian hypotexts, Camões's poem
proves unsuccessful as a serious epic. As we have seen, *The Lusiads'*
style lives up to its noble models, and its formulaic diction, with its
'roving stereotypes, hemistichs, hexameters, groups of verses which
the bard shamelessly reuses' (Genette 15) allows for universal comprehension. However, according to Gozzano, Camões involuntarily acts
as a parodist, because his epic contents stray from the norm of epic
sublimitas. Dido ends up looking too much like Dona Inês de Castro,
Adamastor is a meager copy of Poliphemous, and Vasco da Gama is
an early version of Blackbeard attempting to impersonate Ulysses.
Reduced to an empty shell, only a mask and a disguise, the seafaring
hero is divided into a series of details that cannot be organically combined into a whole, an incongruous jumble of disparate elements (boots,
a pirate's patched outfit, a suit of armour, a Roman helmet) that expose all their conventionality. Camões's characters, in other words, do
not measure up to their superhuman predecessors. The 'total indi-

viduals' of the past are 'contemporized,' fragmented, and 'brought low' (Bakhtin 21).

The *Lusiads*' caricatural and parodic elements that Gozzano emphasizes are not inherent to the poem itself (Camões did not mean to make us laugh). They stem instead from a discrepancy between authorial intentions and readers' responses. Gozzano is not discussing, here, the failure of the epic as a genre. He leaves the Homeric and Virgilian originals untouched, and acknowledges the initial success of what he calls '[uno dei] capolavori piu completi che il Rinascimento abbia dato alla letteratura europea' (22).[13] But he is also keen on recording the changed reception of *The Lusiads*. If Camões intended to seriously imitate two epic models, the *Odyssey* and the *Aeneid*, today's disenchanted readers cannot but view this imitation through a distorting lens, creating unanticipated and meaningful reversals. Modern times impose a change in the readership's attitude, and the downgrading standards applied to the grand epics of the past cause a debasing of the sacred (Dido as Inês de Castro) rather than a sacralizing of the profane (Inês de Castro as Dido). No longer seen in its unreachable totality and self-enclosed unity, Camões's epic poem appears as an absurd collection of different world systems. Intermixing classic and Christian myths, *The Lusiads* produce an assortment of sacred and profane elements, again according to a principle of involuntary caricature:

> Tutto l'Olimpo Pagano e Cristiano presiede alla gesta. La Vergine Maria da una parte – una Vergine troppo paganeggiante – e Venere dall'altra – una Venere che sa di sacrestia e di Santa Inquisizione – si contendono a volta a volta l'eroe navigatore. (22)

> [The entire pagan and Christian Olympus presides over the feast. The Virgin Mary on one side – an excessively paganized Virgin – and Venus on the other – a Venus who smacks of the sacristy and the Holy Inquisition – contend from time to time for the navigator-hero.] (Marinelli 79)

Gozzano's metatextual strategy – his commentary on *The Lusiads* – draws attention to the contextual factors responsible for a significant textual transformation: the original generic contract is breached, and Camões's epic is refunctionalized to be read in a parodic mode. Gozzano thus highlights the contractual nature of the relationship between reader and text. Pertaining to 'a conscious and organized pragmatics' (Genette 9), this relationship is not stable and fixed once and for all, but is bound to evolve in space and time.[14] In *The Lusiads'* case, the discrepancies between original authorial intentions and modern readers' interpretations shatter the exegetic totality that epic discourse requires. Gozzano's reader, in other words, accomplishes a typical modernist gesture, rejecting tradition's sway over the reception of all epic discourses: 'Epic discourse is a discourse handed down by tradition. By its very nature the epic world of the absolute past is inaccessible to personal experience and does not permit an individual, personal point of view ... Evaluated in the same way by all and demanding a pious attitude toward itself [epic discourse demands ...] a commonly held evaluation and point of view which excludes any possibility of another approach' (Bakhtin 16). By transforming the sublime into the grotesque, Gozzano's readers abolish epic distance and leave the epic subject bare under the power of tight scrutiny and close examination. What was heavenly becomes a caricature. Parody and caricature, however, have no place in a world of Saints and Heroes and cannot narrate the feats of the cross and the sword. Gozzano's impertinent smile overturns the respectful devotion that the epic genre demands. It is the first signal of that desecrating process which forces the great and the powerful of the past to be demoted from their dignified status and plunged into a present that is vulnerable to humour and irony. Gozzano's close-ups on single details imply the perceptive familiarity that empowers humour and parody: 'Laughter has the remarkable power of making an object come up close, of drawing it into a zone of crude contact where one can finger it familiarly on all sides, turn it upside down, inside out, peer at it from above and below, break open its external shell, look into its center, doubt it, take it apart, dismember it, lay it bare and expose it, examine freely and experiment with it.' (Bakhtin 23) Nothing is left intact in the epic image of the absolute past: 'the entire world and everything sacred in it is offered to us without any distancing at all' (Bakhtin 26).

Gozzano's demythologizing of the epic code in *The Lusiads* and his opening it up to the relativity of the present has none of the liberating, pluralistic, and anti-totalitarian features that Mikhail Bakhtin attributes to this process. Gozzano remains the bearer of those values of purity, harmony, and cohesive unity, which become real judgments of value when he transposes them upon the extraliterary reality, as in this description of the Goanese *mestiços* he sees in the Old City:

[Q]uesta folla numerosa [è] così diversa dalla corretta eleganza degli Inglesi e dalla grazia dignitosa degli Indu, folla di meticci portoghesi che si riprodussero come la gramigna sotto questo cielo [...] e che si chiamano pomposamente *Toupas* [sic], cioè europei 'che portano il cappello,' ma che d'europeo non hanno più nulla, con quelle spalle gracili, le gambe smilze, il volto olivagno, angoloso, dagli occhi vivi, ma scimmieschi sotto la fronte depressa; e hanno atteggiamenti grotteschi di cavalleria, sono lisciati, impomatati, portano in giro sigari enormi e compagne languide. (29–30)

[[This] large throng [is] so different from the correct elegance of the English and the dignified grace of the Hindus, a crowd of Portuguese *mestizos* who in this climate reproduce like weeds [...] and who pompously call themselves *Toupas* – that is, Europeans 'who wear hats.' Yet there is nothing European about them, with their delicate bones, their slight legs, their angular, olive-hued faces with vivid simian eyes under their prominent brows. They have a grotesque chivalric bearing, are well-groomed and pomaded, smoke huge cigars, and have languid female companions.] (Marinelli 88)

Gozzano borrows this peculiar piece of information from Édouard de Warren, a French officer in the British army in India and author of two volumes on British India, originally published in Paris in 1844:

[H]éritant des vices plus souvent que des qualités des deux races dont ils sont le produit, les half-castes ont en général toute la lubricité de l'Indien et toute l'ivrognerie de l'Anglais, et cette combinaison en amène un grand nombre à un fin prématurée et sans reproduction. S'il y a progéniture, elle se confond le plus souvent avec les Topassies ou Topas, pour se perdre à la longue parmi les indigènes. On appelle Topas ou Topassies des indigènes qui portent chapeaux, mais qui n'ont rien de commun avec les Européens qu'une partie de l'habillement et le plus souvent la religion catholique. Il descendent généralement des ancien métis français, portugais et hollandais. (121–2)[15]

[Having inherited the vices more often than the virtues of the races that have produced them, the half-castes are, generally, as lustful as the Indian and as intemperate as the English, and this combination leads a great many of them to an early and childless demise. If they do have children, they most often resemble the *Topassies* or *Topas*, and ultimately disappear among the indigenous people. We call *Topas* or *Topassies* the indigenous people who wear a hat, but who do not have anything in common with the Europeans, except for this article of clothing and, more often, the Catholic religion. They generally descend from the ancient French, Portuguese, and Dutch mestizos.]

Inspired by de Warren's description of Indo-Portuguese dressing habits, Gozzano renders de Warren's racist statements with a caricatural vignette, the primary function of which is, of course, derision. Degraded to laughable acts and exterior poses, this debased Goanese chivalry bears no relation to its noble European origins other than those of parodic distortion. Gozzano confronts the surfacing of the material and corporeal, which Bakhtin relates to the vitality of popular culture, with all the duplicitous distance of vulgarization and irony. He examines sexuality from a position of contemptuous intellectual superiority, and then demeans it with the trite humour of an obvious double-entendre (enormous cigars). Behind the scornful smile and the clichéd image, begging the readers' complicity, remains a fundamental aversion, a visceral fear, of all that is felt as hybrid, as *métissage*.

Race relations in Portuguese India have been the subject of wide controversy, with praise or censure bestowed upon the practices of intermarriage and interbreeding, and much discussion about the nature and effects of acculturation and assimilation, and about the extent of the intermingling between the 'cultures and societies of the Portuguese and the local people with whom they interacted' (Pearson 104). Positions on this issue vary greatly according to the ideological and cultural make-up of those who held them.[16] Overall, Gozzano's stance parallels earlier or contemporary British racial attitudes. In 1847, British explorer and orientalist Richard Burton wrote:

The reader may remember that it was Albuquerque who advocated marriages between the European settlers and the natives of India. However reasonable it might have been to expect the amalgamation of the races in the persons of their descendants, experience and stern facts condemn the measure as a most delusive and treacherous political day dream ... As soon as intermarriage with the older settlers takes place the descendants become Mestici – in plain English, mongrels. [...] It would be, we believe, difficult to find in Asia an uglier or more degraded looking race than that which we are now describing. The forehead is low and flat, the eyes small. [...] Their figures are short and small ... The mongrel men dress like Europeans, but the quantity of clothing diminishes with the wearer's rank. Some of the lower orders, especially in the country, affect a full-dress costume, consisting *in toto*, of a cloth jacket and black silk knee breeches. (87–8, 97)

In a typically Victorian tone, William W. Hunter claimed, in 1899, that 'the Goanese became a byword as the type of an orientalised community, idle, haughty, and corrupt' (157). Interbreeding, in particular, was seen as one of the main causes of Portuguese decline in India. John Fryer, an English visitor to Goa in 1909, draws a picture that chillingly contradicts any idea of racial tolerance as well as the myth of the progressive and peaceful assimilation of two races within one Luso-tropical civilization based on miscegenation and Catholicism: '[In Goa] the Mass of the People are Canorein, though Portuguezed in Speech and Manners; paying great Observance to a White Man, whom when they meet they must give him the Way with a Cringe and Civil salute, for fear of a *Stochado* [rapier's blow]' (27). In all of these descriptions, including Gozzano's, the racist disdain for hybrids manifests itself through caricature: the mestizos' physique is caricatured by emphasizing lack of (classic) proportions. The behaviour and dress code is deemed to demonstrate exaggerated mimicry and distorted movements, as in Gozzano's description of the Goanese boy who shows 'una mimica eccessiva che rivela il rampollo di razza bastarda' (27).[17] The 'strange melange of European and Asiatic peculiarities' (Burton 100) is seen as a monstrosity indeed.

If Gozzano's metatextual analysis decrees the impossibility of the epic in the modern word, his parodic revisions, with their mixtures of high and low registers, their tendency towards caricature, and their contamination of the serious with the profane, have no egalitarian inspiration. On the contrary, they function to showcase differences within a hierarchical setting, rather than to celebrate or abolish them. Parody, in Gozzano, rests on ambiguous epistemological grounds, as it stylistically and structurally exploits the very forms that it ideologically condemns. As one of the classic genres, Gozzano implies, the epic establishes a norm designating a typology and an interdiction, and parody is culpable of defying precisely this norm. As Jacques Derrida argues, tongue in cheek, whenever the notion of genre is at stake, whether it is a matter of *physis* or *techne*, one must not risk 'impurity, anomaly, or monstrosity,' lest it cause the demise of the genre itself: 'If a genre is what it is, or if it is supposed to be what it is destined to be by virtue of its *telos*, then "genres are not to be mixed"; one should not mix genres, one owes it to oneself not to get mixed up in mixing genres. Or, more rigorously, genres should not intermix. And if it should happen that they do intermix, by accident or through transgression, by mistake or through a lapse, then this should confirm, since, after all, we are speaking of "mixing," the essential purity of their identity' (204). Gozzano's metatext, his commentary on the epic, reveals that genres are not exclusively literary phenomena but also demonstrations of the ways in which literature processes and interprets historical reality. Arguably, literary genres order the system of literature in accordance with the contemporary interpretations of the world outside of literature. Shaped by socio-historical reality, genre structures have a telling story to narrate, that of the history of mentality, as they reflect the conceptual systems – and reveal the inner tensions and contradictions – which order, and thus attempt to control, social and textual spaces.[18]

Gozzano comments on the same impossibility for the epic at the intertextual level. By degrading the epic code, Gozzano exploits, and melancholically subverts, one of its fundamental themes, that of the quest. To the colossal pursuits of epic heroes (*sapientia mundi* and immortality, *salus et amor, virtute e canoscenza*), Gozzano opposes his own degraded and modest quest. Leaving his friends in Bombay, he travels alone, in an absurd and inexplicable search for 'il fratello sconosciuto di un amico dimenticato' (29),[19] a Franciscan missionary by the name of Vico Verani. Gozzano's *Descensus ad Inferos* does not appear to have clear ethical or epistemological motives and must, rather, be related to the vague and irrational nostalgia for an unknown person whose last name contains the root of the word truth (*verità*): '[n]on ho altra mèta, altra indicazione in questa solitudine di piante e di ruine che il nome di un italiano non conosciuto mai: e lo ripeto a tutti i rari passanti' (27).[20] Pathetic pilgrim, Gozzano follows an equally unepic guide, whom he presents according to the racist caricatural model discussed earlier: '[era] un monello goanese che si [interessava] a quella ricerca con grandi esclamazioni grottesche, e agitar d'occhi e di braccia' (27).[21] Gozzano's wanderings in the nightmarish city reveal that all that appears familiar is only a hollow surface, pervaded by sinister sadness:

La nostra malinconia ritrova [...] a Goa lo spettro di cose nostre: conventi, palazzi, chiese del Cinquecento e del Seicento: una vasta città che ricorda a volte una via di Roma barocca o una piazza dell'Umbria. [...] La città è vastissima, ma sono pochi gli edifici completi. Avanzo a caso, senza una mèta. [...] Un edificio m'attira, un palazzo del Seicento, imponente, dalle grate panciute, dai balconi a volute aggraziate, recanti al centro, in corsivo, un monogramma o uno stemma padronale; e lo stemma è riprodotto in pietra sul vasto androne d'ingresso. Il cortile è circondato da un doppio loggiato barocco, a colonne spirali; ma il loggiato è crollato per una buona metà e s'apre sopra la campagna selvaggia. Seguo il portico a caso, entro nella vasta dimora. Ohimè! Vedo il soffitto; e, attraverso il soffitto, larghe chiazze azzurre: il cielo del tropico. Dei tre ripiani, delle fughe interminabili di sale e corridoi, non resta più traccia, tutto è crollato, e il palazzo non è che una scatola, una topaja deserta, che serve di magazzino per le noci di cocco. In terra, fino a vari metri d'altezza, sono accumulati i grossi frutti chiomati che fanno pensare a piramidi di teste tronche. (25–6)

[Still we find in Goa the specter of our own civilization: sixteenth- and seventeenth-century convents, palaces and churches, a vast city that at times reminds one of a street in baroque Rome or a square in Umbria. [...] The city is endless, but few of the buildings are still whole.

I walk haphazardly, without a destination. [...] One building attracts me, an imposing seventeenth-century palace with curved window gratings, pretty balconies, and volutes bearing in the center, in italics, a monogram or proprietor's coat of arms; and the coat of arms is also reproduced in stone in the vast entrance hall. The inner court is surrounded by a baroque open double gallery with spiral columns. At least half of the open gallery has collapsed and one sees the vast countryside above it. I wander along the arcade, enter the vast dwelling. Alas, I gaze up at the ceiling, and through the ceiling at broad patches of blue: the tropic sky. There is no trace of the three landings, of the interminable suites of rooms and corridors. Everything has tumbled down, and the palace is nothing more than a box, a deserted rats' nest used as a storehouse for coconuts. On the ground, up to the height of several meters, are piled the large, hairy fruit, which make me think of pyramids of severed heads.] (Marinelli 83)

By 1915, the legendary palaces that the Portuguese had built during the height of Goa's splendour (the mid-seventeenth to the mid-eighteenth century) had long disappeared, due to the slow decline of the empire and the harshness of the tropical weather. However, Gozzano captures here an interesting architectural hybrid – an example of a colonial Portuguese/Italianate building – that has notable symbolic value. The exterior stairway protected by a colonnaded porch, leading to the first floor and opening onto a walled courtyard, like the one which Gozzano describes, was the defining element of early colonial buildings. Characterized by rigour and austerity, these imposing and martial-looking palaces, originally conceived by military engineers, were meant to convey Portuguese strength and permanence to the peoples recently conquered:[22] 'In colonial Portuguese architecture, [the colonnaded porch] was used primarily as a means for illustrating the policy of global power and social dominance developed by the Portuguese. The viceroy placed his guards, outfitted in blue livery and halberds along the stairs. The nobility, and even the archbishop, imitated the viceroy's practices to the finest detail, with the number of their servants and the luxury of their presentation' (Carita 17).

When a more elaborate practice of formal display replaced the earlier policy of force at the end of the sixteenth century, buildings began to reflect an Italian Mannerist influence, which lasted throughout the eighteenth and nineteenth centuries (Carita 19). Built for leisure and ostentation, these palaces were physical manifestations of the economic power of the Church and the Society of Jesus. Architectonic features that the Jesuit Fathers imported from Italy included a variety of ornamental elements decorating the buildings' façades, such as elaborate molding and fluting, capitals, balcony windows, and family insignia. While Gozzano's 'volute aggraziate' and 'grate panciute,' with their noble family crests inscribed in cursive script, may have less to do with real Goa than with his own fascination with contemporary European art nouveau style, his description nevertheless reveals the powerful alliance between military and religious powers while bearing witness to these powers' dismal decay. The image of the gutted palace transformed into a desolate mausoleum of truncated head-like coconuts provides a chilling contrast to the deceptive sense of permanence offered by another art form, that of celebratory portraiture:

> [immagino] una tela di Velasquez o di Van Dyck [raffigurante] uno di quei *conquistador* mezzo mercanti, pirata, guerriero, esploratore che s'avanza in tutta la pompa delle sete, delle piume, dei velluti, recando la consorte per mano, una pingue signora a riccioli simmetrici, sorridente nonostante il ferreo busto a imbuto, la gorgiera crudele; e la prole li segue in bell'ordine, già tutta imbustata e corazzata come i genitori, e un servo negro reca una scimmia sulla spalla e un pappagallo nell'una mano, sollevando con l'altra una cortina di velluto, e tra le due colonne appaiono le galee potentissime d'innanzi al porto di una città favolosa: Goa. (26)

> [[I imagine] a portrait by Velazquez or Van Dyck, one of the conquistadors, half-trader, half-pirate, warrior and explorer, who advances in all the pomp of silks, plumes, and velvets, holding his consort by the hand, a plump lady with symmetrical curls, smiling in spite of her iron corset and cruel gorget;

and the offspring, all proper, all corseted and armored like their parents; and a Negro slave carrying a monkey on his shoulder and a parrot in one hand, with the other holding up a velvet curtain; and between the two columns the mighty fleet lies at anchor before the fabled city: Goa.] (Marinelli 84)

Gozzano's *ekphrasis*, more than describing a specific artwork, identifies here the conventions of a style, that of seventeenth-century celebratory painting. Devoted to the commemoration of military victories or the celebration of aristocratic and royal families, these paintings contained thematic and formal elements akin to Gozzano's description. Naturally, given their function and the circumstances under which they were commissioned, the paintings were intended to glorify their sitters, and often allegorized the events they depicted. In particular, the celebratory paintings of aristocratic families demonstrated the close connections between art and the illustration of socioeconomic power. These connections had nonetheless to be mediated, and financial worth was often converted, and idealized, into the representation of military distinction for the male sitters, and opulent, regal elegance for the women. Discussing Rubens's œuvre, Giorgio Doria humorously recalls the vogue of portraying 'meticolosi contabili su cavalli rampanti, mogli di oculati prestatori di denaro [vestite come] principesse' (24).[23] In Van Dyck's Genoese works, powerful aristocratic families such as the Dorias, Spinolas, and Lomellinis translate the wealth amassed through trade and banking into the elegance of military postures, precious fabrics, and sumptuous decors, and in the sheer dimensions of paintings where the sitters were often painted from below, to increase the sense of their power and size. The royal portraits were, understandably, even more ambitious. Rubens and Velázquez's portraits of the Spanish royal family underscore the conventional tendency to 'regard the king as a quasi-divine person, as a "deity" or "demi-god on earth"' (Lopez-Rey 57). A telling example, which Gozzano may have seen at the Uffizi gallery in Florence, is the allegorical equestrian portrait of Phillip IV of Spain, in which Velázquez and his workshop painted allegorical figures descending from the skies and presenting the majestic king mounted on horseback with a cross, a laurel twig, and a globe. From below, a richly clad and solemn-looking black youth offers Phillip a helmet. Painting black characters, usually servants, and usually extravagantly dressed to emphasize the wealth of the sitter's family, was also a pictorial convention of the times, as attested, for example, by Van Dyck's portrait of Elena Grimaldi Cattaneo. By placing the diminutive black servant between two slender white columns and Elena's imposing figure, Van Dyck emphasizes Elena's height and the classic splendour of her surroundings.

In his description of the imagined painting by Van Dyck or Velazquez, Gozzano overturns such painterly idealizations through parodic redundancy and debasement. The representation of the black servant offering the viewer a first glance of the Portuguese conquest of Goa, while holding a parrot as well as a monkey, accentuates the colonialist notion of the natives' grateful submissiveness. This image is just as redundant a representation of exotic clichés as the portrayal of little children as miniature copies of their self-satisfied parents is of the advance of Western conquest. In what has become a familiar move in 'Goa: "La Dourada,"' Gozzano peers closely at the *conquistador*, brings him down, so to speak, thus revealing his composite nature. With a brilliantly ironic chiasmus ('uno di quei conquistador mezzo mercanti, pirata, guerriero, esploratore' [one of those conquistadors who were part merchant, pirate, warrior, and explorer]), Gozzano tightly interweaves commerce with economic exploitation, and political aggression with exploration. As with Camões's epic celebration, Gozzano's analysis of the imagined painting rests upon an interpretative change that activates a parodic register absent from the original intentions. Modernity, Gozzano implies, is bound to favour close scrutiny rather than idealized distance, in all realms of human experience:

Ancora una volta tocco l'ultimo limite della delusione, sconto la curiosità morbosa di voler vedere troppo vicina la realtà delle pietre morte, di voler constatare che le cose magnificate dalla storia, dall'arte, cantate dai poeti, non sono più, non saranno mai più, sono come se non siano state mai! (26–7)

[Once again I am disappointed and pay the price of wanting to see the reality of the dead stones too close up, wanting to verify, to ascertain that the things glorified by art and history, sung by the poets, no longer exist, will never again exist, are as if they had never existed.] (Marinelli 84–5)

Against the intention of celebratory art to bestow permanence and timeliness, Gozzano's futile yet stubborn quest in the Baroque Inferno of Goa yields only one revelation: the *sic transit* which art itself cannot overcome.

For Gozzano, depleting the present of heroic possibilities also means negating the temporal model upon which the epic plot is traditionally organized. Once in the cradle of the world, Gozzano fails to decipher the code revealing the origins of all that is to come. In a world where the first Word is absent or incomprehensible, history cannot follow a progressive order. The only Word that permeates this repetitive history states the disquieting, because rationally undecipherable, presence of an absence: 'nessuno conosce Vico Verani. [...] La solitudine mi par pi completa, [...] ora che so di aver seguita la traccia d'un morto nella città morta' (27; 29).[24] If the epic 'was the form through which classical antiquity, Christianity and the feudal world had represented the basis of civilizations, their overall meaning, their destiny' (Moretti 36),[25] and if *The Lusiads* sang in epic form 'the Portuguese achievement [as ...] part of a great providential design to win the world for the true faith' (Atkinsons 25), Gozzano interprets the history 'bestowed' upon the world outside of Europe as a heritage of ruins. For Gozzano, these ruins bear testimony to the distant achievement of epic dreams, as well as to the overall futility of those very achievements. Ultimately, Gozzano's approach is steeped in ambiguity: oscillating between the destructive powers of irony and nostalgia's conservative drives, Gozzano nurses a sense of emotional loss for what he himself helped to analytically destroy.

It is precisely this sense of loss that Gozzano chooses to emphasize by concluding his journey to Goa with a sonnet by José Maria de Heredia:

Morne Ville, jadis reine des Océans!
　Aujourd'hui le requin poursuit en paix les scombres
　Et le nuage errant allonge seul des ombres
Sur la rade où roulaient les galions géants.
Depuis Drake et l'assaut des Anglais mécréants,
　Tes murs désemparés croulent en noirs décombres
　Et, comme un glorieux collier de perles sombres,
Des boulets de Pointis montrent les trous béants.
Entre le ciel qui brûle et la mer qui moutonne,
　Au somnolent soleil d'un midi monotone,
　Tu songes, ô Guerrière, aux vieux Conquistadors;
Et dans l'énervement des nuits chaudes et calmes,
Berçant ta gloire éteinte, ô Cité, tu t'endors
　Sous les palmiers, au long frémissement des palmes. (143)

[Sad city, of old time the Ocean's queen!
  To-day the shark in peace pursues his prey,
  And in thy road where giant galleons lay
Shadows of drifting clouds alone are seen.
Since Drake's assault, his miscreants' rapine,
  Thy walls have crumbled in a black decay
  And seem, where Pointis rent them, to display
A zone of glorious pearls of somber sheen.
Between a burning sky and fleecy sea,
  While the sun sleeps through noon's monotony,
  Thy dream is of the old Conquistadores;
In enervating nights of tropic calm,
Beneath the unending shudder of the palm
  Thou slumberest, cradled in thy vanished glories.] (O'Hara 125)

However extensive, Gozzano's citation is incomplete. By eliminating the poem's epigraph (*Cartagena de Indias* 1532 – 1583 – 1697), Gozzano transforms Cartagena, the city that Heredia's ancestor, Don Pedro de Heredia, founded in 1532 in what is now the country of Colombia, into Portuguese Goa. Gozzano thus eliminates Goa's un-heroic and prolonged decline by inventing a dramatic defeat at the hands of Sir Francis Drake's army. If, in the preceding examples, Gozzano subverted the epic model by way of parody, here he bluntly relativizes it, by emphasizing the sudden replacement of one colonial power with another.

Gozzano overcomes the impasse created by his desire to dismantle the epic model and his nostalgic longing for that very model by delegating to another voice the representation of that longing. Through the filter of Heredia's poetic persona (the implicit 'Je' of the sonnet), Gozzano effects a drastic change in textual perspective. The elegy for the defeated replaces the victor's epic, and the gaze of a sympathetic observer substitutes for the parodist's close scrutiny. The resulting vision, broad enough to span the ages, identifies the existence of a permanent natural law guiding the course of all human history. As exemplified by Heredia's second verse, Nature, which outlives History, effectively and calmly paraphrases the Darwinian law of the survival of the fittest. While Goa has exited from the progressive historical models imposed by the West, no independent historical scheme takes the place of Western rule. Having reverted to the rhythms of Nature, Goa is now a ghostly home to the 'peoples without history,' as

Hegel would have called them. The city's sole identity is cast in the dream-like and passive remembrance of the heroic times when Goa, the *Guerrière*, had been invested with the individuality of its *Conquistadors*. The rhythms of the French poem superimposed upon Gozzano's Italian prose narrative, and the evocation of a separate poetic persona omnisciently addressing a 'tu' who has no voice of its own, effectively cast an aura of remoteness and difference upon Goa. Alien and estranged in its spatial, temporal, and aesthetic distance, the city of which Heredia sung shares its silence with Gozzano. Having renounced the creation of new meanings through the parodic transformation of the voices of the past, Gozzano completes his troubled journey to discover 'il senso della *cosa nuova*' by entrusting the construction of the elsewhere to the conservative notes of the already said.

NOTES

1 Within the general heading of transtextuality, Genette identifies numerous categories, such as intertextuality (defined as the 'copresence between two texts or several texts,' which includes the literary practices of quoting, plagiarism, and allusion); paratextuality (or the relationship between texts and elements such as their titles and subtitle, prefaces, postfaces, blurbs and illustrations, covers etc.); metatextuality (or commentary, which defines the critical relationship of a text that speaks about another text); archtextuality (defining the general categories to which the text belongs, such as genre and type of discourse); and hypertextuality (the relationship uniting a text A, or hypotext, to a text B, or hypertext) (Genette 1–10).
2 This volume was published in Milan by Fratelli Treves in 1917.
3 I am referring, specifically, to Alida D'Aquino Creazzo's splendid edition of Gozzano's Indian narratives: *Verso la cuna del mondo: Lettere dall'India*. In this volume, D'Aquino Creazzo collects Gozzano's texts following the sequence that Antonio Borgese adopted for the first edition of Gozzano's *Lettere*, and adds a number of previously uncollected narratives. For each narrative, D'Aquino Creazzo identifies and cites extensively multiple sources.
4 Gozzano originally published 'Goa: "La Dourada"' in the Milanese periodical *Bianco rosso e verde*, in 1915.
5 On India as literary construct, see Weinberger-Thomas (11).
6 For an analysis of Gozzano's ironic use of poetic tradition see Bongie (118–19).

7   The page number in parenthesis after the citation in Italian refers to Alida
    D'Aquino Creazzo's edition of Gozzano's *Verso la cuna del mondo*. The
    number in parenthesis following the English version refers to David
    Marinelli's translation of Gozzano's text. I have used D'Aquino's text and
    Marinelli's translation throughout this essay.
8   On the obvious discrepancies between Gozzano's real itinerary and his
    narrative inventions, see De Rienzo and Grisay.
9   To keep closer to the original, I rendered Gozzano's 'il senso della cosa
    nuova' with 'the sense of novelty' rather than retaining Marinelli's more
    idiomatic 'the sense of the unheard-of.'
10 See Camões's proud opening of *The Lusiads*: 'This is the story of heroes
    who, leaving their native Portugal behind them, opened a way to Ceylon,
    and further, across seas no man had ever sailed before' (39).
11 'The world of the epic is the national heroic past: it is a world of "begin-
    nings" and "peak times" in the national history, a world of fathers and of
    founders of families, a world of "firsts" and "bests"' (Bakhtin 13).
12 The epic, Bakhtin argues, 'is the environment of a man speaking about a
    past that is to him inaccessible, the reverent point of view of a descendent.
    [...] The represented world of the hero stands on an utterly different and
    inaccessible time-and-value plane, separated by epic distance' (14).
13 'One of the most perfect masterpieces of the European Renaissance'
    (Marinelli 79).
14 In more universalizing terms, Genette argues that parody is inherent to all
    epic discourse: 'In truth, the epic style, by its formulaic stereotypicality,
    isn't simply a designated target for jocular imitation and parodic reversal;
    it is constantly liable, indeed exposed, to involuntary self-parody and
    pastiche. Pastiche and parody are inscribed in the very text of the epic:
    [...] as a daughter of rhapsody, parody is always already present and
    alive in the maternal womb; and rhapsody, nourished constantly and
    reciprocally by its own offspring, is [...] the daughter of her daughter. [...]
    Parody is the reverse of rhapsody and vice versa, [...] and everyone
    remembers what Ferdinand de Saussure said about the relationship
    between *recto* and *verso*. Similarly, of course, the comic is only the tragic
    seen from behind' (15).
15 Édouard de Warren's book had a considerable fortune and was repub-
    lished with extensive additions soon after the Sepoy rebellion in 1858.
16 Pearson effectively compares the two renowned and widely differing
    interpretations by Brazilian sociologist Gilberto Freyre and British
    historian Charles R. Boxer. With other apologists of the Portuguese
    empire during the Salazar dictatorship, Freyre argued that centuries of

interbreeding had created a remarkable racial harmony in India. He thus justified the retention of Portugal's colonies in the twentieth century. Conversely, Boxer provided a far less idyllic picture of early racial tensions between *reinoes* (Portuguese born in Portugal) and *indiáticos* or *castiços* (Portuguese born in India), *mestiços* or *descendentes* (people of Indo-Portuguese ancestry).

17 'excessive mimicry revealing that he is the offspring of a bastard race' (Marinelli 86)

18 For an interpretation of genre taking into consideration socio-historical issues see Steinmetz.

19 'the unknown brother of a forgotten friend' (Marinelli 87).

20 'I have no goal, I have nothing to guide me in this solitude of plants and ruins other than the name of an Italian I never knew. I repeat it to every one of the few passersby' (Marinelli 85).

21 '[It was] a Goan urchin [who showed interest] in my search ... with loud exclamations accompanied by grotesque gestures, rolling his eyes and waving his arms' (86).

22 On the symbolism of space in the Portuguese palaces in India see Kubler.

23 'meticulous accountants riding rampant horses, wives of shrewd money-lenders [dressed like] princesses.' On Van Dyck's Genoese paintings see also Barnes et al.

24 'Nobody knows Vico Verani ... The solitude seems more complete ... now that I know that I have been following the trail of a dead man in a dead city' (85; 87–8).

25 Moretti (36).

WORKS CITED

Atkinson, William C. Introduction. *The Lusiads*. By Luis de Camoens. Trans. William C. Atkinson. Harmondsworth: Penguin, 1980.

Bakhtin, Mikhail M. *The Dialogic Imagination*. Ed. M. Holquist. Trans. C. Emerson and M. Holquist. Austin: U of Texas P, 1981.

Barnes, Susan J., Piero Boccardo, Clario Di Fabio, and Laura Tagliaferro, eds. *Van Dyck a Genova*. Milan: Electa, 1997.

Benjamin, Walter. *Illuminations: Essays and Reflections*. Ed. and intr. Hannah Arendt. New York: Schocken, 1968.

Bongie, Chris. *Exotic Memories: Literature, Colonialism, and the Fin de Siècle*. Stanford: Stanford UP, 1991.

Boxer, Charles R. *Portuguese India in the Mid-Seventeenth Century*. Delhi:

Oxford UP, 1980.

- Race Relations in the Portuguese Colonial Empire, 1415–1825. Delhi: Oxford UP, 1963.

Burton, Richard. Goa and the Blue Mountain, or Six Months of Sick Leave. Berkeley: U of California P, 1991.

Camões, Luis de. The Lusiads. Trans. and intr. William C. Atkinson. Harmondsworth: Penguin, 1980.

Carita, Helder. Palaces of Goa: Models and Types of Indo-Portuguese Civil Architecture. London: Cartago, 1999.

Derrida, Jacques. 'La loi du genre/The Law of Genre.' Glyph: Textual Studies 7 (1980): 176–232.

De Rienzo, Giorgio. Guido Gozzano. Milan: Rizzoli, 1983.

Doria, Giorgio. 'Un pittore fiammingo nel "secolo dei genovesi."' Rubens e Genova. Genoa: La Stampa, 1977. 13–29.

Freyre, Gilberto. The Portuguese and the Tropics: Suggestions Inspired by the Portuguese Methods of Integrating Autocthonous Peoples and Cultures Differing from the European in a New, or Luso-tropical, Complex of Civilisation. Trans. Helen M. D'O. Matthew and F. de Mello Moser. Lisbon: Executive Committee for the Commemoration of the Vth Centenary of the Death of Prince Henry the Navigator, 1961.

Fryer, John. A new Account of East India and Persia. Vol. 2. London: Hakluyt Society, 1909.

Genette, Gérard. Palimpsestes: Literature in the Second Degree. Trans. Channa Newman and Claude Doubinsky. Lincoln and London: U of Nebraska P, 1997.

Goethe, Johann Wolfgang von. Faust. Ed. and trans. Stuart Atkins. Cambridge, MA: Suhrkamp/Insel, 1984.

Gozzano, Guido. Verso la cuna del mondo: Lettere dall'India. Ed. Alida D'Aquino Creazzo. Florence: Olschki, 1984.

Grisay, Aletta. 'L'India di Guido Gozzano e quella di Pierre Loti.' La rassegna della letteratura italiana (Sept.–Dec. 1967): 427–37.

Heredia, José-Maria de. Les Trophées. Paris: Belles Lettres, 1984.

Hunter, William W. A History of British India. Vol. 1. London: Longmans, Green, 1899.

Kubler, George. Portuguese Plane Architecture between Spices and Diamonds, 1521–1706. Middletown, CT: Wesleyan UP, 1972.

Lopez-Rey, José. Velázquez: catalogue raisonné. Vol. 1. Köhln: Taschen, 1999.

Loti, Pierre. L'Inde (sans les Anglais). Paris: Calmann-Lévy, 1903.

Marinelli, David, trans. Journey toward the Cradle of Mankind. By Guido

Gozzano. Evanston, IL: Marlboro P/Northwestern, 1996.

Moretti, Franco. *Modern Epic: The World-System from Goethe to García Màrquez*. Trans. Quintin Hoare. London: Verso, 1996.

O'Hara, John M. Trans. *The Trophies*. By José-Maria de Heredia. Westport, CT: Hyperion, 1978.

Pearson, Michael N. *The Portuguese in India*. Cambridge: Cambridge UP, 1987.

Scammell, Geoffrey V. *The World Encompassed: The First European Maritime Empires, c. 800–1650*. London: Methuen, 1981.

Spitzer, Leo. 'La enumeración caótica en la poesia moderna.' *Lingüistica e Historia Literaria*. Madrid: Gredos, 1961. 247–91.

– 'Interpretation of an Ode by Paul Claudel.' *Linguistics and Literary History: Essays in Stylistics*. New York: Russell and Russell, 1962. 193–236.

Steinmetz, Horst. 'Genres and Literary History.' *General Problems of Literary History: Proceedings of the 10th Congress of the International Comparative Literature Association, New York 1982*. Ed. Anna Balakian et al. Vol. 1. New York: Garland, 1985. 251–5.

Warren, Édouard de. *L'Inde anglaise avant et après l'insurrection de 1857*. Vol. 2. Paris: Kailash, 1994.

Weinberger-Thomas, Catherine. 'Introduction. Les yeux fertiles de la mémoire: Exotisme indien et réprésentations occidentales.' *L'Inde et l'imaginaire/India in Western Imagination*. Centre d'études de l'Inde et de l'Asie du Sud 11. Ed. Catherine Weinberger-Thomas. Paris: École des Hautes Études en Sciences Sociales, 1988. 9–32.

Wilde, Oscar. *Epigrams and Aphorisms*. Boston: John W. Luce, 1905.

PART III

Avant-Garde

7 Modernism in Florence: The Politics of Avant-Garde Culture in the Early Twentieth Century

WALTER L. ADAMSON

Quando l'arte è in uno l'innervatura pulsante della sua anima, e vede che nel consenso comune essa è diventata una borsa dove banchieri e sensali mercanteggiano, deve sentire arroncigliarsi le sue dita e tremar del bisogno di abbrancare il collo di codesti lordatori. E così!: strangolarli.

[When art becomes a pulsating nervousness inside your soul, and you see that in the common opinion of the day art has become a commodities exchange where bankers and brokers haggle, you should feel your fingers tightly curl and tremble before the need to seize these filthy beasts by the neck: to strangle them!]

Scipio Slataper ('Ai Giovani' 1)

La Voce non è un giornale politico, non può, nè farà mai dichiarazioni socialiste, repubblicane o radicali; ma ricorderà sempre che i problemi della cultura nostra non si risolveranno che in relazione a quelli politici ed economici. [...] Quel divorzio funesto fra l'attività politica e le altre attività intellettuali e morali dello spirito umano [...] che è stata sempre una delle malattie peggiori della nostra patria, non esiste nella nostra coscienza.

[*La Voce* is not a political journal – it cannot and will not make socialist, republican, or radical declarations – but it will always remember that the problems of our culture can be resolved only in relation to political and economic ones. [...] That ruinous divorce between political activity and the other intellectual and moral activities of the human spirit [...] that has always been one of the greatest maladies in our country, does not exist in our consciousness.]

Giuseppe Prezzolini ('Perché siamo anticlerical,' 1; 'Da Giolitti,' 1)

Nineteenth-century bourgeois societies emancipated art in the sense that experience no longer had to be forced into a priori genres and period styles but was allowed to give birth to artistic form. This emancipation made possible an oppositional art, but it also unleashed a process of commodification which, by the century's close, threatened to redefine art as entertainment and to integrate it even more effectively than in pre-bourgeois societies. Thus arises the paradox of an art freed in principle and yet neutralized in practice. It is this paradox which provides the context for, and in a general way defines, the phenomenon of modernism in art.[1]

Modernism, however, was not merely a movement in the arts. It was also an effort to use the aesthetic realm to reinvigorate modern society and culture. Modernists were acutely aware of the social and cultural wounds opened by the disruptions of commodification, urbanization, and secularization. Modernism, as I, following Adorno, understand it, is the effort to overcome this crisis through the conviction that art has a fundamental role to play in restoring, or reinventing, the qualitative dimension of human experience. If commodification undermines experience by reducing it to the quantitative and fungible, art can restore or reinvent qualitative experience by coming to understand itself in its own terms, that is, by pursuing autonomy independent of all external functions, whether cognitive (like representation) or social (like entertainment). Only art pursues that which lies outside exchange and cannot be reduced to exchange value – such is modernism's fundamental premise.

For modernists, then, art pursued autonomously is the key to the reinvigoration of experience both private and public. While modernists prized the solitary, individual, and unique, they also aimed to use art to reinvigorate the public sphere. Modernism's restless, questing character – what Poggioli has called its 'agonism' (65–8) – should be treated, in my judgment, not simply as an internal characteristic of the modernist avant-garde, but also as a reflection of, and a response to, a late-nineteenth-century public sphere reconstituting itself under the impact of a new mass politics. As many recent historians have shown, much of Europe experienced a new vibrancy of public life after 1880, as mass-circulation newspapers expanded; 'little reviews' proliferated; 'leagues,' parties, and mass-entertainment industries developed; and new social types (the 'new woman,' the 'intellectual') were born.[2] Not only did modernist intellectuals play important roles in this new public life, but they helped to define it in a new way, one in which the aesthetic is not subordinated to society, which itself becomes an integrated totality (Friedrich Schiller's model of a century earlier), and in which autonomous art becomes in some ways the model for a performative politics of the self. In Italy, the role of art in defining a new politics of performance is perhaps most closely associated with Gabriele D'Annunzio.

In short, modernists responded to their perception of a civilization in crisis and, insisting that we must look forward rather than back, argued that autonomous art as the fundamental locus of qualitative experience was the key to overcoming it. In this way, modernism was inherently political. Yet, above all among modernists of the generation that came into its own about 1900, and thus after the heyday of aestheticism, politics was fused with culture in the way indicated by the epigraph taken from Prezzolini. Indeed, perhaps the most fundamental characteristic of that generation's modernism was its refusal to pursue either politics or culture in isolation. Committed politically to leading an aestheticization of the public sphere that challenged all parties, left and right, that failed to face up to the crisis of values in the social and political world, the early modernists were also committed culturally to a politicization of art. Cultural against actually existing politics, they were also political against actually existing cultures.

One further, general point about the politics of modernism must be made before we can turn to the Florentine experience. The bourgeois societies that produced commodification and oppositional art also, for related reasons, produced nationalism. As George Mosse has shown for Germany, nationalist thinking was often intensely aesthetic because it aimed to restore meaning to a sundered experiential life, and because aesthetic politics proved to have broad appeal in the new era of mass politics. Nationalism's ideal, like that of most romanticisms and post-Kantian idealisms, was that of a retotalized social world in which separations between the secular and religious, rational and emotional, public and private sides of life would be overcome. Although their ideal of autonomous art made modernists more wary of reconciling art and culture with the contemporary economy and state, their assessments of the problems in modern life and their emphasis on the aesthetic often brought them close to nationalist aesthetic politics. Indeed, although the point is insufficiently appreciated, modernism and nationalism can be said to have been engaged in a pas de deux. Even where nationalists were most intensely aligned against them, as in Germany and France, modernists commonly developed nationalist sentiments of their own – if only to protect themselves – while they explored the univeralist, cosmopolitan logic of their creative pursuits. Indeed, as we will soon see, the putative universalism of modernist art as well as its association with cosmopolitan cities like Paris could serve to intensify nationalist sentiment in a place like early-twentieth-century Florence.

The Coming of Avant-Garde Modernism in Florence

Florence may seem like a strange venue for a modernist movement. If one thinks of Paris as the archetypical city of modernism, then Florence – in its provincial backwardness – would seem to be the very opposite. Yet the fact that the wider European world around Florence was undergoing such rapid change, coupled with the exposure of its emerging intellectual avant-garde to that wider world and some of the developmental pressures Florence itself was beginning to experience, helps to explain why the city experienced the explosion of modernist vitality that it did shortly after 1900. The city's old aristocratic elite and its patronizing culture of *moderatismo* (middle-of-the-roadism) had prevented the emergence of anything approaching a vibrant public sphere, and the changes the city had undergone in the late nineteenth century increased the tensions between that elite and the vast majority of Florentines. Thus were planted the seeds not only of an avant-garde counter-culture but of a potent working-class opposition and, as would become fully apparent in 1921, a peasant-based opposition to the status quo as well. Moreover, in resting on its Renaissance laurels, the city's elite had made Florence into a Mecca for foreigners, further stimulating resentments among potential rebels of all kinds who were tired of seeing their city regarded as nothing but a tourist destination where one could not escape the 'nefando parlare anglo-, o franco-italiano d'albergo e di guida e di dizionario da viaggio [abominable Anglicized or Frenchified Italian of the hotels, guidebooks, and travel dictionaries].[3] Even in creating a university, the old Florentine elite had been so out of touch with the more advanced currents of European intellectual life that it had cultivated positivism at a time when this outlook was elsewhere under siege. In this sluggish, provincial climate, the avant-garde that the new university unintentionally helped to spawn counterattacked with ideals of masculinism, nationalism, and modernism, ideals necessary, in its view, to overcome the reigning obsession with material well-being and restore a sense of greatness to the public world.

The main vehicles of Florentine modernism were the journals *Leonardo* (1903–7), *La Voce* (1908–14), and *Lacerba* (1913–15); and their main protagonists, Giovanni Papini, Giuseppe Prezzolini, and Ardengo Soffici.[4] While they did not enter the city's cultural scene entirely without forerunners – the aestheticist *Il Marzocco* of Alfredo and Adolfo Orvieto and Giuseppe Pescetti's socialist movement dominated the cultural landscape of the 1890s – they consciously defined themselves against the ideals of these movements and, above all, against what they saw as a debilitating division of labour among opposition forces. A bohemian refinement based on an ideal of 'pure beauty' and a political activism based on a narrowly materialist appeal without a deeper cultural grounding – that was the split which, in their minds, defined the generation of their older brothers. It was a split to be overcome at all costs. For not only did it make no sense strategically – cultural and political imperatives were always inextricably linked – but it led inevitably to pessimism and defeatism. As Prezzolini reflected in his book, *Italia 1912*, 'la generazione di prima, era una generazione non credente, scettica. Ora questa gente de *La Voce* era diversa: essa credeva, bene o male, arbitariamente o razionalmente, sforzandosi verso l'universale o restringendosi in sé, con pregiudizi o senza, con un contenuto dogmatico o filosofico, ma credeva [the previous generation was a generation of unbelievers, of sceptics. These new people from *La Voce* were different: they believed, badly or well, arbitrarily or rationally, pushing towards the universal or restricting themselves to the particular, with prejudices or without, with dogmas or more philosophical beliefs – but they believed].' (83–4).

At the centre of this generation's beliefs, Prezzolini recalled, was that 'un movimento doveva essere *totale*, ossia doveva parlare all'uomo, all'uomo di oggi, all'italiano d'oggi con una sua lingua, con un suo modo di esprimersi; doveva essere tutto collegato, intieramente radicato con l'arte: e non con l'arte in genere, ma con quell'arte che meglio si stringeva a quel modo idealistico di vedere [a movement ought to be *total*, it ought to speak to people, to contemporary people, to today's Italians in their own language, in their own modes of expression; it ought to be wholly integrated with, wholly rooted in art – and not just art in general but with those forms of art most closely tied to idealist ways of seeing]' (*Italia 1912* 85–6). While he did not indicate the source of this belief, he could have done so with a single word: Paris. All of the key figures in the Italian modernist avant-gardes, including Marinetti, Papini, Soffici, and Prezzolini, had crucial formative experiences in Paris, imbibing its art and philosophy as well as the culture of its soirées and revues. Important as the heritage of the previous generation – D'Annunzian Decadentism and, above all, Crocean Idealism as expressed in the *Estetica* (1902) – was for them, it was from their experiences in Paris that they came to appreciate the role of the aesthetic for modern cultural renewal.

Paris, it must quickly be added, did not mean exactly the same thing for each of them. Soffici's Paris was the most bound up with art and poetry. It was he who introduced the readers of *La Voce* and *Lacerba* to the Paris art scene with early articles on Gustave Courbet, Henri Rousseau, Auguste Renoir, and Pablo Picasso, in addition to his topical pieces on Impressionism; it was also Soffici who introduced them to French avant-garde poetry with his 1911 study of Arthur Rimbaud, the first such book published in Italy. The Paris of Papini and Prezzolini, in contrast, was much more centred on philosophy and social thought; theirs was the Paris of Sorel, Péguy, and Rolland. Far more than Soffici's, this was a Paris of émigrés from the various regions of France – Sorel from Cherbourg, Péguy from Orléans, Rolland from Clamecy – and, perhaps in part because of those provincial origins, it was a Paris of moralism and high intellectual seriousness, of the Sorbonne rather than Montmartre. Yet there was one Parisian figure who influenced everyone, precisely because he straddled and overcame the division of art and philosophy in thought as well as in life. That man was Henri Bergson.

Bergson was the inspirational figure not only for Sorel's social philosophy but also for many of the Cubists.[5] For what Bergson had discovered was an inspiration to activists and creators of all sorts: that there were two fundamental modes of human knowing, intuition and analysis, but that only the former was absolute and in harmony with reality, while the latter was relative and conceptual, a mere tool for manipulating reality for human ends. Intuition lies deep within us, while analysis is external; intuition involves not so much the discovery of new knowledge as the revelation of what at some deep level we already know. Intuition is the vital source of life and of qualitative rather than quantitative experience. Bergson's concepts of life and experience overcame the oppositions of reason and faith, science and art, cosmos and psyche, in a way that satisfied the yearnings of the Florentine modernists for a unified cultural renewal and a new secular religion. It also led them to an appreciation of that art which did not paint or write as if the world existed independently of our consciousness but which understood that the world is apprehended differently by each of us, and that at the centre of all genuine art must lie a vision at once individual, interior, and intimate. Bergson alerted them precisely to the nature of those forms of art that partook of 'idealist ways of seeing.'

Modernism and Nationalism in *Leonardo*

In linking art and religion through an indepth analysis of intuition as a mode of knowing, Bergson was giving philosophical shape to the modernist imperative of cultural renewal via secular religion that is receiving increasing historical attention.[6] It was certainly an imperative in full force among the writers for *Leonardo* – or the *leonardiani*, as they were called. No word recurred more often in that journal's pages than 'renewal' and its various near-equivalents: 'rebirth,' 'reawakening,' 'renaissance,' 'regeneration,' 'resurgence,' and 'resurrection.' Nor was any attitude more deprecated there than the one that simply contemplated the world rather than seeking to remake it.[7] Theirs was a philosophical quest for faith inspired by Bergson, William James, F.C.S. Schiller, and other philosophers aiming to uncover a primal self buried beneath the debilitating incrustations of a decadent civilization. In so probing spiritual depths, they explicitly hoped to locate the basis for a 'nuova era spirituale dell'umanità [new spiritual era of humanity]' ... 'la nuova religione che doveva succedere al cristianismo [the new religion that should succeed Christianity]' (Papini, 'Mazzini' 1). Yet, supposing that such a religion could be created, would the people accept it? Could cultural renewal, once conceived, be put into practice? Doubts about such questions constantly plagued the *leonardiani*. On the one hand, they frequently appealed to a kind of cultural populism in which the falseness, corruption, and backwardness of Italian cultural life were traced to control by the academy and in which the hope for renewal was linked to liberating the 'potenza personale, segreta [secret personal power]' or 'subliminal selves' of the common people (Papini, 'Atena e Faust' 1).[8] Such sentiments were perhaps strongest in Soffici who, reacting against seven years of life among the 'decadent' Parisian avant-garde, idealized the vigour and quiet strength of the Tuscan peasantry after his return in 1907, thereby creating the ideal of *toscanità*.[9] On the other hand, they often imagined a 'sleeping' and 'ignorant' people who might never be 'awakened' or 'changed.' Much of their writing evoked an ideal of solitude that seemed aimed at consoling them, as it had Nietzsche's Zarathustra, for their inability to reach the unblinking herd. Thus, for example, they had pictured Leonardo as loving 'l'opera solitaria [solitary work]' (Papini, 'Il segreto' 1), Bergson as having conceived the good life as that of 'uno spettator solitario [a solitary spectator]' (Prezzolini, 'Vita trionfanti' 1), and André Gide as being 'uno dei compagni della solitudine che amiamo di più per il suo spirito semplice e profondo [one of the companions in solitude whom we love most for his simple and profound spirit]' (Papini, Review of 'Saül' 1).

The ambivalence about the Tuscan *popolo* among the *leonardiani* was reflected in a division within their notions of cultural renewal itself, for they aimed to reinvigorate both the public and the private spheres, both collective and individual life. While many, probably most of their preoccupations were self-consciously 'spiritual,' that is, on a higher plane than mere 'politics,' they were also quite clear about the need for the integration of a political moment into their concept of cultural regeneration. Both Papini and Prezzolini wrote several expressly political articles during the first year of *Leonardo*, and when Enrico Corradini founded *Il Regno* late in 1903, they contributed substantially to the effort; indeed, Papini served as its first editor. Moreover, from the beginning it was clear that their political ideas turned on a nationalist commitment. In 1904, for example, Papini devoted considerable time to giving speeches in various towns and cities on his 'programma nazionalista' [nationalist program]'.[10] Yet while they made common cause with Corradini, they could not accept his commitments to what they viewed as anti-modern ideals of *romanità* (Romanness), organic nationalism, and imperial grandeur. These ideals were not only incompatible with their own individualism, but overly traditionalist and bombastic. Rather than build an Italian nationalism on such principles, they preferred to think in terms of a refortified Tuscan regionalism as the grounding for a modernist vision of cultural renewal. They believed that their views were at once intellectually dynamic and rooted in textures of local life.

Soffici was the *leonardiano* who gave the fullest and most emotionally charged expression of this synthesis. When Papini had trumpeted his 'campagna per il forzato risveglio [campaign for a reawakening by force]' in a 1906 issue, Soffici contributed a woodcut, 'Don Chisciotte in Toscana [Don Quixote in Tuscany],' for its cover. The image suggested a cultural renewal spearheaded by lone-crusading, idealist intellectuals who would eventually make contact with the peasant masses, restoring genuine spirituality to the world while simultaneously overcoming Italian backwardness by linking intellectual and popular vitalities. It was an image that both Soffici ('Don Chisciotte') and Papini ('Miguel de Unamuno') associated with parallel efforts by Miguel de Unamuno in Spain. However, it also raised all the usual doubts. As Soffici argued in a letter to Papini, 'l'idea invisibile è nell'Arte e nell'Amore e quindi in *noi* [the invisible idea is in Art and in Love and thus in *us*].' Yet,

> Il popolo non può credere al nostro: il suo Dio è un signore con la barba, buono e terribile, un immenso *Padrone* che sorveglia ogni cosa ... Se non crede più a questo Dio, è finita – e ora non ci crede – ed è bene. Ma il popolo non si sgomenta mai, e quando si ritrova senza un Dio, si crea degli Dei. Ora ne ha fra le mani diversi: la Scienza, l'Economia politica, il Progresso generalmente, ecc. Sta a noi, lavorare perché egli cessi di esser politeista e ateo per divenire come noi. Non è forse questo il più etico degli scopi e la più bella speranza della Cultura?

> [The people cannot believe in our God; their God is a master with a beard, good and terrible, an immense *Padrone* who watches over everything ... If this God no longer commands belief, he is finished – and today he is no longer believed in, and that is good. But the people are never daunted, and when they find themselves without a God, they create Gods. Now they have in their hands various ones: Science, Political Economy, Progress generally, etc. It is for us to work to see that they cease this polytheism and atheism and become like us. Is this not perhaps the most ethical of purposes and the most beautiful hope in Culture?][11]

The idea of synthesizing international modernist and Tuscan regionalist perspectives in a call for national 'renewal' remained over the next half-decade the Florentine avant-garde's alternative to the more conservative and narrowly political forms of nationalism proposed by Corradini and his friends, who created the Italian Nationalist Association (ANI) in 1910. But *Leonardo* itself did not last, for reasons having to do primarily with the group's internal politics. As the journal's issues mounted towards the twenty-five they would ultimately number, *Leonardo* looked more and more like the idiosyncratic expression of a few individuals rather than the mouthpiece of an avant-garde group or intellectual generation. Moreover, the issues became increasingly bulky, forbidding in appearance, and remote from the audience they hoped to reach. Ideas the *leonardiani* had, but they had proven unable to institutionalize themselves as a movement or to connect with the people they claimed to champion. The journal was forced to commit a self-described 'suicidio [suicide]' (Papini, 'La fine') in the summer of 1907.

La Voce as Avant-Garde Convention

When the idea of a successor journal to *Leonardo* took shape a year and a half later, it was the principle of tolerating differences in order to forge a unified movement that lay at the centre of the Florentine avant-garde's vision. As Prezzolini wrote shortly after the maiden issue of *La Voce* in December 1908, 'Il *Leonardo*, invece, è stata la più bella espressione del momento arbitrario della coscienza individuale. [...] Ma come Enrico Heine si accorse un giorno che un Dio non poteva aver male allo stomaco, così la coscienza arbitraria si accorge di non esser sola e separata dal mondo, ma di avere nel fondo di se stessa la comunicazione con l'infinito dal quale si sprigionano tutti gli individui [*Leonardo* was the most beautiful expression of the arbitrary moment of individual consciousness. [...] But just as Heinrich Heine recognized one day that God cannot have a stomach ache, so, too, arbitrary consciousness recognizes that it is not alone and separate from the world but has in its depths a communication with the infinite from which every individual emanates]' (*La teoria sindicalista* 31). To coexist as a group, the *vociani* would have to learn to tolerate their internal differences.[12] That was the self-conscious understanding of the group in 1908, and it underlay Prezzolini's characterization of *La Voce* in *Italia 1912)*, even after the crisis of the Libyan War effectively dissolved that unity:

> *La Voce* del primo anno era un convegno di gente molto differente: per origine, per età, per fini, per cultura. I contatti, spesso violenti, le affermazioni, contraddittorie. Gli atteggiamenti in urto fra loro. Eppure come mai il pubblico sentì un'aria di famiglia, un senso di unità, qualche cosa che legava tutti ad un compito? Non si sa come avvenne, ma avvenne. O meglio dire si sa come avvenne: quest'unità, questa famiglia c'era davvero, rispetto alla disorganizzazione delle scuole, dei partiti, delle religioni, di tutto. (83)

> [From the beginning *La Voce* was a convention with many different kinds of people attending, different in terms of origin, aims, and cultural background. The encounters were often violent, the resolutions contradictory.

Attitudes clashed. How was it, then, that the public saw a family atmosphere, a sense of unity, something that tied everyone together? It is not clear how this happened, but it did. Or rather: it is clear how it happened, since there really was this unity, this family, in comparison with the disorganization of the schools, political parties, religions, and all the rest.]

In editing *La Voce* and leading the *vociani*, Prezzolini saw himself as a facilitator rather than a unifier. As he wrote in the journal's 'Progetto [programmatic statement],' the journal's principles would be 'abbastanza larga per ammettere persone di molto varie vedute [sufficiently broad to admit persons of very diverse views],' and the only obligatory commitment for its writers would be that 'quello che scrivono è suscittibile di difesa razionale e non è titillamento delle loro fantasie o uno sfogo dei loro bisogni sentimentali [what they write is capable of rational defence and is not the titillation of their fantasies or the venting of their emotional needs]' (100). For the most part, the principle served him well. All in all, *La Voce* involved more than three hundred different writers ranging across political views and subject matters. Among the more important literary contributors were Scipio Slataper, Piero Jahier, and Emilio Cecchi. In politics and history, Gaetano Salvemini and Giovanni Amendola joined Antonio Anzilotti, Romolo Murri, and Luigi Ambrosini. In philosophy, there were Benedetto Croce and Giovanni Gentile, along with Giovanni Boine and Piero Jahier. Finally, of course, Prezzolini, Papini, and Soffici all wrote voluminously and on many subjects for *La Voce*'s pages.

The blend of diversity and coherence that *La Voce* achieved, especially during its first three years, was all the more remarkable in view of the intellectual itineraries of its major protagonists, who had, if anything, grown further apart since the demise of *Leonardo*. Prezzolini had become a Crocean in 1908 and a Sorelian syndicalist in 1909, choices neither Soffici nor Papini could abide. They, in turn, deepened their interests in avant-garde art, spiritualism, and *toscanità*, ideas Prezzolini shared but with far less passion. Prezzolini remained the philosopher, while Papini moved away from philosophy towards poetry and away from the Parisian intellectual world towards the mountainous countryside just north of Arezzo, where he now spent much of his time. His concepts of a religion of art and of *toscanità* were not the same as Soffici's, but they were no less prominent in his thought.

What primarily held *La Voce* together was the intention of each of its main figures to remain activist, and in that sense avant-garde. When

Papini explained his move away from philosophy ('pura speculazione' – pure speculation) in an 18 May 1908 letter to Prezzolini (*Storia* 1:212– 15), he did so in terms that all of them shared and would continue to share:

> Io sono spinto a modificare qualcosa. [...] Per me il moralista deve essere apostolo – deve prima conoscere ma conoscere per *fare*. E per fare, cioè per agire sugli uomini, non basta la semplice e nuda manifestazione del pensiero. Ci vuol l'arte, cioè qualcosa che più universalmente muova e persuada i nostri simili, e per questo ho deciso di essere un apostolo morale vale a dire un essere pensante [...] e infine un essere artista il quale si giova del ragionamento appassionato e della rappresentazione estetica, della favola o della predica, per muovere fortemente gli uomini, e per indurli a mutar vita.

> [I am driven to change things. [...] For me the moralist should be an apostle – should first know, but know in order *to create*. And to create, that is, to act on men, the simple and bare manifestation of thought is not enough. It is necessary also to have art, that is, something that moves and persuades people like us at a more universal level, and that is why I have decided to become a moral apostle, that is, a thinking being [...] and an artistic being who uses passionate reasoning and aesthetic representation, fables and sermons, to move men forcefully and induce them to change their lives.]

Though Prezzolini preferred to cast this argument in Crocean terms as the importance of the moment '*dell'intuizione* [of intuition]' in preparing the way for the higher moment '*del pensiero* [of thought],' his understanding was substantially the same.[13]

In addition to the unity it derived from its activism, *La Voce* was solidified by a common sense of the desirable relation between Italian and European culture. That Italian intellectual life was viewed by its northern neighbours as backward and, at least in recent times, derivative was clearly a sore point among the *vociani*, and Papini made it the theme of the lead article for the journal's very first issue. There he argued ('L'Italia risponde') that although '*forestieri illustri* [distinguished foreigners]' had until recently heavily influenced Italian culture (Nietzsche was his main example), this tendency was now slowing, and he himself felt a new freedom to speak. At the same time, he was careful not to push to the point of chauvinism the national pride he felt in this liberation. In concluding he wrote: 'Si legga pure Comte, ma anche Galileo – si ammiri Loisy ma anche Sarpi – si citi Hegel ma anche Bruno – si traduca Nietzsche ma si goda anche Macchiavelli ... Si tratta di ridare all'Italia non soltanto il contatto colla cultura europea ma anche la conscienza storica della cultura sua, ch'è pur tanta parte della cultura europea. Io mi contento di poco: Nazionalisti no, ma Italiani sì! [We should read Comte but also Galileo; we should admire Loisy but also Sarpi; we should cite Hegel but also Bruno; we should translate Nietzsche, but we should also enjoy Machiavelli ... We need to give Italy again not only contact with European culture but also historical consciousness of its own culture, which is certainly a significant part of European culture. I shall content myself with a few words: nationalists no, Italians yes!]'[14]

In Soffici and Prezzolini, too, the accent fell frequently on the desirability of reinvigorating national and local creativity by appropriating without simply copying the strongest creative forces operating internationally. Thus Soffici ('L'impressionismo' 1) saw in French Impressionism 'la possibilità di un ammaestramento virile, che raccolto dalla nostra gioventù potrebbe servirle come di spinta verso ricerche personali, di carattere tutto nostro e capaci di rendere un frutto vitale [the possibility of a vigorous education that, absorbed by our youth, might serve them as an impulse towards personal quests that can produce vital results while also being completely Italian].' Prezzolini reacted similarly to German Expressionism, the first stirrings of which had coincided with his sojourn in Munich during the summer of 1905. National traditions and the rootedness of one's perceptions in local experience need not be protected from the creative forces operating internationally. On the contrary, they ought to be nurtured by them, thus raising the prospect of a powerful cross-fertilization between innovations in high culture and volkish rootedness. Nationalism, they sensed, was often a defensive reaction but it was most vital when open to foreignness and inclusive.

The point may be further clarified by a comparison of the nationalism of the *vociani* with that of one of their avant-garde compatriots in France, Guillaume Apollinaire. Apollinaire, born in Italy of an Italian father, was a good friend of Soffici's and would collaborate on *Lacerba*. Yet he felt himself to be Parisian through and through, and, unlike Soffici, he had no 'local' attachment to balance his Parisian avantgardism. Nonetheless, he was very much the French nationalist. In part, his nationalism was a response to being viewed as 'other' by the French ethnic nationalists, such as the critic Georges Duhamel, who dismissed him as running a 'boutique de brocanteur [second-hand furniture store]' in a 1913 review of his newly published *Alcools*. But it also reflected the strong nationalist current that had run through the French avant-garde ever since the *Naturisme* [naturism] of the late 1890s, a current this avant-garde developed largely in order to defend itself against charges of anti-Frenchness by the cultural right. In the very different environs of Florence such defensive nationalism was unnecessary, and the nationalism of its modernist avant-garde was, on the contrary, part of their effort to take the cultural offensive. Still, as in France, so here, too, the modernists made a point of distinguishing their nationalism from the extreme right versions of a Corradini or a Charles Maurras.

A final commonality among the *vociani* emerges when one probes more deeply into the differences between their nationalism and that of the cultural right. Unlike Corradini and the ANI, who saw themselves as a party of order and who represented the conservative side in their alliance with the Fascists in 1923, the *vociani* were committed more or less equally to anarchy and order, to creativity and control. This precarious combination is well-illustrated by Scipio Slataper, a *triestino* who had moved to Florence and who would die in the early days of the First World War. His anarchic attitude and the anger it represented, which are fully evident in the words cited in the epigraph to this chapter, were extreme enough to lead him to criticize his fellow *vociani* on this point. 'Il torto della *Voce*,' he wrote just after the outbreak of the war in Libya, 'è stato di schematizzare la vita. [...] Prezzolini manca sopratutto di giocondità. Manca d'abbandono, di scampagnate all'aria, di discorsi facili e magari un poco imbecilli. Prezzolini è sempre serio [The mistake of *La Voce* has been that it schematizes life. [...] Prezzolini lacks above all a certain joyousness, a sense of abandon, an openness to outings in the country and to conversation that is casual or even a bit silly. Prezzolini is always serious].'[15] Life, for Slataper ('Quando Roma' 1), was instinctive and primitive, best lived in the manner of 'le lontane terre barbariche [distant barbarous lands].' Yet his 'barbarism' also had a self-consciously moralistic side, one committed to values such as sacrifice, discipline, and – above all – work. As his friend Giani Stuparich would later write (99), work for Slataper 'vuol dire vivere [...] di convincere, d'insegnare, di amare, di creare. La cosa divina, l'amicizia degli uomini, la felicità [means *to live* [...] to persuade, to teach, to love, to create. The divine, human friendship, happiness],' and Slataper himself often spoke of the value of work, though of 'un lavoro più intenzionale, di sprone e invito, che lavoro proprio lavoro [a more intentional kind of work that spurs and invites rather than work for the sake of work]' ('Il silenzio' 1).

Art and Philosophy, Anarchy and Order

But Slataper was only the most extreme representative of that compound of anarchy and order that can be found in the outlook of all the major figures of *La Voce*. Unstable in the best of times, it was the source of the group's rapid unravelling when powerful external events like the war in Libya and the rise of the Futurist movement overtook them. Differences over each of these events and their relative significance led to the defection of Gaetano Salvemini from *La Voce* in October 1911 and increased tensions among those who remained over the proper relation between culture and politics in a modernist review. Should the group aim to develop a culture through which the masses are genuinely educated for practical political action, even if this culture becomes divorced from the international avant-garde and its conceptions? Or should the aim be to create a new culture in the most avant-garde way, even if it does not engage the masses – or *does* engage them, but in a politically irrational manner? If the former aim is chosen, how can the group continue to think of itself as a modernist avant-garde; if the latter, how can it continue to maintain that the artistic, poetic, and philosophical efforts of the various individuals associated with it are bringing about the intellectual and moral redemption of Italy? This was the fundamental question that would be posed with increasing insistence in 1912 and that would mark the dividing line between *La Voce* and *Lacerba* after the founding of the latter in 1913.

Florentine avant-garde modernism did not end in the fall of 1911, nor did *La Voce*. But the 'convention' Prezzolini had spoken about in connection with the early *La Voce* certainly did. More and more over the next three years, the Florentine avant-garde became split between the intense, if short-lived, Futurism and ribald irreverence of the *lacerbiani* and the philosophical and high moral seriousness of *La Voce*, which was now increasingly identified with Prezzolini alone. While *La Voce* promoted the Croce-Gentile debate and offered Prezzolini's own philosophical reflections on modernity, *Lacerba*'s inaugural manifesto declared that 'tutto è permesso [everything is permitted]'; rejected 'serietà [seriousness]' and 'dimostrazioni razionali [rational demon-

strations]'; promoted art as the 'giustificazione del mondo [justifica-
tion of the world]'; and voiced its preference for 'il bozzetto più della
composizione, il frammento più della statua, l'aforisma più del trattato
[the sketch over the composition, the potsherd over the statue, the
aphorism over the treatise]' (Papini, 'Introibo' 1). *Lacerba's* articles were
slapdash and marked by colloquialisms and playful, sometimes mor-
dant polemic. The journal insisted on catering to a popular, and even
working-class audience, while also printing as much as possible of the
Parisian and Futurist avant-gardes and aiming to be 'un foglio stonato,
urtante, spiacevole e personale [a journal that is jarring, irritating, un-
pleasant, and personal]' (Papini, 'Introibo' 1). And it had undeniable
success. Though it rejected *La Voce's* project of elevating the masses
through education, it managed to gain their attention far more effectively (as print-run figures attest) than *La Voce* ever did. The young
Antonio Gramsci may have read *La Voce*, but it was *Lacerba* that, according to him (53), was read by the industrial workers he organized.

After Europe was plunged into war in the summer of 1914, the two
wings of Florentine modernism united again by virtue of their common enthusiasm for Italian intervention on the side of the Entente.
Over the next nine months, they all became immersed in interventionist politics, *Lacerba* taking an expressly political turn (it ended in May
1915 when Italy entered the war) at the same time that Prezzolini
moved to Rome to join Mussolini's new *Il Popolo d'Italia*, as well as to
put out a Roman edition of *La Voce*, which he called *La Voce politica*.
Yet this solidarity would last only so long as Italy did not enter the
war. Once that occurred, the Florentine avant-garde died an instant
death, at least for the generation that had created it. Had the war
proven to be the reinvigorating and 'revolutionary' event that the avant-
garde had anticipated, their own end as an expression of a collective
culture might not have mattered. But before Italian participation was
many weeks old, it was clear to all of them that the war was doing far
more to kill than to realize the ideals with which they had invested it.
Although they had imagined the war as the long-delayed fruit of a
decade of cultural activism, it proved in reality to mark a new beginning in which each of the major participants in that activism would go
his separate way and all common efforts would be abandoned.

The campaign for intervention, then, marked the last chapter in
what had begun to unfold in Florence with the debut of *Leonardo* in
1903. Although it reunited that generation with a common sense of
purpose that they had not shared since the early days of *La Voce*, it
also demonstrated that there was a certain trade-off between their

own solidarity and their belief in the collective power of the popular masses they were seeking to influence. Never had their view of the masses reached such despairing depths. To understand why Italy was attracted by the neutralist appeal, Papini argued ('Due nemici' 1), one had first to recognize that its *popolo* was 'il più gretto, più meschino, più incerto, più avaro che vivi e moltiplichi sulla faccia della terra [the most narrow-minded, petty, uncertain, and niggardly that lives and multiplies on the face of the earth].' And while Prezzolini and Soffici never used language this extreme, they too argued for the war far more in terms of its capacity to 'make Italians' than in terms of any territorial or other more tangible benefits for Italy. Nearly four years later, when the war finally came to an end, they saw that among its few favourable effects was that the Italian *popolo* had come into its own and was now ready to play a more mature role in public life. Soffici, especially, rhapsodized ('Principî' 1) about his new-found respect for the creativity of 'i miei operai [the workers around me],' and came to feel even that 'gli uomini sono destinati a divenire, col tempo, tutti artisti; e che l'espressione artistica propriamente detta poteva rivelarsi alla fine inutile e quindi cessare [all men were destined to become artists over time, and therefore that artistic expression in the proper sense of the word would ultimately become useless and cease].' Yet, seemingly, as their enthusiasm for those they addressed increased, their own unity fell apart, and each went his separate way. Papini became a born-again Christian, albeit at least initially of a highly idiosyncratic sort. Prezzolini relinquished modernism and gave himself over to a straightforwardly political embrace of Mussolini's Fascism, even if he often despaired at the antics of the Fascist *squadristi*. And Soffici renounced all varieties of pre-war avant-gardism in favour of a post-war 'return to order,' only to rededicate himself by the mid-1920s to a new sort of regionalist avant-gardism, the *'strapaese'* movement associated with Mino Maccari's *Il Selvaggio*.

Politicization and Dissolution

But let us return for a moment to 1915. The most immediate result of the European conflagration for Florentine modernism was the movement's politicization. *Lacerba* moved abruptly from art to politics. New political newspapers and journals were born, and the locus of collective concern shifted from Tuscany to Rome. Prezzolini abandoned *La Voce*, and its editorship was assumed by Giuseppe De Robertis, who transformed it into a purely literary journal devoid of political projects or involvements. In short, the pressure of international events split apart the cultural and political synthesis of Florentine modernism. Art recoiled from the catastrophe of public life and became self-reflective; modernist politics lost their wider cultural reference and felt the need to ally with the emerging political movements the war had spawned, above all Bolshevism and Fascism.

The one exception to this picture was the journal *L'Italia futurista*, created by a group of young Florentines born in the early 1890s, hence standing in relation to the generation of Papini and Prezzolini more or less as they had stood in relation to the aestheticism of *Il Marzocco*. Born out of the depths of war in June 1916, *L'Italia futurista* never achieved the prestige of *La Voce* or the notoriety of *Lacerba*, but the young collective who ran it was determined to perpetuate the cultural-political synthesis of its modernist forebears, indeed, to best them at their own game. As the journal's name suggests, the group had close ties with Marinetti, and that fact, coupled with generational rivalry, led them to an immanent critique of *Lacerba* as failing to live up to its own ideals. As one member of the group expressed the point, '*di fronte a noi, i futuristi di* Lacerba *apparivano un po' come dei professori convertiti* [...] *come il residuo di un bagaglio tradizionalista da rifiutare* [compared with us, the futurists of *Lacerba* appeared a bit like converted professors [...] like the remains of a traditionalist baggage to be discarded]' (Conti 131). And they did in fact sharpen their technological edge – in typography, photography, and film – in a way that appeared to date the *lacerbiani*. Moreover, *L'Italia futurista* proved able to draw strength from war itself (as against merely feeding on the prospect of war), strength sufficient to forge itself into a collective unit, a protopolitical party, in a way that not even the early *La Voce* had achieved.

Yet the bloom of *L'Italia futurista* endured only until February 1918. As the military tide turned in Italy's favour and expectations about post-war politics grew more intense, some of its stalwarts also felt the need to move to Rome and to begin more strictly political enterprises. While the larger Futurist movement to which *L'Italia futurista* belonged might have appeared to be bringing the fruits of pre-war modernism to a resplendent harvest, the idea of an alliance of Futurism and Fascism as co-equals, which Marinetti fantasized in 1919, ultimately provoked the fracturing of Futurism into divergent political and aesthetic roads, just as the war had fractured the Florentine avant-garde that *L'Italia futurista* sought to supersede. By 1923, with his Futurist movement in complete disarray, Marinetti publicly ceded (560–9) Futurism's political moment to the new regime by accepting the notion that a narrowly 'aesthetic' Futurism could offer loyal support for the 'political revolution' of Fascism in return for a kind of state sanction. However successful one may judge Marinetti's 'second Futurism,' it was a very different sort of avant-garde than its heroic, pre-war counterpart.

In the second half of the 1920s and into the early 1930s, the group around Maccari's *Il Selvaggio* may have appeared to have revived the fusion of culture and politics upon which all pre-war Italian modernism had been based, but it did so only at the cost of an increasing irrelevance to the regime and the populace it sought to influence. Its lack of a substantial audience and its inability to enter into the regime or the party in administrative roles meant that no one was obliged to take its pronouncements seriously, and the group's shrill, anti-American pose as Tuscan *'selvaggî* [savages]' turned its members into quaint curiosities rather than the cultural leaders that the pre-war Florentine modernists had been.

In the end, then, one is driven to the conclusion that the fusion of culture and politics that had given pre-war Italian modernism its distinctive character was unable to survive the war and the political forces it unleashed. For Florentine modernism in particular, one is therefore led to further reflection upon the context of the local *moderatismo* in which it had taken root. In addition to stimulating the cultural adventurism that led the young avant-gardists to Paris and the anger that provoked their modernist critiques, the stagnant provincialism of fin-de-siècle Florence seems to have offered the sort of neglectful and passively liberal environment in which a potent opposition can thrive. Once more powerful external forces overwhelmed that environment, sending it into turmoil and provoking new, expressly political forces of opposition, Florentine modernism fragmented and lost its original character. During the interwar years, modernist movements would survive only in those environments not overwhelmed by new political movements, that is, only in relatively provincial places like *moderatista* England.

NOTES

1 The classic formulation of this argument is Adorno 225–9.

2 For France, where this vibrancy is especially evident and has been most studied, see the studies by Rearick, Weber, Kleeblatt, Silverman (1989), Charle, and Schwartz.
3 See Prezzolini ('I miei fiorentini') and Papini ('Contro Firenzi').
4 For the full story, see Adamson. In its original form under Prezzolini's editorship, *La Voce* ended in 1914, but it continued as a more strictly literary journal under the editorship of Giuseppe De Robertis through 1916.
5 For the latter connection, see Antliff.
6 See especially Silverman, 'Weaving Paintings.'
7 See, for example, Papini, 'Marta e Maria.'
8 Papini's notion of 'subliminal self' appears in English in the original. See also Papini, 'Campagna.'
9 See, for example, Soffici's letter of 31 May or 1 June 1908 to Papini in their *Carteggio* (237–8).
10 This program appeared in print only a decade later when Papini and Prezzolini recycled their early 'spiritual-nationalists' writings for the intervention campaign of 1914–15.
11 Soffici, letter to Papini of 7 Sept. 1908 in their *Carteggio* (341–2); emphasis in original.
12 See Prezzolini's letter to Papini of 6 Mar. 1908 in their *Storia* 1:181.
13 See his letter to Papini of 28 May 1908 in Gentili (229–30).
14 The article impressed Romain Rolland, who translated it into French.
15 Letter from Slataper to Gigetta of 17 Dec. 1911 in Slataper, *Lettere*, 3:119.

WORKS CITED

Adamson, Walter L. *Avant-garde Florence: From Modernism to Fascism.* Cambridge: Harvard UP, 1993.
Adorno, Theodor W. *Aesthetic Theory.* Trans. R. Hullot-Kentor. Minneapolis: U of Minnesota P, 1997.
Antliff, Mark. *Inventing Bergson.* Princeton: Princeton UP, 1993.
Charle, Christophe. *Naissance des Intellectuels 1880–1900.* Paris: Éditions de Minuit, 1990.
Conti, Primo. *La gola del merlo.* Florence: Sansoni, 1983.
Duhamel, Georges. Review of Guillaume Apollinaire, *Alcools. Mercure de France* (16 June 1913).
Gentili, Sandro. 'Prezzolini e Soffici e Papini (1902, 1908, 1912).' *Giovanni Papini: L'uomo impossibile.* Ed. Paolo Bagnoli. Florence: Sansoni, 1982. 220–51.

Gramsci, Antonio. *Selections from Cultural Writings*. Ed. D. Forgacs and
G. Nowell-Smith. Trans. W. Boelhower. Cambridge: Harvard UP, 1985.
Kleeblatt, Norman L., ed. *The Dreyfus Affair: Art, Truth, and Justice*. Berkeley,
Los Angeles, and London: U of California P, 1987.
Marinetti, F.T. 'I diritti artistici propugnati dai futuristi italiani: Manifesto al
governo fascista.' *Teoria e invenzione futurista*. Ed. L. De Maria. Milan:
Mondadori, 1983. 560–9.
Mosse, George L. *The Nationalization of the Masses*. New York: Howard Fertig,
1975.
Papini, Giovanni. 'Atena e Faust.' *Leonardo* (Feb. 1905).
– 'Campagna per il forzato risveglio.' *Leonardo* (Aug. 1906).
– 'Contro Firenze.' *Lacerba* (15 Dec. 1913).
– 'Due nemici.' *Il Popolo d'Italia* (9 Feb. 1915).
– 'La fine.' *Leonardo* (Aug. 1907).
– 'L'Italia risponde.' *La Voce* (20 Dec. 1908).
– 'Introibo.' *Lacerba* (1 Jan. 1913).
– 'Marta e Maria (dalla contemplazione all'azione).' *Leonardo* (March 1904).
– 'Mazzini è stato tradito.' *Leonardo* (June-Aug. 1905).
– 'Miguel de Unamuno.' *Leonardo* (April-June 1907).
– 'Un programma nazionalista' [1904]. Papini, Giovanni and Giuseppe
Prezzolini, *Vecchio e nuovo nazionalismo*. Milan: Studio Editoriale Lombardo,
1914. 1–36.
– Review of '*Saül, Le Roi Candaule*.' *Leonardo* (June 1904).
– 'Il segreto di Leonardo.' *Leonardo* (19 Apr. 1903).
Papini, Giovanni, and Giuseppe Prezzolini. *Storia d'un amicizia*. 2 vols.
Florence: Vallecchi, 1966.
Papini, Giovanni, and Ardengo Soffici. *Carteggio, I, 1903–1908: Dal 'Leonardo'
a 'La Voce*.' Ed. M. Richter. Rome: Edizioni di Storia e Letteratura, 1991.
Poggioli, Renato. *The Theory of the Avant-garde*. Trans. G. Fitzgerald. Cam-
bridge: Harvard UP, 1968.
Prezzolini, Giuseppe. 'Da Giolitti a Sonnino.' *La Voce* (16 Dec. 1909a).
– *Italia 1912: Dieci anni di vita intellettuale (1903–1912)*. Ed. C.M. Simonetti.
Florence: Vallecchi, 1984.
– 'I miei fiorentini.' *La Voce* (7 and 21 Apr., 14 July 1910).
– 'Perché siamo anticlericali.' *La Voce* (21 Jan. 1909).
– 'Progetto di una rivista di pensiero in Italia' [1908]. Prezzolini, *Italia 1912*.
97–103.
– *La teoria sindacalista*. Naples: Perrella, 1909.
– 'Vita trionfante.' *Leonardo* (4 Jan. 1903).
Rearick, Charles. *Pleasures of the Belle Epoque: Entertainment and Festivity in
Turn-of-the-Century France*. New Haven: Yale UP, 1985.

Schwartz, Vanessa. *Spectacular Realities: Early Mass Culture in Fin-de-siècle Paris*. Berkeley, Los Angeles, and London: U of California P, 1998.

Silverman, Debora L. 'Weaving Paintings: Religious and Social Origins of Vincent van Gogh's Pictorial Labor.' *Rediscovering History: Culture, Politics, and the Psyche*. Ed. Michael S. Roth. Stanford: Stanford UP, 1994. 137–68.

– *Art Nouveau in Fin-de-siècle France: Politics, Psychology, and Style*. Berkeley, Los Angeles, and Oxford: U of California P, 1989.

Slataper, Scipio. 'Ai giovani intelligenti d'Italia.' *La Voce* (26 Aug. 1909).

– *Lettere*. 3 vols. Ed. G. Stuparich. Turin: Buratti, 1931.

– 'Quando Roma era Bisanzio.' *La Voce* (20 Apr. 1911).

– 'Il silenzio.' *La Voce* (24 Mar. 1910).

Soffici, Ardengo. 'Don Chisciotte in Toscana.' *La Riviera ligure* (Dec. 1908).

– 'L'impressionismo e la pittura italiana.' *La Voce* (6 May 1909).

– 'Principî di un'estetica futurista.' *La Raccolta* (15 Aug.–15 Oct. 1918).

Stuparich, Giani. *Scipio Slataper*. Milan: Mondadori, 1950.

Weber, Eugen. *France Fin de Siècle*. Cambridge: Harvard UP, 1986.

8 Back to the Future: Temporal Ambivalences in F.T. Marinetti's Writings

ENRICO CESARETTI

The future is a territory of the past.

W. Ong

There is still a widespread and commonly accepted notion in much of the critical literature on Italian Futurism that deals with Futurism's relationship to the category of time. According to this view, which is well summarized by Stephen Kern, Futurists 'voiced the most passionate repudiations of the past ... celebrated the here and now and created an art that was perishable and ephemeral.' 'Their most energetic spokesman. [...] F.T. Marinetti,' continues Kern, 'vowed to mock everything consecrated by time' and 'in 1914 [...] announced the funeral of all *passéiste* beauty, including its nefarious ingredients of memory, legends, and ruins' (57). Publications such as 'Contro Venezia passatista [Against Past-Loving Venice]' (1910), 'Contro la Spagna passatista [Against Past-Loving Spain]' (1911), or 'Contro Roma passatista [Against Past-Loving Rome]' (this latter a section of *Guerra sola igiene del mondo* [War, the World's Only Hygiene] (1915)) exemplify, even in their repetitive and unambiguous titles, the kind of antagonistic attitude that Kern is describing and that Marinetti would continue to revive, under various formal guises.

It is hardly a surprise, therefore, that even after recent acknowledgments of the multifaceted character of Futurism,[1] Marinetti, the founding father of the movement, is still consistently perceived by critics as someone who lived a predominantly mono-directional life, advocating in his works a voluntary rejection of the past and its myths and championing an aggressive dismissal of tradition. In other words, he was somebody whose perception of the present and the future, of historical development, was limited, since he tended to interpret these dimensions exclusively from the perspective, the theoretical framework and the needs of his movement.

The validity of the central tenets of this critical position cannot really be called into question, since they are grounded, well beyond Italy, in the wider context of the birth and proliferation of the avant-garde and in the poetics of modernity itself. In this period, at the turn of the twentieth century, as the historian Hayden White writes, a 'hostility towards the historical consciousness and the historian gained wide currency among intellectuals in every country of Western Europe' (qtd. in Kern 61). The time of the avant-garde, including Futurism, is the present: avant-garde movements celebrate vital intensity, the extemporaneousness of the new, of contingency, while expressing a hostility towards whatever is spread through time, such as the idea of a book, a masterpiece, a museum, or any object that offers itself to reproducibility and memory. The supremacy of the powers of oblivion over those of memory is therefore one of the essential traits of modernity; and one that stems directly from Nietzsche's (and later Benjamin's) philosophy, with its rejection of tradition and its denial of the powers of the historical conscience to interpret and 'read' the present time (Guglielmi, *La parola* 172).

Guido Guglielmi, whose work in *La parola del testo*[2] has inspired this initial section of my paper, makes an interesting and thought-provoking distinction between the concepts of 'avant-garde' and 'modernism' (both of which are said to belong to and shape 'modernity') – a distinction which is based primarily on how each perceives the category of time. Simplifying his position, while the avant-garde, as I have suggested, is synchronic, since it detaches itself from the past in favour of the immediacy of the present, modernism – Guglielmi argues, quoting from and extensively commenting on T.S. Eliot's essay 'Tradition and the Individual Talent' (1919), rediscovers diachrony. It aims to restore the distance of the past but only by re-inventing and modifying it. Eliot significantly spoke of a 'simultaneous order,' of a 'living unity' between different eras. An 'authentic' poet is someone, he said, who is able to speak an anterior word, who can recreate and produce the present of the past: 'the historical sense involves a perception not only of the pastness of the past but of its presence; the historical sense compels a man to write not merely with his own generation in his bones, but with a feeling that the whole of the literature of

Europe from Homer and within it the whole of the literature of his own country has a simultaneous existence and composes a simultaneous order' (Eliot 49). Eliot's insistence on the need for a 'historical sense' for anyone who 'wants to be a poet beyond his twenty-fifth year' implies a constructive dialogue between the present and the past, and exemplifies an important aspect of the modernist poetic. Eliot was not alone, one might add, in sustaining this kind of argument. An echo of his words is found, for example, in another modernist writer, Ezra Pound, who had his own version of the concept of 'simultaneous existence.' Pound's idea of the 'eternal present,' as it emerges in *The Spirit of Romance*, and through which he presents and justifies his program to re-evaluate the Western (medieval) literary tradition, seems in fact to share more than a few similarities with Eliot's perspective.[3]

The positions of these two masters of modernism are, apparently, as distant as one can possibly imagine from Marinetti's avant-gardist magniloquent statements, with their total dismissal of history, tradition, the past and its various materializations. They are equally distant from Marinetti's and his friends' vision of what the ideal fate of poets should be: to be replaced and thrown 'nel cestino, come manoscritti inutili [into the waste basket, like useless manuscripts]' before turning forty (Marinetti, *Teoria e invenzione*, hereafter *TIF* 13). Italian Futurism, therefore, especially in its first revolutionary, strongly *antipasséiste* phase, seems perfectly to exemplify the rhetoric of the avant-garde regarding time that has been outlined to this point.

One cannot help, however, but to challenge such a seemingly unproblematic and transparent distinction between the avant-gardist and modernist poetics. It is undeniable that the concepts of modernity and, by extension, of avant-garde, are often best defined through their contradictions ('la contraddizione è inscritta nella modernità [contradiction is inscribed in modernity]') (Guglielmi, *La parola* 181), through the discrepancies and the inconsistencies that exist between their theory and practice. If, for example, it is true that it is possible to try to forget the historical past, and then also forget having forgotten it, this does not necessarily mean or imply that what has been forgotten and discarded has been completely annihilated.[4] That the past is perceived as an obstacle, a hindrance that prevents the development and the growth of the present, is one side of the coin; but the other side is that – whichever way one chooses to approach this dimension, either trying to forget or, paradoxically, trying to remember in order to be able to exorcise the past and so 'move on' – it is actually impossible to totally get rid of it. As Nietzsche wrote, the idea that man could ever free himself from the burden of history is an illusion. The destiny of man will always be that of being a successor, an 'epigone' (cfr. Guglielmi, *La parola* 158/183).

Luciano De Maria, in his 'Nota sull'autobiografismo marinettiano' which prefaces *Una sensibilità italiana nata in Egitto* [An Italian Sensibility Born in Egypt] (1943) and *La grande Milano tradizionale e futurista* (1943) – the latter a text whose revealing, 'oxymoronic' title (*The Great Milan Traditional and Futurist*) could well emblematize the focus of this essay – was among the first critics to notice the existence 'sin dall'inizio [from the beginning]' in Marinetti's works, of a contradictory 'dimensione apologetica e memorialistica che contrasta il [...] moto antimnestico ['apologetic and memorialistic dimension which contrasts with the [...] antimnestic tendency]' (in Marinetti, 'La grande Milano, 23); and De Maria encouraged other scholars to analyse this intriguing feature.[5]

In what follows, I too should like to take up De Maria's invitation and examine the presence in Futurism, and especially in some of Marinetti's texts, of an ambiguous and problematic rhetoric regarding time. More particularly, and in line with the latest critical studies in the field of Italian Futurism, I should like to argue that the emergence of a rhetoric of nostalgia and memory in some early texts, such as 'Uccidiamo il chiaro di luna' [Let's Murder the Moonshine] (1909), as well as in later ones, such as *Gli indomabili* [The Untamables] (1922), *Spagna veloce e toro futurista* [Fast Spain and Futurist Bull] (1931) and *Il fascino dell'Egitto* [The Allure of Egypt] (1933), calls into question Futurism's 'original' rejection of the 'old' and its overall relationship with the 'three ecstasies of temporality,' as Guglielmi calls the present, the past, and the future (*La parola* 182).

While it may be true that it is the second phase of Futurism in particular – often dismissed as 'a more pragmatic, less innovative' period, or seen as 'an involution and return to tradition,' or both (Sartini Blum 126) – that presents the kind of works most useful for the analysis I am undertaking here, I would like to begin by proposing that at least some aspects of the 'recycling of the past,' or the appeal to memory, are not limited to texts that belong to the later years of the movement. In my view, such aspects actually constitute one of the structuring principles of much of Futurism's rhetorical and ideological practice, whether of the first or the second phase, and are deeply engrained in its poetics. A first, empirical way to begin looking at this question could, for example, recognize that Marinetti, throughout his 'career' as a poet and a cultural icon, was constantly 'moving back' in time and appealing to memory. That is, he was recapitulating and reconnecting his present poetical and cultural discourse to his past initial inventive moments. I do not believe it is necessary to cite any specific textual proof of this; every reader of Marinetti's oeuvre has surely noticed how the writer tends not only to reiterate at every possible opportunity the names of his 'compagni futuristi' and the events they organized/participated in, but also how a series of original, core concepts of Futurism ('syntheticism,' the 'religion of speed,' the 'idolization of the machine,' etc.) continue to repropose themselves, under different guises, from the first Manifestos to the texts and programs of the thirties and the forties.[6] This attitude is, one may object, merely evidence of the propagandistic genius of Marinetti, of his ability to 'sell his product' by repeating himself over and over. This may very well be the case; however, from another perspective, one could also interpret this behaviour as a sort of 'fear of forgetfulness,' that is, a fear that his audience would forget what he had already said or written, his past life and accomplishments, a situation to which he reacts by drilling words into our memory in the attempt to keep alive something (a past, a tradition which has just been formed) that he is condemning on more general, theoretical terms. When, moreover, Eliot wrote that an authentic poet is one who is able to resume and recapture an anterior world, I cannot help but notice that his statement could very well be adapted to Marinetti's situation. With one major modification, of course: Marinetti tended to repeat and summarize his (and his friends') own previous words (and actions and enterprises) rather than those of others not affiliated to his movement. His retrieval of the past, of history, of memories, even though a retrieval of *a* very specific and selective past, history, and set of memories *is not*, nonetheless, insignificant, since it is our first step in the attempt to gain a more balanced perspective on any discourse dealing with Futurism's understanding of time.

At this point, I must challenge my own somewhat restrictive initial statements on Marinetti in the hope of demonstrating that the ambiguities present in his perception of time are more complex than a mere circular recycling of his own past rhetoric.

When, in the section 'Nascita di un'estetica futurista [The Birth of a Futurist Aesthetics]' in *Guerra sola igiene del mondo*, Marinetti writes:

'Noi abbiamo quasi distrutta la concezione di spazio e singolarmente diminuita la concezione di tempo. Noi prepariamo così l'ubiquità dell'uomo moltiplicato. Noi arriveremo così all'abolizione dell'anno, del giorno e dell'ora[7] [We have almost destroyed the concept of space and singularly diminished the concept of time. We are preparing the ubiquity of the multiplied man. In this way we shall reach the abolition of the year, the day and the hour]' (Marinetti, *TIF* 315), he is neither literally repudiating the past, nor praising the immediacy of the present (or the excitement of the future). He is also not merely and aggressively advocating the annihilation of the categories of space and time. What I believe he is doing is echoing, if not virtually quoting verbatim, Henri Bergson's groundbreaking ideas about the concepts of space and time as they are expressed in *Time and Free Will* (1889), *Matter and Memory* (1896), and *Creative Evolution* (1907). For Bergson – whose irrationalist and intuitionist philosophy draws significantly on Symbolist and especially Nietzsche's thought, and whose influence on Futurism's poetics is well known[8] – time, analytically and quantitatively, is only a succession of instants that follow one another in a determined linear order (past, present, and future). In other words, 'scientific time' for him (the choice of words is revealing when read together with Marinetti's) 'is represented as an extended homogeneous medium, composed of normative units (years, hours, seconds)' (qtd. in Antliff 44). However, qualitatively and empathetically, that is, from the perspective of the subject's consciousness, time is irreducible to the moment, it is durée, a fluid process that simultaneously treasures the past and creates the new. The 'proposals' of 'abolishing the year, the day and the hour' and substituting them, in Marinetti, with 'the ubiquity of the multiplied man' (a man that is everywhere, at every time, *simultaneously*) and, in Bergson, with the durée, have so many implications that it would be futile even to try to summarize them here. Among these, nevertheless, two considerations are particularly relevant for my discussion. The first is that if the aggressive words Marinetti writes regarding the destruction of space and time deal with and refer to questions of aesthetics, then we can perhaps say that they target a very specific kind and image of time: not time as a general category, but 'scientific time,' only the kind of time which is quantifiable, homogenized, utilitarian, regulated. A time which, basically, has negative effects on the (Futurist) artist's inspiration and creative abilities and prevents him/her from behaving and creating according to his/her inner experience.[9] The second implication – strictly related to the first – is that, in this 'Bergsonian' perspective, 'with regard to our own activity, we gain an intellectual perspective [...] only in retrospect' (Antliff 45). As a consequence, 'real' knowledge (that is, the knowledge claimed to be possessed by the Futurist artist) is not based on an intellectual, linear, 'scientific time,' but rather on durée, or, translating the concept in Futurist terms, on the 'ubiquitous' and the 'simultaneous,' which, therefore (and this is what really matters), implies the contemporary presence in man's interiority of the dimensions of the past, the present, and the future. I would like to stress that I am not here implying that the concepts of durée and 'simultaneity' are synonymous, but only that the premises of a particular epistemology, of the kind of knowledge I delineated above, seem to be possible only when drawing on both of these inclusive interpretations of time.

Confirmation that my interpretation of Marinetti's position on the concept of time is consistent, and that he is actually giving a clear voice to a pervasive 'Bergsonian' attitude within Futurism and the avant-garde, may be found if we briefly turn our attention to the field of Futurist painting.[10]

When Gino Severini (1883–1966), one of the signatories of the *Manifesto of Futurist Painters* and of *Futurist Painting: Technical Manifesto* (1910),[11] painted *Souvenirs de voyage* (a.k.a. *Memories of a voyage*; 1910–11, oil on canvas, 81.2 x 99.9 cm, Private collection) and described the picture by affirming, 'I destroyed time and space, reuniting in a single plastic ensemble realities perceived in Italy, in the Alps, in Paris, etc.' (in Hanson 35), both the 'Bergsonian flavour' and the rhetorical affinities with Marinetti's statements in *Guerra sola igiene del mondo* appear evident.[12] They also re-emerge when Severini 'insisted on the historical necessity of portraying successive memories' by claiming that: 'In this epoch of dynamism and simultaneity one cannot separate any event or object from the memories [...] which its expansive action calls up simultaneously in us' (in Hanson 35). Likewise, the other Futurist Luigi Russolo (1885–1947),[13] in a similar perspective, depicted his *Souvenir d'une nuit* (*Memories of a Night*, 1911, oil on canvas, 100 x 101 cm, Slfika Coll., New York) with images of the past 'scattered about the picture surface as they are in reality scattered a-chronologically about the mind.'[14] The attitudes and affirmations of these Futurist painters thus conformed with G. Apollinaire's pronouncement that the avant-garde painter must 'encompass in one glance the past, the present and the future' (qtd. in Kern 83–4). But they also expanded the meaning of one of Futurism's key concepts, that of 'simultaneity,' beyond its initial 'technical' range – a synthesis of sensations or places in time or 'an experience that had spatial as well as temporal aspects' in which recent technology often plays a role (Kern 315) – into one that, along with Bergson's theory, revalorizes the notions of remembrance and bygone experience and emphasizes the importance of *all* temporal dimensions.

There are, of course, substantial differences between this expanded concept of Futurist 'simultaneity' of Bergsonian derivation and the 'simultaneous order' proposed by Eliot in his 1919 modernist essay. One could point out, for example, that Eliot's interpretation of 'tradition' seems to validate only classical, ancient poetic traditions and to exclude more recent ones. Or, we could say that he is dealing strictly with an attempt to redefine poetry, while Bergson's general notion of time is more comprehensive and has a much wider range of consequences that affect a whole 'real' world and not only the literary one. It is not my intention, therefore, to propose vague comparisons between them, even if, ultimately, one of my intermediate goals is to reduce the gap between the two and emphasize their similarities. At present, I am simply drawing attention to the versatility and diffusion of the concept of 'simultaneity.' During the first three decades of the twentieth century, across various disciplines, currents, and 'isms,' 'in the cultural sphere no unifying concept for the new sense of the past or future could rival [simultaneity's] coherence and popularity ...' (Kern 314). In other words (and this is my second and last goal), rather than emphasizing the disjunctions between past, present, and future within the Futurist movement and the avant-garde, I would consider to have made my point if I could finally say that Marinetti's 'invention' derives its lasting influence and power exactly from a conscious (but also at times involuntary) re-appropriation of the past, from an excellent understanding of the present, and from a utopian vision of the future, that is, a 'simultaneous' (or 'ubiquitous') and comprehensive vision of all three categories.

A critical statement such as 'reality became increasingly alien to Marinetti's fiction of power. He responded by investing his fantasies in the past' (Sartini Blum 137) aptly brings to our attention the escapist, aestheticizing aspects of the rhetoric of nostalgia and memory which is undoubtedly present in Marinetti's later works. But it also marginalizes the possibility that over the years Marinetti actually engaged in a more 'realistic' and 'constructive' revision of his (and his movement's) overall relation with time. A passage from a short article by the Futurist Bruno Sanzin, from Trieste, which appeared in 'Stile futurista' in 1934, for example, may well represent Marinetti's position in its attempt to more concretely redefine the concept of tradition in a way that is no longer antithetical to and incompatible with Futurism:

> Tradizione è il perpetuarsi nel tempo dei valori eminentemente costruttivi che nelle varie epoche hanno eccelso, portando lustro e vantando meriti giammai dimenticabili. [...] È sbagliato credere che i valori tradizionali tendano a produrre un influsso retroattivo. [...] La tradizione è invece una forza eminentemente positiva. Le grandezze del passato brillano al sole eterno perché gli uomini nuovi le superino, perché le loro quote siano di partenza, non di arrivo. [...]
> (qtd. in D'Ambrosio 10–11)

> [Tradition is the perpetuation in time of the eminently constructive values that have excelled in the various ages, bringing lustre and boasting never forgettable merits. [...] It is wrong to believe that traditional values tend to produce a retroactive influx. [...] Tradition is instead an eminently positive force. The greatness of the past shines in the eternal sun so that new men may exceed it, so that its height be a point of departure, not of arrival ...]

What I consider to be really significant, therefore, is that if it is true that Marinetti's destructive rhetoric is not directed towards time in general but against a specific kind of time, and if some of his writings present a retrieval of the past and an ambivalence towards change and modernity, then such an awareness may authorize an interpretation of Futurism not merely as an avant-garde movement, but also as one that overlaps and coincides to a deeper extent with European modernism. Without pretence of performing in this essay the impossible task of thoroughly redefining Futurism's position vis-à-vis the poetics of the avant-garde and of modernism, one may perhaps begin by suggesting that the former shares with modernist poetics a rediscovery of diachrony, an attempt, to paraphrase Eliot, to retrieve the distance of the past and tradition by re-inventing and modifying them.

An early text by Marinetti like 'Uccidiamo il chiaro di luna' (1909) already demonstrates some ambivalence and ambiguity as far as temporality is concerned. On the one hand, we find the appeals to 'far saltare in aria tutte le tradizioni, come ponti fradici! [blow up all traditions, like rotten bridges!]' and to '[sbeffeggiare] tutto ciò che è consacrato dal tempo [mock everything that is consecrated by time]'.

On the other, we hear the fictionalized voice of Ermanno Cavacchioli – one of the 'fratelli futuristi [Futurist brothers]' whose task is to destroy 'Paralisi' and 'Podagra' – saying: 'Io sento ringiovanire il mio corpo ventenne! ... Io ritorno, d'un passo sempre più infantile verso la mia culla ... Presto rientrerò nel ventre di mia madre! [I feel my twenty-year-old body rejuvenate! ... I return, with an always more infantile step towards my cradle ... Soon I shall re-enter my mother's womb!]' (Marinetti, *TIF* 18), words that betray a regressive, 'back to the origins,' nostalgic rhetoric.

In her analysis of this text, Marzia Rocca perceptively notes how the narration offers us the image of the sun (a symbol of clarity, of the language of logic and reason, in opposition to the blurred, indefinite atmosphere in which poetry and art are said to flourish) followed by Marinetti's invitation to his 'fratello futurista [futurist brother]' Paolo Buzzi to guide the sun's 'ruota [wheel]' as if it were an 'automobile da corsa [racing car]' in order to become 'guidatore del mondo! [the driver of the world]' (Marinetti, *TIF* 18–19) by drawing strength from its powerful, blinding energy and light. Nonetheless, the same sun is described later as a flickering light, a star that is fading away (for instance, in the references to the 'vecchio sole europeo [old European sun]', with its 'tremulo e rosso volante di fuoco [flickering and red wheel of fire],' as well as the work's concluding lines: 'Sì, noi sapremo riscaldarti fra le nostre braccia fumanti, o misero Sole, decrepito e freddoloso, che tremi sulla cima del Gorisankar! ... [Yes, we shall be able to warm you in the embrace of our smoking arms, oh wretched Sun, decrepit and cold suffering, trembling on the top of Gorisankar!]') (Marinetti, *TIF* 26). Rocca's interpretation, therefore, stresses that 'Uccidiamo il chiaro di luna' presents a deep ambiguity between a striving towards the future and a fascination with the end, between the insistence on images of light and the subtle, subterranean interest in the decline and the disappearance of a whole world (41–2).

Such a reading is confirmed elsewhere in the text, where we find a farewell to Europe, a Western world that is only a landscape of ruins ('attraversammo le rovine dell'Europa [we crossed the ruins of Europe],' followed by the entrance into the different, Eastern, ancient world of Asia. Marinetti's appeals to destroy the past and its traditions, therefore, have to be read as the rejection exclusively of the past and the traditions of the Western world (the ones that correspond to a 'scientific,' 'capitalist' time, or to a sort of 'profane time,' to use Mircea Eliade's expression), which cannot bring real knowledge or permit the birth of a truly innovative artistic creation. The essential search through-out the text coincides therefore with the attempt to return to a distant origin, to a 'notte piena ... quasi in cielo, su l'altipiano persiano, sub-lime altare del mondo [deep night ... almost up in the sky, on the Persian plateau, sublime altar of the world]' (Marinetti, *TIF* 21), that is, to a time and space less dominated by the 'blinding' light of reason. It is a sort of 'backward' movement towards a 'sacred time' which, none-theless, allows the 'poeti incendiarî [incendiary poets]' and the 'fratelli ... futuristi' to move forward, towards the 'costruzione del gran Binario futurista [construction of the great Futurist Track]' (Marinetti, *TIF* 17). The 'usignoli [che] bevevano l'ombra odorosa [nightingales [that] drank the fragrant shadow],' the 'favolosa foresta [fabulous forest]' stirred by a slow breeze and immersed in a 'diluvio di profumi [shower of perfumes]' help to define the originary spatial/temporal coordinates of a nocturnal dimension that one must retrieve and re-access in order to create new artistic forms. This dimension seems in fact not only temporarily to prevail over the modern 'trecento lune elettriche [three hundred electric moons],' but also to constitute the necessary premise for those 'lune [moons]' to be able to erase 'coi loro raggi di gesso abbagliante l'antica regina verde degli amori [with their dazzling chalk-white rays the ancient green queen of the loves],' and for Futurism to 'ricolorare le aurore ammalate della Terra [recolour the sick dawns of the Earth]' (Marinetti, *TIF* 22/26).

Marinetti's deep fascination with this ancient, exotic, eastern world filled with seductive and primitive meanings cannot easily be erased (Rocca 42–4). Furthermore, it is likely to recall exactly that 'tradition' that, once appropriated, reinvented and modified, will allow us to 'create the future.' If Marinetti's Futurist revolt is officially a refusal of the 'old' and an idolization of the 'new,' paradoxically, in 'Uccidiamo il chiaro di luna' it has to begin in an 'old,' intact space-time, which becomes essential if that same revolt is to have the possibility of exist-ing in the first place.[15] This kind of ambivalence between the old and the new, together with a recurrent attraction to the exotic, links this early text with the later ones I mentioned earlier.

In *Spagna veloce e toro futurista* (1931), the temporal dimension, as the early appearance of 'gli invisibili ma sensibili fantasmi del Passato [the invisible but sensitive ghosts of the Past]' attests (Marinetti, *TIF* 1022), is still a central issue for its author. This time the task is to fight the 'Vento Burbero comandante delle Forze del Passato [Surly Wind, chief of the Forces of the Past]' while travelling between Barcelona and Madrid, and at the same time to 'inscatolare uno spazio X in un tempo X [box a space X in a time X],' in what seems like a desperate attempt to control and to freeze something that is actually uncontrollable. The impossible striving to frame an extended present and the emphasis on coincidence and identity (X=X and not, as one might expect from the geometrical Cartesian axes, X and Y), is an operation, moreover, that only momentarily flattens the category of time into a single, comprehensive, undifferentiated dimension. While accomplishing this attempt, the sudden, unexpected emergence of other dimensions of time and their consequent acknowledgment is problematic and a source of anguish for the author. It is, indeed, quite destabilizing for someone who imagines himself to be constantly moving forward, towards the future, and who believes that he is able to control and master both time and space, to realize, not without some self-irony, that such an enterprise can easily be undermined: 'Improvvisa sosta forzata./Subito, il Tempo e lo Spazio che tenevo impacchettati fra le mie mani strette lacerano l'involucro./Subitaneo terrore/Tremano le Logiche [Sudden forced stop./Immediately, the Time and the Space which I kept packed between my tight hands tear the wrappings./ Sudden terror/the Logics are trembling]' (Marinetti, *TIF* 1027). The episode of the forced stop, then, is little more than the account of a mechanical car failure that delays the poet's arrival in Madrid, because it provides him with the realization that a vision of the world which is based primarily on a single temporal dimension is actually impossible ('Tremano le logiche').

Ultimately, the real struggle will be against a future which coincides with old age, senility, death: 'fiuto i profumi corrotti del potere e della gloria senili [I smell the corrupted scents of senile power and glory].' The real challenge of the bull/poet who is 'ferito, non vinto [wounded, not conquered]' is to stay alive, against all the odds; to fight against what has still to come – 'È lei che debbo uccidere! [...] La Morte [It is her who I must kill! [...] Death]' (Marinetti, *TIF* 1049) – and, at the same time, to savour and remember the past, epitomized by the 'fresca [...] gioventù lontana [fresh [...] distant youth]' (Marinetti, *TIF* 1044).

Elsewhere, Marinetti seems to suggest that the way one can actually challenge and oppose death is by fighting it with a coalition made up of the forces of both the past and the future. In *L'alcova d'acciaio* (1921), Marinetti's account of his experience in the First World War, we read of 'dolori e piaceri passati [che] corazzano i combattenti [past pains and pleasures [which] harden the fighters],' as if past experiences could provide a shield from death and constitute a bridge-head into their future lives. In addition, we also find the admission that:

> Il segreto complesso del passato e del futuro nella stessa coscienza si rivela a coloro che tutto il passato hanno vissuto, sudato, pianto, baciato, morso e masticato e che vogliono fra le carezze e le gomitate della morte vivere, baciare, masticare e soffrire il loro futuro. (ch. 3)

> [The secret complex of past and future in the same conscience is revealed to those who have lived, sweated, cried, kissed, bit and chewed all the past and who want to live, kiss, chew and suffer their future among the caresses and the elbow blows of death.]

Here, the secret of the relationship between past and future is actually something worth looking for, in order 'futuristically' to live life to the full.

It is in *Il fascino dell' Egitto* (1933), however, as the title immediately suggests, that travel impressions made in the exotic land of Marinetti's childhood – an 'Africa [which] is not merely the distant, exotic setting typical of much orientalist literature' (Sartini Blum 138) – most effectively combine with the theme of nostalgic remembrance. The title of the first chapter, 'Ultimi brandelli nostalgici di una sensibilità futurista [Last Nostalgic Shreds of a Futurist Sensibility],' immediately reveals that the reader is going to be engaged in a literary voyage not only in space but also through time. These pages are dominated by memory, by an active and conscious effort to revive the past following the 'filo nostalgico della [...] carne [nostalgic thread of [...] flesh]' (Marinetti, *TIF* 1054), as well as the eagerness to 'far rinascere nuovi ricordi verdi salienti [revive new green salient memories]' (Marinetti, *TIF* 1055).[16] The effects of Western progress and modernity upon the centuries-old traditions in the city of King Fuad are described ambiguously, with a language that oscillates between excitement and admiration for the 'machine aesthetic' and regret for something that is going to be irretrievably lost:

> ... il Mex che ha distrutto i suoi molini a vento per macinare a vapore [...] i gonfi mercati di stoffe gioielli pasticcerie già sventrati dalle velocità meccaniche, le indolenze concentrate degli arabi nei tram che sembrano rapirli via nel mare, l'ostinata pigiatura di odori colori sapori profumi e fetori che si difendono eroicamente contro la modernità europea nei suk del

Cairo. Mi dicevo non gusterò più avidamente le fresche e polpose ostriche dei miei quindici anni fra le cabine di legno turchine sbilenche del piccolo stabilimento di bagni di Ramleh che tremolava ad ogni ondata sui suoi pali di ferro! Non avrò più negli occhi e nelle nari quel bel mare di cristallo verde salatissimo in cui mio padre aveva brutalmente lanciato il mio corpicino di pupo per insegnarmi a disprezzare i salvagente.
[...]
Ma le ardenti e sensuali gaggie della mia adolescenza erano sparite! In loro vece entrava nelle mie nari un forte odore di catrame che veniva dalla chiglia di un barcone sovraccarico di cotone. [...] Con un ronzìo gemente ma tenace di ape bellicosa, l'apparecchio mi sorvola. Flauto nero di guerra, ferì musicalmente l'azzurro. Aveva per ali le mani stesse mozzate del suo musicista, abbandonato sulla terra. (Marinetti, *TIF* 1056/1058–9)

[... the Mex that destroyed its windmills [in order] to grist with steam ... the swollen markets of clothes jewels pastry-shops already demolished by the mechanic speeds, the concentrated indolences of Arabs in street-cars that seem to steal them into the sea, the obstinate cramming of smells, colours, flavours, perfumes and stenches that heroically defend themselves against European modernity in the suk of Cairo. I said to myself that I shall not avidly taste any more the fresh and succulent oysters [I ate when I was] fifteen years old between the wooden deep blue crooked cabins of the small bathing establishment in Ramleh which trembled as every wave [hit] its iron poles! I shall no longer have in my eyes and in my nostrils that beautiful crystal green very salty sea where my father had roughly thrown my little child's body to teach me how to despise life-buoys.
[...]
But the ardent and sensual cassias of my adolescence were gone! Instead a strong smell of tar coming from the keel of a barge overloaded with cotton penetrated into my nostrils. [...] With the lamenting but tenacious drone of a bellicose bee, the plane flies over me. A black flute of war, it musically wounded the blue. Its wings were the very hands severed from its musician, abandoned on earth.]

Marinetti's choice of words is particularly revealing. Whereas the expressions related to images of modernity have the negative connotations of harshness and alienation (mechanical speeds that 'demolish,' street-cars that 'kidnap' their passengers, a 'strong smell of tar,' an airplane that 'wounded' the sky, 'hands severed'), those evoked by remembrance are associated with feelings, emotion, and natural beauty ('fresh and succulent oysters,' 'beautiful, crystal green, very salty sea,' 'the ardent and sensual cassias'). Thus, 'although the destructive effects of colonialism seem to be accepted as an inevitable fate, the triumph of productive, geometric, militaristic modernity over the past is figured in gloomy tones that culminate in an emblematic image of mutilation' (Sartini Blum 139). The airplane, previously the idolized symbol of modern technology, has here been transformed into a symbol of the evils of progress, a menacing, dangerous object that abandons its maimed pilot on the ground.

The conflict between the new and the old is, in Marinetti's words, 'la tragica lotta che si svolgeva nelle mie vene tra quel passato gemente e il magnifico futuro che lo strangolava [the tragic fight that was taking place in my veins between that moaning past and the magnificent future that was strangling it]' (Marinetti, *TIF* 1056), and I believe that for him this was not a completely irresolvable struggle. When the character of King Fuad talks to Marinetti about the destiny of his country, he arouses the interested comments of his interlocutor. His project of 'conserv[are] le vecchie tradizioni artistiche e insieme suscit[are] nuove originalità creatrici [...] in una sintesi armoniosa che fosse insieme artistica e politica [preserving the old artistic traditions and together kindling new creative originalities [...] in a harmonious synthesis that was both artistic and political]' (Marinetti, *TIF* 1057) is an ambitious, utopian, yet also transparent enterprise that aims exactly at the sort of 'simultaneity' we have previously encountered, as mirrored in Bergson's durèe and advocated by modernist poetics: an operation which aims to recycle and modify the past in order to influence the present and the future, not to discard it, as the first avant-gardes were advocating. Marinetti's position – if my interpretation is plausible – seems to convey at the same time a moderately optimistic outlook on the future and the acknowledgment, by an older and wiser poet, of a setback, in the sense that his previous proposals, his revolutionary action, his repudiation of tradition, were not sufficient to achieve his goals.

This 'discovery,' that the 'incendiary, iconoclastic rhetoric ... fired against the ruins of the past' (Sartini Blum 139) was not enough 'artistically' (but also politically) to change the world, is not exclusive to the autobiographical and nostalgically permeated *Fascino dell'Egitto*. Earlier incarnations of this idea can be recognized in a much more complex work such as *Gli indomabili* (1922), with which I would like to conclude my article.[17]

This enigmatic allegorical novel set on an island in 'the African seas,' 'la vetta suprema di Marinetti prosatore "tradizionale" [the supreme achievement of Marinetti as a "traditional" prose-writer]' (in Marinetti, *TIF* lxxxiii), according to Rocca's insightful close reading, deals with the recognition of the failure of the utopian dream that art can change society for the better. In other words, it exposes the nefarious effects of the language of reason and rationality at the expense of that of poetry. The theme of remembrance or, better, of the impossibility of remembering, is crucial to an understanding of this text, since the appeal to the past, to memory and tradition, ultimately represents the only possibility of change in an otherwise utterly negative fictional universe.

At the beginning of the novel we learn that both the 'degraded' intellectuals who have become the primitive, muzzled 'indomabili [untamables]' (including the priest Curguss, the school teacher Kurotoplac, and the surgeon Mirmofim) and their guardians, 'i negri [the blacks]' Mazzapà and Vokur, cannot remember what they see during the night, the time when they ritually move from the infernal pit in the desert where they are confined to the Oasis and the Lake of Poetry and Sentiment. It is Mazzapà who, in the first chapter, entitled 'La Duna dei Cammelli,' says to Vokur:

> A che serve entrare nell'Oasi ogni notte, se l'indomani non ci ricordiamo di nulla? Non possiamo neanche dire che cosa ci sia, nell'Oasi. Anche gl'Indomabili sono incapaci di ricordarsi di ciò che hanno visto nella notte. Eppure sono dei sapienti. [...] Raccontano, raccontano la loro vita passata, ma non possono raccontare ciò che avvenne ieri o la notte scorsa. (Marinetti, *TIF* 932)

> [What is the point of entering the Oasis every night if, the day after, we cannot remember anything? We cannot even say what there is in the Oasis. The Untamables too are unable to remember what they saw during the night. And yet they are wise. [...] They tell, they tell their past life, but they cannot tell what happened yesterday or last night.]

As Rocca observed, there is apparently a significant difference between the warders and the prisoners, since the latter are said to be 'sapienti [wise].' Their knowledge, however, belongs to a remote past and, as such, it has no particular meaning for or visible effect on their present situation. It is a knowledge, moreover, that does not have anything to do with poetry and art, since the untamables' symbolic plunge into the lake of poetry seems only to have the effect of creating simulacra, a 'pseudo-poetry,' an operation that Mirmofim himself describes negatively: 'Facciamo un rumore infernale senza ottenere il più piccolo effetto musicale [We make a hellish noise without obtaining the faintest musical effect]' (Marinetti, *TIF* 975). The inability to remember, for the untamables, is then directly linked to their inability to create art. Apart from the diversity in their hierarchical status, therefore, there is no true difference between the 'negri [blacks]' and their prisoners. The memories of both are only superficial, related as they are to their dull, repetitive daily rituals, which are marked by a time that is quantifiable and analytical. They cannot descend to the depths, where true remembrances are possible; those remembrances that are associated with a time that is durée and, consequently, with the foundation myths and with the ancient, primal inspirational motifs that allow real story-telling and the creation of real poetry.[18] Two very different kinds of 'sapienza [knowledge]' are thus outlined in these opening pages of *Gli indomabili*: the one possessed by the intellectuals at the beginning of their quest, which is linked to reason and history (and which we could then associate with Bergson's exterior, empirical form of knowledge), and the one that derives from memory and identifies itself with poetry (or Bergson's 'interior' knowledge, which advocates the contemporary presence in our consciousness of the past and the present, of the remembrance which projects itself onto and is able to condition the present, making it appear to us under different shapes and circumstances) (Rocca 118–19).

It is particularly significant, in the light of this reading, that when the untamables, in one of the stages of their nightly journey, arrive in the city of 'i Cartacei' (the Paper People, a symbol for the Futurist artists), where they find 'i grandi libri di Spinoza, Pascal, Machiavelli, Vico, Nietzsche, Kant, Marx [the great books of Spinoza etc.],' their first, pressing need is to 'ad ogni costo conoscere il maggior numero di quei meravigliosi libri coricati [at all costs know most of those wonderful books laying down flat]' (Marinetti, *TIF* 996–7), namely, to find out the content of ancient, classical books belonging to the Western cultural tradition that, the older they are ('più lacerati, sciupati e quasi senza fogli) [more torn, damaged and almost without pages]' the higher the spiritual life they are said to possess ('avevano una più potente vita spirituale) [they had a more powerful spiritual life]' (996). This would seem to be, therefore, the first step in a transformation, in a process of rediscovery of tradition, of a specific cultural past whose appropriation and re-elaboration may permit the untamables once again to move 'Verso il Futurismo [Towards Futurism]' (interestingly, the title of the section immediately following), towards a birth of a new, truly 'futuristic' art.

In the last chapter of *Gli indomabili*, entitled 'L'arte,' the question of memory and the problem of time circularly reappear through the words of the leader of the untamables, Mirmofim, who shouts: 'Ecco! Ecco! Ecco! vedo dentro di me tutto ciò che avvenne questa notte nell'Oasi e sulle sponde del Lago [Here! Here! Here! I see inside me all that happened this night in the Oasis and on the shores of the Lake]' (1011). His assertion thus re-affirms the positive role of memory – 'a means of redemption and escape into the consoling realm of aesthetic catharsis' (Sartini Blum 130) – which is now capable of reaching even beyond the 'simple' past of the Paper People and their books into an 'absolute' origin, where 'real' knowledge is possible and a truly new, Futuristic aesthetic/artistic experience can begin. The metamorphosis undergone by the untamables – from men into artists – at the conclusion of the novel is made possible only through an act of remembering, a specifically Bergsonian remembering we may add, in which the primordial is retrieved and re-expressed in order to infuence the present and the future.[19] The 'sovrumana frescalata Distrazione dell'Arte [superhuman coolwinged Distraction of Art]' (Marinetti, *TIF* 1011–12) becomes the moment when an original unity between man and memory is rediscovered; a unity which allows the untamables to finally possess a new form of creative knowledge that also constitutes the basis for their new identity (Rocca 130).

At the end of *Gli indomabili*, the 'simultaneous' balancing between past, present, and future is thus the hidden *quid* that allows artistic creation and, ultimately, as I have been trying to argue in these pages, also what may help us to begin redefining Marinetti and Futurism's position in the poetics of avant-garde and modernism. The best conclusion to my essay, however, can be found in Marinetti's own words in 'Una lezione di Futurismo tratta dall'*Orlando furioso*,' one of the essays in a collection significantly (and we may now realize how appropriately) entitled *Commemorazioni in avanti* [Commemorations Forward]: 'Talvolta il passato ben intuito e accettato frammentariamente può consigliare e dirigere il ribollente oggi e insegnarci a domare l'impetuoso domani che si avventa contro di noi [Sometimes a well-guessed and fragmentarily accepted past may council and direct the boiling present and teach us how to tame the impetuous tomorrow which rushes upon us]' (in D'Ambrosio 61). Marinetti's statement finally brings together the 'three ecstasies of temporality,' in the ultimate realization that perhaps it is only through cooperation and understanding, and not their limiting opposites, that art and life can prosper.

NOTES

1 Cfr. Sartini Blum (125–6). The author notes how 'The map of Italian futurism becomes more complex as we trace the movement's expansions into factions and provincial diffusion,' and how 'Scholars have tended to simplify matters by drawing a boundary between a utopian, experimental first phase (the so-called first or heroic futurism) and a more pragmatic, less innovative second phase (the so-called second futurism).' While I generally agree with Sartini Blum's statements, I still believe that the distinction between a first and a second Futurist phase may possess some practical usefulness.

2 I refer in particular to chapter 7, 'Memoria e oblio della storia.' On modernism and its experience of time, see also the more recent book by Ronald Schleifer, in particular the pages where he discusses 'the collision of past and present' which characterizes this historical moment (109–12).

3 Pound writes: 'All ages are contemporaneous. [...] This is especially true of literature, where the real time is independent of the apparent, and where many dead men are our grandchildren's contemporaries, while many of our contemporaries have been already gathered into Abraham's bosom, or some more fitting receptacle' (6). It may be of some relevance to note that the same concept present in Pound appears also in *La Vie de l'espace* (1929), an enigmatic work by M. Maeterlinck, who was an important representative of the fin-de-siècle Symbolist avant-garde in Belgium and France. In *La Vie de l'espace*, however, it is the spatio-temporal fourth dimension of eternity which is said to significantly coincide with a 'perpetual and universal simultaneity, or the eternal present' (Maeterlinck 85).
Maeterlinck's interpretation, with its mystical undertones, in turn, seems to fall into what Mircea Eliade would characterize as 'sacred time,' that is, 'a time essentially different from the profane succession which preceded it' and in whose dimension of a 'mythical' or 'eternal' present, the possibility of 'revealing what we may for convenience call the *absolute*, the supernatural, the superhuman, the superhistoric' may be realized (388–9).

4 On this point, it is worth remembering Lyotard's observations in the chapter 'The Sublime and the Avant-Garde': 'The secret of an artistic success, like that of a commercial success, resides in the balance between what is surprising and what is "well-known". [...] This is how innovation in art operates: one re-uses formulae confirmed by previous success, one throws them off-balance by combining them with other, in principle incompatible, formulae, by amalgamations, quotations, ornamentations, pastiche' (106–7).

5 Cinzia Sartini Blum has heeded De Maria's exhortation. See esp. the chapter on 'Transformations in the Futurist Mythopoeia' (Sartini Blum 125–62). De Maria continues: 'Il memorialismo marinettiano esplode, da ultimo, letteralmente, nei due "poemi" autobiografici di cui trattiamo: quel ritorno del rimosso [...] assume qui una veste lirica conclamatamente autobiografica [Marinetti's memorialism explodes at last, literally, in the two autobiographical "poems" we are dealing with: that return of the rejected [...] takes here a lyrical and clearly autobiographical form]' (qtd. in Marinetti, *La grande* 23).

6 It may be appropriate to recall here Deleuze's ideas about the concept of repetition. The implications of a statement such as, 'The ideal constitution of repetition thus implies a kind of retroactive movement between [the] two limits [those of the object and the subject]' (71), for example, empha-size the inextricability of a past temporal dimension from the act of repeating, and therefore they indirectly reinforce the general premises of my essay. On this point, see also Somigli: 'the past resurfaces in the very language of Futurism, in the tropes and figures which are deployed to sketch an outline of the program of the movement' (256).

7 This passage, it is incumbent on me to note, is the same one that Kern quotes in order to exemplify Marinetti's *antipasseiste* attitude.

8 Curi (115–23); De Maria, in his introduction to *TIF* (lxix); Sartini Blum (59, 200 note 23); Antliff (169); Calvesi (428–30); Rocca (118 ss). Bergson's influence on Futurism is widely acknowledged (especially as mediated through the Bergsonian/nationalist theories of G. Sorel). Marinetti, for his part, repeatedly denied or minimized such a connection (Rocca 122).

9 See Antliff (177), where the author also discusses Rabelais's vision of a utopist commune without clocks, which apparently was 'eulogized' by several avant-garde movements. It may be relevant, in this context, to recall also Aldo Palazzeschi's 'philosophy' of 'controdolore' which rejects, by means of a parodic reversal, precisely whatever prevents human beings from satisfying their deeper instincts and desires. Also interesting, for the general topic of my essay, is the fact that Marinetti, writing about

Palazzeschi, actually stated that 'Palazzeschi ricavava futurismo (una disposizione attiva verso il futuro) dal passatismo [Palazzeschi obtained Futurism (an active disposition towards future) from passatism]' (qtd. in Guglielmi, *L'udienza* 65).

10 In the wider context of the avant-gardes, I am reminded of some of Salvador Dalì's works that specifically deal with questions of temporality. A Surrealist painting such as *La Persistence de la Mémoire* (1931), for example, shows a limp clock and a dress hanger hanging from a dead tree branch and could be a representation of one of the phenomenological dimensions of time – memory – which persists beyond death. *La Noblesse du Temps*, where the image of the limp clock appears again, is another representation of the flexibility of time and of the indivisibility of space and time. The latter is not rigid, but fluid. The unexpected and shocking limpness of the clock reflects the psychological experience of the passing of time. The limp clock cannot 'keep' time anymore; it cannot measure its course. The speed of our time depends only on us; the limp clock measures the time of life, so it must free itself from conceptuality, from the rigidity of linear time and be able to 'melt,' to adhere to the 'truer' reality it measures.

11 Severini (and Balla) did not participate in the writing of the *Manifesto*. The actual authors were Boccioni, Carrà, and Russolo. For an analysis of the specific influence of Bergson on Boccioni, see the article by Petrie. Boccioni, in the *Prefazione al Catalogo della Ia Esposizione di Pittura Futurista*, wrote that 'the picture must be a synthesis of what one remembers and what one sees' (Petrie 143).

12 Antliff notes that in this painting, which 'by his own admission, Severini painted [...] in response to his reading of Bergson's *Introduction to Metaphysics* [... he] selected a vast array of memory images related to travel and distributed them around a central image of a well, taken from his home town. [...] The work is a paradigmatic example of simultaneity: the scale of these images defies "perspectival" logic; they are disparate, yet bear a thematic relation to each other; and their radial arrangement suggests the idea of "convergence." To arrive at his conception, Severini had an intuition of the idea of travel, and since he had been reading Bergson, and Bergson equated consciousness with memory, Severini's internal meditation on the theme resulted in the welling up of an array of remembered images bearing a synthetic relation to the intuition of travel' (Antliff 53–4).

13 Russolo, from his experiments with sounds (the Futuristic sound machine called 'intonarumori' was his invention) gradually turned to philosophy and painting in the later stages of his life.

14 Even though Russolo's painting is structured very differently from Severini's, its images (some faces in a crowd in the right lower corner, electric lights on the right and the top left corners, a horse silhouette in the distance, shadows of men walking and, in central-top position, the 'phantasmatic' features of a woman's face) intend to convey the same sense of scattered memories retrieved (and painted) simultaneously. For an in-depth discussion of Russolo's painting, see Martin (89).

15 At the same time, one might add that such an 'old time' had been previously forgotten, or erased from the collective memory, and therefore it is now 'new' in a different way (which would explain even more, perhaps from a psychoanalytical perspective, Marinetti's fascination with it).

16 For Bergson 'the past collects in the fibers of the body as it does in the mind and determines the way we walk and dance as well as the way we think' (qtd. in Kern 41).

17 The argument that Marinetti's 'nostalgic' view of the past is possible only in Asia or in Egypt precisely because they are exotic extra-European realities, alien from modernity and progress, may also be relevant to my study. In the present analysis, however, I am not going to venture into a discussion that would require me to deal extensively with the complex subject of Marinetti's vision of colonialism.

18 Again, Eliade's conception of a 'sacred time,' opposed to a 'profane time,' when a total regeneration in search of an 'eternal moment' becomes possible, seems to be appropriate not only to the final pages of *Gli indomabili*, and may well complement my reading, while opening new lines of research and analysis. I am thinking, for example, of the ritualistic aspects of the novel, and how the initial scenes in the 'fossa' could be interpreted in light of Eliade's statements according to which 'The wish to abolish time can be seen even more clearly in the "orgy". [...] An orgy is also a regression into the "dark," a restoration of the primeval chaos, and as such precedes all creation' (399).

19 In order to reach such a future dimension which, as previously noted, often coincides with a utopian one, it is interesting to note that Marinetti has been using the setting of the island, that is, the consolidated, classical space of utopia. Once again, what we find is another look at the past, another return to tradition.

WORKS CITED

Antliff, Mark. *Inventing Bergson: Cultural Politics and the Parisian Avant-gardes.* Princeton: Princeton UP, 1993.

Calvesi, Maurizio. 'Boccioni, Umberto.' In *Futurismo & Futurismi.* Ed. P. Hulten. Milan: Bompiani, 1986. 428–30.

Curi, Fausto. 'Nota su Marinetti e Bergson.' In *Tra mimesi e metafora: studi su Marinetti e il futurismo.* Bologna: Pendragon, 1995. 115–23.

D'Ambrosio, Matteo. *Le 'Commemorazioni in avanti' di F.T. Marinetti – Futurismo e critica letteraria.* Naples: Liguori, 1999.

Deleuze, Gilles. *Difference and Repetition.* Trans. P. Patton. New York: Columbia UP, 1994.

Eliade, Mircea. *Patterns in Comparative Religion.* Trans. R. Sheed. U of Nebraska P, 1996.

Eliot, Thomas Stearns. 'Tradition and the Individual Talent.' In *The Sacred Wood. Essays on Poetry and Criticism.* London: Methuen; New York: Barnes & Noble, 1960.

Guglielmi, Guido. *La parola del testo. Letteratura come Storia.* Bologna: Il Mulino, 1993.

– 'The Paradoxes of Literary Modernity.' *Yale Journal of Criticism* vol. 5, n.1 (1991): 217–33.

– *L'udienza del poeta. Saggi su Palazzeschi e il futurismo.* Turin: Einaudi, 1979.

Hanson, Anne Coffin. *Severini futurista: 1912–1917.* New Haven: Yale University Art Gallery, 1996.

Kern, Stephen. *The Culture of Time and Space: 1880–1918.* Cambridge: Harvard UP, 1983.

Lyotard, Jean François. *The Inhuman: Reflections on Time.* Trans. G. Bennington and R. Bowlby. Stanford: Stanford UP, 1991.

Maeterlinck, Maurice. *La vie de l'espace.* (Trans: *The Life of Space,* 1929) (Publisher unknown).

Marinetti, Filippo Tommaso. *L'alcova d'acciaio.* Milan: Serra e Riva, 1985.

– *La grande Milano tradizionale e futurista – Una sensibilità italiana nata in Egitto.* Milan: Mondadori, 1969.

– *Teoria e invenzione futurista [TIF].* Ed. L. De Maria. Milan: Mondadori, 1990.

Martin, Marianne W. *Futurist Art and Theory.* Oxford: Clarendon P, 1968.

Mongardini, Carlo. *La cultura del presente – Tempo e storia nella tarda modernità.* Milan: F. Angeli, 1993.

Petrie, Brian. 'Boccioni and Bergson.' *The Burlington Magazine* 114 (March 1974): 140–7.

Pound, Ezra. *The Spirit of Romance*. New York: New Directions, 1968.

Rocca, Marzia. *L'oasi della memoria – Estetica e poetica del secondo Marinetti*. Naples: Tempi Moderni, 1989.

Sartini Blum, Cinzia. *The Other Modernism: F.T. Marinetti Futurist Fiction of Power*. Berkeley and Los Angeles: U of California P, 1996.

Schleifer, Ronald. *Modernism and Time: The Logic of Abundance in Literature, Science, and Culture, 1880–1930*. Cambridge: Cambridge UP, 2000.

Somigli, Luca. 'On the Threshold: Space and Modernity in Marinetti's Early Manifestoes and *Tavole parolibere*.' *Rivista di studi italiani* Anno XVII, n. 1 (June 1999): 250–74.

9 Ungaretti, Reader of Futurism

ANTONIO SACCONE

I

On more than one occasion, and in particular in the decade between 1920 and 1930, Ungaretti expressed his opinions on Futurism, each time with the clear intention of redefining the fundamental lines of his poetics. In almost all of his writings of those years – the years in which the revision of *Allegria di naufragi* [The Happiness of Shipwrecks] coincided with the preparation of *Sentimento del tempo* [The Sentiment of Time] – the expressive results and the theoretical elaborations of the Marinettian avant-garde undeniably appear as Ungaretti's implicit frame of reference, even when he is not explicitly concerned with them. In 1919, in a text originally conceived as a preface to a second edition of *Porto Sepolto* and which could be described as a real manifesto of poetics for 'un'arte nuova classica [a new classic art],'[1] his call for a 'return to order' (articulated in peculiar terms which cannot be assimilated to the paradigm of *La Ronda* [The Patrol])[2] entailed a direct confrontation with the period of Futurist experimentalism.

In 'Verso un'arte nuova classica' the necessity of a reciprocal conversion of tradition and modernism, of establishing a tight connection between the two notions, is inscribed under the sign of the Petrarch-Leopardi nexus: 'Chi sappia meditare sulle cose dell'arte, vedrà che dal Petrarca, le esperienze occorse e tesoreggiate, in cinque secoli, non si trasmutano in poesia che con l'apparizione di Leopardi [Those who can consider artistic matters will see that, after Petrarch, the experiences which had occurred and had been treasured over five centuries were transformed into poetry only with the appearance of Leopardi]' (*VUS* 13).[3]

For Ungaretti, it was crucial to revive the archetype determined by the two poetic systems – two interdependent referential models – in order to bring to an end the 'epoca di sfacelo e di esageramenti nella quale ancora brancoliamo [period of decline and exaggerations in which we still grope]' (VUS 14), that is to say, decadent art and the art of the avant-garde. The goal was the return 'verso un'arte nuova classica [towards a new classic art],'[4] towards a horizon that needs to be created, but in which the terms of the opposition are nevertheless already clear: an opposition resting on the equilibrium of innocence and memory, of the ephemeral and the eternal, of renewal and tradition, on the attempt, as he wrote in a later essay, of 'accordare modernamente un antico strumento musical [tuning in a modern way an ancient musical instrument].'[5] The creativity of the present can be realized exclusively through regulated freedom, through the intimate conjugation of experimentation and norm, of vitality and discipline, of the impatient projection ahead and the reconstructive return towards the origins:

> E mi pare che l'estro oggimai si muova per misterioso incontro d'inquiet-udine e di nostalgie, allo stesso modo dicessi che dattorno a me il presente altro non sia che un riflesso di passato e di avvenire, di abbandono e di azzardo, di rimpianti e di desiderio, di tradizioni e di scoperte, di logica e d'intuizione, di stile e di fantasia; come se il passato fosse la carne e l'avvenire l'idea, ma fossero un tutt'uno nell'immagine viva dattorno a noi. ('Verso un'arte nuova classica,' VUS 14).

> [And it seems to me that inspiration is now moved by the mysterious encounter of restlessness and nostalgia, in the same way as I would say that around me the present is nothing more than a reflex of past and future, of surrender and chance, of regrets and desire, of traditions and discoveries, of logic and intuition, of style and fantasy; as if the past were the flesh, and the future the idea, but they were both one in the living image around us.]

This passage foregrounds the perspective already assumed in 'Lucca,' the last (chronologically) of the works collected in *Allegria di Naufragi* and thus the conclusive episode of the first period of Ungaretti's poetry. Such a perspective follows almost to the letter the thought expressed by Apollinaire in the last of his *Calligrammes*, 'La Jolie Rousse,'[6] in which the exclusive idea of the new cultivated up to that point by Ungaretti's favourite master gives way to the intellectual and psychological demand of an agreement between invention and canon, adventure and order. After *Allegria di Naufragi*, the same agreement fostered and governed the discovery of the 'sentiment of time,' the rekindling of memory and of tradition. For the poet, this is the way towards the constitution of a classical dimension of the modern, of a new infused with memory. However, only those who (like himself) had assimilated and overcome – one could almost say metabolized – the lesson of Futurism could have aspired to become an authoritative leader in it:

> E se non giunsi ad adottare i rumori in libertà, uno stupore contemplativo mi avvinse in confronto alla parola, la quale mi si risuscitava in tutta la sua vita millenaria, tale che provai la necessità di fermarla nel compimento, staccata in pause. ('Verso un'arte classica,' *VUS* 15)

> [And if I did not come to the point of adopting noises in freedom, a contemplative stupor overwhelmed me with regards to the word, which revived in me in all its millenary life, to such a point that I felt the need to stop it in its fulfilment, loosened into pauses.]

It is significant that, in making reference to the history of his literary identity, Ungaretti contrasts Futurism with that which by then he considered the inaugural phase of his production (*L'Allegria*, and specifically the first two episodes of its complex stratigraphy:[7] *Il Porto Sepolto* and *Allegria di Naufragi*), in which he had contracted a few debts with the procedures of the so-called historical avant-garde. Ungaretti distances himself from 'words in freedom,' the main technique of creative writing invented by Marinetti, and dismisses it as 'noises in freedom,' as mimesis of disorder, thus emphasizing their onomatopaeic dimension, their vocation for the mimetic reproduction of sounds and sensations. The crisis of the word does not lead him to adopt the solution proposed by the Futurists, which involved liberating oneself from the hindrances of the past, from the heritage of memory, from the ties to the world of the fathers, in the name of a temporality founded on the continuous renewal of the new, on absolute presentification, on the never-ending expansion of the present.[8] Ungaretti's perspective in both the recent past of his poetic production and in his current poetic journey is precisely the opposite. In his earlier works, the astonished isolation in which the 'word' had been suspended and parsed, the rhythmic order governing it, already aimed at returning to its original essentiality through temporal depth, by means of memory. The avant-garde had also intended to find a primordial condition, to bring into play a moment of origin. In that case, however, the issue had been not so much that of recovering the initial hour as much as of constituting a new beginning, of inventing origins, of becoming the forefathers and thus, according to the law of an Oedipal, permanent discontinuity, of breaking with the past, of articulating an aesthetics of communication and of spectacular, non-contemplative, immediately pragmatic presence, thus interrupting any temporal continuity. For Ungaretti, on the contrary, the objective was restoring that continuity and reinstating within it the poetic word, reconstructed and refunctionalized in its mechanisms, thus putting its duration back into play: 'Fu un raccattare i frantumi dell'orologio per provare d'intenderne il congegno, per provare di rifargli segnare il tempo [It was like picking up the pieces of the clock to try to understand its mechanisms, to attempt to make it mark time once again]' ('Verso un'arte classica,' *VUS* 15).

The meditation on time became the decisive turning point in Ungaretti's implicit or explicit antagonistic confrontation with the Futurist heritage. In this sense, in the backward journey towards the sources of Italian and European poetry, Petrarch and Leopardi played the role of guardian deities of the values of time and memory, around which Ungaretti's poetry concentrated at the time in which the poetics that oriented *Sentimento del tempo* began to take shape.[9] Ungaretti's critical essays are full of references to the modernity of the poet of Laura,[10] to the strong mark he left upon 'la poesia europea sino al romanticismo, con Mallarmé e a Valéry [European poetry up to Romanticism, including Mallarmé and Valéry]' ('L'esportazione letteraria,' *VUS* 141). The inaugural character, the 'novelty' of Petrarch – as he writes in one of the lessons of the Brazilian period, when the Ungarettian interpretation of the fourteenth-century poet, which had begun in the 1920s, received its organic definition – consisted in having emphasized that one cannot 'avere coscienza di sé se non per il fatto che i suoi atti divengono memoria [have conscience of oneself if not for the fact that one's actions become memory]' ('Sui sonetti del Petrarca,' *VUS* 114). Petrarch is 'in poesia l'inventore del tempo [in poetry, the inventor of time],' the discoverer of the 'profondità del tempo [profoundness of time],' that is, of the fact that 'nell'essere presente di ciascuno sono compresi tutti gli infiniti del suo essere attraverso il tempo, tutte le sue età [within the present being of each and every individual, are included all the infinities of his being through time, all of his ages]' ('Sui sonetti del Petrarca,' *VUS* 118). The concept of time is complementary to the concept of absence, to the 'coscienza di minuto in minuto rinnovata, d'una felicità irreparabilmente rinnovata [consciousness renewed at every moment of an irreparably renewed happiness].' In Petrarch, man is in 'exile from the past:' 'le cose del mondo, solo quando sono passate, si fanno compiute, perfette, atte a risorgere nella memoria [only when they have passed, the things of the world are completed, perfect, suitable to rise again in memory]' ('Sui sonetti del Petrarca,' *VUS* 114–15). From *Sentimento* on, Ungaretti consciously built his own 'inspiration' upon the closely interrelated Petrarchan concepts of memory and absence ('L'idea di assenza [...] è soprattutto rottura delle tenebre della memoria [the idea of absence [...] is above all, a fracture of the shadows of memory]'), completely antiphrastic with respect to the Futurist preaching, founded on the dissolution of memory and on the supremacy of presence.[11]

The theory of time that Petrarch, the poet of memory, transmits to Ungaretti, is linked to the 'duration' strenuously investigated and pursued by Leopardi:

> Il Leopardi principalmente valuta la parola nella sua durata e nella sua variabilità. La parola, come ogni altro corpo vivo, invecchia continuamente e quindi costantemente è diversa, ma continuamente s'accresce anche la sua durata, la sua profondità temporale. ('Idee del Leopardi,' *VUS* 32)

> [Leopardi mainly values the word in its duration and in its variability. The word, as all other living bodies, ages continuously and therefore is constantly different, but its duration, its temporal depth continues to grow.]

But the idea of 'duration,' that is, of 'temporal depth,' also brings into play Henri Bergson, who in the 1920s acted as a filter for the assimilation of the pair Petrarch-Leopardi and of the other ancient and modern authors between the extremes formed by that pair – Plato, St Augustine, Mallarmé – whom Ungaretti used and combined in the elaboration of his poetics of memory.

Ungaretti had attended Bergson's lectures at the Collège de France during the years of his first stay in Paris, and had assimilated a notion of duration that was psychological in character, and parsed by the internal time of consciousness. About ten years later, on the occasion of the publication of *Durée et simultaneité* and of Albert Thibaudet's four volumes of *Trente ans de vie française*, two of which were devoted to Bergsonianism, Ungaretti wrote a few pieces on the French philosopher which offered him the opportunity of another dialectic confrontation with Futurism.[12] He appeared to be well aware of the aesthetic implications of Bergsonian thought ('Il bergsonismo ha lasciato un'impronta nell'arte [Bergsonianism has left a mark in art]' ('L'estetica di Bergson,' *VUS* 80)) and of the influence of the French thinker on the culture of the early years of the twentieth century, in particular on the theories of the Italian avant-garde ('qui da noi, non ci volevan occhi di lince per discernere nei concitati manifesti futuristi, e nelle diffuse dissertazioni futuristiche, spunti e insistenze bergsoniani [here in Italy, it didn't take a particularly keen eye to discern in the impassioned manifestos and in the widely circulated dissertations of Futurism, Bergsonian ideas and preoccupations]' (*VUS* 80)). Ungaretti's concern was nevertheless to show how consistent Bergson's ideas on time were with his own poetics and how substantially different they were from the artistic perspectives elaborated by the Futurists. When speaking about 'il posto che occupa il tempo nella struttura della lingua d'un popolo [the place of time within the structure of the language of a people]' (a sign of the 'grado di civiltà di detto popolo [degree of civilization of said people]') (*VUS* 83), he dwelled upon the ample treatment that the grammars of the past dedicated to the distinction between the various conjunctions of time, instilling in this way, 'assieme al senso del tempo insinuatosi nella stessa trama della lingua, il senso della storia, il senso del muoversi del tempo, il senso della genesi e della forza di sviluppo della lingua, il senso del tempo e dello slancio vitale contenuti nella sostanza della lingua [in addition to the sense of time that penetrated within the very texture of language, the sense of history, the sense of the movement of time, the sense of the birth and of the strength of development of language, the sense of time and of the *élan vital* enclosed within the substance of the language]' (*VUS* 84). There could be no clearer reference *e contrario* to the unrelated contemporaneousness imposed by Futurist words-in-freedom through the abolition of the hierarchies of verb tenses, the exclusive emergence of the infinitive mode, and the ensuing disempowerment of contemplative or recalling subjectivity.[13] To the 'adventurous disciple' who 'non ancora aveva avuto il presentimento degli abissi d'anima dai quali trae origine l'apparente inconseguenza delle azioni umane [had not yet had the premonition of the abysses of the soul from which the apparent inconsequence of human actions originates],' those old grammars precociously transmitted 'il senso della profondità dell'uomo [the sense of the depth of man]' (*VUS* 84).

Ungaretti reproposed Bergson's rejection of the spatialized and reversible time of physics, which relied upon the succession of static instants and was indifferent to the qualitative nature of the facts contained within them. Bergson opts for a time that is concretely lived by consciousness,[14] understood as the real duration in which the present psychic state preserves the process from which it originates and is, at the same time, invention, that is to say, something new and unpredictable, not referable to the pre-existing elements. There is no solution of continuity in the unstable 'states' of consciousness. They interpenetrate, giving life to a continuous creation, to a perennial flow where the past projects itself into the present, amalgamating with it. Here is Ungaretti's paraphrase:

Il tempo è la primordiale intuizione della qualità, è la melodia dell'universo, di ciò che dura costantemente mutando, ed è nuovo costantemente, e mutando crea, di ciò che non può esser raffigurato da quantità, perché cesserebbe, se potesse esserne interrotto il corso, d'esser il segno della vita e diverrebbe materia inerte. ('L'estetica di Bergson,' *VUS* 84)

[Time is the primodial intuition of quality. It is the melody of the universe, of that which lasts, while constantly changing, and is constantly new, and, changing, creates; thus, it cannot be represented by quantity, because if its course could be interrupted, it would cease to be the sign of life and it would become inert matter.]

However, in making the model of Bergsonian time correspond to the poetic and theoretical system that he was delineating during the 1920s, Ungaretti once again clearly distinguished it from the precepts of Futurism:

Non dico una figura spaziale, ma la parola quasi non riesce, per Bergson, malgrado poco fa si diceva della lingua, a aderire al moto del tempo, e non perché non possa esser fulminea nel riferire, ma perché necessariamente ha una certa fissità e una certa rigidità. ('L'estetica di Bergson,' *VUS* 84)

[Although we were discussing language a little while ago, in Bergson not only a spatial figure, but even the word is almost unable to adhere to the movement of time, not because it cannot refer instantaneously, but because it has necessarily a certain degree of immobility and of rigidity.]

It seems to me that this is a further confutation of the Futurist axioms, particularly of the claim that the word, freed from any (psycho)logical-syntactic mediation, can reach 'life,' become one with its inexhaustible dynamism, and imitate it with immediacy. Obviously, by denying any possible agreement between the Futurists and Bergson, Ungaretti tried to distance his own poetry from the paths beaten by the avant-garde. If, as has been rightly pointed out, Ungaretti, following Bergson, understands memory as the 'impossibility that the present be present if it is not, at the same time, past, continuity with the past that *yesterday* was the present,' and thus sees poetry as the 'epiphany not of the instant, but of psychic continuity, of emotional duration' (Curi 244), it becomes obvious that he is distancing himself from a perspective like that of Futurism, which aims at adhering to the moment, to its presence, and at making it immediately become future.

Later in 'L'estetica di Bergson' the dissociation of the thought of the author of *Matière et mémoire* from the devices of Futurist words-in-freedom is affirmed in clear and unequivocal terms:

> Senza dubbio, di questo tempo bergsoniano, non il dinamismo plastico che pigliava una questione di qualità per un problema di meccanica, con i mezzi dell'arte, né la simultaneità lirica che si lusingava di far contemporaneamente funzionare, come fa un giornale, fatti successi ai quattro canti del globo, dovevan aver la pretesa d'aver trovato la formula estetica. (*VUS* 84–5)

> [Without a doubt, neither plastic dynamism, which, with the means of art, mistook a question of quality for a problem of mechanics, nor lyric simultaneity, which deluded itself into believing it could make events taking place in the four corners of the globe function contemporarily, as a newspaper does, can claim to have found the aesthetic formula of this Bergsonian time.]

The irreconciliability of Futurist dynamism and simultaneity and Bergson's conception of time stems from the movement's insistence in mixing aesthetic problems, which have to do with quality, with problems that concern matter, that is to say, quantity. Furthermore, Futurism grants a privileged place to the synchronic, ubiquitous human being, endowed with mass mediatic[15] sensitivity, at the expense of depth, of the human being plunged into the abyss of memory, who is, in Ungarettian terms, 'brutally'[16] cancelled.[17]

For Ungaretti, those who perceive Bergsonian influences on 'pure' art or poetry are closer to the truth: 'Bergson allude di quando in quando a una sensazione purgata d'ogni torbido affettivo. Quella sensazione, sgorgando in una pura forma, e rinnovandosi, e sempre tornando a fiorire, e germinando ancora, in una perfetta continuità, non attuerebbe il tempo bergsoniano? [From time to time, Bergson alludes to a feeling purged of any affective disturbance. That feeling, flowing out in a pure form, renewing itself, and always coming back to flourish, and germinating again, in a perfect continuity – would that not bring about Bergsonian time?]' ('L'estetica di Bergson,' VUS 85). The Cubists follow this path, but 'its traces could already be perceived' in Baudelaire, Mallarmé, and in the Valéry who is the heir of Leopardi,[18] the inventor of a 'lyric of the intellect': 'Può darsi, anzi avviene, che gli estremi si tocchino e che suscitando la perfezione, insieme si susciti l'evoluzione perpetua dell'effimero [It may be, and in fact it is the case, that the extremes touch one another, and that, by giving rise to perfection, they also cause the perpetual evolution of the ephemeral]' ('L'estetica di Bergson,' VUS 85). The extremes are temporal ones: immutability and transitoriness, the eternal and temporality. In his theoretical considerations (but even more so in his poetic practice) Ungaretti pursues their 'miraculous' reconciliation, thus attempting to give, in Guido Guglielmi's words, a 'decisive form to the indecisive figure of modernity (73).'[19]

In a conference held in the year when 'L'estetica di Bergson' was published, Ungaretti confirmed his polemic against Futurism, although he recognized its 'straordinari meriti [...] per varietà di esperimenti audaci e per fecondità d'attuazioni originali [extraordinary merits [...] because of its variety of daring experiments and because of its fertility of original accomplishments]' ('Punto di mira,' VUS 295). The years of the triumph of the 'onomatopoeia' (pursued by Pascoli and by Marinetti) had led to the 'sfacelo della parola, o almeno a un punto dal quale si ricomincia' [ruin of the word, or at least to a point from which one begins again]: in other words, to the point from which Ungaretti had begun again. Interested in defending 'la gravità della parola [the seriousness of the word],' in opposing himself 'all'abuso della sensazione verbale [to the abuse of the verbal sensation],' Ungaretti could not avoid looking at Leopardi as to the 'unico dal quale si potesse procedere con qualche profitto [only one upon whom one could build with some benefit]' ('Punto di mira,' VUS 295). Ungaretti makes it clear that already in his first period, that of Il Porto Sepolto, and even in those compositions aimed at giving 'delle sensazioni, simultanee o successive, [...] l'elenco [the list of simultaneous or subsequent [...] sensations], he had worked on the word to give it 'una pienezza di contenuto morale [a fullness of moral content],' detaching it from the pure 'impressionabilità fisica [physical impressionability]' ('Punto di mira,' *VUS* 295) that had been the ultimate goal of the Futurists.[20]

II

In the history of Ungaretti's rereadings of the Futurist phenomenon, a central place is occupied by an important statement of poetics whose title, of great semantic significance, was destined to become one of the most famous emblems of the Egyptian poet.[21] I am referring to the 1926 examination, in three different versions (two in Italian, the third in French), of the concepts of 'innocence' and 'memory,'[22] defined as 'le persone del nostro dramma, di artisti del primo Novecento [the *personae* of our drama, of us artists of the beginning of the twentieth century].' Here, it seems to me that the term '*persona*' is to be understood in its etymological sense,[23] as a mask worn on the literary scene of the first decades of the century. These two disguises are thus to be placed alongside the others to which Ungaretti entrusts the representation of his poetic 'I' (from the wanderer to the soldier, from the shipwrecked to the man in anguish). The author of *Sentimento del Tempo* aims at reconstructing the alternation of those two dramatis personae through the representative development of his personal artistic and intellectual experience:

> L'innocenza, abbiamo saputo com'è fatta. Ci è apparsa, e ci ha tenuto sotto le sue ali già grandi, nei rivolgimenti di questi anni. La memoria aveva gli occhi bendati, poteva dirsi abolita. Persino la nozione del tempo era nuova. Il tempo pareva eterno, non per modi di dire. Non ci è stato nascosto l'orrore dell'eternità. Non contava più che l'istinto. Si era in tale dimestichezza con la morte, che il naufragio era senza fine. ('Innocenza e memoria,' *VUS* 133–4)

> [We know what innocence is like. It appeared to us and kept us under its already wide wings in the upheavals of these years. Memory had its eyes blindfolded, it could have been considered abolished. Even the notion of time was new. Time seemed to be eternal, and not in a manner of speaking. The horrors of eternity were not hidden from us. Nothing but instinct mattered anymore. Our familiarity with death was such that the shipwreck was without end.]

Modernity belongs to the dimension of innocence, and, therefore, so does the horizon of the avant-garde originated on – and from – the characteristics of that modernity: the death of memory, the dissolution of tradition, the absolute cult of the new, the new concept of time. Ungaretti reads the condition of innocence (which he experienced with *Allegria*) in relation to death. The (Futurist) idea of an art which conceives its own dissolution, which makes use of the onslaughts of death against itself to renew and increase its creativity, appears as an apocalypse, a horrifying eternalization of time (which is equivalent to its suspension), a perpetual crisis ('the shipwreck was without end').

Innocence is thus the opposite of memory. However, Ungaretti perceives a new conclusive possibility for modernity: bringing together innocence and memory, finding the former in the 'duration' of the latter:

> Credo che la poesia di domani sarà felice. A poco a poco, il dramma si scioglierà. Saranno andati in fumo anche i tentativi di affidare la parte del burattinaio alla memoria, e all'innocenza quella dell'oracolo. E dell'innocenza, tornata nella memoria al suo posto oscuro, le lusinghe saranno vane. ('Innocenza e memoria,' *VUS* 134)

> [I feel that the poetry of tomorrow will be happy. Step by step, the drama will unfold. The attempts of entrusting the roles of puppeteer to memory and of oracle to innocence will also be fruitless. And the temptations of innocence, now returned to its dark place in memory, will be in vain.]

We thus have the fulfilment of 'Blake's miracle,' that is to say, of the author whose translation Ungaretti began to work on in 1930. '[R]icercando affannosamente vie smarrite della tradizione [in his restless quest for the lost roads of tradition],' Blake had oriented his expositive technique 'verso il recupero dell'originale innocenza espressiva [towards the recovery of the original expressive innocence]':

> Il miracolo, come facevo a dimenticarmene, è frutto, me l'aveva insegnato Mallarmé, di memoria. A furia di memoria si torna, o ci si può illudere di tornare, innocenti. L'uomo che tenta di arretrarsi sino al punto dove, per memoria, la memoria si abolisce e l'oblio illuminante: estasi, suprema conoscenza, uomo vero uomo – è dono di memoria. E il miracolo è parola: per essa il poeta si può arretrare nel tempo sino dove lo spirito umano risiedeva nella sua unità e nella sua verità, non ancora caduto in frantumi, preda del Male, esule per vanità, sbriciolato nelle catene e nel tormento delle infinite fattezze materiali del tempo. ('Discorsetto su Blake,' *VUS* 597)

[The miracle – how could I forget – is the product of memory, as Mallarmé had taught me. By dint of memory one returns, or so one can delude oneself, to a state of innocence. The man who attempts to move back to the point where, through memory, memory is abolished and oblivion is illuminating: ecstasy, supreme knowledge, man true man – is a gift of memory. And the miracle is word: through it, the poet is able to go back in time to the point where the human spirit dwelled in its unity and in its truth, and had not yet fallen to pieces, in the clutches of Evil, in exile as a result of vanity, shattered in the chains and torments of the infinite material features of time.]

III

A year after the publication of 'Innocenza e memoria,' Ungaretti returns to the question of the avant-garde with more explicit arguments. In 'Commemorazione del Futurismo' (a title that, if one pays careful attention to the text that follows, is much more semantically meaningful than Ungaretti suggests in his preliminary justification),[24] Marinetti is praised for having identified the 'also aesthetic' role (*VUS* 171) assumed by the machine in modern life:

> Guardando un'automobile, un transatlantico, un velivolo, un imbrigliamento idroelettrico, una mitragliatrice, una strada ferrata metropolitana, ecc., sono colto dallo stesso diletto che provo davanti a un cavallo da corsa, a un ulivo, a una saetta, a una libellula. Non perché vedo in quei mezzi umani i simboli della volontà occidentale d'emulare la natura, di carpire senza pace segreti alla natura, ma perché quegli oggetti, come le opere della natura, sono comandati da leggi meticolose e rigorose, da esattezza numerica. (*VUS* 171)

> [Looking at a car, a transatlantic, an airplane, a hydro-electric plant, a machine-gun, a tramway line, etc. I am seized by the same pleasure that I get from a racing horse, an olive tree, a thunderbolt, a dragonfly. Not because I see in those human instruments the symbols of the Western desire of emulating nature, of restlessly stealing the secrets of nature, but because those objects, like the works of nature, are ruled by meticulous and rigorous laws, by numeric exactness.]

In displaying his 'pleasure' before the new wonders of modern technology, Ungaretti seems to have in mind Marinetti's manifesto of 1914, 'Lo splendore geometrico e meccanico e la sensibilità numerica [Geometric and Mechanical Splendour and Numeric Sensibility]':

Nulla è più bello di una grande centrale elettrica ronzante che contiene la
pressione idraulica di una catena di monti e la forza elettrica di un vasto
orizzonte, sintetizzate nei quadri marmorei di distribuzione, irti di conta-
tori, di tastiere e di commutatori lucenti. Questi quadri sono i nostri soli
modelli in poesia. (*Teoria e invenzione* 100)

[Nothing is more beautiful than a great humming central electric station that
holds the hydraulic pressure of a mountain chain and the electric power of
a vast horizon, synthesized in marble distribution panels bristling with
dials, keyboards and shining commutators. These panels are our only
model for the writing of poetry.] (*Let's Murder* 106)

As a matter of fact, the new aesthetic paradigm that Futurism had
assigned to the machine, to its functionality, to the 'perfezione
scintillante dei suoi ingranaggi precisi [sparkling perfection of precise
gears]' (*Teoria e invenzione* 100 / *Let's Murder* 106), clashes with the
critical and theoretical system within which Ungaretti had framed his
idea of poetry since the 1920s. For Ungaretti, too, the objects of technology can be 'modelli agli artisti; modelli di metrica, di simmetrie, di
funambolismi, e soccorrere a conoscere nuove risorse [models for the
artist – models of metrics, of symmetries, of acrobatics – and help in
becoming familiar with new resources]' (*VUS* 171). The problem is
that Futurism was 'flawed' by an initial misunderstanding: 'ha creduto
che, a conseguenza dei suoi principi, fosse missione dell'arte *imitare* la
macchina, o piuttosto l'umanità che stava adattandosi a questa sua
ultima creatura [it believed that, as a result of its principles, the mission was *imitating* the machine, or, rather, that humanity was adapting
to its latest creation]' (*VUS* 171). The issue is not establishing that the
'geometric splendor' of the machine is 'centomila volte più interessante
della psicologia dell'uomo, con le sue combinazioni limitatissime [a
hundred thousand times more interesting [...] than human psychology
with its very limited combinations],' as Marinetti had proclaimed (*Teoria
e invenzione* 99/*Let's Murder* 106), but rather 'scoprire ciò che in essa vi
è racchiuso di naturale, di permanente, d'universale [discovering that
which is contained in it, made up of what is the natural, the permanent, the universal]'. This 'initial error' produced the 'incredible' proposal of words in freedom, 'cioè la cieca fiducia nella materia grezza,
nella sensazione, nella materia caotica [that is to say, blind faith in raw
matter, in the sensation, in chaotic matter]' (*VUS* 172). The Futurists
thus did not understand that the model of the machine is the model of
'una materia formata, severamente logica nell'ubbidienza d'ogni

minima fibra all'ordine complessivo, frutto d'una catena millenaria di sforzi coordinati [formed matter, strictly logical in the obedience of the minutest of its fibres to the overall order, the product of a millenary chain of coordinated effort]' (*VUS* 172). The machine signifies measure, order, equilibrium, mystery and above all, continuity of memory ('millenary chain'). This last aspect could not have been grasped by the Futurists who were interested in 'non vedere della realtà che l'aspetto estemporaneo, provvisorio, futile [seeing in reality only its extemporary, provisional, futile aspects],' thus 'dimentichi che ogni atto profondamente umano (e quindi anche la poesia) emana dall'illusione di vincere la morte [forgetting that any profoundly human act (and thus, also poetry), derives from the illusion of overcoming death]' (*VUS* 173). Without this indispensable illusion, Ungaretti concludes, 'trascureremmo di trasfondere le nostre aspirazioni in qualche sostanza di durata, e saremmo dannati a produrre opere vuote di qualsiasi mistero [we would neglect to instil our aspirations into some substance of duration, and we would be condemned to produce works empty of any mystery]' (*VUS* 173).

It does not seem to me an exegetic hazard to recognize in Ungaretti's aspiration to create works of substance, valorized by duration, a polemic allusion to the refusal of the imperishable 'masterpiece,' of the enchantment of the aura, of a beauty that is not transitory, of the sacredness of the aesthetic product, preached by Futurism. A further confirmation comes from a text of the following year, 'Arte e affari e abracadabra [Art, and business, and hocus pocus],' which is clearly hostile to a redefinition of artistic practice in terms of pure professional status.[25] Here, Ungaretti clearly still recalls the echoes of a 1914 manifesto written by Bruno Corra and Emilio Settimelli, 'Pesi, misure e prezzi del genio artistico [Weights, measures, and prices of artistic genius],' in which the value of artistic creation is identified in terms of its quantity of exteriorized energy. The job of the Futurist 'measurer' would be to calculate the artistic talent and fix its weights and prices, with the aim of bringing about its thorough socialization, its integration in the dynamics of the market, in the context of useful economic activities. As can easily be imagined, such prescriptions are completely incompatible with the poetics of Ungaretti, who on the one hand declares that he is aware that 'c'è una frattura oggi tra l'arte e il pubblico [there is a fracture today between art and the public],' but on the other affirms that nevertheless the '"industrializzatori" dell'arte ["industrializers" of art]' cannot be the ones to heal it:

L'arte non rientra nel criterio della statistica, non si misura a metro, implica un giudizio estetico, storico e morale a lungo incerto e mutevole, che si forma attraverso mille vagli indefinibili, che non può venire espresso dal numero. [...] L'arte, s'è detto, non può prosperare e dar frutto che nell'ambito della qualità. (*VUS* 190)

[Art does not follow the criteria of statistics. It cannot be measured with a metre. It implies an aesthetic, historical or moral judgment, uncertain and mutable in the long run, that is formed through a thousand undefinable judgments that cannot be expressed by numbers. [...] Art, it has been said, cannot prosper and give fruit except within the domain of quality.

Even in the 1929 interview with G.B. Angioletti, 'La poesia contemporanea è viva o morta? [Is contemporary poetry dead or alive?],' Ungaretti reproposed, in a way that was anything but marginal, the question of Futurism.[26] After stating that he was not inclined to glorify either technological objects or the images of nature – 'non mi faccio un Dio dell'aeroplano, né dell'albero [I make neither the airplane, nor of the tree into a God]' (*VUS* 190) – he put forward once again a proposition originally formulated by Marinetti, even though he seemed (or most likely pretended) not to recall its paternity:

Non ricordo più chi, uno diceva, e diceva bene, che la poesia moderna si propone di mettere in contatto ciò che più è distante. Maggiore è la distanza, superiore è la poesia. Quando tali contatti danno luce, è toccata poesia. In breve uso, e forse abuso, di forme ellittiche. Come vede, anche la poesia corre dietro, oggi, alla velocità. (*VUS* 191)

[Someone – I no longer recall who – said, and it was well said, that modern poetry aims at putting into contact that which is most distant. The greater the distance, the better the poetry. When such contacts give light, poetry is revealed. In short, I use, and perhaps abuse, elliptical forms. Evidently, today poetry too runs after speed.]

Ungaretti was clearly referring to the analogical procedure proposed in 1912 by Marinetti in the 'Manifesto tecnico della letteratura Futurista' to connect 'le cose distanti, apparentemente diverse e ostili [distant, seemingly diverse and hostile things]' (*Teoria e invenzione* 48/*Let's Murder* 93). In fact that procedure, reactivated as a de-syntacticizing practice, was part of the broader assault against any mediation that would hinder a direct contact between the poetic word and the otherness that emerged with the developments of technology. Ungaretti's position, on the contrary, was the result of an argument that once again recognizes the need for a correspondence between the benefits of tradition and the new paths of research and of experience:

> La difficoltà è di non turbare l'armonia del nostro endecasillabo, di non rinunziare ad alcuna delle infinite risorse che nella sua lunga vita ha conquistato, e insieme di non essere inferiori a nessuno nell'audacia, nell'aderenza al proprio tempo. (*VUS* 191)

> [The difficulty is not to disturb the harmony of our hendecasyllable, not to renounce any of the infinite resources that in its long life it has conquered, and at the same time not to be inferior to anyone in audacity, in adherence to one's own time.]

The positions are, as always, distant, although Ungaretti indicates the experience of the new, and therefore also the lesson of Futurism, as a necessary premise of his 'classicism.' It is not by chance that, further on, the text confirms the end of the age of Marinettian immediacy, heteronomy, and pragmatism:

> Ci fu un momento, nel pieno dell'ora apocalittica del dopoguerra, quando più non contava che l'attimo e tutto pareva precipizio, quando non solo il concetto della relatività aveva varcato ogni ragionevolezza della negazione, quando il poeta si sentiva più che mai soverchiato e attratto e travolto dalla necessità dell'azione, quando non solo sentiva in crisi il concetto di letteratura, e spregiava il vano lavoro delle parole cui irrimediabilmente era inchiodato dalla sua vocazione, ci fu persino un momento in cui, dell'azione che lo stordiva e lo salvava, si sorprendeva a dirsi: a che pro? (*VUS* 195)

> [There was a moment, in the apocalyptic hour after the war, when nothing but the instant mattered and everything seemed to precipitate, when not only the concept of relativity had overcome all reasonable denial, when the poet felt more than ever overwhelmed and attracted and swept away by the necessity of action, when he not only felt that the concept of literature was in crisis, and disdained the useless work of the words to which he was inevitably shackled by his vocation; there was even a moment in which he would catch himself saying, regarding the action that stunned and saved him: What is the use?]

IV

In 'Ragioni di una poesia,' a text of the late 1940s built through an assemblage of lectures and texts conceived in the 1920s and the 1930s, we find a confirmation of Ungaretti's loyalty to the perspective and technical orientations of modernity:

> Se il carattere dell'800 era quello di stabilire legami a furia di rotaie, e di ponti e di pali, e di carbone e di fumo – il poeta d'oggi cercherà dunque di mettere a contatto immagini lontane senza fili. Dalla memoria all'innocenza, quale lontananza da varcare; ma in un baleno. (*VUS* 760)

> [If the characteristic of the nineteenth century was that of establishing connections by means of railways, of bridges and poles, of coal and smoke – today's poet will seek to join distant images without strings. From memory to innocence, what a distance to overcome: but in a flash.]

The reference to the Futurist conception of analogy, understood by Marinetti as 'immaginazione senza fili [imagination without strings]' (*Teoria e invenzione* 53/*Let's Murder* 97) is almost to the letter: analogy, and more generally, art as 'synthetic expression,' cannot, however, eliminate the necessity of 'comunicare il senso d'una durata [communicating the sense of a duration]' (*VUS* 759). 'Today's poet' (a formula that recurs often in Ungaretti's essays, used by the poet to speak about himself and about his relationship with the new emerging in the present), in other words, the poet who 'per risvegliare l'innocenza, [...] non ha negato la memoria [in order to awaken innocence, [...] did not refute memory]' (*VUS* 756), has resolved the question in these terms:

> [...] oggi, ridotta la parola quasi al silenzio, spezzati all'estro analogico i ceppi, s'ottiene, nell'ordine della fantasia, cercando quell'analogia atta ad essere il più possibile, illuminazione favolosa; s'ottiene dando tono, nell'ordine della psicologia, a quella sfumatura propensa a parere fantasma o mito; s'ottiene scegliendo, nell'ordine visivo la combinazione di oggetti meglio evocanti una divinazione metafisica.
>
> Illuminazione favolosa, fantasmi e miti, divinazione metafisiche, non sono forse illusioni di tempo domato, o meglio di tempo abolito? E inoltre, l'affaticarsi alla perfezione dell'opera, rinnovandone da capo a fondo i mezzi come ogni vero poeta d'oggi fa, non è volontà che l'opera duri? Non è volontà che l'opera duri per singolare bellezza? Che duri cioè, per la più

alta qualità di durata, in un'opera di poesia. Tutto ciò più che ricerca
d'illusione d'immortalità, è brama d'eterno. (*VUS* 759–60)

[[...] now that the word has been almost reduced to silence, and the fetters
of analogical inspiration have been shattered, one succeeds, on the level of
fantasy, by looking for the analogy most likely to be fabulous illumination;
one succeeds by emphasizing, on the level of psychology, the nuance liable
to appear as a ghost or a myth; one succeeds by choosing, on the visual level,
the combination of objects which best evokes a metaphysical divination.

Fabulous illumination, ghost or myth, metaphysical divination – are
these not illusions of a domesticated, or better, abolished time? And
furthermore, does not labouring to perfect the work, renewing from top to
bottom its means as every true poet does, reveal the will to make the work
last? Is not this will that the work endure due to its unique beauty? In other
words, that it endure due to its superior quality of duration, in the case of
a work of poetry? More than a quest for the illusion of immortality, this is
a craving for the eternal.]

Notions such as 'fabulous illumination,' 'myth,' and 'metaphysical divination,' all closely related to Ungarettian analogy understood as allusive word, as the vertigo of the absolute, bring into play a sacred idea
of language, entrusted with the task of revealing, of bringing light to
mystery, of immobilizing the moment, of exalting the experience of time.

In 'Influenza di Vico sulle teorie estetiche d'oggi [Vico's influence
on contemporary aesthetic theories],' a lecture published in 1937 and
dedicated to the consecration of memory ('Tutto, tutto, tutto è già
memoria [Everything, everything, everything is already memory]' (*VUS*
345)), Ungaretti coherently developed further his interpretation of Futurism. The machine is reconfirmed as the vehicle for millennial
memory, a model of harmony and rhythm. Futurism was unable to
attribute such meaning to the signs of modernity. Ungaretti does so,
thus proposing himself as the 'counterpart' (Guglielmi 12) of the the
avant-gardes, the authentic image of the 'Poeti d'oggi, cioè [di] tutta
l'ultima poesia italiana d'oggi, nata nel 1917, in trincea, nel *Porto Sepolto*
[poets of today, that is, [of] all the recent Italian poetry of today, born
in 1917, on the front lines, in *Porto Sepolto*]' (*VUS* 357). Ungaretti emphasizes that the Futurists had been exclusively concerned with 'rendering' the machine 'mimeticamente nella sua travolgente brutalità
[mimetically in its overwhelming brutality].' Thus, in their art 'il mito

della macchina era rimasto inespresso [the myth of the machine remained unexpressed].' Since their 'intuition' was 'caotica e non chiara
e distinta [chaotic and not clear and distinct],' 'l'espressione non poteva
essere se non puerile, e difatti era onomatopeica [its expression could
be only puerile, and in fact it was onomatopoeic]' (VUS 357). It seems
to me that in certain points, Ungaretti's argument refers to the
doubts on Futurism expressed by the protagonists of Lacerba after
the first period of cooperation with Marinetti. As is well known,
Giovanni Papini blamed Marinettian Futurism not only for considering art as a 'simple action,' but for bringing art back to the state of
'raw nature':

> Marinetti, colle parole in libertà, spezza e distrugge le articolazioni logiche
> del discorso (la sintassi: conquista lunga dello spirito sopra l'incoerenza
> esclamativa del linguaggio primitivo) – ricorre alle immagini visive
> (realistiche, concrete) sotto forma di parole o frasi disposte tipografica-
> mente in modo da suggerire per ideogramma la visione di cui si parla – e fa
> grande uso di suoni imitativi, che sono pezzi di natura vocale allo stato
> nativo trasportati di peso nel quadro lirico. (VUS 49)

> [With words in freedom, Marinetti breaks and destroys the logical articula-
> tions of discourse (syntax: the long conquest of the spirit over the exclamative
> incoherence of primitive language); he uses visual images (realistic, con-
> crete) in the guise of words or phrases typographically inclined in such a
> way as to suggest ideogramatically the vision referred to; and he makes
> great use of imitative sounds, which are pieces of vocal nature dropped
> directly into the lyrical context.]

In an article signed together with Aldo Palazzeschi and Ardengo
Soffici, Papini had rejected not only the 'naturalization of art,' the
return to 'primal matter,' to pure sensation, of Marinettism, but also
its indiscriminate disconnection with the past (which had resulted,
incidentally, in the substantial impossibility of a real step forward):

> Rifiutando ciecamente il passato esso tende ciecamente all'avvenire, ma
> poiché non si dà arte o pensiero che non sia una propaggine sublimata di
> un'arte o di un pensiero anteriori, il marinettinismo si trova come un
> fenomeno isolato senza reale attinenza col futuro, appunto perché non l'ha
> col passato. (Palazzeschi et al. 50)

[Blindly refusing the past, it blindly goes towards the future, but since there is no art nor thought that is not a sublimated offshoot of a past art or thought, Marinettism is an isolated phenomenon without a real connection with the future precisely because it does not have one with the past.]

It is important that Ungaretti rejected both the sensorial realism of Marinetti, functional to the recording of external matter, and the automatic writing of the Surrealists, linked to dreams, the unconscious, the profound depths of the self:

Per fare un ultimo esempio: oggi si sente tanto questo bisogno di rivelazione che i Surrealisti in Francia hanno pensato di poterci arrivare, cercando un linguaggio che fosse in diretto contatto coll'inconscio. Hanno trovato la scrittura automatica. Hanno commesso, rovesciandolo, il medesimo errore dei Futuristi. Per i Futuristi, occorreva imitare il cieco oggettivo, per i Surrealisti, occorreva imitare il cieco soggettivo. (*VUS* 361)

[One last example: today, this need for revelation is felt so strongly that the Surrealists in France thought they could achieve it by finding a language that was in direct contact with the unconscious. They found automatic writing. They committed the same error of the Futurists, but upside-down. For the Futurists, it was necessary to imitate blind objectivity, for the Surrealists, it was necessary to imitate blind subjectivity.]

By excluding 'the blind subjectivity' of the Surrealists and the 'blind objectivity' of the Futurists, Ungaretti indicated as a future solution a poetics of memory and of waiting, founded on the balancing of subject and object, of the internal and the external, and thus capable of determining 'il trasformarsi della parola in rivelazione [the transformation of the word into revelation]' (*VUS* 361). In recuperating the initial moment, the author reaffirms the 'institutional sacredness of poetic writing' (Ossola 22), which reveals its original magical-religious meaning, bringing into it the here and now of the present, of the temporary, of the mutable.

Redeemed in memory, modernity and the experiences of the new continue to exercise, at the end of the 1930s, their irresistible attraction on Ungaretti's literary ideology. They entail and produce an emptiness, which, being also fear of emptiness (in keeping with the Baroque culture that Ungaretti encountered by retracing the genealogy of European Petrarchism), calls for a revelation. Absence, the necessary condition for the birth of poetry, is the conscience of a loss: it therefore points to a waiting illuminated by memory. The sign of the dramatic force of modern art and of its expressive boldness consists in this. To those who speak of the 'tragedy of the word,' of the fact that 'essa non significa più nulla [it does not mean anything anymore],' Ungaretti replies by remembering and commenting on 'ciò che [gli] diceva una volta un giovane scultore [what [he] was once told by a young sculptor]':

> Mi diceva: Michelangelo vedeva statue prigioniere in ogni blocco di pietra che incontrava ed era preso allora dall'impazienza atletica di liberarle a furia di scalpellate. Per noi, invece, la scultura riempie il vuoto che invochi un'apparizione. Ecco infatti non più la tragedia della parola, o ancora tragedia in quanto la vita è sempre tragica; ma ecco la potenza dell'arte moderna. (*VUS* 362)

> [He told me: Michelangelo saw statues imprisoned in every block of stone that he encountered and was then taken by the athletic impatience of freeing them with his chisel. For us, instead, sculpture fills the void that invokes an apparition. This then is no longer the tragedy of the word – or tragedy only insofar as life is always tragic. This is the power of modern art.]

NOTES

This essay has already appeared in Italian in the miscellaneous volume *Quando l'opera interpella il lettore. Poetiche e forme della modernità letteraria. Studi e testimonianze offerti a Fausto Curi* (Bologna: Pendragon, 2000). I would like to thank the publisher, Pendragon, for having authorized its translation into English.

1 'Verso un'arte nuova classica' [Towards a New Classical Art] was first published in *Il Popolo d'Italia* on 10 Mar. 1919, with the subtitle 'Preface to the Second Edition of *Il Porto sepolto*.' As is well known, the 'second edition' of *Il Porto Sepolto* was published that same year, with the title *Allegria di Naufragi* and without the preface.

2 On the extreme mobility and restlessness of Ungaretti's 'rappel à l'ordre,' and on the vitality of his project which was not limited to a return to tradition, see the recent study by Baroncini.

3 Unless otherwise stated, all page references for Ungaretti's essays are from *Vita d'un uomo. Saggi e interventi*, and are indicated with the abbreviation *VUS*.

4 In *Avanguardia e tradizione. Ezra Pound e Giuseppe Ungaretti*, Ernesto
   Livorni has written: 'That title is, so to speak, Ungaretti's equivalent of
   Pound's motto "Make it New": however, the newness of that art inherits
   the classicism of the lineage that leads from Baudelaire to Mallarmé and
   finally to Valéry' (184).
5 The expression is found in a text of 1935, in which Ungaretti, recalling his
   'concerns' in the years immediately following the war, speaks about,
   among other things, memory as an 'ancora di salvezza.' See 'Riflessioni
   sulla letteratura,' in *La Gazzetta del Popolo*, 13 Mar. 1935, now in
   VUS 274–5.
6 As has been demonstrated with great specificity by Luciano Rebay in *Le
   origini della poesia di Giuseppe Ungaretti*, esp. 94–103.
7 Thoroughly analysed by Carlo Ossola in *Giuseppe Ungaretti*, esp. 227–33.
8 Recall the eighth point of Marinetti's founding manifesto: 'Noi siamo sul
   promontorio estremo dei secoli! [...] Perché dovremmo guardarci alle
   spalle, se vogliamo sfondare le misteriose porte dell'Impossibile? Il
   Tempo e lo Spazio morirono ieri. Noi viviamo già nell'assoluto, poiché
   abbiamo già creata l'eterna velocità onnipresente (*Teoria e invenzione* 10–
   11) [We stand on the last promontory of the centuries! [...] Why should
   we look back, when we want to break down the mysterious doors of the
   Impossible? Time and Space died yesterday. We already live in the
   absolute, because we have created eternal, omnipresent speed]' (*Let's
   Murder* 49).
9 'Quand je me suis mis au travail du *Sentimento del Tempo*, deux poètes
   étaient mes poètes favoris: Leopardi et Petrarque [When I began writing
   Sentimento del tempo, my preferred poets were two: Leopardi and
   Petrarch]' (Ungaretti and Amrouche, *Propos improvisés* 98).
10 In an essay written at the end of the 1920s, and which contains an obvious
   reference to 'Verso un'arte nuova classica,' Ungaretti writes: 'Vogliono
   ch'io rilegga Petrarca. Il sottoscritto crede di essere stato tra i primi, e
   precisamente nel 1919, in un articolo pubblicato dal "Popolo d'Italia," a
   segnalare l'attualità del Petrarca. E continuò, il sottoscritto, a segnalarla
   ostinatamente in tutti questi anni, in conferenze e scritti [They want me to
   reread Petrarch. Yours truly believes that he was among the first to point
   out Petrarch's actuality, to be specific in 1919, in an article published by
   the *Popolo d'Italia*. And yours truly has continued to point it out stub-
   bornly all these years, in conferences and writings]' ('Risposta
   all'anonimo,' *VUS* 204).
11 As one reads in the *Notes* to *Sentimento del Tempo* (*Vita d'un uomo. Tutte le
   poesie* 535). On 'abscence' in the poetry of Ungaretti and on its inescapable

relationship with memory, see Mario Petrucciani's observations in 'Della memoria: il prodigio dell'effimero (Prolegomeni a "La Terra Promessa")': 'only when those figures, and man with his passions, are dead, and therefore absent, memory arises: in the moment, that is, in which, by leaving the biological flux, they are at risk of being pulverized and of disappearing in the neverending space of forgetting – to be lost forever. "Absence" is precisely the *condition sine qua non* of the genesis of memory' (*Petrucciani* 66). Ungaretti annotates the poem "Ritorno" in these terms: 'In questa poesia compare forse per la prima volta la parola *assenza*; dal *sentimento* in poi la mia ispirazione parte dal ricordo, cioè da momenti interamente scomparsi, consumati, assenti. [In this poem the word *absence* appears, perhaps for the first time; since *Sentimento*, my inspiration comes from memory, in other words, from moments that have completely disappeared, that are consumed, absent]' (*VUS* 526).

12 I am referring to 'L'estetica di Bergson [Bergson's aesthetics]' and 'Lo stile di Bergson [Bergson's style],' both published in *Lo Spettatore Italiano*, the first in issue 7, 1 Aug. 1924, 60–6, and the second in issues 8–9, 15 Aug. – 1 Sept. 1924 (now in Ungaretti, *Vita d'un uomo. Saggi e interventi*, 79–86 and 87–9). The second part of 'Lo stile di Bergson' essentially takes up again the conclusive part of 'Una filosofia dell'effimero e Bergson umorista [A philosophy of the ephemeral and Bergson the humorist]' published in *Nuovo Paese* 24 Apr. 1923 (now reprinted as an appendix to Montefoschi's *Ungaretti*, 183–7). The article was then reprinted, with a new introductory statement, in 'Di palo in frasca / Lo stile di Bergson [From one subject to another / Bergson's style]' in *Il Mattino*, 8–9 July 1926.

13 'Si deve usare il verbo all'infinito, perché si adatti elasticamente al sostantivo e non lo sottoponga all'*io* dello scrittore che osserva o immagina [One should use infinitives, because they adapt themselves elastically to nouns and don't subordinate them to the writer's *I* that observes or imagines]' (Marinetti, *Teoria e invenzione* 46/Marinetti, *Let's Murder* 92).

14 'Il tempo reale è uno solo: il tempo psicologico [There is only one real time: psychological time]' (Ungaretti, 'Lo stile di Bergson,' *VUS* 89).

15 Cfr. F.T. Marinetti, 'Distruzione della sintassi. Immaginazione senza fili. Parole in libertà' (1913): 'Il Futurismo si fonda sul completo rinnovamento della sensibilità umana avvenuto per effetto delle grandi scoperte scientifiche. Coloro che usano oggi del telegrafo, del telefono e del grammofono, del treno, della bicicletta, della motocicletta, dell'automobile, del transatlantico, del dirigibile, dell'aeroplano, del cinematografo, del grande quotidiano (sintesi di una giornata del mondo)

non pensano che queste diverse forme di comunicazione, di trasporto e d'informazione esercitano sulla loro psiche una decisiva influenza [Futurism is founded on the complete renewal of human sensitivity that has come about as a result of the great scientific discoveries. Those who, today, use the telegraph, the telephone and the grammophone, the train, the bicycle, the motorcycle, the car, the transatlantic, the dirigible, the airplane, the cinema, the great newspaper (synthesis of a day in the world) don't think that these diverse forms of communication, of transport and of information exercise a decisive infuence on their psychic-psyche]' (*Teoria e invenzione* 65–6).

16 Ungaretti often connotes as 'brutal' the mimetic adherence to the concerns of technological civilization, the belligerent extroversion, the pragmatic reconversion of art proposed by Marinetti. As an example, see his 1920 essay on *Lacerba*, in which Ungaretti distinguishes the merits of the Florentine artists Papini, Soffici, Palazzeschi (not by chance indicated as his '*compagnons de route*') from the limitations of the inventor of Futurism: 'Les problèmes techniques sont posés brutalment par Marinetti. Subjugué par la civilisation mécanicienne, il se proposait de découvrir, ou mieux d'adapter, les formes de l'expression au tumulte extérieur qui moule la société naissante. Ses effortes s'exaspéraient en un ordre exclusivement musculaire [Technical problems are brutally posed by Marinetti. Captivated by mechanical civilization, he intended to discover, or better, to adapt the forms of expression to the external commotion which moulds rising society. His efforts were exasperated in exclusively muscular terms]' ('La doctrine de "Lacerba",' *VUS* 41).

17 Recall the emphatic proclamation of irrational voluntarism with which, in the conclusive propositions of the founding manifesto of Futurism, Marinetti exorcizes the doubts on the impossibility of completely annihilating a reasoned relationship of continuity with tradition: 'Ci opponete delle obiezioni? ... Basta! Basta! Le conosciamo ... Abbiamo capito! ... La nostra bella e mendace intelligenza ci afferma che noi siamo il riassunto e il prolungamento dei nostri avi. – Forse! Sia pure! ... Ma che importa? Non vogliamo intendere! ... Guai a chi ci ripeterà queste parole infami! [You have objections? – Enough! Enough! We know them ... we've understood! ... Our fine deceitful intelligence tells us that we are the revival and extension of our ancestors – perhaps! ... If only it were so! – But who cares? We don't want to understand! ... Woe to anyone who says those infamous words to us again!]' (*Teoria e invenzione* 14/*Let's Murder* 52).

18 Cf. Ungaretti's article 'Va citato Leopardi per Valéry?,' in *Il Mattino*, 3–4 June 1926, now in *Vita d'un uomo. Saggi e interventi*: 'Dopo Leopardi,

nessun altro poeta ha dato tanto peso al pensiero [After Leopardi, no other poet has given such weight to thought]' (*VUS* 105).

19 Guglielmi further notes: 'Therefore, in Ungaretti's terms, modernity is incomplete and without form. It is like "an infancy." No language. It is aphasic. (And aphasia is precisely the "insatiable hope of innocence"). While the world of tradition is a world no longer alive, by now ancient. Now, the ambition to reconcile innocence and memory, modernity and tradition – which, in the end is the ambition of speaking aphasia through the means proper to emphasis – would lead to a strenuous search for "measure"'(73–4).

20 I thus agree with Mario Diacono's argument that 'Futurism finally seems to him [Ungaretti] an *e contrario* moving force which, in its excessive absence of memory and its adherence to matter, makes the poet of *L'Allegria* realize the necessity of memory from the point of view of ideology, and of the de-physicization of the word from the point of view of technique' (Introduction to *Vita d'un uomo. Saggi e interventi*, xxxviii).

21 The first collection of Ungaretti's critical essays, published in France in 1969, was entitled *Innocence et mémoire*; in that title lies the key to his critical (and poetic) discourse.

22 The first version of the text appeared in *Il Mattino*, 21–2 May 1926; the more extensive second version was published in *L'Italiano*, n.12–13, 7 Oct. 1926; the third, 'Innocence et mémoire,' which is essentially the French translation of the second, was published in *La Nouvelle Revue Française*, 1 Nov. 1926. All three versions are found in Ungaretti, *Vita d'un uomo. Saggi e interventi*, 129–38.

23 Recall the verse of 'Monologhetto': 'Poeti, poeti, ci siamo messi/ Tutte le maschere/ Ma uno non è che la propria persona [Poets, poets, we have put on /All the masks/ But one is none other than one's own persona].' This declaration is to be understood, as Mengaldo has rightly suggested, 'to the letter (that is, literally *and* in its reverse)' (188).

24 'Si commemorano i morti. Il futurismo ha 19 anni sulle spalle, ma non credo sia vicino a morire. Dirò anzi che, in arte, contiene una delle rare idee viste nascere nel nostro secolo. Questo lo posso dire senza ambagi, non avendo mai aderito a quel movimento, né essendo in procinto di mettermi sulla sua strada. Dico commemorazione per quel senso di distacco che va crescendo in me (sarà un senso passeggero) e che mi fa considerare tutto (salvo qualche mio sogno) sotto sembianza d'un appiglio per la memoria: – per quel senso, e per il carattere di semplice meditazione che vorrei avessero anche per gli altri queste mie note [One commemorates the dead. Futurism is nineteen years old, but I do not

think that is near death. I would even say that, in art, it expressed one of
the rare ideas that have been born in this century. I can say this openly,
since I never joined the movement, nor am I about to embark on that
path. I use the word commemoration because of the feeling of detachment
that is growing within me (it is probably a passing feeling) which makes
me consider everything (except for some dreams of mine) as a pretext for
memory; for that feeling, and for the character of simple meditation that I
would like my words to assume]' (*VUS* 170). 'Commemorazione del
futurismo' first appeared in *Il Mattino*, 27–8 Aug. 1927.

25 The article was first published in *Il Resto del Carlino* on 23 Aug. 1928.

26 The interview was first published in *L'Italia letteraria* on 16 June 1929.

WORKS CITED

Baroncini, Daniela. Ungaretti e il *sentimento del classico*. Bologna: Il Mulino,
1999.

Curi, Franco. *Il possibile verbale. Tecniche del mutamento e modernità letteraria.*
Bologna: Pendagron, 1995.

Guglielmi, Guido. *Interpretazione di Ungaretti*. Bologna: Il Mulino, 1989.

Livorni, Ernesto. *Avanguardia e tradizione. Ezra Pound e Giuseppe Ungaretti.*
Florence: Le Lettere, 1998.

Marinetti, Filippo Tommaso. *Let's Murder the Moonshine. Selected Writings.* Ed.
R.W. Flint. Trans. F.R. Flint and Arthur Coppotelli. Los Angeles: Sun &
Moon P, 1991.

– *Teoria e invenzione futurista*. Ed. Luciano De Maria. Milan: Mondadori, 1968.

Mengaldo, Pier Vincenzo. 'Giuseppe Ungaretti.' *Poeti del Novecento*. Ed.
Mengaldo. Milan: Mondadori, 1978.

Montefoschi, Paola. *Ungaretti. Le eclissi della memoria*. Naples: Scientifiche
Editrici, 1988.

Ossola, Carlo. *Giuseppe Ungaretti*. Milan: Mursia, 1982.

Palazzeschi, Aldo, Giovanni Papini, and Ardengo Soffici. 'Futurismo e
marinettismo.' *Lacerba* 3.7 (1915).

Papini, Giovanni. 'Il cerchio si chiude.' *Lacerba* 2.4 (1914).

Petrucciani, Mario. *Il condizionale di Didone: studi su Ungaretti*. Naples:
Scientifiche Italiane, 1985.

Rebay, Luciano. *Le origini della poesia di Giuseppe Ungaretti*. Rome: Edizioni di
storia e letteratura, 1962.

Ungaretti, Giuseppe. *Invenzione della poesia moderna. Lezioni brasiliane di
letteratura* (1937–1942). Ed. P. Montefoschi. Naples: Scientifiche Italiane,
1984.

- *Lezioni su Giacomo Leopardi*. Ed. Marco Diacono e Paola Montefoschi. Rome: Presidenza del Consiglio dei Ministri, 1989.
- *Vita d'un uomo. Saggi e interventi*. Ed. Mario Diacono e Luciano Rebay. Milan: Mondadori, 1974.
- *Vita d'un uomo. Tutte le poesie*. Ed. Leone Piccioni. Milan: Mondadori, 1969.

Ungaretti, Giuseppe, and Jean Amrouche. *Propos improvisés*. Paris: Gallimard, 1972.

10 Of Thresholds and Boundaries: Luigi Pirandello between Modernity and Modernism

MANUELA GIERI

A me la coscienza moderna dà l'immagine di un sogno angoscioso attraversato da rapide larve or tristi or minacciose, d'una battaglia notturna, d'una mischia disperata, in cui s'agitino per un momento e subito scompaiano, per riapparirne delle altre, mille bandiere, in cui le parti avversarie si sian confuse e mischiate, e ognuno lotti per sé per la sua difesa, contro all'amico e contro al nemico. Mi par che tutto in lei tremi e tentenni. (Pirandello, 'Arte e coscienza' 880)

[Modern consciousness appears to me as a distressful dream traversed by swift shadows, now sad, now threatening; a night battle, a desperate melée in which thousands of flags flutter for a moment and immediately disappear to be replaced by others, in which the enemies are confused and mixed, and everyone fights for himself, for his own defence, against both friend and foe. It seems as if everything in it trembles and wavers.]

This disquieting statement comes from one of Luigi Pirandello's most engaging essays, 'Arte e coscienza d'oggi' (1893).[1] In fairly apocalyptic terms, the Sicilian author discusses the nature of consciousness as it approaches the end of the nineteenth century and experiences one of its most devastating crises. He also reviews, and eventually rejects, both the philosophical outcomes of such a crisis and the new artistic models generated by it, models which, as stated by Pirandello himself, are best exemplified by Ibsen and Wagner. The author then proceeds to provide his own definition of modernity, quoted above. For Pirandello, modern consciousness is characterized by a feeling of confusion, an inability to find a sense of direction, and this was indeed his negative preoccupation in the last decade of the nineteenth century.

His position, in fact, may be interpreted as close to that of the decadents. Yet, in his study of the relationship between Pirandello and Decadentism, Stefano Giovanardi rightly states that we can comfortably and legitimately use the adjective 'decadent' only in relation to Luigi Pirandello's early writings,[2] speficially to what he wrote in the last two decades of the nineteenth century. Indeed, as he entered the new century, Pirandello became one of the most sensitive and influential representatives of modernism, even though he often engaged in a critical dialogue with modernity and its technological innovations. He was constantly both attracted to and repulsed by those novelties that forever transformed our lives. A poignant example of his ambivalence was his view of the cinema, a new artistic form of expression and a new medium, for which he entertained an intense love-hate relationship that lasted for over thirty years.[3]

One of the most prominent figures of modern Western culture, Luigi Pirandello lived in two centuries. In his dramatic and narrative works he thoroughly overcame most nineteenth-century poetics, including Romanticism and Naturalism, and over the course of the first three decades of the new century, Pirandello eventually came to occupy, albeit restlessly, the threshold between modernism and postmodernism, as exemplified by some of his most compelling later works, such as the unfinished theatrical piece, *I giganti della montagna* [The Giants of the Mountain] (1930–3).

In his volume dedicated to Antonine Artaud, entitled *Teatro e corpo glorioso*, Umberto Artioli commented perceptively that 'the passage from irony to humor would mark the introduction of a tragic note, widely confirmed by all those twentieth century poetics that, from Jarry to Pirandello and Beckett, have assigned a central role to humor' (85, n.51). In his artistic works, Pirandello not only aimed at achieving new narrative and dramatic strategies, he also addressed several issues central to modernist discourse, such as the nature of the novel subject in his/her relationship with reality; the rapport between illusion – that is, fiction – and reality; the diverse roles that author, character, and spectator/reader perform in the artistic process; and the complex nature of both 'narrativity' and 'theatrality.'[4]

From this particular perspective, Pirandello's narrative and dramatic works constitute not simply a breaking away from Naturalism and, more broadly, from the *mimetic* tradition, but also significant stages in the founding of a new poetics and a new tradition, or 'counter-tradition,' if you will, in Western culture. They also constitute a *self-reflexive* stage in the development of both theatre and narrative, as his theatre reflects on the nature of theatrical representation and his narrative works on that of narration itself. Key Pirandellian texts, such as the novels *Il fu Mattia Pascal* [The Late Mattia Pascal] (1904), *Si gira ...* [Shoot!] (1914–15), and *Uno, nessuno e centomila* [One, Nobody and One Hundred Thousand] (1925–6), and the plays of his famous trilogy, *Sei personaggi in cerca d'autore* [Six Characters in Search of an Author] (1921; 1925), *Ciascuno a suo modo* [Each in His Own Way] (1924), and *Questa sera si recita a soggetto* [Tonight We Improvise] (1930) thus become momentuous steps in the unveiling of a true rupture between past and present, here and there, subject and object. The fatal split is generated by the employment of a specific type of estrangement, which is defined by applying humour not merely to the text but to the entirety of the dramatic and/or narrative representation. In the case of theatre, the humoristic dissociation is considered not only or simply an instance of poetics, but a structuring principle of the mise en scène, a dramatic strategy that produces both a dislocation in space and time and a true misplacement of the character and the fabula itself; that is, it produces not 'effects' but genuine 'cases of estrangement,' which are cause and effect of the continuous and incessant sliding of meaning as well as of the very act of signification.

In his search for aesthetic distance Pirandello aimed at representing human beings in their incongruence and internal division. Throughout his artistic production he constantly portrayed the tragic inevitability of the impossibility of recomposing the unity, and thus the aura, of the tragic hero that Walter Benjamin so thoroughly discussed in his 'The Work of Art in the Age of Mechanical Reproduction.' This impossibility is a typical feature of a time without heroes, as observed by Jürgen Habermas in both *Etica del discorso* and in *The Philosophical Discourse of Modernity*. Now that Orestes will forever be Hamlet, Pirandello's narrative and dramatic works become a place in which the awareness of the dislocation between humans and nature, and of human beings' internal division, produces infinite reflections and mirrorings, so that in the end a polyphony of voices ultimately prevails. So thoroughly redefined, Pirandello's discourse is no longer the product of an isolated voice in the Chaos, but 'regains' its place as an integral part of a counter-tradition of a *critical*, if not negative thought which developed within modernity and eventually paved the way to postmodernity.[5]

As I first argued at one of the annual meetings of the Centro Studi Pirandelliani in Agrigento,[6] the shift towards a new, 'modern' consciousness and a thorough revision of contemporary poetics that eventually led to Luigi Pirandello's revolutionary work unquestionably begins with Charles Baudelaire. As Octavio Paz stated in the speech he delivered in accepting the Nobel Prize, 'Baudelaire was the first to touch [modernity] and to discover that she is nothing but time that crumbles in one's hands.' It would not be too arduous a task to establish intertextual correspondences between Pirandello and Baudelaire, or to construct a net of syntagmatic chains common to both authors, of which the 'dream-vision-enstrangement' chain would seem to be the most relevant. Yet, it would perhaps be even more intriguing to establish esoteric correspondences between the author who died in August 1867 (Baudelaire) and the one born in June of the same year (Pirandello). That is, I could easily assess the influence of Baudelaire on Pirandello, but I would rather resort to the physical sense of the term 'source,' 'a vein of water in constant flux.' As I stated in Agrigento, I believe that by moving from Baudelaire to Pirandello we can trace the birth and genesis of the modern consciousness, its aesthetics and its poetics, and in general its existential and artistic utterances.

In the nineteenth century, profound mutations in our perception of the world and our place in the 'order of things' occurred. Revolutionary discoveries forever modified our relationship to nature, as well as the relationship between reality and its artistic representation. In the mid-1800s, artists became deeply aware of the fissure that had opened in that perfect synthesis between object and subject which had once stood as a foundation of dramatic and narrative forms. In his renowned study of modern drama,[7] Peter Szondi maintains that this fundamental crisis was due to the introduction of an epic element – 'the tendency toward the epic in Drama' (59) – in a traditional form, ultimately producing the relativization of the absolute. Szondi maintains that this 'epic relativization' is due to a split in the synthesis between subject and object that was typical of drama. The two terms enter into an oppositional relationship (34–5; 37–8). One of the characters becomes a reflection, and later a true projection of the author's 'I,' and the others become its object. With the appearance on the stage of the figure of the narrator, or rather, of the Pirandellian *raisonneur*, an epic relationship is then substituted for the traditional dramatic one.[8] 'Since modern theatrical works develop out of and away from the Drama itself, this development must be considered with the help of a contrasting concept. "Epic" will serve here. It designates a common structural characteristic of the epos, the story, the novel, and other genres – namely, the presence of that which has been referred to as the "subject of the epic form" or the "epic I'" (6).[9]

According to Peter Szondi, then, the crisis of drama begins around 1860, and it is the result of the appearance of an epic theme within an established form. Several attempts were made to solve this crisis by such artists as Ibsen and Chekov, Strindberg, Maeterlinck, and Hauptmann. However, it is in Luigi Pirandello, and later, Bertolt Brecht, that the European theatrical scene finds two of its most original and influential protagonists.[10] In many ways, as Wladimir Krysinski remarks in his most thorough study of Pirandello's work, *Le paradigme inquiet. Pirandello et le champ de la modernité*, 'Pirandello is a significative vector [vecteur significatif] at the beginning and at the end of the diverse narrative and theatrical modalities of reality and of the work of art insofar as his discourse, more than any other's, makes formal and thematic codes explode' (55).

Indeed, according to Krysinski, it is possible for us to trace a typical series of problematic categories in Pirandello's theory and praxis, such as 'humor, perspect-ivism, irony, fragmentation, self-reflexivity, self-thematism, proliferation' (55). Quite clearly, the tracing of such categories can shed light on the role and place of the Sicilian author's work in a general history of the theatre. Krysinski then continues by suggesting that Pirandello's theatrical theory and praxis are historically identified both in the long-term perspectives of Cervantes, Shakespeare, and Romantic irony and the short-term perspective of 'modern' theatre – Expressionism, Dadaism and Surrealism, Futurism, the theatre of the absurd, Antonin Artaud's theatre of cruelty, and even the theatre of Bertolt Brecht. Unquestionably, if it is true that the main antinomy inherent in dramatic art is that between text and performance, it is also true that this paradoxical relationship has haunted and, to a certain extent, still troubles most of our contemporary dramatists. The development of twentieth-century theatre itself recorded various attempts either to accentuate the irreconcilable nature of the antinomy, or to harmonize it.

Yet, these two attitudes cannot be limited to drama. In modernity, both the theatrical stage and the written text become the forum for an irreparable conflict of significations and, thus, of interpretations. The history of twentieth-century theatralogy becomes nothing more than a series of attempts to redefine the somewhat paradoxical relationship between text and performance. Two different approaches develop in relation to the artistic representation of reality or, more precisely, two dissimilar interpretations of history and subjectivity. One envisions the possibility of a 'mimetic' and thus harmonious relationship between art and nature; the other records the impossibility of such a pacified relationship and verifies the fundamental division of the subject. The search for meaning becomes not only the objective and the true content of any artistic production, but also its form. Within this second perspective Luigi Pirandello's complex discourse develops, and his disquieting paradigm provokes the true *explosion* of pre-existing thematic and formal codes.

It is well known that Luigi Pirandello's discourse is organized according to the paradigms outlined in his essay *L'Umorismo* [On Humor] (1908). Yet we should recall that humour, in opposition to both comedy and tragedy, and because it results from the juxtaposition of both, is profoundly transgressive, as Mikhail Bakhtin observed in his study of Dostoevsky's poetics. Umberto Eco explained with some eloquence that humour is more transgressive than comedy and tragedy precisely because it works within the interstices between narrative and discursive structures, and thus necessarily redefines the roles of the various participants in the production of meaning.[11] This is the reason why, since the Romantic Age, much attention has been given to that particular mode of discourse that was variously defined as irony or humour. As previously observed, the fracture takes place in the Romantic and post-Romantic period, and Charles Baudelaire can easily be identified as the artist who initiated an investigation that inevitably led to the particular discourse on humour which was to characterize most twentieth-century poetics.

One of Baudelaire's almost forgotten essays, entitled 'De l'essence du rire,' is of particular use here. This short and yet extremely enlightening piece was written in July 1855, that is, in the heart of the nineteenth century, when, according to Peter Szondi, the crisis of traditional theatrical forms which would lead to the avant-garde of the twentieth century began. Here Baudelaire makes visionary and engaging comments on the nature of laughter, and these observations may prove pertinent to our discussion of Pirandello's concept of humour. Baudelaire first states that laughter is profoundly human and essentially contradictory, since it is simultaneoulsy the sign of infinite grandeur and infinite misery. He then states that 'c'est du choc perpétuel de ces deux infinis que se dégage le rire [it is from the perpetual shock between these two infinites that laughter bursts out]' (709), and underlines that the 'puissance du rire [the power of laughter]' (709) resides in the one who laughs, not in the object of laughter. It is impossible here to forget the moment of reflection that seizes the Pirandellian humourist when he looks at the old woman's 'masked' and, thus, disfigured face as she attempts to preserve the favours of her much younger husband. For both Pirandello and Baudelaire, the process of humoristic dissociation takes place in the one who laughs, that is, in the one who 'looks,' in other words, in the spectator. Baudelaire continues by saying that only 'le philosophe ... ait acquis ... la force de se dedoubler et d'assister comme spectateur désintéressé aux phénomènes de son moi [the philosopher ... has acquired ... the capacity to double himself/herself and to witness as an uninterested spectator to the manifestations of his/her own self]' (709). Yet, the *raisonneur*, the typical Pirandellian humourist, is nothing but an exasperated form of the Baudelairian philosopher; in the complex paradigm which stands at the very heart of Luigi Pirandello's text/s, he is the one who is not only able to split himself in two, but internally divided, unrestrained, unable to live and totally absorbed in seeing himself live. Many examples of such split subjectivity can be found in Pirandello's dramatic and narrative works, since this is the very nature of the typical Pirandellian character.[12] In establishing parallelisms between Baudelaire's study of laughter and Pirandello's interpretation of humour, we should also remember that Baudelaire subsequently maintains that laughter is nothing but a symptom, the expression of an internally doubled and contradictory feeling.[13] Pirandello similarly maintains that the difference between humour and comedy resides in that *feeling of the opposite* which is the result of the act of reflection that necessarily follows the *perception of the opposite*, which characterizes comedy.[14]

In 'De l'essence du rire,' Baudelaire then proceeds to make a necessary distinction between comedy and the grotesque in the work of art; while the former is *imitation*, the latter, the grotesque or 'absolute comedy,' is *creation* (712). 'Absolute comedy,' according to Baudelaire, is one of those artistic phenomena that denote the coexistence of two beings within each and every human being, that is, 'l'existence d'une dualité permanente, la puissance d'être à la fois soi et un autre [the existence of a permanent duality, the possibility of being oneself and another at the same time]' (720). This is clearly a Pirandellian theme as well since there are many internally divided beings, and many 'humourists' in the Sicilian author's world. In closing his essay, Baudelaire states that the artist is such only provided that he or she is doubled, and does not ignore any of the characteristics of his or her divided nature (720). The very fact of not ignoring this doubled and irreconcilable nature of his being, his existing and his becoming, introduces a tragic note in Pirandello's humourist, as testified by Mattia Pascal, Serafino Gubbio, and Vitangelo Moscarda in the narrative works, but also by Henry IV, Leone Gala, and most of the other characters in Pirandello's plays. Being, as they are, internally divided, these characters are fundamentally unable to establish a harmonious relationship with the world of experience.

As previously discussed, 'estrangement' in Pirandello's disquieting theatrical imagination does not simply function at the level of character but also at the level of the fabula, and it does not refer to the Brechtian tension towards the recomposition of a narrative and epic, and thus historical, continuity between the stage and the orchestra. In Pirandello's case, estrangement means the attentive recording of a reciprocal, contingent, and thus also historical extraneousness, that is, of an unrecoverable hiatus between the 'being' (the world of author and director, of actors and spectators), the 'appearing' (the world of the characters),[15] and the 'becoming' itself of the production of meaning. The same hiatus can also be found between the self and the other contemporarily present in the subject of enunciation, but also between the 'I' and the others, between the stage and the audience, between the theatrical event, that is, art and life.

Luigi Pirandello belongs to Charles Baudelaire's 'constellation,' that is, that particular 'constellation' that Walter Benjamin first talked about.[16] In this constellation, estrangement is not simply the effect of a psychological condition, but a true and unavoidable element of the 'allegorical signification,' to use Luperini's terms. Estrangement becomes form and content, and thus a true strategy of the mise en scène and of theatrical discourse in its entirety. Because of this particular discursive and signifying strategy, the stage in Sei personaggi in cerca d'autore, and in Ciascuno a suo modo and Stasera si recita a soggetto as well, the orchestra, the foyer, the hallways leading to the theatrical event, and ultimately even the outside itself – everything becomes the forum for the conflict of 'meanings.' In this progressive spatial dislocation from inside to outside and back, this constant temporal sliding, the incessant alluding to the 'past' of the 'drama,' the 'other' time in which it was still feasible 'to imitate an action,' to represent 'romantically,' or more generally, in which tragedy was still possible – that is, in the time of modernity – emphasis is necessarily placed on that 'existence d'une dualité permanente, la puissance d'être à la fois soi et un autre [existence of a permanent duality, the power of being at once oneself and another]' (Baudelaire 720).

In the eternal present of the Pirandellian stage, nothing remains but the play of the futile attempt to represent the drama, as Pirandello himself states in the famous preface to *Sei personaggi in cerca d'autore* (*Maschere nude* 40). Thus, the strident laughter of the Daughter at the end of the text is a last act of enunciation, and ultimately represents the invasion of the grotesque in the Baudelairian sense: a form of 'absolute comedy' that means creation rather than imitation. In the closing of *Sei personaggi*, an ultimate enstranging stance ratifies the already staged representation of that 'futile attempt,' that *quête* or incessant search for meaning that is at the heart of the allegorical discourse in modernity. It would indeed be intriguing to speculate on the fact that the strident laughter, that last act of enunciation, coming from the one character who had long refused to 'narrate,' takes place outside the traditional space of representation, the stage, and invades the space of 'narration,' the orchestra. It eventually goes so far as to invade the outside, the very place where the supreme narrative act, history itself, unfolds.[17] It would be equally interesting to reflect on the fact that the one who had long refused to 'represent,' the Son, remains frozen on the stage with the other characters, all of them reduced to phantasmatic images, mnemonic traces of the just-concluded staging of the impossibility itself of representation.[18]

In the essay which opens the collection *Maschere nude* [Naked Masks], Pirandello provides us with a 'humoristic' preface not only to *Sei personaggi in cerca d'autore* but to his entire theatrical production. Written in 1925, after various stagings of the dramatic text (including the Parisian production by the Pitoeffs that almost certainly inspired and to a certain extent influenced the writing of the final version of the play), the preface almost becomes a critical and ideological afterword to *Sei personaggi* and a necessary premise to *Stasera si recita a soggetto*, the last play of the trilogy. There is no real fracture between the pre-1925 production and the following one, as some have wrongly concluded, but rather an unstoppable progression and a diverse articulation of the same critical-negative discourse which informs Pirandello's work in its entirety. The genetic chain is the same and leads inexorably to *I giganti della montagna*, which, in this perspective, is not simply the myth of art and artistic creation but the all-encompassing myth of Pirandello's entire cosmogony.[19] From this point of view, the relationship between the earlier theatre and the theatre of the 'myths' seems extremely fertile.

After the *choc* produced first by the perception and then by the understanding of an unrecoverable hiatus, nothing remains but the vertigo of the grotesque, the 'absolute comedy' that, as Baudelaire remarked, is *creation*, in constrast to the mere imitation of 'comedy.' An 'intertextual magnetism' links Pirandello to Baudelaire, but also to Beckett, Artaud, and ultimately to later theatrical experiments, such as Carmelo Bene's theatre of pure *phoné*.[20] The 'genetic trace' is that critical and negative discourse which finds form and content in the humoristic division; it is through true enstranging strategies that such discourse produces a constant 'contamination' – and certainly not a parthenogenesis – between comedy and tragedy, allegory and symbolism, but also and perhaps more significantly, between the various genres. This is the revolutionary ground of Luigi Pirandello's contribution to our modern consciousness.

NOTES

This essay has been inspired by my work on the Pirandellian mode in cinema published in *Contemporary Italian Filmmaking*, as well as my recent article, 'Pirandello e il cinema' (87–114). Only brief passages are here reported verbatim.

1 'Arte e coscienza d'oggi' was first published in *La Nazione Letteraria* I.6 (Florence, Sept. 1893).
2 See Giovanardi, 'Pirandello e il decadentismo' (134).
3 On this issue, see the first two chapters of *Contemporary Italian Filmmaking*.
4 The neologism 'theatrality' is used here instead of the more normal 'theatricality' for several reasons. The term is directly borrowed from Jean Alter's article, 'From Text to Performance.' As Alter maintains, the very concept that 'theatricality' identifies is relatively new and not uniformly defined, and within its linguistic and conceptual confusion, it has already acquired undesirable connotations that the use of 'theatrality' might help us to avoid. Alter's neologism was inspired by the French word 'théâtralite' (which finds a parallel in the Italian 'teatralità'), which, in modern critical practice, antedates 'theatricality' and has gained widespread acceptance. By 'theatrality,' Alter refers to total theatre, that is, a system composed of

two categories of signs corresponding to its two pragmatic media of expression: text and performance. I maintain that Pirandello's conception of theatre as a total artistic experience accounted for both of these two media.

5 On this matter, Luperini's long essay on Pirandello in *L'allegoria del moderno* (221–58) is illuminating. See also, by the same author, 'L'atto del significare allegorico in *Sei personaggi* e in *Enrico IV*,' and *Introduzione a Pirandello*.

6 In 'Effetti di straniamento come strategia della messa in scena nella trilogia.' See also my essay 'Pirandello e Brecht.'

7 Szondi's *Theorie des modernen Dramas* [Theory of Modern Drama] first appeared in 1956, and was revised in 1959. The text was translated into English quite late, in 1987. The Italian edition was published by Einaudi in 1976.

8 These and other concepts are investigated throughout Szondi's work. For a critical synopsis of this seminal study on modern drama, see Cesare Cases's preface to the Italian edition (1976).

9 Szondi here borrows the expression 'subject of the epic form' from Georg Lukács, and the term 'epic I' from Robert Petsch.

10 On a parallel comparison between the positions expressed by Brecht and Pirandello, see my article 'Pirandello e Brecht.'

11 See Eco's 'The Frames of Comic Freedom.' In this essay, Eco defines the constitutive elements of Pirandello's concept of humour, outlining the differences between the modalities of comedy, tragedy, and humour.

12 On the Pirandellian humourist as *raisonneur*, see Paolo Puppa's numerous studies of Pirandello's narrative and dramatic writings, among which two seem to have the utmost relevance here: *Fantasmi contro giganti* and *Dalle parti di Pirandello*.

13 See 'De l'essence du rire' (710).

14 See Pirandello's *L'umorismo* (127).

15 See Lugnani's essay 'Teatro dello straniamento ed estraniazione dal teatro in *Questa sera si recita a soggetto*.'

16 See Benjamin, *Angelus Novus. Saggi e frammenti* (85–154).

17 See Luperini, 'L'atto del significare allegorico in *Sei personaggi* e in *Enrico IV*' (14–15).

18 On the unsettling role of the Son and its centrality in the elaboration of theatrical discourse as expressed by Pirandello in *Sei personaggi*, see Santeramo's 'Text and Performance: Pirandello and Bene.'

19 See Lugnani's 'In margine ai *Giganti*,' in Lauretta, ed., *Pirandello e il teatro*.

20 On the subject of the apparently incongruous comparison between these

two disquieting personalities of our dramaturgy, see Santeramo, 'Text and Performance: Pirandello and Bene.'

WORKS CITED

Alter, Jean. 'From Text to Performance: Semiotics of Theatrality.' *Poetics Today* 2:3 (1981): 113–39.

Artioli, Umberto. *Teatro e corpo glorioso. Saggio su Antonin Artaud*. Milan: Feltrinelli, 1978.

Bakhtin, Mikhail. *Problems in Dostoevsky's Poetics*. Minneapolis: U of Minnesota P, 1985.

Baudelaire, Charles. 'De l'essence du rire et généralement du comique dans les arts plastiques.' *Oeuvres complètes de Baudelaire*. Paris: Gallimard, 1951. 702–20.

Benjamin, Walter. *Angelus Novus. Saggi e frammenti*. Turin: Einaudi, 1976.

Eco, Umberto. 'The Frames of Comic Freedom.' *Carnival*. By Eco, V.V. Ivanov, and Monica Rector. Ed. Thomas Sebeok. Berlin, New York, and Amsterdam: Mouton, 1984. 1–9.

Gieri, Manuela. *Contemporary Italian Filmmaking: Strategies of Subversion: Pirandello, Fellini, Scola and the Directors of the New Generation*. Toronto: University of Toronto Press, 1995.

– 'Effetti di straniamento come strategia della messa in scena nella trilogia: appunti e spigolature sulla "poetica della scena" di Luigi Pirandello.' *Pirandello e il teatro*. Ed. Enzo Lauretta. Milan: Mursia, 1993. 335–42.

– 'Pirandello e Brecht: il teatro *en r/évolution*.' *Pirandello e le Avanguardie*. Ed. Enzo Lauretta. Agrigento: Centro Nazionale di Studi Pirandelliani, 1999. 269–88.

– Pirandello e il cinema. Al convegno Volta per fare il punto su un rapporto durato più di trent'anni.' *Biblioteca teatrale* (Oct.–Dec. 1999): 87–114.

Giovanardi, Stefano. 'Pirandello e il decadentismo: un incontro "preistorico".' *Pirandello e la cultura del suo tempo*. Ed. Stefano Milioto and Enzo Scrivano. Milan: Mursia, 1984.

Krysinski, Wladimir. *Le paradigme inquiet. Pirandello et le champ de la modernité*. Montreal: Préambule, 1989.

Lugnani, Lucio. 'In margine ai *Giganti*.' *Pirandello e il teatro*. Ed. Enzo Lauretta. Milan: Mursia, 1993. 117–29.

– 'Teatro dello straniamento ed estraniazione dal teatro in *Questa sera si recita a soggetto*.' *La trilogia di Pirandello*. Ed. Enzo Lauretta. Agrigento: Centro Nazionale di Studi Pirandelliani, 1980. 53–114.

Luperini, Romano. *L'allegoria del moderno. Saggi sull'allegorismo come forma artistica del moderno e come metodo di conoscenza*. Rome: Editori Riuniti, 1990.

- 'L'atto del significare allegorico in *Sei personaggi* e in *Enrico IV*.' *Rivista di studi pirandelliani* 3.6/7 (1991): 9–19.

- *Introduzione a Pirandello*. Rome and Bari: Laterza, 1992.

Pirandello, Luigi. 'Arte e coscienza d'oggi.' Pirandello, *Saggi, poesie, scritti varii* 865–80.

- *Maschere nude*. Vol. 1. Milan: Mondadori, 1978.

- *Saggi, poesie, scritti varii*. Milan: Mondadori, 1960.

- *L'umorismo*. Pirandello: *Saggi, poesie, scritti varii*, 15–160.

Puppa, Paolo. *Dalle parti di Pirandello*. Rome: Bulzoni, 1987.

- *Fantasmi contro giganti: scena e immaginario in Pirandello*. Bologna: Pàtron, 1978.

Santeramo, Donato. 'Text and Performance: Pirandello and Bene.' *Pirandello e la Sicilia nella cultura europea*. Ed. S. Milioto, L. Pepe, and A. Pompeo. Rome: Dimensione Europea, 1992. 102–16.

Szondi, Peter. *Theory of Modern Drama*. Ed. and trans. Michael Hays. Cambridge: Polity Press, 1987.

PART IV

The Return to Order: *Metafisica, Novecentismo*

11 Modernism and the Quest for the Real: On Massimo Bontempelli's *Minnie la candida*

LUCA SOMIGLI

The Two Modernities

In this, our postmodern condition, the categories of 'modernity' and 'modernism' may have lost some of their topicality, obscured by the fortune of their more up-to-date successor, but they have certainly not ceased to be sites of contested meaning, signifiers whose relationship with the construction of a certain historical period and cultural production is subject to periodic shifts and redefinitions. Linked by the dictionary,[1] if not by the vagaries of history, on whose stage they appear at very different moments, 'modernity' and 'modernism' thus find themselves locked in a complex dance in which the dislocations of one reflect and respond to those of the other. In this essay I intend to consider one such configuration, as it takes shape in the works of Massimo Bontempelli, a novelist, playwright, and cultural organizer whose oeuvre traverses Italian modernism from the Futurist avant-garde (and, even earlier, nineteenth-century *Carduccianesimo*) to the 'return to order' in the post-First World War period and the culture of Fascism. In particular, I will suggest that in the play *Minnie la candida* (1927) Bontempelli, in taking up one of the great themes of late nineteenth- and early-twentieth-century literature, namely the conceit that technology may be used to reproduce human life, ends up by staging the ambiguous and contradictory relationship among modernity, modernism, and, *avant la lettre*, postmodernism.

Modernity is best understood as a phase in Western history characterized by the emergence and hegemony of the capitalist mode of production, with its ensuing social and economic transformations, the rise of science as the regulating paradigm of knowledge and technology as its translation in the practice of everyday life, and the advent of mass political movements. But, at least since Charles Baudelaire first used the term to speak of a certain character of contemporary art – 'La modernité, c'est le transitoire, le fugitif, le contingent, la moitié de l'art dont l'autre moitié est l'éternel et l'immuable [Modernity is the transient, the fleeting, the contingent; it is one half of art, the other being the eternal and the immovable]' (*Œuvres Complètes* 2: 695/'The Painter of Modern Life' 403) – 'modernity' has also entered the discourse of aesthetics. As Matei Calinescu has demonstrated in his extensive study of the declensions of the term, it is precisely with Baudelaire that 'the two modernities' find themselves in a conflictual relationship. If the artist in modernity has lost his halo, to recall Baudelaire's well-known parable, that is, his function in the celebration of the rituals of power, now that capital finds its justification in itself and its reproduction, the advantage is that he is free to penetrate incognito into bourgeois reality to bring to light its contradictions, 'to reveal the poetry hidden behind the most horrifying contrasts of social reality' (Calinescu 54). It is at this point that the 'great divide,' to use Andreas Huyssen's term, fractures the field of artistic production along a major fault line, separating industrial literature, which obeys the demands and rules of the marketplace, from high art, which finds in the rejection of the norms of bourgeois society its own validation.[2]

It is this critical and at times radically anti-bourgeois thrust that defines, in broad strokes, modernist literature. Certainly, as Raymond Williams has remarked, this oppositionality can be articulated in a number of ways, including reactionary tendencies whose arrière-, rather than avant-, garde attack on modernity, far from bringing into focus its contradictions, seeks to resolve them in an 'other' space, that of myth and of tradition (cf. Williams 76–7). And yet, what modernism has in common even with the ideologies of the right, with which some of its exponents have allied themselves, is the rejection of the mores and in particular of the utilitarian logic of bourgeois society. For example, the appeal of Fascism to intellectuals as diverse as Ezra Pound and F.T. Marinetti (one should also not forget the genuine fascination felt by figures like the young Elio Vittorini, who would later, and quite coherently, find a more suitable ideological home in Communism) was rooted in the fact that the regime presented itself as the restorer and defender of 'strong' community values such as national identity or corporative solidarity, rhetorically (though not practically) opposed to the bourgeois values of self-reliance and economic success.[3]

But modernism is a multifaceted phenomenon. In addition to the form I have just described, there is another whose articulations 'engage with history and with specific social formations' (Williams 77). Modernism is thus also characterized by a revolutionary, anti-institutional thrust which becomes most evident in the avant-garde movements of the 1910s and 1920s, from Futurism to Dada to Surrealism, whose aim, as Peter Bürger has convincingly argued, was to demolish the institutions and the conventions of nineteenth-century bourgeois art and to reintegrate art in the praxis of life. This conflictual relationship is best described by Marshall Berman in *All That Is Solid Melts into Air*. In his words, modernity is 'a mode of vital experience,' 'an environment that promises us adventure, power, joy, growth, transformation of ourselves and the world – and, at the same time, that threatens to destroy everything we have, everything we know, everything we are' (15). Modernity is thus another name for the epistemic shift that characterizes late-eighteenth- and early-nineteenth-century European culture, in which positivist science and the faith in progress become the paradigmatic narratives structuring human experience. But modernity also entails a profound and radical change in the relationship between human beings and their world, in particular through the transformation in labour relations which characterizes the advent of capitalism and the parallel rise of modern technology. In Berman's account, 'modernism' is that complex grouping of visions and ideas aimed at making 'men and women the subjects as well as the objects of modernization, to give them the power to change the world which is changing them' (16).

It is this second aspect of modernism that will inform my reading of Bontempelli's *Minnie la candida*, in particular as a thematization of the transformations wrought by modernity in the way that human beings relate to each other and with the world. Technology plays both a thematic and a metaphorical function in the cultural production of modernism; it figures as both a narrative device and a trope through which are articulated the anxieties of the human subject confronted by the processes of modernization. The fear of technology beyond human control is not simply a literary conceit, as is demonstrated by some curious attempts, in the nineteenth century, to re-establish the distance between it and the human, or to give it, so to speak, a human face. For instance, it is difficult not to feel a certain sympathy for the British 'Locomotive Act' of 1861 which limited the speed of vehicles to '4 miles/hour and obliged owners to have on board at least three people capable of operating it, and furthermore to have the car preceded in all its travels by a pedestrian carrying a red flag' (Robillard 23). Technology here is literally brought down to a human dimension, its potential seen not as an enhancement of human capabilities but rather inscribed and limited by them. But this is of course also a rearguard action, the superficial domestication of a technological drift which was already inscribing human beings in the inhuman rhythm of industrial production. Against this feeble attempt to humanize what remains ultimately a leisure use of technology, one can set the mechanized tempo of industrial production: the automobile industry, for instance, was among the first to adopt the model of the assembly line and turn the production of individual products into the *re*production of a standardized model. In the first decades of the twentieth century the trope of the worker as a purely mechanical being, or as a small cog in the social machinery, proliferates in cultural production, and in particular in cinema and the theatre: Charlie Chaplin's alienated factory worker literally robbed of his freedom by the rhythm of the assembly line in *Modern Times* (1936) is the comical counterpart of the transformation of the factory into a man-eating Moloch, its maws gaping to devour the robot-like workers, in Fritz Lang's *Metropolis* (1926).[4]

Metropolis, we may recall, played with both possibilities of the identification between the human being and the machine: not only did it offer the vision of human beings transformed into creatures of machine-like precision and repetitiveness, locked in a deadly struggle with the tools they manoeuvre, and forced to become more and more like them in order to survive, but it also imagines a science capable of constructing machines that can pass for and replace actual human beings. It is to this latter motif that Bontempelli turned in *Minnie la candida* in order to stage his own modernist critique of modernity. In so doing Bontempelli also tapped into a theme which had exerted its fascination on Western culture since its very origins, and which, since the late eighteenth century, had found a privileged place in the theatre: the theme of the artificial being.

Puppets and Automata: On the Permutations of a Modernist Trope

The landscape of modernism is littered with automata, puppets, mannequins – mechanical beings whose presence calls into question both the relationship of the modern subject to him/herself and to the social body. In a circular movement, the process of inscription of the subject into the rhythms of capitalist production results in a progressive reification of the human being, in his/her (its?) ever-increasing identification with the tools and machinery of technological modernity. As the example of Chaplin's alienated worker makes clear, this subjection of the individual to the machine is a totalizing one which invades every corner of both the physical and the psychological self, as mind and body are shaped to function according to the rigidly choreographed measures of the factory and the assembly line. Repetition undoes the dualism of body and mind, and the Cartesian knot of *res cogitans* and *res extensa* is cut and dissolved by subordinating both to the logic of industrial production. And yet, automata, robots, and other artificial beings also remain ambiguous figures. They have been used, as Sharon King reminds us, 'to symbolize the threat of technology to escape man's control, to alienate him from his world, to precipitate his loss of humanity' (99). However, in more recent and reassuring guises – the *Star Wars* droids, the android Data in the television series *Star Trek: The Next Generation*, or the Robin Williams character in the film *Bicentennial Man* (1999), – automata have also been the vehicle for a more subtle vindication of some kind of ineffable essence – a soul, perhaps – which supposedly characterizes not only living beings but also apparently cold machines, once they experience human feelings like love or hatred or even lust. With these comforting and domesticated repropositions of the tale of Pinocchio, the circle seems to have closed: initially figures for the commodification of the human subject in modernity, mechanical beings have become the metaphoric site for a more complex and ambiguous discourse in which the question of what it means to be human is shifted away from the social realm and squarely thrust upon the individual. The artificial being becomes a consolatory myth:[5] no matter how alienating the relations of production may be in the world of late capitalism, human nature, defined as the capacity to elicit the proper emotional response to a given situation, constitutes the bedrock which distinguishes the human from the artificial. Such is the resilience of this store of feelings and emotion that, in addition to providing an effective antidote to the Chaplinesque mechanization of the individual, it is even powerful enough to infiltrate the mechanical workings of the human machines.

Of course, the theme of the artificial being predates modernity, and can be traced as far back as the myth of Pygmalion. It thus perhaps witnesses to a recurrent concern in Western culture with the reproduction of natural phenomena, and even to the obsessive resurfacing

of a misogynistic desire on the part of the male artist/*artifex* to reproduce without female involvement.[6] However, there are also evident
and significant differences between pre-modern configurations, from
the golem of Jewish legend to the homunculus, and their Enlightenment successors, such as the real automata with which inventors like
Jacques de Vaucanson and Pierre and Henri-Louis Jacquet-Droz delighted and astonished the European aristocracy of the eighteenth century.[7] These wonders of mechanical engineering, relatives and contemporaries of the steam engine and the power loom,[8] were in fact
precisely the opposite of their legendary predecessors: not inert matter
endowed with life, but rather mechanisms which reproduced the movements and gestures of human beings. The golems and the homunculi
of medieval legends still needed the spark of the divine in order to
come to life, and thus paradoxically attested to an order in which only
God can bestow life, whether through direct intervention or through
the use of already living material.[9] Modern automata, in contrast,
bracket the question of life and foreground that of representation: the
wonder of the automaton is that it acts *as if* it were human, and the
issue thus becomes how to distinguish between the human and the
artificial. In the taxonomic system of the eighteenth century, as Michel
Foucault describes it in *The Order of Things*, 'life does not exist: only
living beings. [...] [I]t is usual to divide things in nature into three
classes: minerals [...]; vegetables [...]; and animals, which are capable
of spontaneous movement. As for life and the threshold it establishes,
there can be a slide from one end of the scale to the other according to
the criteria one adopts' (160). Thus, the difference between human
beings and automata may be a matter of degree rather than of nature,
and the former may simply be far more perfect forms of the latter,
'produced by a mechanic who surpasses by far all his human competi-
tors, mere descendants of Prometheus,' as Lieselotte Sauer says discussing Julian Offray de La Mettrie's *L'Homme Machine* (1747). Blair
Campbell's careful analysis of La Mettrie's use of the machine as a
model to interpret both the individual and society demonstrates that it
is related to a very localized debate within French Enlightenment, as it
served to carry out a critique of humanitarianism that gained La Mettrie
the antagonism of the French philosophes. And yet the pervasiveness
of the metaphor itself is significant, as it marks the emergence of what
we can call, with Harald Weinrich, a 'metaphorical field' which links
together in an analogical relationship 'two linguistic spheres of meaning' (40).[10] In this case the receiving metaphoric field, that of human

beings as individuals and as social units, is brought into relation with and interpreted through the emitting metaphoric field of the new products of nascent modern technology, with the result that human beings become inscribed in its economic logic. Metaphorically, the man-machine anticipates the culmination, in the late nineteenth and early twentieth century, of the logic of industrialism, the Fordian assembly line in which individuality is completely erased as each worker must perform with clockwork precision and repetition the same sequence of gestures[11] (it is significant that at this point the machine is no longer the tool but the rival of the human subject, threatening his/her livelihood with its superior mechanical performance, as demonstrated by the process of automation in modern industry).

Finally, in the nineteenth century, androids become disquieting machines, more often protagonists of cautionary tales about the hubris of modern science, as in the case of Frankenstein's monster, than symbols of its triumphs.[12] Furthermore, the artificial beings of Romanticism and Decadentism are still constructed in a sort of artisan fashion. They are unique products of the activities of inventors like Professor Spalanzani in E.T.A. Hoffmann's 'The Sandman' (1817) or Thomas Alva Edison in Villiers de l'Isle-Adam's *Future Eve* (1880), who envision their products as replacements for 'natural' beings rather than as mechanisms. Instead of being mass produced, they are tailored to individual tastes and even appear, on the surface, to have a personality of their own, as if to mask their kinship with the serialized commodities of rising industrial production.

In turn-of-the-century Italian culture – and in particular in the theatre – the theme of the automaton intersects with that of the puppet or the marionette, which had been popular in European theatre since at least the Romantic period.[13] Bontempelli appropriates this tradition, although, as we will see, *Minnie la candida* is the crucible of numerous influences. If Collodi's Pinocchio may be interpreted as an early and pre-technological configuration of the theme (Pinocchio's 'father,' Geppetto, is a mere carpenter rather than an inventor like de l'Isle-Adam's Edison), it is with Futurism that the automaton makes its entrance on the Italian cultural scene. In *Mafarka le futuriste* [Mafarka the Futurist] (1909), the first novel of Filippo Tommaso Marinetti, the founder of the movement, the eponymous protagonist creates a mechanical son, Gazurmah, which destroys its own father as it transcends humanity. Variously interpreted as a staging of the Futurist 'fiction of power' (Sartini Blum), of Marinetti's own biographical psychodrama (Baldissone), or of 'the homophobic fantasy of male autarky' (Spackman 76), this text constitutes a *locus classicus* of the convergence, in the poetics of the movement, of the fascination with technological modernity and the theme of the advent of a new anthropological condition through the merging of the natural and the mechanical. Nineteenth-century suspicion of the replacement of nature by the machine is thus overcome by the appeal to 'l'uomo moltiplicato e il Regno della macchina [multiplied man and the kingdom of the machine],' as Marinetti entitled the manifesto in which he envisioned the cyborg-like 'imminente e inevitabile identificazione dell'uomo col motore [imminent and inevitable identification of men and engines]' (*Teoria e invenzione* 299).[14] But Marinetti is interesting for another reason. In his play *Poupées electriques* [Electric Puppets] (1909),[15] originally written in French, like *Mafarka*, the traditional triangle of bourgeois drama – whose sides in this case are constituted by John Wilson, an engineer like Edison (here *Future Eve* is clearly a source), his wife Mary, and the officer Paul, who is linked to Mary not only by a more or less undeclared love, but also by the memory of Mary's friend Juliette, who committed suicide, possibly because she herself was in love with Paul – is complicated by the introduction of two 'electric puppets' into John and Mary's ménage. The puppets, named Monsieur Prudent and Madame Prunelle, represent the bourgeois conventions that stifle the free display of desires and instincts. Indeed, John has created the puppets to flout the traditional social mores they represent and to spice up his and Mary's sexual life by pretending to be making love surreptitiously behind their back. In an interesting reversal, however, John himself ends up identifying with the puppet of Monsieur Prudent when he suggests to Mary that she will betray him with Paul. The metaphor of the modern individual as a marionette moved by the invisible strings of social conventions is thus literalized in the play, in which both human beings and electric puppets share the subjection to the apparently inescapable norms of bourgeois society. Indeed, the very fact that even the extraordinary man of genius, the inventor Wilson, is unable to rise above them seems to suggest that the internalization of such a moral structure is precisely what constitutes the modern subject, and that only a total anthropological (r)evolution involving all aspects of social, ethical, aesthetic, and political life can break the automatisms that modernity inscribes in the individual. In this sense, then, *Poupées electriques* can also be read as the outline of the condition which Futurism seeks to overcome.

On a specifically literary level, however, the double use, literal and metaphoric, of the puppet, and the openly parodic appropriation and overturning of the conventions of bourgeois drama, also make it possible to read *Poupées électriques* as a precursor of the 'teatro grottesco,' a theatrical current whose birth is marked by the first performance of Luigi Chiarelli's programmatically titled *La maschera e il volto* [The Mask and the Face] on 29 May 1916 in Rome.[16] The critical objective of the works associated with the grotesque, as Gigi Livio has noted, is 'the final phase of bourgeois comedy, centered on the husband-wife-lover triangle' (*Il teatro in rivolta* 60), but its final goal is not so much to introduce new formal structures within the Italian theatrical canon, as was the case with Futurism, but rather to turn the genre inside out 'to lay bare its decay' (58). The two cardinal tropes of the grotesque theatre, enshrined in its imaginary by the very titles of two of its major texts, are that of the mask and that of the marionette (Rosso di San Secondo's *Marionette, che passione!* was first performed in 1918). If the mask points to the themes of the fragmentation of the modern subject, the dialectic between being and appearance, and the layered and dialogic nature of identity, which fills and conceals the emptiness at the core of the self – in other words, the themes brought to their greatest and most nuanced expression by Luigi Pirandello, who entitled his collected plays *Naked Masks* – the marionette constitutes a further articulation of the motif of the mechanicalness of human relations in the bourgeois world whose declensions we have been following. Rosso, like Marinetti, plays with the metaphorical and literal implications of the notion when, in the 'Note for the actors' which opens the play, he writes:

Tengano presente gli attori che questa è una commedia di pause disperate. [...] Pur soffrendo, infatti, pene profondamente umane, i tre protagonisti del dramma, specialmente, sono come marionette, e il loro filo è la passione. Son tuttavia uomini: uomini ridotti marionette.
E, dunque, profondamente pietosi! (73)

[The actors should keep in mind that this is a comedy of desperate silences. [...] In fact, although they suffer profoundly human sorrows, the three protagonists of the play, in particular, are like marionettes, and their string is passion. And yet they are human beings: human beings reduced to marionettes.
And as such, profoundly pitiful!]

The 'grottesco' obviously flows within the great river bed of post-Ibsenian drama, in which the enclosure of the domestic space is exploded by the conflict between the anarchic power of individual desire and the normative force of social conventions, thus staging the impossible equilibrium of the separation of the private and the public spheres in bourgeois society. What the 'grottesco' brings to this European theme is the profound stylization of the characters, the flattening of the dichotomy of being and appearing on the surface of the latter. Thus, the adoption of the metaphor of the puppet links the crisis in the social and moral institutions of bourgeois society with the alienating effect of its economic structures, also metaphorized by the mechanization of human beings and human relations.

Bontempelli's Puppets and Čapek's Robots

Born in 1878, Massimo Bontempelli arrives at the avant-garde gradually and relatively late, rejecting most of his early production, which consisted of several volumes of poetry in traditional closed forms, plays, and short stories.[17] Bontempelli's engagement with the theme of the mechanical being begins with his brief flirtation with the Futurist movement during the First World War.[18] The poem 'Automi [Automata],' published in 1919 in *Il purosangue – L'ubriaco*, Bontempelli's only work acknowledged as Futurist, projects the theme onto a cosmological level, in which God himself is declared an Automaton – albeit a perfect one. In his later production, the theme is initially approached from a perspective consistent with that of the grotesque. The play *Siepe a nordovest* [Hedge to the Northwest] (1919), in which Bontempelli stages two parallel but mutually imperceptible worlds, one populated by marionettes, the other by human beings, can even be read as a literal translation of the poetics of the marionette of the grotesque theatre. In the play, the marionettes inhabit a world of heroic ideals and passions, and display the supposedly human characteristics of honour, courage, passion, and so on, while the human characters, locked in the predictable and formulaic love triangle, are characterized by world-weariness and apathy, and thus live both their emotional and their physical lives mechanically. The exchange of roles is underlined by the comments of the figures on the stage: for instance, Carletto, the 'other man' in the human triangle, comments that 'Noi non siamo Dèi, siamo povere cose: non siamo che marionette tirate da un filo [we are not Gods, we are poor things: we are nothing but marionettes pulled by strings]' (50), implicitly and unknowingly reversing the previous existential musings of the marionette Hero, who had proclaimed to his companions: 'Noi non siamo miseri strumenti in mano di un operaio: siamo faville divine, siamo padroni o signori del nostro volere e della nostra riflessione [We are not miserable tools in the hands of a labourer: we are divine sparks, we are lords and masters of our own will and our own thought]' (48). Finally, Bontempelli adds, as a kind of chorus, two puppets who observe and comment on the scene. To one of them, Colombina, is entrusted this nugget of critical wisdom: 'E gli uomini hanno un che di marionetta [The human beings have something of the marionette]' (64).[19]

If the play suffers from the 'intellectualistic and affected development' that, as Luigi Fontanella has remarked (*Il surrealismo italiano* 140), is a recurrent weakness in Bontempelli's theatrical production, it can also be read as an early parodic comment on the already conventional overturning of the narrative structures of bourgeois theatre; as such, it opens the way to a more original use of the motif of the puppet in the 1920s.[20] In those years, Bontempelli almost obsessively stages the confrontation between human and mechanical beings not only in his theatrical works, but also in his short fiction (the most direct source for the plot of *Minnie la candida* was his 1924 short story 'Giovane anima credula') and in the two 'metaphysical fables' *La scacchiera davanti allo specchio* [The Chessboard before the Mirror] (1921) and *Eva ultima* [Ultimate Eve] (1923).[21] *Eva ultima* in particular represents an important turning point in Bontempelli's narrative which indicates the way towards overcoming the somewhat contrived use of the trope in his previous works. The critique and parody of bourgeois mores become secondary to an existential probing of the boundaries between human and artificial, and of the complex configurations that the conceit of the human as machine might assume.

If the title establishes an intertextual link with Villiers de l'Isle-Adam's *Eve Future*, the relationship between the two works might best be described in terms of a repeated inversion of the motifs which structured the decadent text.[22] De l'Isle-Adam's novel took scientific and technological modernity as the point of departure for a quest which, in its yearning for the absolute, leaves social reality behind; Bontempelli's novel, set from the beginning in the indefinite space and time of fables,[23] finally turns upon the socially constructed nature of the self and of identity.

Eva ultima tells the story of a young and innocent woman, Eva, and her mysterious abductor Evandro, who spirits her to his villa. There she meets and becomes fond of the marionette Bululù, created by

Evandro to serve her.[24] A curious and unusual restoration of the love triangle is thus established. In her relationship with Evandro, Eva is relegated to a passive role.[25] But with Bululù she is able to establish a more complex and satisfying relationship, which leads both the woman and the puppet to a mutual questioning and redefinition of their identity. On the one hand, Eva's attention grounds Bululù's existence:

Eva

Sono calma. Quando ti parlo, sono calma. Invece pensare a te mi turba. Evandro lo ha capito. Perché mi turba? Tu devi saperlo, Bululù. Perché non ti commuovi alla mie parole?

Bululù

Perché sono fatto d'albero, signora Eva, oppure di niente.

Eva

Per questo rifiuti di darmi la tua mano? Forse temi ch'io mi accorga che non esisti? Che cosa importa, se ti sento, ti sento in me? E perché ti sento come in me? Sei forse mio figlio tu? (76)

[Eva

I am calm. When I speak with you, I am calm. But thinking about you disturbs me. Evandro has understood that. Why does it disturb me? You must know, Bululù. Why aren't you moved by my words?

Bululù

Because I'm made of wood, lady Eva, or of nothing.

Eva

Is this why you refuse to hold my hand? Perhaps you are afraid that I will realize that you don't exist? What does it matter, since I can feel you, I can feel you within me? And why do I feel you within me? Are you my son, perhaps?]

On the other hand, Bululù's existence as a marionette whose wires are manipulated by an unknown puppeteer leads Eva, who 'non [ha] mai voluto star a pensare se c'è qualche cosa più su della [sua] testa [has never wanted to think about whether there's something above [her] head]' (78), to re-evaluate her own existential condition. The climactic event of the novel, after which Bululù returns to the background, occurs when Eva concedes to the puppet's solicitation to touch the wires which move him:

Brancolò un poco con le mani, tutto il suo corpo barcollava, brancolò sopra il capo di Bululù; e d'un tratto dette un urlo acutissimo e ritrasse la mano

come se l'avesse sentita bruciare, e con tutto il corpo balzò indietro, e ria-
prì gli occhi, sbarrati. Bululù era come inanimato e un poco piegato su un
fianco. (79)

[She groped with her hands, her whole body was shaking, she groped above
Bululù's head. Suddenly she gave a shrill scream and pulled back her hand
as if she had been scalded; her whole body jumped back, and she opened her
eyes wide. Bululù appeared lifeless, slightly sagging on one side.]

The scene recalls a vision that Eva had had in a previous chapter, in
which she had found herself surrounded by people from her past,
'persone care perdute da tempo, creature dimenticate del suo passato
disperso. [...] D'un tratto le pareva veder l'aria scialba corsa da una
specie di obliqua pioggia rigida dal cielo fin sopra le teste delle larve,
le quali non sembravano accorgersene, e quella massa di fili ogni tanto
crollare [beloved persons lost a long time ago, forgotten creatures from
her scattered past. [...] Suddenly she thought that she saw the faded
air crossed by a sort of slanted, rigid rain all the way to the heads of
the ghosts, who seemed to be unaware of it, and that the tangle of
wires at times shook]' (67). Is this some sort of divine revelation as to
the nature of the invisible puppeteer, of the 'something above' about
whose presence Eva had refused to think? Perhaps: after all, Eva's
vision closes with the apparition of 'un vecchio grave con la barba
bianca, che a cenni riordinò quelle torme di larve, e le fece volgere, e
disposte in lunghe file lentamente le avviò [a heavy old man with a
grey beard, who, gesturing, gathered together the ghosts, and turned
them, and ordered them in lines which he slowly set on their way]'
(67) – a figure which certainly resembles the iconography of the biblical God, all the way to his not-so-metaphorical shepherding of souls.[26]
In any case, the fable-like atmosphere carefully cultivated by the author serves to deflect the possibility of any rationalist interpretation,
according to the principles of that 'magical realism' which Bontempelli
would soon theorize as the programmatic foundation of the poetics of
Novecentismo in the journal *900* (1926–9), which he co-founded and
directed, and in his later writings on aesthetics.[27] As he wrote in an
article of November 1929,

[s]e è vero che dobbiamo, a sanarci dei miasmi delle vecchie letterature
che ci stanno putrefacendo tra le mani da trent'anni, dobbiamo, come ha
fatto la politica, cancellare senza paura e tornare primitivi – allora l'arte

narrativa del nostro tempo deve – almeno come tentativo, almeno come tendenza, almeno come gusto – volgersi a colorire gli uomini in figure di mito, a costruire i racconti come favole, a fare della nostra letteratura una lucida veste a mezz'aria sopra la crosta terrestre. (*L'avventura novecentista* 188)

[[i]f it is true that, in order to be cleansed of the miasmas of the old literatures which have been rotting in our hands for the last thirty years, we must – as has been done in politics – erase without fear and return to being primitive, then the art of our times must – at least as an attempt, at least as a tendency, at least as a taste – go back to painting human beings as mythical figures, to turning our literature into a bright apparel suspended in mid-air over the surface of the earth.]

This transubstantiation of life into myth, this consummation of history not into a utopian technological future but into the timeless present of primitive mythologies certainly makes it difficult to articulate, through the figure of the artificial being, a social critique of modernity. The reference to Fascism in the 1929 article is not simply a necessary homage to the new Mussolinian system, but a revealing interpretation of both magical realism and the regime. In both instances, the contradictions of social and economic life are dissolved through their transfiguration into the timelessness of myth – individual archetypes in the case of Bontempelli, collective ones (the nation, the race) in the case of Fascism.[28]

Minnie la candida was written by Bontempelli between 1925 and 1927 for Luigi Pirandello's theatrical company 'Teatro dell'Arte,' although it was not staged until 28 December 1928 (cf. Tinterri, '*Minnie la candida*'). According to the author's note to the play (*Minnie la candida* 217–18), Pirandello had suggested that Bontempelli adapt for the stage one of his short stories, as the Sicilian playwright had done himself with great success. As Bontempelli recalls the episode, Pirandello even selected the appropriate story: 'Ho cercato tra le tue novelle [...], *Giovane anima credula* è adattissima, falla, anche il titolo può stare tale e quale [I looked through your short stories [...], "Giovane anima credula" is very appropriate, do it, even the title can stay as it is]' (217). Whether or not Pirandello was aware of the fact, the story that had attracted his attention had itself a theatrical origin, which Bontempelli's friend Nino Frank recalled half a century later, reminiscing about their days together in Paris in 1924: 'One evening we went to the theater to see Čapek's *R.U.R.*, which was enjoying great success. That evening, struck by the *robot* invented by the Czechoslovakian author, Massimo's imagination found what it had been looking for, and, between acts he told me the story [*novella*] of *Minnie la candida*, which he wrote the following day and which later turned into a joyful and cruel comedy for Pirandello's *Teatro dei dodici.*'[29] Certainly Frank's description does justice to the play. Bontempelli himself – always very careful in such matters – defined the play as a '*dramma*' to underscore its substantially different dramatic atmosphere from his previous two plays, *Siepe a nordovest* ('farce in prose and music') and *Nostra Dea* ('historical comedy'). The suspension of the contradictions of modern society which *Eva ultima* had effected through its escape into the atmosphere of the fabulous and the 'metaphysical' is no longer possible. While Bululù had constituted a kind of consolatory myth for Eva – a paradoxically 'real' albeit artificial person to set against the unreality of Evandro and his associates – the artificial beings whom Minnie encounters (or, rather, believes she encounters) represent the logical conclusion of a process of dehumanization that has its roots in the social and economic conditions of modernity.

For this reason, the intertextual link with one of the most influential articulations of the motif of the artificial being, Karel Čapek's play *R.U.R. (Rossum's Universal Robots)* – famous, among other things, for introducing what has become the generic term for artificial beings, the word 'robot'[30] – can be an interesting point of departure for an analysis of Bontempelli's play. In both works the 'robots' are no longer submissive or in any case benevolent figures, but turn into a threatening presence whose ultimate aim is the infiltration and replacement of humanity. *R.U.R.* stages the Marxist thematics of workers' alienation by imagining a society founded upon a strict division between two classes of beings, real humans and artificial humanoids, in which the latter are literally tools in the service of their masters (the word 'robot,' we should recall, derives from the Czech *robota*, 'hard labor'). Paradoxically, however, the human characters too initially appear as machines capable only of functioning according to specific parameters of efficiency, so that when the female protagonist Helena first meets the management team at the factory in which the action takes place she initially mistakes them for robots.[31] Other textual elements suggest that the difference between robots and humans is more labile than the humans themselves might be willing to admit: if nothing else, both are plagued by the same menace to their future, their inability to reproduce. Humans and robots are alike regimented into the structures of the capitalist machinery, which has spun completely out of the control of any human agency and become a self-enclosed, self-feeding apparatus that ultimately threatens the virtual extinction of life. Thus, behind the war between robots and humans which constitutes the basis for the science-fiction plot it is easy to read an allegory of the struggle between proletariat and capital, in which the former triumphs when it finally manages to deny the validity of, and to transcend the utilitarian logic and the inhuman and mechanical rhythms imposed by, technology-driven capitalist production. Significantly, however, the robots 'inherit the earth' only at the moment when, in a final reversal of roles, they discover emotions (love in particular), that is, something unquantifiable and not reducible to the simple law of efficiency.[32]

R.U.R. thus seems to offer the positive side of the modernist crisis: according to its narrative, modernity is a phase, a deviation, perhaps, in the march of (some kind of) humanity towards the realization of its full potential. The damages it has wrought upon human beings and their relationship with the world – in particular, the transformation of human relations into relations of use and exchange – can and must be reversed. In taking up Čapek's theme, Bontempelli offers in *Minnie la candida* its dark side, in spite of the playful and comical moments that characterize at least the first two of the three acts of the play. Bontempelli shifts the site of the conflict away from the literal stage (and the symbolic stage of history) to situate it in the inner space of his protagonist's mind. Thus, the confrontation with the machine becomes the ground for a process of questioning of self-identity: Minnie's *dramma*, to use Bontempelli's genre definition, is that of the impossibility of representing herself to herself as human according to the parameters that underlie the ideology of positivism, that is, as a unique subject endowed with the capacity for self-knowledge.

Between Representation and Simulation: The Drama of the 'Candido'

Briefly, the plot of *Minnie la candida* is as follows. In an unspecified Italian city, a woman of uncertain origins and even more uncertain language, Minnie, becomes the victim of a childish prank played on her by her fiancé Skagerrak and his friend Tirreno. While waiting for Skagerrak in a café, Tirreno and Minnie spot a man who is carrying a tub of goldfish to be released into a nearby fountain. Tirreno convinces the woman that the fish are not real animals, but artificial electrical creatures indistinguishable from the real thing. Furthermore, Tirreno says, the electrical fish are not the only artificial beings made by their mysterious creators: the experiment culminated with the fabrication of twelve human beings, six men and six women, who have recently escaped and infiltrated human society, indistinguishable from other people and unaware of their artificial nature. Minnie's initial astonishment quickly gives way to anguish and terror: even after Tirreno and Skagerrak explain that the whole thing was a joke, the worm of doubt has burrowed deeply into Minnie's imagination, as she begins to suspect everyone around her of being artificial. Pushing her relentless and iron-clad logic to its extreme conclusion, Minnie realizes that she cannot be sure of her own humanity and commits suicide.

The central issue of the play, then, is the question of the relationship between reality and representation – or rather, the procedures whereby the two can be distinguished. It is for this reason that the play can be considered the most 'Pirandellian' in Bontempelli's oeuvre.[33] The meta-theatrical subtext, used elsewhere (for instance, in *Siepe a nord-ovest*) as a plot device, becomes here a structural motif that offers an interpretative key to the whole play. Act I opens in a panoramic square. In the foreground are the entrance to a café and several tables. Towards the backstage, two tables are occupied by a man alone and by a couple, who, as we will later discover, are actors paid to play the part of customers. The scene is surveyed by the waiter Astolfo, who '[g]uarda un momento intorno, poi va a diversi tavolini, accendendo di qualcuno le lampadine, d'altri no, riprovando ecc., come per ottenere un effetto pittorico [looks around for a moment, then goes to several tables, lighting the lamps at some but not at others, then trying again etc., as if to obtain a pictorial effect]' (175). The opening line is Astolfo's: 'La scena è bella. Speriamo che non venga nessuno. Gli uomini guastano, quasi sempre [The scene is beautiful. Let's hope nobody comes. People spoil things, almost always]' (175). Then, like any good artist, he proceeds to close off his world of simulation from any real-world intrusion – in this case, a bourgeois family out for some ice-cream. This meta-theatrical moment, this staging of the act of staging a representation whose function remains unclear, introduces into the play the question of the lability of the border between reality and representation, spectacle and life.

The question that haunts Minnie is how one can differentiate between real and artificial human beings. To make their prank more effective, Tirreno and Skagerrak initially tell her that the distinction is impossible, both in the case of the goldfish and of the counterfeit men and women:

Minnie: E a levarli dall'acqua, che cosa accade?
Tirreno: Come i veri, sempre: sono fatti alla perfezione: boccheggiano, dànno due o tre strappi, e poi irrigidiscono e non si muovono più. Come se morissero.
Minnie: E poi?
Tirreno: E poi si buttano via.
Skagerrak: E dopo qualche giorno fanno come se marcissero. (185)

[Minnie: And what happens if you take them [the goldfish] out of the water?
Tirreno: Same as with the real ones, always. They're perfectly crafted: they gasp, give a tug or two, then become stiff and stop moving. As if they had died.
Minnie: And then?
Tirreno: And then you toss them out.
Skagerrak: And a few days later, it's as if they had rotted.]

The same, according to Tirreno, is true of the fabricated humans: 'Erano perfetti. Impossibile distinguerli dagli uomini e dalle donne vere. Pensate Minnie: forse qualche volta ne abbiamo incontrato uno, senza saperlo. Forse qualche volta un vostro vicino, in trattoria, o in treno, vi ha guardata ... [They were perfect. It's impossible to tell them apart from real men and women. Imagine, Minnie: we might have met one without realizing it. At some point, someone sitting near you on a train or in a restaurant may have looked at you ...]' (186). What becomes hopelessly entangled and fused in Minnie's imagination is the distance between world and subject, matter and intellect. However, Minnie does not surrender to this apparent impasse but devises a system of signification that should allow her to re-establish the order which the doubt sowed in her mind by Tirreno and Skagerrak has shattered. Subverting the Platonic notion that representations are imperfect copies of a perfect original, Minnie argues that, on the contrary, flaws and imperfections are the mark of authenticity: 'Volete vedere ora capisco tutto e non sbaglio più? Ecco. Pesciolino fabbricato è tutto molto molto perfetto, ma quello vero uno ha la testa un poco grossa, uno cammina un poco storto: e cosí gli uomini debbono essere:

uomini e donne, quando sono veri tutti hanno una cosa un po' buffa che non va proprio bene e fa ridere, chi ne ha una e chi un'altra [You want to see now I understand everything and don't make mistakes anymore? Here. Man-made little fish is all very very perfect, but the real one, one has a head a little too big, one walks a little crooked. And men must be the same: men and women, when they're real, all have something a little funny which doesn't look good at all and makes you laugh, and each have their own]' (197). As products of industrial technology, the artificial beings obey the laws of efficiency and productivity, whereas what distinguishes the 'real' humans is that 'excess of signification' which cannot be translated into those terms.[34]

Minnie's newly found certainty is, however, short-lived, as a new character, Skagerrak's uncle, deals it a crushing blow. The uncle refuses to define himself in the terms devised by Minnie, and responds to her cautiously probing questions in a way which leads the woman back to her desperate condition of un-knowledge: 'Mi accorgo che la mia nipotina vorrebbe trovare in me qualche cosa da criticare,' Skagerrak's uncle tells Minnie. 'Sarà difficile. Prima per la benignità di Dio, poi soprattutto per la mia potente volontà, sono riuscito a foggiarmi in modo che, sí, oso dire perfetto [I see that my little niece would like to find something to criticize in me. It will be difficult. First, thanks to God's kindness, and above all thanks to my own powerful will, I have managed to forge myself into something which I dare to call perfect]' (200). Even his 'flaws' – his slightly crooked tie, his slight lack of punctuality – are carefully studied so as to strike an efficient balance between the extremes of life: his is a world of studiously considered effects and timetables to minimize risks and maximize results in every situation. The principles of technological modernity have spilled into everyday life and govern its very construction: it is not so much a question of distinguishing between real and machine-like human beings, but rather of recognizing that within the horizon of modernity human beings have to perform according to the principles which govern industrial production. Of course, there are no artificial men and women – and in this lies the crucial difference from a work like *R.U.R.*, in which the robots on stage can become an allegorical representation of something else (for instance, the proletariat). It is rather the boundary between the human and the mechanical that has been redrawn. Act I ends with the following tableau: 'Entrano da sinistra sei uomini e sei donne in tenuta di globe-trotter e quasi a passo di marcia silenziosamente traversano la scena e scompaiono a destra. [...] Si sente la loro marcia smorzarsi e perdersi nella lontananza [Enter from stage left six men and six women in tourist uniforms, they march silently across the stage and vanish stage right. [...] Their marching steps can be heard faintly in the distance, then are lost]' (188). Minnie takes them for the artificial beings, but whether they are or not is a moot point. Like the workers in Lang's *Metropolis* or Walter Ruttmann's *Berlin: Symphony of a City* (1927), who march mechanically to their place of employment, these twelve world-travellers, the representatives of the equally regimented leisure industry,[35] visually represent the neat inscription of the modern individual into the rhythm of capitalism in all realms of activity.

The play emphasizes the fact that Minnie is an outsider: hence, her shaky control of language and her uncertain origin. Hence also her 'candore,' a spiritual category which Bontempelli, in his 1937 eulogy of Pirandello, defined as follows:

> [A]ffacciandosi al mondo il candido non accetta e dapprima quasi non intende il giudizio altrui intorno alle cose. Conosciutolo, immediatamente ne vede fino all'ultimo le consegeunze, e senz'altro le denuncia, qualunque scompiglio ne possa accadere. (*Introduzioni* 14–15)[36]

> [[L]ooking into the world, the candid does not accept, and initially does not understand other people's assessment of things. Once he grasps it, he immediately sees to the very end its consequences, and sternly denounces them, no matter what confusion may result.]

Minnie follows the three steps delineated above: lack of understanding (Act 1), non-acceptance (Act 2), and finally, extreme consequences (Act 3). In Act 1, Minnie's misrecognition of the values which govern the social world in which she finds herself is brought into relief by an early exchange with Tirreno, in which she suggests that he could easily escape his despondency over going to Germany to earn 'molti marchi, negli uffici del suo nobile suocero e a fianco alla sua giovane moglie [lots of marks in the office of his noble father-in-law and next to his young bride]' (181) by making 'le cose difficili. Voi piantate matrimonio, e marchi e nobile suocero e domani venite con noi in America [the difficult things. You drop marriage, and marks, and noble father-in-law, and tomorrow come with us to America]' (181). Tirreno of course demurs, responding that '[o]gnuno deve prendere la sua vita come la trova. Chi incontra la fortuna, deve affrontarla tal quale come chi incontra gli ostacoli [[w]e all must take our life the way we find it. Those who encounter fortune, must face it just like those who encounter obstacles]' (182). In Act 2, Minnie seeks to impose upon the world her own system of signification, which evinces the impossibility of grasping reality directly. Indeed, as Jacques Derrida reminds us in 'Différance,' systems of signs are always a detour through which we engage this impossibility: 'When we cannot take hold of or show the thing, let us say the present, the being-present, when the present does not present itself, then we signify, we go through the detour of signs. We take up or give signs; we make signs' (138). Minnie's invention of her own system of signs through which she can articulate the differ- ence between human and artificial – 'io capisco i segni, credi a me [I understand the signs, believe me]' (202), she desperately tells Skagerrak once she becomes convinced that his uncle is an artificial man – in fact never allows her to grasp 'the real,' but rather further pushes her into an interpretative practice whose aim is quite simply to create the very difference – real/artificial, natural/mechanical – which it ought to identify. Signs create (her) reality, rather than vice versa.

So, what remains of the 'real' which Minnie so urgently and vainly seeks? For Minnie, the real should be a place (metaphorical and other- wise) in which the difference between human and mechanical can be established clearly and unequivocally – in other words, a place in which human beings are not inscribed in the rhythm of capitalist pro- duction and consumption, in which some ineffable but ascertainable essence distinguishes them from the technological tools of modernity. The real is finally a site in which the subject may enjoy an authentic relationship with the world and with itself but, as we have just seen, access to it is always deferred by the necessity of approximating it through semiotic systems whose relation to the real is conventional and therefore artificial. Furthermore, in the course of the play things have become more complicated. Minnie's doubt has turned from epis- temological to ontological, and her initial question, 'How do I tell apart two beings – one artificial and one real – whose origins are certainly different?', has by the third act become 'How do I establish my own identity as human?' In this shift, the issue of the real becomes conflated with the issue of origin; Minnie's doubt about her own genu- ine (that is, non-artificial) nature leads her to question her own inner world, and memory itself as that which endows the subject with co- herence and continuity. This is the final blow, which immediately precedes, and justifies, her suicide:

Ma però, però [...] io mi ricordo tante cose vecchie. E allora? [...] Ma, ma anche ricordare può essere finto. Sì, cosí: cosí hanno messo dentro, dentro, dentro insieme questo ricordare, quelli che m'hanno fabbricata, per ingannarmi di più. Si vede. Si capisce tutto. E non lo sapevo! Oh tante cose ora capisco, tutto capisco. (215)

[But yet, yet ... I remember so many old things ... So what? [...] But, but even remembering can be fake. Yes, that's it: that's how they put inside, inside, inside together this remembering, those who made me, to deceive me more. It's obvious. Everything is clear. And I didn't know! Oh, I understand now so many things, everything I understand.]

The concept of origins, as Foucault argues in his reading of Nietzsche's notion of '*Ursprung*,' is slippery: it can be both a point of departure, a foundation ('Nietzsche, Genealogy, History' 140–1), and a point of arrival, that which, by being the source of the play of representations, of the copies of the Ideas, is the object of inquiry of the philosopher. Foucault writes: 'This search is directed to "that which is already there," the image of a primordial truth fully adequate to its nature, and it necessitates the removal of every mask to ultimately disclose an original identity' (142). But, as Pirandello had already theorized in his works, there is no core behind the mask. There is always another mask, or rather an emptiness momentarily filled by the mask(s), as Vitangelo Moscarda, the protagonist of the novel *Uno, nessuno e centomila* [One, No One and One Hundred Thousand] remarks in a rhetorical question which sums up the implications of the title: 'Ma che altro avevo io dentro, se non questo tormento che mi scopriva nessuno e centomila? [What else did I have inside me, except this torment that revealed me as no one and as a hundred thousand?]' (*Uno, nessuno* 860 / *One, No One* 120).[37] As Moscarda learns, personal history is not the result of a coherent existential trajectory from a starting point – a point of origin, precisely – in space and time, but of a process of suppression of the multiple selves behind the grimace of a single mask to which is assigned the role of 'I'. But *Minnie la candida* emphasizes from the very beginning the uncertain and labile identity of its protagonist, born, as Tirreno says flippantly, 'qua e là [here and there]' (178). Minnie's answer to him underlines her problematic, nomadic identity:

Prego, non ero nata io qua e là, io ero nata tutta insieme in un luogo solo, che è in una città di Siberia. Ma se ho detto 'sono io di Siberia,' qualcuno

comincia a parlare lingua siberiana, e poi domanda ha veduto questo, ha
veduto quello, e io invece niente sapevo perché ero venuta via molto
piccolina. [... E] io con mia madre insieme siamo sempre cambiate di paese
finché ella era viva; e Skager conoscevo a Costantinopoli e insieme siamo
partiti, ma io parlo solamente bene linguaggio italiano, come mia madre.
(178)

[Please, I was not born here and there, I was born all together in one place,
which is a city in Siberia. But if I have said 'I am of Siberia,' someone starts
speaking the Siberian tongue, and then asks you saw this, you saw that, and
instead nothing I knew because I left very little. [... A]nd I with my mother,
together we always change country when she was alive; and I was meeting
Skager in Constantinoples and together we left, but I only speak well the
Italian language, like my mother.]

Minnie has literally no place of origin, no 'mother country' or 'mother
tongue' (her Italian is far from correct, both grammatically and lexi-
cally),[38] and she is unable to reconstruct a coherent history of her own
self. However, her nomadism, far from being liberating, puts her in a
position of constant doubt, as she finds herself disconnected from the
coordinates of space and time that seem to regulate the existence of
the other characters. After asking Tirreno the name of the city where
they are, she explains: 'Io e Skager partivamo pochi giorni fa da
Costantinopoli. Io sempre dormo, mangio, guardo dal finestrino,
sentivo in stazioni lingue diverse: ma non sono stata attenta quando
Skager prendeva biglietti; poi io dimenticavo contare i giorni e notti [I
and Skager were leaving from Constantinoples a few days ago. Always I sleep, eat, look outside the window, heard different languages
in stations. But I didn't pay attention when Skager got the tickets; then
I was forgetting to count the days and nights]' (178). But when Tirreno
comments on the happy lot of being unaware of where one is, she
replies: 'No, no. A non sapere, non si è mai felici. Eravamo sempre
infelici per le cose che non sapevamo. A saperle, si diventa tutti felici
[No, no. When we don't know, we are never happy. We were always
unhappy for the things we didn't know. When we know, then we
become happy]' (178).[39] The quest for origins, for the truth of origins,
becomes a way to bring together the fragments of Minnie's identity,
and it is precisely the failure to carry out this operation and to accept
fragmentation itself as the condition of the modern subject that leads
her to suicide. Death, the annihilation of the self, appears as the only
antidote to its scattering, as it is the reciprocal and complementary

aspect to the originary moment: a *storia*, hi/story, has a beginning and an end, and the end validates the beginning. The play, however, does not offer such consolations, and in death there is no respite from the ontological doubt that has plagued Minnie in life: after all, as Skagerrak had said in Act 1, the artificial goldfish die and rot just like real ones.

Thus, in the transition from Act 1 to Act 3 the emphasis of the play has shifted from the question of representation to that of simulation, which hinges precisely on the question of origins. Gilles Deleuze's definition of the simulacrum in *The Logic of Sense* is especially relevant at this point: 'the copy is an image endowed with resemblance, the simulacrum is an image without resemblance' (257). Resemblance entails an original of which the copy is a copy, and the dualism of original and copy – or, in the terms of Deleuze's critique of Platonism, Idea and image – is the building block upon which Western thought is constructed. The characteristic of original and copy is that they reciprocally validate one another through resemblance: the Idea can be represented only by means of images that are necessarily decayed even when good; the copy founds its identity on the degree to which it resembles the Idea. With the simulacrum, on the other hand, the origin is absent, and there is nothing behind the mask of the image: 'The simulacrum is not a degraded copy. It harbors a positive power which denies *the original and the copy, the model and the representation*' (262). There is no real external to the simulacrum, to which the latter refers by means of resemblance and which endows it with meaning. The question of origin, which for Minnie had become conflated with that of truth, ceases to operate precisely because the 'regime of representation'[40] has been suspended and replaced by that of performance: 'Simulation,' writes Deleuze, 'designates the power to produce an *effect*' (263). This aspect of Deleuze's theory – the idea that being human might be an 'effect,' not an essence that can be ascertained, grasped, and recovered – constitutes the threat to Minnie's modernist 'candore.'

In the play, there is no space free of the virus of simulation – the artificial beings could be everywhere, and even Minnie's 'real' is a simulation, the result of sign production. In the words of Jean Baudrillard, the lyric bard of the passing of the real, 'To simulate is to feign what one hasn't. [... S]imulation threatens the difference between "true" and "false," between "real" and "imaginary"' (5–6). How this might happen is obvious. In the dichotomies referred to by Baudrillard, as in the case of those of signified and signifier, referent and sign, reality and map, the former is that which is produced, as an effect or perhaps as a performance (in the sense that it is nowhere present except in the here and now of the reception of the signs), by the play of semiosis – hence Baudrillard's argument that in the regime of simulation 'the map precedes the territory' (2). What is feigned, that is produced, ultimately, is the existence of a reality lying outside the domain of simulation, and the notion of difference continues to operate only if it is understood in the sense in which it is used in structural linguistics, namely, as that which distinguishes elements *within* the system, and therefore makes the system close upon itself.

Thus, to use a classic passage from Baudrillard, we can compare the world of Bontempelli's play, with its apparently neat distinction between representation (Astolfo's café) and reality (Minnie's world), to the French philosopher's description of America: 'Disneyland is there to conceal the fact that it is the "real" country, all of "real" America, which *is* Disneyland. [...] Disneyland is presented as imaginary in order to make us believe that the rest is real. [...] It is no longer question of a false representation of reality (ideology), but of concealing the fact that the real is no longer real, and thus of saving the reality principle' (25). Likewise, the invisible, 'non-existent' artificial men and women initially serve to inoculate the others, the humans, against the fear of their own mechanicalness.[41] But the difference between Minnie and her friends lies precisely in her unwillingness to take the signs of reality for reality itself. When Minnie asks Skagerrak what one of the fabricated beings would do if he knew what he was, he answers 'Ma niente. Andrebbe a spasso. E se tutto il mondo fosse fabbricato da qualcuno? Chi dice che non sia così? [Nothing. He'd go for a stroll. What if the whole world had been fabricated by someone? Who can say that's not the way things are?].' And Tirreno adds: 'A me non me ne importerebbe proprio niente. E neanche a te, non è vero, Skagerrak? [I wouldn't care at all. And you wouldn't either, right, Skager?]' (212). In other words, Skagerrak and Tirreno accept what Minnie strenuously, and in the end vainly, seeks to resist, namely, the vanishing of the real, and their own inscription in the regime of simulation.

Is the point simply that Bontempelli's play in some way anticipates the postmodern motif of the vanishing of the real and the dissolution of the human subject in the precession of simulacra? If that were all, I think one could be understandably disappointed – a 'postmodern' Bontempelli would add very little to our comprehension of Italian modernism. What I would like to suggest is, I believe, more interesting. It seems to me that Bontempelli can help us see that postmodernism belongs to the same cultural horizon as modernism: it is, like its antecedent, a response to the problems posed by modernity, and in particular to the question of what happens to the real in a social environment governed by exchange, in which there is no moment of authenticity – of truth, one might say – to halt the circulation of signs and products and to endow the whole structure with meaning. Postmodernism is the moment of celebration of the supposed openness of this condition, of abandoning oneself to the ebbs and lulls of the flow, as Fredric Jameson has cogently if apocalyptically suggested. Indeed, Jameson is correct in insisting that the homologies between the rhetoric of the marketplace and that of the 'precession of simulacra' should at least arouse a modicum of suspicion.[42] But while the postmodernist theorists of the simulacrum seem to be uninterested in this question – for Deleuze the simulacrum is the lever through which he can 'reverse Platonism' (253), while Baudrillard's dizzying *mise en abîme* of the real leaves no space for a critical moment – for the modernist Bontempelli that relationship becomes central to understanding Minnie's existential crisis. In the scene that precedes Tirreno and Skagerrak's admission that it makes no difference whether they are human or artificial, and just before the climactic moment of the protagonist's suicide, the two men, exhausted and worn out by their constant watch over an increasingly delirious Minnie, observe the cityscape and see 'frammenti di pubblicità luminose, alcune si muovono; in lingue diverse; alcune fatte di sillabe senza significato [fragments of illuminated advertisements, some of which move; in different languages; some made up of meaningless syllables]' (211). 'Tutta finta. Non c'è più cielo [It's all fake. There is no sky anymore],' says Tirreno, to which Skagerrak responds:

> Quante scritte! C'è tutta la vita! No, tutta no. Ma le cose più importanti: (*additando*) alberghi ... tacchi elastici ... spumante ... un dentifricio ... automobili, il grammofono ... cani di Pekino ... spumante, automobili ... tutti di luce, tutta luce. È bello. Tutto a stelle. Sarà un miliardo di stelle.
> Tirreno: Sono pianeti nuovi, Skager. Una volta non c'erano.
> Skagerrak: Ce n'erano degli altri. Queste qui hanno scacciato le vecchie costellazioni dal cielo. Sono costellazioni finte: forse sono più belle? Guarda.
> Tirreno: Il cielo s'è dato il rossetto. (211–12)

[How many signs! The whole of life is there! No, not all. Only the most
important things: (*pointing*) hotels ... elastic heels ... champagne ... a
toothpaste ... automobiles, the gramophone, Peking dogs ... champagne,
automobiles ... all made of light, all light. It's beautiful. All stars. There
must be a billion of stars.
Tirreno: They are new planets, Skager. Once, they didn't exist.
Skagerrak: There were others. These pushed the old constellations out of
the sky. They are fake constellations: perhaps they are more beautiful.
Look.
Tirreno: The sky is wearing lipstick.]

In this nightly reflection of the capitalist market, the natural and the
artificial world are collapsed together, erasing the dividing line between reality and its representation: the advertising images of consumer products literally loom larger than life, no longer signs referring to 'real' objects, but a new kind of reality altogether, new artificial
constellations which have spilled over the old natural ones, like the
foam of the champagne advertisement, 'ed è tutta luce, luce che si
muove ... senza fine, senza fine ... [...] E dal bicchiere cala giù, sulla
città [light, light which moves ... [...] endlessly, endlessly ... And it
flows down from its glass, over the city] (213).[43] In this new condition,
in which there is no inside and outside, since every possible space has
been colonized by capitalism and its logic, and in which everything is
inserted into a loop of circulation whereby use value is completely
replaced by exchange value, in the dazzling beauty of the advertising
image, of the simulacrum of a product which is itself the simulacrum
of a need constructed by the market, surrender appears the only possible alternative to Minnie's despair.[44]

The problem in the modernism/postmodernism debate, as Sanford
Schwartz has recently observed, is that the latter has been used as a
theoretical tool to construct a certain image of the former ('Modernism
was associated with identity, unity, and homogeneity, postmodernism
with difference, multiplicity, and heterogeneity' (11)), often losing sight
of the more nuanced relations that connect the two cultural moments.
But can we also think of modernism as a critical anticipation of exactly
those themes and metaphors which structure the self-understanding
of postmodernism? For instance, the famous essay on mechanical reproduction by Walter Benjamin – a figure who thoroughly belongs
within a modernist horizon – shows that the alternative between iden-

tity and difference is a false one or, to put it differently, that it is possible to carry out a critique of the 'aura,' of identity and authenticity, and still articulate a critical and political program. Likewise, *Minnie la candida* could be read as the confrontation between two modes of self-construction, one represented by Minnie's impossible and yet necessary quest for a real outside the self and the other by Skagerrak and Tirreno's acceptance of the model of the simulacrum. If we want to use shorthand formulas, we can even call these two modes modernist and postmodernist: what matters, however, is that by staging them simultaneously, this reading of Bontempelli allows modernism to emerge as postmodernism's critical other, not simply its historical predecessor but, more importantly, its moment of critique. The play counters the glee of postmodernism with nostalgia, the desire for an already lost state of plenitude and of meaning.

Minnie's tale is the symbolic locus of that loss, insofar as Minnie does not renounce the project of inhabiting modernity on human terms, rather than letting the ideology of modernity inhabit her. To return to Berman's definition, Minnie's 'candore' is precisely the faith that the human being can – or at least should – become subject as well as object of modernization, its producer as well as its product. Thus, Minnie's is not simply the tragedy of the estrangement of the individual in an alienated and alienating world, which many commentators have seen as the main theme of the play;[45] it is above all the tragedy of the impossibility of finding new criteria whereby one can validate one's sense of self and establish a relationship with the world. Minnie, in true high modernist fashion, remains bent upon finding a still point, a centre which does hold. Her attempt to push beyond the boundaries of modernity, pursued with the rigorous single-mindedness of the 'candido,' only leads to death – which, as we have noticed, is no more authentic than life. Minnie's tragedy is the tragedy of a subject confronted with the vacuum left by the disappearance of (the belief in) the authenticity of the real, and by the impossibility of locating a truth which is not already implicated in the regime of simulation, a truth which is nevertheless longed for. If postmodernism comes to terms with and even celebrates the Nietzschean death of God as the ultimate guarantor of (the belief in) 'hard' reality, Minnie may well be interpreted as the last sacrificial victim.

NOTES

Sections of this essay were first presented in 1999 at the conference 'Spectacle in Italian and Italian-American Culture' at the Center for Italian Studies, S.U.N.Y. Stony Brook, and as a lecture sponsored by the Samuel Clemens Chair and the Department of Modern Languages and Literatures at S.U.N.Y. Buffalo. I thank Fred Gardaphé and Marìa Elena Gutiérrez, respectively, for their invitation to share my work. Thanks are also due to Max Statkiewicz, who read various versions of this paper and always came up with insightful comments, to my colleagues Rocco Capozzi and Manuela Gieri, and to my research assistant Elana Commisso, especially for some interesting discussions on golems. I also gratefully acknowledge the financial assistance of the Social Sciences and Humanities Research Council of Canada and of the Connaught fund, which sponsored the research project on modernism of which this essay is a further development. Unless otherwise noted, all translations are mine.

1 Renato Poggioli notes their common relation to the concept of '*la mode*' (216).

2 See also Bourdieu.

3 One of the recurrent figures of ridicule in post-First World War literature in Italy is the 'pescecane,' the war profiteer who has benefitted financially from the social and human sacrifices of the soldiers in the trenches and the honest civilians on the home front. See, for example, the character of Tono in Enrico Pea's *La Maremmana* (1937), or Bontempelli's own short story 'Pescecanea' in *La vita operosa*. It should also be noted that the comparison between Soviet Russia and Fascist Italy, on the basis of their common opposition to bourgeois democracy, was not infrequent, especially in the early years of the regime. Bontempelli himself makes it in the first 'Preamble' of *900*: 'Oggi abbiamo in Europa due tombe della democrazia ottocentesca. Una a Roma, l'altra a Mosca [There are now two tombs of nineteenth-century democracy. One is in Rome, the other in Moscow]' (*L'avventura novecentista* 12).

4 *Metropolis* and *Modern Times*, in their turn, translate literally Marx's analysis of the mechanization of the worker in *Capital*: 'To work at a machine, the workman should be taught from childhood, in order that he may learn to adapt his own movements to the uniform and unceasing motion of an automaton' (*Marx-Engels Reader* 408).

5 I use the notion of myth in the sense described by Roland Barthes, as the ideological transformation of History into Nature, or, to use his incisive definition, the 'disease of thinking in essences' (75). In fact, Barthes's

foundational myth of humanism described in the essay 'The Great Family of Man,' on the exhibition of photographs of the same title, functions in a way not unlike the one I am suggesting here. He writes: 'This myth functions in two stages: first the difference between human morphologies is asserted, exoticism is insistently stressed. [...] Then, from this pluralism, a type of unity is magically produced: man is born, works, laughs and dies everywhere in the same way; [...] Of course this means postulating a human essence, and here God is re-introduced into our Exhibition' (100). Likewise, the initial difference from and diffidence for robots is precisely what makes it possible to appeal to a higher human essence, of which however they also partake, once their fundamental similarity of 'life' experiences is established.

6 See Sauer (287–8), and Woesler de Panafieu, who studies the three motifs of 'a man's aim to create life by himself, to produce his image of women and to create an identity as modern man' (129) in Romantic and decadent literature, but traces the roots of these concerns to medieval cabalists' and alchemists' dream of 'procreation without female help' (140, n. 2). The 'ultimate technological fantasy' of 'creation without mother' (70) is analysed in detail by Huyssen in his essay on *Metropolis* in *After the Great Divide*. Although not always accurate, Cohen's *Human Robots in Myth and Science* provides an extensive overview of the theme of the artificial being in Western culture. Finally, on the tension between artistic creation and procreation in modernist culture, see also Lucia Re's essay in this volume.

7 On Vaucanson's flute player, which has been called 'the first [example] of which we have any detailed knowledge, of what is now called an androide [sic]' (Lasocki), see Vaucanson's own description in *An Account of the Mechanism of an Automaton*. On automata see also Chapuis and Droz's monumental study, which includes extensive descriptions of the functioning of such machines from antiquity to the late 1950s, and Chapuis's own *Automates*, which is of documentary interest because it was published in 1928, just one year after Bontempelli's play. An observation on Vaucanson in Chapuis and Droz's study is particularly revealing. They write: 'People in the seventeenth and eighteenth century wanted to make mechanical men in human form; now in our own era we try to make the machine as primarily something of practical value, no longer copying the mere movement of a human being but imitating his actions and replacing him in the fulfillment of his work' (387). The ideological value of the android, the machine in the shape of a human being, is thus laid bare: its symbolic function, to reassure a human audience that man remains the measure of all things, serves to conceal precisely its replacement by the machine –

including computers – in the productive realm. (On the opposition between symbolic and productive, see Eagleton 377).

8 Significantly, Vaucanson introduced 'the first elements of mechanical looms [into silk manufacturing] before Hargreave's spinning jenny (1767)' (Woesler de Panafieu 141).

9 The fashioning of the golem, for instance, requires the manipulation, on the part of the initiate, of the letters of the alphabet, which have magical and creative power, and which, as God's instrument for creation, are directly linked with the divine (cf. Scholem 166–7). On the other hand, according to Paracelsus's 'recipe,' the creation of a homunculus requires an organic component, human sperm, thus confirming the impossibility of creating life *ex nihilo*. For a comparison of these two artificial beings, see also Rowen. Some interesting reflections on the relationship and differences between 'the golem and the robot' are also found in Plank's essay of that title.

10 On the heuristic potential of the machine metaphor, see also Caronia, who notes how 'the comparison of the human body to a machine is the analogy on which can be based a conception of the body as formed by organs which can be observed and studied as such, and whose workings can be described. Scientific discourse is founded on it' (49). If Descartes is the first influential proponent of this analogy, its origins can be traced back, according to Caronia, to the sixteenth-century anatomist Andrea Vesalio and his anatomic tables (*De humani corporis fabrica* 1537–43).

11 According to Campbell, La Mettrie's earliest formulation of the man-machine in *L'Homme Machine* aimed precisely at annulling 'the uniqueness and spontaneity of the individual in his relationship to society (or culture): mechanism hangs upon the human personality as a symbol of humiliation, an invitation for society to chastise all elements of individuality' (557). Campbell also discusses the later significant transformations of the doctrine of the mechanism in La Mettrie's thought. On the introduction of mechanistic metaphors in modern thought with Descartes, see also Woesler de Panafieu (130–1).

12 In any case, Frankenstein's experiment is an ambiguous one, more concerned with returning life to dead matter than with creating life *ex nihilo*. As Rowen has observed, the monster is in a certain way as much a throwback to pre-modern golems and homunculi as he is a precursor of the robot.

13 For a history of the influence on European theatre of the figure of the puppet and related forms such as the marionette, and a thorough survey of its articulations in the theatre of modernism, see Segel's *Pinocchio's*

Progeny. As Segel makes clear, the theme emerges in Western literature as early as Cervantes' *Don Quixote* (and indeed puppet and marionette shows date back to antiquity), but does not become a recurrent literary motif until the late eighteenth century. Unlike Segel, I am somewhat reluctant to consider puppets and automata as mere 'kin' figures, although the distinction that I suggest is by no means observed rigorously by the authors under discussion and is offered here mainly for its heuristic value. The automaton is an object which is made to appear like or pass for a human being: from Vaucanson's machines to the replicants in *Blade Runner*, the uncanniness of these figures lies in the fact that they mimic (or replicate) human actions to the point that they appear indistinguishable from the 'real' thing (which, as we will see, is precisely what is at issue in *Minnie la candida*). With the puppet or marionette, on the contrary, we are already in the realm of theatrical representation: the puppet's artificial nature, the fact that its strings are pulled by a puppeteer behind the scenes, is foregrounded rather than concealed. Thus, the metaphorical implications are subtly different. With the automaton, what is called into question is the ontological status of the human subject, the difference between reality and simulation. In the case of the puppet, what is often at stake is the question of individual freedom, whether the puppeteer is God or, as in the *teatro grottesco*, mere social conventions.

14 The manifesto, dated 1910, was published in 1915 in *Guerra sola igiene del mondo*.

15 The play was probably written in 1906; cf. Lista (39–42). Lista suggests Offenbach's *Tales of Hoffmann* as Marinetti's source of inspiration for the theme of the automaton.

16 On the history of the 'grotesque theatre' see in particular chapters 4 and 5 of Livio's *Il teatro in rivolta*, which also discuss the question of whether it can be considered a school or movement. For a more theoretical analysis of the parodic dimension of the works of the movement, see Livio's 'Il grottesco in Italia.' Verdone's 'Il problema del grottesco' is a useful comparative study of the 'grotesque' which situates it in the context of European expressionism. On marionettes see also Puppa.

17 After over forty years since his death (21 July 1960), the critical bibliography on Bontempelli remains limited. For an overview of the writer's career, especially useful are the monographic studies by Baldacci, Tempesti, Airoldi Namer, Urgnani, and Fontanella.

18 The reasons for Bontempelli's rapprochement with Futurism during the First World War and the terms of his later polemic with the historical avant-garde, which provided the point of departure of the program of

Novecentismo, are best discussed by Antonio Saccone in his '«La trincea avanzata» e «la città dei conquistatori».'

19 On the relationship between *Siepe a nordovest* and the grotesque theatre, see Nuciforo Tosolini (32–6) and Lapini (98–101). Lapini (93–5) also notes the influence of Futurism on the *pièce*, especially in the simultaneous staging of two separate planes of reality, and that of Edward Craig's theorization of the super-marionette. As is well known, Craig resided in Italy and published his journal *The Mask* in Florence.

20 Fontanella further remarks on the affectedness of Bontempelli's forays into the fantastic in his latest study of the author, *Storia di Bontempelli* (e.g., 40; 50–1).

21 'Due favole metafisiche' was the collective title under which the two works were republished by Mondadori in 1940. The reference to the coeval 'Metaphysical School' of Giorgio De Chirico, Carlo Carrà, and Alberto Savinio in painting was most certainly intentional, and Bontempelli had made explicit the relationship between his 'magic realism' and Metaphysical painting in the opening article of the second issue of *900*, 'Fondamenta' (cf. *L'avventura novecentista* 16). The theme of the automaton also resurfaces in other works of the period, for instance, in the play *Nostra Dea* (1925); cf. Barsotti.

22 Other aspects of the relationship between the two texts are discussed by Airoldi Namer, 'L'Émergence du formes théatrales' (177 and 181), and Pinto (xi).

23 Even the homodiegetic narrator to whom is remitted the function of witnessing to the reality of the events recounted is forced to admit the lability of the 'factual' proofs mustered. See in particular the 'Note' in which the narrator explains his involvement:

> A questo proposito desidero anzi segnalare, che quando Eva mi faceva il suo minuzioso racconto (e io ogni sera tornato a casa mia prendevo appunto d'ogni cosa ch'ella m'aveva narrata e descritta) avrei voluto metterne insieme una esposizione asciutta, vera e propria relazione, con tono quasi di documento scientifico. Fu lei Eva, romantica com'era, a non permettermelo, anzi a comandarmi che dessi al racconto l'intonazione di romanzo inventato. Tuttavia io non volevo nulla alterare. Per questa ragione volli, dopo la morte di Eva, visitare i luoghi dell'avventura. [...] Mi occorre anche avvertire che sia il Duiblar sia Hramazé [the locations mentioned in the text] hanno più tardi cambiato nome; e che quando io vi fui ho riconosciuto il villaggio dove Eva incontrò la Tricomante e la pineta e la pianura e il monte e la campagna collinosa e chiara; ma non ho trovato traccia della villa di Evandro.

[I must point out that when Eva told me in great detail her story (and every night I, in my turn, noted down everything that she had told and described to me as soon as I arrived home), I would have liked to put it together in a brief statement, almost with the tone of a scientific document. It was Eva, as romantic as ever, who did not allow me to do that, and even ordered me to give the story the form of a made-up novel. And yet, I did not want to change anything. This is the reason why, after Eva's death, I decided to visit the places where she lived her adventure. [...] I must also point out that both Duiblar and Hramazé later changed name; and that when I was there I recognized the village where Eva encountered the Hair Reader, and the pine wood, the planes, the mountain and the hilly and bright countryside. But there were no traces of Evandro's villa.] (111–12)

24 It should be noted that in Spanish the word 'bululú,' attested as early as 1603, means 'an actor who performed alone, changing voice according to the persons supposed to speak through his mouth' (Corminas and Pascual 1: 694). In Spanish playwright Ramón del Valle-Inclán's *Esperpento de los cuernos de Don Friolera* (1921), the 'bululú' is in fact a puppeteer (cf. Segel 155).

25 Consider for instance the following exchange in the course of the first encounter between Eva and Evandro:

Egli taceva, ed ella, imitando la voce della scomparsa indovina, disse:
– Coraggio: ci vuole coraggio, per fare il tricomante.
– Perché – rispose. [...] Evandro – dirti il tuo futuro? Non sarebbe più bello che io te lo creassi?
Eva non comprendeva, rispose con una diversione:
– Come potrei ricambiartelo?
– Tu – disse Evandro- mi seguirai nella mia creazione.
– Non sono docile – ribatté Eva.
– E mi intimidisci – aggiunse l'uomo. – Vedi come la situazione è poco soprannaturale. Non sali?

[He was silent, and she said, imitating the voice of the vanished fortune teller:
'Courage: it takes courage to be a Hair Reader.'
'Why should I tell you your future?' Evandro answered. [...] 'Wouldn't it be better if I created it for you?'
'How could I repay you?'
'You will follow me in my creation,' Evandro answered.

'I am not obedient,' Eva replied.
'And you intimidate me,' the man added, 'You can see how the situation is a bit supernatural. Won't you climb on?'] (15)

This passage also points to the biblical subtext of the novella. Eva differs from her namesake in *Genesis* at the moment in which she refuses to simply 'follow' Evandro (whose name derives from the coupling of Eve and the Greek *andros*, 'male') in order to establish a relationship on her own terms with Bululù.

26 Bontempelli is certainly an author haunted by a series of 'obsessive metaphors.' The piercing of the screen of mimesis, and the revelation of the puppeteer moving the characters on the stage, occurs also at the conclusion of *Siepe a nordovest*, after which the marionettes, like the ghosts in Eva's vision, become lifeless.

27 The journal, subtitled 'Cahiers d'Italie et d'Europe,' was initially published in French (issues 1–5, Fall 1926–Fall 1927). Under pressure from the Fascist regime, Bontempelli began a 'new series' in Italian in 1928, which lasted twelve issues (July 1928–June 1929). On the journal, see Saccone, *Massimo Bontempelli*, ch. 4, and Airoldi Namer, 'Gli scritti teorici.' On the ideological implications of *Novecentismo*, see also Cecchini.

28 Hence Bontempelli's stern rejection of nineteenth-century realism/naturalism in his articles on the importance of journalistic writing, apparently in contradiction with his 'magical realism': 'Ho detto *realismo magico* e non rinuncio a nessuno dei due termini. [...] La trovata del racconto come *documento umano*, come *tranche de vie*, è del vecchio realismo zoliano o post-zoliano, e ne è la parte più caduca. *Il realismo è stato ed è interessante soltanto dove, senza accorgersene, tradisce se stesso* [I said *magic realism* and I do not intend to give up either term. [...] The contrivance of the story as a *human document*, as a *tranche de vie*, belongs to Zolian and post-Zolian realism, and is its short-lived part. *Realism was and is interesting only when it betrays itself, without realizing it*]' (*L'avventura* 56, note 1).

29 Pirandello's 'Teatro dell'arte' was also known as 'Teatro degli undici' or 'dei dodici,' from the number of its founding members (of which Bontempelli himself was one). As Airoldi Namer has noted in 'Lettura di «Minnie la candida»,' Bontempelli borrowed elements from other short stories for the play, in particular 'Cataclisma' (the 'advertising metropolis' in Act 3 of the play), and 'Avventura disonorevole con una bella crimeana' (Minnie's uncertain language). Mariella Mascia Galateria has recently analysed the transition from the short story to the play and the

1941 operatic adaptation of *Minnie la candida* by Riccardo Malipiero junior in her essay, 'Dal racconto di terza pagina al dramma teatrale.'

30 The term was in fact invented by Karel Čapek's brother Josef, with whom he co-authored several works. Cf. Harkins (84) and Clute (585) (but Naughton has pointed out that 'robot' does not appear in Josef's story 'Opilec,' as Harkins claims. It thus appears that the attribution of the term to Josef rests solely on his brother's declaration; cf. Naughton 73).

31 For a discussion of this scene, see Harkins (89) and Eagle (37).

32 It is this humanist strain in the text that makes it impossible to read the play as an orthodox Marxist allegory of class struggle – a reading which, in any case, Čapek himself rejected (cf. Harkins 89).

33 On the reciprocal influences of Bontempelli and Pirandello, see Bosetti. On their collaboration more specifically, see Tinterri, *Pirandello capocomico*.

34 In one of the earliest and most perceptive critical readings of the play, Pullini had already remarked on the fact that Minnie understands identity in terms of the subject's irreducible unicity: 'Having a personality means, for her, possessing some sign which differentiates us and makes us different from others' (310).

35 Note that when the uncle proposes to join Skagerrak and Minnie on their trip to the United States, he is dressed like 'un perfetto viaggiatore [a perfect traveller]' (202).

36 In this sense, Minnie's 'candore' is more than a combination of 'innocence, simple-mindedness, and gullibility,' to use Segel's terms (296). It is rather an *other* logic, a way of relating to the world which sets Minnie apart from all the other characters in the play.

37 Cf. Deleuze on simulation: '[Simulation] is intended [...] in the sense of a "sign" issued from a process of signalization; it is in the sense of a "costume," or rather a mask, expressing a process of disguising, where, behind each mask, there is another' (263).

38 Lia Lapini rightly points out that, in addition to isolating her from the other characters, Minnie's language, with its frequent inversions, the constant use of coordination over subordination, and the improper use of the definite article, tends to 'return words to their originary fullness of meaning' (176). In other words, Minnie believes that words relate to real things in the world. As she says when Skagerrak tells her that she always believes everything, 'Io credo le cose che sono vere [I believe the things that are true]' (180).

39 In Act 3, confronted by the new tenant of the apartment that Minnie and Skagerrak were supposed to vacate, and where instead the two men have become virtual prisoners of Minnie's madness, Tirreno says again:

'Signore, se non sa niente, e non vuol saper niente, lei è l'uomo felice [Sir, if you don't know anything and don't want to know anything, you are a happy man]' (206). But his flippant attitude from Act I has now turned into 'desolata dolcezza [desolate gentleness],' as the stage direction tells us.

40 I take this expression from Max Statkiewicz's unpublished essay *'Représentation* under Erasure.'

41 On the concept of 'inoculation,' see Barthes's *Mythologies*: '*[I]noculation* ... consists in admitting the accidental evil of a class-bound institution the better to conceal its principal evil. One immunizes the contents of the collective imagination by means of a small inoculation of acknowledged evil; one thus protects it against the risk of a generalized subversion' (150).

42 Cf. *Postmodernism, or the Cultural Logic of Late Capitalism*: 'Appropriately enough, the culture of the simulacrum comes to life in a society where exchange value has been generalized to the point at which the very memory of use value is effaced' (18).

43 This scene is also a barb at the 'advertising metropolis,' to use the expression coined by Iengo (187), imagined by Futurism and exemplified by texts such as the freeword composition added by Marinetti to his manifesto 'Il Teatro del varietà' in 1914 (cf. *Teoria e invenzione* 89–91).

44 Cf. Jameson (37–8), and (260–78).

45 See in particular Baldacci (119–29), Lapini (197–8), and Airoldi Namer ('Lettura' 83–4).

WORKS CITED

Airoldi Namer, Fulvia. 'L'Émergence du formes théatrales dans le roman «Eva Ultima» de Massimo Bontempelli.' *Le Rôle des formes primitives et composites dans la dramaturgie européenne*. Ed. Irène Mamczarz. Paris: Klincksieck, 1992. 175–94.
– 'Lettura di «Minnie la candida».' *Rivista italiana di drammaturgia* 3.7 (1978): 81–8.
– *Massimo Bontempelli*. Milan: Mursia, 1979.
– 'Gli scritti teorici di Massimo Bontempelli nei «Cahiers du '900'» e la ricostruzione mitica della realtà.' *Studi novecenteschi* 12 (1975): 249–70.
Baldacci, Luigi. *Massimo Bontempelli*. Turin: Borla, 1967.
Baldissone, Giusi. *Filippo Tommaso Marinetti*. Milan: Mursia, 1986.
Barsotti, Anna. '«Nostra Dea», l'automa liberty.' *Massimo Bontempelli scrittore e intellettuale*. Ed. Corrado Donati. Rome: Riuniti, 1992. 237–57.

Barthes, Roland. *Mythologies*. Trans. Annette Laveers. New York: Farrar, Straus & Giroux, 1972.

Baudelaire, Charles. *Œuvres Complètes*. 2 vols. Ed. Claude Pichois. Bruges: Gallimard, 1990.

– 'The Painter of Modern Life.' *Selected Writings on Art and Literature*. Trans. P.E. Charvet. London: Penguin, 1992. 390–435.

Baudrillard, Jean. *Simulations*. Trans. Paul Foss, Paul Patton, and Philip Beitchman. New York: Semiotext(e), 1983.

Benjamin, Walter. 'The Work of Art in the Age of Mechanical Reproduction.' *Illuminations*. Ed. Hannah Arendt. Trans. Harry Zorn. New York: Schocken, 1968. 217–51.

Berman, Marshall. *All That Is Solid Melts into Air. The Experience of Modernity*. 2nd ed. Harmondsworth: Penguin, 1988.

Bontempelli, Massimo. *L'avventura novecentista*. 1938. Ed. Ruggero Jacobbi. Florence: Vallecchi, 1974.

– *Eva ultima*. Rome: Lucarini, 1988.

– *Introduzioni e discorsi*. Milan: Bompiani, 1964.

– *Minnie la candida*. Bontempelli: *Nostra Dea e altre commedie* 171–218.

– *Nostra Dea e altre commedie*. Ed. Alessandro Tinterri. Turin: Einaudi, 1989. 171–218.

– *Il purosangue*. Ed. Vanni Scheiwiller. Milan: Scheiwiller, 1987.

– *Siepe a nordovest*. Bontempelli: *Nostra Dea e altre commedie* 89–169.

– *La vita operosa. Opere scelte*. Ed. Luigi Baldacci. Milan: Mondadori, 1978. 147–285.

Bosetti, Gilbert. 'De la poétique de mythe de Bontempelli aux «Géants de la montagne» de Pirandello.' *Revue des études italiennes* 28 (1982): 40–71.

Bourdieu, Pierre. *The Field of Cultural Production*. Ed. Randal Johnson. New York: Columbia UP, 1993.

Bürger, Peter. *Theory of the Avant-Garde*. Trans. Michael Shaw. Minneapolis: U of Minnesota P, 1984.

Calinescu, Matei. *Five Faces of Modernity. Modernism, Avant-Garde, Decadence, Kitsch, Postmodernism*. Durham, NC: Duke UP, 1987.

Campbell, Blair. 'La Mettrie: The Robot and the Automaton.' *Journal of the History of Idea* 31 (1970): 555–72.

Čapek, Karel. *R.U.R. (Rossum's Universal Robots). Toward the Radical Center. A Karel Čapek Reader*. Ed. Peter Kussi. Trans. Claudia Novack-Jones. Highland Park, NJ: Catbird P, 1990.

Caronia, Antonio. *Il cyborg. Saggio sull'uomo artificiale*. Rome and Naples: Theoria, 1985.

Cecchini, Carlo. *Avanguardia mito e ideologia. Massimo Bontempelli tra futurismo e fascismo*. Rome: Il Ventaglio, 1986.

Chapuis, Alfred. *Automates. Machines automatiques et Machinisme*. Geneva: S.A. des Publications Techniques, 1928.

Chapuis, Alfred, and Edmond Droz. *Automata: A Historical and Technological Study*. Trans. Alec Reid. Neuchâtel: Éditions du Griffon; New York: Central Book Company, 1958.

Clute, John. 'Karel Čapek.' *Science Fiction Writers: Critical Studies of the Major Authors from the Early Nineteenth Century to the Present Day*. Ed. E.F. Bleiber. New York: Scribner, 1982. 583–9.

Cohen, John. *Human Robots in Myth and Science*. London: Allen & Unwin, 1966.

Corominas, Joan, and José A. Pascual. *Diccionario crítico etimológico castellano e hispánico*. 6 vols. Madrid: Editorial Gredos, 1980.

Deleuze, Gilles. *The Logic of Sense*. Ed. Constantin V. Boundas. Trans. Mark Lester. New York: Columbia UP, 1990.

Derrida, Jacques. 'Differance.' *Speech and Phenomena*. Trans. David B. Allison. Evanston: Northwestern UP, 1973. 129–60.

Eagle, Herbert. 'Čapek and Zamiatin – Versions of Dystopia.' *On Karel Čapek*. Ed. Michael Makin and Jindžich Toman. Ann Arbor: Michigan Slavic Publications, 1992. 29–41.

Eagleton, Terry. *The Ideology of the Aesthetic*. Oxford: Basil Blackwell, 1990.

Fontanella, Luigi. *Il surrealismo italiano. Ricerche e letture*. Rome: Bulzoni, 1983.

– *Storia di Bontempelli. Tra i sofismi della ragione e le irruzioni dell'immaginazione*. Ravenna: Longo, 1997.

Foucault, Michel. 'Nietzsche, Genealogy, History.' *Language, Counter-Memory, Practice. Selected Essays and Interviews*. Ed. Donald F. Bouchard. Trans. Donald F. Bouchard and Sherry Simon. Ithaca, NY: Cornell UP, 1977. 139–64.

– *The Order of Things: An Archeology of the Human Sciences*. New York: Random House, 1970.

Frank, Nino. 'Con Bontempelli cinquant'anni fa.' *L'osservatore politico letterario* 20.10 (1974): 118–19.

Harkins, William E. *Karel Čapek*. New York and London: Columbia UP, 1962.

Huyssen, Andreas. 'The Vamp and the Machine: Fritz Lang's *Metropolis*.' *After the Great Divide: Modernism, Mass Culture, Postmodernism*. Bloomington and Indianapolis: Bloomington UP, 1986. 65–81.

Iengo, Francesco. *Cultura e città nei manifesti del primo futurismo (1909–1915)*. Chieti: Vecchio Faggio, 1986.

Jameson, Fredric. *Postmodernism or, the Cultural Logic of Late Capitalism.* Durham, NC: Duke UP, 1991.

King, Sharon D. 'A Better Eve: Women and Robots in Čapek's *R.U.R.* and Pavlovsky's *El Robot.*' *Women in Theatre.* Ed. James Redmond. Cambridge: Cambridge UP, 1989. 99–107.

Lapini, Lia. *Il teatro di Bontempelli. Dall'avanguardia al novecentismo.* Florence: Vallecchi, 1977.

Lasocki, David. Preface. Vaucanson n. pag.

Lista, Giovanni. *La Scène futuriste.* Paris: Éditions du Centre National de la Recherche Scientifique, 1989.

Livio, Gigi. 'Il grottesco in Italia tra linguaggio della scena e scrittura drammatica.' Scrivano 109–19.

– *Il teatro in rivolta: futurismo, grottesco, Pirandello e pirandellismo.* Milan: Mursia, 1976.

Marinetti, Filippo Tommaso. *Teoria e invenzione futurista.* Ed. Luciano De Maria. Milan: Mondadori, 1968.

Marx, Karl, and Friedrich Engels. *The Marx-Engels Reader.* Ed. Robert C. Tucker. New York and London: Norton, 1978.

Mascia Galateria, Marinella. 'Dal racconto di terza pagina al dramma teatrale al libretto d'opera. Le metamorfosi di «Minnie la candida».' *La lotta con Proteo. Metamorfosi del testo e testualità della critica. Atti del XVI congresso A.I.S.L.L.I.* Ed. Luigi Ballerini, Gay Bardin, and Massimo Ciavolella. Florence: Cadmo, 2000. 1027–34.

Naughton, James D. 'Futurology and Robots: Karel Čapek's *R.U.R.*' *Renaissance and Modern Studies* 28 (1984): 72–86.

Nuciforo Tosolini, Barbara. *Il teatro di parola, Massimo Bontempelli.* Padua: Liviana, 1976.

Pinto, Paolo. Preface. Bontempelli, *Eva Ultima* vii–xiii.

Pirandello, Luigi. *One, No One and One Hundred Thousand.* Trans. William Weaver. New York: Marsilio, 1992.

– *Uno, nessuno e centomila. Tutti i romanzi.* Ed. Giovanni Macchia. Milan: Mondadori, 1973. 2: 737–902.

Plank, Robert. 'The Golem and the Robot.' *Literature and Psychology* 15 (1965): 12–28.

Poggioli, Renato. *Theory of the Avant-Garde.* Trans. Gerald Fitzgerald. Cambridge: Harvard UP, 1968.

Pullini, Giorgio. *Teatro italiano fra due secoli 1850–1950.* Florence: Parenti, 1958.

Puppa, Paolo. 'La marionetta, l'anima e il sonno.' *Quaderni di teatro* 8 (1980): 30–40.

Robillard, Pierre. 'A quoi sert le permis de conduire?' *L'Histoire* 235 (1999): 22–3.

Rosso di San Secondo, Pier Maria. *Marionette, che passione! Teatro grottesco del Novecento*. Ed. Gigi Livio. Milan: Mursia, 1965. 67–117.

Rowen, Norma. 'The Making of Frankenstein's Monster: Post-Golem, Pre-Robot.' *State of the Fantastic: Studies in the Theory and Practice of Fantastic Literature in Film*. Ed. Nicholas Ruddick. Westport, CT: Greenwood P, 1992. 169–77.

Saccone, Antonio. '«La trincea avanzata» e «la città dei conquistatori». Bontempelli e l'avanguardia futurista.' *«La trincea avanzata» e «la città dei conquistatori». Futurismo e modernità*. Naples: Liguori, 2000. 123–39.

– *Massimo Bontempelli. Il mito del '900*. Naples: Liguori, 1979.

Sartini Blum, Cinzia. *The Other Modernism: F.T. Marinetti's Futurist Fiction of Power*. Berkeley: U of California P, 1996.

Sauer, Lieslotte. 'Romantic Automata.' *European Romanticism: Literary Cross-Currents, Modes, and Models*. Detroit: Wayne UP, 1990. 287–306.

Scholem, Gershom. 'The Idea of the Golem.' *On the Kabbalah and Its Symbolism*. Trans. Ralph Manheim. New York: Schocken, 1965. 158–204.

Schwartz, Sanford. 'The Postmodernity of Modernism.' *The Future of Modernism*. Ed. Hugh Witemeyer. Ann Arbor: U of Michigan P, 1997. 9–31.

Scrivano, Enzo, ed. *Pirandello e la drammaturgia tra le due guerre*. Agrigento: Centro nazionale studi pirandelliani, 1985.

Segel, Harold B. *Pinocchio's Progeny: Puppets, Marionettes, Automatons, and Robots in Modernist and Avant-Garde Drama*. Baltimore and London: Johns Hopkins UP, 1995.

Spackman, Barbara. *Fascist Virilities: Rhetoric, Ideology, and Social Fantasy in Italy*. Minneapolis: U of Minnesota P, 1996.

Tempesti, Fernando. *Massimo Bontempelli*. Florence: La Nuova Italia, 1974.

Tinterri, Alessandro. '*Minnie la candida*.' Bontempelli, *Nostra Dea e altre commedie* 271–80.

– ed. *Pirandello capocomico: la Compagnia del teatro d'arte di Roma, 1925–1928*. Palermo: Sellerio, 1987.

Urgnani, Elena. *Sogni e visioni. Massimo Bontempelli fra surrealismo e futurismo*. Ravenna: Longo, 1991.

Vaucanson, J[acques] de. *Le Mécanisme du fluteur automate / An Account of the Mechanism of an Automaton or Image Playing on the German-Flute*. 1738/1742. English trans. J.T. Desaguliers. Buren: Frits Knuf, 1979.

Verdone, Mario. 'Il problema del grottesco nel teatro europeo.' Scrivano 99–107.

Weinrich, Harald. *Metafora e menzogna: La serenità dell'arte.* Ed. Lea Ritter Santini. Trans. Paola Barbon et al. Bologna: Il Mulino, 1976.

Williams, Raymond. *The Politics of Modernism: Against the New Conformists.* London and New York: Verso, 1989.

Woesler de Panafieu, Christine. 'Automata – A Masculine Utopia.' *Nineteen Eighty-four: Science Between Utopia and Dystopia.* Ed. Everett Mendelsohn and Helga Nowotny. Dodrecht, Boston, and Lancaster: Reidel, 1984. 127–45.

12 De Chirico's Heroes: The Victors of Modernity

KEALA JEWELL

In this essay I enter into the subject of modernism as it appears in the literary works and paintings of Giorgio de Chirico through an analysis of the theme of heroism in general and the figure of the gladiator in particular. As a founder of the Italian Metaphysical School of painting in the first decades of the twentieth century, de Chirico is known for his strange atmospheres, dislocated spaces, and hybrid characters, from the mannequin to the androgyne. His uncanny works engage, it would seem, a modern 'alienation' in which epic thematics have little place. At the same time, however, de Chirico exhibits clear links to classical traditions (as well as Renaissance and Baroque ones), both in subject matter and style. His treatment of heroic myths contributes significantly to his distinctive depiction of a modernity anchored in an aged culture. Too often, however, critics have attempted to explain the contradiction inherent in the modern/classical combinations typical of metaphysical texts by cataloguing *sources*, formal or thematic. In other words, the puzzling male combatant is understood to have revealed its significance when genealogical links to 'tradition' are forged. If, to give a related example, an androgynous, marbleized being appears in an architectural niche and half-hidden by a black sail, this might be explained by linking it to Hermaphroditus in the Greek pantheon or in Ovid.

This essay has a different aim. Rather than looking for the key that would unlock the secrets of metaphysical texts, I ask what is at stake in constructing enigmas in the first place. My hypothesis is that mystery is inseparable from another problematic: that of cultural mastery. De Chirico does not just belong to a great European tradition which informs his opus, he invokes the cultural heritage as leverage on the future. His way of deploying the past becomes the basis of a unique concept of cultural action. Cultural wealth and a renewed 'Italianicity' are inseparable in this logic. De Chirico in fact fashioned his classical themes in accordance with his notions of cultural mastery. He focused his attention on the vexed question of the value of the past to avant-garde movements and to the future of Italian culture as it moves into modernity. What can modernity do with the tradition of 'great Masters'? This is a great riddle in de Chirico, one that has taxed many a European intellectual, writer, and painter in both the modern and postmodern periods. Italy as a country appears in de Chirico's works as an astounding, exemplary pastiche of traditions. The Italian Piazza paintings are just one example. Italy seems there to assemble traces of a deep history which in other places has long since disappeared, so that the classical lives on in the present in uncanny ways (a ruin at a train station, for instance). In de Chirico's view, avant-garde thinkers must turn a discriminating gaze on the past and engage in a savvy remixing of traditions.

The greatest modern artists in this perspective inhabit a milieu favourable to the enterprise. Geography and art are inseparable when it comes to cultural abundance and artistic mastery. New identities in the modern period must be based on a shared sense of the cultural past and its power in the present. In that shared tradition is to be found the mastery of what I call 'veteran' cultures, Italian and European alike. De Chirico can be understood to display just what long-lived, well-trained cultures believe they know about the world. What they know gives them a sense of what 'Italy' is. In de Chirico's case, this knowledge is linked to what he called the 'polymorphic' traditions. In short, national identity and agency are at stake in our artist's representations of enigmatic mixed beings and spaces – and his heroes are just such mixed beings. De Chirico's heroes effectively assert the traits 'longevity' and 'accumulation,' which for him are the hallmark of cultural protagonism.

Displacing War

De Chirico was certainly intent on the redefinition or transvaluation of the systems of meaning that metaphysical thought in the Western tradition had evolved. Among the pre-eminent myth systems that served to 'work out' how the physical world and some metaphysical one might be conceived as contiguous was that of the Agon, the great battle. It is not just that in epics such as the *Iliad* or the *Aeneid* the gods mingle in the fray at every turn in an effort to turn the tides of battle. The agon is a way of dramatizing the 'solutions' worked out in mythic dialectics of victory and defeat. A partisan and interfering pantheon of gods figure into the Western conceptualization of the specifics of super-human power and, by contrast, inferior or limited human powers. When the relations between human beings and deities are spatialized, a culture constructs the conjunctions and divergences between a physical and a metaphysical world. A principle of contrast and a principle of conflict overlap.

Importantly, battle narratives bequeath to cultures a legacy of principles governing human 'agency' – the ability to act and to achieve something through action. They also work to govern ideas of interagency, interaction. Epic narratives of conflict between two sides set up, in other words, sides or 'worlds' distant from and different from each other. And only one side can, in these agonistic stories, through victory gain a position as the 'superior' world, the one with greater powers.

None too surprisingly, combatants heavily populate the works of the Metaphysical School. Mythic heroes such as Castor and Pollux, Jason, and Hector appear in myriad visual and literary texts by both de Chirico and his brother Alberto Savinio. Yet we would not call these works 'epic.' The recasting of tradition is made clear in distinctly deforming representations of the heroes. For example, we do not find the trait of 'power' clearly displayed. In fact, in the case of de Chirico, the artist seemed to favour the least powerful of the classic heroes as an iconographical subject. His favourite warrior was Hector, who not only lost his life and was dragged around Troy in pieces, but whose side lost the war to the Greeks, thanks more to the trickery and betrayal of the immortals than anything having to do with Hector's physical prowess. Second is Jason, who needed Medea's potions to garner martial glory and who spent as much time rowing and shouldering his ship, the Argo, as he did in combat – as we learn from Apollonius of Rhodes. We can say that de Chirico set out to articulate a divergence from the traditional narrative epic and its brand of heroism and at the same time to reconceptualize 'metaphysics.' If the epic tradition articulates different levels of power and forms of agency, recasting it can mean recasting human agency itself. De Chirico's representations show a keen awareness that agonistic narratives found a dialectics of difference and that the epic genre, with its representations of combat, constitutes a discourse functional to defining the prerogatives a culture arrogates to itself. How 'we' conceive epic heroism defines 'our' collectivity and its ability to act. Revision of the epic in de Chirico thus bears upon the achievement of a new 'national' position.[1]

In his novel *Ebdòmero* de Chirico's recasting of male heroes requires him to redefine the nature of 'action.' The novel's phantasmatic land-scapes, oneiric characters, and fragmentary plot displace its readers' attention away from the battle genre and the kinds of themes we usually associate with the combat narrative: males duelling for scarce resources, cunning strategy decisions with reversals of fortune, tragic truncations of masculine bodies and psyches, male bonding or tragic betrayals, entry into adulthood, patriotism and its illusions. But the fact remains that a swarm of combatants – from centurions, to cavalry, to gladiators – fill nearly every page in 'falangi di soldati fanatizzati [phalanxes of fanatical soldiers]' (49). Yet there is not a single bona fide battle scene in the text, nor a defined war going on. The familiar themes I have just outlined appear deformed and distant, in an obses-sional recounting of the fears of the main character, Ebdòmero, and of the assuagement of them, usually by escape from a foggy menace.

All of the groups of combatants in this novel are men, largely sepa-rated from a barely present civilian population of older people, women, and children, who appear in forts and towns. Constantly migrating soldiers pass by these people on ill-defined marches or defend them from ill-defined enemies. Males become a separate category, divided from the rest of the social group. Yet within their own realm, the strangely phantasmatic men in this fiction evince differences, for they do not all hail from the present. Many appear in military dress of ancient times or the nineteenth century, in sailing ships or on horses, and some of the combatants are gladiators rather than warriors. An-cient warriors with out-of-date arms materialize in modern times, as in this one-sentence episode:

Uomini risoluti e truci, condotti da una specie di colosso dalla barba di dio antico, lanciavano ad uso di catapulte contro le porte blindate dei grandi alberghi, enormi travi tolte ai cantieri. (*Ebdòmero* 86)

[Fierce determined men led by a man like a colossus with the beard of an ancient god, snatched huge wooden beams from building sites and hurled them like catapult missiles at the armor-clad doors of the hotels.] (*Hebdomeros* 82)

These many different sorts and ages of warriors provoke temporal chaos and generic confusion. The epic seems like theatre, since people might be dressing up. But when narrative elements are subtracted, the prose shades into a lyric style. The text about war itself becomes the site of hermeneutic strife and conflict, so much so that the theme of combat is packaged in pastiche as an artistic form. The text is itself a war of styles and forms.

That 'poetics,' convictions about the nature of art, become a 'battle ground' is a notion de Chirico, with some resentment, expressed in his memoirs, where the painter represents himself as under attack from many quarters: by jealous Surrealists and venial phonies without talent or discipline, by other artists ill-versed in the lessons of the great masters or ignorant of the bases of modern art (in Romanticism). While he scoffs at the notion that art is a 'battle' in his book *Ricordi di Roma* (1944), de Chirico describes disputes in detail. Some of these concern his views as a prominent supporter of the two literary/art journals, *La Ronda* [The Patrol] and *Valori plastici* [Plastic Values]. Others are explicitly political. The author recalls, for example, the early nineteen twenties in Rome, shortly after the famous Fascist 'march on Rome' (1922). Painting a verbal picture of thugs with guns who invade a movie theatre and force the public to chant slogans, de Chirico distances himself from Fascist politics (*Ricordi di Roma* 111). The author also carefully notes that he left Rome to live in Paris in 1925 because of Italian 'hostility' to his views and his work. Thus though de Chirico does not want to make art in the twentieth century a terrain of battle – and he mocks those who do – the artist does allude to what he calls 'i cosidetti tempi eroici [so-called heroic days],' which he appears to treat in all seriousness: 'si profilavano all'orizzonte avvenimenti destinati ad aprire nuove strade e soprattutto ad additare agli italiani la via retta dell'arte e della letteratura [on the horizon loomed events whose destiny was to open new roads and, above all, to indicate to the Italians the route straight to art and literature]'.

When fate is invoked, any antagonists are duly excluded from the glorious future and are unworthy of heroics. They are the sissies and 'pederasts.' Thus masculinity of some sort, although recast in important ways with respect to the 'warring' motif, is inextricable from poetics and artistic greatness. A certain revised representation of masculinity is in fact in this logic highly instructive; it is necessary to 'indicate [...] the route' (De Chirico, *Ricordi* 111).

The reasons why de Chirico might choose selectively to twist or deform epic battle narratives in his own work are complex and invest several symbolic areas. First and foremost is this modern construction of masculinity in tandem with an aesthetic position. At issue is the proper 'form' for modernity. On a second, more historical level, the text also inscribes anxieties about the changing nature of warfare in modernity, and hence anxieties about a newly ungraspable masculinity. War is no longer epic, but fought as mass war, as the hopeless trench warfare where combatants have no hope of individual distinction, but may be sent with bayonets against artillery. Yet even in mechanized modern warfare, men are held to epic models of manhood that measure each individual's courage and ability. This is the most autobiographical key of *Ebdòmero*, since de Chirico was a soldier during the First World War. He spent it largely in Ferrara, painting. The First World War coincided with the birth of the Metaphysical School of painting; an era of historical violence and changing ideologies of masculinity coincided in de Chirico's life with an outpouring of creativity. The war also brought de Chirico to Italy, whereas he had grown up in Greece, studied in Germany, and begun his artistic career in France. Wartime drew de Chirico into issues of Italianicity, and the war novel thus superimposes interrelated themes: masculine identity, Italian identity, artistic identity.

Still in a historical vein, the subject of revised gender identities must be linked to the ways in which Italy was being transformed by modernization. The modernization of Europe brought not only the rise of singular national identities, but also a rigidification of sexual and gender identities – a phenomenon described in George Mosse's influential book, *Nationalism and Sexuality*. The Metaphysical School, with its enigmatic males, counters this rigidity with an ideology of ungraspability. In this way de Chirico also revises certain nationalist ideologies which mark the first decades of the century.[2]

The male body in de Chirico is certainly different from what appears in traditional iconographies of prowess and in the literary epics composed by the likes of Ariosto and Tasso in the Renaissance. The gladiator in particular is not elegant, beautiful, or well-proportioned; he is nothing like the famous 'man in a circle.' Grotesque and of indeterminate nature, looking like marble or terracotta, the gladiator is inserted in crowded, off-scale perspectives which seem to parody the harmonious spaces of Renaissance compositions. His body appears *on view* together with a multitude of other familiar signs in Metaphysical paintings and literary texts. What might be at stake in retrieving gladiators and, as with other revised heroes, building into their representations what I have called tropes of 'inaction'?

The Gladiator and Cultural Politics

First, the gladiator is cast by de Chirico as a figure of enigma. The sense of mystery de Chirico orchestrates derives in part from the sheer temporal displacement from antiquity to modern settings, but it also derives from the puzzling quality of the longevity the figure brings to the present. The gladiator appears in the present but he has undergone transformations. His being is spectral and phantomatic. Yet he represents the fullness and multiplicity of history's long haul. An 'impossible' being for modernity, he brings together disparate temporal elements, just as de Chirico's cityscapes do. Marcel Duchamp provided an astute explanation of the term 'metaphysical' when he wrote that de Chirico 'organized on his canvas an encounter of things that could only be joined in a "metaphysical world".'[3] The gladiators inhabit just such a place.

The gladiator is always portrayed as a mysterious but powerful veteran who is projected into the future:

> Giunsero sulla soglia d'una sala vasta e alta di soffitto, ornata secondo la moda del 1880. Completamente vuota di mobili questa sala, per la luce e il tono generale, faceva pensare alle sale da gioco di Montecarlo; in un angolo due gladiatori dalle maschere di scafandri si esercitavano senza convinzione sotto lo sguardo annoiato d'un maestro, ex-gladiatore in ritiro, che aveva il profilo d'un avvoltoio ed il corpo coperto di cicatrici. 'Gladiatori! questa parola contiene un enigma,' disse Ebdòmero rivolgendosi a voce bassa al più giovane dei suoi compagni. E pensò ai teatri di varietà, il cui soffitto illuminato evoca le visioni del paradiso dantesco; pensò anche a quei pomeriggi romani, alla fine dello spettacolo, quando il sole declinava e l'immenso velario aumentava l'ombra sull'arena da cui saliva un odore di segatura e di sabbia inzuppate di sangue. (*Ebdòmero* 11)

> [They were coming to the threshold of a vast, high-ceilinged room, decorated in the style of the 1880s; the lighting and general atmosphere of the room, which was completely bare of furniture, reminded one of the gaming rooms at Monte Carlo; in a corner two gladiators wearing diving helmets were practicing half-heartedly, watched by a bored instructor, a retired

gladiator with eyes like a vulture and a body covered with scars. 'Gladiators! There's an enigma in that word,' said Ebdòmero, speaking in a low
voice to the younger of his companions. And he thought of the music halls
whose brightly lit ceilings conjure up visions of Dante's paradise; he also
thought of those afternoons in Rome, when the games would be over for the
day and the sun sinking lower in the sky, the immense canopy over the arena
augmenting the evening shadows, and smells floating up from the sawdust
and blood-soaked sand.] (*Hebdomeros* 3)

Here de Chirico, through his use of anachronism, subverts the linear narrative of history by bringing gladiators, wearing diving helmets no less, to an 1880s parlour. He also presents us with men engaged not in combat but in teaching: they are 'bored instructors.' He
foregrounds not action but a repetitive temporality attached to 'prac-
ticing half-heartedly.' De Chirico conjures up an alternative combatant, the aged, scarred gladiator with a prowess of his own unrelated
to the epic. Absent are any climactic moments of violent death. While
this passage evokes the Roman circus, it turns the Coliseum into a
distant historical memory of the protagonist who observes the new
breed of combatant. Importantly, only the moment when the games
were over is invoked. The shady, canopied arena of Roman days exists as a stage emptied of events.

Other scenes in the novel go a step further in subverting classic
representations of gladiatorial-style combat by displacing fighting
scenes from any familiar arena into *tableaux vivants* performed for
provincial audiences in the modern world. Performance remains but
the theatre is displaced. In one long episode, a whole town is celebrat-
ing the return of a 'prodigal son' named Locorto, and the festivities
include a combat play on an outdoor stage Locorto senior has built at
his villa (82). De Chirico narrates how one night amid the great pomp
one of the actor/fighters on stage breaks the theatrical illusion and
actually pounds his fellow actor out of exasperation over some undis-
closed disagreement. A series of 'salon' encounters and conversations
follow the scandalous episode. The text then veers into a discussion
first of the political uses of spectacle and then the politics of aesthetics
as well. Some vaguely anti-Fascist remarks are offered up by the protagonist of the novel. For example, Ebdòmero expresses irritation with
a 'demagogue' who speaks from a balcony before 'delirious crowds'
(93), as Mussolini was famously wont do. He launches in the same
breath into a denunciation of the 'volontà [will]' of political fanatics

who prefer only 'le forme e i piani rettilinei, assetata di purezza deleteria [straight forms and planes, thirsting for a deleterious purity]' (92). The Metaphysical aesthetic favours, we know, the polymorphic accumulation of forms, and the theatrical combat performance provides an occasion for de Chirico to articulate that discourse. At the same time, he acknowledges that aesthetic and political questions are intertwined.

In an episode following on the heels of Locorto's return, Ebdòmero tells of another performance which seems of a piece with the villa spectacles (although de Chirico leaves out the precise links in terms of place and time). As the day of the spectacle in question draws near, the inhabitants of the town are in an uproar. Everyone knows there will be violence on stage because the male troupe is engaging in 'esercizi brutali [brutal exercises]'. Significantly, major characters in this episode are political figures: the mayor and the wife of the mayor ('prefetto'). The town's first lady begs her spouse to order the suppression of the most violent scenes. De Chirico pointedly gives his readers a spectacle of violence seen in a socio-political context. Ebdòmero is drawn to the events and hopes to learn from the troupe something about the social upheavals ('rivolte,' 94) he says he regularly witnesses about him:

> Avrebbe voluto interrogare quegli asceti del muscolo che allora si riposavano dei loro esercizi brutali in pose piene di stile e di nobiltà, come se anche sfiniti dallo sforzo, non avessero voluto mostrare né al compagno di lotta, né al rivale, né al profano la stanchezza che torturava le loro membra pesanti come la ghisa. Ma gli asceti del muscolo di certo non avrebbero risposto. Essi guardavano Ebdòmero con aria di sprezzante ironia poi, all'uscita dallo stadio, si spingevano con i gomiti e ridevano tra di loro quando l'incontravano. Il loro fare cattivo, taciturno ed indispettito era del resto molto spiegabile. Il mestiere era duro e, malgrado gli spettacoli d'una bellezza indiscutibile che essi offrivano agli abitanti della città, non si poteva dire che nuotassero nell'oro. Di domenica, quando essi organizzavano quei simulacri di combattimenti ai quali il prefetto assisteva con sua moglie, cominciano ad allenarsi dalle cinque del mattino, e d'inverno alla luce delle lampade. (*Ebdòmero* 94–5)

> [He would have liked to interrogate those muscular ascetics who, momentarily resting from their brutal exercises, fell into styled and noble poses as though they wished to show neither to their brother fighters nor to the profane onlookers the weariness that tortured their leaden limbs. But these

muscular ascetics certainly would not reply. They looked at Hebdomeros with contemptuous irony, and, outside the stadium, nudged each other and snickered when they met him. This attitude, malicious, taciturn and irritated, was quite understandable. The profession was difficult, and despite the undeniable beauty of the performances they gave the citizens, one could hardly say that they rolled in riches. On Sundays, when they organized sham fights in front of the prefect and his wife, they began training at five o'clock in the morning and during the winter months by lamplight.] (*Hebdomeros* 91)

This long rehearsal episode effectively establishes male combat as a beautiful, demanding, repetitive performance. The muscle-bound men represented here are clearly superior in training and preparedness. De Chirico has his fighters scoff at Ebdòmero or ignore him, using his protagonist as a foil. When the performers snigger at the character, their behaviour cannot be deciphered by the uncomprehending spectator. The male behaviour of the actors (fighting, posing) is made unfamiliar even to the protagonist, who becomes a prime witness to the 'enigma' of the combatants. If they scoff at Ebdòmero, the most learned and wise of all in the novel, then the other spectators too must be outsiders to the kind of expertise this well-muscled, ascetic group possesses. How will the protagonist fulfil his desire to learn about 'social upheaval' by watching the spectacle offered to the public in a modern circus?

No literary naif, de Chirico artfully allows his protagonist to turn the situation around in order to grant Ebdòmero an epiphanic moment of clairvoyance with regard to these arresting fighting men. Despite the pleas of the mayor's wife and 'quelli che detestavano gli esercizi violenti [those who detested violent exercises]' (92), the prefect insists that the show will take place, and de Chirico can orchestrate his protagonist's crucial moment of illumination, thereby giving his readers a dose of instruction:

Allora bisognò inchinarsi davanti all'inevitabile. La sera circondato dai suoi amici Ebdòmero assistette solo all'ultima parte dello spettacolo; ai quadri viventi *e capì tutto*. L'enigma di quell'ineffabile gruppo di guerrieri, di pugili, difficili a definirsi e che formavano in un angolo della scena un blocco policromo e immobile nei loro gesti di attacco e di difesa, non fu in fondo capito che da lui solo; se ne accorse subito vedendo la faccia che facevano gli altri spettatori. Il fatto d'essere solo a rendersi conto d'una cosa tanto rara e profonda lo turbò. (*Ebdòmero* 96) [emphasis in the original]

[So he had to bow before the inevitable. That evening, surrounded by his friends, he attended the performance and understood everything. The riddle of this ineffable composition of warriors, of pugilists, difficult to describe and forming in a corner of the drawing room a block, many-colored and immobile in its gestures of attack and defense, was at bottom understood by himself alone; he realized this when he saw the facial expression of the other spectators. The fact of being the only person present to comprehend a thing so rare and profound worried him.] (*Hebdomeros* 93)

Just what does Ebdòmero grasp? What the episode gives us is the protagonist's new ability to *read* something out of what appears as indeterminate and mixed. It is important that the enigma Ebdòmero confronts is the difficult-to-define nature of combatants who form a 'many-colored block,' a unique entity composed of many parts. What Ebdòmero sees, furthermore, are pugilists and warriors at once – a composite of things that are divergent yet similar. De Chirico chooses to portray a sport, boxing, which suits his discourse. It is clearly a game unto itself, separable from combat, for it is played with no weapon but the fist. It entails no military formation or formal grouping of men and it has no collective status. The activity veers in fact in the direction of gladiatorial combat. Boxing constitutes a 'violent exercise.'

The indetermination the author has his protagonist take note of multiplies in yet other ways in the passage. The men's gestures are frozen into one pose of 'attack and defense' at once. The men are paradoxically 'arrested' in action. They might also be considered 'in between' because they are both classical (they enact Greek subjects) and modern. These polymorphs are precisely the opposite of the 'pure' forms favoured by those lovers of 'straight forms and planes.' Ebdòmero recognizes the value of polyvalent representations. And de Chirico may be giving us his alternative to what he views as a restrictive, misguided modernism to be associated with the culturally 'poor.'

Gladiatori

The motif of the 'arrested' is particularly important in the painting 'Gladiatori' (figure 12.1). Were it not for titles, one might be hard pressed in some cases even to define the fighters one sees as gladiators rather than the more undefined combatants of the performance troupe in *Ebdòmero*. In some cases, the accoutrements of the gladiator are clearly present: tridents, leg-armour, helmets, nets. These signs, even though they permit identification of the subject matter, do not explain the artist's choice of it. And de Chirico's gladiator paintings have been a trying mystery to art historians, in part, I would argue, because the motifs of masculinity and combat and their ties to Metaphysical aesthetics have not been fully explored.

Discussion of the motif often begins by describing how de Chirico (along with Ernst, Picabia, Savinio, and Severini) chose to decorate the home of the art dealer Léonce Rosenberg in Paris with the gladiator motif.[4] It then passes quickly to note the strangeness of these visual texts. We read, for example, in the prestigious catalogue of the show *De Chirico: Gli Anni venti*: 'When it appears suddenly in his painting, the theme of gladiators is almost a surprise: all thematics have a probable beginning in the Metaphysical or Romantic epoch [of his work]: this theme is born from a disturbed mind' (154).[5] The author cites possible sources from Salomon Reinach's 'repertoire' of classical sculptural motifs but declares the paintings an 'enigma' (*De Chirico: Gli Anni venti* 154). Authors of another important exhibition catalogue, *On Classic Ground*, detected no madness but simply asserted in all honesty: 'It is not known why de Chirico became interested in the subject of gladiators, but inevitably it carried connotations of the classical world' (Cowling and Mundy 84). Italian and European critics generally have laboured over the years to uncover pertinent iconographic genealogies, noting, for example, echoes of a late imperial frieze style and a certain kinship with the 'immobility' found in Piero della Francesca. Some scholars delved specifically into the theme of combat and war, interpreting the paintings as a meditation on the drama of life and death or documenting how de Chirico drew in his paintings from epic themes in literary sources – Domenico Guzzi's volume *Arma virumque cano* is notable here. It is as though de Chirico's citing of classical subjects led his interpreters to expect classical narratives, but the expectation is amply disappointed.

When the politics of representation are invoked, the critical discourse which developed in the decades after the gladiator paintings were done quickly becomes more profound. Robert Motherwell, known for his support of the Spanish Republic and his opposition to Fascism, boldly politicized the gladiatorial motif, linking it to useless classical paraphernalia and collusion with Fascist programs that promoted virile violence. Charmion von Wiegand, writing in *New Masses*, felt instead that the classical motif in de Chirico was 'related to the façade of classicism with which fascism masks its naked brutality and intellectual bankruptcy.'[6] In her view, de Chirico's work holds up a mirror to Fascist degeneracy and is not at all in sympathy with Fascist discourse. In yet another view, the gladiators might signal the welcome end of ideology altogether, appearing, as Waldemar George felt, as 'paltry actors who have ceased to believe in the role that they interpret.'[7] Thus they might be seen to disavow *all values*. Recently, Emily Braun has emphasized the parodic quality of de Chirico's work in the twenties in the important catalogue entitled *De Chirico in America*. In it we find Ellen Adams's opinion that the gladiator paintings can best be understood as a *parody* of the Fascist cult of virility.[8] In this view the grotesque, deformed bodies which appear in the gladiator paintings (noted originally by George) would be intended to debunk classical ideals of male perfection and beauty as the sign of a superior order and power. Furthermore, a less-than-martial masculinity would serve as a correction of Fascist masculinity myths and possibly as evidence of de Chirico's 'notably ambiguous' sexual identity, as Braun has noted (20–1). As ever in parodies, although a critique is evident, the parodist's preferred alternative is less obvious.

Braun's views go a long way in helping us to distinguish de Chirico's own positions from those of his contemporaries. Yet they might be expanded in order to understand not only what the artist wanted to reject but also what he wanted to propose. I would argue, maintaining an emphasis on the politics of representation, that de Chirico does propose something. By representing and troping the male body in a particular way he actively revises the epic and redefines the agency of men in his gladiator paintings.

In the case of de Chirico's gladiators, we must note, taking a cue from gender and narrative theory, the specific divergence between gladitorial and epic combat as forms of cultural signification. With gladiators, the outcome of the *agon* is quite different from the outcome of warfare. For the lone combatant, the stakes in the battle may be the same, life or death. For the collectivity that commissions the combatants, the stakes are quite different. Gains in the arena were never territorial, or exactly national. De Chirico, in selecting this motif, chooses to stage rites of training (rehearsal, practice) and the idea of sacred games over the staging of the triumph and victory of an emperor, king, or state. We know that the earliest gladiatorial games were associated with funerary rites and that later they were linked to social and political displays, the *munus*, and to the generation of collective values

such as bodily courage and the justice of punishment.[9] The gladiatorial combat therefore entailed a social function that did not coincide
with a martial one.

The gladiatorial combat in de Chirico represents male prowess quite
differently from war narratives.[10] And it is significant specifically that
Italian paintings and sculptures of male combat have gravitated over
the centuries away from the Roman *topos* of gladiatorial combat,
favouring instead the battles portrayed on Roman triumphal arches
and columns, such as Trajan's column, and themes such as the defeat
of the Dacians and the destruction of Jerusalem. De Chirico's compositions recall Pollaiuolo's famous battle scenes, yet one cannot readily
cite any specific allusion to gladiators per se in the art historical tradition. Even the Fascists, so drawn to masculine prowess, would not
touch the subject of gladiators. And it is not terribly surprising that
Italians have not been keen on recalling their 'pagan' roots in this case.
De Chirico dared instead to show the Roman arena in a fresco painted
in Milan in 1933 in honour of the Fifth Triennium of Fascism, which
had as its subject 'Italian culture.' What kind of Italianicity might de
Chirico suggest? What revisions to beliefs about Italy's supposed roots
in classical culture?

As in *Ebdòmero*, the gladiator motif undermines traditional representations through a series of displacements. The painting 'Gladiatori'
(figure 12.1) like the prose text, removes combat from the fighting
arena and places it in a room or a theatrical set. De Chirico virtually
banishes in this way the horror of death and the gloating of one victor
or victorious side. If the combatants are in a strange room, they must
be 'playing' at gladiators. Absent are tragic salutations to the emperor
which would build drama ('morituri te salutant! [we who are about to
die salute you!]' And there is none of the melodrama of sacrifice that
will characterize many cinematic treatments of gladiators.[11]

To undercut the climactic, tragic moments and moralities attached
to them, de Chirico has also chosen uncannily humdrum scenes from
gladitorial life. In 'Gladiatori,' the men wield weapons but their poses
are non-belligerent. The still poses highlight the lack of movement, the
'frozen' quality. This deferral of action contrasts not only epic action
but a 'moving' modernism we associate with Futurism and Cubism.
Citing Greenberg's view that 'the avant-garde moves, while
Alexandrianism stands still,' Emily Braun has noted how 'De Chirico
deliberately rejected the modernist drive to "supersede" in favor of a
postmodernist "deepening" that arrests time in a continuous back-

Figure 12.1: Giorgio de Chirico, *Gladiatori* [Gladiators]

and-forth of associations, citations, and repetitions' (18).[12] Again, victory and defeat are displaced. In de Chirico, tellingly, there are no 'sides,' only the accumulation of men and their maleness to focus our attention on a revised 'collectivity,' on the 'many-colored block' Ebdòmero came to understand. The presence in 'Gladiatori' of many male bodies in a single cohort is crucial because it erases the agency of single men. Gladiators in veritable pile-ups, or the 'block,' are a frequent motif, as for instance in 'La vittoria [the victory]' (figure 12.2).

As part of a pointed revision of masculinity as the gendered signifier of a revised aesthetic, de Chirico also uses representations of male muscularity to suggest the power of the polymorphic. Muscularity appears on canvas as a vast series of lights and darks, of bulges and valleys of flesh, which pattern the surface of the painting across the combatants' bodies. Separate, well-defined male bodies almost disappear as muscular limbs and trunks mingle in a continuous cohort.

Figure 12.2: Giorgio de Chirico, *La Vittoria* [The Victory], 1928

Tints also expand uniformly across the bodies. Endless muscles appear almost as an expanse of folds, not of drapery but of flesh, which can hardly be differentiated from the folds of the loincloths.

Observers have read the signifieds one might associate with the trope of muscularity here in profoundly different ways. Adams, in a commentary on the painting 'Gladiators and Lion' in *De Chirico in America*, associates these gladiators' bodies with impotence, stating that 'de Chirico's fighters have pasty, almost jelly-like bodies, paunchy stomachs, and decidedly flaccid physiques' (Braun 219). This representation constitutes, according to the author, an anti-Fascist move since it negates any cultural power that might accrue from 'dressing up' as Augustans. Romanity is emptied of prowess when its 'muscle' is deflated. Accordingly, the author calls de Chirico's combatants 'apathetic' (219). To view one's own cultural tradition as weakened and impotent is also to relinquish one's own position of cultural power. But what if these flabby muscle men signal a different kind of power?

If the value of combat is seen to have been emptied out in the gladiator paintings, as Adams seems to assert, then the *production* of values is obscured by what appears as nihilism, negativity, and self-detraction. De Chirico's gladiators may very well be the antithesis of any ideal 'Greek' athletic, singular male body, and of most Renaissance sculptural and painted depictions of the male body. Yet de Chirico labours in his treatment of gladiators to represent a kind of male heroism based on preparedness and precaution rather than action. The 'inaction' hero does not require brute strength. The *different* bodily 'muscularity' can be seen to *produce* cultural values and not merely to reject Fascist ones. De Chirico's representations of male combat produce value for a powerful non-singularity, for a potent indetermination linked to a bountiful, diverse accumulation. They are a metaphor for multiplicity that only certain cultures possess by virtue of their longevity and their 'long view.'

This non-singularity/accumulation appears not only in the contiguous, interlocking, male bodies in the painting I have just described, but also in many other 'heap' compositions, such as 'Combattimento di gladiatori nella stanza [Combat of gladiators in the room]' and 'La scuola di gladiatori [Gladiator school].' In them de Chirico adopts still other compositional strategies for subtracting agency from the singular male body. For example, he frequently chooses only partial, dramatically incomplete views of male bodies. Half-portraits and odd, three-quarter-length views are common. 'Gladiatori nella stanza [Gladiators in a room]' illustrates another typical composition in which de Chirico places one gladiator with his back to us while another is viewed frontally (figure 12.3). Although it is a painterly convention, this choice emphasizes the notion that each gladiator's body is a perfect half and therefore decidedly unwhole.

Focus on the partial foregrounds how each body is only an element of a larger cohort, where strength and power are to be located. The power of these figures derives in part from the placing of large, over-sized bodies right at the front of the picture plane in a room that recedes into smallness.[13] The particular configuration and positioning of bodies appears in verbal form in *Ebdòmero* in yet another passage evoking a multiplicitous group of men, here called 'many-headed:'

> Ancora una volta i razzi silenziosi salirono laggiù nella grande notte oscura, gruppi compatti di filosofi e di guerrieri, veri blocchi policefali dai colori teneri e brillanti, tenevano conciliaboli misteriosi negli angoli della camera, sotto il soffitto basso, là ove la cornice che unisce le pareti al soffitto formava un angolo retto. (*Ebdòmero* 67)

> [Once again the flares rose silently in the distance into the great, dark night; compact groups of philosophers and warriors, like polycephalic blocks in soft, luminous colors, hold mysterious secret meetings in corners of the low-ceilinged rooms.] (*Hebdomeros* 62)

Missing in the paintings, as here, are the ordered ranks of an army and the deployment of bodies in military 'divisions.' What we see is hardly a fighting formation. The group of men is not formed into the 'fascistic' ranks made so visible and spectacular in Mussolini's regime. Yet it is a group and it is powerful.

The Cultural Spoils: 'Trofeo'

Having established the value de Chirico arrogates to gladiators as signs of the polymorphic, I would like to comment on the section of *Ebdòmero* that depicted a city of trophy-builders and to examine a series of paintings of trophies. We usually think of 'trophies' as signs of achievement. Etymologically, however, 'trophy' has a more precise meaning – the heap of captured arms and booty a victor places on a battlefield as a memorial. Figuratively, a trophy is therefore a sign of a glorious past worthy of respect. Tellingly, this root meaning is also

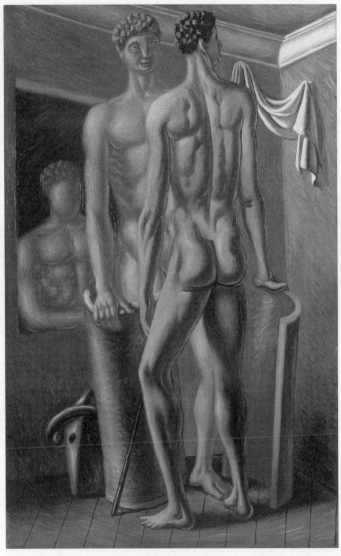

Figure 12.3: Giorgio de Chirico, *Gladiatori nella stanza* [Gladiators in the Room]. 1928–9

Figure 12.4: Giorgio de Chirico, *Gladiatori-trofeo* [Gladiators-Trophy]. 1930

used by de Chirico to articulate his discourse of accumulation (the heap) through the trophy series, begun in 1926. One of these paintings was destined to decorate Léonce Rosenberg's home in Paris. Another, 'Gladiatori-trofeo [Gladiator-trophy]' (1930), presents fighters quite literally as a tall pile of limbs, shields, heads, weapons, and drapery (figure 12.4). These unusual compositions are a clue to the significance in de Chirico's visual and literary texts of the amassification of objects and beings.

The passage quoted below, taken from *Ebdòmero*, foregrounds the importance of the semantic element 'wealth' in de Chirico's discourse. Wealth is obviously something which grants power on the basis of accumulation. While de Chirico pointedly avoided representing individual agency or epic subjectivity in the paintings at hand, he called into existence a surreptitious 'subject' of wealth, a presumptive owner of the cultural wealth the Metaphysical School makes it its business to represent in so many paintings, from the piazzas series to the 'metaphysical interiors,' with their enigmatic towers of things. The significant impersonal pronoun ('we' and 'our' in English translation), while unutterable in the visual text, appears in this long and crucial passage of *Ebdòmero*, where the title character speaks precisely on the subject of a cultural wealth that belongs to 'our' civilization:

A poco a poco, con l'età e l'esperienza, la disciplina, il sapere ed il mestiere predominano sull'istinto; si piglia un fare da chirurgo di gran classe, si diventa nel tempo stesso fine e potente; vi è una certa lentezza apparente in ciò che si fa, specialmente se si pensa alla foga della gioventù; ma dietro a questa lentezza, a pacchi, a serie, le creazioni si ammucchiano le une sulle altre; formano capitali formidabili, fondi di riserva inauditi; ci si costruisce punti d'appoggio d'una solidità a tutta prova; si apre un credito illimitato a quelli che danno le garanzie richieste; si fanno circolare a traverso il vasto mondo le proprie creazioni-capitali; si mandano persino assai lontano, in quei paesi ancora mal esplorati ove la nostra millenaria civiltà non ha ancora che ben debolmente imposto i suoi sigilli e i suoi stampini; perciò io vi dico, amici miei: metodizzatevi, non sprecate le vostre forze [...] tanto più che voi tutti siete allenati da lungo tempo al giuoco difficile del rovesciamento del tempo ed a girar l'angolo del vostro sguardo; [...] voi che in fondo credete ancora meno allo spazio che al tempo, voi speraste sempre in questa marcia cadenzata che trascina in avanti le grandi razze umane, marcia alla quale nulla può opporsi. (*Ebdòmero* 48–9)

[At the beginning, we founder about and get dirty as we work, we spatter the walls around us, we get our things into a mess, crumpled papers and grimy rags bestrew the floor. [...] Then gradually with age and experience, discipline, knowledge and skill prevail over instinct; we begin to have the air of top-flight surgeons, we become at once subtle and forceful; a certain slow deliberation can be seen in everything we do, particularly if one thinks of the ardor of youth; but behind this slowness, in batches, in series, creations pile up one on top of the other, they form an impressive capital, unheard-of reserves; we build supports of a solidity to withstand all tests; we grant unlimited credit to those furnishing the requisite guarantee; we circulate throughout the wide world creations from our stock; we even send them far away to those still little explored lands which our millenary civilization has as yet but faintly marked with its seal and trademarks; this is why I say to you, my friends: be methodical, don't waste your strength [...] particularly as you all have long been involved in the difficult game of reversing time and switching your angle of vision; [...] you have always had faith in the rhythmical march which carried forward the great human races, a march which nothing can resist.] (*Hebdomeros* 42–3)

Who is the subject of 'our millenary civilization' and the owner of these copious potential cultural exports? What culture marches ahead while overturning time?[14] Only the most aged, veteran cultures possess the history which generates the diversity and accumulation necessary to the manufacturing of 'trophies.' These heaps of diverse elements from many eras supplant that untrustworthy space/time of current metaphysics (untrustworthy to those 'who at heart believe even less in space than in time'). What is suggested is a temporality that is produced by representations, and these circulate. De Chirico also theorizes a paradoxical cultural 'race,' a potent, dominant collectivity which circulates its culture through the 'wide world' in a virtual act of colonization. Oddly, this imperialist movement occurs without resort to war and its mode of conquest. What works is 'gradual,' 'slowness,' 'heaping,' the 'march' over the battle.

What 'we' are we reading about here? The 'Manuscript from the collection of Paul Eluard,' a collection of de Chirico's prose pieces which deal primarily with aesthetics, depicts a trip to Rome that dramatically influenced de Chirico's work and his concept of a collectivity:

[A]près avoir lu les ouvrages de Frédéric Nietzsche, je m'aperçus qu'il y a une foule de choses étranges, inconnues, solitaires, qui peuvent être traduites en peintures. [...] Je compris alors certaines sensations vagues que je ne m'expliquais pas avant. Le language qu'ont quelquefois les choses en ce monde; les saisons de l'année et les heures du jour. Les époques de l'histoire aussi. – La préhistoire, les révolutions de la pensée à travers les âges [...], les temps modernes, tout me parut plus étrange et plus lontain. (*Il meccanismo* 17)

[After having read the works of Friedrich Nietzsche, I became aware that there is a host of strange, unknown, solitary things which can be translated into painting. [...] Then I understood certain vague sensations which I had previously been unable to explain. The language that the things of this world sometimes speak; the seasons of the year and the hours of the day. The epochs of history too: pre-history, and the revolutions in thought throughout the ages, modern times: all appeared strange and distant.] (*Hebdomeros* 185)

De Chirico visits Rome, reads Nietzsche, and notices that time is inscribed in the material world in concrete representations that 'speak' as though the physical world were a 'language.' Their messages become the artist's inspiration, as de Chirico 'discovers' the perfect subject for art in the Italian landscape: here Rome, its creations, its artistic capital. The power of a culturally wealthy 'world' appears a few sentences ahead:

Se représenter tout dans le monde comme des énigmes, [...] comprendre l'énigme de certaines choses qui sont considérées en général comme insignifiantes. Sentir le mystère de certains phénomènes des sentiments, des caractères d'un peuple, arriver au point de se figurer même les génies créateurs comme des choses, des choses fort curieuses que nous retournons de tous les côtés. Vivre dans le monde comme dans un immense musée d'étrangété, plein de jouets curieux, bariolés, qui changent d'aspect. [...] Le lien invisible qui unit un peuple avec ses créations. (*Il meccanismo* 17–18)

[One must picture everything in the world as an enigma [...] understand the enigma of things generally considered insignificant. To perceive the mystery of certain phenomena of feeling, of the character of a people, even to arrive at the point where one can picture the creative geniuses of the past as things, very strange things that we examine from all sides. To live in the world as if in an immense museum of strangeness, full of curious many-colored toys which change their appearance. [...] The invisible tie that joins a people to its creations.] (*Hebdomeros* 186)

Here 'enigma' is clearly linked to certain 'peoples.' Do not modern Italians become the 'we' which possesses the cultural wealth necessary to artistic production? We must remember that just what the 'New Italians' might be is still a significant question in the nineteen-twenties; the *Risorgimento*, the national unification movement, continued to play a great role in the cultural imaginary of the nation and in de Chirico's own paintings. The gladiatorial motif, so crucial to the representation of that cultural capital, is therefore connatural with defining a political entity, and a collective identity for Italy. I have quoted at some length above in order to highlight the key words related to that paradoxical national entity: 'a people,' the 'creations of a people,' the 'character of a people.' A people need not be defined by a land or a birthright; what they have is simply culture in all of its being there. The 'accumulation' and 'inaction' I have uncovered as ideologemes in de Chirico are in no way innocent. Metaphysical texts, visual and literary, display their symbolic wealth in a highly ideological way.

De Chirico believed that all of Europe had their eyes on his art, and he may have been right.[15] Influential critics have dubbed him the precursor of a postmodern aesthetic, and Italy's artistic past bequeathed him the materials for a new kind of national identity based on the trope of accumulation. Linda Hutcheon has noted that 'postmodernist texts are [...] specifically parodic in their intertextual relation to the traditions and conventions of the genres involved' (251). If 'parody' is based on the summing of several traditions and therefore on the 'accumulation' trope, then postmodern texts might also be seen to build identities of a certain kind. If they typically display their cultural superiority, they may produce a cultural self-definition based on the assumption that European modern culture has no reason and no necessity either to assert or to defend itself. The victory has already occurred, and it can be evoked endlessly.

Cumulative and hybrid textualities are not necessarily transgressive and progressive because they break down received categorizations of masculinity or cultural agency. In the process of grappling with the problem of the directions of twentieth-century culture, de Chirico laboured to imagine and define a counter-modernity. The motivations for the type of text he produces cannot be seen to be singular. On the one hand, modernity and modernism can be challenged by texts that favour the 'long view' and its powerful, polymorphic conglomerates of representations. Yet on the other hand, a dominant cultural identity can be forged that asserts the superiority of one national identity – the Italian one – over others precisely for its modernity. Challenge to and the conservation of traditions come together. De Chirico's legacy may be fruitfully addressed in those terms.

NOTES

1 Pia Vivarelli discusses de Chirico's 'classicism' as 'filtered through the tradition of Humanism and the Renaissance in such a way that nationalism increases.' 'Classicisme et arts plastiques en Italie entre les deux guerres,' in the catalogue of Les Realismes 1919–1939, Centre Pompidou 1980–81 (Rubin 66–8). Vivarelli characterizes de Chirico's work as a 'dialogue' with the classics marked by distance and 'dépaysement.' Yet, at the same time, the self becomes an aesthetic formation, since 'ego pictor classicus [I, classical painter]' in the famous phrase of the painter.

2 A useful analysis of patriotism and aesthetics is found in Kenneth Silver's Esprit de Corps, especially the discussions on Jean Cocteau and Guillaume Apollinaire, two figures with close ties to de Chirico and Savinio.

3 Duchamp also noted how the joining of disparate things into impossibility, but within a 'traditional perspective,' was a trait de Chirico passed onto the Surrealists and which also constituted an anti-abstract gesture. Cited in Fioravanti (263).

4 See Derouet (111–12).

5 'Quando appare alla ribalta nella sua pittura il tema dei gladiatori è quasi una sorpresa: ogni tematica ha un probabile inizio in epoca metafisica o romantica: questa nasce da un cervello esaltato.'

6 Motherwell and von Wiegand are both cited by Jennifer Landes (Braun 40–1).

7 De Chirico in America outlines Waldemar George's commentaries on this period (here 219), but see also the essay by Karen Kundig, 'Giorgio de Chirico, Surrealism, and Neoromanticism' (Braun 106).

8 See Emily Braun's essay, 'Introduction: A New View of de Chirico,' in De Chirico in America, (14), for a general view of parody in de Chirico and p. 219 for a specific commentary by Ellen Adams on gladiators as parodic.

9 See Brown.

10 For the debate on reading the male body, and especially the penis/ phallus, in the context of the social generation of authority and negotiating conflict see the essay by Norman Bryson, 'Géricault and "Masculinity",' and Ernst Van Alphen's response to it, 'Strategies of Identification.'

These essays concentrate on sexual members, while I will be more concerned with the trope of muscularity.

11 See Maria Wyke's *Projecting the Past* for an account of highly symbolic transformations of the gladiator's body as an emblem of the 'body politic' in cinema, esp. pp. 34–72 on various Spartacus films.

12 Braun also finds that de Chirico chooses periods of 'feminine excesses,' such as the Baroque, and Kitsch, to evoke in countering 'hard-edged' male modernism. For an analysis of de Chirico's 'critique of modernity' see also Jean Clair, 'Dans la terreur de l'Histoire.'

13 Thanks to Kathleen Corrigan of Dartmouth College for a bibliography on gladiators and insights into the significance of de Chirico's compositional choices. Thanks also to Adrian Randolph, also of Dartmouth College, for advice on the subject of masculinity in current art historical debates.

14 Hal Foster has linked the 'revision of time' to 'the deferred action of primal fantasy' in his de Chirico chapter, 'Convulsive Identity,' in *Convulsive Beauty* (61). Foster finds that 'petrification' in de Chirico should not be linked to 'nostalgia' for Italy, which critics have overemphasized, but to an aesthetics which founds itself on tropes of sexual trauma and therefore the uncanny. I am looking at de Chirico's use of tradition not as 'nostalgia' but as cultural legitimization.

15 See 'Autopresentazione,' *Il meccanismo del pensiero* (76–7).

WORKS CITED

Braun, Emily, ed. *De Chirico in America*. Exh. cat. New York: Hunter College of the City University of New York, 1996.

Brown, Shelby. 'Death as Decoration: Scenes from the Arena on Roman Domestic Mosaics.' *Pornography and Representation in Greece and Rome*. Ed. Amy Richlin. New York and Oxford: Oxford UP, 1992. 180–211.

Bryson, Norman. 'Géricault and "Masculinity".' *Visual Culture: Images and Interpretation*. Ed. Bryson, Michael Ann Holly, and Keith Moxey. Hanover and London: Wesleyan UP, 1994. 228–71.

Clair, Jean. 'Dans la terreur de l'Histoire.' *Giorgio de Chirico*. Ed. William Rubin and Wieland Schmied. Exh. cat. Paris: Centre Georges Pompidou, 1983.

Cowling, Elizabeth, and Jennifer Mundy, eds. *On Classic Ground: Picasso, Léger, de Chirico and the New Classicism 1910–1930*. Exh. cat. London: Tate Gallery, 1990.

De Chirico, Giorgio. *Ebdòmero*. Genoa: Il melangolo, 1990.
– *Hebdomeros, with Monsieur Dudron's Adventure and other Metaphysical Writings*. Trans. John Ashbury et al. of *Hébdomeros: le peintre et son génie chez écrivain*, 1929. Cambridge: Exact Change, 1992.
– *Il meccanismo del pensiero: critica, polemica, autobiografia 1911–1943*. Ed. Maurizio Fagiolo. Turin: Einaudi, 1985.
– *Ricordi di Roma: 1918–1925*. Rome: Cultura Moderna, 1945.
Derouet, Christian. 'Un problème du Baroque italien tardif à Paris.' *Giorgio de Chirico*. Ed. William Rubin, Wieland Schmied, and Jean Clair. Exh. cat. Paris: Centre Georges Pompidou, 1983.
Fioravanti, Fiora. 'De Chirico: Bibliografia di un decennio.' *De Chirico: gli anni Venti*. Ed. Massimo and Massimo Simonetti Di Carlo. Exh. cat. Milan, Palazzo Reale. Milan: Mazzotta, 1987.
Foster, Hal. *Convulsive Beauty*. Cambridge: MIT P, 1993.
Guzzi, Domenico. *Arma virumque cano: Giorgio de Chirico, il mito classico dell'eroe guerriero*. Exh. cat. Montecatini Terme. Rome: Leonardo Arte, 1989.
Hutcheon, Linda. 'Beginning to Theorize Postmodernism.' *A Postmodern Reader*. Ed. Joseph Natoli and L. Hutcheon. Albany: State U of New York P, 1993. 243–72.
Rubin, William, Wieland Schmied, and Jean Clair, eds. *Les Realismes: entre révolution et réaction 1919–1939*. Exh. cat. Paris: Centre Georges Pompidou, 1982.
Silver, Kenneth. *Esprit de Corps: The Art of the Parisian Avant-garde and the First World War, 1914–1925*. Princeton: Princeton UP, 1989.
Van Alphen, Ernst. 'Strategies of Identification.' Ed. Bryson, Michael Ann Holly, and Keith Moxey. *Visual Culture: Images and Interpretation*. Hanover and London: Wesleyan UP, 1994. 228–71.
Wyke, Maria. *Projecting the Past: Ancient Rome, Cinema and History*. London: Routledge, 1997.

13 Gender, Identity, and the Return to Order in the Early Works of Paola Masino

ALLISON A. COOPER

What happens to literary writing and intellectual reflection in Italy when, in the wake of the modernist epistemological and metaphysical crisis in Europe, the external universe increasingly appears to be a subjective and unstable concept? When the objective reality of time and space and even identity seem to collapse? What happens when philosophy, traditionally dedicated to the examination of ideas like truth, existence, history, and reality, determines these to be nothing other than mythic constructs? Where – in a vacuum not convincingly filled by either science or religion – can one turn for a semblance of truth and order?

These questions, central to the literary and artistic movements of Italy's post–First World War 'return to order,' emerged out of the turbulent historical moments and cultural developments of early twentieth-century Europe – a growing crisis of consciousness stimulated by the writings of such thinkers as Nietzsche, Bergson, and Freud, the rise of Italian Futurism and the French avant-gardes, and the 'Great War' itself. The increasingly subjective nature of modern experience, for example, was a theme of the plays and narratives of Luigi Pirandello and Italo Svevo, who explored with irony the notion of a fixed and knowable self in works such as *Enrico IV* [Henry IV] (1922) and *La coscienza di Zeno* [Zeno's Conscience] (1923). The Futurist avant-garde, which sought to liberate Italy from its past through new and experimental art forms, introduced radical and fluid notions of time and space through its various aesthetics, substituting previously distinct metaphysical categories of subject and object with the destabilizing Bergsonian notions of flux and interpenetration. Finally, the First World War, with its unprecedented horrors and disappointing outcome, stripped many of their faith in religion, country, technology, and even, as suggested in the wartime poetry of Giuseppe Ungaretti, of faith in the ability of language to correspond to and communicate experience. Caught somewhere between the intense subjectivism of the thinkers and movements described above and the post-war search for a new objectivity, modernist women authors like Paola Masino and Anna Maria Ortese countered their contemporaries' efforts to construct a stronger metaphysic with literary innovations designed to draw attention to psychological and spiritual realities. This essay focuses in particular on Paola Masino's early work to demonstrate how it reacts to and critiques the post-war search for epistemological 'certainties' and the very notion of a return to order and tradition.

Slowly taking shape during the war and then gaining momentum in the volatile period that followed it, Italy's 'return to order' was comprised of diverse movements linked by a common desire to correct the metaphysical and epistemological instabilities produced by the historical moments and cultural developments of the previous thirty years. Frequently, this project had less-than-subtle political overtones, as for example in the case of Margherita Sarfatti's *Novecento* movement, which attempted to combine traditional and modern pictorial elements to create an art representative of a new, Fascist Italy. While the desire to recover the artistic patrimony that Futurist painters had once polemically denounced as 'tarlato, sudicio [moth-eaten, dirty]'[1] and 'corroso dal tempo [corroded by time]' ('Manifesto dei pittori futuristi' 23) often translated into art that lent itself to the politicized search for *italianità* [Italianicity], in some cases it also evolved into a more philosophical exploration of the metaphysical relationship between subject and object, as in the art of Giorgio de Chirico and others involved with the so-called *scuola metafisica* [Metaphysical School] and the journal *Valori Plastici* [Plastic Values] (1918–22). For these, recourse to the kinds of traditional forms rejected by the avant-garde constituted only one aspect of a sophisticated investigation into the relationship between the modern individual and the external world – the world of objects, materials, and discernible forms.[2]

As Italy's post-war return to order found graphic illustration in the visual arts, important literary figures of the period were also drawn to the idea of recuperating the past. This interest led to the creation of several publications of a collaborative nature in which artists and writers contributed with an equal sense of urgency to debates regarding the relationship between the past and the present. Among these were journals such as *La Ronda* [The Patrol] (1919–23) and *900* (1926–29). The former, published by a group of intellectuals headed by former *La Voce* [The Voice] contributor Vincenzo Cardarelli, supported a return to the classical forms of the past as a means of expressing modern ideas.[3] In contrast to the avant-garde of the pre-war period, which had sought to effect socio-political change through art, *La Ronda*'s writers proposed a renewed separation of society and politics on the one hand, and art on the other. But where the *rondisti* advocated hermetic art and literature that reflected Italy's illustrious past, those who contributed to *900* promoted art forms that continued to depart from tradition – forms often of non-Italian origin. Founded by Curzio Malaparte and Massimo Bontempelli, *900* sought to renew Italian culture through the introduction of fresh and innovative writers and movements, and its international contributors included Anglophone writers like James Joyce and members of the Surrealist, Dada, and Expressionist movements.

For Bontempelli, who assumed sole control of *900* after Malaparte's departure in 1927, the notion of a return to order was closely tied to what he considered the profoundly incapacitating 'malattie spirituali [spiritual illnesses]' of the nineteenth and early twentieth centuries. Aestheticism, Impressionism, Idealism, Freudian psychology, and the democratic spirit were, in his opinion, different symptoms of a 'paurosa decadenza [dreadful decadence]' that prized appearance over substance, intuition over perception, the unconscious over the conscious and finally, individual or collective interests over greater laws or truths (*L'avventura novecentista* 26–7). Bontempelli suggested that this frightening decadence, by causing the individual to retreat ever further from the material world into his or her own self, had brought about the destruction of the natural and reassuring boundaries of time and space. 'L'orgia metafisica dell'Io,' he wrote in 1928, 'come misura unica del mondo, prima, poi come unica verità, portava fatalmente l'individuo a non credere più nemmeno a se stesso, cioè spingeva l'umanità al suicidio morale [The metaphysical orgy of the self as the only measure of the world, first, and then as the only truth, inevitably led the individual to no longer believe even in himself, that is it pushed humanity to moral suicide]' (27). Thus the return to order proposed by Bontempelli was one that had as its primary task the reconstruction of time and space – a task he theorized would subsequently lead to 'il ritrovamento dell'individuo [the recovery of the individual],' and presumably also to greater cultural stability (9).

At the heart of the *900* project was an artistic practice that Bontempelli identified as *realismo magico* [magic realism], which proposed the magical interpretation of everyday human experience and familiar objects as a means of reaffirming the relationship between the individual and the external world. 'Questo è puro "novecentismo",' he wrote in 1927, 'che rifiuta così la realtà per la realtà come la fantasia per la fantasia, e vive nel senso magico scoperto nella vita quotidiana degli uomini e delle cose [This is pure *novecentismo*, that rejects reality for the sake of reality just as it does fantasy for the sake of fantasy, and lives in the magical sense discovered in the everyday life of men and things]' (22).[4] Bontempelli cited the art of the Quattrocento as an example of *realismo magico*, for its evocation of the tension between the material world (as depicted through precisely rendered everyday objects) and an implied world beyond the merely physical (21). The appeal of such artists as Masaccio, Mantegna, and Piero della Francesca for Bontempelli lay in their ability to create a suggestive atmosphere through the representation of the quotidian. In drawing analogies between his own project and the art of Italy's past, Bontempelli was not suggesting that the return to order be predicated upon a return to any particular tradition (Italian or otherwise), but rather upon a renewed artistic effort to evoke a mysterious reality beyond our own, a reality he felt had been destroyed by the various forms of decadence described above, and which philosophical inquiry, spent with the idealism of the early twentieth century, could no longer address (28).

900 became an important vehicle for news and illustrations of literary and artistic innovation throughout Europe, many of which developed out of a growing interest in the same inward turn of consciousness described by Bontempelli in the early issues of the journal. In its first volume (published in the autumn of 1926) the journal featured a broad selection of works from authors such as Joyce, the Spanish avant-gardiste Ramón Gomez de la Serna, and the German Expressionist playwright Georg Kaiser – all of whom also served as members of its editorial board. What linked these authors' diverse contributions – an excerpt from a novel, a phantasmagoric series of images evoked through brief tableaux, and a one-act tragedy – was a common interest in exploring the intersection of modern, chaotic life and individual consciousness.

While many of the authors and artists who contributed to *900* over the course of its three-year lifespan had already established reputations, or were rapidly building them, at least one was a newcomer to the modernist intellectual scene. Paola Masino (1908–1989), whose short story 'Ricostruzione [Reconstruction]' appeared in the journal in 1928, was twenty years old at the time of its publication, making her one of its youngest contributors. Masino's work had never been published before and she was one of only two female writers to have her work included in *900*.[5] Like her fellow *novecentisti*, the Roman writer was interested in exploring the ambiguous relationship between the real and the imaginary. Her work, however, is distinguishable from that of her peers for its innovative presentation of the modernist crisis of consciousness in light of the psychological and socio-political implications of gender.

Creative and intellectually curious, Masino was an ambitious writer who had shown interest at an early age in making original use of the literary medium in order to explore the relationship between gender and society. This appears to be true even of her first work of fiction, a play written in her adolescence entitled *Le tre Marie* [The Three Marias], which reportedly revolved around three women – Maria, Marta, and Maddalena – who were 'variamente innamorate e soggiogate e condizionate' by 'un grand'uomo [variously in love with and subjugated and conditioned by a great man]' (*Io, Massimo e gli altri* 21).[6] Evidence of Masino's early concern with gender, *Le tre Marie* seems to constitute her first investigation of society's enduring attachment to female archetypes and the principal characteristics – love, sacrifice, sexual appeal – that these often embody. With the emblematic names of the play's female protagonists and the description of its single male character as 'un grand'uomo,' Masino linked these archetypes to the Christian, patriarchal society that would become her focus in successive works.

Le tre Marie was never produced, but Masino's youthful determination to stage it brought her into contact for the first time, in 1924, with Luigi Pirandello, a figure who would become an important influence on her subsequent development as a writer.[7] A dramatist of international renown by the early 1920s, Pirandello had brought to life, perhaps more effectively than any other Italian of his generation, the early-twentieth-century preoccupation with the 'inaccessibility of truth.'[8] In his plays of the period, which included *Sei personaggi in cerca d'autore* [Six Characters in Search of an Author] (1921) and the previously mentioned *Enrico IV*, he presented a series of memorable characters caught up in a futile struggle to reconcile reality with appearances. The modern crisis of consciousness that these plays depicted would become an important theme in Masino's work as well, particularly the Pirandellian principle – originally outlined in *Umorismo* [On Humour] (1908) and applied in works such as *Così è (se vi pare)* [So It Is (If You Think So)] (1917) and the novel *Uno, nessuno e centomila* [One, No One and One Hundred Thousand] (1925–26) – of the tragic conflict between our own individually created realities and the realities assigned to us by others, or by society at large. In Masino's fiction the tension between the former and the latter was to be interpreted with special regard to the plight of modern woman who, driven by desire, seeks to create her own reality but is confronted at every turn with society's entrenched and inflexible images of woman.

Pirandello's theory of the constructed and fictitious nature of identity provided Masino with a valuable starting point from which to explore the relationship between women and society, but it was undoubtedly Surrealism that provided inspiration for her unique representation of that relationship. Presented to the public in André Breton's 1924 *Manifeste du surréalisme* [Manifesto of Surrealism], the movement was largely based upon the aesthetic interpretation of Freudian theories, which led it to embrace the disturbing, the fantastic, and the bizarre in its efforts to depict the workings of the subconscious. Masino's realistic depiction of the chaotic inner world of her characters stems from a similar emphasis on dreams and the uncanny, but in her work the desires of the female subconscious are continuously played out against societal mandates of femininity – a situation that transforms her characters' consciousness into a battleground of gendered impulses and sublimations. The psychological and sociopolitical implications of this battle were the subject of both 'Ricostruzione' and Masino's first novel, *Monte Ignoso* [Mount Ignoso] (1931).

In 'Ricostruzione,' the short story of 1928 that signalled the beginning of her writing career, Masino examines the interlaced themes of love, society, and female subjugation that she first explored in *Le tre Marie*, but with a new interest in the role of the conscious as mediator between subjective and material worlds. A melodramatic story about a girl who literally appears to die of heartache after her disapproving parents cause her to sever relations with her lover, its title refers to its temporarily reanimated protagonist's efforts to understand her own death by rebuilding her confused memories of the events leading up to it.[9] Though the story's thematic concerns are common to the work of many of Masino's female predecessors and contemporaries, from

Sibilla Aleramo's *Una donna* [A Woman] (1906) to Alba de Céspedes *Nessuno torna indietro* [There Is No Turning Back] (1938), an examination of the story itself reveals Masino's early rejection of the conventional narrative forms through which these were often presented in favour of the more radical styles of her modernist contemporaries.

The radical transformation of traditional narrative elements such as structure, setting, and tone in 'Ricostruzione' occurs from the story's outset, which begins, for example, where most other stories end: with the death of its central character. 'La giovane morta,' we are told by an anonymous narrator in the opening line, 'si alzò a sedere nella bara e ... guardò la tomba dove l'avevano chiusa [The dead young woman raised herself up to sit in the coffin and ... looked at the tomb in which they had enclosed her]' (77). This matter-of-fact presentation of an otherwise remarkable event, consistent with *realismo magico*'s practice of juxtaposing the real and the fantastic, sets the story in precisely the sort of literary reality-beyond-our-own that Bontempelli promoted in *900* and in his own fiction.[10] The departure from the classic conventions of storytelling – beginning where a story would normally end – is a calculated effort to surprise and confound the story's reader from the start by putting him or her in a position not unlike that of the protagonist, who is equally confused by her abrupt return to life. Masino perpetuates her reader's sense of disorientation through the use of a limited narrative point of view that permits his or her slight understanding of events to grow only apace with the protagonist's, a fact that ultimately causes the reader to share the protagonist's sense of discovery as her memories eventually fall into order to reveal the broader context of her death.

Masino continues to challenge traditional narrative structure with the short story's unusual exposition. By linking the development of its action to its protagonist's fragmented memories of her past, Masino creates a narrative form that mimics the processes of the psyche as it simultaneously moves backwards and forwards in time, progressing towards a denouement only as its protagonist reaches into her past and allows the chaotic flow of her memories to wash over her and rise to the surface of her conscious mind. As the flashes of memory come together and become increasingly intelligible – images likened in the story to 'quadri cinematografici [cinematographic pictures]' (79) – the young woman becomes progressively aware of the circumstances of her death. This literary experimentation with the representation of the processes of the subconscious and conscious calls to mind not just the

work of the modernist authors who were Masino's contemporaries –
Woolf, Joyce, and, in Italy, Italo Svevo – but also that of contemporary
artists like Giorgio de Chirico (with whom Masino was acquainted),
who had made the question of how we perceive the world and our
own experiences the subject of numerous paintings and theoretical
writings.

De Chirico's 1919 *Valori Plastici* article entitled 'Sull'arte metafisica'
is one such work. In it, the painter explores the relationship between
memory, experience, and art, metaphorically presenting memory as
'un rosario continuo di ricordi dei rapporti tra le cose e noi e viceversa
[a continuous series of memories of relations between things and ourselves and vice-versa]' (16). Describing what he believed would take
place if the thread that held memories together – the thread giving
them context and making them useful tools for sorting and organizing
experience – were to break, de Chirico declared that though the material world would not change, our perception of it would, revealing
what he called 'l'aspetto metafisico delle cose [the metaphysical aspect
of things].' '[O]gni cosa,' he wrote, '[ha] due aspetti: uno corrente
quello che vediamo quasi sempre e che vedono gli uomini in generale,
l'altro lo spettrale o metafisico che non possono vedere che rari
individui in momenti di chiaroveggenza o di astrazione metafisica
[Every thing has two aspects: a common one that we almost always
see and that men in general see, the other the spectral or metaphysical
one that only rare individuals can see in moments of clairvoyance or
of metaphysical abstraction]' (16). Metaphysical art, implied de Chirico,
ought to capture or suggest the perceptions of a mind loosened from
the moors of memory in order to reveal the previously unknown aspects of things – a goal that allied it to *realismo magico*, which similarly
attempted to evoke the 'magical' aspects of everyday things and human experience. De Chirico's effort to escape the ordering influence of
memory was also echoed by Breton in the *Manifeste du surréalisme*,
where – revealing the influence not just of de Chirico, but also of
Freud's work on sleep and dreams – he proposed that 'Man, when he
ceases to sleep, is above all at the mercy of his memory [...],' an opinion that led Breton to view 'the waking state' as little more than a
'phenomenon of interference' (12).

Something akin to de Chirico and Breton's rejection of the ordering
function in memory operates in Masino's 'Ricostruzione,' the plot of
which turns on its protagonist's escalating awareness of the circumstances of her death – an awareness made possible by her increasingly

clear memories, which eventually reveal to her and to the reader the subjugation she suffered in life, particularly in her relationship with her parents. Memory slowly discloses that her mother and father 'le avevano insegnato che è meglio la morte che il disonore [had taught her that death is better than dishonour]' (80) – a not-unfamiliar patriarchal axiom evidently invoked to curtail the young woman's sexuality and independence. The extreme consequence of this lesson, we read, is that 'perchè aveva sempre rispettato gli insegnamenti ricevuti [...] ne moriva [because she had always respected the teachings she received [...] she was dying from them]' (80). The protagonist's horrified reaction to the realization that her own feelings had been sacrificed in the name of family honour is compounded by a revelation that the lover for whom she died had never loved her. Eventually, her rage and disgust lead her to choose death a second time, described in the story's closing line as a form of sleep: 'si riadagiò nella bara morbida e, scacciato l'incubo, entrò nel sonno pesante che precede il risveglio [she sank back down into the soft coffin and, having squashed the nightmare, entered into the heavy sleep that precedes waking up]' (81). Yielding to death (metaphorically sleep) once again, Masino's protagonist rejects not only her own memories, but also symbolically the role of the conscious, the external world, and society altogether.

The second, self-imposed death of the protagonist of 'Ricostruzione' metaphorically suggests her spiritual and psychological death – a self-obliteration resulting from extreme self-denial – and indicates Masino's ongoing concern with society's efforts to define and regulate female sexuality. Condemned to suppress her own needs in order to fulfil those of others, Masino's protagonist is depicted as a victim of a patriarchal society that consigns its female members to the roles historically prescribed for them, checking their desires and limiting their self-determination in the process. Pirandello had alluded to the consequences of this predicament in his play *Così è (se vi pare)*, where the mysterious and elusive Signora Ponza finally identifies herself to her inquisitors as both the daughter of Signora Frola and the second wife of Signor Ponza, adding that for herself, however, she is 'nobody' (138). Here and in other works, such as the short story *Candelora* (1917, republished 1928) and the play *Diana e la Tuda* [Diana and Tuda] (1925), Pirandello's female characters – fabricated as they are according to the desires of others – uniquely embody the Sicilian author's theory of the constructed and fictitious self. And while male characters such as Henry IV and Mattia Pascal grapple with the implications of this theory, they do so of their own accord, not because forces set in motion by gender-based distinctions have imposed the struggle upon them. Pirandello's acknowledgment of the affinities between his own notion of the fluid self and modern woman's struggle to free herself from static and binding notions of femininity anticipates and, to a certain extent, enables Masino's modernist representation of woman's fight for self-determination.[11]

Even a brief look at 'Ricostruzione' suggests the wide variety of modernist figures and movements that exerted their influence on the young Masino: Pirandello, Bontempelli's *realismo magico*, de Chirico's *arte metafisica* [Metaphysical art], Surrealism, and stream-of-consciousness writing all appear to have affected Masino's early efforts to develop a style capable of representing the inner turmoil of the modern female subject. Yet despite this plurality of influences, and despite the originality of her work, Masino's creative inquiry has been superficially and often solely identified with Bontempelli's – a surprising fact considering that Masino adopted the techniques of *realismo magico* to depict the isolated and alienated psyches of her characters, a use of the fantastic that linked her work to the very 'orgia metafisica dell'Io' that Bontempelli sought to counter. It is for this reason that Masino's innovative approach to writing should be reconsidered, and viewed perhaps as Lucia Re has suggested, as part of a 'different and unusual experimental register, a modernist realism infused with surrealist and expressionist elements' ('Futurism and Fascism' 203). Masino's stylistic innovations would arguably become the most compelling aspect of *Monte Ignoso*, her critically acclaimed novel of 1931, which offered readers a powerful and disturbing portrayal of one woman's struggle against the oppressive patriarchal structures and female archetypes that conspire to construct, interpret, and crystallize female identity.

The most striking technique that Masino developed in *Monte Ignoso* was one that she had already experimented with in 'Ricostruzione,' and involves the deployment of what Freud had termed the 'uncanny' as a means of accessing and depicting the inner reaches of her protagonist's psyche. The uncanny played an important role in the return to order, in both Bontempelli's *realismo magico* and de Chirico's *pittura metafisica* where, in admittedly simplified terms, the presence of the unnatural or the bizarre was intended to suggest the existence of a reality beyond our own. Freud's exploration of the uncanny, however, focused on its relationship to previously repressed thoughts or traumatic experiences, leading him to argue in 1919 that the uncanny could be generated when 'infantile complexes which have been repressed are once more revived by some impression, or when primitive beliefs which have been surmounted seem once more to be confirmed' ('The Uncanny' 150). Linked in this manner to the workings of the subconscious mind (charged in Freudian psychoanalysis with the safe-keeping of repressed thoughts), the uncanny became one of the most important tools of the Surrealist movement – a fact convincingly demonstrated by Hal Foster in *Compulsive Beauty*, where he describes it as 'a concept that comprehends surrealism,' and links it to the political goals of the avant-garde movement, defining it as 'a concern with events in which repressed material returns in ways that disrupt unitary identity, aesthetic norms, and social order' (xvii).

Many of Freud's works were published (and translated into French, if not into Italian) in the years surrounding the First World War, when Masino was a young girl.[12] However, her close relationship with Bontempelli and *novecentismo* and her interest in Surrealism would have exposed her to at least two (very different) interpretations of Freudian psychology. Though one might be tempted to downplay Masino's receptivity to Freudian theories by invoking her relationship with Bontempelli (who condemned Freudian psychology, claiming that it reduced individuals to what he called 'larve vaganti,' wandering shadows forced to relinquish a stable sense of self), Bontempelli himself, in the pages of *900*, had provided the Surrealists with an Italian forum in which to express their ideas. This fact indicates Bontempelli's willingness to suspend his criticism of Freud in the name of promoting revolutionary forms of literature and art. Thus it is probable that Masino became familiar with the Surrealists and their aestheticized forays into the subconscious as a result of her relationship with Bontempelli, rather than despite it.

This last point is significant, because Masino's recourse to the uncanny in *Monte Ignoso* is best understood in a Surrealist and psychological key; instead of suggesting a reassuring reality beyond our own, the novel's uncanny elements plunge its reader into the psyche of its protagonist – focusing attention once again on the subjective, internal world that Bontempelli had denounced in the pages of *900*. The novel's uncanny effects are owed to a series of seemingly animated paintings of female biblical characters, which Masino uses not only to reveal the

enduring and destructive power of deeply repressed female archetypes, but also to criticize the aesthetics of Italy's return to order and
the nascent Fascist regime's increasingly narrow view of women.

The novel, which describes the dissolution of a family in a dramatic
tale of adultery, madness, and murder, has as its protagonist a woman
named Emma, who is haunted by biblically themed paintings that
hang in a room in her family home (whose *unheimlich* nature is immediately apparent). The uncanny role that these will play in the story is
prefigured in the opening chapter of the book, which utilizes a discon-
certing technique not unlike cinematic slow disclosure to reveal the
various stories that the paintings depict. As a small candle flame slowly
illuminates the surfaces of the paintings, their biblical subjects come to
life and the reader is figuratively (and ironically) 'enlightened' by
their stories, which are described not as the bearers of the moral and
spiritual values of Judaeo-Christian culture, but as tales marked by
perversion, betrayal, lust, violence, and revenge. As the candle illuminates a broader portion of each tableau, its flame frankly reveals, 'senza
misericordia [without mercy],' the actions of those traditionally held
to be the progenitors of Judaeo-Christian culture, from Jacob and Esau
to Joseph and Moses, from Lot and his daughters to Mary and the
infant Jesus.

Like 'Ricostruzione,' which also featured a strategically disconcert-
ing opening, *Monte Ignoso* immediately throws its reader into a state of
confusion. Perplexed by the mysterious and iconoclastic references to
the biblical stories and denied contextual relief by the opening scene's
enigmatic presentation of them, our discomfort anticipates Emma's
eventual reaction to the paintings. This is described shortly after the
first chapter, after the pictures are presented in a more formal manner.
'Tra un armadio e l'altro,' we are told, 'erano appesi quadri immensi
di scene bibliche. Pitture primitive e monotone di nessun valore. Le
persone erano più grandi del vero. Alcune sbiadite, altre fatte nere dal
tempo. Ogni mano sembrava avere sei dita, tutti i piedi erano stortati
[Between one armoire and another were hung immense paintings of
biblical scenes. Primitive and monotonous paintings of no value. The
people were larger than in reality. Some faded, others made black by
time. Every hand seemed to have six fingers, all of the feet were
twisted]' (16). Grotesque, with their colours mottled by time, the paintings become visual metaphors of the monstrous nature of the archetypes that they represent. Passing through the room where they hang,

Emma keeps her eyes fixed ahead, 'come,' we read, 'uno che cammina su un abisso e ha paura delle vertigine [like somebody who walks over an abyss and is afraid of becoming dizzy]' (16).

Before long, the source of Emma's troubled relationship with the paintings is revealed. After discovering a diary in which her parents recounted their sexual activities in minute detail, Emma had apparently learned that the act leading to her own conception was inspired by the violent biblical stories that were presented obliquely in the novel's opening chapter. Standing in front of one of the pictures, Emma relates in an agitated monologue that every evening her father (under the influence, she believes, of the paintings) required her mother to assume the identity of a female biblical character, after which, she continues, 'si mettevano in terra, qui davanti [they lay down on the ground, here in front]' (22), presumably to re-enact the violent sexual acts hinted at in the paintings. In the pages of her parents' journal Emma discovered 'il modo orribile del suo concepimento al quale ... i personaggi dipinti avrebbero presieduto [the horrible means of her conception over which the painted characters would preside]' (35). The knowledge of the connection between the paintings and her own birth led Emma to consider herself 'una emanazione dei quadri misteriosi, una materia in loro potere, non più una vita libera [an emanation of the mysterious paintings, a material in their power, no longer a free life]' (35) – a conviction so powerful that it causes her to interact, through a series of vivid hallucinations, with the characters in the paintings as though they were alive.

Brought to life in this manner, the paintings become a mechanism that permits Masino to evoke her protagonist's inner world. Emma's surreal interaction with the spectral biblical characters, which alternately mock her and sympathize with her reveals her unconscious desire for release from the violent historical figures and events that she believes presided over her birth, and from the stifling and unyielding female archetypes crystallized in the paintings – archetypes that she has internalized to the extreme point of believing them to be integral parts of her biological and spiritual make-up. Through the uncanny animation of biblical characters like Amnon and Tamar and Lot and his daughters, Masino vividly evokes the hold that the history of Judaeo-Christian culture – and its reliance upon female sacrifice in particular – has on her protagonist. Reiterating ideas first presented in 'Ricostruzione,' this dramatic confrontation between modern woman's desire to be self-determining and the immobilizing power of history or tradition also critiques articulations of the return to order that relied heavily upon the latter, such as Carlo Carrà's 1919 painting *Le figlie di Lot* [The Daughters of Lot].

Like de Chirico, Carrà was involved in the development of *pittura metafisica* and was a founding member of the journal *Valori Plastici*. Originally an active contributor to the Futurist avant-garde movement, during the First World War the Piedmontese painter developed an interest in the masters of the Trecento and Quattrocento – particularly Giotto, Piero della Francesca, and Paolo Uccello – eventually publishing several articles in which he praised the formal and transcendental qualities of their works (*On Classic Ground* 56). His growing effort to recover and build upon the artistic innovations of the Renaissance arose out of a desire to add a spiritual dimension to modern painting: a dimension he felt had been ignored by Futurist aesthetics. Attracted to de Chirico's metaphysical compositions, Carrà collaborated with the painter for several months in the spring of 1917. However, as the art historian Emily Braun has pointed out, his continuing emphasis on the primacy of Italian artistic traditions 'aligned the style of plastic values with a nationalist agenda' – a view that distanced his painting from de Chirico's, whose ironic incorporation of a similar iconography constituted a 'radical break with traditional representation' ('Renaissance and Renascences' 39). The two artists continued to work together on *Valori Plastici*, but by 1919 Carrà had moved away from metaphysical iconography in favour of a distinctly archaic, or primitive style (*On Classic Ground* 52).

An important work from Carrà's *Valori Plastici* period, *Le figlie di Lot* (figure 13.1) demonstrates how post–First World War artists engaged in the aestheticization of a biblical past in the name of a return to tradition and order. As its title indicates, the painting's subjects are the daughters of Lot. Believing themselves the sole survivors of the destruction of Sodom and Gomorrah, they were said to have made their father drunk so that they could lay with him and preserve the human race. While they are typically depicted in the act of inebriating their father, Carrà unusually portrays the two young women engaged in a private colloquy.[13] In a scene that seems suspended in time and space, the artist's treatment of the well-known biblical characters evokes the transcendental qualities that he admired most in works of the past. The fact that this painting was reproduced alongside an article Carrà had written on Giotto for *Valori Plastici* is not insignificant, since the fourteenth-century master's influence is particularly noticeable in its

Figure 13.1: Carlo Carrà, *Le figlie di Lot*, 1919. Oil on canvas, 110 x 80. Museum Ludwig, Cologne.

simply defined masses, shallow space, use of light and colour, and stage-like setting. The almost monumental, or heroic quality of Carrà's figures is conveyed by their simple, sculpted forms, the rigidity of their posture and gaze, and even in the ordered folds of their skirts. Their positioning in the extreme foreground of the narrow picture plane intensifies their imposing stature. The unnatural, cerulean blue sky and the suggestion of distant lands just beyond the painting's craggy hills also contribute to its timeless, otherworldly atmosphere. With references to the classical past in the pedestal to the extreme right of the picture plane and in the indistinct rotunda in its background (reminiscent of the one featured in the fifteenth-century *View of an Ideal City*, attributed to Urbino architect Luciano Laurana and painter Piero della Francesca), Carrà also pays homage to his Renaissance predecessors.

The painting's socio-political message, however, is not to be found so much in its formal elements as in its use of symbolism and allegory, which prefigure the charged biblical imagery of *Monte Ignoso* in meaningful ways. Carrà engages his audience at the rhetorical level by means of a serpentine perspective that obliges us to consider several symbols in the work's iconography. Naturally scanning from left to right, the viewer's eye lingers first on the figure of the standing daughter, whose hand rests on her slightly swelling abdomen in a gesture that strongly suggests imminent motherhood. Moving downwards and to the right, the eye falls on the dog, traditionally a symbol of faithfulness, whose presence here serves as a reminder of the responsibility the two women have assumed with their actions (to preserve and continue the species or race), and their devotion to father and family. The posture of the kneeling daughter with her outstretched hand suggests both submission and humility. The pedestal behind her right shoulder bears the pinecone, traditionally a symbol of fertility for people of the Near East, and foretells for her a fate similar to that of her elder sister. These symbols ask the viewer to meditate on the scene, and transform it into an allegory of female obedience, duty, and of sanctified pregnancy.[14] The purity of this allegory is preserved by Carrà's decision to depict the daughters outside of the presence of Lot, seemingly after (or in the case of the younger daughter, possibly just before) the incestuous act has been committed. Unlike customary representations of the story, in which the daughters are depicted as instigators of a forbidden sexual act, Carrà's painting defuses their sexuality by focusing on their maternal roles, visually linking them to the domesticated animal that attends them.

Le figlie di Lot, with its aestheticized depiction of a biblical past in which women were obsessively represented as virgins, mothers, or prostitutes, reveals the sort of problem that Masino confronted as a female author writing in the years of Italy's return to order.[15] By 1930, the year in which *Monte Ignoso* was written, the question of female identity was beginning to assume new socio-political dimensions as the Fascist regime formulated social programs and policies that reinforced the mythologizing, essentialist view of womanhood suggested in Carrà's painting.[16] Masino's animated biblical subjects (who bear an eerie resemblance to the primitive and ill-proportioned figures in *Le figlie di Lot*) challenge not only Carrà's image of woman, but also Fascist efforts to define women solely in terms of their maternal and procreative functions. However indirectly and symbolically, *Monte Ignoso* addresses and critiques the patriarchal foundations of Fascist ideology.

The animation of the otherwise two-dimensional biblical women who are the subjects of the novel's paintings allows Masino to explore the ideological and psychological implications of their existence for modern woman – implications that are repressed in Carrà's static treatment. In a process that seems to have been inspired by early-twentieth-century theories of repression, Masino's protagonist internalizes the symbolic value of the figures, and links that internalization to their traumatizing presence at her conception. She then peoples her house with the disturbing figures, again essentially meeting her psychological processes outside herself.[17] This uncanny phenomenon enables Masino to demonstrate the enduring effects of the historical archetypes on Emma (and, by extension, on modern woman), for as Freud had written in 1913: 'distance is of no importance in thinking – since what lies furthest apart both in time and space can without difficulty be comprehended in a single act of consciousness [...] the world of magic has a telepathic disregard for spatial distance and treats past situations as though they were present' (*Totem and Taboo* 106).

Paola Masino was a proponent of *realismo magico*; however, her unique interpretation of the genre ought to be distinguished from Bontempelli's. As this discussion of *Monte Ignoso* has demonstrated, the 'magic' elements of her early works are above all else a reflection of her interest in incorporating emerging theories of the psyche into her exploration of the psychological and socio-political implications of gender. Seen in this light, the uncanny collapse of time and space in

Monte Ignoso serves to identify a continuum of Judaeo-Christian gender politics whose relevance to modern female experience could only be demonstrated through the intimate and relentless exploration of its protagonist's inner world.

In conclusion, it is worthwhile to recall an American text – now considered a classic – that preceded Masino's early writings by nearly forty years; a short story by Charlotte Perkins Gilman entitled 'The Yellow Wallpaper.' Like *Monte Ignoso*, 'The Yellow Wallpaper' explored female suffering, memory, and madness as its protagonist peopled the walls of the room to which she was confined with the figure of a creeping woman seeking to escape imprisonment in a two-dimensional world. Gilman's compelling psychological drama augured the twentieth century's interest in the alienated self, and related this alienation to female oppression by linking its protagonist's condition to the authoritarian and subordinating voice of her husband, who dismissed her anxiety as a 'temporary nervous depression – a slight hysterical tendency,' telling her that thinking about her condition would only worsen it (639). Masino's work picks up these threads and interweaves them in a dense literary style that reflects the complicating influences of her time and milieu; Freudian psychoanalysis, *realismo magico, arte metafisica*, and Surrealism. In her writing, as in Gilman's, the fantastic is not a means of suggesting the presence of a reassuring external world, it is a means of bringing to light issues of female persecution and oppression, and of relating those issues to the epistemological crisis that played a central role in modern culture.

NOTES

1 Unless otherwise noted, these and subsequent translations are my own.
2 For an overview of Italian culture in the early years of the 'return to order' see Emily Braun's 'Renaissance and Renascences' (21–48).
3 For more on Classicism and politics in post–First World War Italy, see Braun's 'Political Rhetoric and Poetic Irony.'
4 For more on the relationship between magic realism and *novecentismo* in the visual arts and literature of early- twentieth-century Italy, see Maurizio Fagiolo dell'Arco's 'Realismo magico' and Paolo Baldacci's 'Il mito del realismo magico (arte e letteratura).'
5 The other woman writer whose work appeared in the journal was Amelia Della Pergola (writing under the pen name 'Diotima'), who contributed

two short pieces in the winter of 1926 and spring of 1927. Della Pergola and Bontempelli had been married in 1909 but were subsequently separated.

6 Masino discusses *Le tre Marie* in her posthumously published autobiography *Io, Massimo e gli altri*. As noted above, the play was never published, nor does it appear among the letters and works of Masino preserved in the Getty Research Institute's Massimo Bontempelli Papers archive. For this reason I limit my comments on it to that which can be inferred from Masino's mention of it in *Io, Massimo e gli altri*.

7 Introduced to Roman theatre by her father, a civil servant with a passion for literature, drama, and music, it is certain that Masino was highly aware of the work of Pirandello, whose radical dismantling of traditional notions of truth and reality had caused a stir both in Italy and abroad. Her initial, brief visit with the playwright in 1924 (described in *Io, Massimo e gli altri* 21–5) was to be the first of many meetings between the two – a fact that was no doubt due in part to Masino's romantic involvement, from 1927 on, with Bontempelli, Pirandello's colleague and partner in the Teatro d'Arte di Roma in 1924 and 1925.

8 In his *Modernisms: A Literary Guide*, Peter Nicholls presents this notion and its metaphysical consequences as key aspects of modernist writing.

9 The tumultuous love story at the heart of 'Ricostruzione' was almost certainly inspired by contemporary events in Masino's own life. The story of Masino's and Bontempelli's relationship, which lasted until Bontempelli's death in 1960, deserves closer attention than I am able to give it here. Briefly, however, Masino's family disapproved of her relationship with the author, who was thirty years her elder and still married to (though separated from) Amelia Della Pergola. Attempting to avoid a scandal, Masino's parents sent their daughter to Paris in the summer of 1929, where she lived for the better part of a year and a half, working at first for the French magazine *La Nouvelle Europe* [The New Europe], and then as a liaison between Italy's Fascist government and French artists and intellectuals. Despite her parents' objections, Masino spent much of her time in Paris with Bontempelli, and in December 1930 was reunited with him permanently in Milan. These events are documented in the correspondence of Masino and Bontempelli, part of the Massimo Bontempelli Papers, 1865–1990, Getty Research Institute, Research Library, Accession no. 910147, 910147*.

10 Both Masino and Bontempelli may have been influenced by the work of Edgar Allan Poe; see, for example, Poe's short story, 'The Facts in the Case of M. Valdemar' (1845).

11 Masino's adoption of a plot device that features the unsettling resurrection of a central character may also have originated with Pirandello, who
used a similar trope with great success in his one-act play *All'uscita* (1916,
republished 1926).
12 The dissemination of Freud's works and theories in Italy is the subject of
Michel David's study *La psicanalisi nella cultura italiana*. According to
David, Freud's introduction to Italian culture was facilitated by a series of
articles published by Giovanni Papini and Giuseppe Prezzolini in *La Voce*
in 1910. Beyond these, Italians interested in learning more about Freudian
psychoanalysis had to look to the French for treatments and translations
of his ideas, since Italian translations of Freud's texts remained scarce
until after 1945 (248).
13 The subject of Carrà's painting is likely the moment in which the elder of
the two daughters commands her younger sister to sleep with Lot. 'Next
day the elder said to the younger, "Last night I lay with my father. Let us
ply him with wine again tonight; then you go in and lie with him. So we
shall preserve the family through our father." ... In this way both of Lot's
daughters came to be pregnant by their father' (Gen. 19:34).
14 A different interpretation of *Le figlie di Lot* can be found in Paolo Fossati's
Storie di figure e di immagini, which offers an extensive formalist reading of
the painting, but fails to consider its content and significance from the
point of view of ideology or gender.
15 For more on the Bible's portrayal of women, see Mieke Bal's *Lethal Love* or
Anti-covenant: Counter-Reading Women's Lives in the Hebrew Bible.
16 Victoria De Grazia has studied extensively the Fascist regime's treatment
of women in her *How Fascism Ruled Women*.
17 For Freud's early-twentieth-century study of this phenomenon, see *Totem
and Taboo*: 'Spirits and demons ... are only projections of man's own
emotional impulses. He turns his emotional cathexes into persons, he
peoples the world with them and meets his internal mental processes
again outside himself ...' (115).

WORKS CITED

Bal, Mieke. *Lethal Love: Feminist Literary Readings of Biblical Love Stories*.
Bloomington: Indiana UP, 1987.
– ed. *Anti-covenant: Counter-Reading Women's Lives in the Hebrew Bible*.
Sheffield, Eng.: Almond, 1989.
Baldacci, Paolo. 'Il mito del realismo magico (arte e letteratura).' In *Realismo
magico: pittura e scultura in Italia*. Milan: Mazotta, 1998. 103–10.

398   Allison A. Cooper

Boccioni, Umberto, et al. 'Manifesto dei pittori futuristi.' 1910. *I manifesti del futurismo*. Florence: Edizione di 'Lacerba,' 1914. 23–6.

Bontempelli, Massimo. *L'avventura novecentista*. Ed. Ruggero Jacobbi. Florence: Vallecchi, 1974.

Braun, Emily. 'Political Rhetoric and Poetic Irony: The Uses of Classicism in the Art of Fascist Italy.' In *On Classic Ground: Picasso, Lèger, de Chirico, and the New Classicism 1910–1930*. (London: Tate Gallery Publications, 1991).

– 'Renaissance and Renascences: The Rebirth of Italy, 1911–1921.' *Masterpieces from the Gianni Mattioli Collection*. Milan: Electa, 1997. 21–48.

Breton, André. 'Manifesto of Surrealism.' 1924. *Manifestoes of Surrealism*. Trans. Richard Seaver and Helen R. Lane. Ann Arbor: U of Michigan P, 1972.

Cowling, Elizabeth, and Jennifer Mundy. *On Classic Ground: Picasso, Léger, de Chirico and the New Classicism 1910–1930*. London: Tate Gallery Publications, 1990.

David, Michel. *La psicanalisi nella cultura italiana*. Turin: Boringhieri, 1966.

De Chirico, Giorgio. 'Sull'arte metafisica.' *Valori Plastici*. Apr.–May, 1919: 15–18.

De Grazia, Victoria. *How Fascism Ruled Women: Italy, 1922–1945*. Berkeley: U of California P, 1992.

Fagiolo dell'-Arco, Maurizio. 'Realismo magico. Ragioni di una idea e di una mostra.' In *Realismo magico: pittura e scultura in Italia*. Milan: Mazzota, 1998. 13–34.

Fossati, Paolo. *Storie di figure e di immagini: da Boccioni a Licini*. Turin: Einaudi, 1995.

Foster, Hal. *Compulsive Beauty*. Cambridge: MIT Press, 1993.

Freud, Sigmund. *Totem and Taboo: Some Points of Agreement between the Mental Lives of Savages and Neurotics*. Trans. James Strachey. New York: Norton, 1950.

– 'The Uncanny.' Trans. Alix Strachey. *Psychological Writings and Letters*. Ed. Sander L. Gilman. New York: Continuum, 1995. 120–53.

Masino, Paola. *Io, Massimo e gli altri*. Ed. Maria Vittoria Vittori. Milan: Rusconi, 1995.

– *Monte Ignoso*. 1931. Genoa: Il melangolo, 1994.

– 'Ricostruzione.' *900*. 1 Aug. 1928: 77–81.

Massimo Bontempelli Papers, 1865–1990, Getty Research Institute, Research Library, Accession no. 910147, 910147*.

Nicholls, Peter. *Modernisms: A Literary Guide*. Berkeley: U of California P, 1995.

Perkins Gilman, Charlotte. 'The Yellow Wallpaper.' *Anthology of American Literature, Volume II: Realism to the Present.* Ed. George McMichael. New York: Macmillan, 1989. 637–49.

Pirandello, Luigi. *It Is So! (If You Think So). Naked Masks.* New York: Meridian-Penguin, 1952. 61–138.

Re, Lucia. 'Futurism and Fascism, 1914–1945.' *A History of Women's Writing in Italy.* Ed. Letizia Panizza and Sharon Wood. Cambridge: Cambridge UP, 2000. 190–204.

PART V

Towards the Postmodern

14 Representing Repetition:
Appropriation in de Chirico and After

JENNIFER HIRSH

Now, however, a feeling overcame me which I can only describe as uncanny, and I was glad enough to find myself back at the piazza I had left a
short while before. [...] Other situations which have in common with my
adventure an unintended recurrence of the same situation [...] also result in
the same feeling of helplessness and of uncanniness.

Sigmund Freud, 'The Uncanny' (237)

Appropriation represents one of the strongest trends in the practice of
visual arts of the last thirty years.[1] Artworks operating under this
artistic strategy are often understood as manifesting the belated legacy
of the work of Marcel Duchamp, best remembered for his 1917 ready-
made sculpture *Fountain*, the inverted urinal that he deemed a sculpture by christening it with the fictitious signature 'R. Mutt' (figure
14.1). Art historians have nominated Duchamp as the principal father
of appropriation, thus baptizing him into the critical discourse as the
progenitor of an entire legion of artistic producers.[2] Many contemporary artists interested in strategies of appropriation are quick to acknowledge their debt to Duchamp by copying his most memorable
ready-made object, as seen, for example, in Mike Bidlo's *Not Duchamp*
(1986) or Sherrie Levine's *After Duchamp: 1* (1991).[3] Such representations, reproductions of an original work authored by another artist
exploring the possibility of reproductive artistic strategies, both reinforce and destabilize the status of their artistic ancestor, as they postu-
late a postmodern critique of this and other canonical images that
constitute the history of modern art as it has been written.[4] Duchamp's
spectre looms large in this discourse, which repeats not only his gesture but his very likeness, as figured in Yasumasa Morimura's 1988

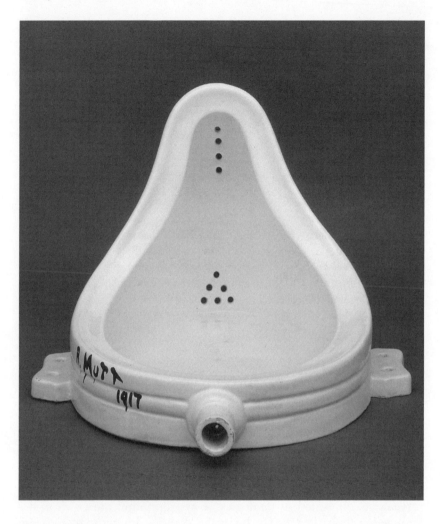

Figure 14.1: Marcel Duchamp, *Fountain*, 1917. Tate Gallery, London. Art Resource, NY.

Figure 14.2: Yasumasa Morimura, *Doublonnage*, 1988. Museo Nacional Centro de Arte Reina Sofia, Madrid. Courtesy of the artist and Luhring Augustine, New York.

Doublonnage, a clever restaging of Man Ray's 1923 photograph of an ambiguously gendered Duchamp in the guise of his alter ego Rrose Sélavy, here replaced by Morimura, who masquerades as the already elusive Duchamp (figure 14.2).[5]

The central concern of this essay, however, is not Duchamp. Instead, I shall be talking about an artist still rather neglected in the history of appropriation: Giorgio de Chirico, the itinerant Italian artist most familiar for his so-called Metaphysical compositions, which are replete with fragments of classical antiquity and architectural arcades coupled with disparate references to modernity.[6] Made famous by oneiric paintings such as his *Enigma of a Day* (1914) and *The Soothsayer's Recompense* (1913), canvases figuring hauntingly empty Italian *piazze*, simultaneously meaningful and meaningless, de Chirico left behind numerous examples of his appropriative strategies. Enigmatic combinations of classical and modern objects and monuments are deprived of their expected meanings and recast as parts of a cryptic visual code to which the viewer has no access.[7] The central concern of this essay is the sense in which de Chirico's approach to representation can be analysed in terms of its appropriative function.

At the core of what I maintain is a critical misrepresentation of de Chirico's contribution to twentieth-century art lies the reception (or complicated misperception) of de Chirico's post-Metaphysical art, or art produced after 1918. Remembered for the ways in which his Metaphysical style prefigured the Freudian motifs that fascinated his Surrealist followers, de Chirico was memorialized in the history of art not only as the progenitor of *pittura metafisica* but also as the father figure of the Surrealist movement, which in turn rejected him in an Oedipal gesture in the late 1920s, thus tainting the critical reception of the artist's post-Metaphysical production.[8] Since his roles as Metaphysical painter and proto-Surrealist have overshadowed other, in my view no less salient, characteristics of his oeuvre, the aspect of de Chirico's work associated with the appropriation of studied art objects remains obscured in the art-historical discourse, hardly discussed and invariably glossed over.[9] This essay addresses these lacunae, arguing that these omissions have limited not only our understanding of the art of de Chirico, but our perception of the contemporary moment as well.

Melancholy and the *Maestro*: A History of Critical Consideration

Crucial to my argument is the concept of melancholia, a concept not unfamiliar to de Chirico scholarship, and indeed essential to de

Figure 14.3: Giorgio de Chirico, *Melancholy* (Alternatively known as *Solitude*), 1912. Eric Estorick Collection. London. © 2004 Artists Rights Society (ARS), New York/SIAE, Rome.

Chirico's iconography. His famous *Melancholy* (1912) is merely one example of the many works whose titles openly invoke this sentiment and which restage ancient sculptures, in this case the mythological figure of Ariadne (figure 14.3). Inscribed with the word 'Melanconia,' the misplaced figure in the artwork signals the spectator to account for and mourn a loss that is unidentified.[10] Such paintings elude explanation by virtue of their seemingly random sampling of objects in illogical settings.[11] Writing about how his autumn stay in Turin influenced his works between 1912 and 1915, de Chirico notes that even he suffered from 'una crisi di melanconia' upon realizing the burden of Metaphysical vision (cited in Baldacci, *De Chirico. 1888–1919* 127; de Chirico, *Il meccanismo* 320–2).

Building on the notion of the melancholic as invoked by established critics of de Chirico, and as defined psychoanalytically by Sigmund Freud in his 1917 essay on 'Mourning and Melancholia,' the present analysis reconsiders de Chirico's works as symptomatic of a melancholic condition of mourning in the iconic configuration of traces of histories no longer recuperable, which in turn signals an inability to deal with a recurrent loss, that of meaning. My essay relies on a psychoanalytic framework that maps out artistic practice, both past and present, as the impossible recovery of lost objects, arguing that de Chirico's status as an appropriation artist must be re-evaluated in order to present a more comprehensive view of his work. Hence, I reject the problematic Metaphysical/post-Metaphysical split in de Chirico's work as asserted by the Surrealists and then canonized by historians of twentieth-century art, with a view towards formulating a more focused analysis of de Chirico's contemporary artistic legacy. After reviewing the history of critical readings of melancholy in these artworks, I will look forward, rather than back, to see how this crisis of meaning, as first articulated by de Chirico, continues to manifest itself in the appropriative work of later artists who acknowledge their debt to him. Critics have repeatedly made melancholy a concern of their analyses in reaction to its literal and metaphorical presence in paintings by de Chirico. In what follows, I will review other scholars' readings and then add my own, arguing that the very act of accounting for meaning in de Chirico's works has itself become melancholic, with each de Chirico critic unable to move beyond the loss already inherent in his pictorial representations, thus producing criticism that replicates the elusive flavour of the work itself.

In his early study of de Chirico's work (first published in 1941, then expanded in conjunction with a de Chirico exhibition organized by Soby in 1955 at the Museum of Modern Art in New York), James Thrall Soby interprets the presence of Ariadne in paintings such as *Melancholy* as related to two aspects of de Chirico's background: 1) the artist's upbringing in Greece, the source of classical culture, and 2) the artist's great appreciation of Friedrich Nietzsche and that philosopher's repeated invocation of the figure of the forsaken Ariadne (*Giorgio de Chirico* 52–6). De Chirico's most prolific critic, Maurizio Fagiolo dell'Arco, has read melancholy as figured in the antique statue as a personification of Nietzsche's 'gay science,' linking the painter's artistic philosophy to Nietzsche's nihilistic view of history (*Classicismo pittorico* 116–17).

In his essay on 'De Chirico and Modernism,' William Rubin asserts that the '*Stimmung* of melancholy and lassitude' links the artist's works with a rhetoric of Romanticism, rather than with the Classicism to which they seem to allude explicitly (56).[12] In attempting to account for a modern painter whose iconography included traditional signposts of the classical tradition, Rubin insists that their invocation results in an emptying of meaning that negates their original context. In other words, by perverting classical icons, de Chirico breaks abruptly with tradition and abstracts pictorial logic in a way that mimics, for example, Cubism's formal disruption of the laws of representation. Rubin struggles, however, with a reading of de Chirico's contribution as properly modernist. Rubin refers, for example, to de Chirico's mannequins, with their deformed, featureless heads and bodies replete with wooden fragments and tools, as pictorial paraphrases of synthetic Cubism's physical inclusion of wooden forms as part of its multimedia collage aesthetic. Rubin suggests that de Chirico's employment of classical iconography as a means of disrupting temporal logic parallels Cubism's abstracting of the picture plane; moreover, he views de Chirico's modernism as beholden to the rules of avant-garde French artistic practices contemporary to his first phase of Metaphysical activity. Such a view becomes problematic, however, when applied to de Chirico's stylistic shift in the 1920s, a shift that Rubin writes off as simply qualitatively poor work. As he writes: 'My own resistance to the late de Chiricos has finally something to do with a perception of the pictures that goes beyond aesthetics – a response to something I will have to call the "ethos" of the work. It does not follow from anything I know about the paintings or their author ...' (73). Paradoxically, Rubin himself criticizes the notion of a split between the Meta-physical and post-Metaphysical works, although his 1982 exhibition rearticulates much of what Thrall Soby had already said about de Chirico in the 1955 show, which also promoted almost exclusively the artist's earlier works. I challenge this limited view of de Chirico's oeuvre, which locates the melancholic exclusively in de Chirico's first phase of production; in my view, the melancholic disposition towards representation itself can be seen as guiding the dramatic stylistic shifts *throughout* de Chirico's oeuvre.

In her psychoanalytic rereading of a selection of de Chirico's early canvases that depict statuary, Nancy Stokes defines melancholy as the artist's or spectator's search for something lost. In her reading, what is lost (both to the canvases and in the spectatorial experience) is an entire generation of artworks, that is, the nineteenth-century casts of ancient sculptures that were copies themselves. Based on historical and biographical evidence, Stokes argues that de Chirico's engage-ment with antiquity was already mediated by the casts he would have encountered in Munich, while he studied at the Academy of Fine Arts, and then later at Versailles, when he resided in France. Stokes intelli-gently observes the complicated nature of de Chirico's relationship to antiquity, one in which antiquity is lost and rediscovered repeatedly in the history of representation, taking on new meaning in each new context of artistic production and spectatorial reception. Inherently foreign to the modern period, antiquity is discovered by de Chirico as an entity already lost and rediscovered by generations of artists prior to him.[13]

As noted by critics as early as Soby, de Chirico – confronted by copies and originals (which themselves, if Hellenistic, were copies of classical Greek statues) – engages with a Classicism that is present and absent in both real and simulated forms, re-manifestations of antiquity that map out a tradition which modernism's tenets of authenticity and originality resist.[14] As a modernist, then, de Chirico already behaves as a postmodernist, demonstrating a sensitivity to the cyclical nature of historicity through his traditional iconography, insisting on history's inevitable self-repetition, rather than presenting the modernist vision of innovation and progress. I would argue that herein lies the heart of the real problem in de Chirico's reception: modernism, as typically defined, fails to accommodate a view of history that insists on the absent presence, or the present absence, of tradition.[15] De Chirico stages this aspect of historicity through repetition of self and other, prefiguring postmodernist conceptions of history in his resurrection of the antique and Old Master traditions. In other words, de Chirico not only inserts himself into a tradition of copying but also presents his works as masterworks that he himself copied, hence establishing a precedent for those who illicitly copy his works as early as the 1920s, as I shall review below.

In a psychoanalytic reading of *Mystery and Melancholy of a Street*, Milly Heyd links melancholy to de Chirico's inability to process the loss of his older sister, whose premature death left him 'not only with a sense of loss but also [...] envy and [...] guilt.' For Heyd, the resulting melancholy is a 'melancholy of death' and the work, by extension, 'the mystery and melancholy of perfection, which for de Chirico remained unattainable throughout his artistic life' ('De Chirico: The Girl with the Hoop' 91–2).[16] In a second essay on de Chirico's work, Heyd focuses on the theme of doubling, as seen in de Chirico's iconographic choices of pairs of horses on the beach, gladiators, and even the ancient *dioscuri*, as the two de Chirico brothers (Giorgio and Andrea, later renamed Alberto Savinio) were known. Heyd even considers the reference to de Chirico's lost sister as a feminized replacement for his rivalry with his brother ('De Chirico: *The Greetings of a Distant Friend*').[17]

In his well-documented account of de Chirico's early period, Paolo Baldacci analyses melancholy as figured in the sculpture of Ariadne. Appropriated by de Chirico from Nietzsche's philosophical musings on the triangular dynamic of Ariadne-Theseus-Dionysus in classical literature, she is the second Ariadne, or the one already abandoned on Naxos by Theseus, after he has confronted the enigma of the Labyrinth (*De Chirico. 1888–1919* 127–44).[18] Interpreting the myth as the ultimate dramatization of a spatial and temporal crisis symbolized by the minotaur and the labyrinth, Baldacci traces the presence of the melancholic in the early works, underlining the fact that the painter, in exploring possible compositional strategies, positioned the statue of Ariadne within miniature dioramas, hence copying his own sculpted copies even in the early painted works (131).[19] Further, Baldacci links the iconography of melancholy to the death of the father, noting that the closed window shutters in the painting signal mourning to the viewer, according to Western customs (132). In accounting for the presence of Ariadne in de Chirico's Metaphysical works, Baldacci turns to Giorgio Agamben's analysis of Freud's theory of mourning and melancholia, a particularly sensitive reading of the ways in which unhealthy mourning occurs (134). Of particular interest in Agamben's interpretation of Freud's argument is his stipulation that the beloved object mourned in the melancholic condition need not even exist, as in those objects included in de Chirico's iconography, objects available only as fictitious representations of objects already long lost, ghosts rather than beings. Moreover, Agamben points to those objects that are 'not capable of being appropriated'; hence Baldacci's invocation of such a reading nicely parallels de Chirico's fragmentation of lost objects that are likewise both real and imagined (Baldacci, *De Chirico. 1888–1919* 134; Agamben 7–35).[20]

In her book on Mario Sironi, building on the earlier work of Jean Clair, Emily Braun uses the term 'melancholy' in the context of a compelling argument about the failure of signification in de Chirico's Metaphysical paintings, as she reassesses the way in which de Chirico's metaphysical iconography figures visually the role of melancholy in the construction of modern allegory (68–89). Braun nominates de Chirico's work as the first in the visual arts to acknowledge the loss of meaning inherent in allegory, and indeed, by extension, in all representation, thus providing a visual parallel to similar assertions made in relation to drama and the loss of meaning in the literary arts in Walter Benjamin's *The Origin of German Tragic Drama*. She analyses de Chirico's amalgamations of disparate, fragmented elements, both classical and modern, in order to point to the ways in which an appropriative strategy necessarily empties objects of expected meanings, underlining a loss of meaning incurred as the signifier no longer points the viewer to the signified. In her argument, melancholia, traced from the medieval period through to modernist texts, is invoked as the explanation of how the Metaphysical iconography functions by paralysing the viewer in the oscillation between the disparate temporalities of the referents and the randomness of the combinations, as seen, for instance, in the *Song of Love* (1914) (figure 14.4). Bombarding the beholder with signs drawn from past and present, history and his own memory, de Chirico creates a pastiche (in postmodern terms) that upsets the act of viewing on many levels. While a red glove, a fragmented head of the *Apollo Belvedere*, and a green ball create a confusing and nonsensical iconography, de Chirico simultaneously juxtaposes history (that is, art history) with personal memory (as seen in the railways and the contemporary architecture that represents his present). De Chirico also takes on the rules of painting in the Western tradition, as he undercuts the rule of perspectival unity with paintings

Figure 14.4: Giorgio de Chirico, *Song of Love*, 1914. Nelson A. Rockefeller Bequest, Museum of Modern Art, New York. Scala/Art Resource, NY.

replete with multiple perspectival mechanisms. Whereas Braun's analysis links melancholy to de Chirico's (and then Sironi's) awareness of the loss of meaning in the modern world as shown through their representation of modern allegory, my analysis here underlines the melancholic aspect of de Chirico's personal disposition towards the act of representation itself. This disposition becomes evident in his painterly practice throughout his oeuvre in both early and 'late' paintings: it is engendered not only by the iconography of his early paintings, but also by the repetitious production of his later paintings, a legacy renewed by the contemporary artists who in turn reassert the importance of the copy in their own subsequent repetitions. Hence, my study shifts the focus on melancholy from its role in the structure of allegory in the modern world to its role as a strategy of repetition, a practice that, in the case of de Chirico, amounts to sixty years of returns and copies, made first on rare occasions and later with more regularity.[21]

In his account of Surrealism, *Compulsive Beauty*, Hal Foster includes de Chirico as a key voice (58–73). Asserting the relevance of developments in psychoanalytic thought contemporary to the development of Surrealism for his study, Foster views the presence of melancholic elements in de Chirico's paintings as indicating not only 'a nostalgia for Italy, neoclassical styles, old master techniques, and so on,' but also as constituting '[p]sychically [...] charged [...] representatives of the dead father,' linking such symbols as the trains to de Chirico's father's career as a railway engineer in Thessaly (71).[22] Returning to a Freudian psychoanalytic framework, Foster provides a psycho-biographical interpretation of melancholy as reflected in an iconography filled with lost objects, projecting this reading onto the already standard art-historical criticism of de Chirico as longing for a past now available only in fragments and traces, as figured in the metaphysical works, or 'images of the dead (dead father, traditional motifs, old master methods) [...] [whereby] melancholy seems to pass over into masochism' (73). Yet while Foster reads de Chirico's melancholy as a kind of nostalgia for that which is lost, my own employment of the term will consider the practice of painting itself, expanding his iconographic argument in order to highlight what is melancholic not only in de Chirico's approach to artistic activity but also in those more recent artists who return to both the formal and practical components of de Chirico's artistic production.

Mourning and Melancholy in the Contemporary Moment: Two Case Studies

Although many contemporary figures can be linked to de Chirico, this essay will focus on Andy Warhol and Mike Bidlo, two post-war American artists who repaint de Chirico, in order to show how this common interest evidences a perpetuation of the inability to mourn the loss of meaning already figured in de Chirico's own paintings.[23] In considering works inspired by de Chirico, I interpret them as an extension of de Chirico's own works, since they resuscitate certain aspects of his original pictorial project and revitalize his original impulse to negotiate visually the status of this artist and his works, as well as the value of what de Chirico's rhetoric did, and indeed will have done, to revolutionize modern art. Whereas Warhol slips into a manic production, or insistent reproduction in response to de Chirico's own images of loss, Bidlo expresses a depressed melancholic disposition, recreating many of de Chirico's paintings exactly, thereby cancelling himself in the process, as he defines himself not as what he is, but as what he is not. Pitting Andy Warhol's 1982 multiplication of de Chirico's *Hector and Andromache* against Mike Bidlo's 1989 *Not de Chirico (Hector and Andromache)* – both copies of the same 1917 de Chirico image (an image that de Chirico himself repainted on numerous occasions) – this essay concentrates on two instances of contemporary visual appropriation with a view towards asserting a new art-historical framework for de Chirico, insofar as the verbal (that is, art-historical) discourse, in my view, still lags far behind its visual counterpart in its appreciation of de Chirico's artistic practice (figures 14.5–14.7).[24] In short, my mournful essay will assert a psychoanalytic reading of the work of the present in order to allow for a reappraisal of the past. My reading itself thus becomes a rereading, as it too represents an uncanny return to the ghost of tradition that continues to haunt the art-historical discourse today.

Andy Warhol is best known as the Pop artist who reproduced commodified images and icons drawn from popular culture, as seen in two of his works from 1962: *200 Campbell's Soup Cans* and *Marilyn Diptych* (a work executed, mournfully, in the immediate aftermath of her death).[25] Retrospectively, art historians have come to call Warhol's art appropriative, since he compulsively steals images (and their emptiness) from the popular culture around him. Pertinent to this discus-

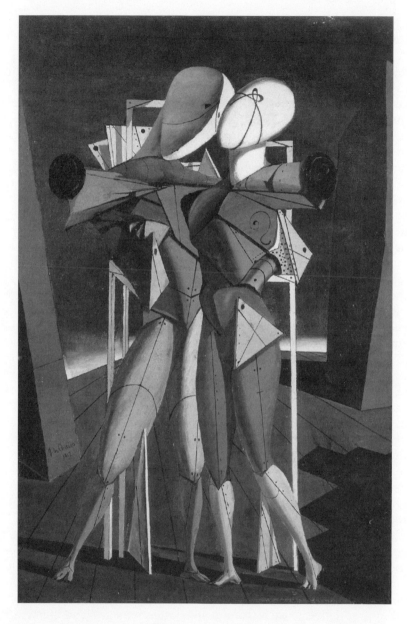

Figure 14.5: Giorgio de Chirico, *Hector and Andromache*, 1917. Mattioli Collection, Milan. Scala, Art Resource, NY.

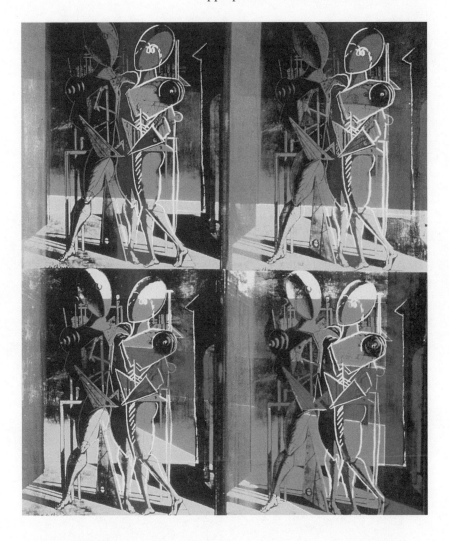

Figure 14.6: Andy Warhol, *Hector and Andromache*, 1982. Andy Warhol
Foundation, Pittsburgh. © 2004 Andy Warhol Foundation for the Visual
Arts/ARS, New York.

Figure 14.7: Mike Bidlo, *Not de Chirico (Hector and Andromache)*, 1989. Private Collection.

sion are Warhol's multiple reproductions of a number of de Chirico's best-known images, such as his *Piazza d'Italia* of 1982, images that had already acquired the status of problematic commodities. In calling them 'problematic,' I refer to the history of de Chirico copying his own painted images, a gesture not well received by the art market.[26] De Chirico's copies of his own images are the basis for his strategy of denying originality, a gesture prefiguring the championship of the copy and parody in postmodern discourse. These multiples are further multiplied, as the already repeated de Chirico image within each Warhol canvas is re-repeated in multiple editions or screenings of the same Warhol painting, suggesting a remedy to melancholia that combats the notion of an irretrievable originality by simultaneously overwriting it in different directions, wildly enacting a kind of mania of creativity-as-reproduction.

Warhol began to make his silk-screened series of multiple *Shadows* just days after de Chirico's death, suggesting a direct connection between the death of de Chirico and the contemporary master of repetition.[27] In a second 'uncanny' gesture, Warhol's exhibition of a series of silk-screened images derived from trade-mark de Chirico paintings opened on the day after the four-year anniversary of the *Maestro*'s death. Warhol thus enacts a second eulogization of the artist and his work as a testament to the fact that he 'love[d] [de Chirico's] art and [...] the idea he repeated the same paintings over and over again [,...] [he] thought it would be great to do it [himself].' Shown at the Campidoglio in Rome in 1982, at the Marisa del Re Gallery in New York in 1985, and at the Palazzo delle Prigioni Vecchie in Venice in 1987, this exhibition included paintings by de Chirico alongside Warhol's drawings or copies of the same works. Still more dramatic were Warhol's large-scale, silk-screened canvases generated from those sketches, images that include either four or eight copies of each de Chirico on each Warhol canvas. As Kim Levin notes, 'Warhol compresses a lifetime of [de Chirico's] repetitions into each piece' (252). Warhol put into paint a series of repetitions that echoed de Chirico's own repetitions of the same image over time, visually echoing the final textual illustration accompanying curator William Rubin's essay on 'De Chirico and Modernism,' which was published in the catalogue accompanying the 1982 de Chirico retrospective held at the Museum of Modern Art. This illustration, itself a visual appropriation in the form of a facsimile, reproduces the layout of the eighteen versions of the *Disquieting Muses* painting as included in Carlo Ragghianti's

1979 essay that attacked de Chirico for his practice of repetition. Further complicating matters, Warhol returned to images that de Chirico himself had reproduced on several occasions during his career, making his gesture of repetition still more poignant (Foster 248–9, n. 44). 'What he repeated regularly, year after year,' Warhol said, 'I repeat in the same day, in the same painting' (Bonito Oliva 50). Hence, what appears a crisis of temporality in the modern stagesets of de Chirico's diachronic iconography is revisited in Warhol's images that speed up the clock of representation, collapsing the space and time traditionally present between copies by making almost simultaneous multiple editions of the already multiplied images. In serializing de Chirico, Warhol appropriates already appropriated paintings, hence intensifying the self-reflexivity of the gesture in his acknowledgment – by virtue of continuing the repetitions already initiated by de Chirico – of the meaning-emptying commodification of de Chirico's works as originally produced. Here, we must be careful with the word 'original,' as the early paintings by de Chirico, in their initial production, were not seen to be equalled, for the public or private collector, in the later paintings or replicas he created in the same form.[28] In a similar but belated act, Warhol's repetitions of de Chirico's paintings, though not identical, remain indistinguishable, with their like forms and equal monetary value. In other words, Warhol's editions were each produced as a group of Warhol reproductions of de Chirico, each silk-screen differing from the next arbitrarily and each an equally valued piece at the time of entry onto the art market, whereas the different de Chirico repetitions – that is, the reproduced individual paintings – had different values at different moments on the art market, with the early, made-to-order copies for the Surrealists in the 1920s considered to be fine works of art, while later editions came to be deemed frauds. Although even de Chirico's later copies continued to sell on the market, their value never equalled that of the originals whose trade-mark quality they reproduced and reinforced. Eliminating the artistic hand with mechanical means of reproduction, Warhol underlines the impossibility of his own gesture of originality as he calls attention to the reenactment or restaging of de Chirico's melancholic drama of repetition. As Thomas Crow argues, 'Warhol, though he grounded his art in the ubiquity of the packaged commodity, produced his most powerful work by dramatizing the breakdown of commodity exchange,' an exchange, in the case of de Chirico, already destabilized by repeated originals (51). Perhaps Crow's analysis is more appropriate for de

Chirico, however, given that it was his works – and here I refer to the 'late' works of the early style – that failed to sell at the high prices equal to those of the genuine early works, while Warhol's, in their reproduction of the ubiquitous and the infamous – as in Marilyn – drew high prices from the market precisely because of their reproduced nature. In economic terms, the shift from the modern to the postmodern dramatically inverted how the art market would receive what seem to be similar artistic gestures. Although de Chirico surreptitiously made later copies in his earlier style, many of his copies were produced in response to individual requests from collectors. As a result, we can also view Warhol's gesture of reproducing de Chirico as a kind of creative and productive misunderstanding, or indeed, representation, of de Chirico's gesture that underlines the ironic shift in reception, both critically and economically.

In order to situate my argument psychoanalytically, I turn now to Freud's 'Mourning and Melancholia.' Freud distinguishes between healthy mourning that allows one to grieve the loss of the loved one and move on in time and an unhealthy mourning that results in the pathological fixation of melancholia, or the inability to accept the beloved's loss, often manifested in the subject's own loss of self-esteem resulting from the introjection of the lost object of love. In invoking Freud, I am not asserting a diagnosis of clinical depression for the late Andy Warhol; rather, in seeking to account for the 'multiple' aspect of his repainting of de Chirico, I suggest that his repetitions envision one possible outcome of the melancholic condition: 'its tendency to change round into mania – a state which is the opposite of it in its symptoms' (253). While suffering from melancholia, one may slip into a manic phase of hyperactivity as the depression associated with melancholia is replaced 'by the signs of discharge of joyful emotion and by increased readiness for all kinds of action' (254). Rather than the loss of 'self-regard' typically experienced by the self-effacing subject while in the depressed state of melancholia, the stricken subject here reverts to a manic state in which unrealistic grandiosity replaces the equally unrealistic absence of 'self-regard' as experienced by the depressed.

Such a psychoanalytic framework facilitates a reading of Warhol's renditions as a kind of mania by virtue of their sheer multiplicity. Warhol's numerous reproductions replace de Chirico's already melancholic and, as I will later suggest, also manic works. Substituting a pictorial gesture predicated on the grandiosity required to repaint de

Chirico's famous images repeatedly, Warhol, in a paradoxical gesture, simultaneously asserts uniform and random qualities in his revisions of de Chirico's individual/multiple masterpieces, thus exchanging master machinist for master artist. Abstracted by Warhol's wild and random applications of colour that render the replicated image into an empty repetitious pattern on each canvas, Warhol's images not only perpetuate de Chirico's images in an excited gesture full of exuberance and energy, but also elide the individuality of the particular image multiplied. In other words, Warhol's own signature, the mechanically driven reproduction that made him famous, both immortalizes and erases, preserving and yet defacing the master's images in a postmodern fantastic gesture that says as much (if not more) about Warhol as it does about de Chirico. De Chirico has become another potent commodity for Warhol, much like images of the Campbell's soup can and Marilyn Monroe, in this new pictorial rhetoric that extends Warhol's ambivalent critique of consumer culture to include images created under the artistic rubric of Italian modernism. The mania in Warhol's execution of the mechanical multiple, as opposed to the single, carefully executed hand-painted work, points to a particular aspect of the melancholic condition. In Freudian terms, '[i]n mania, the ego must have got over the loss of the object' (255), suggesting that in his own attempt to mourn the loss (or impossibility) of originality, Warhol in this case manically reproduces the work of an artist for whom the impossible issues of originality and authenticity had already been central for decades (Tully).

In order to balance out what I have labelled 'manic' in the melancholic legacy of de Chirico, I turn now to the work of Mike Bidlo, a contemporary New York painter and sculptor, whose artworks I interpret as figuring the 'depressed' side of the melancholic predicament. Between 1989 and 1990, Bidlo painted single copies of de Chirico's works – all titled *Not de Chirico*, with the respective proper titles as given by de Chirico following in parentheses. In 1990, he exhibited the canvases together at the Galerie Daniel Templon in Paris and the Galerie Bruno Bischofberger in Zurich in an exhibition entitled *BIDLO (Not de Chirico)*, suggesting an ironic retrospective of artworks that, though created within a span of two years, also recreate a lifetime's work. Unlike the 1982 retrospective, *BIDLO (Not de Chirico)* did include later (or should I say *Not* later) works, thus overwriting William Rubin's prejudice against paintings created by de Chirico 'late' in his career. Bidlo copied works from the artist's entire career, rather than just his early Metaphysical period, repainting works from that period up to and including later works, such as de Chirico's 1969 canvas, *The Departure of Hebdomeros*.[29] In reviewing Bidlo's retrospective exhibition of *Not de Chirico* paintings, we do not see de Chirico's *Mystery and Melancholy of a Street* (1913), we do not see de Chirico's *Uncertainty of the Poet* (1913), and we do not see de Chirico's *Archaeologists* (1929) (figure 14.8–14.10). One particular painting, Bidlo's *Not de Chirico (Metaphysical Interior with Piazza d'Italia)*, stages an ironic critique of not only the artist, but also of the unfortunate problem of inauthentic works within de Chirico's oeuvre. Presented as a copy of a de Chirico image, this image is really *not* a copy of a painting by de Chirico, insofar as the original de Chirico painting on which Bidlo based his image has been deemed to be a fake, though it had slipped into a serious art collection (figure 14.11).[30] This image copied by Bidlo was in fact one of the false paintings, judged by Baldacci to be a Dominguez fake and included in the Allard show, that entered into the collection of the Sprengel Museum in Hannover, Germany (Baldacci and Schmied, 91).[31] Given that Baldacci's exhibition and catalogue were not produced until 1994, that is, after Bidlo had completed his *Not de Chirico* project, it seems unlikely (though it remains possible) that Bidlo would have been aware of his (mis)copying. That said, perhaps this painting represents Bidlo's most genuine replication of de Chirico, his act intensifying the fate and fortune not of de Chirico's canvases, but of those which were *not*. Thus, at the level of the art-historical discourse, Bidlo re-inscribes his own voice as the progenitor of a generation that will have re-evaluated de Chirico's work as a whole, eschewing the artificially imposed split in his oeuvre between the Metaphysical and post-Metaphysical works and confronting the pervasiveness of the fake paintings and the instability of what exactly constitutes a de Chirico painting.

As an appropriation artist who strives to create exact copies of studied modernist masterworks, Bidlo returns to the attempt to process loss that we have already noted in both de Chirico and Warhol, only now creating works which, in their self-effacement of the artist always labelled as 'not,' articulate the depression and loss of self-esteem associated with melancholia as defined by Freud. In painting these repaintings of another artist's works, Bidlo embeds his own identity, or self, as artist within the images that figure the traces of another; in inscribing his own artistic enterprise within these already extant texts, he weds his ego to that of the other. In my psychoanalytic reading of Bidlo's works, he does not avoid an inability to come to terms with the

Figure 14.8: Mike Bidlo, *Not de Chirico (Mystery and Melancholy of a Street)*, 1989–90. Private Collection.

Figure 14.9: Mike Bidlo, *Not de Chirico (Uncertainty of the Poet)*, 1989–90.
Private Collection.

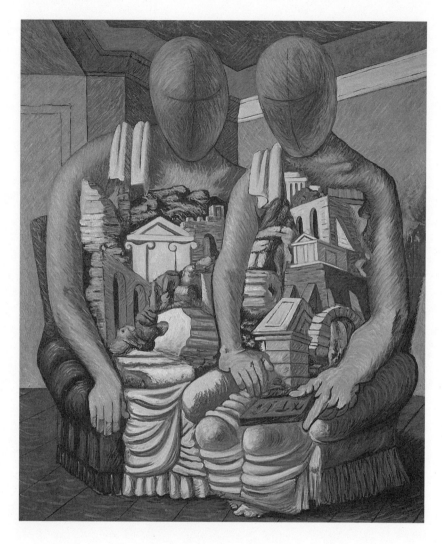

Figure 14.10: Mike Bidlo, *Not de Chirico (Archaeologists)*, 1989–90. Private Collection.

Figure 14.11: Mike Bidlo, *Not de Chirico (Metaphysical Interior with Piazza d'Italia)*, 1989–90. Private Collection.

loss that those works represent, the loss of meaning as figured in the fragments of history (and of art history) that haunts de Chirico's canvases, early and late, and inspires the transference of melancholia from artist to spectator. Bidlo labels his works as what they are *not*, rather than as what they are: '(Not de Chirico),' rather than Bidlo's de Chirico. What may be read as manic about the depressed production of Bidlo is the shifting of identities in his insistent imposter syndrome. Manically masquerading as memorialized modernist heroes, Bidlo was *Not Picasso* in 1983 (figure 14.12) and *Not Cézanne* in 1986. Never maintaining one non-persona for long, Bidlo has created an artistic identity for himself that continues to gain meaning as he asserts what he is *not*, rather than what he is.[32]

Bidlo's work thus expresses a depressed melancholia, as it 'displays something else besides which is lacking in mourning [...] an extraordinary diminution in his self-regard, an impoverishment of his ego on a grand scale. [...] The patient [or Bidlo] represents his ego to us as worthless [and] incapable of any achievement [...]' (Freud, 'Mourning and Melancholia' 246). Bidlo performing (or reperforming) de Chirico's work cannot move beyond the loss, fixates upon the loss of the object, and replicates it as already lost. As in Warhol, Bidlo's large-scale endeavours (evidenced by the sheer numbers of the canvases in each project), also suggest a manic pole that oscillates with the depression of his artistic gesture of self-effacement. The fact that Bidlo eventually moves on to the next lost modernist points to a kind of manic pattern in his unquenchable desire always to shift to the next bereavement ... and the next ...

Of Bidlo's appropriations of modernist masters, however, his appropriation of Warhol – as seen in his *Not Warhol* series of 1984–6 – remains most interesting for my purposes here, given that it occurred before his *Not de Chirico* series of 1989–90, and yet after Warhol's screening of de Chirico in 1982 (figure 14.13). In considering critically Bidlo's repainting of de Chirico, we must acknowledge as well his prior reworking of Warhol in the mid-1980s. Bidlo repeated both production and product, having replicated not only trade-mark Warhol objects, but also the very Factory setting itself, which made Warhol (in)famous. Bidlo's engagement with Warhol suggests a careful study of that artist, linking him before *Not de Chirico* to a repetition of the master repeater. Thus, the question arises: did Bidlo plagiarize Warhol, who has already plagiarized icons that have been stolen from popular and elite culture? In his 1990 series of 'Not de Chirico' images, then,

Figure 14.12: Mike Bidlo, *Not Picasso (Demoiselles d'Avignon)*, 1983. Private Collection.

Figure 14.13: Mike Bidlo, *Not Warhol (Brillo Boxes)*, 1984. Private Collection.

Bidlo showed further consideration of Warhol's artistic critique of art criticism and the history of art. And so, when we consider Bidlo's *Not de Chirico* series, we must ask if it is only *Not de Chirico*, or if it is instead a second (or even extended) artistic articulation of *Not Warhol*, that is, an expression of de Chirico necessarily complicated by his already completed project *Not Warhol*. Therefore, we may see Bidlo repainting de Chirico already repainted by Warhol as Bidlo's impersonation of the artist Warhol in the form of a performance piece, much like his impersonation of Jackson Pollock's act of urination on Peggy Guggenheim's fireplace.[33] Copying not only the work but also the Pop artist's enigmatic behaviour, Bidlo too pursues the shadows and shades of the deceased, engaging with de Chirico not only directly, but also in a way that is mediated by his earlier engagement with Warhol. Moreover, through an act of triangulation, Bidlo mediates his desire to reproduce de Chirico through Warhol's earlier reproductions. As an appropriation artist sensitive to the ways in which the history of art has been constructed by a history of criticism, Bidlo necessarily asserts his own critique of that history by repeating de Chirico, whose critical fortune has already been artistically altered by Warhol's images, images inserted not only into the history of de Chirico's legacy, but which entered Warhol's list of problematic commodities deserving documentation. In other words, this triangular model of desire figures not only Bidlo's comment on de Chirico, but also on de Chirico in Warhol and Warhol on de Chirico, forging a circular and also cyclical relationship among all three artists as Bidlo's gesture further blurs the limits between the compulsive reproductions of an artist whose memory has been permeated by a discourse of forgeries and fakes. This rereading of de Chirico thus hinges on a delicate matrix mapped between Warhol and Bidlo as artists who highlight de Chirico's own melancholic artistic practice.

Commodification and the Canvas: Forgeries and Fakes as de Chirico's Fortune

Forgeries and fakes have affected the history of de Chirico reception and scholarship in complicated and elusive ways, for not only have other artists passed off their own work as that of de Chirico, but the artist himself passed off later paintings as earlier ones, retroactively inserting into his Metaphysical oeuvre paintings dated from 1910–18. As history has shown, both the artist himself and his connoisseurs have rejected works formerly believed to be authentic, both for faulty authorship and faulty dating.[34] As Emily Braun has asserted, '[f]uture scholarship will also need to prove, as defenders of de Chirico's integrity maintain, that de Chirico himself never forged his work; that is, he never reproduced images with the intention to pass them off as the original for financial gain' ('Kitsch and the Avant-Garde' 74). The series of lawsuits launched by de Chirico against the Venice Biennale in 1948 is merely one example of the artist's own invective regarding authenticity and his paintings.[35]

Judd Tully summarizes how forgeries by other artists, and de Chirico's own falsified dates, have thrown the critical discourse on, as well as the practice of collecting paintings by, de Chirico into disarray. Without a relatively stable consensus as to what constitutes de Chirico's oeuvre, scholars will continue to find difficulty in reassessing the artist's contribution.[36] In recalibrating an appreciation of de Chirico's later works this uncertainty is particularly problematic, given that the bulk of 'false' and misdated works fall within the so-called post-Metaphysical period of his career. Tully notes how some critics have actually played off of the theme of faking as an ironic gesture within their own critical discourse. For example, *Giorgio de Chirico: Betraying the Muse – De Chirico and the Surrealists*, shown at the Paolo Baldacci Gallery in New York in 1994, faced the de Chirico forgery problem head on, including actual fakes in that exhibition of de Chirico's work.[37]

Most recently, William Robinson, curator of Modern Art at the Cleveland Museum of Art, has confronted this problem of 'Verifalsi or Falsifalsi' in relation to a 1981 acquisition, entitled *Metaphysical Interior*, which members of the authentication committee of the Fondazione Giorgio e Isa de Chirico in Rome declared a forgery shortly thereafter.[38] In search of the proper attribution of the Cleveland painting (in Baldacci's view an Oscar Dominguez canvas), Robinson hypothesizes that Surrealist painters, acting as double agents, produced fake de Chiricos and sent them to Nazi collectors, hence creating a market for the fakes that in turn supported the French Resistance movement in the 1940s, a theory in his view bolstered by the large number of fakes in German collections.[39] Robinson's thesis seems improbable, however, given that the majority of false paintings made by Oscar Dominguez were sold at the end of the Second World War, more specifically, post–1944, when Paris had already been liberated. By that time, there would no longer have been a need to finance a resistance.[40]

In a recent work that theorizes about authenticity in the history of art, Sándor Radnóti is careful to distinguish between fakes and forgeries, using the criminal metaphors of theft and fraud to flesh out how acts of plagiarism are different from forgeries (109–10). When an artist creates a forgery, he passes off the work of another as his own, whereas when an artist creates a fake, he passes off his own work as that of another. De Chirico's compelling position here is that, aside from the artists who copy him (that is who make fake de Chirico's, forging his signature), de Chirico himself commits both crimes: he steals other artists' artworks in creating Old Master remakes, plagiarizing, and hence forging them, as noted in his memoirs; simultaneously, he fakes his own works, replacing later dates with earlier ones in order to insert paintings anachronistically into the earlier phase of his oeuvre.

Old Master or Old Modernist?
Mourning and Melancholia in Italian Modernism

To round out my interpretation of mourning and melancholia in de Chirico's contemporary legacy, I return to the artist himself in order to note the ways in which both manic and depressed behaviours were already present in his oeuvre. In copying endless numbers of Old Masters,[41] de Chirico suppressed his own ego, much as Bidlo would go on to do in his *(Not de Chirico)* project. De Chirico turned back to the materiality of paint, eliminating his own artistic 'originality' – his trade-mark Metaphysical style – and choosing instead the images that had already been owned by his predecessors. De Chirico became increasingly interested in technique and material, as evidenced by his 1928 treatise, *Piccolo trattato di tecnica pittorica*. Moreover, in replicating Old Masters, de Chirico prematurely inscribed himself into the canon of Western art, impersonating the Old Masters, or, can we say, becoming a New Master.[42] In copying himself, de Chirico, the living artist, reproduces de Chirico, the perhaps already dead, and hence memorialized, artist. Much as he had staged his *Self-Portrait* of 1920, now at the Toledo Museum of Art, de Chirico functions as both living and dead artist, as both the anxious, practising painter and the already monumentalized, and hence dead artist, fixed in a marble portrait bust of himself (figure 14.14).[43] Indeed, this image is a pictorial analog of my own analysis of de Chirico's artistic practice as both Old Master (the dead bust) and Old Modernist (the anxious artist who confronts the problematic condition of engaging in an artistic activity associated with artists who are no more). What remains to be studied more care-

Figure 14.4: Giorgio de Chirico, *Self-Portrait*, c. 1922. Toledo Museum of Art, Toledo. © 2004 Artists Rights Society (ARS), New York/SIAE, Rome.

fully are the differences between the Old Masters whom de Chirico copies. Copying Raphael is not necessarily the same as copying Rubens, while reproducing Fragonard does not equal replicating Delacroix.[44] Much as Bidlo manically shifted from one Modernist Master to the next, so too had de Chirico altered his own identity as he slipped between one Old Master and another, somehow, if only briefly, occupying their places, acting as a kind of living (or perhaps resurrected) double for each, becoming a living shadow for the now dead and memorialized artists whose canvases he repainted, creating works that were not Raphael, not Rubens, not Fragonard, and not Delacroix. Moreover, the flamboyance, monumentality, and garish colours manifested in the styles and brushwork associated with de Chirico's later, Baroque-style reworkings that rely on Old Master models betray the kind of elation and mania that I attribute to the Warhol works that serialize de Chirico. Thus, I include de Chirico's engagement with the Old Master tradition not only as exemplary of how his works expressed a mourning that was nostalgic, as Hal Foster has argued, but also as exemplary of the ways in which melancholic behaviour, both manic and depressed, already existed within his works, not only in terms of repetition, but also in terms of self-cancellation. De Chirico's copies of his own works can then be read as manically driven series that insist on a certain authenticity (as early paintings) but undermine their own worth (as late copies). Returning again and again to his *Piazze d'Italia*, de Chirico illustrates Freud's condition of endlessly returning to a site, as described in 'The "Uncanny"' (237). Reproducing his own originals, yet problematizing their authenticity by misdating them, de Chirico, as New Master, creates a problem for the esteemed tenets of high modernism that are predicated on originality and authenticity.

Conclusion

This mournful analysis of de Chirico's postmodern legacy returns me, ultimately, to de Chirico's artistic practices, as I attempt to account for the art-historical discourse on de Chirico's work that has been destabilized by the repetition that exists within his oeuvre, exemplified by the now-famous example of his *Disquieting Muses*. By repetition, I refer to many aspects of de Chirico's artistic production, as this term condenses many phenomena into one observation. As Braun has explained, de Chirico included studied art objects in his metaphysical painting, emptying these copies of their expected meanings and creating a new visual language that denied those same meanings: the signifier no longer secured the signified, in a dangerous game of allegorical and melancholic renegotiation of meaning that destabilizes the modernist viewer in search of pictorial unity (*Mario Sironi* 68–89). De Chirico also reproduced, or repainted, his own images, initially to satisfy the desires of patrons, but ultimately with the effect of challenging as well the prevailing esteem that modernism has embedded in originality and authenticity. In recopying the copy, Warhol and Bidlo, as postmodern artistic practitioners, enact a multivalent homage to de Chirico, copying not only the image, but also the practice of copying itself. In thus denying the status of 'the original,' de Chirico anticipates their postmodern artistic contribution.

Insofar as his art already figured a melancholic disposition towards signs and their meanings, de Chirico was already expressing both depressed and manic behaviours. The depressed de Chirico repainted other artists' works and, indeed, entire stylistic stances, owning them, yet cancelling his own role as artist in his designs of disparate combinations, prefiguring Warhol and Bidlo's postmodern critiques in his copied and serialized Metaphysical and Old Master-style canvases. The manic de Chirico repeated his own works throughout his career, making version after version of the same image, implying an increase in his skill whose market value was (and continues to be) evaluated as inversely proportionate to the number of copies executed.

In light of de Chirico's practices of repetition, we can make yet another diagnosis of melancholia, for the collector, whether private or public, also comes to suffer from a loss of 'self-regard,' this time in economic terms, upon realizing that a 'de Chirico' painting is really *not* a de Chirico.[45] This diagnosis can be extended further to include the very work of art itself, since the material object itself triggers a loss for the collector, given the destabilization of its status and the devaluation of its worth. This melancholia of endless repetition remains present throughout de Chirico's oeuvre, insofar as he recycles not only classical monuments but also Renaissance, Baroque, and nineteenth-century icons, techniques, and styles, as well as his own images (and their inherent figuration of the loss of meaning), simultaneously granting and denying them the status of canonical images. This disturbance of repetition is not only figured in the work, but also *figures* the images themselves, as the reworking itself is symptomatic of such a condition. In this essay, both painting and painter have come under analysis, each, however, in differently mournful ways.

NOTES

This essay began as a paper delivered at the April 2000 American Association for Italian Studies annual conference in New York City. I owe many thanks to my adviser, Steven Z. Levine at Bryn Mawr College, for his careful and patient reading and rereading of my essay during all stages of my writing. In addition, thanks are due to Emily Braun at Hunter College, City University of New York, who, in serving as the respondent to the panel at which the essay was originally presented, encouraged me to expand it to include not only de Chirico's artistic legacy but also his engagement with the Old Master tradition. My colleagues Jon Seydl and Isabella Wallace also provided thoughtful suggestions for this essay.

1 Most recently, the National Gallery in London held the 'Encounters: New Art from Old' exhibition (14 June–17 Sept. 2000) on the theme of appropriation, in which twenty-five contemporary artists were commissioned to create individual artworks derived from Old Master works in the museum's collection, staging 'snatches of dialogue' between artists much like the 'similar conversations [already] go[ing] on in the galleries where Rembrandt talks to Titian, Velázquez looks at Rubens, Seurat nods to Piero della Francesca, and Turner, by his own express wish, hangs forever beside [...] Claude Lorrain' (Rosenblum, *Encounters* 7). See Robert Rosenblum's introduction to the accompanying catalogue for a discussion of the thematics of art about art. See also Leo Steinberg's 'The Glorious Company,' his introduction to *Art about Art*, the 1978 exhibition at the Whitney Museum for American Art in New York City, which brought together American artworks that engage in a dialogue with the history of art. Steinberg points out how contemporary artists, much like their predecessors, take from nature and from other artworks in a similar fashion, erasing distinctions between past and present. What motivated this particular exhibition was the way in which this kind of appropriation has become rampant and self-conscious in (what we now label) the postmodern period, generally, and in the American context, specifically.

2 In a reassessment of Duchamp's place in the postmodern debate, Amelia Jones points to the irony of identifying Duchamp as the father of this discourse, given that postmodernism, by definition, is a critique of origins (esp. 63–109).

3 Udo Kultermann includes Bidlo and Levine in his analysis of contemporary American artists who confront the problem of originality. See Mike Bidlo, *Mike Bidlo: The Fountain Drawings*, for a full selection of Bidlo's study of Duchamp and Bidlo, *Masterpieces*, for discussions of Bidlo's practices of copying, including interviews with the artist.

4 Rosenblum notes that a) 'such replications seem totally subservient to history, a catechism of venerable images, like the copies of sacred manuscripts made in a medieval scriptorium' or b) '[l]ooked at another way, their fascination with virtual reality, with reproductive images, seems to embrace fully the visual environment of the late twentieth century' ('Remembrance of Art Past' 22).

5 See Norman Bryson for a reading of the ways in which Morimura's photographs call into question the history of Western art as he deconstructs the binaries of Western representation, such as male versus female, occidental versus oriental, both of which can be seen in Morimura's re-presentation of Duchamp's image as staged by Man Ray, an image that already blurred the boundaries between genders.

6 In his essay published in conjunction with the *De Chirico* exhibition that he curated at the Museum of Modern Art in New York in 1982, William Rubin compares de Chirico with Duchamp by interpreting de Chirico's citations of antiquity as a re-viewing, much as he considers Duchamp's *The Large Glass* as a literal presentation of a kind of lens (with its glass) through which to reconsider representation. The two artists are hence linked through their common interest in the self-conscious figuration of re-examination of artworks (57).

7 For an example of an appropriated icon that is both ancient and modern, see Milly Heyd's psychoanalytic interpretation of *Mystery and Melancholy of a Street* (1914), in which she links the figure of a young girl with a rolling hoop both to a classical, textual source, the Latin poet Ovid (*Tristia* III, Elegy 12), and to modern visual artworks (Georges Seurat's *Sunday Afternoon on the Island of the Grand Jatte* (1896), Henri Rousseau's *War* (1894), and Kirchner's *Street* (1907) ('De Chirico: The Girl with the Hoop' 87)). Soby had already noted the iconographical link between Seurat and de Chirico (*Giorgio de Chirico* 74, citing Soby, *The Early Chirico*).

8 By 1928 de Chirico's ties with the Surrealists had fallen apart; indeed, André Breton, Paul Eluard, and others mounted a show of early de Chirico works in their collections as a protest again the artist's 1928 show at the Léonce Rosenberg's Galerie L'Effort Moderne, which was offering his contemporary (and hence post-Metaphysical) paintings (Tully 155). As Emily Braun has noted, a movement to reconsider de Chirico's later works has begun in Europe, although much work remains to be done (*De Chirico and America* 14). See, for example, Maurizio Clavesi and Mario Ursino for a reconsideration of the neo-Metaphysical works.

9 Robert Rosenblum has begun a revisionist account of de Chirico's work, in which he explores de Chirico's influence on American artists, ranging from painters to architects ('De Chirico's Long Shadow'). Although Rosenblum

considers de Chirico's appropriative practices as an attractive strategy for postmodern artists invested in pursuit of the fragment, he does not analyse de Chirico's absence from the discourse of appropriation, which is couched primarily in Duchampian terms. Rosenblum discusses both Charles Moore's *Piazza d'Italia* (1975–8) and Philip Johnson's *AT&T Building* (now owned by the Sony Company) (1978–84) in order to show how postmodern architecture picks up on the displacement of historical references so rampant in de Chirico's oeuvre. Moreover, Rosenblum notes that Wieland Schmied has conducted a parallel study of de Chirico's influence on European artists.

In her introduction to the catalogue published on the occasion of the 1996 *De Chirico and America* exhibition held at Hunter College in New York City, Braun suggests that rereading de Chirico from a post-modernist perspective thematizes, along with the problematic of the copy, the ways in which his later works can be read through the lenses of parody and pastiche. Renato Barilli has also suggested rereading the Old Master works as a postmodernist renegotiation of the history of art and its canonical formulation. See also Zdenek Felix's essay on 'Pittura Metafisica und Postmoderne' for a consideration of how Metaphysical painting translates fragmented antiquity into a prefiguration of postmodernity.

10 Baldacci notes that this painting contains the first figure to be labelled *Melanconia* (dated in his account to the fall of 1912), but that the figure without such an inscription appears earlier that year (spring 1912) in the painting *La Lassitude de l'infini* (*De Chirico. 1888–1919* 133).

11 As a matter of fact, up to late 1913, when de Chirico discovers the famous 'solitude of signs,' his compositions, despite their increasingly oneiric atmosphere, are relatively plausible from an ordinary point of view. It is his later, Metaphysical works, combining completely implausible combinations of objects (bananas, trains, artichokes, canons), that resist traditional pictorial logic. Hence, his later paintings entitled 'melancholy' make their use of the word more poignant.

12 Baldacci considers the influence of Romanticism on de Chirico vis-à-vis Leopardi ('La siepe di Leopardi e il muro metafisico').

13 Cornelia Syre interprets Metaphysical (and later) painting by both Carrà and de Chirico as representations of both Trecento and Quattrocento themes and visual strategies. In this sense, these works invoke classical antiquity in a way that is consciously mediated by the renovation of antiquity orchestrated by Early Renaissance forms.

14 Soby notes that de Chirico would have worked from his own plaster model of Ariadne, echoing the method of Old Masters such as Nicholas

Poussin, as evidenced by Poussin's model now preserved in the Musée du Louvre (*Giorgio de Chirico* 52ff).

15 Exhibitions in Europe continue to challenge de Chirico's position in the history of art. In fall 2001, an exhibition of works by both de Chirico and his brother, Alberto Savinio, entitled 'Die andere Moderne. Giorgio de Chirico und Alberto Savinio,' curated by Paolo Baldacci and Wieland Schmied, was shown first at the Kunstsammlung Nordrhein-Westfalen in Düsseldorf and then, in early 2002, at the Städtische Galerie im Lenbachhaus in Munich.

16 In continuing her reading of de Chirico's work as a form of mourning, Heyd considers the three Parisian canvases, *The Anguish of Departure* (1913–14), *The Mystery and Melancholy of a Street* (1914), and *The Enigma of the Day* (1914), as a linked series in which de Chirico 'began to work through the mourning process' with respect to his sister ('De Chirico: The Girl with the Hoop' 92)

17 The hoop, as a pictorial sign rich with allusions that both demand and frustrate interpretation, has been reinvoked by Federico Fellini in his film *The Satyricon* (1969), in which such a figure rolling a hoop appears. In a future work that lies outside the scope of this essay, I will argue that the strong and prominent presence of de Chirico's visual strategies and iconography in post-war Italian cinema is responsible to a significant extent for shaping it as a richly self-reflexive genre of Italian representation that relies heavily on the history of Italian art, whether of the classical, Renaissance, or modern period. De Chirico's presence is evident as well in the works of Luchino Visconti, Giuseppe Tornatore, Mario Martone, and other contemporary Italian filmmakers, all of whom, I argue, take on the metaphysical as central to their cinematic discourse.

18 The theme of Ariadne in de Chirico's oeuvre was the focus of an exhibition organized by Michael Taylor at the Philadelphia Museum of Art, which opened in November 2002 and then in January 2003 at the Estorica Collection in London.

19 Baldacci discusses Giorgio de Chirico's use of sculpture, both real and imagined, in his introductory essay published in conjunction with *De Chirico. The Centenary sculptures/Le sculture del Centenario*.

20 De Chirico, insofar as he included his own version of copied statues of Ariadne in his metaphysical canvases, was featured in the exhibition *Nachbilder. Vom Nutzen und Nachteil des Zitierens für die Kunst*, which was held at the Kunstverein Hannover in 1979 (35–6).

21 In referring to de Chirico's '60 years of copies and returns,' I acknowledge that this practice, although begun in the 1920s, became increasingly popular post–1929, and most common even later in his career.

22 Predating Foster's reading of the father in de Chirico's iconography, Nancy Stokes, in her psychoanalytic reading of the presence of nine-teenth-century sculpture in de Chirico's early Metaphysical works, has also suggested that de Chirico's father (or in a wider sense, his fatherland) should be understood as the source for the male statues that occupy his metaphysical *piazze* (51–2).

23 This subject has already been explored, to a certain extent, by Wieland Schmied in his overview of de Chirico's influence in Europe. Moreover, de Chirico's popularity continues to grow with contemporary Italian artists such as Mario Logli, as evidenced by the strong echoes of de Chirico's spatial sensibilities in the works included in *Raccontare il futuro*, the travelling exhibition of Logli's works mounted in honour of the Giacomo Leopardi Celebrations.

24 On the occasion of the Robert Miller Gallery's exhibition (25 Apr.–19 May 1984) of de Chirico's later works, Robert Pincus-Witten calls for a reap-praisal of the post-Metaphysical and Baroque paintings (1920–70) as 'proto-postmodernist.'

25 Thomas Crow discusses how many of Warhol's images (especially early images) were drawn from public events that focused on death, which were of particular interest given the celebrity involved, the notoriety of the cause of death (accidents), or the controversial orchestration of death (the death penalty, as in the electric chair series). Specifically, his essay traces this theme from the specific deaths/tragedies of female celebrities (Marilyn Monroe, Liz Taylor, and Jacqueline Kennedy) to more generic public deaths (caused by the cans of poisonous tunafish) to politically charged deaths (linked to the electric chair, race riots, etc.). Crow then argues that Warhol's later and indeed seemingly less emotionally charged works (those figuring cows, Campbell's soup cans, etc.) had less to do with death, per se, and more to do with consumer culture. I would argue that since Warhol produced the *Shadows* series in 1978, just after de Chirico's death, and the *After de Chirico* series shortly thereafter in 1982, when the art market would have responded economically to this death, these works would have triggered responses linked to both death and consumer culture. Like his images of Marilyn, Warhol's images of de Chirico's works were produced just after the artist's death (Stoichita 206). Moreover, the very notion that the popular artist Warhol chose to make remakes of de Chirico's works would have elicited a response from viewers of those works. See also, for example, the catalogue from the recent Warhol exhibition at the Pennsylvania Academy of Fine Arts, Binstock, *Andy Warhol, Social Observer*, in which his work in categorized into themes, highlighting 'Death and Disaster' (42–5).

26 While it was the requests of collectors that generated many of de Chirico (re)productions, the prices that the canvases fetched continued to be lower than those values granted to the 'originals' of such series. Moreover, de Chirico's practices of copying were harshly criticized by the art historical community as well, as in Ragghianti's famous polemical assessment.

27 Victor Stoichita interprets the *Shadows* series as Warhol's tribute to that *artistic* celebrity. He reads the artist's death as a catalyst, as in earlier celebrity deaths, of Warhol's abstract production that eliminates all traces of de Chirico's figurative works, obscuring them with traces of the metaphysical by figuring *only* the shadows, or one aspect of de Chirico's works that continuously defied pictorial logic (206–17). Stoichita also cites Donald Kuspit, who notes that 'both Warhol and the later de Chirico used serial copying destructively' (67–8). See Denis Hollier for a discussion of how the Surrealists frequently represented unrealistic shadows. In the case of de Chirico (considered for Hollier's purposes a Surrealist), Hollier notes how the clocks frequently figured in the artist's Metaphysical works show times of day that do not correspond with the kinds of shadows thrown by the objects and figures in the compositions.

28 Soby describes Madame Breton's (mislabelled as Gala Eluard) request to purchase the original *Disquieting Muses*. Since it had already been sold, de Chirico proposed re-painting another version for Mme. Eluard (*Giorgio de Chirico* n. 134). De Chirico's self-copying remains a source of great interest for his critics. See, for example, Giuliano Briganti's essay published in conjunction with the de Chirico retrospective mounted at the Galleria Nazionale d'Arte Moderna from 11 November 1981 to 3 January 1982. Briganti notes that in his youth de Chirico would have been surrounded not only by images derived from classical culture, but also by the ubiquitous Byzantine icons of the Greek Orthodox culture that enveloped him, a visual culture that granted high status to copies (26).

29 The very format of the catalogue from Bidlo's exhibition takes on Rubin's 1982 retrospective, offering a similar golden-yellow cover that substitutes an undecorated square with the text 'BIDLO (Not de Chirico)' for the metaphysical image (*Joy of the Return*, 1915) featured prominently on the cover of the Museum of Modern Art exhibition catalogue. A similar yellow-coloured cover design is repeated in 1995 by José María Faerna for the Abrams 'Great Modern Masters' series.

30 See de Chirico's letter to Angioletti – published as 'Truffa a de Chirico' in 1946 – for the artist's invective regarding the show of what he claimed were not his works mounted at the Gallerie Allard, no. 20 Rue des Capucines, in Paris.

31 I am indebted to Gerd Roos for his astute observation of Bidlo's copying a 'false' de Chirico.

32 In considering Bidlo's work as an imposter figure, it seems germane to invoke Thomas Crow's essay 'The Return of Hank Herron: Simulated Abstraction and the Service Economy of Art' [now in *Modern Art*],' in which he treats explicitly the subject of the appropriation artist and imposter-like behaviour. Moreover, his analysis adds yet another dimension to the role of the imposter. Supposedly an appropriation artist much like Sherrie Levine or Elaine Sturtevant, 'Hank Herron' was to have been an artist 'whose exhibited work consisted entirely of exact copies of works by Frank Stella.' Crow shows that Herron too was a fictional creation, an abstract expressionist designed by a simulated art historical account published by a fictional art historian whose identity and credentials themselves were simulations (69–84).

33 Bidlo's 'Peg's Place' at P.S. 1 in 1982, which recreated Pollock's bad-boy act of peeing in Peggy Guggenheim's fireplace, won Bidlo instant notoriety' (Siegel and McCormick).

34 This is especially problematic, given that there is no accepted *catalogue raisonée* for de Chirico's oeuvre, with the exception of Paolo Baldacci's 1997 monograph on the early works, now accepted by many scholars as a period-specific *catalogue raisonnée* for de Chirico's Metaphysical period. Indeed, the *Catalogo generale* (the only attempt ever made at a *catalogue raisonnée* of de Chirico's work), published between 1971 and 1978, included many paintings later deemed fakes by various parties, including the artist, Claudio Bruni Sakraischik, the artist's wife, and various former and ongoing members of the advisory committee of the Fondazione Giorgio e Isa de Chirico in Rome.

35 Maria Cristina Bandera has recently published the correspondence between de Chirico and Rodolfo Pallucchini, the *Segretario generale* of the Venice Biennale, letters that represent the communications regarding the upcoming 1956 Venice Biennale, where de Chirico was to have a *personale*. In these letters, one is reminded of de Chirico's contemptuous attitude towards the 1948 Biennale, which had prompted him to launch his legal attack (lodged 3 July 1948, only resolved in March 1955) against that institution for exhibiting what he had declared a 'falso.' Moreover, Bandera includes additional correspondence from de Chirico to Palluchini (16 January 1956), in which the artist laments the fact that Soby had included reproductions of 'falsi' in his 1941 and 1955 monographic publications on the artist. Notably, the list of works selected by de Chirico for his *personale* at the 1956 Biennale was accompanied by the following disclaimer (both as published in the 1956 Biennale catalogue and in the

actual exhibition space of the works): 'Per espressa dichiarazione dell'artista le opere non hanno indicazione di data; soltanto una porta l'anno di esecuzione sulla tela' (Bandera 300, citing *XXVIII Biennale 1956* 87).

36 See Carlo Accorsi for a listing of works included in the *catalogo generale* that were then claimed as works executed by Peretti. Accorsi divides the fake paintings into two categories: 1) those that are false with positive authentications and 2) those that are false that have been notarized as such. *OP. Settimanale di fatti e notizie* also published a listing of false paintings (*Catalogo dei falsi de Chirico*) in December 1978, just after de Chirico's death.

37 Baldacci included Dominguez fakes as well as Max Ernst copies of de Chirico paintings in his exhibition (Baldacci and Schmied 90–1; 190–6).

38 Baldacci and Schmied included this work in their documentation of 'fakes' at the 1994 show in New York, hence publicizing the purchase as inauthentic (91, figure 82).

39 Robinson originally presented his findings in a paper entitled 'Exquisite Fakes: The Treachery of the Surrealists' at the College Art Association annual meeting held in New York City in February 2000. I thank the author for generously making his argument available to me prior to its publication in the journal *IMFR*.

40 Moreover, as Baldacci pointed out in his *Betraying the Muse* exhibition, the real 'metaphysical interiors' belong to 'a genre that de Chirico painted only in Ferrara between 1916 and 1918, and therefore cannot be painted on French canvases and stretchers, like the works made by de Chirico in Paris between 1912 and 1915.' Baldacci also points out that Dominguez, relying on reproductions of de Chirico's paintings, often inserted certain painted images into his false metaphysical interiors, while he also, having copied the images from reproductions rather than originals, grossly mistook the technique that de Chirico used when completing his pencil drawings within his oil paintings (Baldacci and Schmied 92).

41 Luigi Cavallo provides the most thorough treatment thus far of the 'Baroque' aspect of de Chirico's practice. Less thorough treatments of de Chirico's later work are José María Faerna's discussion of de Chirico's 'Return to Classicism' and 'The Reinvention of Painting' sections of his survey of de Chirico's oeuvre, Giorgio Pillon's consideration of Rubens's influence on de Chirico, and Mario Ursino's analysis of de Chirico's re-presentations of Titian's images and manner.

42 Soby locates the decline in de Chirico's artistic genius to de Chirico's copying of Old Masters, compromising his geometrical distinction and

articulating instead 'the fuzziness of contour borrowed in exaggerated form from the Rubens-Delacroix-Renoir tradition' (*The Early Chirico* 82).

43 For the dating of this painting, I rely on Gerd Roos, who is in the process of compiling a *catalogue raisonée* of de Chirico's more than 250 painted and drawn self-portraits.

44 It would be constructive to compare de Chirico's late works that figure restagings of Delacroix's works in light of what has been said about late Delacroix at the recent exhibition in Paris and Philadelphia, *Delacroix: The Late Work*. Much of Delacroix's later work that was formerly disregarded, as the curators of this exhibition have shown, is concerned with a formalist reconsideration of his own earlier subject matter, hence a kind of artistic precedent for not only de Chirico's self-repetition, but the negative reception thereof. In a future essay, I will be considering how Old Masters figure in de Chirico's art-historical writings, whose opinions and tones shift, much like his own artistic practices.

45 Tully notes a similar case of devaluation, describing one of the pictures that Eric Manesse of the Interart Cultural Exchange investigated on the occasion of the 1990 *Giorgio de Chirico 1920–1950* show held at the Borghi & Company Gallery in New York. Upon accepting expert Paolo Baldacci's endorsement of Maurizio Fagiolo dell'Arco's dating of *Italian Square* (*Apparition of the Locomotive*) to the late 1930s, the value dropped from $3 million to $400,000 (158).

WORKS CITED

Accorsi, Carlo. 'Ecco l'elenco dei falsi riprodotti in catalogo. Peretti ci ha detto: questi li ho fatto io.' *Bolaffiarte. Rivista Mensile di Informazioni*. 10: 91 (Summer 1979): 28–33.

Agamben, Giorgio. *Stanze, la parola e il fantasma nella cultura occidentale*. Turin: Einaudi, 1977.

Ahrens, Gerhard, and Katrin Sello. *Nachbilder vom Nutzen und Nachteil des Zitierens für die Kunst*. Exh. cat. Hannover: Th. Schafer Druckere, 1979.

Baldacci, Paolo. *De Chirico. 1888–1919. La Metafisica*. Milan: Leonardo Arte, 1997.

– 'La siepe di Leopardi e il muro metafisico.' *ON – OttoNovecento. Rivista di storia dell'arte*. (1997). 34–42.

– *De Chirico. The Centenary Sculptures/Le sculture del Centenario*. Turin: Umberto Allemandi, 1995.

Baldacci, Paolo, and Wieland Schmied. *Giorgio de Chirico: Betraying the Muse – De Chirico and the Surrealists*. Exh. cat. New York: Paolo Baldacci Gallery, 1994.

Bandera, Maria Cristina. *Il carteggio Longhi-Pallucchini. Le prime Biennali del dopoguerra 1948–1956.* Milan: Charta, 1999.

Barilli, Renato. 'De Chirico e il ricupero del museo.' In *Tra presenza e assenza. Due Ipotesi per l'età postmoderna.* Milan: Bompiani, 1974. 268–303.

Benjamin, Walter. *The Origin of German Tragic Drama.* Trans. John Osborne. London: Verso, 1985.

Bidlo, Mike. *Masterpieces.* With text by Robert Rosenblum. Zurich: Bruno Bischofberger, 1989.

– *Mike Bidlo: the Fountain Drawings.* Zurich: Galerie Bruno Bischofberger, 1998.

Biennale di Venezia XXVIII. Exh. cat. Venice, 1956.

Binstock, Joseph P. *Andy Warhol, Social Observer.* Philadelphia: Pennsylvania Academy of Fine Arts, 2000.

Bonito Oliva, Achille. 'Industrial Metaphysics.' Interview with Andy Warhol in *Warhol verso de Chirico.* Exh. cat. New York: Marisa del Re Gallery, 1985.

Braun, Emily, ed. *De Chirico and America.* Exh. cat. Turin: Umberto Allemandi, 1996.

– 'Kitsch and the Avant-Garde: The Case of De Chirico.' *Rethinking Images Between the Wars: New Perspectives in Art History.* Copenhagen: Museum Tusculanum, 2001. 73–90.

– *Mario Sironi and Italian Modernism: Art and Politics under Fascism.* New York: Cambridge UP, 2000.

Briganti, Giuliano. 'De Chirico e l'altro se stesso. Il problema delle repliche.' *Giorgio de Chirico 1888–1978.* Vol. 1. Exh. cat. Rome: de Luca, 1981. 24–7.

Bryson, Norman. 'Yasumasa Morimura: Three Readings.' *Art and Text* 52 (Sept. 1995): 74–9.

Calvesi, Maurizio, and Mario Ursino. *De Chirico: The New Metaphysics.* Buffalo: Craftsman House/G & B Arts Int., 1996.

'Catalogo dei falsi de Chirico. Chi li ha fatti. Chi li possiede.' *OP. Settimanale di fatti e notizie.* 1: 37 (26 Dec. 1978): 21–40.

Cavallo, Luigi. 'Il "barocco" di de Chirico ovvero de Chirico il barocco.' In Luigi Cavallo and Maurizio Fagiolo. *De Chirico, il barocco. Dipinti degli anni '30–50.* Florence: Galleria Farsetti, 1991. 5–25.

Clair, Jean. 'Sous le signe de Saturne: Notes sur l'allégorie de la mélancolie dans l'art de l'entre-deux-guerres en Allemagne et en Italie.' *Cahiers du Musée National d'Art Moderne* 7/8 (1981): 179–207.

Crow, Thomas. *Modern Art in the Common Culture.* New Haven: Yale UP, 1996.

De Chirico, Giorgio. *Piccolo trattato di tecnica pittorica.* Milan: Scheiwiller, 1928, 1945, 1983.

– 'Truffa a de Chirico.' *Fiera Letteraria* (25 July 1946).

- *Il Meccanismo del pensiero*. Ed. Maurizio Fagiolo dell'Arco. Turin: Einaudi, 1985.
- *Giorgio de Chirico nelle collezioni della Galleria Nazionale d'Arte Moderna, 78 opere dal 1909 al 1975*. Rome: Galleria Nazionale d'Arte Moderna, 1994.

Faerna, José María. *De Chirico*. New York: Cameo/Abrams, 1995.

Fagiolo dell'Arco, Maurizio. *Classicismo pittorico. Metafisica, Valori Plastici, Realismo Magico e '900'*. Genoa: Costa & Nolan, 1991.

- *Giorgio de Chirico. Metafisica dei Bagni misteriosi*. Milan: Skira, 1998.

Felix, Zdenek. 'Pittura metafisica und Postmoderne.' in *Mythos Italien Wintermärchen Deutschland. Die italienische Moderne und ihr Dialog mit Deutschland*. Exh. cat. Munich: Prestel Verlag, 1988. 53–8.

Foster, Hal. *Compulsive Beauty*. Cambridge: MIT Press, 1997.

Freud, Sigmund. *Beyond the Pleasure Principle*. Trans. and ed. James Strachey. New York: Norton, 1961.

- 'Mourning and Melancholia.' In vol. 14 of *The Standard Edition of the Complete Psychological Works of Sigmund Freud*. Trans. James Strachey with Anna Freud. London: Hogarth Press, 1959. 243–59.

- 'The "Uncanny."' In vol. 17 of *The Standard Edition of the Complete Psychological Works of Sigmund Freud*. Trans. James Strachey with Anna Freud. London: Hogarth Press, 1959. 218–56.

Heyd, Milly. 'De Chirico: The Girl with the Hoop.' *Psychoanalytic Perspectives on Art*, vol. 3. Ed. Mary Mathews Gedo. Hillsdale: Analytic Press, 1988. 85–106.

- 'De Chirico: *The Greetings of a Distant Friend*.' *Psychoanalytic Perspectives on Art*, volume 3. Ed. Mary Mathews Gedo. Hillsdale: Analytic Press, 1988. 107–28.

Hollier, Denis. 'Surrealist Precipitates: Shadows Don't Cast Shadows.' *October* 69 (Summer 1994): 110–32.

Jones, Amelia. *Post-Modernism and the En-gendering of Marcel Duchamp*. New York and London: Cambridge UP, 1994.

Kultermann, Udo. 'Amerikanische Malerei Heute. Der Neubeginn der achtziger Jahre.' *Pantheon* (1991): 167–75.

Kuspit, Donald. *The Cult of the Avant-garde Artist*. New York: Cambridge UP, 1993.

Levin, Kim. 'The Counterfeiters: De Chirico Versus Warhol.' In *Beyond Modernism: Essays on Art from the '70s and '80s*. New York: Harper and Row, 1988. 250–5.

Logli, Mario. *Raccontare il futuro*. Exh. cat. Milan and Los Angeles: Rockwell-Rimoldi, 1988.

Nietzsche, Friedrich. *Thus Spake Zarathustra*. Trans. Thomas Common. Rev., with introduction and notes by H. James Birx. Buffalo: Prometheus, 1993.

Ovid. *Tristia; Ex Ponto.* English trans. Arthur Leslie Wheeler. 2nd ed. rev. G.P. Goold. Cambridge: Harvard UP, 1988.

Pillon, Giorgio. *De Chirico e il fascino di Rubens.* Rome: Serarcangeli, 1991.

Pincus-Witten, Robert. 'Capriccio di de Chirico.' *Giorgio de Chirico. Post-Metaphysical & Baroque Paintings 1920–1970.* Exh. cat. New York: Robert Miller Gallery, 1984.

Radnóti, Sándor. *The Fake: Forgery and Its Place in Art.* Trans. Ervin Dunai. Lanham: Rowman & Littlefield, 1999.

Ragghianti, C.L. 'Il Caso de Chirico.' *Critica d'arte* 14 nuova serie, fasc. 163–65 (Jan.–June 1979): 3–54.

Robinson, William. 'Verifalsi or Falsifalsi? De Chirico Fakes Himself.' *IMFR.* Publication forthcoming.

Rosenblum, Robert. 'De Chirico's Long Shadow: From Surrealism to Postmodernism.' *Art in America* 84 (July 1996): 46–55.

– 'Remembrance of Art Past.' *Encounters: New Art from Old.* London: National Gallery, 2000. 8–23.

Rubin, William. 'De Chirico and Modernism.' *De Chirico.* Ed. William Rubin. Exh. cat. New York: Museum of Modern Art, 1982.

Schmied, Wieland. *De Chirico und sein Schatten.* Munich: Prestel Verlag, 1989.

Serullaz, Arlette, ed. *Delacroix: The Late Work.* Exh. cat. Philadelphia: Philadelphia Museum of Art, 1998.

Siegel, Jeanne, and Carlo McCormick. 'Stealing That Painting! Mike Bidlo's Artistic Kleptomania.' In *Mike Bidlo. Masterpieces.* Zurich: Galerie Bruno Bischofberger, 1989.

Soby, James Thrall. *The Early Chirico.* New York: Dodd, Mead & Co., 1941.

– *Giorgio de Chirico.* New York: Museum of Modern Art, 1955.

Steinberg, Leo. 'The Glorious Company.' In *Art about Art*, ed. Jean Lipman and Richard Marshall. Exh. cat. New York: E.P. Dutton, in assoc. with the Whitney Museum of American Art, 1978. 8–31.

Stoichita, Victor. *A Short History of the Shadow.* London: Reaktion Books, 1999.

Stokes, Nancy. 'The Mystery and Melancholy of Nineteenth Century Sculpture in de Chirico's *Pittura Metafisica.*' *Psychoanalytic Perspectives on Art*, vol. 3. Ed. Mary Mathews Gedo. Hillsdale: Analytic Press, 1988. 49–84.

Syre, Cornelia. 'Versöhnung von Tradition und Revolution. Die Rezeption des italienischen Trecento und Quattrocento bei Carlo Carrà und Giorgio de Chirico.' In *Mythos Italien Wintermärchen Deutschland. Die italienische Moderne und ihr Dialog mit Deutschland.* Exh. cat. Munich: Prestel Verlag, 1988. 65–70.

Tully, Judd. 'Real and Unreal: The Strange Life of de Chirico's Art.' *Artnews* 93 (Summer 1994): 154–9.

Ursino, Mario. 'de Chirico e Tiziano.' *Atti del Convego Tiziano dopo Tiziano.* Treviso, 1991.

Index